Oracle Siebel CRM 8 Installation and Management

Install, configure, and manage a robust Customer Relationship Management system using Siebel CRM

Alexander Hansal

BIRMINGHAM - MUMBAI

Oracle Siebel CRM 8 Installation and Management

Copyright © 2010 Packt Publishing

All rights reserved. No part of this book may be reproduced, stored in a retrieval system, or transmitted in any form or by any means, without the prior written permission of the publisher, except in the case of brief quotations embedded in critical articles or reviews.

Every effort has been made in the preparation of this book to ensure the accuracy of the information presented. However, the information contained in this book is sold without warranty, either express or implied. Neither the author, Packt Publishing, nor its dealers or distributors will be held liable for any damages caused or alleged to be caused directly or indirectly by this book.

Packt Publishing has endeavored to provide trademark information about all the companies and products mentioned in this book by the appropriate use of capitals. However, Packt Publishing cannot guarantee the accuracy of this information.

First published: July 2010

Production Reference: 2190710

Published by Packt Publishing Ltd.
32 Lincoln Road
Olton
Birmingham, B27 6PA, UK.

ISBN 978-1-849680-56-1

www.packtpub.com

Cover Image by Tina Negus (tina_manthorpe@sky.com)

Credits

Author
Alexander Hansal

Reviewers
Michael Weigl
Tim Bull

Acquisition Editor
Amey Kanse

Development Editor
Dhwani Devater

Technical Editor
Ajay Shanker

Indexer
Monica Ajmera

Editorial Team Leader
Akshara Aware

Project Team Leader
Lata Basantani

Project Coordinator
Leena Purkait

Proofreader
Aaron Nash

Graphics
Geetanjali Sawant

Production Coordinator
Adline Swetha Jesuthas

Cover Work
Adline Swetha Jesuthas

About the Author

Alexander Hansal has worked for various companies and governmental institutions as IT instructor and consultant. He started as a Siebel CRM instructor for Siebel Systems Germany in 2001. After the acquisition of Siebel Systems by Oracle, Alexander continues to support European customers as an instructor and consultant for Siebel CRM and Oracle Business Intelligence.

Strongly believing in the power of information sharing, Alexander regularly discusses Siebel CRM and Oracle BI related topics on his weblog (`http://siebel-essentials.blogspot.com`).

> I would like to express my gratefulness to the following wonderful fellow human beings. Without your contributions this book would not have been possible.
>
> Michael Weigl for his review work and for hiring me.
>
> Tim Bull for his invaluable input as native English speaker.
>
> Amey and Leena at Packt Publishing.
>
> All those dedicated people who contribute to the Siebel CRM community.

About the Reviewers

Michael Weigl holds master's degrees in physics and computer science. After having worked as a programmer for several years he has been a technical trainer for Digital Equipment, Siebel Systems, and Oracle, teaching programming languages, operating systems, network technology, databases, Siebel CRM, and finally Oracle BI. This has been interrupted by his participation in various programming projects, Siebel implementations, and end-user training opportunities. He is a happy father of two adult sons who fortunately have not followed him into the computer industry (although they of course love computer games).

Tim Bull has been working with Siebel since joining the company in 1999. Starting life as a Siebel Administrator. He has worked as a consultant and is now a Principle Instructor for Oracle University developing and delivering technical courses in all aspects of Siebel CRM.

For Sarah

Table of Contents

Preface	**1**
Chapter 1: Introducing the Siebel Web Architecture	**7**
The Siebel web architecture	**8**
The Siebel database	10
The Siebel File System	11
The Siebel Enterprise Server	12
The Siebel Gateway Name Server	13
The Siebel Server	13
The Application Object Manager (AOM)	14
Configuration parameters	15
Data Manager (DM)	15
Siebel Repository File (SRF)	15
Siebel Web Engine (SWE)	15
Siebel Web Templates (SWT)	16
The web server	16
The Siebel Web Server Extension	17
The browser and the Siebel user interface	19
Summary	**21**
Chapter 2: Planning and Preparing the Installation	**23**
Planning the Siebel CRM installation	**24**
Sample planning document	25
More planning information	26
Understanding hardware and software prerequisites	**26**
Sizing the Siebel deployment	**27**
Preparing the Siebel database	**28**
Creating the service owner account	**30**
Creating the Siebel File System root folder	**32**
Downloading the Siebel installation archives	**32**
Using a download management tool	34

Table of Contents

Running the Siebel Image Creator	36
Obtaining the license key	38
Summary	39
Chapter 3: Installing Siebel CRM Server Software on Microsoft Windows	**41**
About the Siebel server installer	42
Installation using GUI mode	44
Installation using console mode	44
Installing the Siebel Gateway Name Server	46
Installing the Siebel Server	49
Verifying successful Siebel Server installation	52
Installing the Siebel Database Server Utilities	53
About the Sample Database support module	54
Verifying the successful installation of the Siebel Database Server Utilities	55
Installing support files for the Siebel EAI Connectors	56
Installing the Siebel Web Server Extension	60
Checking the system configuration with the Siebel Environment Verification Tool (EVT)	61
Applying patches for Siebel server software	65
Summary	65
Chapter 4: Configuring Siebel Server Software on Microsoft Windows	**67**
About the Siebel Software Configuration Wizard	68
Configuring the Siebel Gateway Name Server	70
Verifying the successful Siebel Gateway Name Server configuration	72
Configuring the Siebel Enterprise	73
About the Siebel Enterprise name	76
About additional tasks for configuring the Enterprise	77
Verifying the successful Enterprise configuration	78
Configuring the Siebel Web Server Extension logical profile	79
About SWSE parameters	81
Verifying the successful SWSE logical profile creation	82
Installing the Siebel Database schema and seed data	83
Preparing and executing the grantusr.sql file	84
Enter the correct tablespace names	84
Modify default passwords if needed	85
Add additional user accounts	85
Executing the grantusr.sql Script	87
About the Siebel Upgrade Wizard and the Log Parser	87
Steps of the Install Siebel Database task	91
Verifying the successful Siebel database installation	92

Using the Siebel Log Parser	92
Verifying tables and data	94
Restarting the Siebel Upgrade Wizard in the case of errors	94
Configuring the Siebel Server	**95**
Verifying the successful Siebel Server configuration	98
Configuring the Siebel Web Server Extension	**98**
Verifying the successful Siebel Enterprise server installation	**101**
Starting the Windows services	101
Logging on as the Siebel Administrator for the first time	102
Finalizing the Siebel Server installation	**106**
Setting the System Service owner account	106
Copying the Siebel File System Seed files	107
Creating administrative Siebel user accounts	108
Applying additional license keys	110
Synchronizing server components	111
Installing and configuring Siebel server software in unattended mode	**112**
Creating an .ini file for unattended Siebel server installation	113
Creating a response file for the Siebel Configuration Wizard	113
Modifying the .ini file to launch the configuration automatically	114
Executing the installer in unattended mode	115
Summary	**116**
Chapter 5: Installing and Configuring Siebel CRM Server Software on Linux	**117**
Installing the Siebel Gateway Name Server	**118**
Installing the Siebel Server	**121**
Verifying the Siebel Server installation	122
Installing the Siebel Database Server Utilities	**123**
Installing the Siebel Web Server Extension	**124**
Using the Siebel Software Configuration Wizard on Linux or UNIX	**126**
Preparing to run the Software Configuration Wizard	127
Configuring the Siebel Gateway Name Server	**128**
Verifying the Siebel Gateway Name Server Installation on Linux or UNIX	129
Configuring the Siebel Enterprise	**131**
Verifying the successful Enterprise configuration	134
Verifying the ODBC data source	134
Configuring the Siebel Web Server Extension logical profile	**135**
Verifying the successful SWSE logical profile creation	138
Installing the Siebel Database Schema and Seed Data	**138**
Preparing the environment for database configuration	139
Creating the dbenv.sh script	139
Modifying the dbenv.sh script	139

Table of Contents

Executing the dbenv.sh script	141
Verifying ODBC settings using odbcsql	141
Starting the Siebel Configuration Wizard	141
Starting the Siebel Upgrade Wizard	144
Verifying the successful Siebel Database installation	144
Restarting the Siebel Gateway Name Server	144
Stopping the Gateway Name server	145
Modifying the siebenv.sh file	145
Executing the siebenv.sh file	145
Starting and verifying the Gateway Name Server	145
Configuring the Siebel Server	**146**
Verifying successful Siebel Server Configuration	148
Configuring the Siebel Web Server Extension	**149**
Preparing the web server	149
Configuring the Siebel Web Server Extension	150
Verifying the successful SWSE configuration	151
Verifying the successful Siebel Enterprise Server installation	**152**
Starting the services	152
Starting the Siebel Gateway Name Server on Linux or UNIX	152
Starting the Siebel Server	153
Starting the web server	153
Logging on as SADMIN for the first time	154
Final Steps	**154**
Configuring services for automatic start on Linux	155
Editing the siebel_server file	155
Copying the siebel_server file to the init.d folder	156
Setting permissions for the siebel_server file	156
Creating a non-root user file	156
Creating soft links	156
Summary	**157**
Chapter 6: Installing Siebel Client Software	**159**
About the Developer and Mobile Web Client	**159**
User groups and Siebel Client Software	161
Prerequisite software and configuration settings for Siebel Web Clients	**162**
About database client software for Developer Web Clients	162
Installing with administrative user rights	163
Internet Explorer security settings	163
Java Runtime Environment (JRE)	163
Additional software recommendations	164
Installing the Siebel Developer Web Client	**165**
Verifying the Siebel Developer Web Client installation	168

About the Siebel Client configuration file	170
About configuring data sources for the Siebel client	172
Configuring the Local data source for the Mobile Web Client	173
Configuring the Server data sources for the Siebel Developer Web Client	174
Setting up additional data sources	175
Creating Siebel application shortcuts	177
Installing the Siebel sample database	**178**
Verifying successful installation of the Siebel Sample Database	180
Installing Siebel Tools	**182**
Verifying successful Siebel Tools installation	184
Configuring Siebel Tools for the Siebel Sample Database	185
Creating shortcuts for Siebel Tools	185
Applying patches to Siebel client software	**186**
Summary	**187**

Chapter 7: Installing Ancillary Siebel Server Software — 189

Installing and configuring the Visual Mining NetCharts server	**189**
Downloading the Visual Mining NetCharts Server installer	191
Planning and preparing the NetCharts Server installation	191
Installing the Visual Mining NetCharts server on Windows	192
Verifying successful installation of the NetCharts Server	193
Configuring connectivity from Siebel CRM to the NetCharts Server	194
Creating a project folder and file for Siebel	194
Setting Siebel Enterprise parameters	195
Verifying successful setup of Siebel Charts	196
Installing Oracle BI Publisher	**197**
Downloading Oracle BI Publisher Enterprise Server	199
Prerequisites for Oracle BI Publisher Enterprise Server	200
Installing Oracle BI Publisher Enterprise Server	200
Verifying successful installation of BI Publisher	201
Setting up Siebel CRM for BI Publisher reports	202
Siebel CRM version differences	202
Importing Fix Pack SIF files	204
Creating a new outbound web service for BI Publisher 10.1.3.4.1	205
Importing the Siebel inbound web services	207
Creating XMLP responsibilities	208
Configuring the Siebel outbound web service for Siebel 8.2 or higher	208
Copying Siebel java libraries to the BI Publisher server	209
Enabling external file references for BI Publisher	209
Enabling Siebel Server components	210
Setting parameters for the XMLP Java subsystem	212
Setting the BI Publisher Security Model	213

Uploading preconfigured reports	214
Verifying BI Publisher integration for Siebel CRM	216
Assigning BI Publisher roles to the SiebelCRMReports folder	218
Copying fonts for BI Publisher reports (optional)	219
Configuring the BI Publisher Scheduler (optional)	219
Summary	**226** |ರ

Chapter 8: Special Siebel Server Configurations — 227

Installing and configuring additional Siebel servers	**227**
Planning the installation of additional Siebel Servers	229
Installing additional Siebel Servers	229
Verifying the successful Siebel Server installation and configuration	230
About configuring multiple Siebel Servers on the same physical machine	231
Configuring Siebel load balancing	**232**
About Siebel load balancing	232
Single Siebel Server	233
Siebel Native Load Balancing	234
Third-Party Load Balancing	234
Configuring the SWSE for Siebel Native Load Balancing	234
Creating the load balancer configuration file	234
Reconfiguring the Siebel Web Server Extension	235
Validating the eapps.cfg file	237
Verifying the successful load balancing configuration of the SWSE	238
Installing additional language packs	**239**
Downloading Siebel CRM language packs	240
Adding language packs to existing Siebel installation images	241
Installing additional language packs for Siebel Enterprise Server software	242
Adding language support for a Siebel Server	243
Importing language-specific seed data into the Siebel database	244
Installing language-specific seed data	247
Deactivating non-multilingual List of Values (MLOV) seed data	248
Importing language-specific repository metadata	248
Enabling multilingual List of Values	251
Installing additional language packs for the Siebel Web Server Extension	254
Verifying the successful language pack installation for Siebel server software	255
Restarting the Siebel Enterprise	256
Logging on to the new application object manager	256
Verifying UI translation	257
Verifying multilingual List of Values	257
Installing additional language packs for the Siebel Developer or Mobile Web Client	259

Table of Contents

    Verifying the successful language pack installation for the Siebel Developer
    Web Client   260
    About language packs for Siebel Tools   260
  Summary   **260**

Chapter 9: Siebel Server Management   261

  Understanding servers, components, and parameters   **262**
    Servers   263
    Component groups   263
    Component definitions   266
        Component definition run modes   267
        Component types   268
    Enterprise parameters   269
    Enterprise profiles   270
    System alerts   272
    Siebel enterprise hierarchy and parameter inheritance   272
  Using server management screens in the Siebel client   **275**
    Using the Administration - Server Configuration screen   276
        Backing up the Siebel enterprise configuration   276
        Restoring the Siebel enterprise configuration   277
        Enterprise Explorer   277
        Servers view   282
        Job Templates   284
    Using the Administration - Server Management screen   286
        Enterprises view   286
        Servers view   288
        Components view   288
        Tasks view   289
        Sessions view   289
        Jobs view   290
  Using command line tools for Siebel server management   **292**
    About the srvrmgr command line utility   293
    Listing and reviewing information about the Siebel enterprise   295
    Backing up the enterprise configuration   297
    Listing and modifying parameters   297
    Creating and modifying component definitions   298
    Controlling assignment of component groups to Siebel servers   299
    Setting the start up mode of server components   300
    Controlling server components   301
    Running jobs for batch and background components   302
    Using input files   302
  Summary   **303**

Table of Contents

Chapter 10: User Authentication — 305
User authentication concepts in Siebel CRM — 305
Database authentication — 308
Security adapters are defined as enterprise profiles — 308
Associating a security adapter with a server component — 309
Managing user accounts for database authentication — 310
Directory server authentication — 311
Installing the directory server (optional) — 312
Installing the IBM LDAP Client — 312
Creating user accounts in the directory server — 314
    Creating the shared credentials account — 315
    Creating the anonymous user accounts — 317
    Setting access permissions for LDAP accounts — 319
Verifying the proxy account — 320
Configuring the LDAP Security Adapter — 321
Configuring server components — 323
Verifying LDAP authentication — 324
    Registering a new user — 324
Configuring the Siebel Gateway Name Server for LDAP authentication (optional) — 326
    Verifying LDAP authentication for the Siebel Gateway Name Server — 329
Configuring Siebel clients for LDAP authentication (optional) — 329
    Setting the SecThickClientExtAuthent system preference to TRUE — 330
    Creating the central authentication configuration file — 331
    Modifying the client configuration file — 332
    Verifying directory server authentication for the Siebel client — 332
Web Single-Sign-On — 333
Creating a non-anonymous virtual directory on the web server — 335
Creating or verifying user accounts in the external authentication system — 337
Modifying the Siebel Web Server Extension configuration file — 337
Modifying the LDAP security adapter — 339
Verifying the Web SSO configuration — 339
Summary — 341

Chapter 11: User Authorization and Access Control — 343
Understanding Siebel Access Control — 344
Controlling access to Siebel views — 345
The importance of business process analysis — 346
Using responsibilities to control access to views — 347
    Creating or modifying responsibilities — 349
    Understanding the implications of view access — 350
    Controlling view access on local databases — 351
    Controlling read-only behaviour of views — 352

Table of Contents

Controlling the tab layout for screens and views	353
Controlling access to customer data	**354**
Controlling record access for a single user or employee	355
Controlling record access for multiple employees	358
Controlling record access for teams based on positions	360
Controlling record access for different companies based on organizations	362
Controlling access to master data	**364**
Personalized access to features and data	**367**
Controlling access to applets and views based on personalization	368
Controlling data display based on personalization	371
Summary	**373**
Chapter 12: Managing User Accounts	**375**
Understanding divisions and organizations	**375**
Setting up divisions	376
Setting up organizations	378
Setting up and managing the position hierarchy	**380**
Multiple positions for an employee	382
Setting up user and employee accounts	**382**
Creating or verifying user accounts in the authentication system	384
Summary	**385**
Chapter 13: Siebel Remote and the Siebel Development Environment	**387**
Introduction to Siebel Remote	**388**
Differences between developers and end users	390
Setting up mobile clients	**391**
Enabling and configuring Siebel Remote server components	**392**
Creating the database schema files	**394**
Extracting data for local databases	**395**
About Siebel Remote system preferences	396
Running a database extract job for developers	397
Initializing the local database	**399**
Establishing network connectivity for mobile clients	399
Verifying settings in the client configuration files	400
Additional configuration file settings for developers	401
Logging in to the local database for the first time	401
Understanding the Siebel configuration process	**403**
Synchronizing local databases	**405**
Manual synchronization	405

[ix]

Table of Contents

Siebel TrickleSync	406
Monitoring and managing Siebel Remote users	**407**
Managing the transaction components on the Siebel server	407
Monitoring mobile client activity	409
Sending messages to mobile users	410
Re-extracting local databases	410
Deactivating mobile user registrations	411
Summary	**412**
Chapter 14: Installing and Configuring the Siebel Management Server Infrastructure	**413**
Overview of the Siebel Management Server Infrastructure	**414**
Installing and configuring the Siebel Management Server	**415**
Prerequisites for the Siebel Management Server	415
About the cross-enterprise user account	416
Adding the Siebel Server bin directory to the PATH environment variable	416
Installing the Siebel Management Server on Microsoft Windows	417
Verifying the successful installation and configuration of the Siebel Management Server	420
Installing and configuring Siebel Management Agents	**422**
Verifying the successful installation and configuration of a Siebel Management Agent	424
Registering Siebel Management Agents	**425**
Summary	**427**
Chapter 15: Migrating Configuration Changes between Environments	**429**
Overview of Siebel Application Deployment Manager	**430**
Administrative data (Database objects)	430
Repository objects	432
Files on Siebel servers and Siebel Web Server Extensions (SWSE)	432
The Application Deployment Manager Architecture	433
Setting up Siebel Application Deployment Manager	**435**
Enabling the ADM component group	436
Managing ADM components in source and target enterprises	436
Configuring the enterprise profile for ADM	437
Enabling ADM support for the application object manager	437
Activating ADM workflow processes	438
Restarting Siebel Servers	439
Verifying the adm.cli file	439

Creating shared directories	439
Creating the enterprise profile and deployment batch files	440
Exporting and Packaging Configuration Changes	**443**
Creating the ADM package	443
Creating the empty package structure	443
Exporting administrative data using the Application Deployment Manager screen	445
Exporting administrative data using the ADM Batch Processor server component	447
Exporting repository data using Siebel Tools	448
Exporting repository object definitions for Hot-Fixes	449
Exporting repository object definitions for mid-level releases	450
Exporting repository data using the consoleapp utility	452
Copying files to the ADM package	454
About deploying Siebel Repository Files	455
Sealing the ADM package	455
Validating the ADM package	456
Deploying ADM packages	**456**
Other migration utilities	**460**
Siebel Upgrade Wizard—Migrate Repository	460
Deploying enterprise configuration data using the cfgmerge utility	464
Deploying new component definitions from source to target enterprises	465
Using the cfgmerge utility	465
Summary	**467**
Chapter 16: Monitoring Siebel Applications	**469**
Server component event logging	**470**
Using the Siebel Server Manager command line to set event log levels	474
Siebel Application Response Measurement (SARM)	**474**
Enabling SARM	476
Enabling SARM for Siebel servers and components	476
Enabling SARM for other Siebel software units	478
Managing SARM files	480
Using sarmquery to read SARM files	481
Specifying the start and end time	483
Application performance by area and subarea	484
Time histograms	487
Identifying slow performing objects	487
Creating SARM output files	488
Automating SARM data retrieval	489
Siebel Diagnostic Tool	**490**
Client-side logging	**494**
Enabling client-side logging for the application object manager	495
Enabling client-side logging on the client machine	496

Table of Contents

Reviewing the client log file	496
Siebel Usage Collection	**496**
Summary	**499**
Appendix A: Sample Planning Document	**501**
Database server information	501
Siebel File System-related information	502
Web server-related information	502
Siebel Gateway Name Server installation and configuration	503
Siebel Enterprise Server configuration	504
Siebel Web Server Extension logical profile configuration	504
Siebel Server installation and configuration	506
Installing the Siebel database	507
Siebel Web Server Extension installation and configuration	508
Example topology	508
Appendix B: Uninstalling Siebel CRM Software	**511**
Uninstalling Siebel CRM server software on Microsoft Windows	**511**
Verifying the Siebel Server uninstaller	515
Uninstalling Siebel CRM server software on Linux or UNIX	**515**
Uninstalling Siebel CRM client software	**516**
Appendix C: More Information	**517**
Getting trained	**517**
Finding information	**518**
The Siebel Bookshelf	518
Oracle Forums	519
My Oracle Support	519
The Internet community	519
Index	**521**

Preface

Oracle's Siebel CRM is the market-leading Customer Relationship Management software. Unmatched in functionality and scalability, it offers a lot of challenges for the system administrator. This book will be your safe vessel while navigating the deep waters of installing and managing Siebel CRM.

This book is a complete exercise in installing and managing Oracle's Siebel CRM 8 for your organization. You will understand the Siebel architecture and install it piece by piece. In easy-to-follow chapters, the book guides you through the installation of Siebel server, client, and third-party reporting software on Microsoft Windows and Linux. We begin with the planning process, cover downloading the software, and explain the exact installation and configuration tasks.

After reading this book, you will feel fully prepared for setting up multiple Siebel servers and multi-lingual configurations. Not only does the book give you step-by-step instructions, it also fosters your general understanding of the intricate features and functionality of Oracle's Siebel CRM. For example, you will understand how data security works. In addition, you will learn how to support development environments and how to migrate configuration changes between environments using Application Deployment Manager.

Another benefit of this book is that it teaches administrators how to establish system monitoring strategies to identify and avoid performance bottlenecks.

This book provides a practical, hands-on experience. Chapter by chapter, a Siebel CRM self-study environment is created that can be used to follow the examples described in the book and to explore Siebel CRM functionality. The book ensures that you understand what you are doing and why you are doing it. It contains clear step-by-step instructions, explanatory tables, screenshots, and precise diagrams.

What this book covers

Chapter 1, *Introducing the Siebel Web Architecture* lays the foundation for a clear understanding of the Siebel Web Architecture. You will learn about its building blocks and you will be able to describe their functionality and purpose.

Chapter 2, *Planning and Preparing the Installation* introduces you to the planning and preparation process, which ensures that you are able to install and configure Siebel CRM server software flawlessly.

Chapter 3, *Installing Siebel Server Software on Microsoft Windows* guides you through the process of installing Siebel CRM server software on Microsoft Windows step by step.

Chapter 4, *Configuring Siebel Server Software on Microsoft Windows* shows you how to use the Siebel Configuration Wizard to configure Siebel server software and conduct an initial installation of the Siebel server database. The chapter also introduces you to verification and finalization steps.

Chapter 5, *Installing and Configuring Siebel Server Software on Linux* teaches you to install and configure Siebel CRM server software successfully on Linux using step-by-step instructions.

Chapter 6, *Installing Siebel Client Software* guides you through the installation of the Siebel Mobile or Developer Web Client, the Siebel Sample Database, and Siebel Tools. In addition, you will learn how to apply patches to Siebel software.

Chapter 7, *Installing Additional Server Software* explains how to support end users with charting and reporting functionality by installing the Visual Mining NetCharts Server and Oracle BI Publisher.

Chapter 8, *Special Server Configurations* enables you to install multiple Siebel Servers and configure Siebel Load Balancing. You will also learn how to apply additional language packs and support multi-lingual Siebel CRM deployments.

Chapter 9, *Server Management* provides full insight into the configuration and management of Siebel Enterprises. The chapter introduces the structure of a Siebel Enterprise and guides you through typical administrator tasks in the Siebel user interface and the Siebel Server Manager command line.

Chapter 10, *Authentication* makes you an expert in user authentication. Besides understanding the mechanism of database authentication, you will learn how to configure LDAP directory authentication and Web Single-Sign-On.

Chapter 11, *Authorization and Access Control* strengthens your general understanding of Siebel CRM functionality by providing deep insight into the concepts of user authorization, data access, and personalization.

Chapter 12, *Managing User Accounts* enables you to set up the organization and position hierarchy in Siebel CRM and create user accounts.

Chapter 13, *Siebel Remote and the Siebel Development Environment* shows how to support the development team and how the Siebel Remote module allows you to create local databases. In addition, the chapter teaches you how to support mobile users.

Chapter 14, *Installing the Siebel Management Server* explains how the Siebel Management Server and Siebel Management Agents provide the framework for Siebel modules such as Application Deployment Manager and Siebel Diagnostic Tool. You will learn how to install and configure the Siebel Management Server infrastructure in this chapter.

Chapter 15, *Migrating Configuration Changes between Environments* guides you through the complete process of migrating configuration changes from development to test or production enterprises using Application Deployment Manager and the Siebel Upgrade Wizard.

Chapter 16, *Monitoring Siebel Applications* lets you know how to use the following tools to efficiently monitor the performance and usage of Siebel applications: Event Logging, SARM, Diagnostic Tool, Client Side Logging, and Usage Collection.

Appendix A, *Sample Planning Document* supports you with your first steps and contains a complete example planning document.

Appendix B, *Uninstalling Siebel Application Software* shows you how to uninstall Siebel CRM software (if you have to).

Appendix C, *More Information* gives you information on where to find more information on Oracle Siebel CRM.

What you need for this book

This book is for a technical audience. You will get most out of this book if you have a solid information technology (IT) background and familiarity with operating systems and relational databases. If you have experience with enterprise-class information systems, consider this an additional benefit.

It is strongly recommended to use additional resources on your Siebel learning path. The course offerings of Oracle University (http://education.oracle.com) are a perfect start.

Preface

Who this book is for

The book is written with the role of a system administrator in mind who has to ramp up quickly on Siebel CRM, focusing on typical tasks such as installing and managing the Siebel CRM infrastructure.

Conventions

In this book, you will find a number of styles of text that distinguish between different kinds of information. Here are some examples of these styles, and an explanation of their meaning.

Code words in text are shown as follows: "We can include other contexts through the use of the include directive."

A block of code is set as follows:

```
create user GUESTCST identified by 8icJIPZH;
grant sse_role to GUESTCST;
alter user GUESTCST default tablespace SIEBELDB_DATA;
alter user GUESTCST temporary tablespace TEMP;
```

Any command-line input or output is written as follows:

```
list tasks for comp SCC% show CC_ALIAS, TK_DISP_RUNSTATE(10), TK_LABEL
```

New terms and **important words** are shown in bold. Words that you see on the screen, in menus or dialog boxes for example, appear in the text like this: "Click the **Manual Start** button.".

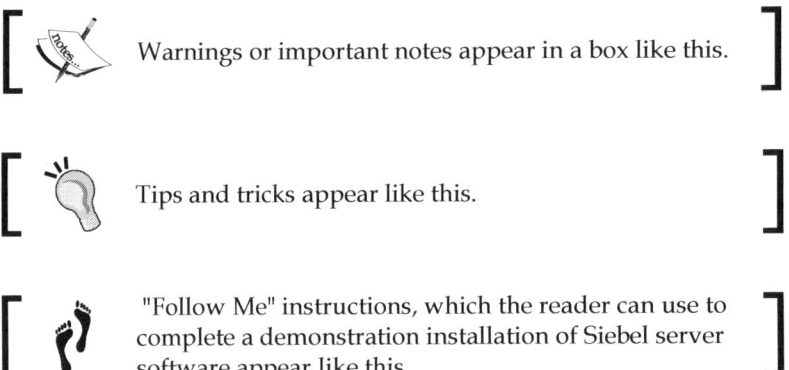

[Warnings or important notes appear in a box like this.]

[Tips and tricks appear like this.]

["Follow Me" instructions, which the reader can use to complete a demonstration installation of Siebel server software appear like this.]

[4]

Reader feedback

Feedback from our readers is always welcome. Let us know what you think about this book—what you liked or may have disliked. Reader feedback is important for us to develop titles that you really get the most out of.

To send us general feedback, simply send an e-mail to `feedback@packtpub.com`, and mention the book title via the subject of your message.

If there is a book that you need and would like to see us publish, please send us a note in the **SUGGEST A TITLE** form on `www.packtpub.com` or e-mail `suggest@packtpub.com`.

If there is a topic that you have expertise in and you are interested in either writing or contributing to a book on, see our author guide on `www.packtpub.com/authors`.

Customer support

Now that you are the proud owner of a Packt book, we have a number of things to help you to get the most from your purchase.

Errata

Although we have taken every care to ensure the accuracy of our content, mistakes do happen. If you find a mistake in one of our books—maybe a mistake in the text or the code—we would be grateful if you would report this to us. By doing so, you can save other readers from frustration and help us improve subsequent versions of this book. If you find any errata, please report them by visiting `http://www.packtpub.com/support`, selecting your book, clicking on the **let us know** link, and entering the details of your errata. Once your errata are verified, your submission will be accepted and the errata will be uploaded on our website, or added to any list of existing errata, under the Errata section of that title. Any existing errata can be viewed by selecting your title from `http://www.packtpub.com/support`.

Piracy

Piracy of copyright material on the Internet is an ongoing problem across all media. At Packt, we take the protection of our copyright and licenses very seriously. If you come across any illegal copies of our works, in any form, on the Internet, please provide us with the location address or website name immediately so that we can pursue a remedy.

Please contact us at copyright@packtpub.com with a link to the suspected pirated material.

We appreciate your help in protecting our authors, and our ability to bring you valuable content.

Questions

You can contact us at questions@packtpub.com if you are having a problem with any aspect of the book, and we will do our best to address it.

Introducing the Siebel Web Architecture

Installing and managing a complex enterprise application such as Oracle's Siebel CRM can be challenging. Whether you consider yourself a seasoned IT professional or a beginner: once we add concepts such as load balancing or multiple language deployment, it is easy to get lost.

The reason why you are reading this book might have been stated above. In this book, we are going to follow a typical Siebel CRM installation procedure. Additionally, we will look under the hood and learn how to manage all those different pieces of software.

Understanding the building blocks of Oracle's Siebel CRM applications as well as knowing how to avoid general pitfalls during installation and system management are of course great benefits. We can then execute our Siebel CRM projects more quickly and subsequently with less cost and risk.

When you finish this book, you will not only be able to successfully master the installation and system management procedures, you will also have the advantage of a deep understanding of the intricacies of Siebel CRM.

Instead of starting the setup program in a rush to see what happens, we should first understand what we are going to install. It is therefore strongly recommended to follow the course of this book. The topics in this book are arranged so that each chapter builds upon the previous one. The following is a list of what we will learn:

- Understanding the Siebel web architecture
- Planning and preparing a Siebel CRM installation
- Installing the Siebel CRM server and client software on different operating systems

- Installing ancillary server software
- Configuring load balancing and installing language packs
- Managing Siebel Servers
- Provisioning external authentication
- Understanding and managing data security
- Supporting developer teams and mobile users
- Deploying configuration changes
- Measuring application performance

This chapter sets the stage with an overview of the Siebel Web Architecture. We will describe the building blocks of the latter in order to be able to lay out a concise planning document and use a structured approach during the installation and configuration procedures.

The Siebel web architecture

In order to allow thousands of users access to critical enterprise data over the web channel, Siebel CRM is based on a typical web architecture. This architecture allows for great scalability and platform compatibility and has been under development for more than a decade.

> In 2001, Siebel released version 7.0 of its CRM suite. This was the first version that was completely web-based. Prior versions (like Siebel 2000) were based on the client-server architecture, which was typical for enterprise applications in the 90s.
>
> However, Siebel 7.0 was not the first version that allowed access to data and functionality from a web browser. Applications like Siebel eService or Siebel eSales were available in earlier versions and the Siebel web architecture as we see it today had its origin in these first customer facing web applications.

The Siebel web architecture consists of the following main building blocks:

- A **relational database** to store customer, administrative, and repository data
- A shared **directory** structure to store binary, non-relational information such as attachment documents and temporary files

- One or more **Siebel Servers**, which are grouped together in a **Siebel Enterprise** server
- The **Siebel Gateway Name Server** to manage and store the enterprise configuration
- A **web server**
- The **Siebel Web Server Extension (SWSE)**, installed on the web server
- A **web browser** to display the graphical user interface

Let us bring these building blocks together in a diagram:

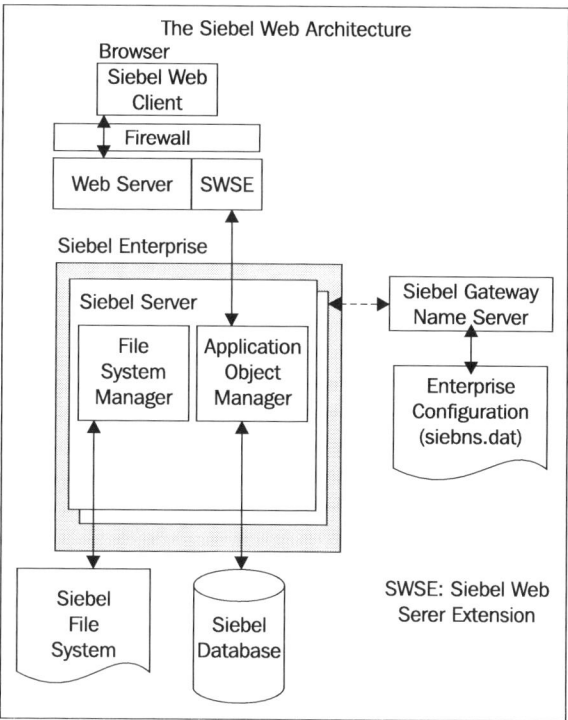

The diagram above depicts the Siebel Web Architecture. In the following section, we will discuss each of the major building blocks in detail.

The Siebel database

Whenever a salesperson looks up customer information, a call center agent enters a new trouble ticket, or a customer drops an item into the shopping cart on the Internet, all this information must be stored in a database. Siebel CRM is no exception to that rule. Relational database management systems (RDBMS) do a great job in storing any type of data and Siebel CRM supports a variety of versions and vendors.

The following table lists database system vendors (in alphabetical order), products, and versions supported by Siebel CRM 8.1 (Source: Siebel System Requirements and Supported Platforms, Version 8.1).

Vendor	Product	Version
IBM	DB2 for Windows and Unix based OS	9.1 FixPak 4 or above
IBM	DB2 UDB for z/OS	8 or above
Microsoft	SQL Server	2005 SP1 or above
Oracle	Enterprise Server	10g
Oracle	Enterprise Server	11g

In addition to the above list, Siebel Remote, Siebel Tools, and the Application Deployment Manager use an embedded database engine from Sybase (Adaptive Server Anywhere). The version currently supported by Siebel CRM 8.1 is 9.0.1. Supported software vendors, platforms, and product versions are listed in the Siebel System Requirements and Supported Platforms document (SR&SP), which is published along with each release of Siebel CRM. SR&SPs can be downloaded from Oracle's Technology Network website at `http://otn.oracle.com` in the Documentation section.

What we need to know about the Siebel database is that it is used to store all the customer, administrative, and repository data. No business logic, such as constraints, primary keys, or foreign key references, is implemented at the database level. So, we can imagine the Siebel database simply as a place to store all the relational data we need in order to run the system.

The Siebel File System

Not all data needed by end users such as salespersons or call center agents can be easily stowed away in a set of tables in a relational database. People often rely on graphical information such as charts or images, additional descriptions, documents downloaded from the Internet, spreadsheets, and so on to get a more complete view of the relational data such as the customer information they see in the Siebel client.

Technically, the Siebel File System is a shared directory with a number of subdirectories. Most of these subdirectories are created during the installation process but some are added manually when specialized modules such as Siebel Search are set up.

Whenever an end user, an external system, or internal processes upload file-based information, the file is compressed, and stored in the directory tree. We can see a typical Siebel File System directory tree in the screenshot below:

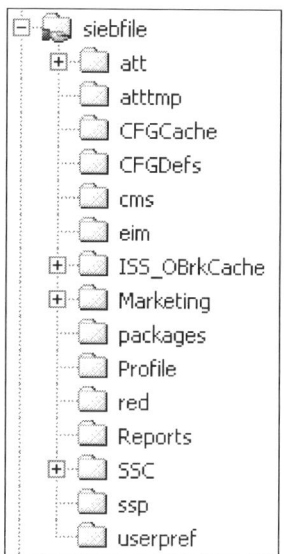

For files that need to be accessed and downloaded by end users or external systems, Siebel CRM creates a record in a database table that points to the file. Because the files are compressed, and stored in a network share that is typically not accessible by the average user, the level of information security is very high. Even if we could locate a file stored in the Siebel File System, we would not be able to read the information contained in the file unless we uncompressed it using either the Siebel application or command line utilities provided by Oracle.

Introducing the Siebel Web Architecture

The following screenshot illustrates how a document attached to a customer record can be located and downloaded from the Siebel Web Client using the Attachments view in the **Accounts** screen.

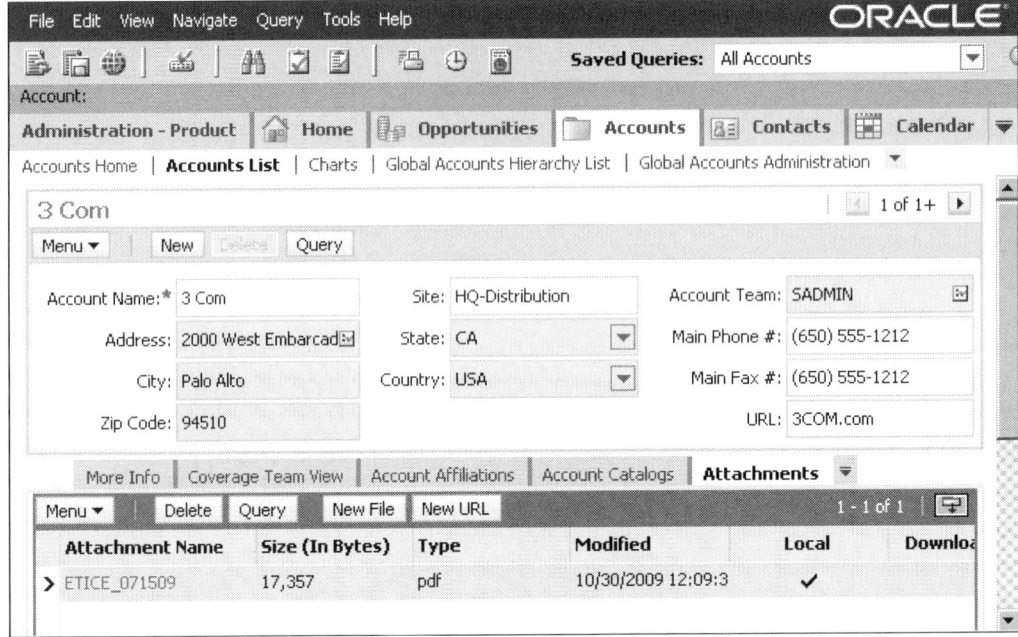

A PDF file has been uploaded using the **New File** button. End users can now access the file by clicking on the hyperlink in the **Attachment Name** column.

The Siebel Enterprise Server

Even though we can install and manage several Siebel Enterprise Servers in our network infrastructure, an Enterprise Server is not a piece of software but merely a logical collection of Siebel Servers that access the same Siebel database and file system, and which are managed by a single Siebel Gateway Name Server.

The Siebel Gateway Name Server

A Siebel Enterprise may consist of dozens of Siebel Servers, each running dozens of components—programs which implement a specific functionality. Each of these components has different parameter values. In order to easily manage all this information across the entire Enterprise, Siebel has developed the Gateway Name Server. It is a service or daemon process that stores the entire enterprise configuration in a text file named `siebns.dat`, hence the official name of the file is "Enterprise Configuration Store".

In order to understand the role of the Gateway Name Server properly, we can examine the following scenario:

A Siebel administrator stops all Siebel services. He then tries to start the Siebel Servers without starting the Gateway Name Server. An error message indicates that the Siebel Server could not start.

This is because the only piece of information that a Siebel Server has at the moment of startup is the hostname of a Gateway Name Server, which it immediately tries to contact in order to retrieve more configuration information.

So, the Gateway Name Server is a critical component of the Siebel Web Architecture because it must be present when any Siebel Server starts up or configuration changes have to be applied. However, if the Gateway Name Server fails during normal operation, end users and external systems will still be able to access the Siebel applications and functionality provided by the Siebel Servers. But, it is of course a good idea to monitor the Gateway Name Server and bring it back to life as soon as possible if it should fail.

The Siebel Server

Processes that interact with end users, or external systems that access data in the Siebel database, or files in the Siebel File System, are all located on one or more Siebel Servers. Each Siebel Server is a member of just one enterprise. In more technical terms, a Siebel Server is an application server. An application server is a generic container for applications or programs that are made available for access by other systems.

Being just that, an application server, the Siebel Server hosts so-called components, that implement the various pieces of Siebel functionality such as providing end user sessions, uploading files to the Siebel File System, exchanging data with external systems, and so forth.

Introducing the Siebel Web Architecture

For the sake of scalability and preventing single points of failure, installing more than one Siebel Server is very common. This allows administrators to assign components to explicit servers and avoid poor performance when end users or external systems produce heavy load.

The software units on the Siebel Server that are needed to support Siebel applications include:

- Application Object Manager (AOM)
- Configuration Parameters
- Data Manager (DM)
- Siebel Repository File (SRF)
- Siebel Web Engine (SWE)
- Siebel Web Templates (SWT)

The Application Object Manager (AOM)

If we look at the Siebel Web Architecture from an end user's perspective, a component must exist on the Siebel Server that handles all requests made by the user as he or she clicks in the browser window. Components of this type are called Application Object Manager. They are programs that handle all user interactions such as authentication, data access, and rendering of the pages passed back to the user's browser. In other words, they execute the complete application logic on behalf of the end user. If we could place an application object manager under a microscope, this is what we would see:

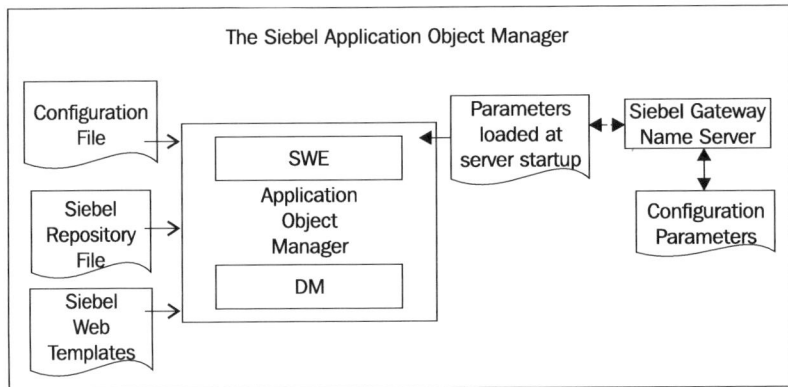

In the following section, we will discuss the software units and files that are constitutional parts of the Siebel application architecture.

Configuration parameters

It is correct to think of the Application Object Manager as a generic program that acts upon a specific set of parameters for each incarnation. These parameters have historically been stored in text files on the Siebel Server. The files, with an extension of .cfg, are still present in modern Siebel CRM versions but only a tiny fraction of the parameters that drive the behavior of the Application Object Manager originate there.

The second and more important portion of parameters is stored and managed by the Siebel Gateway Name Server and loaded into the Siebel Server's memory when it starts up.

Data Manager (DM)

This is the application object manager's access layer against the relational data sources. Using specific dynamic link libraries (dll) on Microsoft Windows or shared objects (so) on UNIX-based operating systems, the data manager layer generates database vendor-specific SQL statements.

Siebel Repository File (SRF)

As we can see in the object manager diagram, the application object manager reads a file with a .srf extension. This file, known as the Siebel Repository File, contains a structured representation of the application metadata, which allows the object manager to quickly derive vital information such as table and column names, business logic, and user interface layout. The Siebel Repository File is consumed not only by the application object manager component type but also by other Siebel Server components that need access to metadata information.

Siebel Web Engine (SWE)

A request coming in from an end user or an external system is basically a set of commands towards the Siebel Web Engine (SWE). The SWE parses the commands and calls functions of underlying programs in order to satisfy the request. Other modules of the application object manager execute the business logic or access the database to retrieve the necessary data. The SWE is also responsible for building the result pages, which are then passed back to the browser.

Introducing the Siebel Web Architecture

Siebel Web Templates (SWT)

Many of the layout elements of the Siebel user interface such as lists or forms are repetitive in their style (for example a list will always contain a top banner with button controls and the columns in the list will always have a header and body text). For this reason, the HTML for these elements does not need to be generated on the fly. It can rather be stored in text files that are read by the Siebel Web Engine.

These files are named Siebel Web Templates and typically have a suffix of .swt. If we examine these files more closely we find that they contain typical HTML tags such as <table> but also tags that are proprietary commands for the Siebel Web Engine. These <swe:> tags are replaced with content rendered by the Siebel Web Engine at runtime.

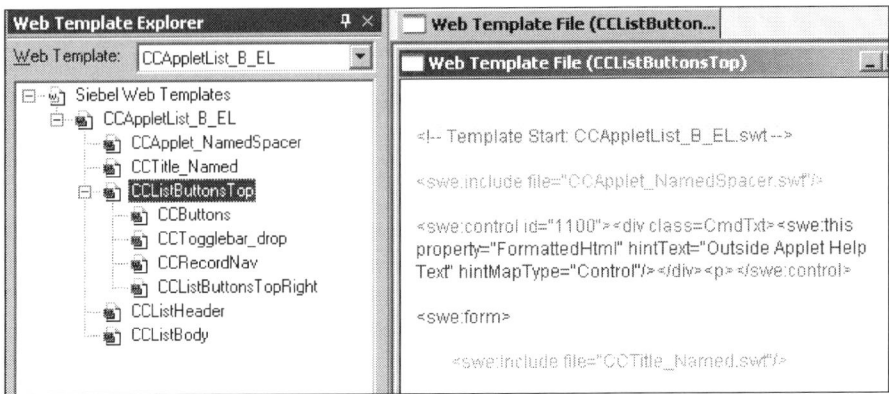

The above screenshot shows a Siebel Web Template opened in the Web Template Explorer provided by Siebel Tools, the development environment of Siebel CRM.

The web server

As the entire communication with the browser on the end user's computer has to be done via http, a web server is a vital part of the Siebel Web Architecture. Siebel CRM supports a variety of vendors and products such as Microsoft's Internet Information Services, HP Web Server (Apache), or Oracle HTTP Server (Apache).

The web server has to exist but does not need to take heavy load. As we have seen above, the Application Object Manager handles all incoming requests. So, the web server's only task is to pass requests to the application object manager and pass the result back to the end user's browser.

[16]

It is exactly at this point where questions should be raised. How can a third-party web server communicate with a proprietary application server? (We learned that the Siebel Server is not a standard application server.) The solution is just at hand in the form of a piece of software that is installed on the web server in order to teach it the internal Siebel protocol. This is where the Siebel Web Server Extension enters the stage.

The Siebel Web Server Extension

The Siebel Web Server Extension (SWSE) enables any supported web server to communicate with the object managers on the various Siebel Servers. The SWSE serves as a plug-in and enables the web server to forward incoming request URLs from the end user's browser to the application object manager session on the Siebel Server.

Among the more interesting capabilities of the SWSE is the authentication of user sessions and load balancing. The SWSE reads a configuration file named `eapps.cfg` that links each virtual directory on the web server to a process on the Siebel Server. This process is implemented as a server component named Siebel Connection Broker.

The following diagram illustrates how the SWSE connects to the appropriate Application Object Manager on one of the Siebel Servers on the network:

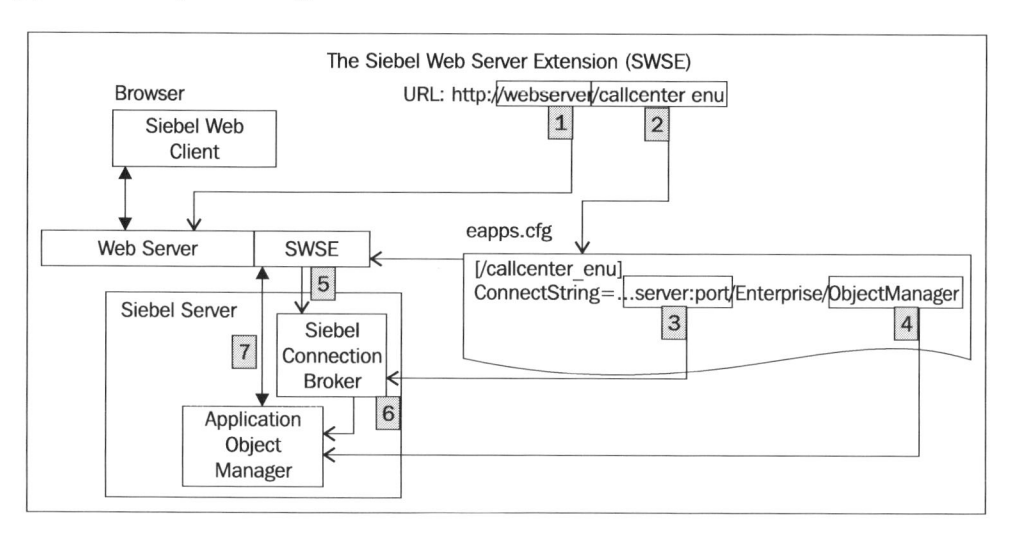

1. The first part of the URL entered into the browser's address bar points to the web server that hosts the Siebel Web Server Extension.

2. The second part of the URL references a virtual directory on the web server. The naming convention (as suggested by Oracle but not written in stone) is "application_language". So, the above diagram shows an example of a connection to the Siebel Call Center application in American English (enu = English—United States). Each "application_language" string is stored as a section in the `eapps.cfg` file read by the Siebel Web Server Extension.

3. In the section in the `eapps.cfg` file, the SWSE can read the Siebel Server hostname and the port number of the Siebel Connection Broker component.

4. In addition, the SWSE reads the internal name of the Application Object Manager instance.

5. The SWSE can now connect to the Siebel Connection Broker component and request a session for the Application Object Manager.

6. The Siebel Connection Broker forwards the request to the appropriate process on the Siebel Server.

7. The connection between the SWSE and the Application Object Manager is now established.

The browser and the Siebel user interface

We cannot discuss web-based architectures without talking about web browsers. As we know, the Siebel Web Engine renders the result pages, which are then passed back to the user's browser window. Siebel applications come with a pre-built user interface that can be distributed in two modes, namely **High-Interactivity (HI)** Mode and **Standard Interactivity (SI)** Mode. HI mode provides for very high usability. For example, drag and drop operations, scrolling through lists of records, the right-click context menu, and the wizard-style Task User Interface are features that are only available in the HI mode. The penalty for this high level of user friendliness is the limited set of supported browsers. In fact—because HI mode uses Microsoft's **ActiveX** technology—Microsoft Internet Explorer is the only browser that is supported for Siebel applications in HI mode. The following screenshot shows the Siebel Sales application in High-Interactivity mode running in Microsoft Internet Explorer:

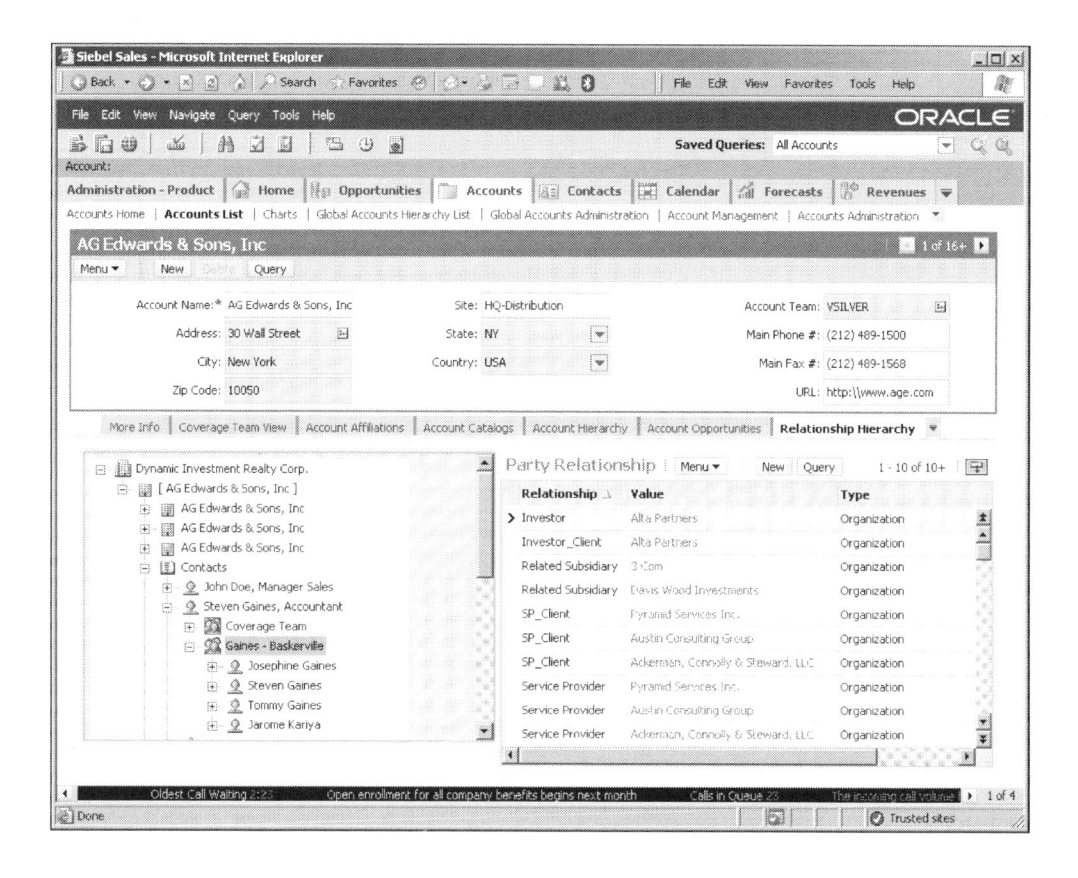

Introducing the Siebel Web Architecture

Other browsers like Firefox or Safari are supported only for Siebel applications in SI mode. The following screenshot shows the Siebel Partner Portal application in Standard-Interactivity Mode in Mozilla Firefox.

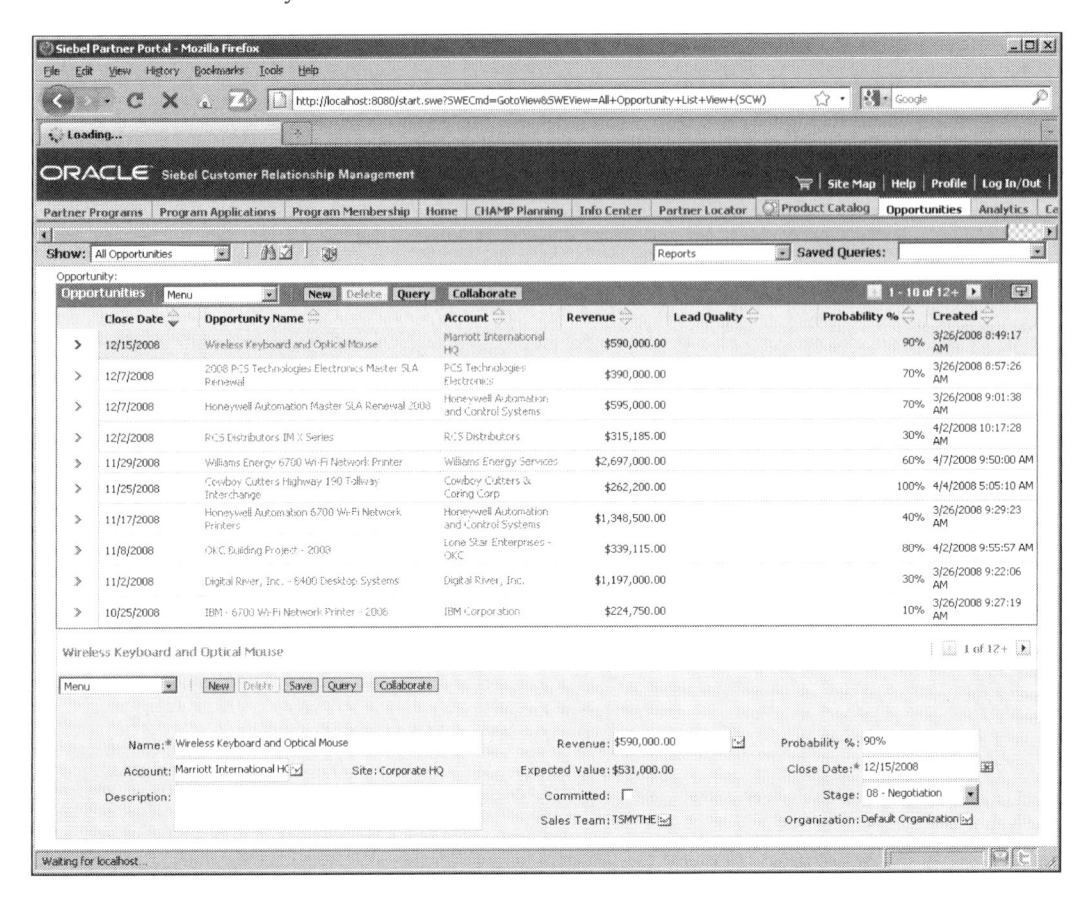

There are even more ways to generate a rich user experience. The Siebel Enterprise Application Integration (EAI) framework provides pre-built web services and capabilities to support any external application, from a simple browser to middleware-based UI generators, to access the Siebel data and business logic in order to generate their own UI.

> A Siebel application can display data from and write data to multiple data sources. including non-relational sources.
>
> Siebel CRM has a proprietary protocol named SISNAPI (Siebel Internet Session Network Application Programming Interface), which allows processes external to the application object manager to communicate with the latter.

Summary

Installing Siebel CRM is a complex endeavour that involves multiple professionals. In this chapter, we learned the fundamentals of the Siebel web architecture and how this infrastructure provides enterprise class applications to large end user audiences.

In this chapter, we named the building blocks that are needed to run Oracle's Siebel CRM applications.

In the next chapter, we will learn how to plan and prepare the installation of the Siebel CRM infrastructure.

Planning and Preparing the Installation

When tackling the complex task of installing and configuring Oracle's Siebel CRM, we should keep in mind that a well-considered approach and proper documentation are key factors for a successful completion.

In this chapter, we will discuss the following steps of the Siebel installation process:

- Planning the Siebel CRM Installation
- Understanding hardware and software prerequisites
- Hardware sizing
- Preparing the Siebel database
- Preparing the Siebel file system
- Creating service owner accounts
- Downloading the Siebel installation archives
- Running the Siebel Image Creator
- Obtaining the license key

The overall process of planning and preparation can be described as follows. The following flowchart describes the major steps of the process of planning and preparing a Siebel CRM installation. In this chapter, we will describe each step in detail.

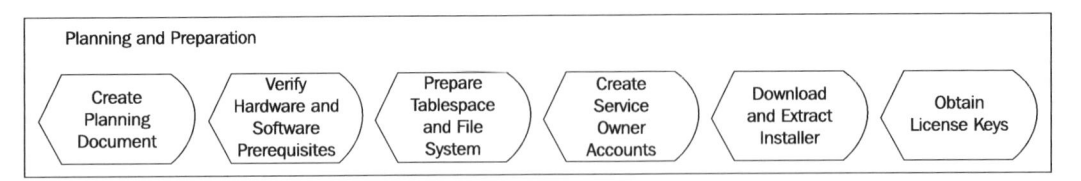

Planning and Preparation: Create Planning Document → Verify Hardware and Software Prerequisites → Prepare Tablespace and File System → Create Service Owner Accounts → Download and Extract Installer → Obtain License Keys

Planning the Siebel CRM installation

Implementing Siebel CRM for thousands of users in corporations that do business across the globe is not something a single person would do on a single day. Sometimes, hundreds of technicians, IT architects and business analysts are involved to fulfil the company's requirements. Siebel CRM projects can be costly, lengthy, and sometimes risky expeditions into rough terrain.

In a typical Siebel CRM project, people from various companies—integrators and IT staff of the customer—work together to install and set up the different Siebel environments from first prototyping areas over the development, test, and training environments, to the final production environment.

Siebel and third-party software for these environments are typically installed on multiple server machines and it is not unusual to find a mix of operating systems.

What is expected from us—being the reliable and trustworthy expert that the customer hired to install Siebel CRM on their systems—is a **planning document**. The key to a useful planning document is knowledge about the customer's IT infrastructure, as well as the Siebel installation and configuration processes.

The following is an example of a typical planning document that provides all the information that is needed to successfully install the Siebel CRM infrastructure on Microsoft Windows machines. The official Siebel Installation Guide includes a Deployment Planning Worksheet, which can serve as a starting point. In a real life project, we can use any spreadsheet application to create and collaborate on this information.

You can find a complete sample planning document in the appendix section of this book.

> For the sake of example and simplicity, passwords in the sample document are written in clear text. In a real life project, we must ensure that no sensitive information is included in the document. Rather, we can use common encryption tools to secure the information or leave references in the planning document to where the information is.

Sample planning document

The following table is a sample planning document for information regarding the relational database management system (RDBMS) to host the Siebel database. We record information about the RDBMS vendor and version as well as the machine hostname and administrative user account. For a typical Siebel CRM installation, we also plan the creation of two tablespaces. Details on how to create tablespaces and undertake other prerequisite installation steps are described later in this chapter.

Component/Parameter	Name/Value Examples	Description
Database Server Vendor	Oracle	
Database Server Version	11gR1	
DB Server System Account/Password	sys/T67PBhtr as SYSDBA	Needed to connect directly to the database to run the grantusr.sql script.
Database Server hostname	dbsrvr1	
DB host admin user	Administrator	
DB host admin user password	XBXfi8F9	See the note on password examples.
Database Server port	1521	
Database Server SID	ORCL	
Siebel DB index tablespace	SIEBELDB_IDX	This tablespace will hold the indexes of the Siebel CRM schema.
Siebel DB data tablespace	SIEBELDB_DATA	This tablespace will hold the data tables of the Siebel CRM schema.

More planning information

Of course, a decent planning document contains more than just a series of tables. Sometimes, we might need to bring specialists on board to define the necessary amount of servers, the hardware configuration, and so forth.

Security-related information such as user accounts, remote access settings, or simply the phone numbers of the firewall administrators, can help the project team to finish a Siebel CRM infrastructure provisioning on time.

Certainly, the project plan will include a timeline. We will not go into details of project management in this book, but we should ensure that our project plan provides enough time and money for training—for both technicians and the end user community.

Understanding hardware and software prerequisites

Many problems in Siebel CRM projects arise from improper planning. As we learned, delivering a decent planning document is a key milestone of our Siebel CRM implementation project.

The success of the installation process we will start in the next chapter relies on the correct installation of third-party software on the correct hardware.

Therefore, it is very important that any person involved in planning and conducting a Siebel CRM installation has access to the **Siebel System Requirements and Supported Platforms** document that can be downloaded from the Oracle Technology Network website: `http://download.oracle.com/docs/cd/E11886_01/srsphomepage.html`.

This document is available for each individual Siebel CRM version and outlines in detail the minimum hardware requirements and software prerequisites.

For example, if we plan to provide a prototype environment for evaluation and testing of Siebel CRM 8.1 and would like to use Microsoft Windows Server 2003 as the operating system, we would have to provision hardware and software as follows:

Siebel Component	Minimum Processor Requirements	Minimum Memory Requirements
Siebel Server	2 PIII XEON 500 MHz	1 GB
Siebel Gateway Name Server	PIII XEON 500 MHz	256 MB
Web Server	PIII XEON 500 MHz	512 MB

(Source: Siebel System Requirements and Supported Platforms, Version 8.1)

If we were to install these components on a single piece of hardware, we would have to provision a 4 CPU unit (2 for the Siebel Server, 1 for the Siebel Gateway Name Server, and 1 for the Web Server) with at least 1.7 GB (1 GB plus 256 MB + 512 MB) of free memory for the Siebel components, which would be a physical minimum of 2 GB of memory as the operating system will also be hungry for memory.

Sizing the Siebel deployment

Installing Siebel CRM for personal evaluation or prototyping is one thing, providing a stable and high performing enterprise application to hundreds or thousands of end users is quite another challenge.

In certain phases of the Siebel CRM implementation project, consultants and IT staff will have to deliver a sizing document that provides insight into the expected number of end users and their concurrent sessions.

The necessary amount of hardware units and software components is dependent on these main factors:

- Maximum number of concurrent user sessions
- Expected volume of data and indexes
- Hardware vendor
- Operating system type
- Database vendor
- Network bandwidth
- High-availability and failover requirements

Each of these has to be considered and evaluated. Customers typically rely on the services of experienced staff from either Oracle or consulting corporations to accomplish this.

Preparing the Siebel database

At a typical customer site, the IT department will already have multiple relational databases in place for their existing enterprise systems. To prepare the installation of Siebel CRM, we have to ensure that sufficient tablespace is provisioned on the RDBMS.

The following is an example for the Oracle database and assumes that the Oracle RDBMS has already been installed and a database instance has been created following the instructions in the Siebel Installation Guide.

We can use an SQL script similar to the sample code below via the command line or any suitable software tool to create two tablespaces, one for the Siebel tables and the other for the indexes. This is a recommended practice as the Siebel installation wizard will prompt us for the names of two tablespaces.

```
rem ================================================
rem create initial tablespace for Siebel data tables
rem ================================================
CREATE SMALLFILE TABLESPACE "SIEBELDB_DATA" DATAFILE 'C:\ORACLE\
PRODUCT\10.2.0\ORADATA\ORCL\SIEBELDB_DATA.DBF' SIZE 500M AUTOEXTEND
ON NEXT 10M MAXSIZE UNLIMITED LOGGING EXTENT MANAGEMENT LOCAL SEGMENT
SPACE MANAGEMENT AUTO;
rem ================================================
rem create initial tablespace for Siebel indexes
rem ================================================
CREATE SMALLFILE TABLESPACE "SIEBELDB_IDX" DATAFILE 'C:\ORACLE\
PRODUCT\10.2.0\ORADATA\ORCL\SIEBELDB_IDX.DBF' SIZE 500M AUTOEXTEND ON
NEXT 10M MAXSIZE UNLIMITED LOGGING EXTENT MANAGEMENT LOCAL SEGMENT
SPACE MANAGEMENT AUTO;
```

When we run this script, one tablespace named SIEBELDB_DATA and a second one named SIEBELDB_IDX with an initial size of 500 MB will be created. Both tablespaces will be automatically extended by intervals of 10 MB with no limit.

Other tasks for the process of preparing the Oracle database for an initial Siebel CRM installation include:

- Setting global parameters for the database
- Sizing the redo logs
- Creating additional tablespaces
- Setting user roles and privileges

We can use the management tools provided by the database vendor to inspect the Siebel database and verify the settings. The following screenshot shows information about the two tablespaces for the Siebel database in Oracle Enterprise Manager:

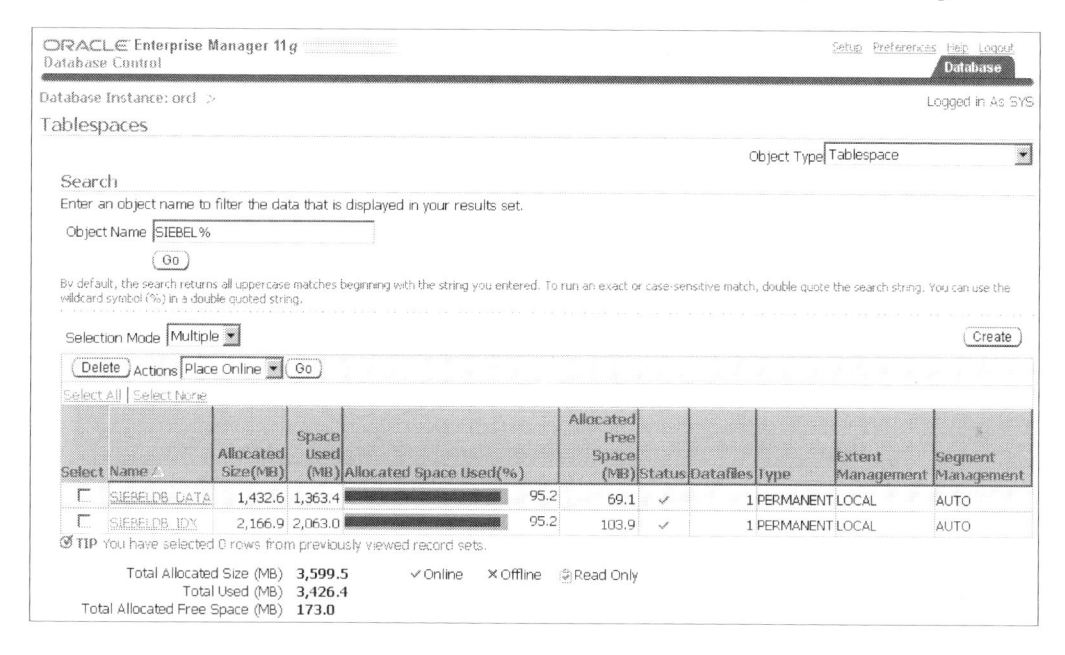

Planning and Preparing the Installation

> If you wish to follow along with your own installation of Siebel CRM, you can use the Follow Me boxes in the chapters of this book.
>
> As we have discussed the database settings, you can start with installing and setting up an Oracle 10g or 11g enterprise database on a machine that suits the hardware requirements for a simple test instance. The author's recommendation is to use a virtual machine with a fully licensed Microsoft Windows Server operating system.
>
> You should run this virtual machine on a physical host machine with at least 2 GB (4 GB is better) of physical memory and sufficient disk space (20 GB of free disk space is a minimum to store the installation, database, and Siebel software installation files). Any modern laptop or desktop model should have sufficient CPU power to support your first Siebel CRM installation. However, you should take care and invest some time to limit the memory footprint of the virtual machine to an absolute minimum. You can do so for example by setting unnecessary services to manual start.
>
> If you need to download the Oracle database installers, visit `otn.oracle.com` and navigate to the download section for the Oracle database software. In the OTN License agreement available at `http://www.oracle.com/technology/software/popup-license/standard-license.html`, Oracle grants us a
>
> "…nonexclusive, nontransferable limited license to use the programs only for the purpose of developing, testing, prototyping and demonstrating…"
>
> Follow the instructions in the Oracle documentation to install the Oracle database server. You might want to check the sample database option, which has the benefit that when the installer finishes, a database instance (ORCL) is already present.
>
> Once you have installed and started the Oracle database, you can modify and run the scripts explained in this chapter or use your tool of choice to create the tablespaces for the Siebel database.

Creating the service owner account

Because the Siebel Gateway Name Server and Siebel Server are implemented as services (on Microsoft Windows-based operating systems) or daemon processes (on UNIX-based operating systems), the processes must run on behalf of an account with certain administrative rights.

On Microsoft Windows-based operating systems, we must ensure that a system user account with the following characteristics is provisioned on each machine that will host the Siebel services and the Siebel File System before the Siebel installation process is started:

- The service owner account must either be part of a Windows domain or identical local accounts will have to be created locally
- Usernames and passwords must not contain any spaces
- The password policy must not be set to "User must change password at next logon" (uncheck this value) and must be set to "Password never expires" (check this value)
- The service owner account must be a member of the Administrators group.
- The service owner account must have the following user rights assigned in the Windows security policies:
    - Log on as a service
    - Act as part of the operating system

The following screenshot shows the local security policy setting "Act as part of the operating system" for the local user account "SIEBELSVC" on Microsoft Windows:

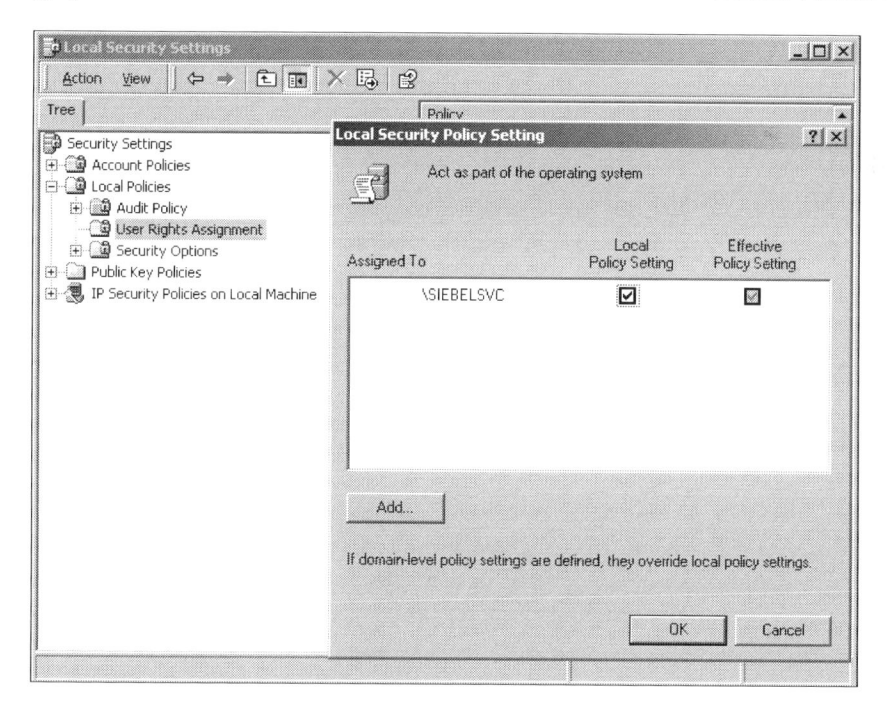

[31]

> Navigate to the user management on your demonstration machine and create a local user account with the settings discussed in the previous section.
>
> Ensure that you add the user account to the Administrators group.
>
> Then, navigate to the local security policy management in the Microsoft Windows Administrative Tools and assign the policies mentioned in the previous section to the newly created user account.

Creating the Siebel File System root folder

As we have learned in the chapter on the Siebel web architecture, the Siebel File System is a set of directories to store non-relational data. Luckily, the generation of these directories is managed by the Siebel installers; we only have to provide a shared directory.

Using the tools provided by the operating system, we create a directory, share it and set user privileges. Granting access only for selected accounts and groups ensures that the Siebel File System is secure and only visible to Siebel system services and administrators.

> On your demonstration machine, create a new directory, share it and set the permissions to "Full Control" for the Administrators group and the service owner account.

Downloading the Siebel installation archives

We have discussed the preliminary steps for the installation of a Siebel CRM demonstration system. Now, it is time to download the Siebel installation files from the Oracle E-Delivery website (http://edelivery.oracle.com).

When we first use Oracle E-Delivery, we must register with our full name, company name, E-mail address, and country information. A new registration is processed by Oracle in typically a day.

Chapter 2

Also, we must ensure that we read and agree to the licensing information. Software downloaded from Oracle E-Delivery must either be licensed or is made available for a limited 30 day trial period.

Once we have successfully filled in the Export Validation Form, we enter the search screen of Oracle E-Delivery. The following screenshot shows the search results for the Siebel CRM product pack on the Microsoft Windows (32-bit) platform:

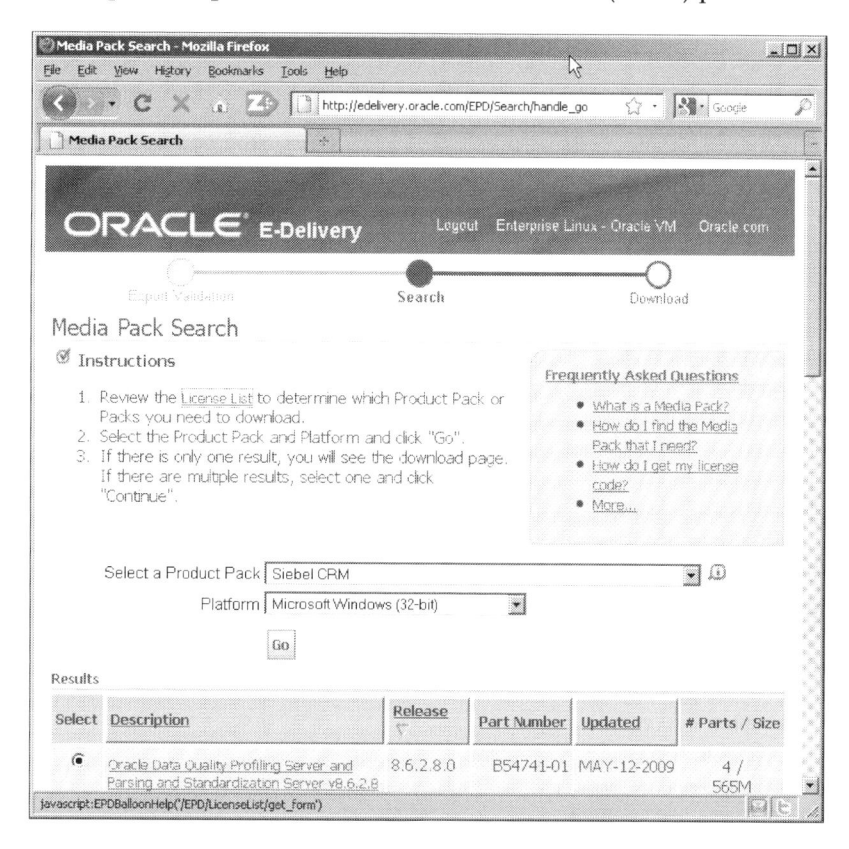

We can also use the **License List** link in the instructions section to conduct a search for the correct product and the associated product pack.

To download the base Siebel CRM software needed for a demonstration system, click on the link for **Siebel Business Applications (with Translations) Media Pack**. There are several links for different versions of Siebel.

Planning and Preparing the Installation

> Siebel CRM is made available in two flavors. The Siebel Enterprise Applications (SEA) is a smaller subset of the Siebel Industry Applications (SIA). The Siebel Enterprise Applications are also widely known as "horizontal" applications that provide functionality across different industries, whereas the Siebel Industry Applications provide industry-specific applications such as Siebel Automotive.
>
> The download link including the acronym SEA takes you to the installers for the horizontal Siebel applications.
>
> Oracle has announced it will discontinue the delivery of two separate flavors in favor of the Siebel Industry Applications.

When we reach the download page for the selected media pack, we should ensure that we download only the bits and pieces that we need. This might prove a little difficult for people who have never done this before and the risk of downloading unneeded language packs or software and therefore clogging our disk drives is high. Oracle provides a Readme file that lists the contents of each download archive file.

We can follow this "shopping list" to download what we need for our first Siebel CRM demonstration installation:

- All parts of the Siebel Business Applications English language pack
- All parts of the Siebel Business Applications Base Applications
- All parts of the Siebel Business Applications Siebel Client
- All parts of the Siebel Business Applications Siebel Tools
- The Siebel Business Applications ImageCreator Files

Using a download management tool

Given the fact that the download files are huge (from several hundreds of megabytes to more than 1.5 gigabytes), the probability of losing our Internet connectivity during the download and therefore having to restart the download is relatively high. In order to avoid this kind of trouble, we should use a download management tool of our choice.

The author (who is not related to the authors of the following software) has used the open-source tool named Free Download Manager (FDM) available at `http://freedownloadmanager.org`. An especially nice feature of FDM is its ability to read the file listing of `.zip` archives and to allow selecting or unselecting certain files within the archive, resulting in a smaller download size. The following screenshot shows the ZIP Preview feature of Free Download Manager:

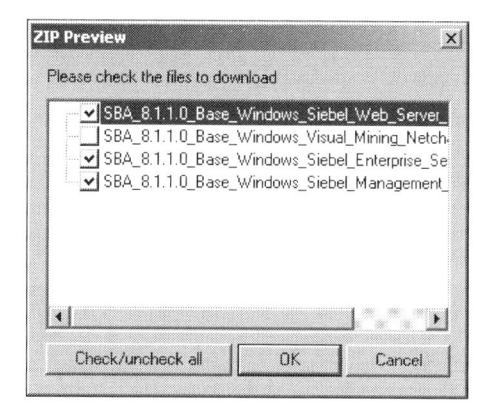

We can see the content of the zip archive for the Siebel Business Applications 8.1.1.0 Base Applications (Part 1 of 2) with the Visual Mining Netcharts installer unselected.

However, if we are in doubt we should download the entire zip archive and store all downloaded archives in a single directory on our hard drive.

Once all zip archives are downloaded, we need to unzip them using our utility of choice. Oracle recommends using the unzip utility on UNIX-based operating systems and warns of using the built-in unzip feature of Microsoft Windows or the commercial WinZip software.

The author has successfully unzipped all downloaded files with 7zip, an open-source utility available at `http://www.7-zip.org`.

We can simply unzip all downloaded zip archives into a single directory. The following screenshot shows the result of unzipping the downloaded zip files, a set of jar archives and the files for the Siebel Image Creator:

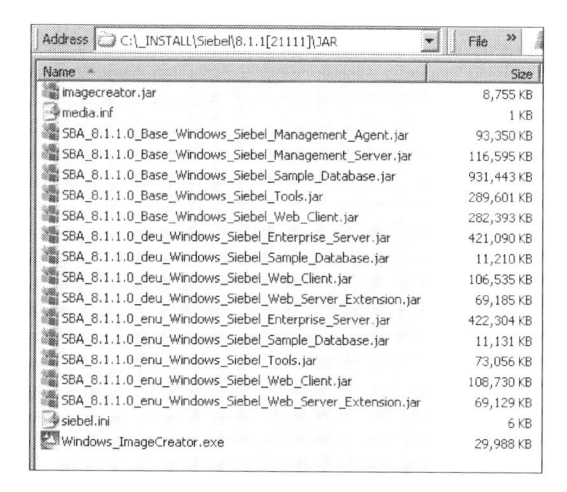

Planning and Preparing the Installation

> If you wish to continue following along with the installation of a Siebel CRM demonstration system, your task is now to download and unzip the Siebel installation archives as described in the above section.

Running the Siebel Image Creator

The Siebel Image Creator is a utility provided for each operating system platform. It is responsible for extracting the installation files from the jar archives and storing them in a directory tree—the image—suitable for the installation. Installing Siebel CRM directly from the zip or jar archives is impossible.

The Siebel Image Creator can be run in graphical mode (GUI) or in command line mode. On operating systems that support graphical user interfaces, we typically use GUI mode.

We can start the Siebel Image Creator on Microsoft Windows by double-clicking the `Windows_ImageCreator.exe` file.

The following table provides step-by-step instructions for how to create a Siebel Installation Image using the Siebel Image Creator.

Step	Description	Tasks and Example Values
1	Start the Siebel Image Creator.	Double-click the `Windows_ImageCreator.exe` file.
2	The Welcome dialog is displayed.	Click **Next**.
3	Display of options.	Choose **Create a new image…** Click **Next**
4	Specify the directory to which the installer images should be copied.	Example: **C:\Siebel_Install_Image** Click **Next**
5	Application type selection.	Select **Siebel Industry Applications** Click **Next**
6	Select operating system platform.	Select **Windows** Click **Next**

Step	Description	Tasks and Example Values
7	Select products.	Select the following:
		Siebel Tools
		Siebel Web Client
		Siebel Sample Database
		Siebel Enterprise Server
		Siebel Web Server Extension
		Click **Next**
8	Specify languages.	Select **ENU – English (American)**
		Click **Next**
9	Progress of the file extraction process is displayed.	Wait for completion
10	Success message is displayed.	Click **Finish**

Now, we can navigate to the directory we specified in step 4 and verify that the Siebel installer files have been created for the selected products and languages. The following screenshot shows the directory tree for a Siebel installation image for various products such as Siebel Tools and Siebel Web Client:

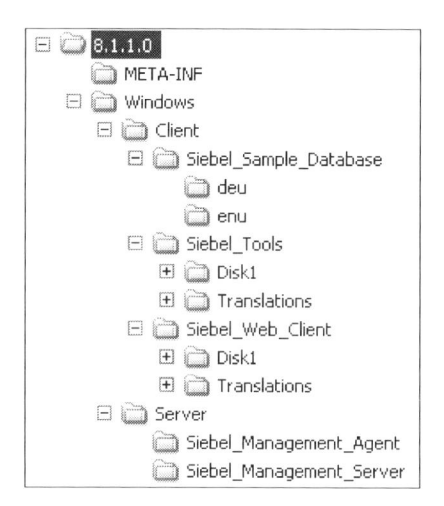

```
8.1.1.0
    META-INF
    Windows
        Client
            Siebel_Sample_Database
                deu
                enu
            Siebel_Tools
                Disk1
                Translations
            Siebel_Web_Client
                Disk1
                Translations
        Server
            Siebel_Management_Agent
            Siebel_Management_Server
```

If we consider a large project setting then it is definitely a recommended practice to copy the Siebel installation image directory to a network location that is accessible by anyone who needs to install Siebel CRM software.

> If you have finished downloading and unzipping the Siebel installation archives from the Oracle E-Delivery website, you can now follow the steps outlined in the above section and create the Siebel installation image on your hard drive.
>
> Ensure that you follow the steps in the table above correctly to extract the installation images for all Siebel CRM products needed for a demonstration environment.

Obtaining the license key

Siebel CRM application functionality is licensed by Oracle on a per-module basis. If a customer does not need, for example, the Siebel Marketing functionality, then he does not have to pay for it.

The interesting part, however, is that when we install Siebel CRM, we install the so-called Siebel Repository, the metadata store holding all pre-built application configurations. This repository is the same for all customers. What customers get when they purchase a Siebel CRM license for the modules they have chosen is the Siebel license key.

Plainly, the license key is a set of numbers that control the availability of the Siebel CRM functionality to the end users. Siebel functionality is accessed by means of Siebel Views, which are simply filtered away if the respective license key is not present in the Siebel database.

For an initial demonstration installation of Siebel CRM, it is therefore important to download the correct license key from the Oracle website. For evaluation purposes, we can download a set of license keys that expire after a certain period.

The URL where Oracle makes the license keys for all applications available is `http://licensecodes.oracle.com`.

On that website, we navigate to the Siebel section and locate the link for the all-inclusive license keys. We find the correct "flavor" of Siebel CRM and copy all lines of the respective license code to our clipboard. It is a good practice to paste the license code in a text file and store it in a safe place.

The license key will be needed during installation of the Siebel database.

> You can use the checklist below to verify whether you have completed all steps in the "Follow Me" boxes.

- Provisioned a Microsoft Windows based operating system (including Internet Information Services) on appropriate hardware
- Installed an Oracle 10g or 11g database server
- Created two tablespaces
- Created a system owner account with correct privileges
- Created and shared a file system root folder
- Downloaded the Siebel installation archives
- Created the Siebel installation images
- Downloaded and stored the correct Siebel license key

Summary

Creating a planning document is one of the first tasks for Siebel professionals who have to install Siebel CRM. This chapter provided information on how to plan the several phases of a Siebel installation using a sample planning document.

In addition, we learned how to execute the prerequisite steps for a Siebel CRM server installation on Microsoft Windows. These steps included the creation of tablespaces on an Oracle database and managing user accounts and file shares.

Finally, the chapter covered the steps to download the installation files, license keys, and to create the installation images using the Siebel Image Creator.

In the next chapter, we will get even more practical and learn to install Siebel CRM server software on Microsoft Windows.

3
Installing Siebel CRM Server Software on Microsoft Windows

In this chapter, we will discuss the concepts of installing Siebel CRM server software on Microsoft Windows-based operating systems in a very practical way. The following topics will be discussed:

- About the Siebel Server Installer
- Installing the Siebel Gateway Name Server
- Installing the Siebel Server
- Installing the Siebel Database Server Utilities
- Installing the Siebel EAI Connector support files
- Installing the Siebel Web Server Extension
- Checking the system configuration with the Environment Verification Tool (EVT)
- Applying patches to Siebel Server Software

The overall process flow of installing Siebel CRM server software can be depicted as follows:

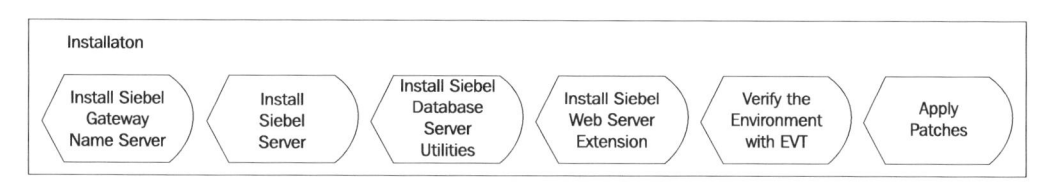

Installaton: Install Siebel Gateway Name Server → Install Siebel Server → Install Siebel Database Server Utilities → Install Siebel Web Server Extension → Verify the Environment with EVT → Apply Patches

About the Siebel server installer

The Siebel CRM installation images provide a setup executable, which is located in the root folder of the respective module we wish to install. When we invoke this executable, an installation dialog will guide us through the installation process. During this process, the application's binary files and other files that provide Siebel CRM functionality are extracted from the installation image files to a directory structure on the disk drive.

The setup executables read a text file named `siebel.ini`, which contains information such as which programs to launch when the file copy process is complete. In the current Siebel CRM releases for example, the `siebel.ini` files are preconfigured to launch the Siebel Software Configuration Wizard immediately after the software files have been extracted.

For the installation of components of the Siebel Enterprise Server on Microsoft Windows-based operating systems, we find the `setup.exe` file among others in the `Siebel_Enterprise_Server` folder as shown in the following screenshot:

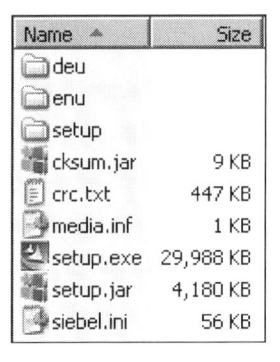

Name	Size
deu	
enu	
setup	
cksum.jar	9 KB
crc.txt	447 KB
media.inf	1 KB
setup.exe	29,988 KB
setup.jar	4,180 KB
siebel.ini	56 KB

For operating systems based on UNIX, the structure of the installation image folders is similar. However, the setup executable name includes the name of the operating system. The following screenshot shows the content of a Siebel installation image root folder for installation on Linux. Note the setuplinux executable.

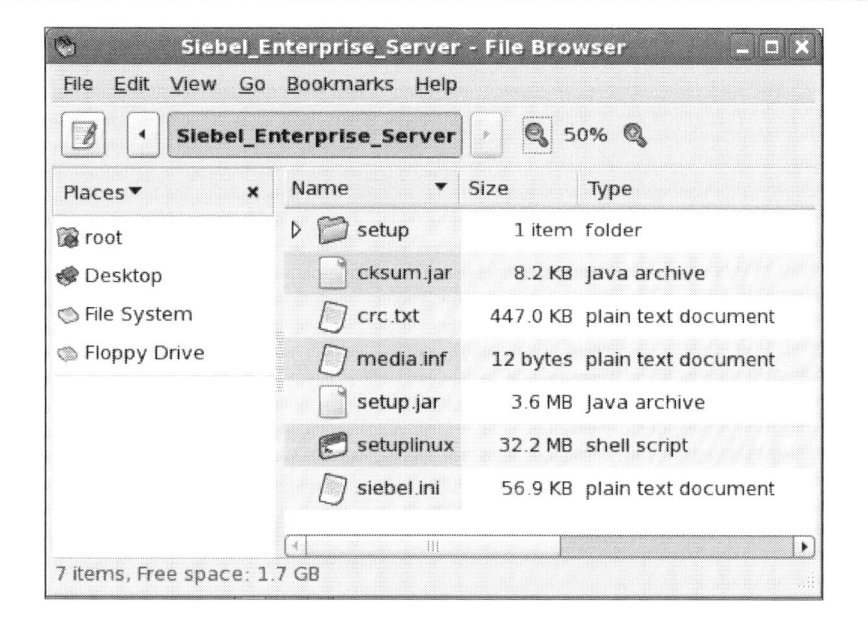

![Siebel_Enterprise_Server file browser showing setup folder, cksum.jar, crc.txt, media.inf, setup.jar, setuplinux, siebel.ini]

Independent of the operating system, the setup executable supports three modes of installation:

- Graphical User Interface (GUI) mode
- Console mode
- Unattended mode

We will discuss the first two modes in this section. The configuration steps for unattended installation are discussed in the next chapter.

Installation using GUI mode

The graphical user interface mode is the default and most used mode of the Siebel setup file. In Microsoft Windows environments, we can simply double-click the `setup.exe` file in the `Siebel_Enterprise_Server` directory and a Java-based installation wizard will start up. The following screenshot shows the graphical Welcome dialog of the InstallShield Wizard for the Siebel Enterprise Server:

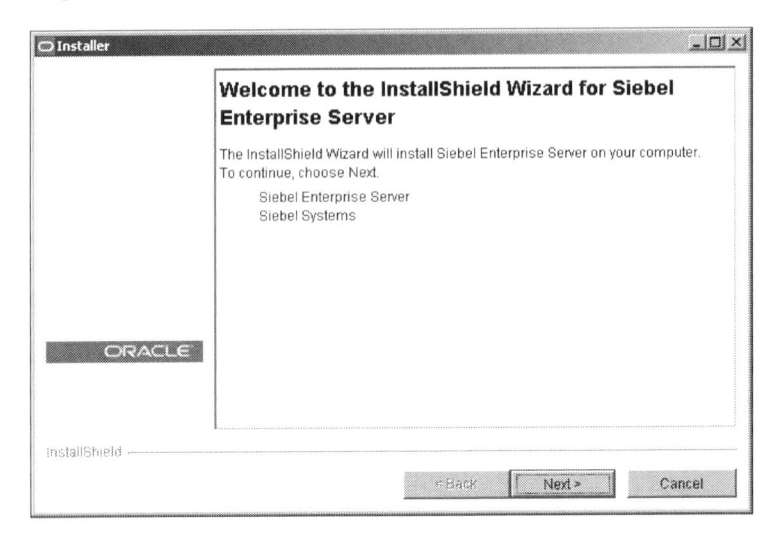

Following the dialogs, the administrator is prompted for several parameter values, such as the target directory to copy the application files to.

Installation using console mode

For certain situations—for example while installing using a remote command shell—the setup executable supports console mode. In console mode, the information display and entry of parameter values is accomplished through the command shell of the operating system.

To invoke the setup routine in console mode, we can use the following command line syntax (example for Microsoft Windows):

`setup.exe -is:javaconsole -console -is:tempdir c:\temp`

The `-is:javaconsole -console` command will invoke the `setup.exe` program in console mode. The `-is:tempdir c:\temp` command directs the `setup.exe` program to use the `c:\temp` directory to store temporary files needed for the execution of the wizard. The following screenshot shows the InstallShield Wizard for the Siebel Enterprise Server in console mode.

```
|----------|----------|----------|----------|
0%        25%       50%       75%      100%
||||||||||||||||||||||||||||||||||||||||||||
--------------------------------------------
Welcome to the InstallShield Wizard for Siebel Enterprise Server

The InstallShield Wizard will install Siebel Enterprise Server on your
computer.
To continue, choose Next.

Siebel Enterprise Server
Siebel Systems


Press 1 for Next, 3 to Cancel or 4 to Redisplay [1] 1
--------------------------------------------
Siebel Enterprise Server Install Location

Please specify a directory or press Enter to accept the default directory.

Directory Name: [C:\sba82]

Press 1 for Next, 2 for Previous, 3 to Cancel or 4 to Redisplay [1]
--------------------------------------------
Please select the products you wish to install.
     [ ] 1 - Gateway Name Server
     [ ] 2 - Siebel Server
     [ ] 3 - Database Configuration Utilities
     [ ] 4 - EAI Connector
To select an item enter its number, or 0 when you are finished: [0]:
```

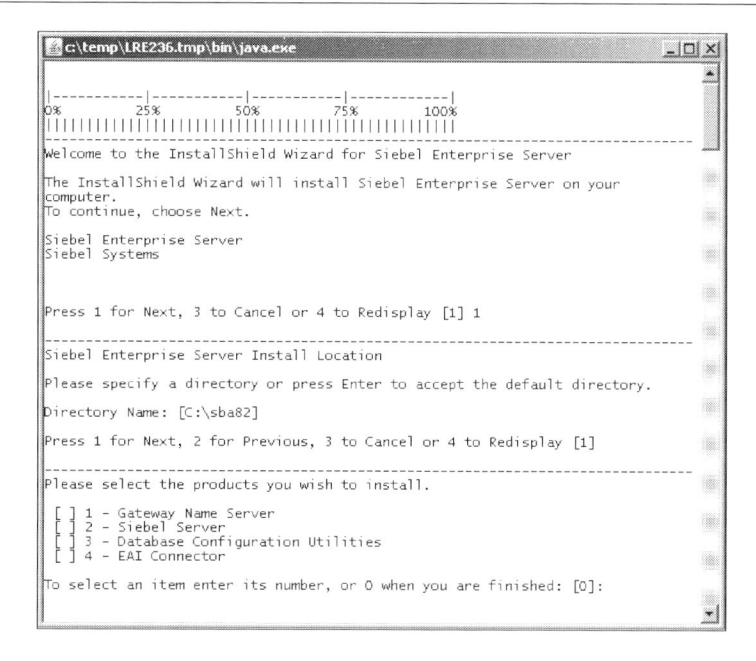

An administrator can still view all the necessary information and will have to enter parameter values such as the install directory using the command shell.

Other command line options for the InstallShield setup executables (including the Network Image Creator discussed in Chapter 2) are listed in the table below.

Command	Description
`-is:javaconsole -console`	Launches the InstallShield Wizard in console mode.
`-is:tempdir <directory>`	Provides a directory location to store temporary files.
`-is:log <logfile path>`	Provides a path to the log file for the installer.
`-args RECORD=<path to response file>`	Runs the installer in record mode. Used for preparing unattended installation mode. Record mode produces a `siebel.ini` file.
`-args SS_SETUP_INI=<path to response file>`	Allows running the installer in unattended mode. Used to read a `siebel.ini` file if it is not located in the installation image root folder.

The Siebel Enterprise Server installer will be used in the following sections to install these building blocks of the Siebel Web Architecture:

- Siebel Gateway Name Server
- Siebel Server
- Siebel Database Server Utilities
- Siebel EAI Connectors

We will now examine the details of each installation procedure.

Installing the Siebel Gateway Name Server

A typical Siebel Enterprise Server installation starts with the Siebel Gateway Name Server. The reason behind this strategy is that when it comes to the step of configuring the Enterprise and the first Siebel Server, the Gateway Name Server has to be up and running.

It is possible to combine the Siebel Gateway Name Server installation procedure with the installation of the Siebel Server, the Siebel Database Server Utilities, and Siebel EAI Connectors. This is a typical scenario for a single-machine installation.

However, a more realistic scenario is to install each component of the Siebel Web Architecture on separate physical machines. For this reason, the following sections discuss the technique of installing the Siebel Enterprise Server components separately.

The installation of the Siebel Enterprise Server components on Microsoft Windows begins with double-clicking the `setup.exe` file in the `Siebel_Enterprise_Server` folder of the Siebel installation image. The following table describes the steps that the InstallShield Wizard guides us through and what entries and actions we have to take in order to install the Siebel Gateway Name Server on the machine that we dedicated for hosting it in our planning document. We described the planning process in the *Planning the Siebel CRM installation* section in Chapter 2.

Chapter 3

Step	Description	Tasks and Example Values
1	Start the InstallShield Wizard	Double-click the setup.exe file in the Siebel_Enterprise_Server folder
2	The Welcome dialog is displayed	Click **Next**.
3	Specify the directory to which the application files should be copied	Example: **C:\SIA8**. **The directory should already have been specified in the planning document.** A subdirectory for the Siebel Gateway Name Server will be created automatically Click **Next**.
4	Select products to install	Select the following: • **Gateway Name Server** Click **Next**.
5	Select setup type	Select **Custom**. Click **Next**.
6	Feature selection.	Keep the default selection. Click **Next**.
7	Language selection.	Select **ENU – English (American)**. Click **Next**.
8	Windows Program Menu Folder	Keep the default menu folder name. Note: The installer will create shortcuts to the Software Configuration Wizard in this folder. Click **Next**.
9	Summary	Check the information in the summary dialog. Click **Next**.
10	The Siebel Configuration Wizard is launched automatically	We will launch the Siebel Configuration Wizard later to finish the configuration of the Siebel Gateway Name Server. Click **Cancel** to close the Siebel Configuration Wizard and confirm with **Yes**.
11	The InstallShield wizard success dialog is displayed	Click **Finish**.

Installing Siebel CRM Server Software on Microsoft Windows

We can verify the installation of the Siebel Gateway Name Server by navigating to the installer target directory. We can observe that the installer has created the following:

- A log file in the target root directory
- A directory that hosts the uninstaller program
- The directories and files needed to run the Siebel Gateway Name Server

The screenshot below shows the directories and files created by the Siebel Gateway Name Server installer:

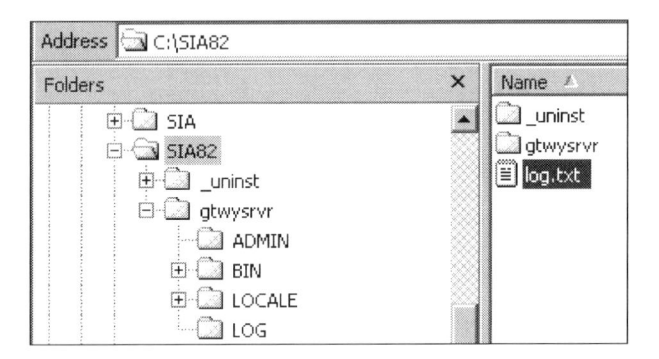

In addition, we can check the Windows start menu for the existence of a program folder that should now contain a shortcut labeled **Siebel Enterprise Configuration**. This shortcut is configured to launch the Siebel Software Configuration Wizard, which we will use later to configure the Siebel Gateway Name Server and the Siebel Enterprise.

The `log.txt` file can be helpful in the case that errors occur during the installation process.

> In this and subsequent "Follow Me" boxes, you are invited to use the steps described in the above section to install the Siebel Web Architecture on a demonstration machine. Instructions on how to prepare this demonstration machine have been given in the previous chapter.
>
> If you wish to follow along with this chapter, complete the following steps:
>
> 1. Run the `setup.exe` program and follow the steps described in the above table to install the Siebel Gateway Name Server on your demonstration machine.
> 2. Follow the verification steps described in the above section.

Installing the Siebel Server

In the following section, we will discuss the process to install the Siebel Server program files on Microsoft Windows-based operating systems. The following table guides us through the dialogs displayed by the InstallShield wizard. We begin by invoking the setup executable on the machine that we dedicated to host the Siebel Server during the planning process. We described the planning process in the *Planning the Siebel CRM installation* section in Chapter 2.

Step	Description	Tasks and Example Values
1	Start the InstallShield Wizard	Double-click the `setup.exe` file in the `Siebel_Enterprise_Server` folder.
2	The Welcome dialog is displayed	Click **Next**.
3	Install new components or add languages	This dialog is displayed when the installer detects any existing Siebel Enterprise Server installations. Keep **Install a new instance or add new components** selected. Click **Next**.
4	Specify the directory to which the application files should be copied	Example: **C:\SIA8**. **The directory should already have been specified in the planning document.** Component subdirectory for the Siebel Server will be created automatically. Click **Next**.
5	Select products to install	Select the following: • **Siebel Server** Click **Next**
6	Select setup type	Select **Custom**. Click **Next**.
7	The selectable features for the Siebel Server are displayed	These features are explained after this table. Deselect **Siebel Management Agent**. Note: We will install the Siebel Management Agent separately. Click **Next**.

Installing Siebel CRM Server Software on Microsoft Windows

Step	Description	Tasks and Example Values
8	Windows Program Menu Folder	Keep the default menu folder name.
		Note: The installer will create shortcuts to the Software Configuration Wizard in this folder.
		Click **Next**.
9	Summary	Check the information in the summary dialog.
		Click **Next**.
10	The Siebel Configuration Wizard for the Siebel Server is launched automatically	We will launch the Siebel Configuration Wizard later to finish the configuration of the Siebel Server.
		Click **Cancel** to close the Siebel Configuration Wizard and confirm with **Yes**.
11	The InstallShield wizard success dialog is displayed	Click **Finish**.

In step 7 of the table above, the installation wizard for the Siebel Server prompts for the following selectable features of the Siebel Server:

- Object Manager Component
- Handheld Synchronization
- Data Quality Connector
- Remote Search Support
- Java Integrator
- PIM Server Integration
- Siebel Management Agent

The following screenshot shows the InstallShield wizard dialog, which allows the selection or de-selection of these features.

[50]

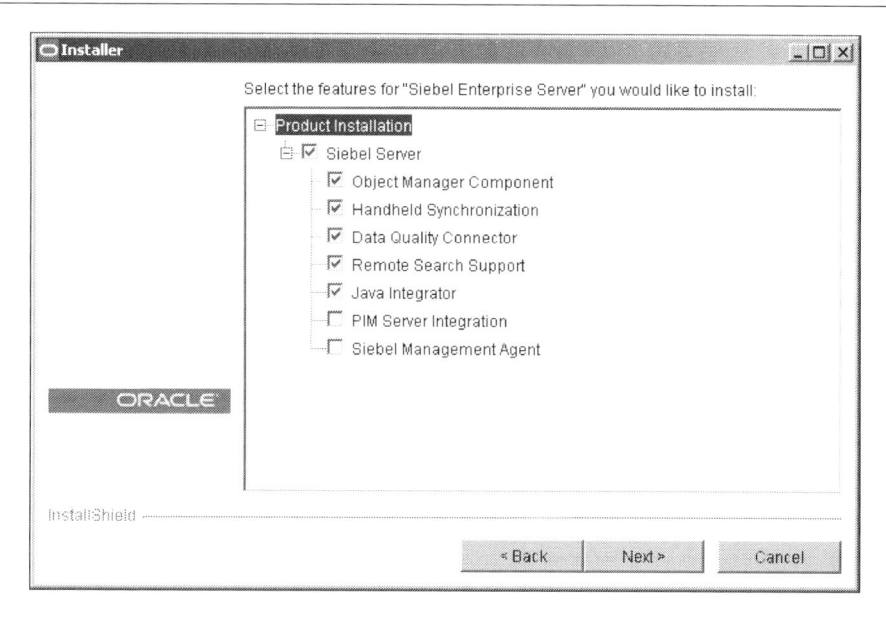

A brief explanation of these features shall be given in the following section. As a general rule of thumb, we should keep the default settings when in doubt. This will ensure that we can simply activate a feature later in the project. Deselecting a feature will require us to run the installer again to make it available.

- Object Manager Component: This option enables the installation of the files necessary to operate the Siebel Application Object Manager components on the Siebel Server. This feature should always be selected.
- Handheld Synchronization: This feature supports data synchronization between the Siebel Server and clients installed on handheld PCs. If our company does not deploy handheld clients we can deselect this feature.
- Data Quality Connector: This feature is needed when your company intends to deploy the Siebel Data Quality module, which provides data matching and data cleansing capabilities by integrating Siebel CRM with third-party data quality software such as Oracle Data Quality, FirstLogic, or Trillium.
- Remote Search Support: If we intend to use Siebel Search using a search server that is not installed on the machine hosting the Siebel Server, we should keep this feature selected.
- Java Integrator: Enabling this feature will copy files needed for integrating Siebel applications with Java-based software using the Siebel Java Data Bean (JDB).

- PIM Server Integration: The abbreviation PIM translates to Personal Information Manager and refers to a program or device that allows storing of calendar and contact information. An example for this is Microsoft Outlook. The server behind Microsoft Outlook is Microsoft Exchange. Selecting this feature will direct the installer to copy the files needed to enable the server-side integration of Siebel CRM with Microsoft Exchange, also known as server-side synchronization for Exchange (SSSE). This feature is not selected by default.
- Siebel Management Agent: The Siebel Management Agent is a part of the Siebel management framework. It enables communication with the Siebel Management Server. Proper installation of the Siebel management infrastructure is needed if we want to deploy configuration changes from development environments to test or production environments using the Application Deployment Manager. Also, the Siebel Diagnostic Tool relies on the Siebel management infrastructure. The Siebel Management Agent can be installed using a separate installer with the benefit of a separate uninstaller being created. For this reason, it is recommended to unselect the feature and install the Siebel Management Agent later using its own installer.

Verifying successful Siebel Server installation

In order to verify the successful installation or troubleshoot problems during installation of the Siebel Server, we can navigate to the installation root folder. The `log.txt` file will contain information about the installation process and a `siebsrv` directory should exist containing the folders and files necessary to operate one or more Siebel Servers on this machine.

Also, we can check the Windows start menu for the existence of a program folder that should now contain a shortcut labeled **Siebel Server Configuration**. This shortcut is configured to launch the Siebel Software Configuration Wizard, which we will later use to configure a Siebel Server.

> In order to continue with the installation of the Siebel Web Architecture on your demonstration machine, you can now complete the following steps:
> 1. Run the `setup.exe` program and follow the steps described in the above table to install the Siebel Server software on your demonstration machine.
> 2. Follow the verification steps described in the above section.

Installing the Siebel Database Server Utilities

Any operation that has to be carried out against the Siebel database is done via the **Siebel Upgrade Wizard**. This utility along with other programs and files such as pre-built SQL scripts are installed using the Siebel Enterprise Server installer option **Siebel Database Server Utilities**.

As the Siebel Upgrade Wizard uses folders and files situated in the Siebel Server installation directory, it is necessary to install the Siebel Database Server Utilities on the **same machine** as the Siebel Server. The Installer shows a warning message when we attempt to install the Database Server Utilities into a root directory that does not include a Siebel Server installation.

The table below describes the steps that the InstallShield wizard guides us through when we install the Siebel Database Server utilities on Microsoft Windows-based operating systems.

Step	Description	Tasks and Example Values
1	Start the InstallShield Wizard.	Double-click the `setup.exe` file in the `Siebel_Enterprise_Server` folder.
2	The Welcome dialog is displayed.	Click **Next**.
3	Install new components or add languages.	This dialog is displayed when the installer detects any existing Siebel Enterprise Server installations. Keep **Install a new instance or add new components** selected. Click **Next**.
4	Specify the directory to which the application files should be copied.	Example: **C:\SIA8**. **The directory should already have been specified in the planning document.** A subdirectory for the Database Server Configuration Utilities will be created automatically. Click **Next**.
5	Select products to install.	Select the following: • **Database Server Configuration Utilities** Click **Next**.

Step	Description	Tasks and Example Values
6	Select setup type.	Select **Custom**.
		Click **Next**.
7	The selectable features for the Database Server Utilities are displayed.	In order to save disk space, we can safely deselect the Microsoft SQL Server and IBM DB2 options as we are installing on an Oracle database.
		Note: Keep the **Sample Database support** option selected. This option is explained in more detail below this table.
		Click **Next**.
8	Windows Program Menu Folder.	Keep the default menu folder name.
		Note: The installer will create shortcuts to the Software Configuration Wizard in this folder.
		Click **Next**.
9	Summary	Check the information in the summary dialog.
		Click **Next**.
10	The InstallShield wizard success dialog is displayed.	Click **Finish**.

About the Sample Database support module

The following screenshot shows the feature options for the Siebel Database Configuration Utilities that we select in step 7 of the above process:

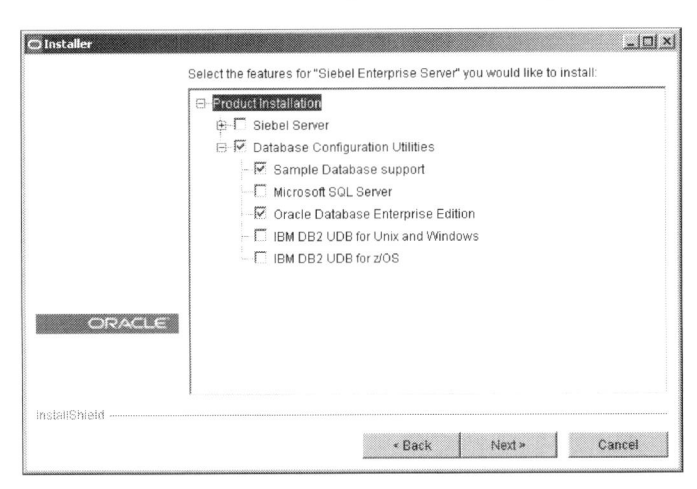

The feature options include:

- Sample seed files (Sample Database support)
- Scripts and utilities for Microsoft SQL Server databases
- Scripts and utilities for Oracle databases
- Scripts and utilities for IBM DB2 databases on Microsoft Windows, Linux, and UNIX-based operating systems
- Scripts and utilities for IBM DB2 databases on the IBM z/OS operating system

If we select the **Sample Database support** option, we ensure that a directory named FILES will be created in the database server utilities installation folder (dbsrvr). Despite the name **Sample Database support**, this option has nothing to do with the Siebel Sample Database, which can be installed with the Siebel Mobile Web Client. The FILES directory contains files that support the sample sales literature, images, and communication templates for use by administrators and end users of the Siebel CRM applications.

We will have to copy these files to the real Siebel File System to complete the Siebel Enterprise Configuration. This step will be discussed in the next chapter.

Verifying the successful installation of the Siebel Database Server Utilities

To verify the successful installation of the Database Server Utilities, we can navigate to the target directory and check whether a dbsrvr directory exists. This directory should contain subdirectories with executables and SQL scripts for the database platforms we have selected during installation.

In addition, the Windows start menu folder should now contain a new shortcut labelled **Database Server Configuration**.

> If you wish to follow along with this chapter and proceed with the installation of the Siebel Web Architecture on your demonstration machine, you can now complete the following steps:
> 1. Run the setup.exe program and follow the steps described in the above table to install the Siebel Database Server Utilities on your demonstration machine.
> 2. Follow the verification steps described in the above section.

Installing support files for the Siebel EAI Connectors

If our company has decided to use any of the platforms or technologies in the list below to integrate with Siebel CRM, we should install the support files for the respective platform using the EAI Connector installation option of the Siebel Enterprise Server installer:

- Microsoft BizTalk Server
- OLE DB
- Oracle eBusiness applications 10.7 or 11i
- COM Data Control
- Java Data Bean

The following screenshot shows the selectable features for the EAI Connector installation option of the Siebel Enterprise Server installer:

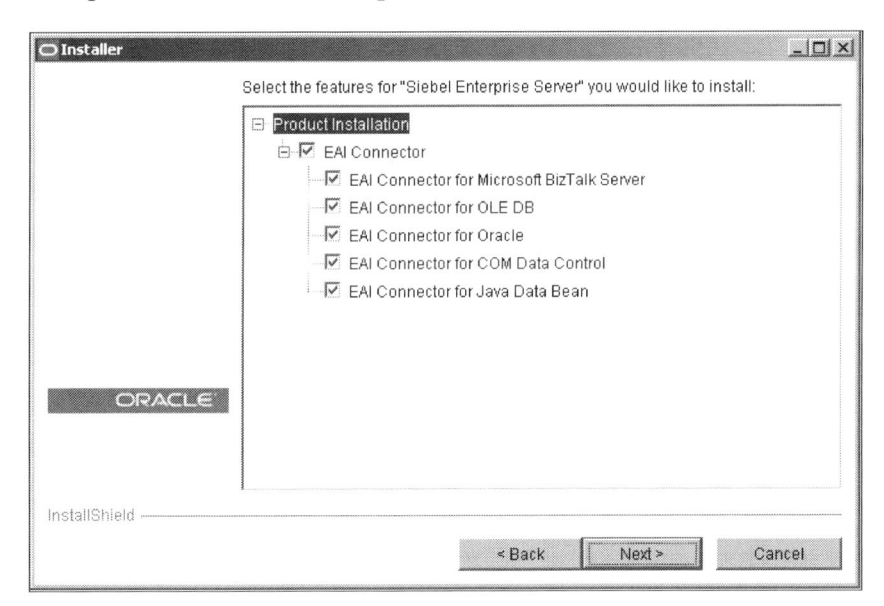

A brief explanation of this option shall be given in the following sections:

- EAI Connector for Microsoft BizTalk Server

    According to the Siebel Installation Guide for Microsoft Windows, the EAI Connector for Microsoft BizTalk Server is not supported in Siebel CRM release 8.1. Oracle will make announcements on its support portal in case the support is re-established. (Source: Siebel Installation Guide for Microsoft Windows, Version 8.1)

    Selecting this feature will result in the creation of a directory that holds files needed to integrate Siebel CRM with Microsoft BizTalk Server, however unsupported it might be to use them.

- EAI Connector for OLE DB

    OLE stands for "Object Linking and Embedding" and is a technology layer established by Microsoft to connect applications. The OLE DB standard is the object linking and embedding technology used to link applications to databases.

    In versions up to Siebel 7.8, the Siebel EAI toolkit included an OLE DB provider option, which would enable so-called OLE DB consumers such as hand-written or standard software to connect to the Siebel business layer using the OLE technology stack. Executing the EAI Connector installer with this option would place the necessary support files onto a machine where the OLE DB consumer would run.

    However, OLE DB has been de-supported by Oracle in Siebel CRM 8.0. So, the feature selection is not of any use if we install Siebel CRM 8.0 or above.

- EAI Connector for Oracle

    When Siebel Systems Inc. was an independent software company, several connectors for other standard enterprise applications were part of the product portfolio. These connectors were made available for:

    - Oracle eBusiness applications 10.7 and 11i
    - SAP R/3
    - PeopleSoft applications

    PeopleSoft and Siebel have been acquired by Oracle in 2004 and 2005 respectively and Oracle has developed the Application Integration Architecture, which provides middleware-based integration for these and other standard enterprise applications.

In the (admittedly rare) case of the need to integrate with one of these applications in a peer-to-peer manner, then only for Oracle eBusiness Suite we would have to run a separate installation process in order to obtain the support files. These files are basically pre-built scripts to create SQL views in the Oracle application's database.

The SAP and PeopleSoft connectors are delivered with the standard installation procedure and do not require a separate installer to be run.

- EAI Connector for COM Data Control

  The Siebel EAI toolkit provides several programmatic options to integrate external applications with Siebel CRM using Microsoft's Component Object Model (COM). If we would have the requirement to run a program written in C++ or .NET on a machine that does not host a Siebel Server installation, we would have to run this EAI Connector installer to create the necessary support files. These would be mainly dynamic link library (dll) files, which enable the developer to connect to the Siebel Application Object Manager and use the Application Programming Interface (API) provided by Oracle.

  If the machine has a Siebel Server installation, then the libraries for COM support are already installed and it is therefore not necessary to run the installer separately.

- EAI Connector for Java Data Bean

  In a similar fashion as writing a C++ program to connect to a Siebel Application Object Manager from a Microsoft Windows machine, the Siebel EAI toolkit provides support for programs written in the Java programming language. These programs run on any operating system. If we need to place the support files—in this case mainly Java libraries to support connectivity to the Siebel Application Object Manager from Java code—on a machine that does not host a Siebel Server, then we would use this EAI Connector installer option to do so.

  During the Siebel Server installation, we noticed the "Java Integrator" feature which, when selected, will direct the Siebel Server installer to create a CLASSES subdirectory containing these libraries.

  Regarding the information about supported EAI connectivity above, we should use the EAI Connector installer whenever we plan to integrate Siebel CRM with Oracle eBusiness applications 10.7 or 11i (also known as Oracle connector) directly (not via middleware) or need to deploy support files for COM or Java-based connectivity on a machine that does not host a Siebel Server.

  The following table conveys the steps and necessary input to install the EAI Connector support files:

Step	Description	Tasks and Example Values
1	Start the InstallShield Wizard	Double-click the `setup.exe` file in the `Siebel_Enterprise_Server` folder.
2	The Welcome dialog is displayed	Click **Next**.
3	Install new components or add languages	This dialog is displayed when the installer detects any existing Siebel Enterprise Server installations. Keep **Install a new instance or add new components** selected. Click **Next**.
4	Specify the directory to which the application files should be copied	Example: **C:\SIA8**. **The directory should already have been specified in the planning document.** A subdirectory for the EAI Connectors will be created automatically. Click **Next**.
5	Select products to install	Select the following: • **EAI Connector** Click **Next**.
6	Select setup type	Select **Custom**. Click **Next**.
7	The selectable features for the EAI Connector are displayed	As indicated above, select the features that suit your needs. Click **Next**.
8	Windows Program Menu Folder	Keep the default menu folder name. Note: The installer for EAI Connectors will **not** create shortcuts in this folder. Click **Next**.
9	Summary	Check the information in the summary dialog. Click **Next**.
10	The InstallShield wizard success dialog is displayed	Click **Finish**.

We can verify the successful installation by navigating to the specified target directory and checking whether a new subdirectory named `eaiconn` has been created. The eaiconn directory will contain the support files for each selected feature in a separate folder.

Installing the Siebel Web Server Extension

As we learned in the previous chapter, not only is a web server such as Microsoft IIS necessary, we must also install the Siebel Web Server Extension (SWSE) on this machine. The SWSE serves as a plug-in to the web server and forwards the URL requests from clients or external systems to the appropriate processes on the Siebel Servers.

The SWSE installer resides in its own installation image and must be run on any machine that should later serve as a Siebel web server.

The InstallShield setup executable is located in the `Siebel_Web_Server_Extension` folder of the Siebel installation image. On Microsoft Windows operating systems, we can simply double-click the `setup.exe` file to invoke the installer.

The table below illustrates the process of installing the Siebel Web Server Extension (SWSE) on a Microsoft Windows-based operating system that has the Microsoft Internet Information Services (IIS) installed and configured.

Step	Description	Tasks
1	Start the InstallShield Wizard	Double-click the `setup.exe` file in the `Siebel_Web_Server_Extension` folder.
2	The Welcome dialog is displayed	Click **Next**.
3	Specify the directory to which the application files should be copied	Example: **C:\SIA8\SWEAPP**. The directory should already have been specified in the planning document. Click **Next**.
4	Language selection	Select **enu – English (American)**. Click **Next**.
5	Windows Program Menu Folder	Keep the default menu folder name. Note: The installer will create a shortcut to the Siebel Software Configuration Wizard in this program folder. Click **Next**.
6	Summary	Check the information in the summary dialog. Click **Next**.

Step	Description	Tasks
7	The Siebel Configuration Wizard for the Siebel Web Server Extension is launched automatically	We will launch the Siebel Configuration Wizard later to finish the configuration of the Siebel Web Server Extension.
		Click **Cancel** to close the Siebel Configuration Wizard and confirm with **Yes**.
8	The InstallShield wizard success dialog is displayed	Click **Finish**.

To verify the successful installation of the Siebel Web Server Extension, we can navigate to the installation target directory and check whether folders and files have been created. Most notably, the **PUBLIC** directory will contain folders that represent the installed language packs. The upcoming configuration steps will place files in each language-specific folder, which constitute the browser-side look and feel and functionality of the Siebel application in the form of style sheets (files with a .css extension), image files, and both JavaScript (.js) and ActiveX (.cab) components.

> Ensure that your demonstration machine hosts a supported version of Microsoft's IIS web server and follow the instructions in this section to install the Siebel Web Server Extension.

Checking the system configuration with the Siebel Environment Verification Tool (EVT)

Now that copying the files that will later enable Siebel CRM functionality into the respective folders is complete, we are ready to set up and configure the system components that constitute the Siebel web architecture.

It is worthwhile to check our future Siebel server machines for full compatibility with the platform requirements as laid out in the document "System Requirements and Supported Platforms" for the version of Siebel CRM we are installing.

In order to provide support for this activity, the installer has placed a small utility named "Environment Verification Tool" (EVT) into the installation folders of the Siebel server software. EVT consists of a command line utility named evt.exe and an accompanying evt.ini file, which holds the configuration information for the program.

Installing Siebel CRM Server Software on Microsoft Windows

The purpose of EVT is to allow frequent checks of the operating system, its settings, and the configuration of Siebel software and third-party software on the various machines that the Siebel infrastructure consists of.

These checks include:

- Version and parameterization of the database server and client software
- Version and environment settings of the operating system and its networking subsystems
- Version and configuration of the web server
- Configuration of the Siebel Gateway Name Server
- Configuration of Siebel Servers and their components
- Configuration of the Siebel Web Server Extension

The `evt.ini` file comes preconfigured for the most critical checks. It can be modified by an administrator to instruct the evt executable to carry out additional checks.

The Environment Verification Tool can be run from any point in time once at least one component of the Siebel Enterprise Server has been installed. In order to execute EVT with the preconfigured `evt.ini`, we navigate to the BIN subdirectory of the Siebel software component. In our example, we run the `evt.exe` from the Siebel Server's `siebsrvr\BIN` directory. We open a Windows command prompt, navigate to the BIN folder, and enter `evt`. The following screenshot shows the result of running the evt command on the Windows command line without any additional parameters:

```
C:\SIA82\siebsrvr\BIN>evt
Running checks defined in file [evt.ini]. Please wait..
-1990, 2006, Oracle. All rights reserved. The Programs (which include both the softwar
Environment Verification Summary Report for [oracle-us]
Report Run by [oracle] on [Mon Nov  9 09:30:48 2009]
Installed Version [NOT DETECTED] Installed Build [NOT DETECTED]
Running a [8.0] version validation with [VAN] flavor

Total Checks   : 7
Checks Passed  : 2
Checks Failed  : 4 (4 critical failures, 0 warnings)
Checks Skipped : 1

Critical Failures:

Network Configuration Checks
Please set TCP parameter TcpTimedWaitDelay to 30 - the current value is not defined
Please set TCP parameter MaxUserPort to 65534 - the current value is not defined
Please set TCP parameter MaxFreeTcbs to 10000 - the current value is not defined
Please set TCP parameter MaxHashTableSize to 2048 - the current value is not defined
Complete list of checks:

Environment Settings
USERDUMP is not installed - It is recommended to install this utility using the follow
Environment variable SIEBEL_STRING_REFCOUNT has correctly not been defined

Network Configuration Checks
Please set TCP parameter TcpTimedWaitDelay to 30 - the current value is not defined
Please set TCP parameter MaxUserPort to 65534 - the current value is not defined
Please set TCP parameter MaxFreeTcbs to 10000 - the current value is not defined
Please set TCP parameter MaxHashTableSize to 2048 - the current value is not defined

Operating System Checks
Operating System version 5.0 is up-to-date

C:\SIA82\siebsrvr\BIN>
```

The EVT has executed seven checks defined in the `evt.ini` for Microsoft Windows operating systems. Two of these checks have been passed, four have resulted in critical failures, and one check has been skipped.

The output on the Windows command line contains information about the critical failures as well as the passed checks. EVT also recommends settings to overcome the critical failures and warnings.

EVT supports a variety of command line arguments that can be listed by entering the following command at the command line:

`evt -help`

The following table lists the available parameters for EVT and their descriptions:

EVT Parameter	Description
-g	Name of the Gateway Name Server.
-s	Name of the Siebel Server.
-e	Name of the Enterprise Server.
-u	Username used to log into Server Manager.
-p	Password used to log into Server Manager.
-o	Output format.(TEXT(default)|TEXTFILE|HTML|HTMLFILE)
-f	Location of the `evt.ini` file.
-q	Query mode. Requires a query string.
-t	Type of server (SWSE|GTWYNS|SIEBSRVR|DBSERVER)
-l	Log file output directory.
-w	Web server Installation Directory.
-d	Debug mode

One example for a useful command line argument is the following:

`evt -o HTMLFILE`

The `-o HTMLFILE` argument directs the evt executable to write the information to an HTML file. The file is created in the current directory and the filename is generated automatically using a timestamp to ensure uniqueness of the name.

The following screenshot shows the html file opened in a browser. The same information as on the command line is conveyed. Color coding, formatting, and the ability to automatically generate these files using scheduling tools provide much more flexibility than the command line option.

Complete list of checks:
Environment Settings | Network Configuration Checks | Operating System Checks |

red = Errors
orange = Warnings
black = Passed/OK
blue = Not Executed/Runtime Failures

Environment Settings
USERDUMP is not installed - It is recommended to install this utility using the following instructions http://support.microsoft.com/?kbid=241215. Please rerun EVT after installation if required.
Environment variable SIEBEL_STRING_REFCOUNT has correctly not been defined

Network Configuration Checks
Please set TCP parameter TcpTimedWaitDelay to 30 - the current value is not defined
Please set TCP parameter MaxUserPort to 65534 - the current value is not defined
Please set TCP parameter MaxFreeTcbs to 10000 - the current value is not defined
Please set TCP parameter MaxHashTableSize to 2048 - the current value is not defined

Operating System Checks
Operating System version 5.0 is up-to-date

In conclusion, we should run EVT at least once with the preconfigured `evt.ini` before we configure the Siebel server components. We should correct all errors that EVT points out in order to properly prepare the Siebel environment. EVT should also be run on a regular basis in order to proactively monitor for changes that might affect the performance or even functionality of the Siebel server software.

> On your demonstration machine, open a command prompt, navigate to the `BIN` subdirectory of the Siebel Server installation folder, and use the EVT as described in this chapter to verify your system is ready for operating Siebel CRM applications.

Applying patches for Siebel server software

For each major Siebel release such as 8.1.1.0, the base installers are made available by Oracle on `http://edelivery.oracle.com`. When new features or bug fixes are rolled out for a major release, registered Oracle customers can download the patches or maintenance releases such as 8.1.1.1 or 8.1.1.2 from the Oracle support portal "My Oracle Support" (`http://support.oracle.com`).

Administrators should review the accompanying maintenance release guide thoroughly in order to understand the implications of the patch.

Installing a patch is a process similar to that of installing the base applications as explained in this chapter in detail. The major difference is that the setup executable checks for existing installations and aborts the patch install if there is no appropriate base version available on the machine.

All software components of the Siebel infrastructure, including the clients such as Siebel Tools, must be on the same patch level. This means that we must plan, test, and execute the patch installation professionally.

In order to streamline the patch process, it is highly recommended to run the patch installers in unattended mode.

In order to enable specific features of the patch, it might sometimes be necessary to apply so-called repository patches using Siebel Tools. This typically involves the development team, testers, and the deployment team and adds to the time necessary to complete the patch. The processes to apply repository patches vary and are described in the respective maintenance release guide.

Summary

In this chapter, we discussed the installation of Siebel server software on Microsoft Windows-based operating systems. Siebel CRM is rich in features and we also took the time to have a closer look at the feature offerings of the installers.

In addition to installing the files for the Siebel Gateway Name Server, the Siebel Server, and the Siebel Web Server Extension, we learned how to use the Environment Verification Tool (EVT) to check the system environment before continuing with the software configuration.

Instructions on downloading and applying patch sets finalized the discussion of installing Siebel CRM server software on Microsoft Windows.

In the next chapter, we will discuss the steps necessary to configure the Siebel server software.

4
Configuring Siebel Server Software on Microsoft Windows

In this chapter, we will discuss the details of configuring Siebel CRM server software on Microsoft Windows-based operating systems. The following topics will be discussed:

- About the Siebel Software Configuration Wizard
- Configuring the Siebel Gateway Name Server
- Configuring the Siebel Enterprise
- Configuring the Siebel Web Server Extension Logical Profile
- Installing the Siebel Database Schema and Seed Data
- Configuring the Siebel Server
- Configuring the Siebel Web Server Extension
- Verifying the successful Siebel Enterprise installation
- Finalizing a Siebel Enterprise installation
- Installing Siebel server software in unattended mode

The overall process of configuring Siebel CRM server software can be described with the following flowchart diagram. In this chapter, we will discuss each of these steps in detail.

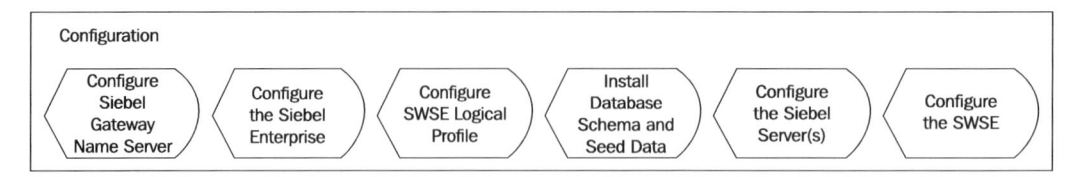

Configuration: Configure Siebel Gateway Name Server → Configure the Siebel Enterprise → Configure SWSE Logical Profile → Install Database Schema and Seed Data → Configure the Siebel Server(s) → Configure the SWSE

About the Siebel Software Configuration Wizard

As we followed the installation process in the previous chapter, we noticed that at the end of the installation of the Siebel Gateway Name Server, Siebel Server, or the Siebel Web Server Extension, the Siebel Software Configuration Wizard was launched automatically.

The purpose of the Siebel Software Configuration Wizard is to provide a safe environment with validation of critical configuration parameter values for administrators. It is mainly used during the initial installation process for a Siebel CRM server environment. The utility can also be used for modifying or removing existing configurations as well as adding configurations at a later time.

When the installer invoked the utility automatically at the end of the installation process, we cancelled the execution and decided to invoke it later. This enabled us to concentrate on the installation of the Siebel Server components and complete the system preparation, for example by using EVT.

We can invoke the Software Configuration Wizard on Microsoft Windows-based operating systems by using the shortcuts that the installer has placed in a Windows start menu folder. The following screenshot shows the Siebel Enterprise Server Configuration start menu:

Chapter 4

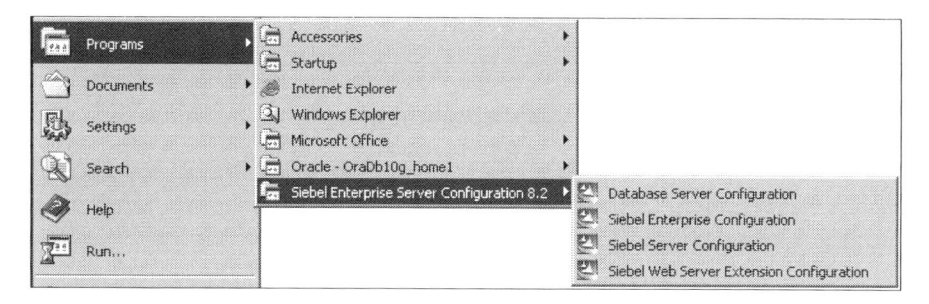

The menu contains shortcuts to invoke the Siebel Software Configuration Wizard for the Siebel server software components installed on this machine.

If we compare the properties of the start menu shortcuts, we find a single executable named `ssincfgw.exe` being invoked with different arguments.

For example, the shortcut labelled "Siebel Enterprise Configuration" contains the following command:

```
C:\SIA82\gtwysrvr\BIN\ssincfgw.exe -args LANG=ENU MODEL_FILE=C:\SIA82\
gtwysrvr\admin\enterprise_console_sia.scm
```

Clicking this shortcut will launch the executable. The `LANG=ENU` argument switches the user interface language to American English. The `MODEL_FILE` argument provides a path to a text file that is preconfigured by Oracle. This text file contains instructions on what parameters need to be collected and what actions are to be carried out by the Software Configuration Wizard. The term "sia" in the name of the model file refers to Siebel Industry Applications, a set of industry-specific applications that are delivered as a single software package.

The `ssincfgw.exe` file is of a similar origin as the InstallShield setup executables and because of that it supports graphical user interface (GUI) mode, console mode, and unattended mode. Using unattended mode to automate Siebel server software configuration will be discussed later in this chapter.

If the need arises, we can launch the Software Configuration Wizard in console mode by appending the `-is:javaconsole -console` command to the shortcut. A command similar to the following, issued at the Windows command shell, will start the Software Configuration Wizard in console mode:

```
C:\SIA82\gtwysrvr\BIN\ssincfgw.exe -args LANG=ENU MODEL_FILE=C:\SIA82\
gtwysrvr\admin\enterprise_console_sia.scm -is:javaconsole -console
```

The following screenshot shows the Siebel Software Configuration Wizard in console mode:

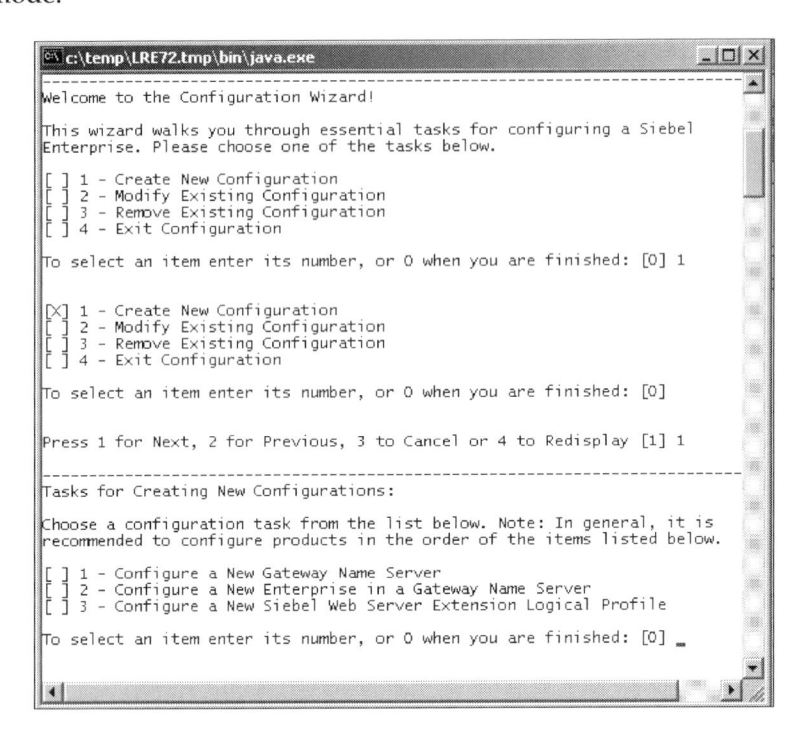

```
c:\temp\LRE72.tmp\bin\java.exe

Welcome to the Configuration Wizard!
This wizard walks you through essential tasks for configuring a Siebel
Enterprise. Please choose one of the tasks below.
[ ] 1 - Create New Configuration
[ ] 2 - Modify Existing Configuration
[ ] 3 - Remove Existing Configuration
[ ] 4 - Exit Configuration

To select an item enter its number, or 0 when you are finished: [0] 1

[X] 1 - Create New Configuration
[ ] 2 - Modify Existing Configuration
[ ] 3 - Remove Existing Configuration
[ ] 4 - Exit Configuration

To select an item enter its number, or 0 when you are finished: [0]

Press 1 for Next, 2 for Previous, 3 to Cancel or 4 to Redisplay [1] 1
-----------------------------------------------------------------------
Tasks for Creating New Configurations:

Choose a configuration task from the list below. Note: In general, it is
recommended to configure products in the order of the items listed below.
[ ] 1 - Configure a New Gateway Name Server
[ ] 2 - Configure a New Enterprise in a Gateway Name Server
[ ] 3 - Configure a New Siebel Web Server Extension Logical Profile

To select an item enter its number, or 0 when you are finished: [0] _
```

However, the more common scenario is to use the utility in GUI mode and enter the parameters from the planning document in the dialogs displayed by the Software Configuration Wizard. Having the planning document that we described in the example in Chapter 2 at hand is of paramount importance to successfully completing the configuration of the Siebel Server components.

The Siebel Software Configuration Wizard works in two phases. In the first phase, parameter values are solicited from the administrator. In the second phase, the utility invokes system commands and other utilities such as registering system services in Microsoft Windows.

Configuring the Siebel Gateway Name Server

As described in Chapter 3, a Siebel Gateway Name Server must be fully installed, configured, and operational in order to carry out any other task in the process of setting up a Siebel Enterprise Server.

After we have successfully installed the Siebel Gateway Name Server software, we launch the Software Configuration Wizard by using the start menu shortcut labelled **Siebel Enterprise Configuration**. Another option is to continue using the Configuration Wizard when it is automatically launched at installation time.

The following table describes the dialogs that the wizard displays and provides details about the parameters that have to be entered from the planning document:

Step	Description	Tasks and Example Values
1	Start the Configuration Wizard	Click the **Siebel Enterprise Configuration** shortcut in the Windows start menu that has been created by the Siebel installer.
2	Select configuration mode	Select **Configure Product in Live Mode**. Click **Next**.
3	Configuration Wizard Welcome Page	Select **Create New Configuration**. Click **Next**.
4	Select tasks for new configurations	Select **Configure a New Gateway Name Server**. Click **Next**.
5	Gateway Name Server TCP/IP port	Keep the default (2320). Note: This value comes from the **planning document**. Click **Next**.
6	Service startup mode	Keep the default (automatic service start). Note: This value comes from the **planning document**. Click **Next**.
7	Final Tasks	References to Siebel Bookshelf and EVT are displayed. Click **Next**.
8	Summary	Verify the selections and values you provided. Click **Next**.
9	Do you want to execute configuration?	Click **Yes**.
10	Execution results are displayed	Click **OK**.
11	The wizard jumps back to the configuration mode selection page	Select **Exit Configuration Wizard**. Click **Next**.

[71]

Verifying the successful Siebel Gateway Name Server configuration

If the wizard indicated successful execution, we should check for the existence of a new Windows service labelled **Siebel Gateway Name Server**. The following screenshot shows the property information of the newly created Siebel Gateway Name Server service on Microsoft Windows.

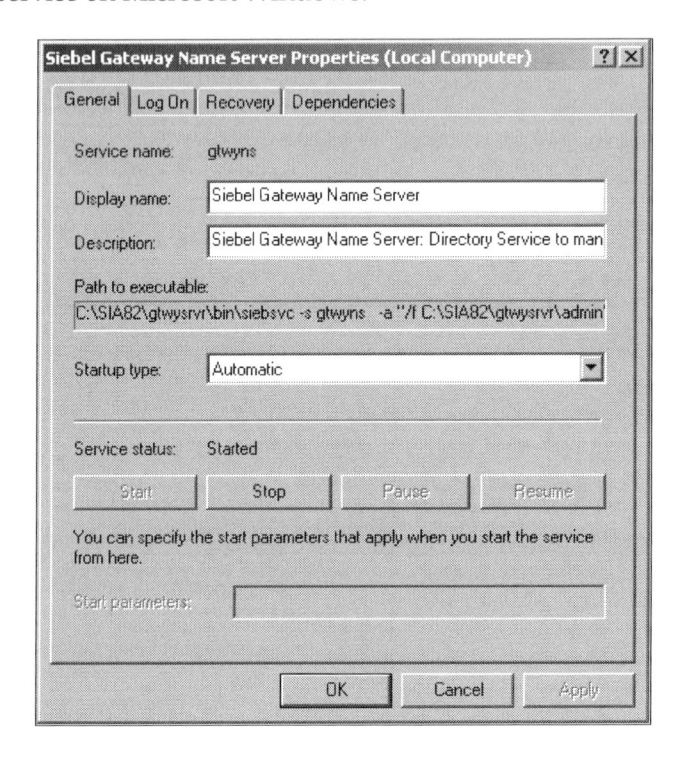

Note that the startup type is set to **Automatic** according to the settings in the configuration wizard.

Apart from a new Windows system service, the configuration wizard has also invoked the creation of files needed to run the Siebel Gateway Name Server, namely the file `siebns.dat`, which we can now find in the ADMIN subdirectory of the Siebel Gateway Name Server installation folder.

The `siebns.dat` file is the location where the Siebel Gateway Name Server stores all configuration information for any component of the Siebel Enterprise. Apart from information about itself, the Gateway Name Server has not yet written any other information to the file. In the next section, we will use the configuration wizard to create a new Siebel Enterprise.

In the case of any errors being reported by the configuration wizard, we should review its log file, which can be found in the LOG subdirectory of the Siebel Gateway Name Server installation. After correcting the cause of the error, we should execute the configuration wizard again.

> On your demonstration machine, launch the Siebel Software Configuration Wizard for the Siebel Enterprise and follow the steps described in the above section to configure a new Siebel Gateway Name Server.

Configuring the Siebel Enterprise

As indicated in the previous section, the Gateway Name Server is now operational. We can now create the definition of a new Siebel Enterprise, which will later contain one or more Siebel Servers.

> It is technically possible but neither supported nor recommended by Oracle to create multiple enterprises in one Siebel Gateway Name Server configuration store.
>
> We can use a utility named nsbrowse.exe (located in the BIN subdirectory of the Siebel Gateway Name Server installation folder) to open the siebns.dat file in read-only mode in order to verify or troubleshoot settings.

To start the configuration of the Siebel Enterprise, we launch the Configuration Wizard for the Siebel Enterprise again. We could also have decided to keep the wizard open once the Gateway Name Server has been configured. It is important that we execute the wizard on the machine where the Siebel Gateway Name Server is running. This is mandatory during an initial installation of a Siebel Enterprise because of the fact that the Siebel Gateway Name Server authentication settings will be changed during the configuration process.

Configuring Siebel Server Software on Microsoft Windows

The table below conveys the details of the process of configuring a new Siebel Enterprise:

Step	Description	Tasks and Example Values
1	Start the Configuration Wizard	Click the **Siebel Enterprise Configuration** shortcut in the Windows start menu that has been created by the Siebel installer.
2	Select configuration mode	Select **Configure Product in Live Mode**. Click **Next**.
3	Configuration Wizard Welcome Page	Select **Create New Configuration**. Click **Next**.
4	Select tasks for new configurations	Select **Configure a New Enterprise in a Gateway Name Server**. Click **Next**.
5	Gateway Name Server Authentication User Account Name	These parameters have no effect during the first configuration. However we set the following: User Account Name: **SADMIN** User Account Password: **TJay357D** Note: These values come from the **planning document**. Click **Next**.
6	Gateway Name Server host name and TCP/IP port	Enter the Gateway Name Server host name and the TCP/IP port used by the service. Host Name: **appsrvrgw1** TCP/IP port: **2320** Note: These values come from the **planning document**. Click **Next**.
7	Siebel Enterprise Name	Ensure that you review the notes on the naming conventions for the name of the Siebel Enterprise. Enterprise Name: **SIEBELEVAL** Note: This value comes from the **planning document**. Description: **Siebel Evaluation Enterprise**. Click **Next**.

Step	Description	Tasks and Example Values
8	Primary Siebel File System	Enter the UNC (Universal Naming Convention) path to the shared directory dedicated for the Siebel File System.
		Primary Siebel File System: \\appsrvrfs1\siebfile
		Note: This value comes from the **planning document**.
		Click **Next**.
9	Database Platform	Select **Oracle Database Enterprise Edition**.
		Note: This value comes from the **planning document**.
		Click **Next**.
10	Table Owner and Oracle SQLNet connect string.	Database Table Owner: **SIEBEL**.
		SQLNet Connect String: **ORCL**.
		Note: These values come from the **planning document**. The parameters required in this step are specific to the database vendor selected in step 9.
		Click **Next**.
11	Siebel Database User Account Name	This user account and password will be provided as an enterprise-wide default for all Siebel Server components that establish connections to the Siebel database.
		User Account Name: **SADMIN**.
		User Account Password: **TJay357D**.
		Note: These values come from the **planning document**.
		Click **Next**.
12	Enterprise Security Authentication Profile	Select **Database Authentication (Default)**.
		Note: This value comes from the **planning document**. Details on Siebel Security Authentication will be discussed in a separate chapter.
		Click **Next**.
13	Security Adapter Name	Keep the default.
		Click **Next**.

Step	Description	Tasks and Example Values
14	Propagate Authentication Settings to the Gateway Name Server	Keep the default (checked).
		Note: As this is the first time setup of a Siebel Enterprise we must ensure that we run the wizard on the Gateway Name Server machine for this feature to work.
		Click **Next**.
15	Additional tasks for configuring the enterprise	As this is the first time setup of a Siebel Enterprise for demonstration purposes, we do not select any options. All these settings can be done at a later time as well.
		Keep all checkboxes unselected.
		Click **Next**.
16	Summary	Verify the selections and values you provided.
		Click **Next**.
17	Do you want to execute configuration?	Click **Yes**.
18	Execution results are displayed	Click **OK**.
19	The wizard jumps back to the configuration mode selection page	Select **Exit Configuration Wizard**.
		Click **Next**.

About the Siebel Enterprise name

The following naming conventions apply when we select a name for our new Siebel Enterprise:

- The name must not be longer than 12 characters
- Alphanumeric characters and underscores are allowed
- No special characters such as hyphens or dashes are allowed
- The name should reflect the purpose of the Siebel Enterprise (for example "SIEBEL_DEV" indicates a development environment)

The first three conventions are actively validated by the Siebel Configuration Wizard and error messages are prompted when the Enterprise name entered violates any of the rules.

About additional tasks for configuring the Enterprise

As part of the process of configuring a Siebel Enterprise, the Siebel Configuration Wizard prompts us to select up to three additional configuration tasks that are related to different features of Siebel CRM. These additional tasks are:

- Setting up the Enterprise Network Security Encryption Type
- Providing Chart Server Settings
- Entering parameters that enable Siebel Data Quality Products and Connectors

The screenshot below shows the Siebel Configuration Wizard prompting for selection of additional tasks:

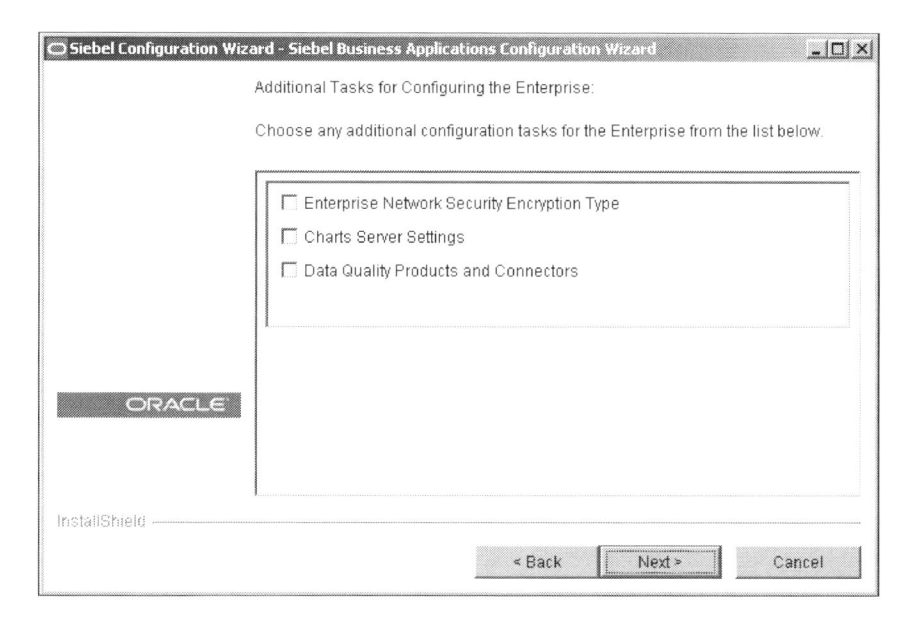

When we select any of these choices, the Siebel Configuration Wizard displays additional dialogs to solicit values for parameters. This is rarely used during an initial installation but can be helpful when—at a later stage of the project—one of these additional features has to be set up. Even if we could set the respective parameters manually, we should use the wizard as it provides input validation and creates log files that allow us to track changes and troubleshoot problems if any arise.

If we choose the **Enterprise Network Security Encryption Type** option, the next dialog allows us to set the SISNAPI (Siebel Internet Session Network API) encryption type, which controls how network packets exchanged between the Siebel Web Server Extension and the Siebel Server processes are encrypted.

When we choose **Chart Server Settings**, the wizard prompts for the chart server hostname and the image format to be used for the rendered charts (GIF, JPG, or PNG). The chart server feature relies on the VisualMining NetCharts server, a third-party product shipped with the Siebel CRM installation archives. Installation of the chart server will be discussed in a separate chapter.

With the third option (**Data Quality Products and Connectors**) selected, we can tell the configuration wizard whether we want to use Siebel Data Matching (based on a third-party product) or not. The wizard will then set the respective parameter accordingly.

Verifying the successful Enterprise configuration

Apart from the success message at the end of the configuration process, we can undertake several checks in order to verify the Enterprise configuration.

First and foremost, the enterprise has been created in the `siebns.dat` file. At the moment, we can only verify this by comparing the file size of the `siebns.dat` file to the size before we started the Enterprise configuration. Because of the propagation of security information, the Gateway Name Server will now authenticate (and audit) any connection. We will have to wait with the connection to the Gateway Name Server (for example using the nsbrowse utility) until we have fully installed the Siebel Database.

The Siebel Enterprise configuration has also created subfolders in the Siebel File System shared folder.

The next check we should do is to navigate to the Microsoft ODBC Data Source Administrator and verify whether a new data source has been created. This data source will be used for the initial installation of the Siebel database. The Microsoft ODBC Data Source Administrator can be found in the `Administrative Tools` folder in the Windows Control Panel.

> In order to proceed with the installation and configuration of the Siebel CRM demonstration environment, you will now execute the Siebel Configuration Wizard and create a new Siebel Enterprise. Use the table provided in the above section and your planning document to enter the correct parameter values.

Configuring the Siebel Web Server Extension logical profile

The web server with the Siebel Web Server Extension (SWSE) plays a vital role in the Siebel web architecture. Because multiple web servers—and therefore instances of the SWSE connecting to the same Siebel Enterprise—might exist, the basic configuration information is stored as a logical profile on a network location. The logical profile contains information such as the Siebel Enterprise name, port numbers, and anonymous user accounts, which will be written into the local configuration files of the SWSE at a later stage in the Siebel installation process.

In order to create the SWSE logical profile, we employ the Siebel Configuration Wizard again and launch the Siebel Enterprise configuration from the Windows start menu.

The following table provides details on the Configuration Wizard's dialogs. As the SWSE configuration includes very specific parameters, a brief explanation of these settings will be given at the end of this section.

Step	Description	Tasks and Example Values
1	Start the Configuration Wizard	Click the **Siebel Enterprise Configuration** shortcut in the Windows start menu that has been created by the Siebel installer.
2	Select configuration mode.	Select **Configure Product in Live Mode**. Click **Next**.
3	Configuration Wizard Welcome Page	Select **Create New Configuration**. Click **Next**.
4	Select tasks for new configurations	Select **Configure a New Siebel Web Server Extension Logical Profile**. Click **Next**.
5	Siebel Enterprise Name and logical profile storage folder	Note: we can enlarge the dialog window if the entry form is not fully visible. Enterprise Name: **SIEBELEVAL** Note: This value comes from the **planning document**. SWSE Logical Profile Name: Keep the default (a subdirectory of the Siebel Gateway Name Server's installation folder). Click **Next**.

[79]

Configuring Siebel Server Software on Microsoft Windows

Step	Description	Tasks and Example Values
6	Collect application-specific statistics	Keep the default (checked). Note: This value comes from the **planning document**. Click **Next**.
7	Compression Type (for traffic between SWSE and Siebel Server)	Keep the default (None). Note: This value comes from the **planning document**. Click **Next**.
8	HTTP 1.1-compliant firewall/enable compression	Keep the default (Checked). Click **Next**.
9	Session timeout values.	Enter 3000 and 9000. Note: These values come from the **planning document**. Click **Next**.
10	HTTP Port Numbers	Keep the default values (80/443) Note: These values come from the **planning document**. Click **Next**.
11	FQDN (Fully qualified domain name)	Keep the default (blank). Click **Next**.
12	High Interactivity or employee user login name and password	User Name: **SADMIN** Password: **TJay357D** Note: These values come from the **planning document**. Click **Next**.
13	Password encryption.	Keep the default (unchecked). Click **Next**.
14	Standard Interactivity or contact user login name and password.	User Name: **GUESTCST** Password: **8icJIPZH** Note: These values come from the **planning document**. Click **Next**.
15	Siebel Enterprise Security Token	Security Token: **TZH65ret** (enter twice) Note: This value comes from the **planning document**. Click **Next**.

Step	Description	Tasks and Example Values
16	Web server statistics page name	Keep the default (_stats.swe)
		Click **Next**.
17	Deploy SSL in the Enterprise	Keep the default (unchecked)
		Click **Next**.
17	Summary	Verify the selections and values you provided.
		Click **Next**.
18	Do you want to execute configuration?	Click **Yes**.
19	Execution results are displayed	Click **OK**.
20	The wizard jumps back to the configuration mode selection page	Select **Exit Configuration Wizard**.
		Click **Next**.

About SWSE parameters

The following parameters entered during the SWSE logical profile configuration shall be explained in greater detail below:

- Collect application-specific statistics
  The respective parameter in the SWSE configuration files (eapps.cfg and eapps_sia.cfg) is named AllowStats and if it is set to "TRUE", application-specific statistics (in addition to system-specific statistics) are collected by the SWSE and displayed in the statistic page (_stats.swe by default).

- Compression type
  The SISNAPI (Siebel Internet Session API) protocol allows compression of messages exchanged between the SWSE and the processes on the Siebel servers. If a smaller network packet size is beneficial (and covers the additional processing cost of compression) then the ZLIB compression can be enabled.

- HTTP 1.1-compliant firewall/enable compression
  If firewall software or hardware secures the Siebel web servers, this parameter can be used to enable packet compression. The firewall must be compliant with the HTTP 1.1 standard if this parameter is set.

- Session timeout values
  If a user session is idle for the specified time (in seconds), the process thread on the Siebel Server will be automatically ended, thus reducing memory consumption on the Siebel server.

- **FQDN (Fully Qualified Domain Name)**
  In order to allow popup blockers to identify the Siebel web server as part of a "friendly" domain, the FQDN parameter—when set to the full domain name—will direct the SWSE to create URLs for popup windows, including the full domain name.
- **Employee user account**
  The employee user is an account that has the privileges to connect to the so-called employee facing applications, which are typically executed in High-Interactivity mode. In order to render the login page, an anonymous user account is required.
- **Contact user account**
  The contact user is any account that logs in to the customer facing or partner applications that provide access to Siebel CRM data and functionality to people outside of the company that owns the Siebel application. Customers and partners can typically browse the website anonymously. In this case, the contact user account is used for session authentication.
- **Siebel Enterprise security token**
  Several commands can be passed to the Siebel Web Engine via URLs. In order to provide a high level of security, these URLs must contain an SWEPassword parameter. The value of this parameter must match the decrypted value of the EnterpriseSecurityToken parameter in the SWSE's configuration files. Otherwise, the connection is refused by the Siebel Web Engine.

> All the passwords that are entered during the configuration process are encrypted before they are written to the configuration files. This ensures that the security of the Siebel application cannot be compromised by accessing the files.

Verifying the successful SWSE logical profile creation

The Siebel Configuration Wizard uses the values provided by the administrator to generate files in the logical profile storage folder. This folder must be made accessible to each machine that hosts a Siebel web server. In order to verify the creation of these files, we can navigate to the profile storage folder specified in step 5. The following screenshot shows the SWSE logical profile directory containing the files generated by the Siebel Configuration Wizard:

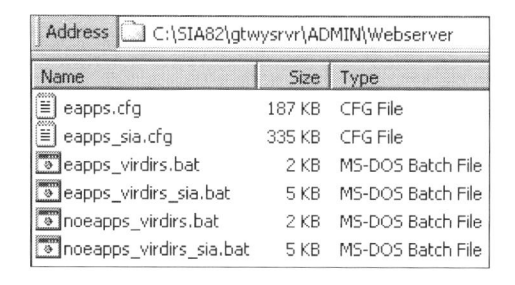

Name	Size	Type
eapps.cfg	187 KB	CFG File
eapps_sia.cfg	335 KB	CFG File
eapps_virdirs.bat	2 KB	MS-DOS Batch File
eapps_virdirs_sia.bat	5 KB	MS-DOS Batch File
noeapps_virdirs.bat	2 KB	MS-DOS Batch File
noeapps_virdirs_sia.bat	5 KB	MS-DOS Batch File

Address: C:\SIA82\gtwysrvr\ADMIN\Webserver

The eapps.cfg (for horizontal applications) and eapps_sia.cfg (for industry-specific applications) files contain the values entered in the wizard's dialogs.

> On your demonstration machine, execute the Siebel Configuration Wizard to create the SWSE logical profile. You can use the table in this section as a guide.

Installing the Siebel Database schema and seed data

If we observe the configuration process for the Siebel Gateway Name Server and the Siebel Enterprise correctly, we find that the Siebel Gateway Name Server authenticates each connection attempt using the account management of the RDBMS that hosts the Siebel Database. This is the default setting. Other authentication techniques such as LDAP or Microsoft Active Directory are also supported.

The only unauthenticated Gateway Name Server session is the first connection that we used to register a new Enterprise with the Siebel Gateway Name Server. Any other connection attempt, such as when we want to register the first Siebel Server, needs to be authenticated.

However, the Siebel Database, which is the default medium for authentication, has not yet been configured. So, the next logical step is to engage the Siebel Configuration Wizard and install the Siebel Database schema.

The Siebel Database configuration process differs from the previous processes in the sense that we first have to prepare and run an SQL script (in a file named grantusr.sql) against the database and that the configuration wizard invokes the Siebel Upgrade Wizard, which itself invokes other utilities and programs to run specific commands against the database.

So, before we launch the Siebel Configuration Wizard, we will discuss both the `grantusr.sql` script and the Siebel Upgrade Wizard.

Preparing and executing the grantusr.sql file

For an initial Siebel CRM installation, it is mandatory to prepare and execute the SQL script provided in the `grantusr.sql` file. We can find this file in the database-specific subdirectory of the Database Server Utilities installation folder. In our example, the file is situated in the ORACLE subdirectory of the `dbsrvr` folder.

The following amendments need to be made to the file before executing it against the Oracle database:

- Enter the correct tablespace names
- Modify default passwords if needed
- Add additional user accounts

We will discuss these steps in the following sections.

Enter the correct tablespace names

The file is prepared for use through Oracle SQL*Plus, which means that tablespace names are represented by placeholders such as `&&siebel_tablespace`. SQL*Plus will stop at these placeholders and prompt the user to enter the names. In order to create a script that is usable with any SQL tool, we will write the tablespace names directly to the file.

We can open the file in any plain text processor such as Microsoft Notepad and replace the text as follows:

1. Replace all the occurrences of `&&siebel_tablespace` with the name of the tablespace for data tables as identified in the **planning document** (in our example `SIEBELDB_DATA`).

2. Replace all the occurrences of `&&temp_tablespace` with `TEMP` (we use the default TEMP tablespace provided during installation of the Oracle database).

3. Find the line `alter user SIEBEL quota unlimited on SIEBELDB_DATA;`. Below this line, create a new line (for example by copying and pasting the line) and change it to "`alter user SIEBEL quota unlimited on SIEBELDB_IDX;`". This ensures that the user SIEBEL (the table owner) will have unlimited quota on the index tablespace.

Modify default passwords if needed

The `grantusr.sql` file contains commands to create three user accounts in the database:

- `SIEBEL` (table owner)
- `SADMIN` (administrative user)
- `LDAPUSER` (proxy user for LDAP authentication)

All three are created in the Oracle database by commands similar to the following:

```
create user SIEBEL identified by SIEBEL;
```

The first occurrence of `SIEBEL` will be the user account name whereas the second occurrence (after the words `identified by`) will be the password. If required to, we must replace the default passwords—which are the same as the account name—with the correct passwords identified in the **planning document**.

Add additional user accounts

If we inspect our planning documentation carefully, we will find that we specified other user accounts besides `SIEBEL` and `SADMIN`. Namely, `GUESTCST` will be used for anonymous access to customer and partner-facing applications.

If any additional accounts have to be established before the database installation, it might be a good idea to add the respective commands to the `grantusr.sql` file.

To accomplish this, we can simply copy and paste the lines that cater for the `LDAPUSER` account and modify the copied lines accordingly to represent the creation of the `GUESTCST` account.

```
create user GUESTCST identified by 8icJIPZH;
grant sse_role to GUESTCST;
alter user GUESTCST default tablespace SIEBELDB_DATA;
alter user GUESTCST temporary tablespace TEMP;
```

The code above shows the lines that were added to the `grantusr.sql` file in order to create the `GUESTCST` account.

In summary, the `grantusr.sql` file now contains commands to direct the Oracle database to do the following:

- Create the `sse_role` role for normal accounts and grant the create session privilege to it:
  ```
  create role sse_role;
  grant create session to sse_role;
  ```

- Create the `tblo_role` role for the table owner account and grant various privileges to it:

  ```
  create role tblo_role;
  grant ALTER SESSION, CREATE CLUSTER, CREATE DATABASE LINK, CREATE
  INDEXTYPE, CREATE OPERATOR, CREATE PROCEDURE, CREATE SEQUENCE,
  CREATE SESSION, CREATE SYNONYM, CREATE TABLE, CREATE TRIGGER,
  CREATE TYPE, CREATE VIEW, CREATE DIMENSION, CREATE MATERIALIZED
  VIEW, QUERY REWRITE, ON COMMIT REFRESH
  to tblo_role;
  ```

- Create the table owner account SIEBEL, associate it to the `sse_role` and `tblo_role` roles and define quotas on the tablespaces:

  ```
  rem Create SIEBEL user
  create user SIEBEL identified by dQ7JXufi;
  grant tblo_role to SIEBEL;
  grant sse_role to SIEBEL;
  alter user SIEBEL quota 0 on SYSTEM quota 0 on SYSAUX;
  alter user SIEBEL default tablespace SIEBELDB_DATA;
  alter user SIEBEL temporary tablespace TEMP;
  alter user SIEBEL quota unlimited on SIEBELDB_DATA;
  alter user SIEBEL quota unlimited on SIEBELDB_IDX;
  ```

- Create three additional user accounts with the `sse_role` role assigned:

  ```
  create user SADMIN identified by TJay357D;
  grant sse_role to SADMIN;
  alter user SADMIN default tablespace SIEBELDB_DATA;
  alter user SADMIN temporary tablespace TEMP;

  create user LDAPUSER identified by BFxR87DT;
  grant sse_role to LDAPUSER;
  alter user LDAPUSER default tablespace SIEBELDB_DATA;
  alter user LDAPUSER temporary tablespace TEMP;

  create user GUESTCST identified by 8icJIPZH;
  grant sse_role to GUESTCST;
  alter user GUESTCST default tablespace SIEBELDB_DATA;
  alter user GUESTCST temporary tablespace TEMP;
  ```

Executing the grantusr.sql Script

After saving the changes we made to the `grantusr.sql` file, we can open the SQL tool of our choice such as Oracle's SQL*Plus, connect to the Oracle database with sufficient privileges, and execute the contents of the `grantusr.sql` file.

In Oracle's SQL*Plus, we use a command similar to the example below to execute the file's content:

`@C:\SIA8\dbsrvr\Oracle\grantusr.sql`

The `@` sign is used to open and execute the SQL script in the given path. Messages such as "user created" and "user altered" indicate successful execution of the script.

About the Siebel Upgrade Wizard and the Log Parser

As indicated at the beginning of this section, any critical database-related tasks such as creating the initial Siebel CRM tables and indices or importing the initial "seed" data are executed by the **Siebel Upgrade Wizard**. This wizard is a specialized software unit that can be invoked from the configuration wizard or manually from the command line.

The utility is mainly used during upgrades from previous versions of Siebel CRM to a newer version, such as when upgrading from Siebel CRM 7.7 to 8.1.1. This is a critical process and the portions of it that involve modifications to the database schema such as creating or altering tables are carried out by the Siebel Upgrade Wizard.

The following are the main actions that the Siebel Upgrade Wizard can execute against the Siebel Database:

- Initial installation of a new Siebel database (described in this chapter)
- Upgrade of an existing Siebel database to a newer version
- Apply additive schema changes as part of an upgrade
- Import the Siebel Repository metadata from a file
- Export the Siebel Repository metadata to a file
- Migrate the Siebel Repository metadata from one database to another
- Run database utilities such as conversion to multi-lingual list of values

Each of these tasks requires various input parameters such as tablespace names and user account names and passwords, which are collected by the Siebel Configuration Wizard. Once the wizard has finished collecting parameter values, it will produce a file with an `.ucf` suffix (upgrade configuration file) containing the parameter values.

The configuration wizard will then launch the Siebel Upgrade Wizard and pass the location of the generated `.ucf` file. The Siebel Upgrade Wizard will read the file and execute the task.

For each task such as installing or upgrading a Siebel database, Oracle provides so-called driver files that contain the detailed steps to carry out the tasks on a specific database platform.

The upgrade wizard will also read these driver files and create a "to-do list". It is important to understand that the Siebel Upgrade Wizard does not connect directly to the Siebel database. To do so and to execute the actions and scripts against the RDBMS, the Siebel Upgrade Wizard invokes command line utilities and programs shipped with the Siebel installer.

During the processes invoked by the Siebel Upgrade Wizard, the utilities and programs direct their log output to files in a folder specified at configuration time. These log files can be big in both amount and size. For this reason, Oracle provides a utility called **Log Parser**, which enables the administrator to monitor a running process or document completed (or failed) processes.

The Log Parser, implemented as the command line utility `logparse.exe`, which is located in the Siebel Server's `BIN` subdirectory, is capable of traversing the log files for a given Siebel Upgrade Wizard process and generating summary files in plain text and formatted HTML. These HTML summaries are useful for documentation and troubleshooting and provide hyperlinks to the original log files.

The following diagram depicts the dependencies between the Siebel Configuration Wizard, the Siebel Upgrade Wizard, and the Log Parser:

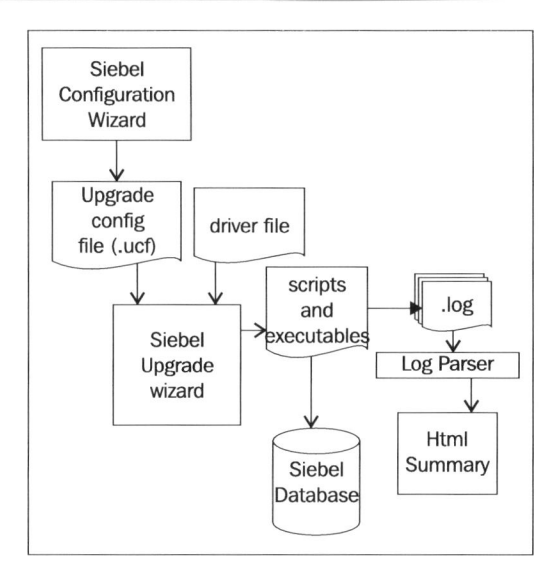

```
┌─────────────────────────────────────────┐
│         ┌──────────────┐                │
│         │   Siebel     │                │
│         │ Configuration│                │
│         │   Wizard     │                │
│         └──────┬───────┘                │
│                │                        │
│       ┌────────┴────┐                   │
│       ▼             ▼                   │
│   ┌────────┐   ┌─────────┐              │
│   │Upgrade │   │driver   │              │
│   │ config │   │  file   │              │
│   │file(.ucf)│  └────┬────┘             │
│   └───┬────┘        │                   │
│       │    ┌────────┴──┐    ┌────┐      │
│       │    │ scripts   │    │.log│      │
│       ▼    │   and     │───▶│    │      │
│   ┌───────┐│executables│    └─┬──┘      │
│   │ Siebel│└─────┬─────┘      │         │
│   │Upgrade│──────┘       ┌────▼─────┐   │
│   │ wizard│              │Log Parser│   │
│   └───────┘              └────┬─────┘   │
│              │                │         │
│              ▼           ┌────▼─────┐   │
│         ┌─────────┐      │  Html    │   │
│         │ Siebel  │      │ Summary  │   │
│         │Database │      └──────────┘   │
│         └─────────┘                     │
└─────────────────────────────────────────┘
```

Now that we know how the Siebel Upgrade Wizard works, we can start the Siebel database installation process by launching the Siebel Configuration Wizard. The following table describes each step of the process:

Step	Description	Tasks and Example Values
1	Start the Configuration Wizard	Click the **Database Server Configuration** shortcut in the Windows start menu that has been created by the Siebel installer.
2	Siebel Server directory	Provide the path to the Siebel Server's installation directory.
		Typically, the default can be kept.
		Click **Next**.
3	Siebel Database Server Utilities directory	Provide the path to the Siebel Database Server Utilities installation folder.
		Typically, the default can be kept.
		Click **Next**.
4	Database Platform	Select **Oracle Database Enterprise Edition**.
		Click **Next**.
5	Task selection	Select **Install Database**.
		Click **Next**.

Configuring Siebel Server Software on Microsoft Windows

Step	Description	Tasks and Example Values
6	Action selection	Select **Install Siebel Database**.
		Click **Next**.
7	Confirmation	Select **Yes I wish to install a new Siebel database**.
		Click **Next**.
8	GRANTUSR.SQL	Select **GRANTUSR.SQL has been run…**
		Click **Next**.
9	UNICODE or NON-UNICODE	Select **UNICODE**.
		Click **Next**.
10	ODBC Data Source Name	Enter **SIEBELEVAL_DSN**.
		Note: This is the name of the System DSN generated during configuration of the Siebel Enterprise.
		Click **Next**.
11	Siebel Database User Name and Password	User Name: **SADMIN**
		Password: **TJay357D**
		Note: These values come from the **planning document**.
		Click **Next**.
12	Siebel Database Table Owner and Password	Table Owner: **SIEBEL**
		Password: **dQ7JXufi**
		Note: These values come from the **planning document**.
		Click **Next**.
13	Index and Data tablespace names	Index Tablespace Name: **SIEBELDB_IDX**
		Tablespace Name: **SIEBELDB_DATA**
		Note: These values come from the **planning document**.
		Click **Next**.
14	License key entry	Select **Yes I would like to enter it now**
		Click **Next**.
15	License key entry	Copy and paste the first line from the **license key file** you generated during the installation preparation process.
16	Oracle parallel indexing	Keep the default ("Does not use…")
		Click **Next**.

Chapter 4

Step	Description	Tasks and Example Values
17	Security group and log output directory	Keep the defaults.
		Note the log output directory will become a subdirectory of the Siebel Server's LOG directory.
18	Apply configuration changes	Select **Yes apply configuration changes now**.
		Click **Next**.
19	Summary	Review the summary information.
		Click **Next**.
20	Do you want to execute configuration?	Click **Yes**.
21	The Siebel Upgrade Wizard is displayed	Click **OK** in the Siebel Upgrade Wizard dialog.
22	During the installation process, several command windows are opened	Ensure that you do not close or make selections in any of the command windows.
		Wait for the Siebel Upgrade Wizard to complete (approximately one hour).
23	The configuration wizard displays a message "Execution successful"	Click **OK** to confirm successful execution of the configuration wizard.
24	The configuration wizard jumps to the Siebel Server directory selection	Click **Cancel** in the Siebel Configuration Wizard dialog.
25	Confirm exiting the configuration wizard	Click **Yes**.
26	Siebel Upgrade Wizard displays "Complete"	Click **OK** in the Siebel Upgrade Wizard dialog.

Steps of the Install Siebel Database task

The Siebel Upgrade Wizard executes the following steps when executing the Install Siebel Database task against an Oracle database:

- Create Siebel tables and indexes
- Import seed data
- Run several predefined SQL scripts
- Create database functions and procedures
- Import the Siebel Repository metadata
- Insert the license key
- Update the history table

We can verify execution of these steps and explore details such as the SQL code by using the Siebel Log Parser.

Verifying the successful Siebel database installation

The following checkpoints exist for verification of a successful Siebel database installation:

- The HTML summary generated by the Log Parser
- Existence of tables and data in the Siebel database

In the following section, we will describe how to use the Siebel Log Parser to monitor or document Siebel Upgrade Wizard processes and we will review tables and their content to verify the Siebel database installation.

Using the Siebel Log Parser

The Siebel Log Parser is implemented as a command line utility named `logparse.exe`. It is situated in the BIN subdirectory of the Siebel Server installation folder.

We can open a Windows command prompt, navigate to the Siebel Server's BIN directory, and type `logparse` to make first contact with the utility. As some required parameters are missing, the utility reports the parameter switches on the command line.

```
/S Siebel Root                     (Required)
/G Language code of log files to be processed (Required)
/R Process Name                    (Required)
/L Log file for this utility       (Default: logparse.log)
/N Number of longest running sqls to show (Default: 10)
/T Threshold time in hh:mm:ss format (Default: 00:10:00)
/E Max number of errors to display in steps summary (Default: 8)
```

The above listing is generated by the logparse utility when it is called with no input parameters. As we can see, the utility requires the path to the Siebel installation root directory (/S), the language code of the log files (/G), and the name of the Siebel Upgrade Wizard process (/R). The name of the Siebel Upgrade Wizard process is the same as the name of the log output directory entered during the configuration process.

So, a correct command line for creating a report on the install process would be as follows:

```
logparse /S D:\SIA8 /G ENU /R install
```

The utility now parses all log files in the install subdirectory of the Siebel Server's log directory and generates a set of HTML files and a text summary file. If a default browser is specified on Microsoft Windows, the start page for the HTML summary is loaded automatically. The following screenshot shows the start page in Microsoft Internet Explorer.

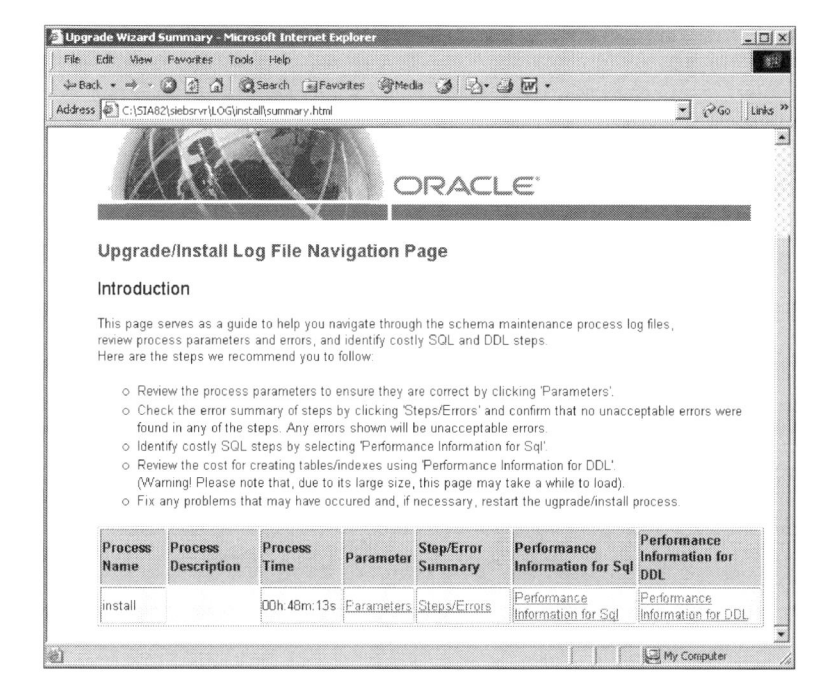

We can click on the **Steps/Errors** hyperlink to see a detailed list of all executed steps and their statuses. If all steps have a status of **Complete** and the Upgrade Wizard has finished successfully, this is an indicator for the successful installation of the Siebel database.

The Siebel Log Parser can be used for any process executed by the Siebel Upgrade Wizard. It is extremely useful to monitor and document complex and lengthy procedures such as upgrading a Siebel database to a newer version.

Verifying tables and data

The following SQL query can be helpful in verifying the successful Siebel database installation. We can run the select statement using the SIEBEL table owner account.

```
SQL> select activity_name, tgt_version from s_inst_upg_hist order by activity_ts desc;
```

The select statement retrieves the list of upgrade (or Siebel Upgrade Wizard) activities from the S_INST_UPG_HIST table. As this is the last action that is carried out by the Siebel Upgrade Wizard, it is a good indicator for success. The ACTIVITY_NAME column contains the name of the driver file used to run the Siebel Upgrade Wizard process.

```
ACTIVITY_NAME                                      TGT_VERSION
-------------------------------------------------- -----------
master_install.ucf                                 V8.2
```

The code above shows the contents of the S_INST_UPG_HIST table after the successful installation of Siebel 8.2.

Restarting the Siebel Upgrade Wizard in the case of errors

There are various sources for errors during the somewhat lengthy process of installing a Siebel database. Whenever errors are encountered, the Siebel Upgrade Wizard will cancel the current task and prompt an error message that has to be acknowledged by clicking **OK**. The Upgrade Wizard window closes upon this action.

It is highly recommended to run the Siebel Log Parser in order to gain insight into the last successful step and to derive and download the correct log file that contains the error message and details about the situation.

In general, the upgwiz.log file generated by the Siebel Upgrade Wizard, which can be found in the output folder of the log directory, is a good starting point for troubleshooting.

The cause for the failure has to be corrected. For example, an error message indicating failure because extents are reached in the database should guide us to increase the extents or set the autoextend parameter to true for the respective tablespace.

Once the corrective action has taken place, we must restart the Siebel Upgrade Wizard from the command line. We must not run the Configuration Wizard again, as this would overwrite the upgrade configuration file.

Instead, we open a command prompt, navigate to the Siebel Server's `BIN` directory, and issue the following command in order to launch the Siebel Upgrade Wizard manually.

`siebupg /m master_install.ucf`

The siebupg executable represents the Siebel Upgrade Wizard. The `/m` switch points to the `.ucf file`—situated in the current directory—which the executable should read. The `master_install.ucf` file has been generated by the Siebel Configuration Wizard.

The Siebel Upgrade Wizard starts and prompts whether we would like to continue an existing upgrade or cancel the operation. We select the option to continue. The Siebel Upgrade Wizard will resume from the last step that was not complete.

> Use the information in this chapter to run the Siebel Database installation on your demonstration machine. Ensure that the installation was successful by carrying out the verification steps outlined above.

Configuring the Siebel Server

The physical (or virtual) machine where the Siebel Server software is installed can be configured to host one or more Siebel Server instances. For a simple demonstration environment, one Siebel Server is sufficient.

Again, the Siebel Configuration Wizard is responsible for prompting the administrator for the correct values for the parameters specific to a Siebel Server. We should highlight the fact that we can undertake the configuration of a Siebel Server only when the following activities have been successfully completed:

- Installing, configuring, and starting the Siebel Gateway Name Server
- Registering a Siebel Enterprise with the Siebel Gateway Name Server
- Configuring the Siebel Database

The following table outlines the steps of the Siebel Server configuration process:

Step	Description	Tasks and Example Values
1	Start the Configuration Wizard.	Click the **Siebel Server Configuration** shortcut in the Windows start menu that has been created by the Siebel installer.
2	Select configuration mode.	Select **Configure Product in Live Mode**. Click **Next**.
3	Configuration Wizard Welcome Page	Select **Create New Configuration**. Click Next.
4	Database Configuration Warning	Review the warning that we must have an existing Siebel Database. Click **Next**.
5	Gateway Name Server Authentication user name and password.	User Name: **SADMIN** Password: **TJay357D** Note: These values come from the **planning document**. Click **Next**.
6	Gateway Name Server hostname and port number.	Hostname: **appsrvrgw1** Port: **2320** Note: These values come from the **planning document**. Click **Next**.
7	Siebel Enterprise Name and Siebel Server logical name.	Enterprise Name: **SIEBELEVAL** Siebel Server Name: **Eval_1** Note: These values come from the **planning document**. Click **Next**.
8	Siebel Server Description	Description: **Siebel Evaluation Server 1** Click **Next**.
9	Enable Component Groups	Select only **CallCenter**. Note: Details on component groups are discussed in a later chapter. Click **Next**.

Chapter 4

Step	Description	Tasks and Example Values
10	Siebel Connection Broker Port	Keep the default (2321).
		Note: This value comes from the **planning document**.
		Click **Next**.
11	Remote Synchronization Manager Port	Keep the default (40400).
		Note: This value comes from the **planning document**.
		Click **Next**.
12	Additional tasks for configuring the Siebel Server.	Select none.
		Click **Next**.
13	Register external Oracle db ODBC driver for the Siebel Connector for Oracle Applications.	Uncheck the selection.
		Click **Next**.
14	Clustering configuration.	Keep the default (Not clustered).
		Click **Next**.
15	Autostart Siebel Server system service.	Uncheck the selection (no automatic start).
		Click **Next**.
16	Start the Siebel Server system service during configuration.	Uncheck the selection.
		Click **Next**.
17	Final Tasks	Review the information on EVT.
		Click **Next**.
18	Summary	Verify the selections and values you provided.
		Click **Next**.
19	Do you want to execute configuration?	Click **Yes**.
20	Execution results are displayed.	Click **OK**.
21	The wizard jumps back to the configuration mode selection page.	Select **Exit Configuration Wizard**.
		Click **Next**.

Verifying the successful Siebel Server configuration

In order to verify the success of the Siebel Server Configuration, we should check whether a new Windows service has been generated. We can do so by navigating to the Windows Services console and verifying that a new service exists. The name of the new service will be "Siebel Server [EnterpriseName_SiebelServerName]", where EnterpriseName is a placeholder for the name of the Siebel Enterprise and SiebelServerName is the logical server name specified in step 7 of the configuration process.

> On your demonstration machine, use the Siebel Configuration Wizard to configure a new Siebel Server. Use your planning document to enter the correct values in the dialogs.

Configuring the Siebel Web Server Extension

During the software installation, we have installed the Siebel Web Server Extension (SWSE) on the machine hosting the web server. As with any Siebel server software, configuration steps must be completed.

In a previous section, we discussed the configuration of the SWSE logical profile, which is typically stored on a shared network folder that must be visible to the web server machine at configuration time.

We will now use the SWSE logical profile as part of the Siebel Configuration Wizard's process. On the machine hosting the web server and SWSE, we start with launching the Windows start menu shortcut for the Siebel Web Server Extension configuration. The following table provides details on the steps of the configuration process:

Step	Description	Tasks and Example Values
1	Start the Configuration Wizard.	Click the **Siebel Web Server Extension Configuration** shortcut in the Windows start menu that has been created by the Siebel installer.
2	Select configuration mode.	Select **Configure Product in Live Mode**.
		Click **Next**.
3	Select configuration task.	Select **Apply an SWSE Logical Profile**
		Click Next.
4	Select a load balancer.	Select **Single Siebel Server**
		Note: Load balancing will be discussed in a later chapter.
		Click **Next**.
5	Siebel Server host name and connection broker port.	Host name: **appsrvrsieb1**
		Siebel Connection Broker Port: **2321** (default)
		Note: These values come from the **planning document**.
6	SWSE logical profile location.	Browse for or enter a UNC path to the directory specified in step 5 of the SWSE logical profile configuration.
		Click **Next**.
7	Final Tasks	Review the information about EVT.
		Click **Next**.
8	Summary	Verify the selections and values you provided.
		Click **Next**.
9	Do you want to execute configuration?	Click **Yes**.
10	A number of command windows are opened as the configuration wizard applies the SWSE logical profile.	Wait for all command windows to close.
11	Execution results are displayed.	Click **OK**.
12	The wizard jumps back to the configuration mode selection page.	Select **Exit Configuration Wizard**.
		Click **Next**.

Configuring Siebel Server Software on Microsoft Windows

We notice that during the execution of the SWSE configuration, a utility named `metabaseedit.exe` is launched several times. This utility is used to generate the virtual directories for the Microsoft Internet Information Server (IIS), and associates those with the Siebel-specific file extensions such as `.swe`. The following screenshot shows the Microsoft Internet Information Services administration console:

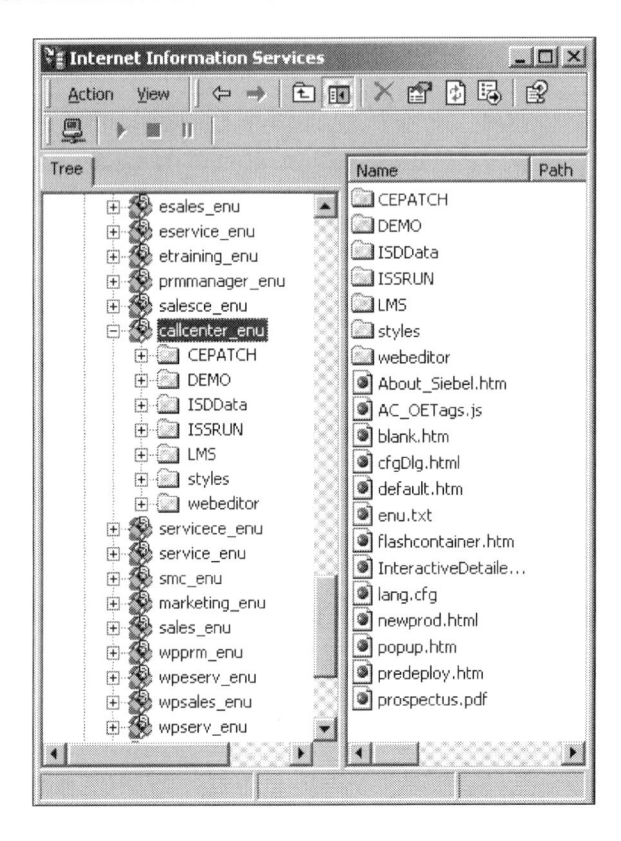

The various virtual directories with a suffix of _enu (for American English) have been created by the metabaseedit utility. Each virtual directory is mapped to the same physical directory PUBLIC/ENU located at the SWSE installation directory.

In order to verify the successful SWSE configuration, we should navigate to the IIS Administration console and check whether a number of virtual directories exist and are mapped as described above.

If the virtual directories do not exist, we must review the files in the SWSE's log directory and repeat the SWSE configuration process after the cause of the problem has been removed.

> Execute the Siebel Configuration Wizard on your demonstration machine and configure the Siebel Web Server Extension. Verify that virtual directories are created on the web server.

Verifying the successful Siebel Enterprise server installation

We can see that installing and configuring a complete Siebel Enterprise is a complex process that involves proper planning and execution of various discrete steps in the correct order. We are now ready to verify that we have successfully completed the basic installation and configuration steps. These verification activities include:

- Starting the Windows services
- Logging on to the Siebel application as the Siebel Administrator

We will then be able to use the Siebel Web Client to undertake the finishing tasks in order to deliver a fully operational Siebel CRM environment.

Starting the Windows services

In order to ensure a fully operational Siebel Server environment, we should ensure that the following Windows system services are started in the sequence they are listed below:

1. Siebel Gateway Name Server
2. Siebel Server
3. World Wide Web Publishing Service

Note that the Siebel Web Server Extension (SWSE) does not have its own service definition. Whenever we need to restart the SWSE, we have to stop and start the according web server (IIS on Microsoft Windows in our example).

Both the Siebel Gateway Name Server and the Siebel Server are implemented as a simple executable named `siebsvc.exe`.

The Siebel Gateway Name Server service calls the `siebsvc.exe` with parameters that "tell" the executable to take over the Gateway Name Server role. The Siebel Gateway Name Server service starts up rather quickly and does not consume a huge amount of memory.

In case of a Siebel Server, the executable takes the role of a Siebel application server, which will establish a connection to its Gateway Name Server in order to read its configuration. Then, it will spawn child processes (one for each server component), which will consume both CPU time and memory.

It is always a good idea to monitor the system (using the Windows Task Manager) or at least wait for a few minutes to allow a Siebel Server to start. The start time is dependent on the amount of enabled components. We will discuss server component management in detail in a later chapter.

After starting the Siebel services, it is beneficial to check the log files for any malicious error message that might indicate an incomplete or failed configuration. The log files for any Siebel software are always situated in the LOG subdirectory of the installation folder.

> On your demonstration machine, navigate to the Windows Services console, stop the three aforementioned services (in reverse order as they are listed), and start them in the sequence they are listed. Ensure that you scan the Siebel log files for errors.

Logging on as the Siebel Administrator for the first time

Now it is time to start Microsoft Internet Explorer (we will log on to a Siebel High-Interactivity application, so this is the only supported browser) and enter the following URL:

`http://localhost/callcenter_enu`

Note that this URL only works on the machine where the web server and SWSE are installed. It is a valid scenario for first tests. If we wish to run our first test from a Windows machine on the network, we will have to replace "localhost" with the hostname or IP address of the web server machine.

The browser will be busy for a noticeable time. As this is the first (or "cold") start of a fresh installation, the application object manager has to load the application metadata into memory. Also, the files that have to reside on the web server, such as images or stylesheets, are now synchronized from the Siebel Server's WEBMASTER subdirectory to the SWSE's PUBLIC directory. This explains the wait time.

Finally, we should see the Siebel login page rendered in the browser, which indicates that the Application Object Manager for Siebel Call Center was able to start and establish an anonymous session. The following screenshot shows the login page for Siebel Call Center loaded in Microsoft Internet Explorer:

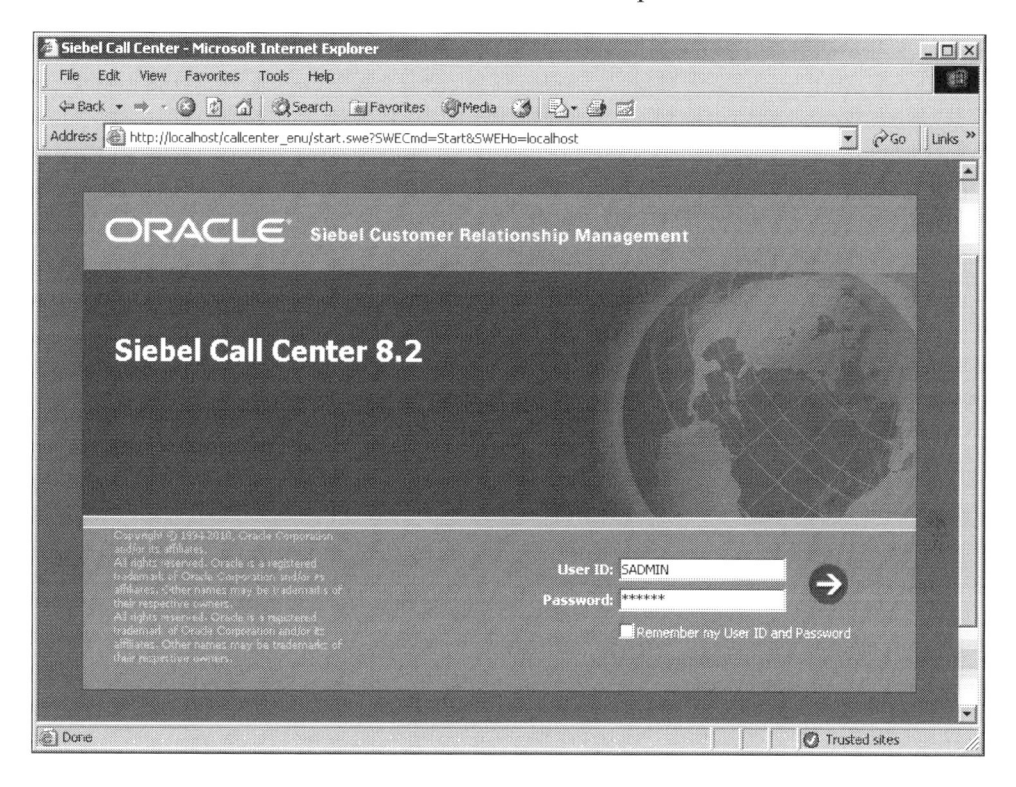

Now we enter **SADMIN** as the user ID and provide the password. We can click the arrow icon or press *ENTER* to continue.

The Siebel Call Center application will now launch. If this is the first launch of a Siebel High-Interactivity application on this machine, we will be prompted to allow the execution of the Siebel High-Interactivity Framework. We should check the box **Always trust content from Oracle USA Inc.** and click **Yes**.

The application continues to launch. One component of the Siebel High-Interactivity Framework is the Web Client Health Check. If any of the critical browser settings are incompatible with the check rules then a dialog similar to the following screenshot is displayed:

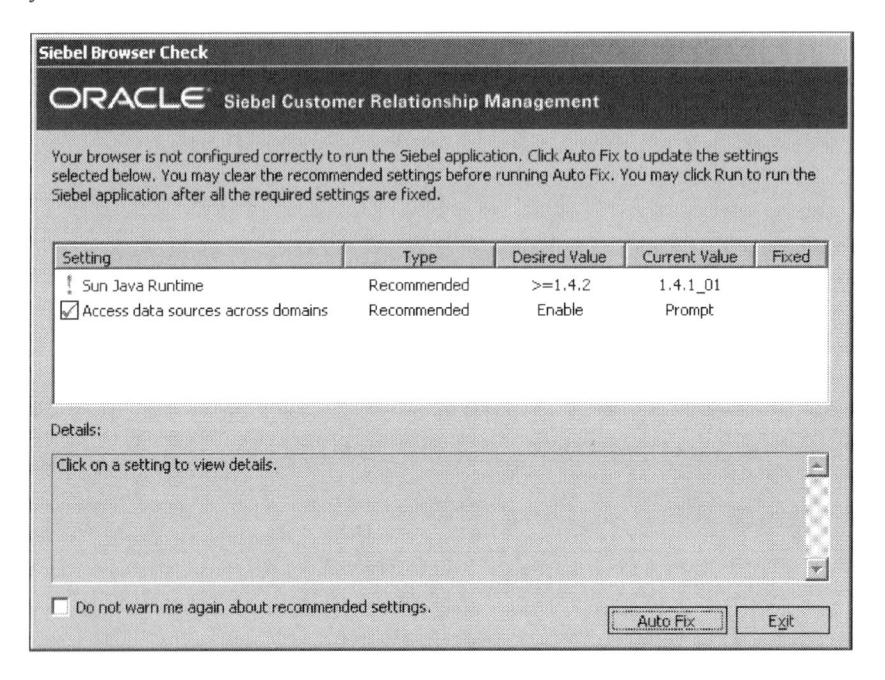

The dialog indicates that the Sun Java Runtime (JRE) does not have the recommended version of 1.4.2 or higher and that the browser setting **Access data sources across domains** is not set to **Enable**. We can click **Auto Fix** to set the parameter (but not install a newer JRE). Then, we click the **Run** button and acknowledge the message that indicates that the Siebel applications might not work as expected.

We will cover the client-side settings in detail in Chapter 6. If problems are encountered during the first application startup, it is generally recommended to add the web server to the browser's trusted sites list.

Finally, we should see the Siebel application's home page view with a greeting message similar to the following screenshot:

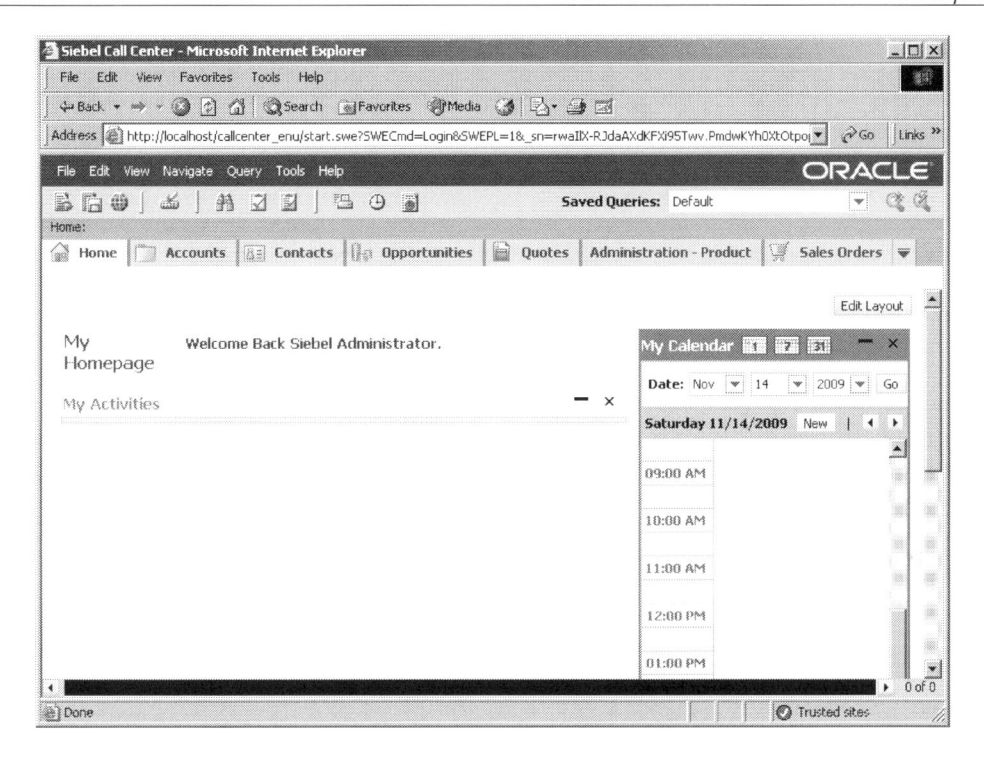

We have now completed the basic steps to install a fully operational Siebel Enterprise.

If we receive an error message instead of the Siebel login page, we must check the log files of the Siebel Server and SWSE thoroughly and verify that we have completed all installation and configuration steps correctly.

> On your demonstration machine, launch Microsoft Internet Explorer and navigate to `http://localhost/callcenter_enu` in order to verify the successful installation of the Siebel Enterprise. Depending on your machine and browser settings, you might receive warnings and messages. However, you should be able to log in as the Siebel Administrator (SADMIN). In the case of errors, you should review the log files and validate the previous steps and processes.

Finalizing the Siebel Server installation

We have successfully logged on to the Siebel Call Center application as the Siebel Administrator (SADMIN), which is the only valid user account at the time of installation.

To finalize the Siebel Enterprise installation and configuration, some small but important tasks are yet to be completed. These tasks include:

- Setting the system service owner account
- Copying the Siebel File System seed files
- Creating an administrative Siebel user
- Applying additional license keys
- Synchronizing Server Components

The process flow of finishing the Siebel CRM server software configuration is as follows:

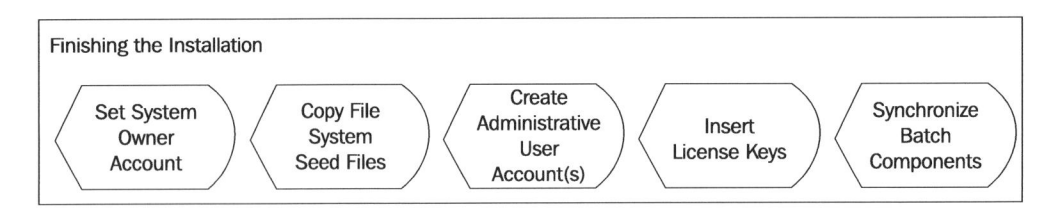

Finishing the Installation

Set System Owner Account → Copy File System Seed Files → Create Administrative User Account(s) → Insert License Keys → Synchronize Batch Components

We will discuss these tasks in the following section.

Setting the System Service owner account

The Siebel Configuration Wizard has created the Siebel Gateway Name Server and Siebel Server system services. These services have the Windows Local System account assigned. In the process of preparing the system for installation of Siebel CRM software, we have created a distinct user account that we now have to assign to the Windows service.

In order to do so, we open the Windows Services console and double-click on the **Siebel Gateway Name Server** service to open its properties dialog box. In the **Log On** tab of the properties dialog, we assign the system owner account that we created earlier. The following screenshot shows the local siebsvc account being assigned to the Siebel Gateway Name Server service. Note that the local domain is addressed using a dot.

Chapter 4

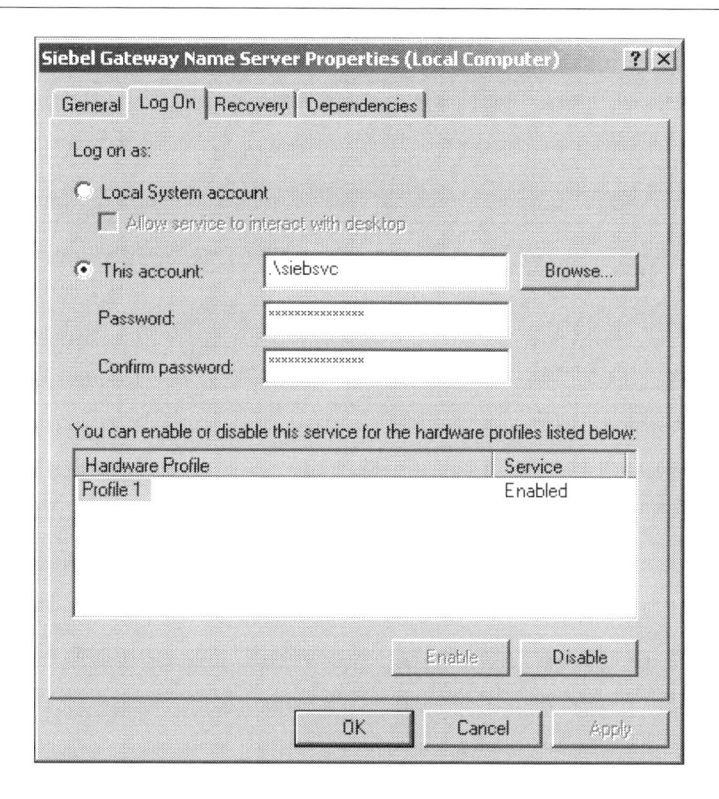

We repeat this procedure for the Siebel Server service. Assigning separate user accounts to the services ensures that we have more control over the user rights assignment for the services and the processes they start. For example, the service account that we assigned to the Siebel Server must have full access to the Siebel File System.

Copying the Siebel File System Seed files

During the installation of the Siebel Database Server Utilities, we chose the feature **Sample Database support**, which caused the creation of a `FILES` subdirectory in the installation folder of the Siebel Database Server Utilities (dbsrvr).

In order to finalize the Siebel Database installation, we navigate to this directory, select all files that have a `.SAF` (Siebel Attachment File) or `.kb` (knowledge base—used for the Smart Answer module) suffix, and copy them to the `ATT` subdirectory of the Siebel File System using the copy utility of our choice.

In order to verify the correct placement of the attachment files, we log on to the Siebel Web Client as **SADMIN** and click the Sitemap (globe) icon to access the **Sitemap**. There we click the **Administration - Document** link and then click the **Correspondence Templates** link to navigate to the Correspondence Templates list view.

In the list of correspondence templates (all imported as seed data during the Siebel database installation), we click the hyperlink for the first template. We should see a dialog box allowing us to choose to open or save the document or cancel the operation. When we click **Open**, the document will be downloaded from the Siebel File System and opened in the associated application.

We must accept the fact that not all seed documents have an associated seed attachment file, but the procedure described above should work for most of the sample correspondence templates and proves that we copied the seed attachment files correctly.

Creating administrative Siebel user accounts

Logging on as the Siebel Administrator (SADMIN) should only be done to verify the installation and to undertake special activities as directed by the Oracle documentation. General administrative tasks should be carried out using our own account, which allows easier tracking and troubleshooting of our activities.

In order to create a new administrative user, we use the Siebel application (where we are logged in as SADMIN) and navigate to the **Administration - User** screen using the Sitemap. In the Employees list view, we use the Query functionality to find the employee with a User ID of "SADMIN" and use the Copy Record command (Right-click and select Copy Record or press *CTRL+B*) to copy the SADMIN employee record.

In the new record, we modify the First Name, Last Name, and User ID fields to reflect our own account. The following screenshot shows a new example employee account for Alexander Hansal with the User ID **AHANSAL** created as a copy of **SADMIN**.

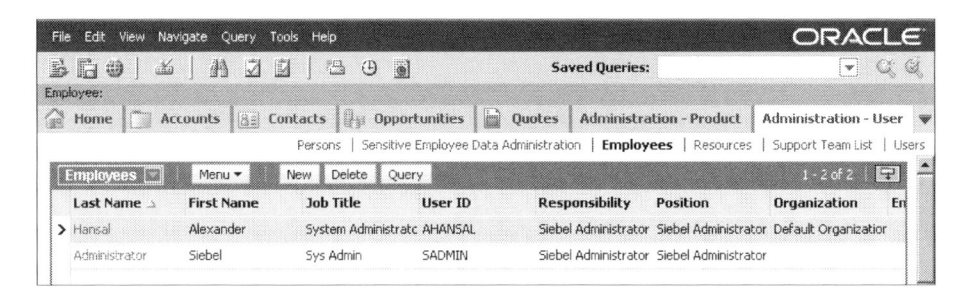

Copying the Siebel Administrator employee ensures that we have the same user rights assigned and can therefore carry out the same administrative tasks.

Before the new user is able to log on, we must register the user ID and password (note that we did not enter a password in the Siebel Client) with the authentication system. As we selected the default authentication via the RDBMS account management in which the Siebel database is located, we have to create a user account in the RDBMS.

We will accomplish this by simply copying the set of commands to create a user account from the `grantusr.sql` file that we used during the Siebel database installation. It is highly recommended to create files and store them in a central location rather than typing the commands directly into the system console. Storing the scripts we used to alter the system configuration allows for easier tracking of changes, troubleshooting, and reuse of the scripts in other environments.

The following code can be imagined as part of a `.sql` input file used to create the AHANSAL user account in an Oracle database.

```
rem Create user account AHANSAL
create user AHANSAL identified by TZ7yxc99;
grant sse_role to AHANSAL;
alter user AHANSAL default tablespace SIEBELDB_DATA;
alter user AHANSAL temporary tablespace TEMP;
```

The script creates a user account whose name matches exactly (case is important) the user ID of the new Siebel employee. The user will have the password **TZ7yxc99** and has the role and tablespace assignment of a typical Siebel user.

Note that this method of creating user accounts in the RDBMS is suitable for small evaluation or development environments. For production environments with thousands of users, companies normally decide to use LDAP or Microsoft Active Directory as the authentication system. User accounts typically already exist in those directories. Setting up authentication via directory services will be discussed in a later chapter.

We can now log off the user SADMIN (by pressing *CTRL+SHIFT+X*) and log in using our new administrative account. We should use that account rather than SADMIN from now on.

> The Siebel Web Client supports keyboard shortcuts.
>
> As we strive for professional and efficient use of the tools provided, we should acquaint ourselves with the most important keyboard shortcuts. A list of keyboard shortcuts can be easily found in the Siebel online help, which can be opened using *CTRL+H*. Click the **Contents** hyperlink and then click **Getting Started: Using Keyboard Shortcuts**.

Applying additional license keys

Even if we are prompted for a license key during the Siebel database installation, a typical Siebel CRM license key contains more than a single line of digits. In order to provide access to all licensed functionality, the administrator must enter the additional license keys.

This can be accomplished using the Siebel Web Client that we used to verify the successful installation and to create new administrative users. Another possibility to manage license keys exists within the Siebel Tools development environment, which we have not yet installed. So, the following section shows how to enter additional license keys using the Siebel Web Client.

Using our own administrative account, we log on to the Siebel application and navigate to the **Administration - Application** screen (using the Sitemap) and then to the **License Keys** view.

In the list, we can use the **New** button to create new records and copy and paste each line from our license key file into the **Key Value** field. This is repeated for each line in the license key file. The following screenshot shows the **License Key** view in the **Administration - Application** screen with additional license key strings entered. Note that the license key values in the following screenshot do not represent real license keys:

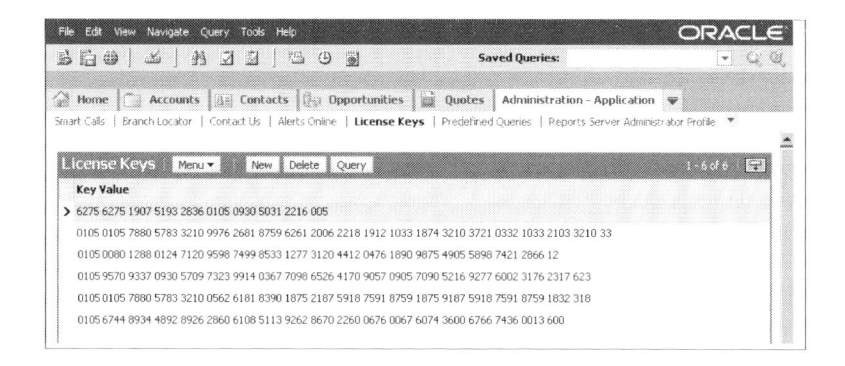

Synchronizing server components

Before the Siebel Server can be used to execute components in batch mode, which is also known as "running jobs", the administrator has to synchronize the batch component definitions from the Siebel Gateway Name Server to the Siebel database. One reason for this is that dropdown lists are used when defining jobs via the graphical user interface (GUI) and these dropdown lists are populated from database tables rather than through a (slower) connection to the Gateway Name Server. Server administration tasks such as running jobs will be discussed in a later chapter in detail.

In the Siebel Web Client, we synchronize the server components by navigating to the site map, the **Administration - Server Configuration** screen, and then the **Synchronize** view. In the empty list, click the **Synchronize** button. The component synchronization takes approximately 20 seconds and we can verify successful synchronization by monitoring the automatic refresh of the components list. The following screenshot shows the Synchronize view after successful synchronization of the server component information from the Siebel Gateway Name server to the Siebel database:

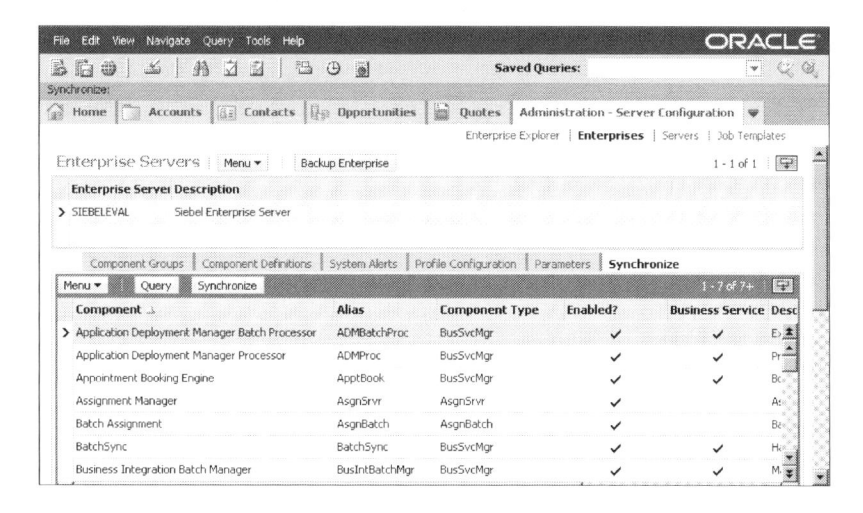

> In order to finalize your Siebel demonstration environment, follow the directions in this section to:
> - Set the system service owner account
> - Copy the Siebel File System seed files
> - Create an administrative Siebel user for yourself
> - Apply additional license keys
> - Synchronize server components

Installing and configuring Siebel server software in unattended mode

For the rather likely event that we have to repeat a Siebel Enterprise component installation and configuration on other systems, the Siebel installer and the Siebel Configuration Wizard support recording our input in response files, which allows us to install and configure the Siebel server software without any manual intervention required.

As the installation and configuration of Siebel server software are separate processes, we have to learn how to:

- Create an `.ini` file for unattended installation
- Create a response file for unattended configuration
- Modify the `.ini` file to launch the configuration automatically
- Execute the installer in unattended mode

Because a Siebel Server is a typical candidate for multiple installations, we use this building block of the Siebel web architecture as an example. In the following section, we will discuss how to create the files needed to install and configure a Siebel Server in unattended mode.

Creating an .ini file for unattended Siebel server installation

When we launch the setup executable for any of the Siebel Enterprise Server components, it reads a file named `siebel.ini`, which is located in the same directory as the executable itself. This file is preconfigured by Oracle to support manual installation using a graphical user interface (GUI). When we wish to run an unattended installation we have to modify the `siebel.ini` file. This can be achieved either through manual editing of the file or by executing the Siebel installer in record mode. We will now discuss the latter option.

First, we should make a copy of the original `siebel.ini` file as a backup.

The next task is to launch the setup executable from the command line similar to the following:

```
setup -args RECORD=D:\ses_install.ini
```

This will launch the installer in record mode. The wizard will proceed through the dialogs as usual. We can perform the steps to install a Siebel server as we did during a real installation. Instead of launching the installation at the end of the process, the wizard will display a message indicating that the response file has been generated in the location indicated by the RECORD argument.

The response file is of similar structure as the regular `siebel.ini` file but it differs from the original file in the following ways:

- All dialog display parameters are set to "no"
- The parameter values entered during recording are part of the default sections

It is a good practice to store the response files in a safe location for later use.

Creating a response file for the Siebel Configuration Wizard

In a similar manner as the Siebel installer, the Siebel Configuration Wizard also supports the recording of response files. We can use the MODE=RECORD argument to invoke the configuration wizard in record mode.

```
C:\SIA8\siebsrvr\BIN\ssincfgw.exe -args LANG=ENU MODE=RECORD MODEL_FILE=C:\SIA8\siebsrvr\admin\siebel_server_sia.scm
```

The above command will invoke the Siebel Configuration Wizard for the Siebel server in record mode. The wizard will execute as in live mode except that at the end of the process it will prompt for a location of the response file. The response file is an XML file that contains the values entered in the wizard's dialogs.

Modifying the .ini file to launch the configuration automatically

The .ini file that we have generated using the Siebel installer's record mode has to be modified in order to invoke the configuration wizard automatically when the installation is complete.

The configuration wizard supports an execute mode, during which it reads a response file. In the sense of a real unattended installation, we have to combine the installation and configuration processes in a single invocation. This can be achieved by adding information to the installer's .ini file.

The following example enables automatic configuration of a Siebel Server on Microsoft Windows after installation.

In the .ini file, locate the **[RunAfter.Windows]** section and set the value of the parameter **ConfigServer.Windows** to **yes**. The following screenshot shows the **[RunAfter.Windows]** section of the **.ini** file after the modification:

```
[RunAfter.Windows]
ConfigGateway.Windows = no
ConfigGatewaySMB.Windows = no
ConfigEnterpriseSMB.Windows = no
ConfigServer.Windows = yes
ConfigAgent.Windows = no
```

Next, we locate the **[ConfigServer.Windows]** section and make the following changes to the Execute and Arg parameters:

Parameter	New Value (Example)
Execute	$(SiebelRoot)\siebsrvr\bin\ssincfgw.exe
Arg	-args MODE=EXECUTE REPEAT=FALSE IN_RESPONSE_FILE=D:\siebel_server_sia.xml -is:javaconsole -console

The Execute parameter contains the relative path to the Siebel configuration wizard executable (`ssincfgw.exe`). The Arg parameter contains the commands to execute the configuration wizard in EXECUTE mode with the `D:\siebel_server_sia.xml` file as input. The wizard will run in console mode and will not repeat itself (`REPEAT=FALSE`). The screenshot below shows the **[ConfigServer.Windows]** section of the `.ini` file after the modification:

```
[ConfigServer.windows]
Condition           = $(SiebelSelected)=yes,$(Patch)=no
Execute             = $(SiebelRoot)\siebsrvr\bin\ssincfgw.exe
Arg                 = -args MODE=EXECUTE REPEAT=FALSE IN_RESPONSE_FILE=D:\siebel_server_sia.xml
workingDirectory    = $(SiebelRoot)\siebsrvr\bin
```

Executing the installer in unattended mode

We are now ready to run the Siebel installer in unattended mode. We must ensure that the response files for both the installer (`.ini`) and the configuration wizard (`.xml`) are stored in the correct folders.

We can then launch the installer using the following shell command:

`setup -args SS_SETUP_INI=d:\ses_install.ini -is:javaconsole -console`

The command invokes the setup executable in console mode and specifies the `d:\ses_install.ini` file as the input file. Console mode is recommended for unattended install because of easier monitoring. The following screenshot shows the command shell window that displays the progress of the Siebel Enterprise Server installer during an unattended Siebel Server installation.

Summary

Configuring Siebel server software correctly is essential for the flawless operation of the Siebel CRM infrastructure. In this chapter, we discussed the procedures to configure the Siebel Gateway Name Server, register a Siebel Enterprise, and configure a Siebel Server within the Enterprise.

Additionally, we discussed the configuration steps for the Siebel Web Server Extension followed by a series of checks and finalizing steps such as entering license keys and synchronizing server components to ensure the availability of all licensed features.

The Siebel installer and configuration wizards can be launched in unattended mode. Preparing and executing an unattended installation of a Siebel Server concluded the discussion on configuring Siebel server software on Microsoft Windows-based operating systems.

In the next chapter, we will learn how to install and configure the building blocks of the Siebel server architecture on Linux.

5
Installing and Configuring Siebel CRM Server Software on Linux

In this chapter, we will explain the concepts of installing Siebel CRM server software on Linux and other UNIX-based operating systems using a practical approach. The following topics will be discussed:

- Installing the Siebel Gateway Name Server
- Installing the Siebel Server
- Installing the Siebel Database Server Utilities
- Installing the Siebel Web Server Extension
- Using the Siebel Software Configuration Wizard on Linux or UNIX
- Configuring the Siebel Gateway Name Server
- Configuring the Siebel Enterprise
- Configuring the Siebel Web Server Extension Logical Profile
- Installing the Siebel Database Schema and Seed Data
- Configuring the Siebel Server
- Configuring the Siebel Web Server Extension
- Verifying the successful Siebel Enterprise installation
- Final steps

Due to the repetitive nature of Siebel installation procedures across different operating systems, this chapter references the previous chapters *Installing Siebel CRM Server Software on Microsoft Windows* and *Configuring Siebel CRM Server Software on Microsoft Windows* when applicable. It is therefore recommended to read the aforementioned chapters first, to understand the complete installation and configuration processes.

This chapter also includes "Follow Me" instructions, which the reader can use to complete a demonstration installation of Siebel server software. The "Follow Me" instructions assume that a virtual machine with **Oracle Enterprise Linux** as the operating system is available. Also, the installation of **Oracle Database 11g R2** and **Oracle HTTP Server** must have been successfully completed on that machine. If you wish to install a demonstration environment for self-study purposes while you follow this chapter, you can download the software packages from Oracle's E-Delivery website at `http://edelivery.oracle.com`. The official documentation libraries for Oracle software—which also include the installation guides—can be found on the Oracle Technology Network website at `http://otn.oracle.com`.

Command examples and procedures in this chapter originate from the **Siebel Installation Guide for UNIX** (Version 8.1), which is available as part of the Siebel documentation at `http://download.oracle.com/docs/cd/E14004_01/books/SiebInstUNIX/booktitle.html`.

Installing the Siebel Gateway Name Server

The installation of the Siebel Enterprise Server components on Linux and other UNIX-based operating systems begins with executing the setup[OS] executable in the `Siebel_Enterprise_Server` folder of the Siebel installation image, where [OS] has to be replaced with a name representing the operating system.

For example, on Linux, the executable is named setuplinux. The following screenshot shows the **Siebel_Enterprise_Server** folder of the Siebel installation image for Linux:

Chapter 5

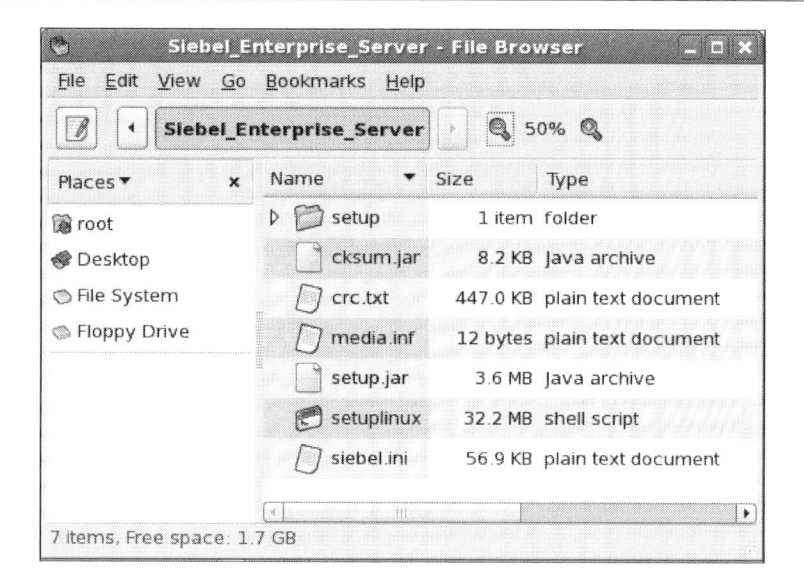

The file named `setuplinux` must be executed to run the InstallShield wizard.

Before launching the setup executable, we must ensure that a directory named `/var/adm/siebel` exists. This directory is used to store files such as `vpd.properties`, which control the state of the installation.

It is also recommended to administer all installation steps under the same non-root user account.

The following table describes the steps that the InstallShield Wizard executes and provides example values for entries an administrator has to make to install the Siebel Gateway Name Server on Linux:

Step	Description	Tasks and Example Values
1	Start the InstallShield Wizard.	Execute the setuplinux file in the `Siebel_Enterprise_Server` folder.
2	The Welcome dialog is displayed.	Click **Next**.
3	Specify the directory to which the application files should be copied.	Example: `/u01/app/siebel/`. **The directory should already have been specified in the planning document.** A subdirectory for the Siebel Gateway Name Server installation will be created automatically. Click **Next**.

[119]

Installing and Configuring Siebel CRM Server Software on Linux

Step	Description	Tasks and Example Values
4	Select products to install.	Select the following: • **Gateway Name Server** Click **Next**.
5	Select setup type.	Select **Custom** Click **Next**.
6	Feature selection.	Keep the default selection. Click **Next**.
7	Language selection.	Select **ENU – English (American)** Click **Next**.
8	Summary	Check the information in the summary dialog. Click **Next**.
9	The Siebel Configuration Wizard is launched automatically.	We will launch the Siebel Configuration Wizard later to finish the configuration of the Siebel Gateway Name Server. Click Cancel to close the Siebel Configuration Wizard and confirm with **Yes**.
10	The InstallShield wizard success dialog is displayed.	Click **Finish**.

We can verify the installation of the Siebel Gateway Name Server by navigating to the installer target directory. We can observe that the installer has created the following:

- A directory `/u01/app/siebel/_uninst`, which hosts the uninstaller program
- The directories and files needed to configure and run the Siebel Gateway Name Server

> If you wish to follow along with this chapter, you can now run the installation wizard for the Siebel Gateway Name Server on a machine that fulfills the prerequisites described at the beginning of this chapter.

Installing the Siebel Server

In the following section, we will discuss the process to install the Siebel Server binaries on Linux. The following table entails the steps of the process and the dialogs displayed by the InstallShield wizard. We start with invoking the setup executable.

Step	Description	Tasks and Example Values
1	Start the InstallShield Wizard.	Execute the setuplinux file in the `Siebel_Enterprise_Server` folder.
2	The Welcome dialog is displayed.	Click **Next**.
3	Install new components or add languages.	This dialog is displayed when the installer detects any existing Siebel Enterprise Server installations. Keep **Install a new instance or add new components** selected. Click **Next**.
4	Specify the directory to which the application files should be copied.	Example: **/u01/app/siebel**. **The directory should already have been specified in the planning document.** A subdirectory for the Siebel Server installation will be created automatically. Click **Next**.
5	Select products to install.	Select the following: • **Siebel Server** Click **Next**.
6	Select setup type.	Select **Custom**. Click **Next**.
7	The selectable features for the Siebel Server are displayed.	Deselect **Siebel Management Agent** Note: It is recommended to install the Siebel Management Agent separately. Click **Next**.
8	Summary	Check the information in the summary dialog. Click **Next**.

Step	Description	Tasks and Example Values
9	The Siebel Configuration Wizard for the Siebel Server is launched automatically.	We will launch the Siebel Configuration Wizard later to finish the configuration of the Siebel Server. Click **Cancel** to close the Siebel Configuration Wizard and confirm with **Yes**.
10	The InstallShield wizard success dialog is displayed.	Click **Finish**.

In step 7 of the table above, the installation wizard for the Siebel Server prompts for the following selectable features of the Siebel Server:

- Object Manager Components
- Handheld Synchronization
- Data Quality Connector
- Remote Search Support
- Java Integrator
- Siebel Management Agent

These features are explained in detail in Chapter 3, *Installing Siebel CRM Server Software on Microsoft Windows*.

Verifying the Siebel Server installation

To verify the successful installation of the Siebel Server, we can navigate to the installation root folder. A siebsrvr directory should exist that contains the folders and files necessary to configure and operate one or more Siebel Servers on this machine. If the siebsrvr directory is not present or the installation aborts with an error, we should check the log file that can be found in the installation root directory. Before repeating the installation process, we should ensure that all previous installations are removed—if possible using the uninstaller utility—and that the respective directories are deleted.

> If you wish to follow along with this chapter, you can now run the installation wizard for the Siebel Server on the demonstration machine.

Installing the Siebel Database Server Utilities

As discussed in Chapter 3, the Siebel Database Server Utilities must be installed on a machine that hosts a Siebel Server.

The following table describes the steps that the InstallShield wizard executes when we install the Siebel Database Server utilities on Linux:

Step	Description	Tasks and Example Values
1	Start the InstallShield Wizard.	Execute the setuplinux file in the `Siebel_Enterprise_Server` folder.
2	The Welcome dialog is displayed.	Click **Next**.
3	Install new components or add languages.	This dialog is displayed when the installer detects any existing Siebel Enterprise Server installations. Keep **Install a new instance or add new components** selected. Click **Next**.
4	Specify the directory to which the application files should be copied.	Example: **/u01/app/siebel**. **The directory should already have been specified in the planning document.** A subdirectory for the Siebel Database Server Configuration Utilities will be created automatically. Click **Next**.
5	Select products to install.	Select the following: • **Database Server Configuration Utilities** Click **Next**
6	Select setup type.	Select **Custom**. Click **Next**.

[123]

Step	Description	Tasks and Example Values
7	The selectable features for the Database Server Utilities are displayed.	In order to save disk space, we can safely deselect the IBM DB2 options.
		Note: Keep the **Sample Database support** option selected to install the files residing in the file system that go along with the Siebel seed data. The sample database support feature and necessary procedures are described in Chapter 3.
		Click **Next**.
8	Summary	Check the information in the summary dialog.
		Click **Next**.
9	The InstallShield wizard success dialog is displayed.	Click **Finish**.

Once the wizard finishes copying the files for the Siebel Database Server utilities, we can verify the existence of the dbsrvr directory in the installation root folder. If the directory is not present, or the installation procedure has encountered an error, we should check the log file, correct the problem, and remove any existing installations before we attempt to repeat the installation.

> On your demonstration machine, execute the installation of the Siebel Database Server Utilities and verify the procedure.

Installing the Siebel Web Server Extension

If we wish to use machines that run on Linux or other UNIX-based operating systems as web servers for our Siebel CRM infrastructure, we have to ensure that a supported version of the Apache HTTP Server is installed. In order to verify the correct HTTP server, we should consult the Siebel System Requirements and Supported Platforms document for the selected Siebel CRM version. This document is available on the Oracle Technology Network website at http://download.oracle.com/docs/cd/E11886_01/srsphomepage.html.

Chapter 5

To run the web server on Oracle Enterprise Linux for example, we have to download and install the Oracle HTTP Server 2.0 as indicated in the official documentation.

The InstallShield setup executable for the Siebel Web Server Extension is located in the `Siebel_Web_Server_Extension` folder of the Siebel installation image.

The following table illustrates the process of installing the Siebel Web Server Extension (SWSE) on Linux:

Step	Description	Tasks and Example Values
1	Start the InstallShield Wizard.	Execute the setuplinux file in the `Siebel_Web_Server_Extension` folder.
2	The Welcome dialog is displayed.	Click **Next**.
3	Specify the directory to which the application files should be copied.	Example: **/u01/app/siebel/sweapp**. **The directory should already have been specified in the planning document.** Click **Next**.
4	Language selection.	Select **enu – English (American)** Click **Next**.
5	Summary	Check the information in the summary dialog. Click **Next**.
6	The Siebel Configuration Wizard for the Siebel Web Server Extension is launched automatically.	We will launch the Siebel Configuration Wizard later to finish the configuration of the Siebel Web Server Extension. Click **Cancel** to close the Siebel Configuration Wizard and confirm with **Yes**.
7	The InstallShield wizard success dialog is displayed.	Click **Finish**.

To verify the successful installation of the Siebel Web Server Extension, we can navigate to the installation target directory and check whether folders and files have been created.

[125]

> Ensure that your demonstration machine hosts a supported web server and follow the instructions in this section to install the Siebel Web Server Extension.

Using the Siebel Software Configuration Wizard on Linux or UNIX

We can invoke the Software Configuration Wizard on Linux or UNIX-based operating systems from the command shell only. For example, the following command will launch the Siebel Enterprise Configuration wizard in the default GUI mode.

```
ssincfgw -args LANG=ENU MODE=LIVE MODEL_FILE=/u01/app/siebel/gtwysrvr/admin/enterprise_console_sia.scm
```

If we do not have a graphical user interface, we can invoke the wizard in console mode using the `-is:javaconsole -console` argument like in the following command.

```
ssincfgw -args LANG=ENU MODE=LIVE MODEL_FILE=/u01/app/siebel/gtwysrvr/admin/enterprise_console_sia.scm -is:javaconsole -console
```

The ssincfgw executable is located in the `BIN` subdirectory of the software installation folder (for example in `/u01/app/siebel/gtwysrvr/bin`). The `-args` switch is followed by argument names and values.

The `LANG` argument takes a valid three-letter language code and controls the language used for the configuration wizard's dialogs (ENU for example is for English – United States).

The `MODE` argument takes one of the following values:

- `LIVE`
- `RECORD`
- `EXECUTE`

In `LIVE` mode, the configuration wizard will directly execute the necessary commands at the end of the configuration process. In `RECORD` mode, the wizard generates an XML file containing the parameter values entered during the process. The XML file can later be used to automate the configuration. This unattended mode is invoked by using the `EXECUTE` value.

The `MODEL_FILE` parameter must point to a text file with suffix `.scm`. These files reside in the `admin` directories of the software installation folders and are provided by Oracle. The `.scm` files contain the necessary information to render the configuration wizards dialogs and entry forms.

The following table lists the model files for each configuration target:

Configuration target	Model file example location
Siebel Gateway Name Server	`/u01/app/siebel/gtwysrvr/admin/enterprise_console_sia.scm`
Siebel Enterprise	Note: This is the model file for Siebel Industry Applications (SIA). For horizontal Siebel enterprise applications, we use the `enterprise_console.scm` file.
Siebel Web Server Extension Logical Profile	
Siebel Database	`/u01/app/siebel/siebsrvr/admin/dbsrvr.scm`
Siebel Server	`/u01/app/siebel/siebsrvr/admin/siebel_server_sia.scm` or `siebel_server.scm`
Siebel Web Server Extension	`/u01/app/siebel/sweapp/admin/swse_server_sia.scm` or `swse_server.scm`

Preparing to run the Software Configuration Wizard

Before we launch the ssincfgw executable, we must set library paths in order for the wizard to execute correctly. The commands to set the paths are provided by Oracle in shell scripts such as `cfgenv.sh` (for Bourne shell).

At the command line, we navigate to the root folder of the software we want to configure (for example `/u01/app/siebel/gtwysrvr`) and execute the shell script.

`. ./cfgenv.sh`

Note that this is the syntax for Bourne shell. We must ensure that there is a space between the dots in order to avoid the script being eventually executed in a different shell.

The script sets the following environment variables:

- `PATH` (appends the bin directory of the Siebel software)
- `LD_LIBRARY_PATH` (appends the lib directory of the Siebel software)

- CLASSPATH (set to the `setup.jar` in the `bin` directory of the Siebel software)

The following screenshot shows the preconfigured `cfgenv.sh` script, which has to be executed before we launch the Siebel Configuration Wizard:

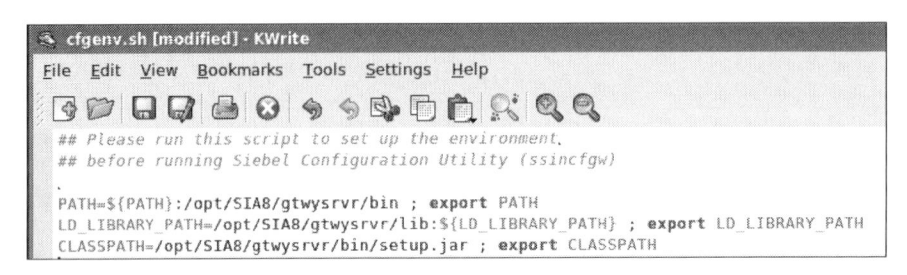

```
## Please run this script to set up the environment.
## before running Siebel Configuration Utility (ssincfgw)

PATH=${PATH}:/opt/SIA8/gtwysrvr/bin ; export PATH
LD_LIBRARY_PATH=/opt/SIA8/gtwysrvr/lib:${LD_LIBRARY_PATH} ; export LD_LIBRARY_PATH
CLASSPATH=/opt/SIA8/gtwysrvr/bin/setup.jar ; export CLASSPATH
```

Configuring the Siebel Gateway Name Server

As we learned in Chapter 3, *Installing Siebel CRM Server Software on Microsoft Windows*, the Siebel Gateway Name Server must be fully installed, configured, and started before we can continue with the configuration process.

As we have successfully installed the Siebel Gateway Name Server software, we can now configure the name daemon (which is another way to describe the Siebel Gateway Name Server) on Linux.

To start the Siebel Configuration Wizard, we open a command console, navigate to the root directory of the Gateway Name Server (for example `/u01/app/siebel/gtwysrvr`) and execute the `cfgenv.sh` script:

`. ./cfgenv.sh`

Next, we navigate to the bin directory:

`cd bin`

Now, we are ready to invoke the configuration wizard for the Siebel Enterprise with the following command:

`ssincfgw -args LANG=ENU MODE=LIVE MODEL_FILE=/u01/app/siebel/gtwysrvr/admin/enterprise_console_sia.scm`

The following table describes the process steps and dialogs displayed by the Siebel Configuration Wizard:

Step	Description	Tasks and Example Values
1	Start the Configuration Wizard.	Prepare and use the ssincfgw executable with the input arguments described above to start the wizard.
2	Configuration Wizard Welcome Page	Select **Create New Configuration**
		Click **Next**.
3	Select tasks for new configurations.	Select **Configure a New Gateway Name Server**.
		Click **Next**.
4	Gateway Name Server TCP/IP port.	Keep the default (2320)
		Note: This value comes from the **planning document**.
		Click **Next**.
5	Final Tasks	References to Siebel Bookshelf and EVT are displayed.
		Click **Next**.
6	Summary	Verify the selections and values you provided.
		Click **Next**.
7	Do you want to execute configuration?	Click **Yes**.
8	Execution results are displayed.	Click **OK**.
9	The wizard jumps back to the configuration mode selection page.	Select **Exit Configuration Wizard**
		Click **Next**.

Verifying the Siebel Gateway Name Server Installation on Linux or UNIX

In order to verify the successful configuration of a new Siebel Gateway Name Server and its operating state, we navigate to its root folder and execute the `siebenv.sh` script.

```
. ./siebenv.sh
```

The `siebenv.sh` script sets the environment variables necessary to execute the Gateway Name Server control commands. These commands are:

- `list_ns`
- `start_ns`
- `stop_ns`

In the following, we discuss how to use these commands to verify the status of the Gateway Name Server.

We can use the `list_ns` command to verify that a Siebel Gateway Server is installed and running. From the Gateway Name Server's installation folder, we enter:

`list_ns`

The script executes and returns a message, which indicates the start up time and process ID of the Siebel Gateway Name Server. If the message indicates that the service is not started, we can use the `start_ns` script to start it. At the command line enter:

`start_ns`

followed by:

`list_ns`

to verify the successful start.

Another way to verify that the Siebel Gateway Name Server is running is by using the `ps` command. The following command would output all process instances in execution by the siebsvc program, which is the executable behind the Siebel Gateway Name Server and the Siebel Server:

`ps- fea | grep siebsvc`

The `-fea` switch ensures that we see full information for all processes. We use the | symbol to direct the output to the "pipe" and the `grep` command to read only those lines from the pipe that contain the string `siebsvc`.

```
[ahansal@ahansaloel ~]$ ps -fea | grep siebsvc
root      10250     1  0 07:27 ?        00:00:01 siebsvc -s gtwyns -a /f /home/ah
ansal/SIA8/gtwysrvr/sys/siebns.dat /t 2320 /c /home/ahansal/SIA8/gtwysrvr/bin/ga
teway.cfg
```

The previous screenshot shows the result of the ps command. We can verify that the siebsvc executable is running and has instantiated the Gateway Name Server by verifying the **-s** switch **gtwyns**.

If we need to stop the Gateway Name Server, we issue the following command at the installation folder:

`stop_ns`

This command will stop the Siebel Gateway Name Server. However, the Siebel Gateway Name Server must be operational before we continue with the installation of a Siebel Enterprise.

Apart from creating a new daemon or service, the configuration wizard has also invoked the creation of the `siebns.dat` file, which we can now locate in the `sys` subdirectory of the Siebel Gateway Name Server installation folder.

> On your demonstration machine, launch the Siebel Software Configuration Wizard for the Siebel Enterprise as described in this section and follow the steps to configure a new Siebel Gateway Name Server.

Configuring the Siebel Enterprise

The Gateway Name Server is now operational. We can now start to create the definition of a new Siebel Enterprise that will later contain one or more Siebel Servers.

To start the configuration of the Siebel Enterprise, we launch the Configuration Wizard for the Siebel Enterprise again on the machine hosting the Gateway Name Server. We could have also kept the wizard open once the Gateway Name Server had been configured.

If we have not yet done so, we prepare to run the configuration wizard by executing the `cfgenv.sh` script from the Gateway Name Server's root directory. Then, we navigate to the `bin` directory and invoke the ssincfgw executable:

`ssincfgw -args LANG=ENU MODE=LIVE MODEL_FILE=/u01/app/siebel/gtwysrvr/admin/enterprise_console_sia.scm`

Installing and Configuring Siebel CRM Server Software on Linux

The following table conveys the details of the process of configuring a new Siebel Enterprise:

Step	Description	Tasks and Example Values
1	Start the Configuration Wizard.	Prepare and use the ssincfgw executable with the input arguments described above to start the wizard.
2	Configuration Wizard Welcome Page	Select **Create New Configuration** Click **Next**.
3	Select tasks for new configurations.	Select **Configure a New Enterprise in a Gateway Name Server** Click **Next**.
4	Gateway Name Server Authentication User Account Name	These parameters have no effect during the first configuration. However, we set the following: User Account Name: **SADMIN** User Account Password: **TJay357D** Note: These values come from the **planning document**. Click **Next**.
5	Gateway Name Server host name and TCP/IP port.	Enter the Gateway Name Server host name and the TCP/IP port used by the service. Host Name: **localhost** TCP/IP port: **2320** Note: These values come from the **planning document**. We can use localhost as the hostname because the wizard is executed on the same machine where the Siebel Gateway Name Server is installed. Click **Next**.
6	Siebel Enterprise Name	Enterprise Name: **SIEBELEVAL** Note: This value comes from the **planning document**. Description: **Siebel Evaluation Enterprise** Click **Next**.

Step	Description	Tasks and Example Values
7	Primary Siebel File System	Enter the path to the shared directory dedicated for the Siebel File System.
		Primary Siebel File System: **/u01/app/siebel/fs**
		Note: This value comes from the **planning document**.
		Click **Next**.
8	Database Platform	Select **Oracle Database Enterprise Edition**
		Note: This value comes from the **planning document**.
		Click **Next**.
9	Table Owner and Oracle SQLNet connect string.	Database Table Owner: **SIEBEL**
		SQLNet Connect String: **orcl**
		Note: These values come from the **planning document**. The parameters required in this step are specific to the database vendor selected in step 8.
		Click **Next**.
10	Siebel Database User Account Name	User Account Name: **SADMIN**
		User Account Password: **TJay357D**
		Note: These values come from the **planning document**.
		Click **Next**.
11	Enterprise Security Authentication Profile	Select **Database Authentication (Default)**.
		Note: This value comes from the **planning document**. Details on Siebel Security Authentication will be discussed in a separate chapter.
		Click **Next**.
12	Security Adapter Name	Keep the default.
		Click **Next**.
13	Propagate Authentication Settings to the Gateway Name Server	Keep the default (checked).
		Note: As this is the first time setup of a Siebel Enterprise, we must ensure to run the wizard on the Gateway Name Server machine for this feature to work.
		Click **Next**.

Installing and Configuring Siebel CRM Server Software on Linux

Step	Description	Tasks and Example Values
14	Additional tasks for configuring the enterprise.	As this is the first time setup of a Siebel Enterprise for demonstration purposes, we do not select any options. All these settings can be done at a later time.
		Keep all checkboxes unselected.
		Click **Next**.
15	Summary	Verify the selections and values you provided.
		Click **Next**.
16	Do you want to execute configuration?	Click **Yes**.
17	Execution results are displayed.	Click **OK**.
18	The wizard jumps back to the configuration mode selection page.	Select **Exit Configuration Wizard**.
		Click **Next**.

Verifying the successful Enterprise configuration

During the configuration of the Enterprise, the wizard does the following:

- Accesses the Siebel Gateway Name Server and register the new Enterprise
- Creates a security profile for the Siebel Gateway Name Server using the information provided in the dialogs
- Creates an ODBC data source

The ODBC data source name is created using the Enterprise's name and a suffix of "_DSN". In our example, the name of the new ODBC data source is SIEBELEVAL_DSN.

Verifying the ODBC data source

The Siebel Configuration Wizard for the Siebel Enterprise creates the `.odbc.ini` file (note the dot at the beginning of the file name, which makes it a hidden file), which contains the library and driver information for the ODBC driver delivered with the Siebel software installer.

We can locate the file in the `sys` directory of the Siebel Gateway Name Server installation folder. The following screenshot shows the `.odbc.ini` file created by the Siebel Configuration Wizard.

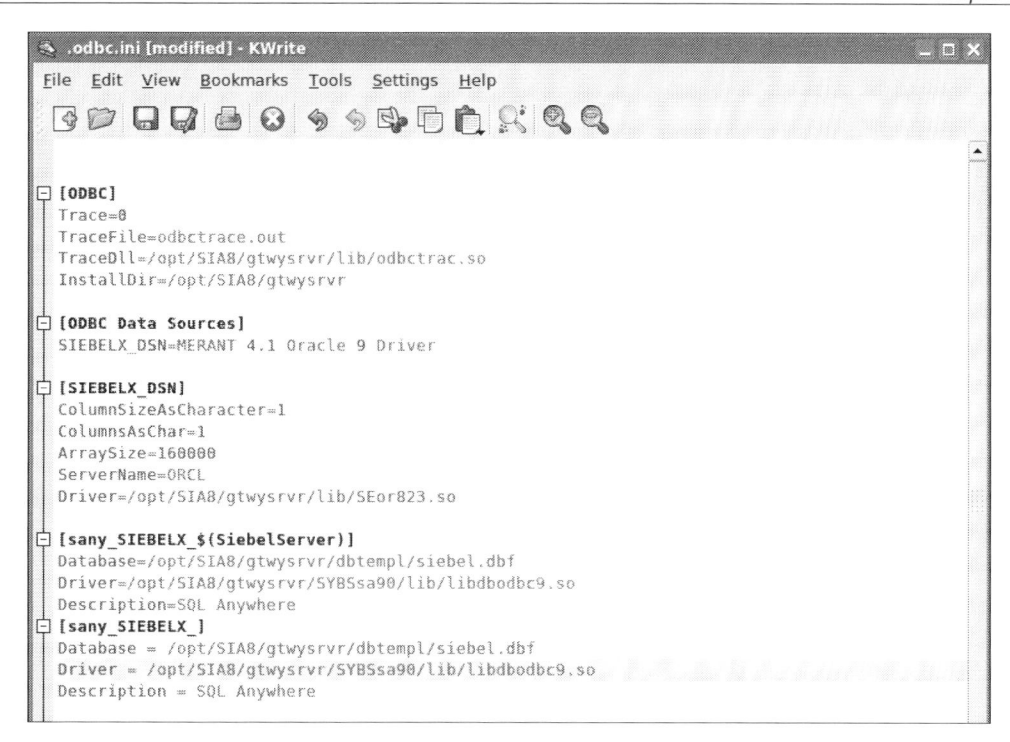

```
[ODBC]
Trace=0
TraceFile=odbctrace.out
TraceDll=/opt/SIA8/gtwysrvr/lib/odbctrac.so
InstallDir=/opt/SIA8/gtwysrvr
[ODBC Data Sources]
SIEBELX_DSN=MERANT 4.1 Oracle 9 Driver
[SIEBELX_DSN]
ColumnSizeAsCharacter=1
ColumnsAsChar=1
ArraySize=160000
ServerName=ORCL
Driver=/opt/SIA8/gtwysrvr/lib/SEor823.so
[sany_SIEBELX_$(SiebelServer)]
Database=/opt/SIA8/gtwysrvr/dbtempl/siebel.dbf
Driver=/opt/SIA8/gtwysrvr/SYBSsa90/lib/libdbodbc9.so
Description=SQL Anywhere
[sany_SIEBELX_]
Database = /opt/SIA8/gtwysrvr/dbtempl/siebel.dbf
Driver = /opt/SIA8/gtwysrvr/SYBSsa90/lib/libdbodbc9.so
Description = SQL Anywhere
```

The **[SIEBELX_DSN]** entry defines the ODBC data source for the Siebel enterprise named **SIEBELX**.

> You can now execute the Siebel Configuration Wizard and create a new Siebel Enterprise. Use the table provided in this chapter and your planning document to enter the correct parameter values.

Configuring the Siebel Web Server Extension logical profile

In order to create the SWSE logical profile, we employ the Siebel Configuration Wizard again and start the Siebel Enterprise Configuration using the ssincfgw executable.

Installing and Configuring Siebel CRM Server Software on Linux

If we have not yet done so, we prepare to run the configuration wizard by executing the `cfgenv.sh` script from the Gateway Name Server's root directory. Then, we navigate to the `bin` directory and invoke the ssincfgw executable:

```
ssincfgw -args LANG=ENU MODE=LIVE MODEL_FILE=/u01/app/siebel/gtwysrvr/
admin/enterprise_console_sia.scm
```

The following table provides details on the Configuration Wizard's dialogs. Please refer to the section on the SWSE logical profile configuration in Chapter 4 for details on the parameters.

Step	Description	Tasks and Example Values
1	Start the Configuration Wizard.	Prepare and use the ssincfgw executable with the input arguments described above to start the wizard.
2	Configuration Wizard Welcome Page	Select **Create New Configuration**
		Click **Next**.
3	Select tasks for new configurations.	Select **Configure a New Siebel Web Server Extension Logical Profile**
		Click **Next**.
4	Siebel Enterprise Name and logical profile storage folder.	Enterprise Name: **SIEBELEVAL**
		Note: This value comes from the **planning document**.
		SWSE Logical Profile Name: Keep the default (a subdirectory of the Siebel Gateway Name Server's installation folder) and ensure that the target folder exists.
		Click **Next**.
5	Collect application specific statistics.	Keep the default (checked).
		Note: This value comes from the **planning document**.
		Click **Next**.
6	Compression Type (for traffic between SWSE and Siebel Server).	Keep the default (None).
		Note: This value comes from the **planning document**.
		Click **Next**.
7	HTTP 1.1-compliant firewall/enable compression.	Keep the default (Checked).
		Click **Next**.

Chapter 5

Step	Description	Tasks and Example Values
8	Session timeout values.	Enter 3000 and 9000.
		Note: These values come from the **planning document**.
		Click **Next**.
9	HTTP Port Numbers	Keep the default values (80/443)
		Note: These values come from the **planning document**.
		Click **Next**.
10	FQDN (Fully qualified domain name)	Keep the default (blank).
		Click **Next**.
11	High Interactivity or employee user login name and password.	User Name: **SADMIN**
		Password: **TJay357D**
		Note: These values come from the **planning document**.
		Click **Next**.
12	Password encryption.	Keep the default (unchecked)
		Click **Next**.
13	Standard Interactivity or contact user login name and password.	User Name: **GUESTCST**
		Password: **8icJIPZH**
		Note: These values come from the **planning document**.
		Click **Next**.
14	Siebel Enterprise Security Token	Security Token: TZH65ret(enter twice).
		Note: This value comes from the **planning document**.
		Click **Next**.
15	Web server statistics page name	Keep the default (_stats.swe).
		Click **Next**.
16	Deploy SSL in the Enterprise.	Keep the default (unchecked).
		Click **Next**.
17	Summary	Verify the selections and values you provided.
		Click **Next**.
18	Do you want to execute configuration?	Click **Yes**

Step	Description	Tasks and Example Values
19	Execution results are displayed.	Click **OK**.
20	The wizard jumps back to the configuration mode selection page.	Select **Exit Configuration Wizard**. Click **Next**.

Verifying the successful SWSE logical profile creation

In order to verify the creation of the SWSE profile files, we can navigate to the profile storage folder specified in step 4 and verify the existence of several configuration file templates such as `eapps.cfg`.

> On your demonstration machine, execute the Siebel Configuration Wizard to create the SWSE logical profile. You can use the table in this section as a guide.

Installing the Siebel Database Schema and Seed Data

The Siebel Database, which also serves as the default authentication mechanism, has now to be installed. The installation will include the creation of tables and indexes as well as the import of seed data, including for example the administrative user SADMIN, responsibilities for controlling access to Siebel Views, List of Values data for dropdown lists, and the Siebel metadata repository.

The Siebel Database configuration begins with preparing and running the SQL script in the `grantusr.sql` file provided by Oracle. The exact steps for preparing and executing this file are described in Chapter 4.

After executing the SQL script in the `grantusr.sql` file, we prepare the environment, launch the Siebel Configuration Wizard, and execute the steps to install a new Siebel database.

To finalize the database configuration, we have to execute the Siebel Upgrade Wizard. The Siebel Upgrade Wizard's purpose and functionality has been described in detail in Chapter 4.

Preparing the environment for database configuration

During an initial installation of Siebel CRM server software on Linux or UNIX-based operating systems, we must verify that database connectivity can be established via ODBC before we are able to continue the installation. This includes the following tasks:

- Creating the `dbenv.sh` script
- Modifying the `dbenv.sh` script
- Executing the `dbenv.sh` script
- Verifying ODBC settings using odbcsql

Creating the dbenv.sh script

Similar to setting environment variables before launching the Siebel Enterprise configuration, we have to execute a script that prepares the environment for running the database configuration. This script is generated by another script named CreateDbSrvrEnvScript. The script is situated in the Siebel Server's directory tree in the `install_script/install` folder. The following command line shows how to execute the script:

```
./CreateDbSrvrEnvScript /u01/app/siebel ENU Oracle
```

This creates the `dbenv.sh` script in the `/u01/app/siebel/siebsrvr` folder with American English (ENU) as the language for installing on the Oracle database platform.

Modifying the dbenv.sh script

A recommended and often times necessary modification to the newly created `dbenv.sh` script is to add the full path to the `/lib` or `/lib32` (if applicable) directory of the Oracle client or database product installation to the `LD_LIBRARY_PATH` environment variable.

Using a text editor of our choice, we add code at the end of the `dbenv.sh` file that sets the `LD_LIBRARY_PATH` environment variable to be similar to the following:

```
LD_LIBRARY_PATH=${LD_LIBRARY_PATH}:/u01/app/oracle/product/11.2.0/
db_home1/lib; export LD_LIBRARY_PATH
```

The path `/u01/app/oracle/product/11.2.0/db_home1/lib` serves as an example for the location of the Oracle `lib` folder.

Installing and Configuring Siebel CRM Server Software on Linux

Also, we should ensure that the ORACLE_SID environment variable is correctly set and exported by adding a line similar to the following to the dbenv.sh file.

```
ORACLE_SID=orcl; export ORACLE_SID
```

This line sets the ORACLE_SID environment variable to a value of orcl, where orcl is a valid service name in the TNS entries of the Oracle database or client product.

The following screenshot shows the dbenv.sh script after the modifications described in this section:

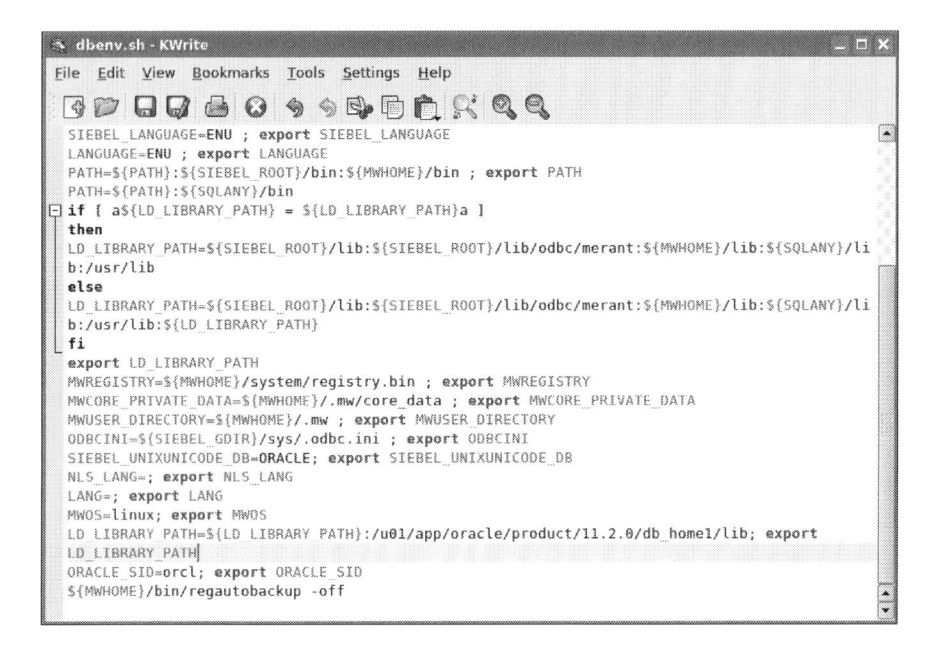

> When you encounter problems with the database connectivity or Gateway Name Server authentication, you should always verify the settings of LD_LIBRARY_PATH and ORACLE_SID in environment scripts such as cfgenv.sh, dbenv.sh, or siebenv.sh.

Executing the dbenv.sh script

We can now navigate to the Siebel Server's installation folder and execute the dbenv.sh script as follows:

```
. ./dbenv.sh
```

The dbenv.sh script now prepares the necessary environment variables for executing the Siebel configuration wizard.

Verifying ODBC settings using odbcsql

Before we launch the Siebel configuration wizard, we should test the ODBC settings using a command line utility named odbcsql. This command line utility is used by the Siebel Upgrade Wizard itself during the database installation and the following command can be executed to create a test connection.

Navigate to the Siebel server's bin directory and enter a command similar to the following:

```
odbcsql /s SIEBELEVAL_DSN /u SADMIN /p TJay357D
```

In this command, the /s switch specifies the name of the ODBC data source that must exist in the .odbc.ini file. The /u and /p switches provide a valid database username and password combination.

The output of the utility should indicate that the login to the data source as the user SADMIN has been successfully executed. The utility now displays an ODBC> prompt.

To exit the utility, enter exit at the prompt.

We must emphasize at this point that the ODBC connection is only used by the programs and utilities invoked by the Siebel Upgrade Wizard. To establish connections to the database at runtime, the Siebel Application Object Manager always uses native database connectivity techniques such as SQL*NET for Oracle databases.

Starting the Siebel Configuration Wizard

We can now navigate to the Siebel server's bin directory and execute the following command to invoke the Siebel Configuration Wizard for the Siebel database configuration process:

```
ssincfgw -args LANG=ENU MODE=LIVE MODEL_FILE=/u01/app/siebel/siebsrvr/admin/dbsrvr.scm
```

Installing and Configuring Siebel CRM Server Software on Linux

The configuration wizard launches and the following table describes each step of the process.

Step	Description	Tasks and Example Values
1	Start the Configuration Wizard.	Prepare and use the ssincfgw executable with the input arguments described above to start the wizard.
2	Siebel Server directory.	Provide the path to the Siebel Server's installation directory. Click **Next**.
3	Siebel Database Server Utilities directory.	Provide the path to the Siebel Database Server Utilities installation folder. Click **Next**.
4	Database Platform	Select **Oracle Database Enterprise Edition** Click **Next**.
5	Task selection.	Select **Install Database**. Click **Next**.
6	Action selection.	Select **Install Siebel Database**. Click **Next**.
7	Confirmation	Confirm that you wish to install a new Siebel database. Click **Next**.
8	GRANTUSR.SQL	Acknowledge that `grantusr.sql` has been run. Click **Next**.
9	UNICODE or NON-UNICODE	Select **UNICODE**. Click **Next**.
10	ODBC Data Source Name	Enter **SIEBELEVAL_DSN**. Note: This is the name of the System DSN generated during configuration of the Siebel Enterprise. Click **Next**.
11	Siebel Database User Name and Password	User Name: **SADMIN** Password: **TJay357D** Note: These values come from the **planning document**. Click **Next**.

[142]

Chapter 5

Step	Description	Tasks and Example Values
12	Siebel Database Table Owner and Password.	Table Owner: **SIEBEL**
		Password: **dQ7JXufi**
		Note: These values come from the **planning document**.
		Click **Next**.
13	Index and Data tablespace names.	Index Tablespace Name: **SIEBELDB_IDX**
		Tablespace Name: **SIEBELDB_DATA**
		Note: These values come from the **planning document**.
		Click **Next**.
14	License key entry.	Select **Yes I would like to enter it now**.
		Click **Next**.
15	License key entry.	Copy and paste the first line from the **license key file** you generated during the installation preparation process.
16	Oracle parallel indexing.	Keep the default (**Does not use...**)
		Click **Next**.
17	Security group and log output directory.	Keep the defaults.
		Note: The log output directory will become a subdirectory of the Siebel Server's LOG directory.
		Click **Next**.
18	Command line for Upgrade Wizard	Take down a note for the command line to invoke the Siebel Upgrade Wizard once the configuration wizard is finished.
		Click **Next**.
19	Summary	Review the summary information.
		Click **Next**.
20	Do you want to execute configuration?	Click **Yes**.
21	Execution results are displayed.	Click **OK**.
22	The Configuration Wizard jumps to the first dialog.	Click **Cancel** and **Yes** to exit the configuration wizard.

After successful completion of the Siebel configuration wizard, we can verify the existence of the upgrade configuration file (.ucf) for the install process. The file can be found in the Siebel server's bin directory and is named master_install.ucf.

Starting the Siebel Upgrade Wizard

The Siebel Upgrade Wizard is the specialized software unit that reads the upgrade configuration files and executes the steps required to complete the process. To install the Siebel database, we launch the upgrade wizard using the following command at the Siebel server's `bin` directory:

```
srvrupgwiz /m master_install.ucf
```

The `/m` switch indicates the path to the `.ucf` file. The Upgrade Wizard will now execute the tasks specified in the driver files provided by Oracle using the parameter values provided during the configuration process. The time for the installation process is approximately one hour.

Verifying the successful Siebel Database installation

We can verify a successful Siebel database installation by using the following checkpoints:

- The HTML summary generated by the Log Parser
- Existence of tables and data in the Siebel database

Both checks are described in detail in Chapter 4.

Restarting the Siebel Gateway Name Server

Before we can continue with the remainder of the Enterprise configuration steps, we must ensure that the Siebel Gateway Name Server is able to authenticate against the Siebel database, which now contains the SADMIN user account and administrative data for the SADMIN employee.

As indicated above, adding two lines that set the LD_LIBRARY_PATH and ORACLE_SID environment variables to scripts such as `siebenv.sh` is recommended to avoid problems with the database connectivity.

The following steps are necessary:

- Stopping the Gateway Name Server
- Modifying the `siebenv.sh` file
- Executing the `siebenv.sh` file
- Start and verifying the Gateway Name Server

Stopping the Gateway Name server

We stop the Gateway Name server—as previously discussed—by navigating to its root installation directory and issuing the following command:

`stop_ns`

The command output indicates that the service is now stopped.

Modifying the siebenv.sh file

Using a text editor of our choice, we open the `siebenv.sh` file situated in the Gateway Name Server's installation root folder and add the following lines at the end of the file:

```
LD_LIBRARY_PATH=${LD_LIBRARY_PATH}:/u01/app/oracle/product/11.2.0/db_home1/lib; export LD_LIBRARY_PATH
ORACLE_SID=orcl; export ORACLE_SID
```

In the above example, the `LD_LIBRARY_PATH` now contains the path to the Oracle database lib folder and `ORACLE_SID` is explicitly set to `orcl`.

We can now save and close the file.

Executing the siebenv.sh file

In order to set the environment variables for the Siebel Gateway Name Server, we execute the `siebenv.sh` script by entering the following command at the console:

`. ./siebenv.sh`

The environment variables are now set.

Starting and verifying the Gateway Name Server

Now, we can use the commands we already know to start and verify the state of the Siebel Gateway Name Server. At the command prompt we enter:

`start_ns`

`list_ns`

The output should indicate that the Siebel Gateway Name Server is now operational.

If, for any reason, the Siebel Gateway Name Server fails to start, we must check its log file to find the error source. Typical problem areas are the ODBC driver or the authentication of the SADMIN user. Some databases such as Oracle 11g treat passwords as case sensitive. If the password is entered incorrectly during the configuration of the Siebel Enterprise, we must use the Siebel Configuration Wizard to remove the Siebel Enterprise and then execute it again to register the Siebel Enterprise again.

> Use the information in this chapter to run the Siebel Database installation on your demonstration machine. Ensure that the installation was successful by carrying out the verification steps outlined above.

Configuring the Siebel Server

We use the Siebel Configuration Wizard to configure one or more Siebel Servers in the new enterprise.

The script to prepare the environment variables for the Siebel server configuration on Linux is `cfgenv.sh` situated in the Siebel server installation directory. To execute the script, we navigate to the Siebel server installation folder and enter:

```
. ./cfgenv.sh
```

Then, we can launch the configuration wizard from the `bin` directory with a command similar to the following:

```
ssincfgw -args LANG=ENU MODE=LIVE MODEL_FILE=/u01/app/siebel/siebsrvr/admin/siebel_server_sia.scm
```

The following table describes the steps of the Siebel Server configuration process:

Step	Description	Tasks and Example Values
1	Start the Configuration Wizard.	Prepare and use the ssincfgw executable with the input arguments described above to start the wizard.
2	Configuration Wizard Welcome Page	Select **Create New Configuration**. Click **Next**.
3	Database Configuration Warning	Review the warning that we must have an existing Siebel Database. Click **Next**.

Chapter 5

Step	Description	Tasks and Example Values
4	Gateway Name Server Authentication user name and password.	User Name: **SADMIN**
		Password: **TJay357D**
		Note: These values come from the **planning document**.
		Click **Next**.
5	Gateway Name Server hostname and port number.	Hostname: **localhost**
		Port: **2320**
		Note: These values come from the **planning document**. We can use localhost as the hostname as long the Siebel Configuration Wizard is executed on the machine which hosts the Siebel Gateway Name Server.
		Click **Next**.
6	Siebel Enterprise Name and Siebel Server logical name.	Enterprise Name: **SIEBELEVAL**
		Siebel Server Name: **Linux_1**
		Note: These values come from the **planning document**.
		Click **Next**.
7	Siebel Server Description	Description: **Siebel Evaluation Server 1**
		Click **Next**.
8	Enable Component Groups	Select only **CallCenter**.
		Note: Details on component groups are discussed in a later chapter.
		Click **Next**.
9	Siebel Connection Broker Port	Keep the default (2321).
		Note: This value comes from the **planning document**.
		Click **Next**.
10	Remote Synchronization Manager Port	Keep the default (40400)
		Note: This value comes from the **planning document**.
		Click **Next**.
11	Additional tasks for configuring the Siebel Server.	Select none.
		Click **Next**.
12	Clustering configuration.	Keep the default (Not clustered).
		Click Next.

Step	Description	Tasks and Example Values
13	Final Tasks	Review the information on EVT.
		Click **Next**.
14	Summary	Verify the selections and values you provided.
		Click **Next**.
15	Do you want to execute configuration?	Click **Yes**.
16	Execution results are displayed.	Click **OK**.
17	The wizard jumps back to the configuration mode selection page.	Select **Exit Configuration Wizard**.
		Click **Next**.

Verifying successful Siebel Server Configuration

In order to verify that the Siebel Server has been correctly configured, we can log in to the Gateway Name Server using the Siebel Server Manager (srvrmgr) command line and check that a Siebel Server definition exists.

In order to do so, we navigate to the `bin` directory of the Siebel Gateway Name Server installation and enter the following at the command prompt:

```
srvrmgr /g localhost /e SIEBELEVAL /u SADMIN /p TJay357D
```

This will log on the user `SADMIN` to the Gateway Name Server on the local machine and open the `SIEBELEVAL` enterprise.

A successful connection is indicated by the existence of the srvrmgr> prompt. We can now enter the following srvrmgr command to list all servers in the enterprise.

```
list servers show SBLSRVR_NAME(20),HOST_NAME(20)
```

The `list servers` command is followed by the `show` command to specify the columns and their display width (in parentheses) in order to provide better readability of the output.

```
srvrmgr> list servers show SBLSRVR_NAME(20),HOST_NAME(20)

SBLSRVR_NAME          HOST_NAME
--------------------  --------------------
Linux_1               ahansaloel

1 row returned.
```

The screenshot shows the output of the `list servers` command. The Siebel server with the logical name of **Linux_1** is hosted on the ahansaloel machine. Outputs similar to this indicate the successful configuration of a Siebel Server.

> On your demonstration machine, use the Siebel Configuration Wizard to configure a new Siebel Server. Use your planning document to enter the correct values in the dialogs.

Configuring the Siebel Web Server Extension

On the machine hosting the web server, we execute the Siebel Configuration Wizard to create the configuration files for the Siebel Web Server Extension (SWSE) and the virtual directories that will later be used to access the Siebel applications. Before we do so, we have to complete some preparation steps for the HTTP server.

Preparing the web server

Before we start the SWSE configuration, we must prepare the HTTP server, which on Linux or UNIX-based operating systems is either based on the Apache web server or the Sun Java System Web Server.

In the following, we outline the preparation steps for the Oracle HTTP Server on Oracle Enterprise Linux. In the `httpd.conf` file, we make adjustments as follows.

Locate and comment the line `AddDefaultCharset ISO-8859-1`. This is how the line should look after editing:

```
#AddDefaultCharset ISO-8859-1
```

Verify the HTTP port number to match the settings in the SWSE configuration. To do so, locate the `Listen` and `ServerName` lines with the web server's IP address and hostname and change the port number if needed.

The following lines serve as an example:

```
Listen 192.168.100.100:8081
ServerName siebelweb.us.ourcomp.com:8081
```

Save the `httpd.conf` file and restart the web server.

Configuring the Siebel Web Server Extension

In order to configure the Siebel Web Server Extension (SWSE), we have to prepare the environment (as usual) by invoking the `cfgenv.sh` script from the software's installation folder. So, we navigate to the SWSE's installation directory and enter the following command:

`. ./cfgenv.sh`

The script prepares the environment variables needed to execute the configuration wizard. We are now ready to launch the Siebel configuration wizard using the following command from the `bin` directory of the SWSE installation folder:

```
ssincfgw -args LANG=ENU MODE=LIVE MODEL_FILE=/u01/app/siebel/sweapp/
admin/swse_server_sia.scm
```

The following table outlines the configuration wizard's dialogs and parameters:

Step	Description	Tasks and Example Values
1	Start the Configuration Wizard.	Prepare and use the ssincfgw executable with the input arguments described above to start the wizard.
3	Select configuration task.	Select **Apply an SWSE Logical Profile**. Click **Next**.
4	Select a load balancer.	Select **Single Siebel Server**. Note: Load balancing will be discussed in a later chapter. Click **Next**.
5	Siebel Server host name and connection broker port.	Host name: **appsrvrsieb1** Siebel Connection Broker Port: **2321 (default)** Note: These values come from the **planning document**.
6	SWSE logical profile location and web server instance location.	Browse for or enter a path to the directory specified during the SWSE logical profile configuration. Browse for or enter the path to the web server root directory. Click **Next**.
7	Restart web server.	Choose **Yes**. Click **Next**.

Chapter 5

Step	Description	Tasks and Example Values
8	Final Tasks	Review the information about EVT.
		Click **Next**.
9	Summary	Verify the selections and values you provided.
		Click **Next**.
10	Do you want to execute configuration?	Click **Yes**.
11	Execution results are displayed.	Click **OK**.
12	The wizard jumps back to the configuration mode selection page.	Select **Exit Configuration Wizard**
		Click **Next**.

Verifying the successful SWSE configuration

The SWSE configuration wizard should have successfully modified the `httpd.conf` file. We can open the file and verify the existence of several new alias entries for virtual directories similar to the following example:

```
Alias /callcenter_enu /u01/app/siebel/sweapp/public/enu
```

This line defines a virtual directory named `callcenter_enu`, which is mapped to the physical `public/enu` directory of the Siebel Web Server Extension. The following screenshot shows a portion of the `httpd.conf` file of Oracle HTTP Server after the SWSE configuration:

[151]

We can see the Alias entries for each Siebel application in each supported language pointing to the `/public` folder of the SWSE installation.

> Execute the Siebel Configuration Wizard on your demonstration machine and configure the Siebel Web Server Extension. Verify that virtual directories are created on the web server.

Verifying the successful Siebel Enterprise Server installation

We are now ready to verify that we have successfully completed the basic installation steps. The verification steps include:

1. Start the services.
2. Log on to the Siebel application as the Siebel Administrator.

We will then be able to use the Siebel Web Client to carry out the final tasks in order to deliver a fully operational Siebel CRM environment.

Starting the services

The following services need to be started in the sequence below:

1. Siebel Gateway Name Server.
2. Siebel Server.
3. Web Server.

The Siebel Web Server Extension (SWSE) does not have its own service definition. We can reinitialize the SWSE by restarting the web server.

Starting the Siebel Gateway Name Server on Linux or UNIX

Before we execute any of the scripts provided by Oracle we must execute the `siebenv.sh` script in order to set the appropriate environment variables. To execute `siebenv.sh`, we navigate to the root folder of the server such as the Siebel Gateway Name Server's root folder and issue the following command:

```
. ./siebenv.sh
```

The command for starting the Siebel Gateway Name Server is implemented as a script named `start_ns`. The script is located in the Gateway Name Server's root folder. At the command prompt, we enter the following to start the service:

`start_ns`

Then, we can use the `list_ns` command to verify that the Gateway Name Server is operational:

`list _ns`

The output of the `list_ns` command allows us to verify whether the Gateway Name Server is started or not.

To stop the service, we use the `stop_ns` command.

Starting the Siebel Server

To start the Siebel Server, we navigate to the Siebel server's installation directory and execute the following commands:

`. ./siebenv.sh`

`bin/start_server all`

The first line executes the `siebenv.sh` script in order to set the environment variables. The second line uses the `start_server` command to start all Siebel servers configured on the machine.

We can use the `list_server` command to monitor the status of the Siebel servers.

The following command will stop all Siebel servers on the machine:

`bin/stop_server all`

Starting the web server

We should use the following command to start the HTTP server:

`startapa`

The `stopapa` command should be used to stop the web server.

> On your demonstration machine, start the Siebel Gateway Name Server, the Siebel Server, and the web server. Follow the instructions in the chapter to verify the successful start.

Logging on as SADMIN for the first time

Chapter 4 describes the process of the first login. As we use the Siebel High Interactivity client, which is only supported on Microsoft Internet Explorer, we must connect to the Siebel application from a machine with a supported version of Microsoft Windows and Internet Explorer. A URL similar to the following will be entered into Internet Explorer's address bar:

```
http://192.168.100.100:8081/callcenter_enu
```

After a short startup period, the browser should display the login page for Siebel Call Center. We can use SADMIN as the username and password as we have specified in the previous tasks.

> On a Microsoft Windows machine, launch Microsoft Internet Explorer and navigate to the `callcenter_enu` virtual directory on your web server. Depending on your machine and browser settings, you might receive warnings and messages. However, you should be able to log in as the Siebel Administrator (SADMIN).

Final Steps

To finalize the Siebel Enterprise installation and configuration on Linux or UNIX-based operating systems, the following steps are necessary:

1. Configure services for automatic start.
2. Copy the Siebel File System seed files.
3. Create an administrative Siebel user.
4. Apply additional license keys.
5. Synchronize Server Components.

Except for the first item in the list, the procedures have been described in detail in Chapter 4, *Installing Siebel CRM Server Software on Microsoft Windows*. As these tasks are not related to the operating system, we will only discuss how to configure the Siebel services for automatic start on Linux.

Configuring services for automatic start on Linux

To ensure automatic start up of the Siebel Gateway Name Server or the Siebel Server services on Linux or other UNIX-based operating systems, we have to register them with the operating system initialization routines.

The following steps are needed on Linux operating systems:

1. Edit the `siebel_server` file.
2. Copy the `siebel_server` file to the `init.d` folder.
3. Set permissions for the `siebel_server` file.
4. Create a non-root user file if necessary.
5. Create soft links.

This procedure has to be carried out under the root user account and is explained in detail as follows.

Editing the siebel_server file

The `siebel_server` file is located in the `bin` directory of the Siebel software installation folder. For the Siebel Server for example, it is located in `/u01/app/siebel/siebsrvr/bin`.

For an automatic start of the Siebel Gateway Name Server, we ensure that the `SIEBEL_GATEWAY_ROOT` variable is correctly set to the root folder of the Gateway Name Server installation.

For any Siebel Server residing on the machine, we add the path to the Siebel Server installation root folder to the `SIEBEL_SERVER_ROOT` variable. We can separate multiple servers using a blank space.

The following example shows the settings for a Gateway Name Server and one Siebel Server:

```
SIEBEL_GATEWAY_ROOT="/u01/app/siebel/gtwysrvr"
SIEBEL_SERVER_ROOT="/u01/app/siebel/siebsrvr"
```

Additional commands such as setting and exporting environment variables like `ORACLE_SID` or `ORACLE_HOME` to ensure database connectivity may be added to the file as well.

Copying the siebel_server file to the init.d folder

On Linux operating systems, we have to copy the `siebel_server` file to the `/etc/init.d` folder.

Setting permissions for the siebel_server file

We can use the `chmod` command to change the permissions for the `siebel_server` file as follows:

```
chmod 755 /etc/init.d/siebel_server
```

Creating a non-root user file

This step is only necessary if the Siebel server software was installed using an account other than root. In this case, we create a second file in the `/etc/init.d` folder named `siebel_server_nonroot` and add a line similar to the following:

```
/usr/bin/su - non_root_account_name -c "/etc/init.d/siebel_server $1"
```

The `non_root_account_name` string has to be replaced with the name of the user account that was used to install the Siebel server software.

Creating soft links

The final step to setting up an automatic start of the Siebel services on Linux is to create two soft links using the `ln` command. The soft links are either created from the `siebel_server` file or (if it exists) from the `siebel_server_nonroot` file. The following example shows the commands for the latter scenario:

```
ln -s /etc/init.d/siebel_server_nonroot /etc/rc3.d/S72siebel_server
ln -s /etc/init.d/siebel_server_nonroot /etc/rc2.d/K32siebel_server
```

In order to finalize your Siebel demonstration environment, follow the directions in this section and Chapter 4 to:

- Configure the services for automatic start
- Copy the Siebel File System seed files
- Create an administrative Siebel user for yourself
- Apply additional license keys
- Synchronize server components

Summary

In this chapter, we learned how to install the Siebel CRM server infrastructure components such as the Siebel Gateway Name Server, Siebel Server, and the Siebel Web Server Extension on Linux and other UNIX-based operating systems.

The focus of this chapter was also on the differences in the configuration process between Microsoft Windows and Linux or UNIX operating systems.

Important steps include preparing and verifying the environment scripts and ODBC connectivity as well as configuring the services for automatic start.

In the next chapter, we will discuss the installation of Siebel client software such as the Siebel Mobile or Developer Web Client, Siebel Tools, and the Siebel Sample Database.

6
Installing Siebel Client Software

The majority of business users access Siebel CRM functionality by means of the Siebel Web client, which can be considered a "small footprint client" because it only relies on files downloaded automatically by the browser. However, there are groups of users who do not have consistent network connectivity, such as travelling sales representatives. Developers, administrators, and testing personnel would also need a secure environment where they could be sure that their changes do not affect other users.

The Siebel client software exists to accommodate these user groups. In this chapter, we will learn how to install, configure, and apply patches to the following software products:

- Prerequisite Software and Configuration Settings for Siebel Web Clients
- Siebel Developer/Mobile Web Client
- Siebel Sample Database
- Siebel Tools

About the Developer and Mobile Web Client

There is a certain source of misunderstanding with the terms "Developer Web Client" and "Mobile Web Client". As this chapter discusses the installation of both varieties of the Siebel client software, we try to distinguish them as follows.

Installing Siebel Client Software

Once the Siebel client software is installed, an executable named `siebel.exe` will be present on the machine. This executable reads a text file with a suffix of `.cfg`, which is known as the client configuration file.

The configuration file contains data source definitions that allow the Siebel executable to connect to different databases. When the database is present on the same machine as the executable and can therefore be accessed without any network connectivity, the client is considered a "Mobile Web Client". The mobile mode is only supported with *Sybase Adaptive Server Anywhere* databases and is widely used to support remote users. The Siebel Remote module provides the necessary functionality to create and synchronize thousands of local databases with the headquarter server.

When the `siebel.exe` file is directed to connect to a relational database over the network—which is only supported for administrators or developers—we call it "Developer Web Client".

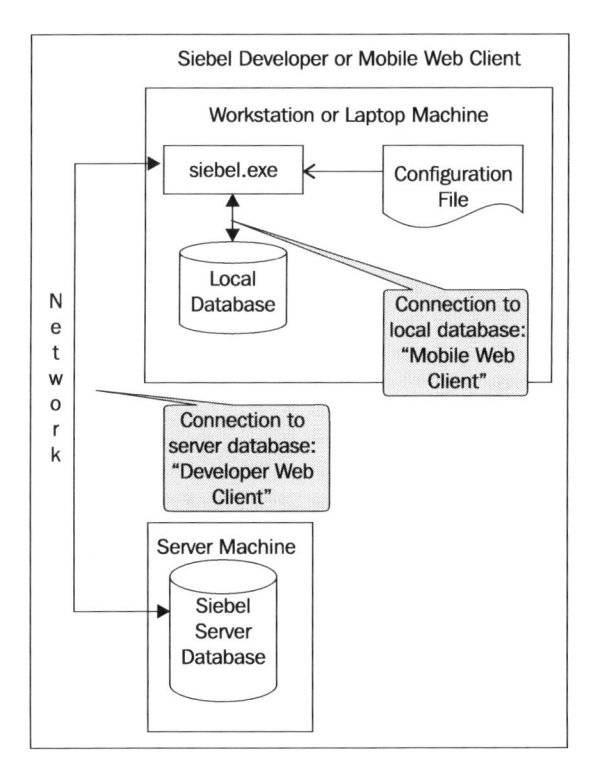

The diagram depicts the difference between the terms "Siebel Mobile Web Client" and "Siebel Developer Web Client". A single instance of the Siebel executable can connect to various data sources at different times. The type of connectivity (local or network) drives the naming convention.

> The Developer Web Client is only supported for technical user groups such as administrators and developers. In earlier versions of Siebel CRM, it was also referred to as "Dedicated Web Client" and many developers refer to it as the "fat client". It can be used to connect directly to the server database, file system, and the Gateway Name Server when there is no web server or Siebel Server running.
>
> Siebel client software is only supported on Microsoft Windows operating systems.

User groups and Siebel Client Software

In a typical Siebel CRM project, different user groups such as office-based users, mobile users, developers, administrators, and testing personnel must be provided with the correct set of Siebel client software to successfully complete their jobs.

The following table can be used to facilitate the installation decisions:

Client Software → Group ↓	Web Client (browser only)	Mobile Web Client	Developer Web Client	Sample Database	Siebel Tools
Office-based User	☑				
Mobile User	☑	☑			
Developer	☑	☑	☑	☑	☑
Business Analyst	☑		☑	☑	☑
Administrator	☑		☑		☑
Testing Personnel	☑		☑	☑	

From the above table, we can derive the following:

- The Siebel Web Client is available to all user groups. This ensures that all end users and project team members have access to the Siebel CRM applications when they are connected to the corporate network.

- The Siebel Mobile Web Client is only distributed to mobile users and developers. Details on setting up and administering the Mobile Web Client are given later in this and other chapters.

- The Siebel Developer Web Client is used by all technical project team members such as developers, business analysts, administrators, and testing personnel. This ensures that members of these groups can access and test Siebel CRM application functionality using a local instance rather than the Siebel Server infrastructure.
- Installing and using the Siebel Sample Database is highly recommended for all people who are involved in the design and development phases of a Siebel CRM project, namely developers, business analysts, and testing personnel.
- Siebel Tools should be provided to all people who need access to the Siebel Repository metadata. This includes developers, business analysts, and administrators. Business analysts should be given access to Siebel Tools because it enables them to explore Siebel standard functionality.

Prerequisite software and configuration settings for Siebel Web Clients

Before we undertake the procedure of installing the Siebel client software on our Microsoft Windows workstations or laptops, we should verify that the following prerequisites are met:

- Database client software is installed (for Developer Web Client only)
- The user account for the installation has administrative rights
- Browser security settings are correct
- The Java Runtime Environment (JRE) is installed

We will discuss the prerequisites in the following subsections.

About database client software for Developer Web Clients

When acting as the software engine behind the Developer Web Client, the Siebel executable must be able to establish a native connection to the server database. As Siebel CRM supports different database vendors such as Oracle, Microsoft, and IBM, the respective client software has to be installed and properly configured on the machine where we intend to operate the Developer Web Client.

The *Systems Requirements and Supported Platforms* document (available on `http://otn.oracle.com`) allows us to identify the correct version for the database client software.

To operate a Mobile Web Client, no further installation of a database client is needed. The Sybase database engine is delivered as part of the Siebel client installation.

Installing with administrative user rights

The user account that is executing the Siebel client installer must have administrative privileges on the Windows machine. The way to set these rights differs depending on the technology used for user administration and the version of Microsoft Windows.

Basically, the user account must be a member of the local Administrators group. This can be achieved by adding the user to the group in the Microsoft Windows Computer Management console or by temporarily granting administrator privileges when prompted at the time of installation.

Internet Explorer security settings

Apart from having the appropriate version of Microsoft Internet Explorer available on the client machine in order to run the Siebel client in High-Interactivity mode, we have to verify the correct browser settings.

Because the Siebel High-Interactivity mode relies on ActiveX technology, we must adjust the browser's security settings in a way that allows automatic download, installation, and execution of ActiveX controls.

The easiest way to do this is to add the local machine's host name to the list of trusted sites. The trusted sites, security level should also be set to Low or Medium-low.

In addition, we should take care that popup windows are allowed for web pages that originate on the local machine.

Java Runtime Environment (JRE)

Some functionality of the Siebel Web Client such as the flowchart editor, expression designer, or organization chart are implemented as Java applets. In order to execute these applets, a local installation of the Java Runtime Environment (JRE) is needed.

If our company does not deploy any of this special functionality, installing the JRE becomes optional.

The version of the JRE should be current but at least 1.5.

> On your demonstration machine, ensure that the prerequisites discussed in this section are met. Adjust settings and download and install additional software if necessary.

Additional software recommendations

Depending on how our company has implemented its business processes, several other software products might have to be installed on the client machine. For example, end users could work with Siebel BI Publisher reports, which can be generated in various output formats, such as Adobe's Portable Document Format (PDF). In order to view the reports in PDF, a PDF reader such as Adobe Reader must be installed.

The following table describes some additional software products that might be needed to allow end users to complete their business processes:

Software Vendor and product	Example Scenario
Adobe Reader or other third-party PDF viewers	For viewing PDF files that are either attached to Siebel records or generated by BI Publisher.
Microsoft Word or other third-party office applications compatible with Word	For working with Word documents generated by the Siebel Document Server or attached to Siebel records.
Microsoft Excel or other third-party spreadsheet tools	For working with data downloaded from Siebel list applets.
Microsoft Outlook	To enable client-side integration between Siebel CRM and Outlook to synchronize calendar and contact data.
Adobe Flash Player (ActiveX)	Needed when Oracle Business Intelligence Enterprise Edition (Oracle BI EE) is deployed. The default chart format of the integrated chart engine in Oracle BI EE is flash (swf).

The above list is not complete. Depending on the business decisions, other software installations might become mandatory.

Installing the Siebel Developer Web Client

After downloading the installation archives from `http://edelivery.oracle.com` and extracting the installation images, we can locate the Oracle Universal Installer (`oui.exe`) in the folder structure. The following screenshot shows the folder structure and contents of the install folder of the Siebel_Web_Client installation image after extraction:

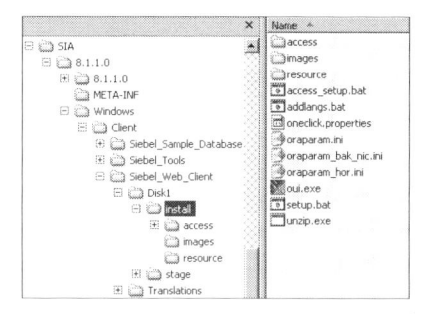

The process of downloading and extracting Siebel CRM software installation images is described in Chapter 2.

While Siebel CRM versions 8.0 and below relied on the InstallShield installation wizard, Oracle decided to use its own Oracle Universal Installer for the installation of the Siebel Developer or Mobile Web Client and Siebel Tools starting with version 8.1.1.0. The following screenshot shows the Oracle Universal Installer during the installation of the Siebel Developer or Mobile Web Client:

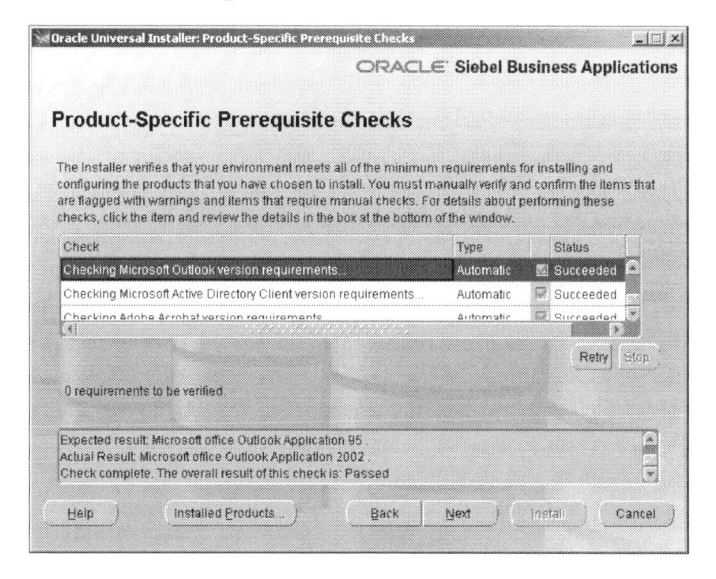

The step displayed is the check for additional prerequisite software such as Adobe Acrobat on the local machine.

The decision to install the Siebel Mobile Web Client or the Siebel Developer Web Client is taken during the setup process driven by Oracle Universal Installer. When we select "Mobile Web Client", the installer asks for the host name of the Siebel Server where the Synchronization Manager component resides. When we select "Developer Web Client", additional parameters such as the database vendor and database server connectivity information are required. We must emphasize here that even if we intend to use both the Siebel Mobile Web Client and the Siebel Developer Web Client on the same machine, we only have to run the installer once.

In the following we will describe the installation process for the Siebel Developer Web Client 8.1.1.0 and above. We start by double-clicking the `oui.exe` file in the `Siebel_Web_Client/Disk1/install` folder that launches the Oracle Universal Installer.

The following table provides details about the installer's dialogs and example parameters. During the installation, we will select "Developer Web Client" as the client type. Later in this chapter, we will learn how to apply the necessary configuration settings to be able to use the client as a Mobile Web Client.

Step	Description	Tasks and Example Values
1	Start the Oracle Universal Installer	Double-click the `oui.exe` file in the `Siebel_Web_Client/Disk1/install` folder.
2	The Welcome dialog is displayed	Click **Next**.
3	Specify the home directory	Example: **C:\Siebel\8.1\Client_1** (default value).
		The directory should already have been specified in the planning document.
		Click **Next**.
4	Prerequisite checks	The installer performs checks for prerequisite checks. Verify that all checks are passed successfully.
		Click **Next**.
5	Select Languages	Select **English**.
		Click **Next**.
6	Welcome to Siebel Business Applications Client Setup	Click **Next**.

Step	Description	Tasks and Example Values
7	Type of Client	Select **Developer Web Client**.
		Click **Next**.
8	Siebel Database Server	Select **Oracle Database Server**.
		Click **Next**.
9	Database Identification	Database Alias: **orcl**
		Table Owner: **SIEBEL**
		Note: These values come from the planning document.
		Click **Next**.
10	File System	Directory Path: **D:\SIA8\siebfile**
		Note: This value comes from the planning document.
		Click **Next**.
11	Siebel Remote Server hostname	Siebel Remote Server: **osappsebl1**
		Note: This value comes from the planning document.
		Click **Next**.
12	Enterprise Server Information	Gateway Name Server address: **osappsebl1**.
		Enterprise Server: **SIEBELEVAL**
		Note: These values come from the planning document.
		Click **Next**.
13	Server Request Broker Information	Request Server Name: **Eval_1**
		Note: This is a logical Siebel server name, not a host name. This value comes from the planning document.
		Click **Next**.
14	Search Server Information	Keep the default values.
		Click **Next**.
15	Summary	Review the summary information.
		Click **Install**.
16	The installation progress is displayed	

Step	Description	Tasks and Example Values
17	Microsoft Internet Explorer is launched	The browser loads the predeploy.htm file in the client's bin directory to load the preconfigured ActiveX controls.
		When the page displays **The download is complete...** we can close the browser window.
18	The installation process continues	
19	Success Message	Click **Exit** and **Yes** to leave the installer.

An important detail of the Siebel Client installer is that it launches the Microsoft Internet Explorer browser during the installation process. The browser is directed to the `predeploy.htm` file in the client's `bin` directory. The purpose of this file is to download and install the preconfigured ActiveX controls. These ActiveX controls are necessary to operate the Siebel High-Interactivity client framework.

Administrators can modify the `predeploy.htm` file to suit their company's requirements. The file can also be used to prepare end users' workstations or laptops for the Siebel Web Client if their user accounts do not have the necessary privileges to download and install ActiveX controls. In such scenarios, administrators would have to provide a script that runs with administrative privileges to open the file once the Siebel client installation is complete.

Verifying the Siebel Developer Web Client installation

In order to verify the successful installation of the Siebel Developer Web Client, we can first navigate to the Windows start menu where we should find a new menu item named **Siebel8_home1**, which contains the Siebel Web Client 8.x item. We can find the shortcuts to several Siebel applications by navigating to **Start** | **Programs** | **Siebel8_home1** | **Siebel Web Client 8.x**.

The next verification step is to launch one of the application shortcuts. For example we can click the Siebel Pharma—ENU shortcut. The login dialog should be displayed.

We can log in as SADMIN (using the password we provided during the Siebel Server installation) to the Server data source. The **Connect to** dropdown box allows us to select from a list of predefined data sources. Note that logging in to the Server data source requires a complete installation of the Siebel database as described in Chapter 4.

Once we click the **OK** button, we should be able to observe that after a while the browser is launched and the Siebel application is loaded. If any prerequisites such as browser security settings are not properly met, messages might pop up indicating the necessity to download and install certain ActiveX controls. We should allow these interactions and adjust the browser security settings as described above to avoid this behaviour in the future.

The following screenshot shows the correctly loaded Siebel Pharma application in Microsoft Internet Explorer:

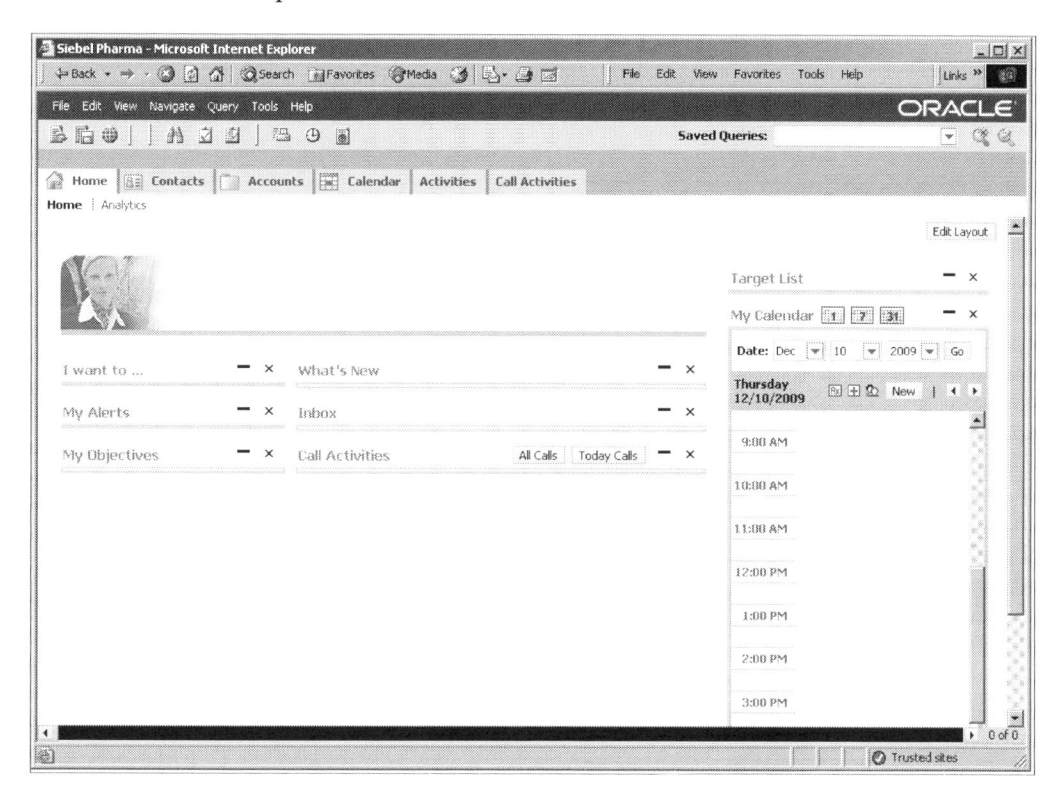

Note that the site icon in the lower right corner of the browser's status bar indicates that the local machine is a member of the **Trusted sites** security zone.

If the verification fails because of database connection problems—often indicated by a **Wrong username or password** message—we must verify the installation of the RDBMS client software and the entries in the Siebel Client configuration file (.cfg). The next section describes how to access and modify the configuration file.

In addition, wrong browser settings can prohibit the successful launch of the Siebel application. If this is the case, we must verify the browser settings as described earlier in this chapter.

> Using the information provided so far in this chapter, install and verify the Siebel Developer Web client on your demonstration machine. In order to test the Developer Web Client, you will need to have a complete Siebel server database installed (as discussed in the previous chapters).

About the Siebel Client configuration file

When we right-click and select Properties on the Windows start menu shortcuts to inspect them more closely, we find that in each of the shortcuts that launch a Siebel application the same executable – siebel.exe – is invoked. The difference between the shortcuts lies within the path to the configuration file (with a .cfg suffix). The following screenshot shows the **Properties** dialog for the **Siebel Pharma – ENU** shortcut:

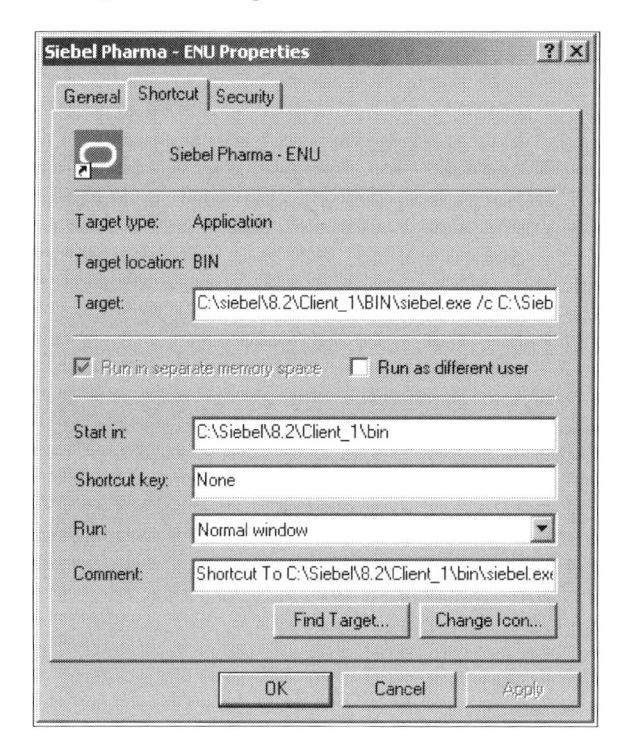

The target of the **Siebel Pharma – ENU** shortcut is similar to the following:

```
C:\siebel\8.2\Client_1\BIN\siebel.exe /c C:\Siebel\8.2\Client_1\bin\enu\
epharma.cfg
```

The `/c` switch directs the Siebel executable to a text file named `epharma.cfg` in the language specific subdirectory (enu for American English) of the `bin` folder. Each Siebel application has its own configuration file. For example, to invoke Siebel Sales we would need to point to the `siebel.cfg` file.

We can open the configuration files with any text editor of our choice in order to inspect or modify them. Before applying major modifications, it is recommended to make a backup copy of the file. The following screenshot shows the `epharma.cfg` file opened in Microsoft Notepad:

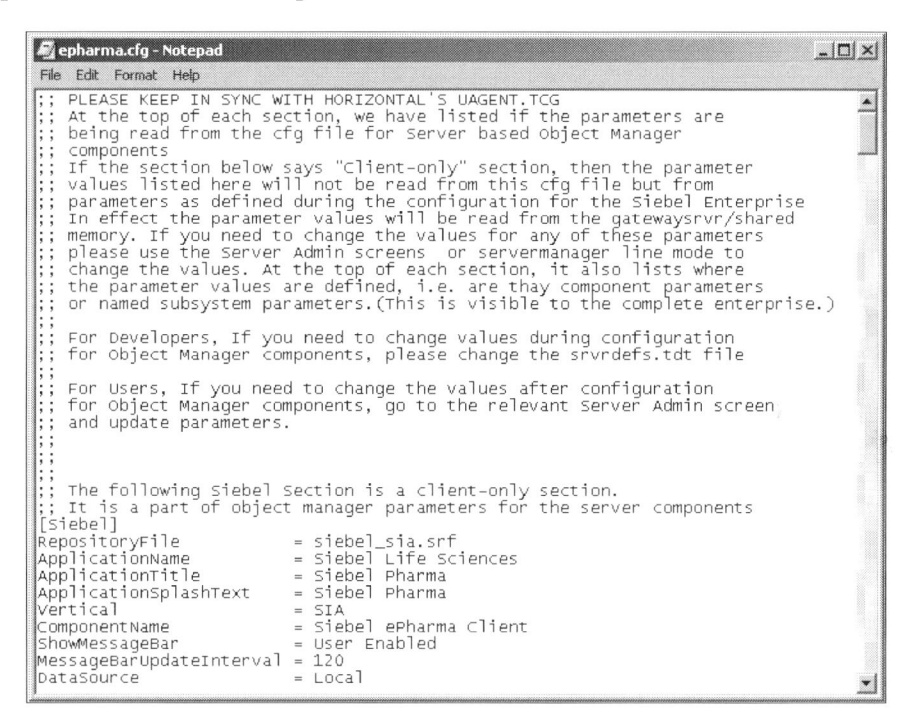

```
;; PLEASE KEEP IN SYNC WITH HORIZONTAL'S UAGENT.TCG
;; At the top of each section, we have listed if the parameters are
;; being read from the cfg file for Server based Object Manager
;; components
;; If the section below says "Client-only" section, then the parameter
;; values listed here will not be read from this cfg file but from
;; parameters as defined during the configuration for the Siebel Enterprise
;; In effect the parameter values will be read from the gatewaysrvr/shared
;; memory. If you need to change the values for any of these parameters
;; please use the Server Admin screens  or servermanager line mode to
;; change the values. At the top of each section, it also lists where
;; the parameter values are defined, i.e. are thay component parameters
;; or named subsystem parameters.(This is visible to the complete enterprise.)
;;
;; For Developers, If you need to change values during configuration
;; for Object Manager components, please change the srvrdefs.tdt file
;;
;; For Users, If you need to change the values after configuration
;; for Object Manager components, go to the relevant Server Admin screen
;; and update parameters.
;;
;;
;;
;; The following Siebel Section is a client-only section.
;; It is a part of object manager parameters for the server components
[Siebel]
RepositoryFile            = siebel_sia.srf
ApplicationName           = Siebel Life Sciences
ApplicationTitle          = Siebel Pharma
ApplicationSplashText     = Siebel Pharma
Vertical                  = SIA
ComponentName             = Siebel ePharma Client
ShowMessageBar            = User Enabled
MessageBarUpdateInterval  = 120
DataSource                = Local
```

The first two parameters in the **[Siebel]** section—**RepositoryFile** and **ApplicationName**—point to a repository file named `siebel_sia.srf` (which is located in the `objects` folder) and direct the `siebel.exe` to load the definition of the Siebel Life Sciences application from that file. The **ApplicationTitle** and **ApplicationSplashText** parameters define the text in the browser's title bar and the login dialog respectively.

The Siebel client configuration file contains dozens of parameters that drive the connectivity and behavior of the Siebel application.

Next, we will discuss one of the most important sections of the configuration file, namely the **[DataSources]** section.

About configuring data sources for the Siebel client

The typical preconfigured configuration files for Siebel clients contain four data source definitions, which are listed in the **[DataSources]** section. The following screenshot shows the **[DataSources]** section of a Siebel client configuration (cfg) file:

```
[DataSources]
Local              = Local
Sample             = Sample
ServerDataSrc      = Server
GatewayDataSrc     = Gateway
```

For each entry in the list, a separate section named after the text to the left of the equals sign exists below this section. The text on the right-hand side of the equals sign is displayed in the login dialog as values in the **Connect to** dropdown box. The following table describes the default data sources and their purpose:

Data source name	Description
Local	Enables connectivity to a local Sybase database created by the Siebel Remote module. When this data source is selected, the client is called a "Mobile Web Client".
Sample	Default data source to the preconfigured Siebel Sample Database (discussed later in this chapter). The sample database is a Sybase database as well.
ServerDataSrc	This connection is configured during the installation of the Developer Web Client and allows for connecting to the server database defined in the installer dialogs. When this data source is selected, the client is called a "Developer Web Client".
GatewayDataSrc	Enables the Developer Web Client to connect to the Siebel Gateway Name Server to give developers and administrators access to the Siebel enterprise configuration and management data. Note: this data source entry is hidden from the **Connect to** dropdown box by having the Hidden parameter set to **True**.

Data source name	Description
`AnalyticsDataSrc` (epharma.cfg only)	This data source enables the Siebel executable to connect to the presentation layer of the Oracle Business Intelligence server, which is part of the Pharma Disconnected Analytics architecture and allows end users to work with Business Intelligence dashboards in offline mode.

Configuring the Local data source for the Mobile Web Client

In order to enable a fully operational Mobile Web Client, the following parameters in the **[Local]** section must be set correctly:

Parameter	Description	Example Value
DockConnString	Host name of the Siebel server that hosts the Synchronization Manager component for Siebel Remote.	osappsebl1
EnterpriseServer	Name of the Siebel Enterprise that the client belongs to.	SIEBELEVAL
RequestServerName	Logical name of a Siebel Server that hosts the Siebel Request Broker component.	Eval_1

These parameters are usually set during the installation procedure but changes are sometimes necessary. The other parameters can usually keep their default values. The following screenshot shows the correctly configured **[Local]** section of a Siebel configuration file as an example.

```
[Local]
Docked                  = FALSE
ConnectString           = D:\SIA81\CLIENT\local\sse_data.dbf  -q -m -x NONE -gp 4096 -c15p -ch25p
TableOwner              = SIEBEL
DockedDBFilename        = CHANGE_ME
DLL                     = sscdw9.dll
SqlStyle                = watcom
MaxCachedCursors        = 16
MaxCachedDataSets       = 16
ReverseFillThreshold    = 100
DockTxnsPerCommit       = 500
DockConnString          = osappsebl1
ChartServer             = localhost:8001
ChartImageFormat        = png
AutoStopDB              = FALSE
EnterpriseServer        = SIEBELEVAL
RequestServerName       = Eval_1
UseCachedExternalContent = TRUE
```

The **ConnectString** parameter points to a path where the local database will be created during initialization of the Siebel Mobile Web client. Creating local databases will be discussed in a later chapter.

Configuring the Server data sources for the Siebel Developer Web Client

When the Siebel client is invoked as a Developer Web Client, it is crucial that all connectivity endpoints can be reached by the Siebel executable. The following parameters must be correctly set in the [ServerDataSrc] section of the Siebel configuration file to accomplish connectivity to the server database and the file system:

Parameter	Description	Example Value
ConnectString	For Oracle databases, this is the service identifier.	ORCL
TableOwner	The table owner in the Siebel server database	SIEBEL
DLL	The Siebel CRM version and database vendor specific dll used to connect to the RDBMS.	sscdo90.dll
SqlStyle	A database vendor specific identifier.	OracleCBO
FileSystem	The path to the ATT subdirectory of the Siebel File System. The user must have read and write permission on the network share.	\\seblfs\SIEBFILE\att

The [GatewayDataSrc] section's parameters must be set as follows to ensure connectivity to the Siebel Gateway Name Server in order to carry out server administration tasks.

Parameter	Description	Example Value
ConnectString	Host name of the Siebel Gateway Name Server.	osappsebl1
PrimaryEnterprise	The name of the Siebel Enterprise.	SIEBELEVAL

When the parameters discussed above are correctly set, we can use the Siebel application as a Developer Web Client. This allows us to access data in the Siebel server database and the Siebel File System even when the Siebel server infrastructure is not available. Furthermore, the Developer Web Client allows us to use the Server Configuration and Server Management screens and administer the Siebel Enterprise. Siebel server administration scenarios will be discussed in a later chapter.

The following screenshot shows correctly configured **[ServerDataSrc]** and **[GatewayDataSrc]** sections in the Siebel client configuration file.

```
[ServerDataSrc]
Docked                  = TRUE
ConnectString           = ORCL
TableOwner              = SIEBEL
DLL                     = sscdo90.dll
SqlStyle                = OracleCBO
MaxCachedCursors        = 16
MaxCachedDataSets       = 16
ReverseFillThreshold    = 100
FileSystem              = \\seblfs\SIEBFILE\att
CurrentSQLID            =
MaxCursorSize           =
PrefetchSize            =
ChartServer             = osappsebl1:8001
ChartImageFormat        = png

[GatewayDataSrc]
ConnectString           = osappsebl1
PrimaryEnterprise       = SIEBELEVAL
DLL                     = sscda10.dll
Hidden                  = TRUE
```

Setting up additional data sources

As a member of a larger Siebel CRM implementation project, we might feel the need to connect the Developer Web Client to different server databases, such as those that support the development, testing, training, or production enterprises.

This can be accomplished by simply copying the existing **[ServerDataSrc]** section and renaming the new section. The name should reflect the purpose, so we could think of a new section named **[TestDataSrc]**.

We must also register the new section in the **[DataSources]** section where we would add an entry like the following:

```
TestDataSrc = Test
```

The string on the right-hand side of the equals sign will appear in the **Connect to** dropdown box in the login dialog.

In the new data source section, we must adjust the following parameters to point to the correct server database. (Source: *Oracle Siebel CRM Bookshelf: Integration Platform Technologies: Siebel Enterprise Application Integration Guide, Version 8.1*)

ConnectString: For Oracle databases, we set this parameter to a valid TNS name entry. For Microsoft SQL Server, IBM DB2, and Oracle BI Enterprise Edition connectivity we enter the name of an ODBC data source.

TableOwner: This parameter must be set to the name of the table owner user for the Siebel database.

DLL and **SqlStyle**: The following table entails the correct settings for the different support database products:

Database Vendor and product	DLL	SqlStyle
IBM DB2	`sscddcli.dll`	DB2
Microsoft SQL Server	`sscdms80.dll`	MSSqlServer
Oracle Database	`sscdo90.dll`	OracleCBO
Oracle BI Server	`sscdsacon.dll`	Siebel Analytics Server Note: Siebel Analytics is the former product name of Oracle BI
Sybase Adaptive Server Anywhere	`sscdw9.dll`	Watcom

The following screenshot shows a new section **[TestDataSrc]** in a Siebel client configuration file and the resulting value display (Test) in the **Connect to** dropdown list:

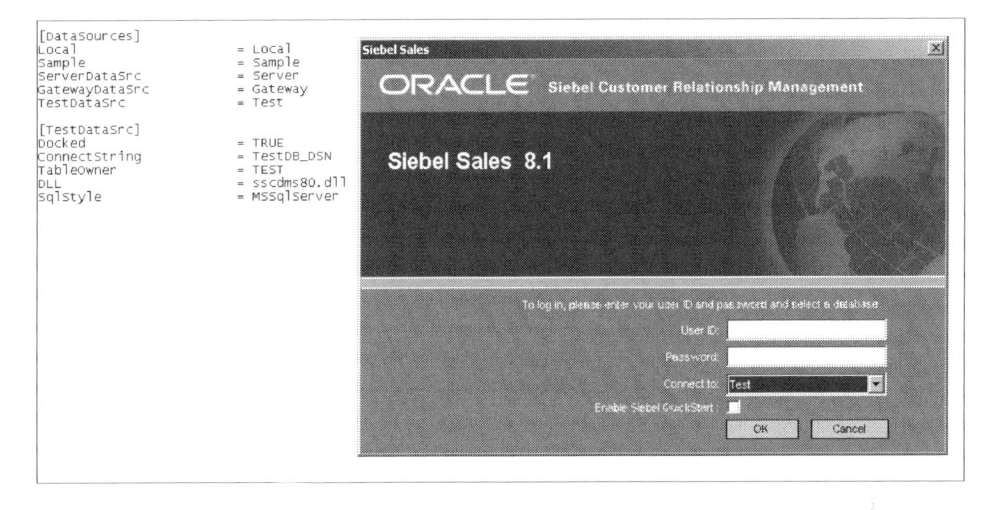

```
[DataSources]
Local            = Local
Sample           = Sample
ServerDataSrc    = Server
GatewayDataSrc   = Gateway
TestDataSrc      = Test

[TestDataSrc]
Docked           = TRUE
ConnectString    = TestDB_DSN
TableOwner       = TEST
DLL              = sscdms80.dll
SqlStyle         = MSSqlServer
```

To bypass the login dialog and to launch certain application configurations faster, we can create Windows shortcuts or batch command files. This will be discussed in the following section.

Creating Siebel application shortcuts

The siebel.exe program can take several parameters that are useful to create shortcuts in locations such as the Windows start menu, the desktop, or the Quick Launch toolbar.

The following table lists the most important parameters and provides examples:

Parameter	Description	Example
/c	The only mandatory parameter directs the siebel.exe to the full path of a Siebel configuration (cfg) file.	/c C:\SIA8\Client\BIN\siebel.cfg
/d	Used to preselect a data source from the [DataSources] section in the .cfg file. The value to the left of the equals sign must follow the parameter.	/d ServerDataSrc
/u	The username.	/u SADMIN
/p	The password (Caution: the password will be stored in clear text in the shortcut).	/p SADMIN
/b	Followed by a path to a browser executable. Useful if Microsoft Internet Explorer is not the default browser on the machine or to test Siebel Standard Interactivity applications with browsers other than Internet Explorer.	/b "C:\Program Files\Firefox\firefox.exe"
/l	Used to specify the language in which the Siebel application should launch. The respective language pack must be installed.	/l DEU
/s	Allows spooling the SQL statements generated by the Siebel executable to a file.	/s c:\temp\spool.txt
/editseeddata	Overrides the seed data protection. Only to be used under specific circumstances.	/editseeddata

Parameter	Description	Example
/ctsim	Enables the communications toolbar (ct) in simulation mode. This parameter is obsolete in Siebel 8.1.1.	/ctsim
/webservice	Followed by a port number. This parameter is supported in Siebel 8.1.1.2 and above. It allows running the siebel.exe program as a listener to inbound web service calls.	/webservice 2330

The following is a typical shortcut command string that launches the Siebel Sales application and logs the SADMIN user in to the test database. Additionally, the SQL statements generated by the application will be written to a text file in the `D:\temp` folder.

```
D:\SIA8\CLIENT\BIN\siebel.exe /c D:\SIA8\CLIENT\bin\ENU\siebel.cfg /d
TestDataSrc /u SADMIN /p SADMIN /s D:\temp\spool.txt
```

The command line above can be used in a Windows shortcut or a shell script to allow fast invocation of the Siebel application.

> Use the techniques described in the previous section to create useful Windows shortcuts to Siebel applications on your desktop.

Installing the Siebel sample database

Oracle provides a sample database that allows us to explore and evaluate Siebel application functionality and usage scenarios. This database is delivered as a Sybase Adaptive Server Anywhere database, which is the same type used for local databases for Mobile Web Clients. For the purposes of evaluating the standard Siebel application functionality against a set of sample data, it is sufficient to install the Siebel Mobile or Developer Web Client and the Siebel Sample Database. No other software installation such as Siebel Server or database software is necessary.

The Oracle Siebel Business Applications Bookshelf Documentation Library contains the **Demo Users Reference** document, which unveils the various predefined user accounts and roles that can be used for evaluation or training purposes. The Demo Users Reference document for Siebel 8.1 can be accessed at the following URL: http://download.oracle.com/docs/cd/E14004_01/books/DemoUser/booktitle.html.

Chapter 6

The sample database installer is delivered as part of the Siebel installation archives. After extraction, we can locate the **install.exe** program that launches the InstallShield installer. As opposed to the Siebel Mobile or Developer Web Client and Siebel Tools, the Siebel Sample Database installation is driven by the InstallShield installer and not Oracle Universal Installer.

The following table describes the procedure of installing the Siebel Sample Database. It is worth mentioning that the sample database can only be installed after a Siebel client and the installation folder must be identical to the client's root directory.

Step	Description	Tasks and Example Values
1	Start the InstallShield Wizard	Double-click the **install.exe** file in the `Siebel_Sample_Database` folder.
2	Choose Setup Language	Select the language that will be used for the remainder of the installation dialogs. Example: **English**. Click **OK**.
3	The Welcome dialog is displayed.	Click **Next**.
4	Setup Type	Select **Custom**. In the Destination Folder section, click **Browse** and navigate to the Siebel client installation directory. Click **Next**.
5	Select Components	Keep **Sample Files** selected. Unselect **Sample Search Index**. Note: The **Sample Search Index** feature is no longer supported in Siebel 8. Click **Next**.
6	Choose Languages	Select **English (American)**. Click **Next**.
7	Select Program Folder	Keep the default. The installer will create a new Windows start menu folder with demo shortcuts. Click **Next**.
8	Installation progress is displayed.	Leave the installer window open and wait for the process to finish.
9	Event Log	Summary information is displayed. Click **Next**.
10	The wizard displays successful completion	Click **Finish**.

Installing Siebel Client Software

Verifying successful installation of the Siebel Sample Database

The installation wizard for the Siebel Sample Database creates a Windows start menu folder with a collection of demonstration shortcuts. The following screenshot shows the Windows start menu generated by the Siebel Sample Database installer (English and German language packs were selected).

More shortcuts can be created manually using the technique described in the previous section.

The demo shortcut command lines use demo user accounts to provide the launch of the application at a single click. For example we can click the **Siebel Marketing Demo - ENU** shortcut.

The Siebel Marketing application should be launched in Microsoft Internet Explorer. The demo user Marion May is logged in automatically. The following screenshot shows the home page view for Marion May in the Siebel Marketing Demo application.

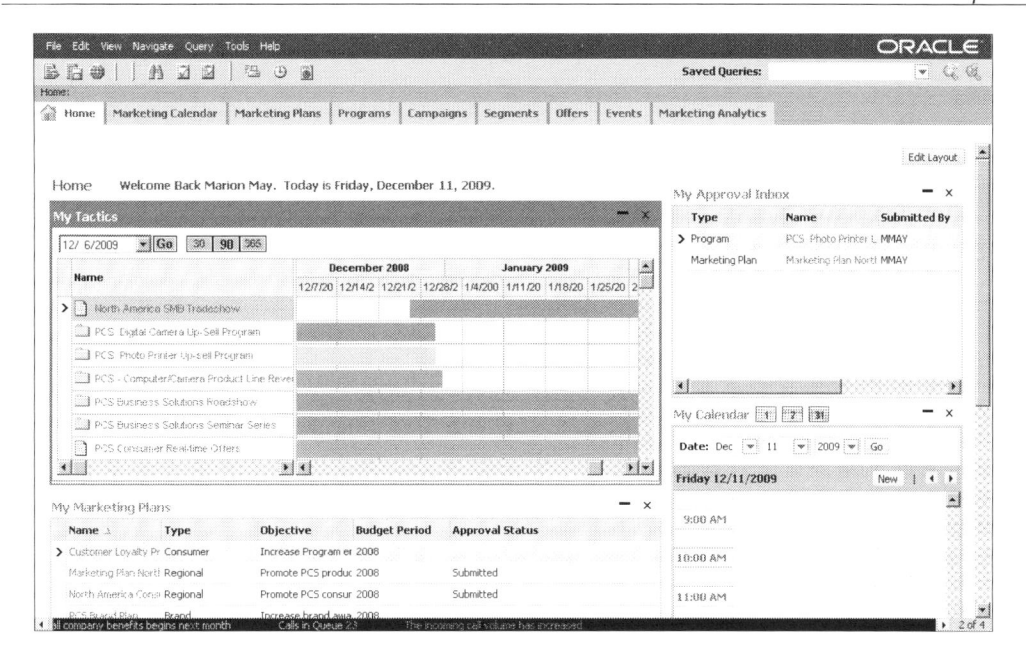

![Screenshot of Oracle Siebel marketing application interface showing Home tab with My Tactics, My Marketing Plans, My Approval Inbox, and My Calendar panels]

We can observe that the Siebel Sample database not only allows different user logins but also contains a great amount of sample data.

If the installation of the Siebel Sample Database is not successful, we should execute the following steps:

1. Uninstall the Siebel Sample Database using the Microsoft Windows **Add or Remove Programs** list (if possible).
2. Delete any remaining `sse_samp.dbf` file in the client's `SAMPLE/UTF8` directory.
3. Close all running programs on the machine.
4. Run the installer again and ensure that no other processes are executed on the machine until the installation is complete.

> On your demonstration machine, install the Siebel Sample Database and invoke a sample application.

Installing Siebel Tools

Siebel Tools is a specialized Siebel CRM application that serves as the integrated development environment (IDE) for customization of all other Siebel applications. Siebel Tools can also be used in conjunction with the Siebel Sample Database for evaluation and research purposes. The executable behind Siebel Tools is siebdev.exe, which acts in a similar way to the siebel.exe program that supports the Siebel Mobile or Developer Web Client. The major architectural difference between Siebel Tools and other Siebel clients is that it executes as a Windows application rather than in a browser. Similar to the siebel.exe, the siebdev.exe program reads a configuration file (`tools.cfg`) and is able to connect to local or network data sources.

Apart from the necessity of having Siebel Tools available on the developer's workstation, it is quite common for Siebel Tools to be installed on computers whose users are not directly involved in customizing Siebel applications, for example business analysts. Also, administrators will find Siebel Tools useful in order to stay current with the development team or adjust object settings themselves.

The Oracle Universal Installer has been used to install Siebel Tools since Siebel CRM version 8.1.1.0. Previous versions of Siebel CRM used the InstallShield wizard. The following table describes the process of installing and configuring Siebel Tools:

Step	Description	Tasks and Example Values
1	Start the Oracle Universal Installer	Double-click the oui.exe file in the `Siebel_Tools/Disk1/install` folder.
2	The Welcome dialog is displayed	Click **Next**.
3	Select a Product to install	Select **Siebel Business Application Tools**. Note: The Siebel Business Rules Developer has been discontinued by Oracle. Click **Next**.
4	Specify the home directory	Example: **C:\Siebel\8.1\Tools_1** (default value). **The directory should already have been specified in the planning document.** Click **Next**.

Step	Description	Tasks and Example Values
5	Prerequisite checks	The installer performs checks for prerequisite checks. Verify that all checks are passed successfully. Click **Next**
6	Select Languages	Select **English.** Click **Next.**
7	Siebel Database Server	Select **Oracle Database Server.** Click **Next.**
8	Database Identification	Database Alias: **orcl** Table Owner: **SIEBEL** Note: These values come from the planning document. Click **Next.**
9	File System	Directory Path: **D:\SIA8\siebfile** Note: This value comes from the planning document. Click **Next.**
10	Siebel Remote Server hostname	Siebel Remote Server: **osappsebl1** Note: This value comes from the planning document. Click **Next.**
11	Enterprise Server Information	Gateway Name Server address: **osappsebl1** Enterprise Server: **SIEBELEVAL** Note: These values come from the planning document. Click **Next.**
12	Summary	Review the summary information. Click **Install.**
13	The installation progress is displayed	
14	Success Message	Click **Exit** and **Yes** to leave the installer.

Installing Siebel Client Software

Verifying successful Siebel Tools installation

To verify the successful installation of Siebel Tools, we navigate to the Windows start menu and locate the new program folder. The name of the program folder is for example **Tools1 8.1**.

We start Siebel Tools by clicking the shortcut. At first launch, the license agreement is displayed, which we should agree to. In the login dialog, we enter **SADMIN** as the username, provide the correct password, and select **Server** in the **Connect to** dropdown box. When the application is completely launched, we should see the Object Explorer window to the left. To verify that repository metadata has been properly loaded into the Siebel server database, we click the **Application** object type in the **Object Explorer** window. A list of applications is displayed. The following screenshot shows the successfully installed Siebel Tools application with the list of application definitions in the Siebel Repository:

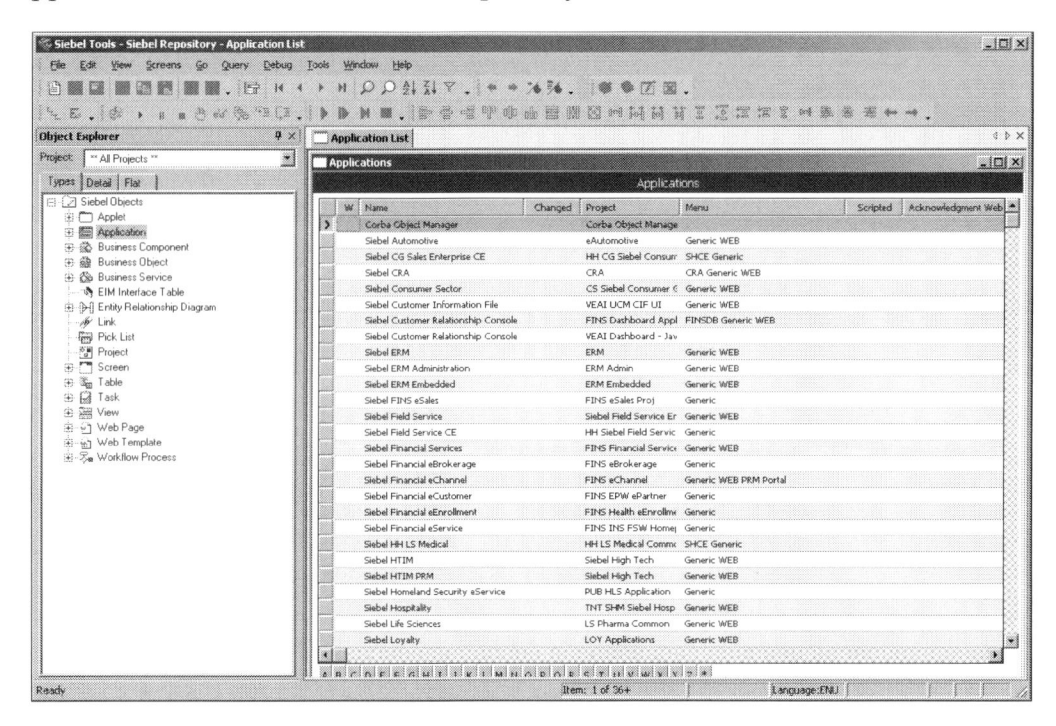

In the unlikely situation that the installation of Siebel Tools has failed, we should consult the installer log file. After correction of the problem, it is recommended to uninstall Siebel Tools (if possible) and attempt the installation again.

Configuring Siebel Tools for the Siebel Sample Database

If we wish to use Siebel Tools to connect to the Siebel Sample Database, we have to modify the application configuration file for Siebel Tools. This file is named `tools.cfg` and resides in the language-specific subdirectory of the Siebel Tools installation's `bin` folder.

We open the `tools.cfg` file with a text editor of our choice and navigate to the **[Sample]** section. The only necessary change is to alter the path to the `sse_samp.dbf` file in the **ConnectString** parameter so that it points to the sample database already installed in the client directory. It is recommended to copy a working path from one of the Siebel client configuration files. The following screenshot shows the altered **ConnectString** parameter in the **[Sample]** section of the `tools.cfg` file:

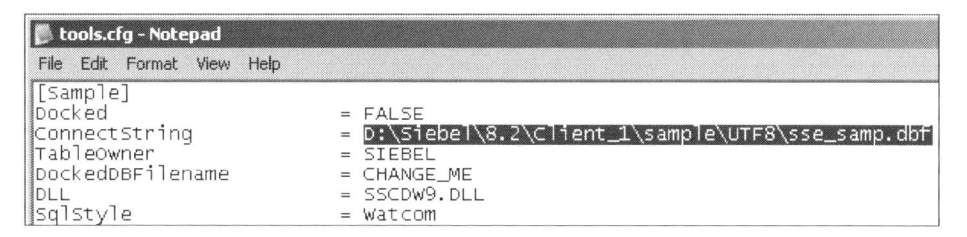

```
tools.cfg - Notepad
File  Edit  Format  View  Help
[Sample]
Docked                = FALSE
ConnectString         = D:\Siebel\8.2\Client_1\sample\UTF8\sse_samp.dbf
TableOwner            = SIEBEL
DockedDBFilename      = CHANGE_ME
DLL                   = SSCDW9.DLL
SqlStyle              = Watcom
```

Now, we can start Siebel Tools and log in as the Siebel Administrator (SADMIN) using SADMIN as the password and choose **Sample** in the **Connect to** dropdown box. The Siebel Sample Database contains exactly the same metadata repository that is imported during a server database installation. Therefore, it is ideal for research and training because any changes made—even erroneous ones—do not affect other users.

> On your demonstration machine, install Siebel Tools and configure the `tools.cfg` file so you can connect to the Siebel Sample Database.

Creating shortcuts for Siebel Tools

In a similar manner as discussed during the Siebel Developer Web Client installation, we can create shortcuts for Siebel Tools.

By opening the properties for an existing default shortcut for Siebel Tools, we can observe that the application executable is different from `siebel.exe`, namely `siebdev.exe`, but takes similar parameters.

In addition to the parameters such as `/d` for the default data source, and `/u` and `/p` for username and password, siebdev.exe can be run from shortcuts or shell scripts with other parameters, which are described in the following table:

Parameter	Description	Example
`/bv`	Validates the entire repository.	`/bv`
`/batchimport`	Used to automate the import of repository metadata from .sif files. The example command will launch the batch import of all archive files in the d:\temp folder, overwriting conflicting object definitions.	`/batchimport "Siebel Repository" Overwrite d:\temp`
`/batchexport`	Used to automate the export of repository metadata to .sif files. The example command will launch the batch export for all objects specified in the input.txt file.	`/batchexport "Siebel Repository" input.txt`
`/bc`	Used for batch compilation of the Siebel Repository File (srf). The example command will compile a new siebel.srf file from all object definitions in the Siebel Repository.	`/bc "Siebel Repository" siebel.srf`

The following is a typical shortcut to launch Siebel Tools as SADMIN against the sample database:

```
D:\SIA8\TOOLS\BIN\siebdev.exe /c "D:\SIA8\TOOLS\bin\enu\tools.cfg" /d sample /u SADMIN /p SADMIN
```

Applying patches to Siebel client software

Oracle makes patch sets for Siebel CRM software available for customers on the My Oracle Support website (`http://support.oracle.com`). The patch sets for Siebel CRM contain bug fixes and enhancements.

Siebel patch sets must be applied consistently for all installed software modules, ranging from server to client.

After downloading and extracting the patch installers, we can launch the Oracle Universal Installer (`oui.exe`), similar to when installing from scratch. The major difference is that we have to select the correct Oracle home location of an existing Siebel client installation. The following screenshot shows the Oracle Universal Installer dialog for specifying the home details for the patch installation:

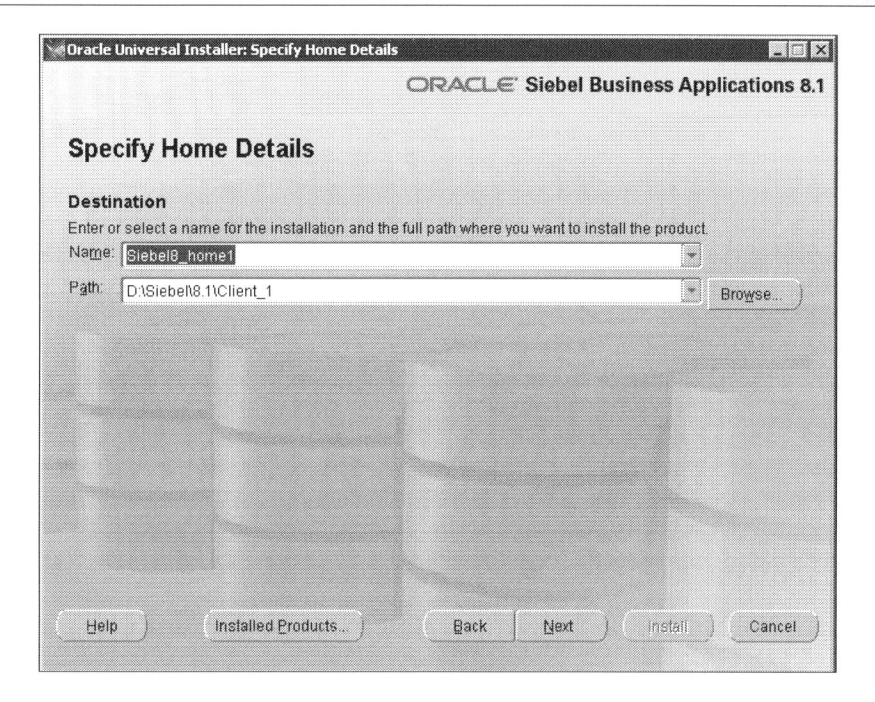

We must select the correct home location from the upper **Name** dropdown box when applying a Siebel client patch.

Summary

In this chapter, we discussed the installation of the Siebel client side software products. We learned to distinguish between the Siebel Developer Web Client and Siebel Mobile Web Client by the location of the database that the Siebel executable connects to.

The chapter discussed the installation of the Siebel Developer Web Client and its configuration as well as the installation and setup of the Siebel Sample Database and Siebel Tools.

Additional information about how to create useful application shortcuts for Microsoft Windows and how to apply software patches for Siebel CRM clients was also given in the chapter.

In the next chapter, we will discuss the installation of ancillary Siebel server software to support charts and reports.

7
Installing Ancillary Siebel Server Software

Siebel functionality is often extended through the integration of other Oracle or third-party software products. In order to enable the functionality as required by the business, administrators have to install and configure the software. In this chapter, we will discuss the installation of two products that support basic data visualization and reporting:

- Visual Mining NetCharts Server
- Oracle BI Publisher

Installing and configuring the Visual Mining NetCharts server

The NetCharts server is a software product of Visual Mining Inc., which allows web-based applications such as Siebel CRM to visualize their data in a chart format. Even in the days of enterprise-wide business intelligence systems such as Oracle Business Intelligence Enterprise Edition (OBI EE), companies either cannot afford or do not want to spend money on systems such as OBI EE.

On the other hand, exporting data to spreadsheet applications such as Microsoft Excel is a lengthy, unsecure, and error-prone process.

The integration of Siebel CRM with the Visual Mining NetCharts Server fills the gap between simple data export and enterprise-scale business intelligence systems. Data can stay where it is and the visualization engine is tightly integrated with the Siebel CRM application. The following screenshot shows the **Revenue by Month by Account** chart in Siebel Sales:

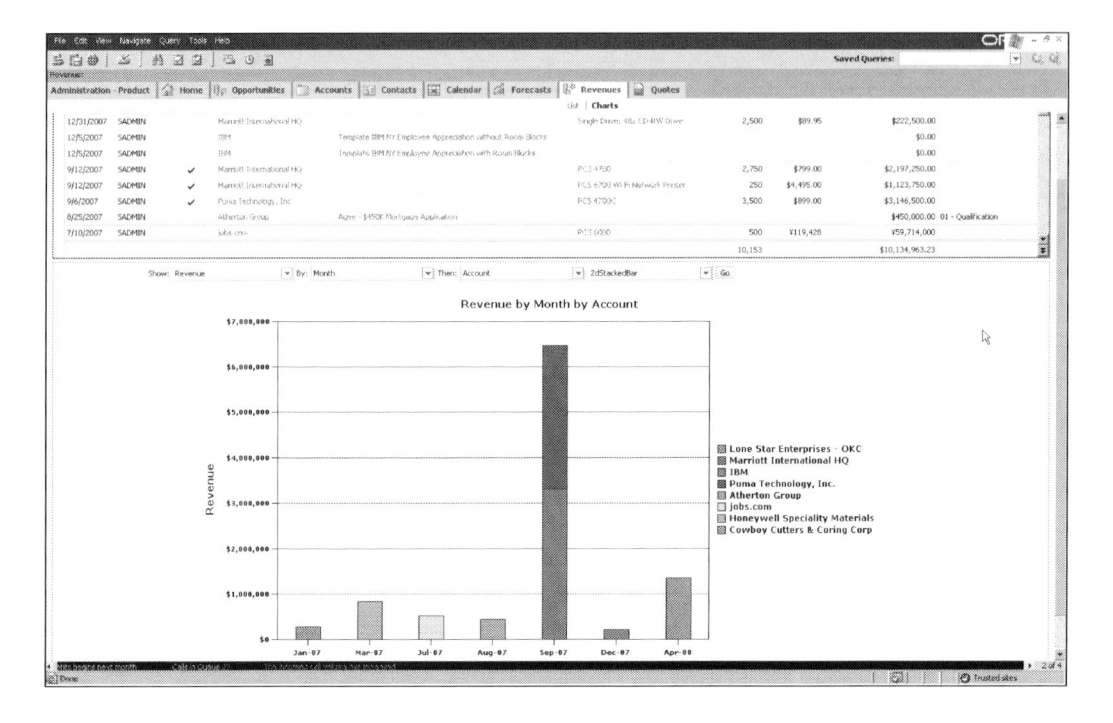

The above screenshot is an example of how the Visual Mining server is integrated into Siebel CRM. End users can filter the data in the Siebel list applet, choose a preconfigured chart applet, and set parameters to control the axis labels and chart display.

The Siebel chart applets also support drilldown mechanisms and can be dragged and dropped into office applications such as Microsoft PowerPoint.

Visual Mining's NetChart server has to be installed to support the web-based infrastructure of Siebel CRM. The Siebel Mobile Web Client that is installed as separate software on the end user's computer includes the NetChart binaries, so a client-side installation is not necessary.

The following section describes how to download, install, and set up the Visual Mining NetCharts Server for Siebel CRM.

Downloading the Visual Mining NetCharts Server installer

The Visual Mining NetCharts Server installer is delivered as part of the Siebel CRM base download archives on `http://edelivery.oracle.com`. The process to download the installer archives and generate the Siebel installers using the Network Image Creator has been discussed in detail in Chapter 2.

After extracting the installers, we can find the NetCharts installer (`NetChartsServer4.6SiebelEdition.exe`) in the `Server_Ancillary` directory of the Siebel installation image folders.

Planning and preparing the NetCharts Server installation

It is recommended to install the NetCharts Server on a Siebel Server machine. If a different machine is chosen, network connectivity must be verified between the Siebel Server machine and the NetCharts machine.

The NetCharts Server uses a port number (default 8001) to enable communication with other systems such as Siebel CRM. We must ensure that this port number is free on the machine we dedicate to host the NetCharts server. The following screenshot shows the NetCharts Server installer prompting for the port number the server will use to listen for requests:

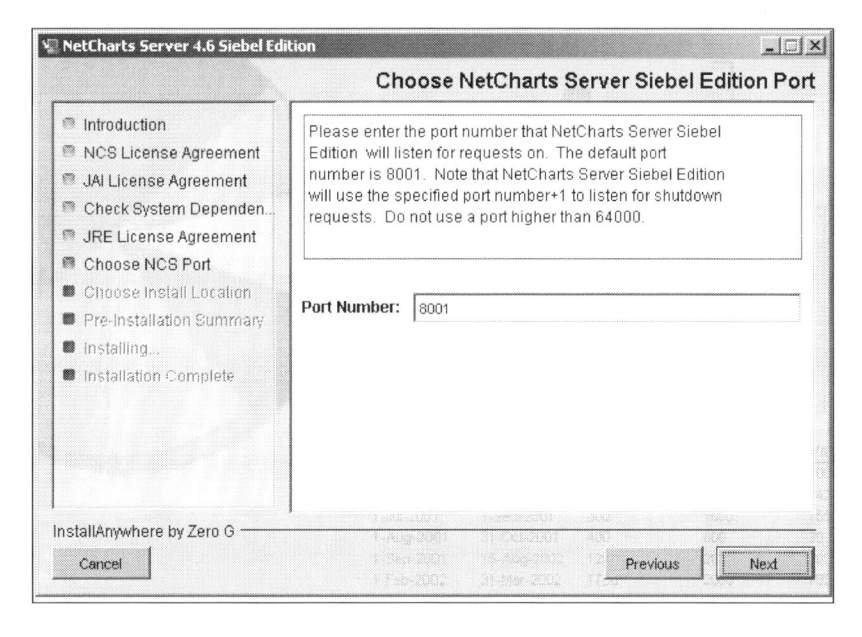

Other port numbers that the NetCharts server uses by default are listed in the following table:

Port number	Description
8002	Used for shutdown requests. Default value is listening port + 1.
1099	Java RMI (Remote Method Invocation) port for the NetCharts administration console.

In Siebel environments, port number 1099 could already be used by the Siebel Management Server. In this case, the RMI port number for the Siebel Management Server must be changed before attempting to install the NetCharts server on the same machine as the Siebel Management Server. Installation and configuration of the Siebel Management Server is discussed in a later chapter of this book.

Installing the Visual Mining NetCharts server on Windows

In order to launch the installer on Microsoft Windows, we simply double-click the executable. The installer dialogs and example parameter values are described in the following table:

Step	Description	Tasks
1	Installer language	Select **English**. Click **OK**.
2	Introduction	Acknowledge the introductory information. Click **Next**.
3	NetCharts License Agreement	Verify the License Agreement and select **I accept the terms of the License Agreements**. Click **Next**.
4	Java Advanced Imaging License Agreement	Verify the License Agreement and select **I accept the terms of the License Agreements**. Click **Next**.
5	Java Runtime Environment License Agreement	Verify the License Agreement and select **I accept the terms of the License Agreements**. Click **Next**.
6	Port Number	Keep the default (8001). Click **Next**.

Step	Description	Tasks
7	Install Location	Example: **C:\SIA8\VMNetCharts**
		Click **Next**.
8	Summary	Verify the summary information.
		Click **Next**.
9	Installation progress display	Wait for the installer to finish.
10	Install Complete	The installer displays the success message.
		Click **Done**.

Verifying successful installation of the NetCharts Server

The following checkpoints exist to verify the successful installation of the Visual Mining NetCharts server on Microsoft Windows:

- Existence of a Windows service
- Connectivity to port 8001

On Microsoft Windows operating systems, we can verify the successful installation of the NetCharts server by navigating to the Windows Services console and checking for the existence of a service named **NetChartsServer4.6SiebelEdition**. The following screenshot shows the Windows service for the NetCharts server generated by the installer:

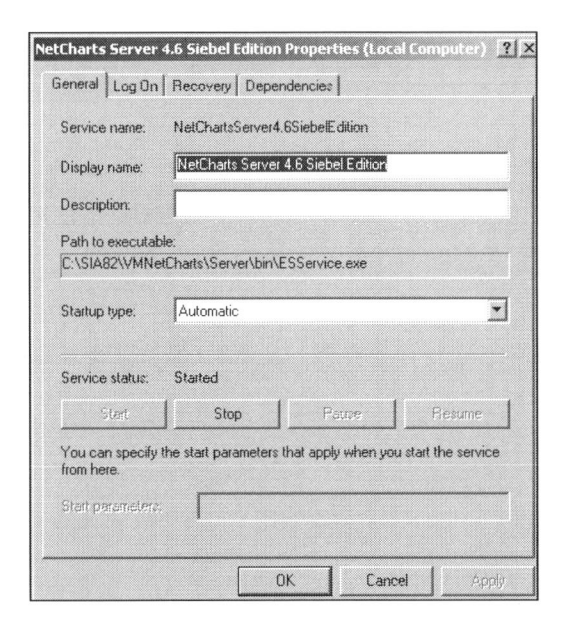

The start-up type is **Automatic** and the service has successfully started.

A final check is to use either telnet or http to connect to port 8001 on the local machine. For telnet, we can use a command such as the following:

```
telnet localhost 8001
```

This will establish a connection to port 8001 on the local machine. If we receive no error message then the connection is established.

In order to verify connectivity using http, we can open a browser window and enter the following address:

```
http://localhost:8001/index.jsp
```

The response from the NetCharts server is a prompt for the license key. For deployments with Siebel CRM, a license key is not needed.

Configuring connectivity from Siebel CRM to the NetCharts Server

Once the NetCharts server is successfully installed and operational, we have to carry out the following setup steps:

1. Create a project folder and file for Siebel.
2. Set Siebel Enterprise parameters for connectivity and image type.
3. Verify the successful setup of Siebel Charts.

These procedures are described in detail in the following sections.

Creating a project folder and file for Siebel

In the NetCharts installation folder, we navigate to the `Server\root\projects` folder. Next, we create a new subdirectory named `Siebel.chart`. Using a text editor such as Microsoft Notepad, we create a new text file within the `Siebel.chart` folder and name it `Siebel.cdx`. In this file, we type the string **CDL** without adding a line break. The following screenshot shows the new `Siebel.chart` folder and the `Siebel.cdx` file:

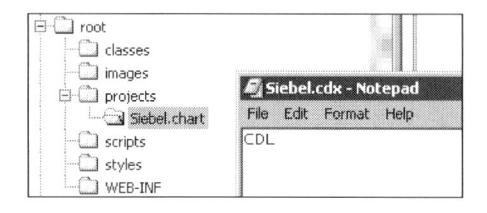

The Siebel.chart folder will later be used to store temporary chart images and HTML files generated by the NetCharts server.

Setting Siebel Enterprise parameters

The following enterprise level parameters must be set in order to enable the Siebel server components to establish the connection to the NetCharts server:

- DSChartServer
- DSChartImageFormat

The DSChartServer parameter must be set to the hostname and port number that the chart server is listening on. The DSChartImageFormat parameter can be set to either gif, jpg, or png, and defines the graphics file type of the chart delivered to the Siebel client.

We can use the Siebel Server Manager command line utility to accomplish this. We log on to the server manager by navigating to the BIN directory of the Siebel server installation folder and entering a command similar to the following:

`srvrmgr /g localhost /e SIEBELEVAL /u SADMIN /p TJay357D`

This will establish a connection to the SIEBELEVAL enterprise (/e) on the local Gateway Name Server (/g) for the SADMIN user (/u and /p for username and password). The Gateway Name Server must be running for successful execution of the login.

At the srvrmgr command prompt, we can enter the following commands to change the two enterprise parameters described above:

`change parameter DSChartServer=hostname:8001 for named subsystem ServerDataSrc`

`change parameter DSChartImageFormat=png for named subsystem ServerDataSrc`

The string `hostname` has to be replaced with the real host name of the machine where the NetChart server is installed.

The first command sets the DSChartServer parameter to the host name and port that the NetCharts server is listening on. The second command sets the image format to png (public network graphics).

After changing the parameters, we use the `exit` command to log off from the Server Manager command line. Finally, we have to restart the Siebel Server service.

Verifying successful setup of Siebel Charts

Once the Siebel Server has restarted, we can log on to the Siebel Web Client. In order to test the chart engine, we should create some test data such as Opportunities. To do so, we navigate to the Opportunities screen and then to the Opportunity Charts list view.

It is sufficient to create a small number (three is sufficient) of Opportunity records and set the Revenue field to any reasonable amount.

Now we select the Pipeline Analysis chart from the dropdown list situated below the record list. A chart that visualizes the data in the upper list should appear correctly. The following screenshot shows the Pipeline Analysis chart by Sales Method:

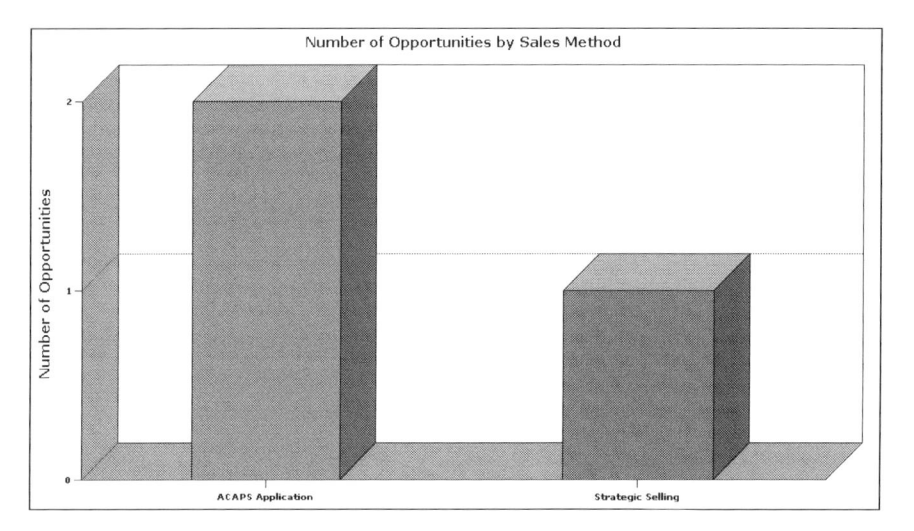

The correct display of a chart in the Siebel Web Client finalizes the installation and setup of Siebel Charts.

Depending on the intended usage of the system we should delete the test data.

> On your demonstration machine, you can now follow the steps described in this section to install the Visual Mining NetCharts server. Use the instructions in the section to verify the successful installation.

Installing Oracle BI Publisher

Oracle BI Publisher—formerly known as Oracle XML Publisher—has been developed to support reporting in Oracle's eBusiness Applications. When Oracle acquired Siebel Systems Inc., the Siebel CRM server infrastructure relied on the Actuate Report Server to provide printable reports to end users.

With Siebel CRM version 8.1.1.0, Oracle started shipping the product to new customers exclusively with Oracle BI Publisher as the pre-integrated reporting tool. Only customers who have been using previous versions of Siebel CRM can choose between Actuate or BI Publisher. However, Oracle started phasing out Actuate as a reporting engine at the end of 2009.

The core features of Oracle BI Publisher are:

- Support for multiple, heterogeneous data sources
- Based on pure Java and XML
- Support for different template types such as rtf or xsl
- Support for multiple output file types such as pdf, rtf, xls, or ppt

Oracle BI Publisher is available either as a standalone product or as a part of Oracle's Business Intelligence Suite Enterprise Edition (OBI EE). Customers who have deployed OBI EE can use the instance of BI Publisher deployed with the suite product (if performance considerations allow).

The reporting facility is pre-integrated with Siebel CRM in two ways. The Siebel Mobile Web Client—supporting offline usage of Siebel CRM functionality—includes the BI Publisher standalone libraries thus providing reporting functionality to disconnected users. To support reporting in the web architecture where users connect to the Siebel web server, we have to establish connectivity to the BI Publisher Enterprise Server.

Installing Ancillary Siebel Server Software

The following diagram depicts the integration touch points of the Siebel CRM server infrastructure with the Oracle BI Publisher Enterprise server:

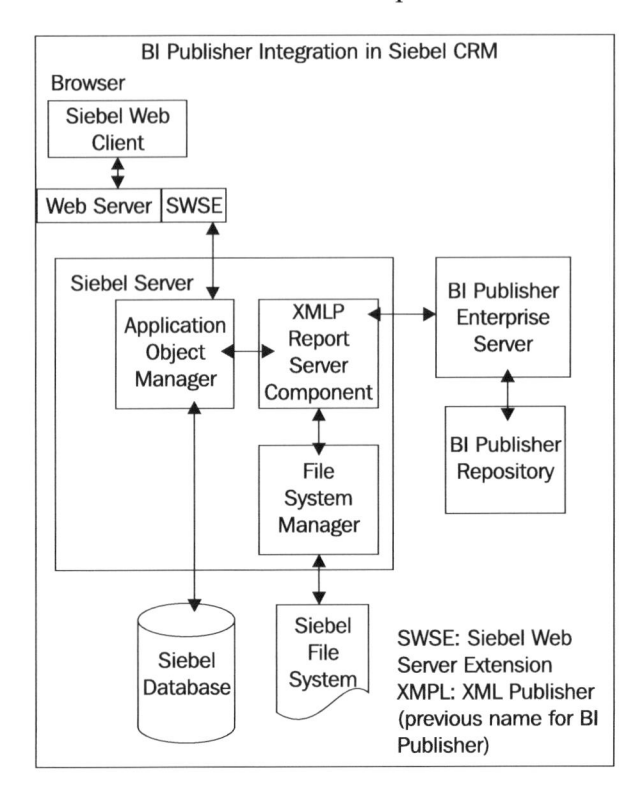

```
BI Publisher Integration in Siebel CRM
Browser
    Siebel Web Client
    Web Server | SWSE
Siebel Server
    Application Object Manager
    XMLP Report Server Component
    BI Publisher Enterprise Server
    BI Publisher Repository
    File System Manager
    Siebel Database
    Siebel File System

SWSE: Siebel Web Server Extension
XMPL: XML Publisher (previous name for BI Publisher)
```

When an end user requests a report, a Siebel server component named XMLP Report Server Component retrieves the necessary data from the Siebel database and submits the data in XML format to the BI Publisher server's web service layer. The reply from BI Publisher includes the generated report file, which is stored in the Siebel File System and presented to the end user as a download. The following screenshot shows the **Opportunity Summary** report generated by BI Publisher in PDF format downloaded to the end user's client:

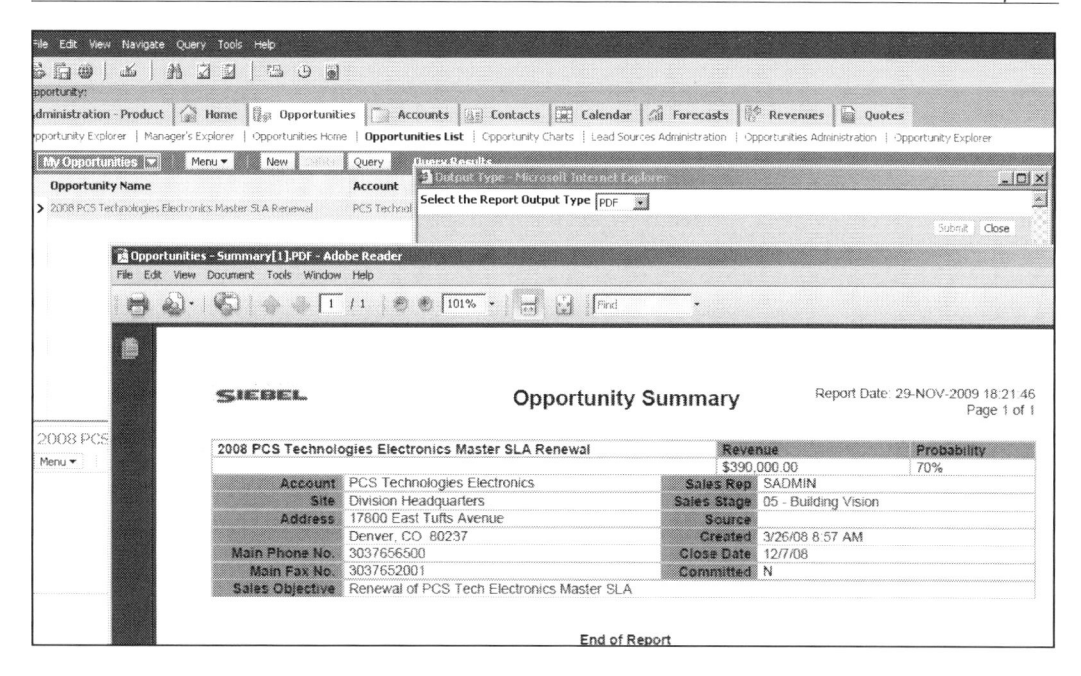

In the following section, we will discuss the download, installation, and configuration procedures necessary to provide reporting functionality to Siebel CRM users.

Downloading Oracle BI Publisher Enterprise Server

If our customer either does not possess the Oracle BI Suite Enterprise Edition or wishes to deploy BI Publisher separately, we must download the correct version of BI Publisher Enterprise before we can begin with the installation.

The following table provides the correct version combinations of Siebel CRM and Oracle BI Publisher as well as the appropriate location for the download:

Siebel CRM Version	Oracle BI Publisher Version	Download Location
8.1.1.0 and below	10.1.3.4.0	`http://edelivery.oracle.com`
8.1.1.1 and above	10.1.3.4.1 and above	`http://otn.oracle.com`

After extraction from the downloaded `.zip` archive, we find an installation image with several directories—including the documentation library—and a setup executable.

Prerequisites for Oracle BI Publisher Enterprise Server

As Oracle BI Publisher is based purely on Java, we must ensure that the **Java Software Development Kit (SDK) 1.5 or higher** is installed on the machine that will host the BI Publisher Enterprise Server as well as any Siebel Server machine hosting the XMLP Report Server component.

If we plan to run BI Publisher as a component of an Oracle Application Server, we must ensure that the application server is properly installed and access privileges are granted to install and publish the BI Publisher component. The default installation of BI Publisher installs the lightweight Oracle Container for Java (OC4J) server to support execution of BI Publisher. In the following section, we will use OC4J as the application container for BI Publisher.

Installing Oracle BI Publisher Enterprise Server

After downloading and extracting the installation image we can invoke the Oracle Universal Installer on Microsoft Windows operating systems by double-clicking the `setup.exe` file.

The following table describes the installation procedure and sample parameters:

Step	Description	Tasks
1	Welcome	The Oracle Universal Installer welcome page is displayed. Click **Next**.
2	File Locations	Keep the source file location settings. Enter a valid path for the destination file location. Click **Next**.
3	Installation Type	Keep the default (Basic). Click **Next**.
4	OC4J Administrator Password	Enter a password for the OC4J (Oracle Containers for Java) administrator account. Click **Next**.
5	Summary	Verify the summary information. Click **Install**.

Step	Description	Tasks
6	Installation progress display	Wait for the installer to finish.
7	Install Complete	The installer displays the success message. Click **Exit** and **Yes**.

Verifying successful installation of BI Publisher

The BI Publisher Server is launched automatically as part of the installation. In order to verify whether the server is operational, we can navigate to the following URL:

```
http://bip_host:9704/xmlserver
```

In the above example, bip_host has to be replaced with the host name of the machine on which BI Publisher Enterprise Server is installed. The port number 9704 is the default port for the lightweight OC4J application server and could differ depending on the type of installation. After a while, we should see a login page similar to the following:

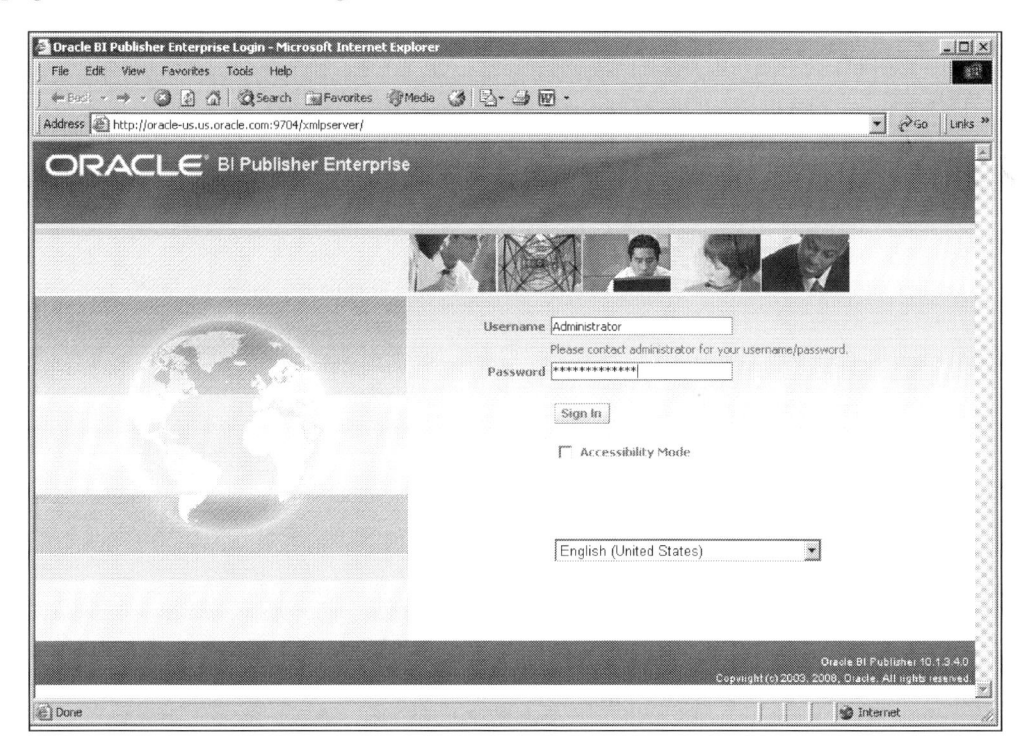

We can log on as the **Administrator** user. The default password for this user is Administrator and should be changed sooner rather than later to a secure password.

If we have installed the BI Publisher Enterprise Server using OC4J as the application server, we must ensure that OC4J is started automatically when the machine boots up.

A command similar to the following starts the OC4J and makes the BI Publisher Enterprise Server available:

```
C:\BIP\oc4j_bi\bin\oc4j.cmd -start
```

The above command is an example for Microsoft Windows installations, but works in a similar way for Linux or UNIX-based operating systems. On Microsoft Windows, program menu shortcuts are provided to start and stop the OC4J.

Using the task scheduler of the operating system, we can invoke a small shell script with the above command any time the host machine boots up. On Microsoft Windows, we can use the Scheduled Tasks feature in the Control Panel to create such a task.

> Follow the instructions in the previous section to download and install the correct version of Oracle BI Publisher Enterprise on your demonstration machine.

Setting up Siebel CRM for BI Publisher reports

Before end users can use the pre-built BI Publisher reports from their Siebel Web client, it is the administrator's duty to complete the setup steps. These steps include setting up web service and Java connectivity between Siebel CRM and BI Publisher and implementing data security. As these tasks require technical expertise in both products, it is recommended that they are carried out by a seasoned professional.

Siebel CRM version differences

Due to the fact that BI Publisher reporting functionality in Siebel CRM version 8.1.1.0 is limited (most importantly, parameterization and scheduling of reports is not available), it is recommended to use at least patch level 8.1.1.1, which includes the missing functionality. Oracle makes patch sets available for licensed customers on My Oracle Support (http://support.oracle.com).

Because a patch set does not alter the Siebel Repository or the seed data, some of the steps described for version 8.1.1.1 will be different from later major releases of Siebel CRM such as 8.2.

The process to enable BI Publisher reports for Siebel CRM depends on the Siebel CRM version we are using.

To prepare Siebel CRM version 8.1.1.1 and above (but below 8.2), we have to complete the following steps:

1. Import Fix Pack SIF files and compile the srf file.
2. Create a new Siebel outbound web service for BI Publisher 10.1.3.4.1.
3. Import the Siebel inbound web services.
4. Create and assign XMLP responsibilities.

For Siebel CRM version 8.2 and above, we can start with this step:

1. Modify the preconfigured Siebel outbound web service

For all Siebel versions (including 8.1 and 8.2), the remaining necessary steps are:

1. Copy jar files.
2. Enable external references for BI Publisher.
3. Enable the Siebel server components.
4. Set the Siebel Java subsystem.
5. Set BI Publisher security.
6. Upload preconfigured reports.
7. Verify BI Publisher reports.
8. Assign BI Publisher roles to the `SiebelCRMReports` folder.
9. Copy fonts to the JRE home (optional).
10. Configure the BIP Scheduler (optional).

Source: *Siebel Reports Guide, Version 8.1 (Oracle Siebel CRM Documentation Library)*

`http://download.oracle.com/docs/cd/E14004_01/books/Reports/booktitle.html`

These procedures will be described in detail in the following sections.

Importing Fix Pack SIF files

This step is only necessary if the Siebel CRM version is a patched version of 8.1 such as 8.1.1.1. We can skip this step if we are using Siebel CRM 8.2 or above as the objects imported during this procedure are already present in the Siebel Repository in these versions.

To add the object definitions that enable the functionality of Siebel Reports for version 8.1.1.1 or higher, we have to import them from Siebel Tools archive files that have a suffix of .sif (Siebel Information File). These files are copied to the REPPATCH subdirectory of the Siebel Tools installation folder when the patch set for Siebel Tools is applied.

The following steps must be executed to successfully import the new object definitions and compile the Siebel repository file (.srf):

1. If necessary, stop the Siebel Server service.
2. Log in to Siebel Tools as SADMIN, connecting to the Server data source.
3. In the **Object Explorer**, select **Project**.
4. In the **Projects** list, query for the XMLP Integration project.
5. Right-click the project and select **Toggle Allow Object Locking**.
6. Check the Locked flag to lock the project.
7. In the **Tools** menu, select **Import from Archive**.
8. In the file selection dialog, navigate to the REPPATCH folder of the Siebel Tools installation folder and select the file named 8111FP_new_feature.sif.
9. Click the **Next** button and continue until the wizard has completed importing the content of the archive file.
10. In the **Tools** menu, select **Compile Projects**.
11. Select the XMLP Integration project.
12. Browse to the Siebel Server's OBJECTS\ENU directory and select the siebel_sia.srf file.

> If you are using Siebel Enterprise Applications (SEA) rather than Siebel Industry Applications (SIA), select the siebel.srf file.

13. Click **Compile**.
14. Keep Siebel Tools open.

Creating a new outbound web service for BI Publisher 10.1.3.4.1

This step is only necessary in Siebel CRM version 8.1.1.1 or a higher patch level. It is not necessary for version 8.2 and above as the web service definition is already part of the prebuilt seed data and repository for these versions.

First, we have to obtain the web service definition file (.wsdl) from the BI Publisher Server. The following steps are part of that procedure:

1. Start the BI Publisher server if necessary.
2. Open a browser window and navigate to the web service URL `http://bip_host.domain:port/xmlpserver/services/PublicReportService_v11?wsdl`

    where `bip_host.domain:port` has to be replaced with the fully qualified host and domain name and the port number where the BI Publisher server resides.

3. Using the browser's file menu, we save the file as `PublicReportService_v11.wsdl` on our disk drive.

The next steps are carried out in Siebel Tools. We use the Siebel Tools WSDL import wizard to create a proxy business service and integration object definitions. In order to avoid conflicts, we have to delete the existing object definitions first.

The following steps serve as a guide to the process:

1. If necessary, stop the Siebel Server service.
2. If necessary, log in to Siebel Tools as SADMIN, connecting to the Server data source.
3. Navigate to the **PublicReportService** business service and delete it.
4. Navigate to the list of Integration Objects and query for all integration objects that have the XMLP Integration project assigned.
5. Delete all Integration Objects in the query result.
6. In the **File** menu, select **New...**
7. In the New Objects wizard, select the **EAI** tab.
8. Double-click the Web Service object. This launches the WSDL Import Wizard.
9. Select the XMLP Integration project
10. Select the **PublicReportService_v11.wsdl** file you created earlier

Installing Ancillary Siebel Server Software

The following screenshot shows the WDSL Import Wizard in Siebel Tools with the settings described in the procedure:

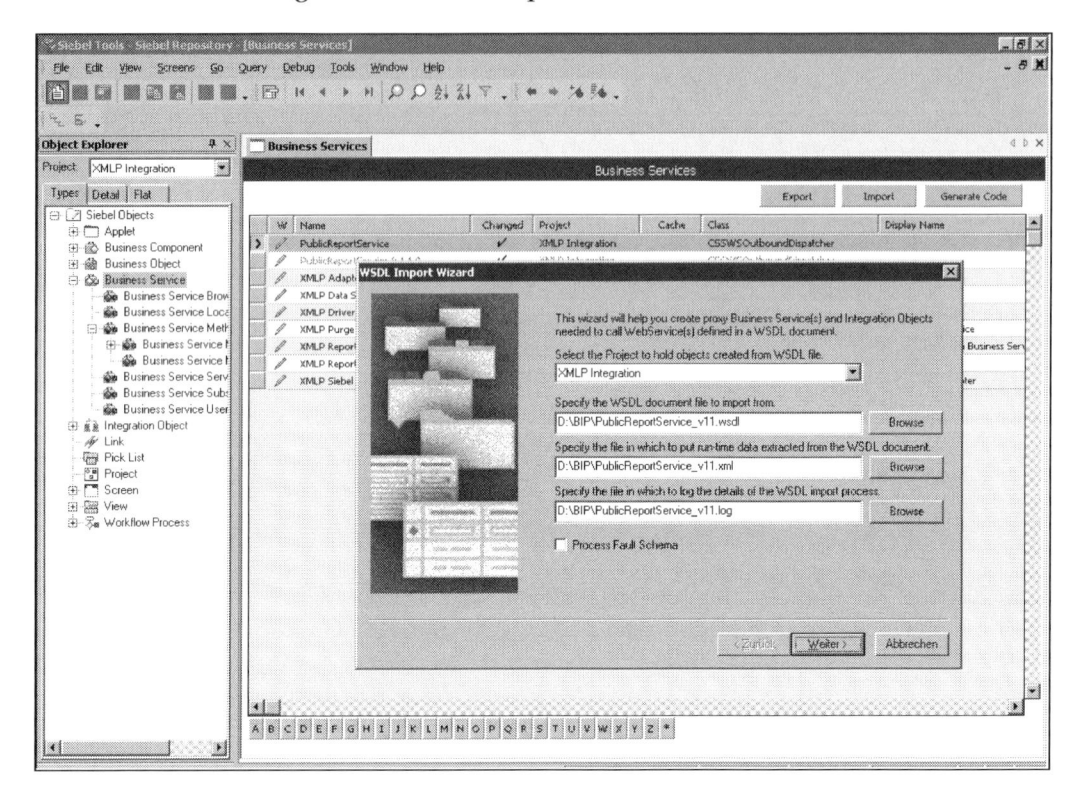

11. Click **Next**.
12. Check the Deploy Integration Object(s) and Proxy Business Service(s) checkbox.
13. Click **Finish**.
14. In the **Tools** menu, select **Compile Projects**.
15. Compile the XMLP Integration project to the Siebel server's `.srf` file.
16. Close Siebel Tools.
17. Start the Siebel server service.

Importing the Siebel inbound web services

This task is only necessary if we implement a patched version of Siebel CRM 8.1, for example 8.1.1.1. In Siebel 8.2 and above, the web service definitions needed for BI Publisher integration are already imported during installation of the Siebel database as part of the Siebel seed data. These web service definitions implement the security and data exchange interface for the integration of Siebel CRM and BI Publisher.

The following tasks have to be completed to import the inbound Siebel web services in a patched version of Siebel 8.1:

1. Log in to the Siebel Web client using an administrative user account.
2. Navigate to the Sitemap and select the **Administration - Web Services** screen.
3. Select the **Inbound Web Services** view.
4. Click **Import** and browse to the Siebel Tools installation folder.
5. Open the REPPATCH directory and select the **BIPSiebelSecurityWS.xml** file.
6. Click **Import**.
7. Repeat the steps above to import the BIPDataService.xml file.
8. In the **Inbound Web Services** list, query for web services that have names starting with BIP.
9. For both web services, modify the address in the Service Ports list to match the web server name, username, and password of the Siebel installation.
10. Click **Clear Cache** in the web services list.

The screenshot below shows the **Inbound Web Services** list and the two imported inbound web services for BI Publisher integration:

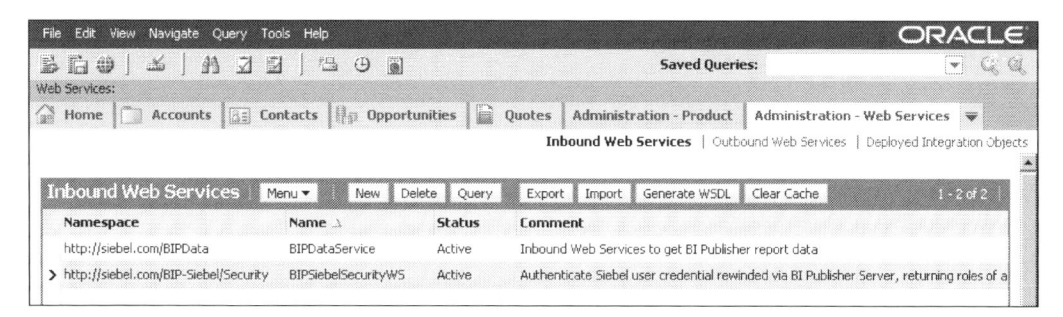

Creating XMLP responsibilities

This step is only necessary for deployments of a patched version of Siebel CRM 8.1 such as 8.1.1.1. As patch sets do not insert seed data into the Siebel database we have to create the view and responsibility records manually. This seed data is already available when we use Siebel 8.2 or above.

We follow the procedure below to accomplish this task:

1. Log on to the Siebel Web Client using an administrative account.
2. Navigate to the Sitemap.
3. Navigate to the **Administration - Application** screen, and then the Views list.
4. Create a new record in the Views list and set the view name to Report Job List View (it is recommendable to copy the view name from Siebel Tools to avoid typing errors).
5. Navigate to the Responsibilities view.
6. Create the following responsibilities (CASE is important):
   - XMLP_ADMIN
   - XMLP_DEVELOPER
   - XMLP_SCHEDULER
   - XMLP_SIEBEL_GUEST
7. Assign the administrative user to each responsibility.
8. Assign the Report Job List View to the XMLP_SCHEDULER responsibility.

We have now finished the necessary tasks to prepare a patched version of Siebel 8.1 such as 8.1.1.1 for BI Publisher Integration. The next step, *Configuring the Siebel outbound web service for Siebel 8.2 or higher*, should be skipped if we implemented Siebel 8.1.

Configuring the Siebel outbound web service for Siebel 8.2 or higher

This step is only necessary when we implement Siebel CRM 8.2 or higher. The preconfigured outbound web service needs to be adjusted to point to the correct host name and port number of the BI Publisher server.

We can accomplish this using the following procedure.

First, we have to log on to the Siebel Web Client using an administrative user account. We can use the Sitemap to navigate to the Administration - Web Services screen and the Outbound Web Services view.

We use the Query functionality to find the web service with the name "PublicReportServiceService". In the Service Ports list we change the address field to reflect the correct path to the BI Publisher machine and port number. The final address should be similar to the following example:

`http://bip_host:9704/xmlpserver/services/PublicReportService_v11`

In the above URL bip_host must be replaced with the host name of the BI Publisher server machine.

Copying Siebel java libraries to the BI Publisher server

This and the following procedures have to be completed for all Siebel CRM versions in order to successfully integrate Siebel CRM with BI Publisher.

In order to enable specialized report functionality, we have to copy Java libraries from the Siebel server installation folder to the `lib` directory of the BI Publisher installation.

We navigate to the CLASSES subdirectory of the Siebel Server's installation folder and copy the following files to the `oc4j_bi\j2ee\home\applications\xmlpserver\xmlpserver\WEB-INF\lib` folder of the BI Publisher installation:

- `XSLFunctions.jar`
- `SiebelCustomXMLP.jar`
- `SiebelCustomXMLP_SIA.jar`
- `iSignBmp.jar`
- `InkToolsLib.jar`

Making these files available to the BI Publisher server ensures that specialized functions integrated in the preconfigured Siebel CRM reports can be executed correctly.

Enabling external file references for BI Publisher

In order to enable the BI Publisher server to execute the custom functions contained in the `.jar` files we copied in the previous step, we have to set the **Disable External Reference** parameter of the BI Publisher server to False.

In order to do so, we log in to the BI Publisher Enterprise Server as Administrator (default password is Administrator) using a URL similar to the following:

`http://bip_host:9704/xmlpserver`

After login, we navigate to the **Admin** tab and click the **Properties** link in the **Runtime Configuration** section. It is a good idea to use the browser's text search functionality to locate the Disable External Reference parameter. We set the value of the parameter to False and then click the **Apply** button on top of the page.

Enabling Siebel Server components

Using BI Publisher reports requires the availability of two components on at least one Siebel server in the enterprise. These components are:

- XMLP Report Server
- EAI Object Manager

The XMLP Report Server is the sole member of the XMLPReport component group and enables communication between the Siebel server and the BI Publisher enterprise server.

The Siebel EAI Object Manager is part of the EAI component group and serves as the inbound listener for web service calls that are made by the BI Publisher when it uses the Siebel security model.

To enable both components on a Siebel server and to ensure that unnecessary components of the EAI component group are set to manual start, we create a text file with content similar to the following. Using text files allows us to repeat the setup in different environments with less effort and also helps during troubleshooting.

```
enable compgrp xmlpreport for server EVAL_AUTO
enable compgrp eai for server EVAL_AUTO
manual start comp BusIntBatchMgr for server EVAL_AUTO
manual start comp BusIntMgr for server EVAL_AUTO
manual start comp CustomAppObjMgr_enu for server EVAL_AUTO
manual start comp EIM for server EVAL_AUTO
manual start comp JMSReceiver for server EVAL_AUTO
manual start comp MqSeriesAMIRcvr for server EVAL_AUTO
manual start comp MqSeriesSrvRcvr for server EVAL_AUTO
manual start comp MSMQRcvr for server EVAL_AUTO
manual start comp SMQReceiver for server EVAL_AUTO
sleep 20
```

We save the file in a folder that is accessible by the Siebel server, using `BIPComponents.txt` as the name, for example.

The first two commands enable the `XMLPReport` and EAI component groups for the `EVAL_AUTO` server.

The manual start command allows us to set the start up type of the components to manual, thus providing for faster start up of the Siebel server as a whole. We set all components except the EAI Object Manager to manual start because they are not necessary for BI Publisher reporting. However, if we need one of the components later in the project we can use the `auto start` command to enable automatic start-up again.

Of course, the logical Siebel server name `EVAL_AUTO` serves as an example and must be replaced by an appropriate name.

The `sleep 20` command lets the command line stay for 20 seconds so we can verify the successful execution.

In order to execute the commands in the file, we ensure that the Siebel Gateway Name Server and Siebel Server services are running. Then, we open a command shell and navigate to the Siebel server's `bin` directory where we enter the following:

`srvrmgr /g localhost /e SIEBELEVAL /u SADMIN /p TJay357D /i D:\BIPComponents.txt`

In the above command, we invoke the server manager utility connecting to the local Gateway Name Server (/g), the SIEBELEVAL enterprise (/e) as SADMIN (/u) using TJay357D as password (/p) and execute the `BIPComponents.txt` file (/i). The following screenshot shows the successful execution of the commands in the `BIPComponents.txt` file for the server `EVAL_AUTO` in the Windows command shell:

```
C:\WINNT\system32\cmd.exe
srvrmgr> enable compgrp xmlpreport for server EVAL_AUTO
Command completed successfully.

srvrmgr> enable compgrp eai for server EVAL_AUTO
Command completed successfully.

srvrmgr> manual start comp BusIntBatchMgr for server EVAL_AUTO
Command completed successfully.

srvrmgr> manual start comp BusIntMgr for server EVAL_AUTO
Command completed successfully.

srvrmgr> manual start comp CustomAppObjMgr_enu for server EVAL_AUTO
Command completed successfully.

srvrmgr> manual start comp EIM for server EVAL_AUTO
Command completed successfully.

srvrmgr> manual start comp JMSReceiver for server EVAL_AUTO
Command completed successfully.

srvrmgr> manual start comp MqSeriesAMIRcvr for server EVAL_AUTO
Command completed successfully.

srvrmgr> manual start comp MqSeriesSrvRcvr for server EVAL_AUTO
Command completed successfully.

srvrmgr> manual start comp MSMQRcvr for server EVAL_AUTO
Command completed successfully.

srvrmgr> manual start comp SMQReceiver for server EVAL_AUTO
Command completed successfully.

srvrmgr> sleep 20
```

Setting parameters for the XMLP Java subsystem

In order to enable the outbound communication of Siebel CRM to the Java-based BI Publisher, we have to set parameters for a parameter collection that goes by the name of XMLPJvMSubsys. These parameter collections are traditionally known as "named subsystems" (subsystems of the name daemon—also known as Siebel Gateway Name Server). In the Siebel user interface, they are labelled "Enterprise profile".

To accomplish this task, we use the server manager command line tool and an input text file similar to the previous section where we enabled server components.

The text file's content should be similar to the following (file paths and server names might vary):

```
change parameter dll=C:\BIP\jdk\jre\bin\client\jvm.dll for named
subsystem xmlpjvmsubsys

change parameter classpath=C:\SIA82\siebsrvr\CLASSES\SiebelXMLP.
jar;C:\SIA82\siebsrvr\CLASSES\xdoparser.jar;C:\SIA82\siebsrvr\CLASSES\
fix6312772.jar;C:\SIA82\siebsrvr\CLASSES\xdocore.jar;C:\
SIA82\siebsrvr\CLASSES\xmlparserv2-904.jar;C:\SIA82\siebsrvr\CLASSES\
versioninfo.jar;C:\SIA82\siebsrvr\CLASSES\share.jar;C:\SIA82\siebsrvr\
CLASSES\jewt4.jar;C:\SIA82\siebsrvr\CLASSES\jdbc12.jar;C:\SIA82\
siebsrvr\CLASSES\i18nAPI_v3.jar;C:\SIA82\siebsrvr\CLASSES\collections.
jar;C:\SIA82\siebsrvr\CLASSES\bipres.jar;C:\SIA82\siebsrvr\CLASSES\
bicmn.jar;C:\SIA82\siebsrvr\CLASSES\Siebel.jar;C:\SIA82\siebsrvr\
CLASSES\XSLFunctions.jar;C:\SIA82\siebsrvr\CLASSES\SiebelCustomXMLP.
jar for named subsystem xmlpjvmsubsys

change parameter vmoptions=-Xusealtsigs for named subsystem
xmlpjvmsubsys

set server EVAL_AUTO

change parameter jvmsubsys=XMLPJvmSubsys for component
xmlpreportserver

unset server EVAL_AUTO

sleep 20
```

We save this text file in a folder reachable from the Siebel server and name it, for example, `BIPConfig.txt`.

The `dll` parameter serves to locate the Java virtual machine (jvm) and must point to the installation of the Java Developer Kit (JDK) on the Siebel server machine (examples are for Microsoft Windows).

The `classpath` parameter must include the full path to the `.jar` files in the Siebel server's CLASSES directory. (Note: This string can be copied from the Siebel documentation and then modified to point to the correct folders).

The `vmoptions` parameter is only necessary on Linux or UNIX-based operating systems and should always be set to the values indicated in the example.

The `set server` command allows us to set the command prompt for a specific server.

The next command in the script assigns the `XMLPJavaSubsys` named subsystem to the XMLP Report Server component.

The `unset server` command undoes the assignment of the command prompt to a specific server.

The `sleep 20` command lets the command line stay for 20 seconds so it is easier to check for successful execution before the window closes.

To execute the commands in the text file, we ensure that the Siebel Gateway Name Server and Siebel Server services are running. Then, we open a command shell and navigate to the Siebel server's `bin` directory where we enter the following:

```
srvrmgr /g localhost /e SIEBELEVAL /u SADMIN /p TJay357D /i D:\
BIPConfig.txt
```

In the above command, we invoke the server manager utility, connect to the local Gateway Name Server (`/g`), the SIEBELEVAL enterprise (`/e`) as SADMIN (`/u`) using TJay357D as password (`/p`) and execute the `BIPConfig.txt` file (`/i`).

Setting the BI Publisher Security Model

When end users run BI Publisher reports, we must ensure that only authenticated Siebel users are able to do so. To accomplish this security check, the BI Publisher server is capable of using Siebel CRM or an LDAP directory that is used by Siebel CRM as its authentication authority. In this section, we discuss how to set the BI Publisher's security model to use Siebel as the authentication system.

In order to set the BI Publisher security model, we have to complete the following tasks:

1. Start the BI Publisher server if necessary.
2. Log in to the BI Publisher server as an administrator.
3. Navigate to the **Admin** tab.
4. Click **Security Configuration**.
5. In the **Local Superuser** section, check the checkbox labeled **Enable Local Superuser**.
6. Enter a username and password for the local super user.

7. In the **Security Model** section, select **Siebel Security** as the security model.
8. In the Siebel Web client, navigate to the **Administration - Web Services** screen, **Inbound Web Services** view.
9. Query for the inbound web service named BIPSiebelSecurityWS.
10. In the service ports list, verify that the web server address is correct.
11. Copy the address string to the clipboard.
12. Navigate back to the BI Publisher security administration page and paste the content of the clipboard to the Siebel Web Service Endpoint field.
13. Enter a valid Siebel username and password (CASE is important) in the Administrator Username and Administrator Password fields.
14. Click the **Apply** button in the upper portion of the security administration page.

The following screenshot shows the settings for the Siebel Security model in the BI Publisher security administration page:

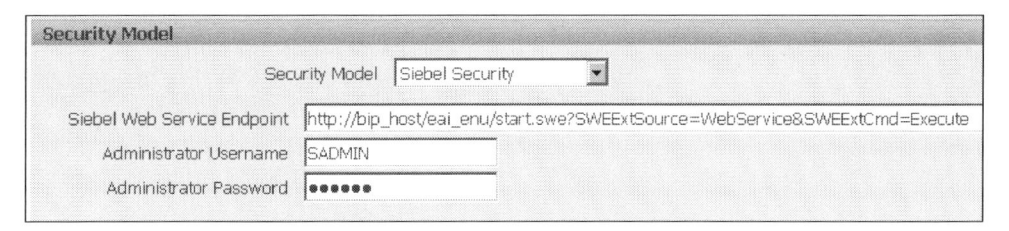

Security Model	
Security Model	Siebel Security
Siebel Web Service Endpoint	http://bip_host/eai_enu/start.swe?SWEExtSource=WebService&SWEExtCmd=Execute
Administrator Username	SADMIN
Administrator Password	••••••

To verify that the BI Publisher security is properly configured, we have to restart the BI Publisher server. Once the BI Publisher server is restarted, we should ensure that the Siebel servers are started. Next, we can try to log in to the BI Publisher Enterprise server using a Siebel user account that has at least one of the XMLP responsibilities assigned (as discussed in a previous step).

If the login is successful, we have correctly configured BI Publisher security.

Uploading preconfigured reports

Siebel Industry Applications are shipped with more than 100 preconfigured BI Publisher report templates that enable end users to create reports in various output formats such as PDF, RTF, or Excel out of the box.

In order to enable the preconfigured reports, we have to upload the templates from the Siebel server to the BI Publisher repository.

This is accomplished from an administrative view in the Siebel client. Before we start, we should verify that both the BI Publisher server and the Siebel server infrastructure are up and running. We can then log in to the Siebel Web client using an administrative user account. Then, we navigate to the **Administration - BIP** screen and the **Report Template Registration** view.

In the view, we query and select (multi-select using the *CTRL* or *SHIFT* key is possible) the reports we wish to enable and click the **Upload Files** button. Some of the preconfigured reports visible in the list might not have an associated template file, which results in an error when we try to upload them. In that case, we should deselect them and continue to upload only the reports we wish to enable in smaller batches. The following screenshot shows the **Report Template Registration** view with the selected report templates:

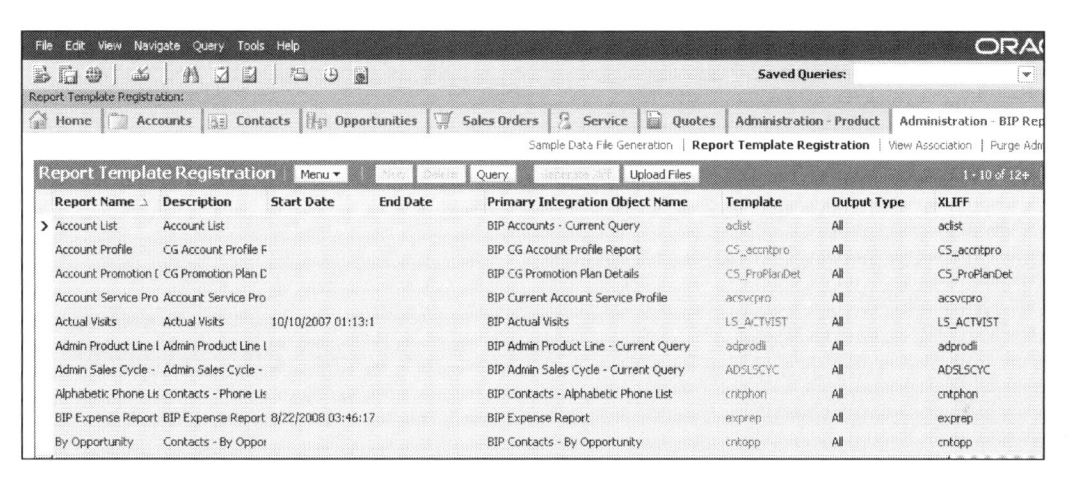

Installing Ancillary Siebel Server Software

We can verify the successful upload by logging on to the BI Publisher Enterprise server as an administrator. Then, we can navigate to the `Shared Folders` directory and we should find a `SiebelCRMReports` folder. This folder is created during the first upload attempt from Siebel CRM. The `SiebelCRMReports` folder should contain the report templates for the reports we uploaded from the Siebel Web client. The following screenshot shows the `SiebelCRMReports` folder in the **BI Publisher Enterprise** administration:

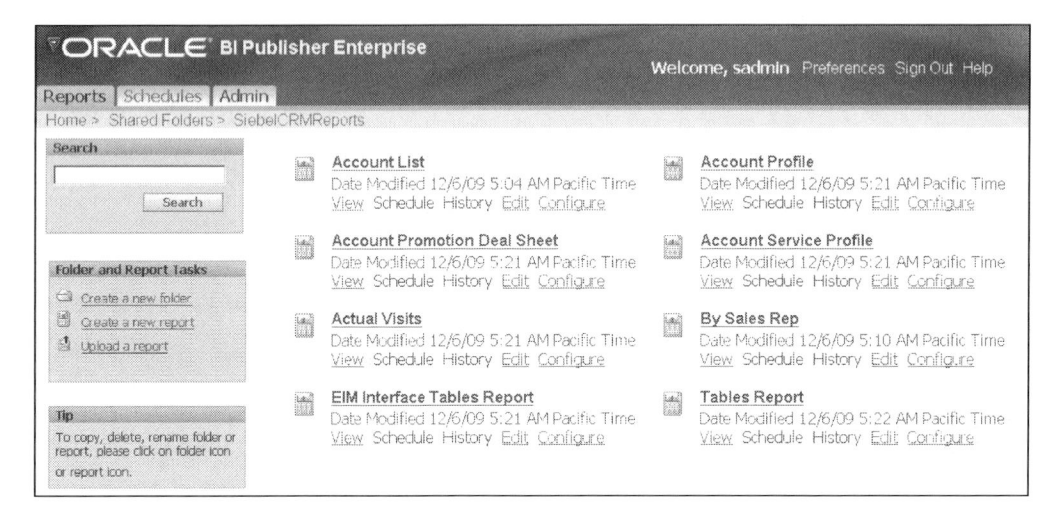

The reports in the folder are available for execution from within the Siebel Web client.

Verifying BI Publisher integration for Siebel CRM

Now that we have completed the fundamental setup procedures, we can test the BI Publisher reporting functionality by running a test report. Logged in to the Siebel Web client as an administrator, we can navigate to the **Administration - Application** screen and the **Tables** view.

In the **Tables** list applet, we query for the **S_CONTACT** table. Enclosing the name in double quotes ensures an exact query. Otherwise, the default wildcard query would result in too many tables for our first test.

In the Siebel CRM toolbar, we click the **Reports** button and select the **Tables Report**. The following screenshot shows the **Reports** button menu expanded and the selection of the **Tables Report**:

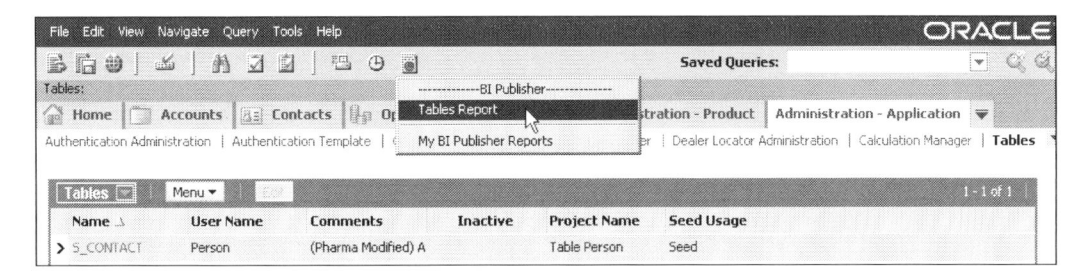

In the pop-up dialog, we select **PDF** as the report output type and click **Submit**.

In the **File Download** dialog box, we can click **Open** to directly open the report in Adobe Reader, which must be installed for this test to work. If Adobe Reader is not present, we can choose HTML as the report output format instead.

As a result, the table report for the **S_CONTACT** table should be displayed.

The following screenshot shows the table report in pdf format for the **S_CONTACT** table:

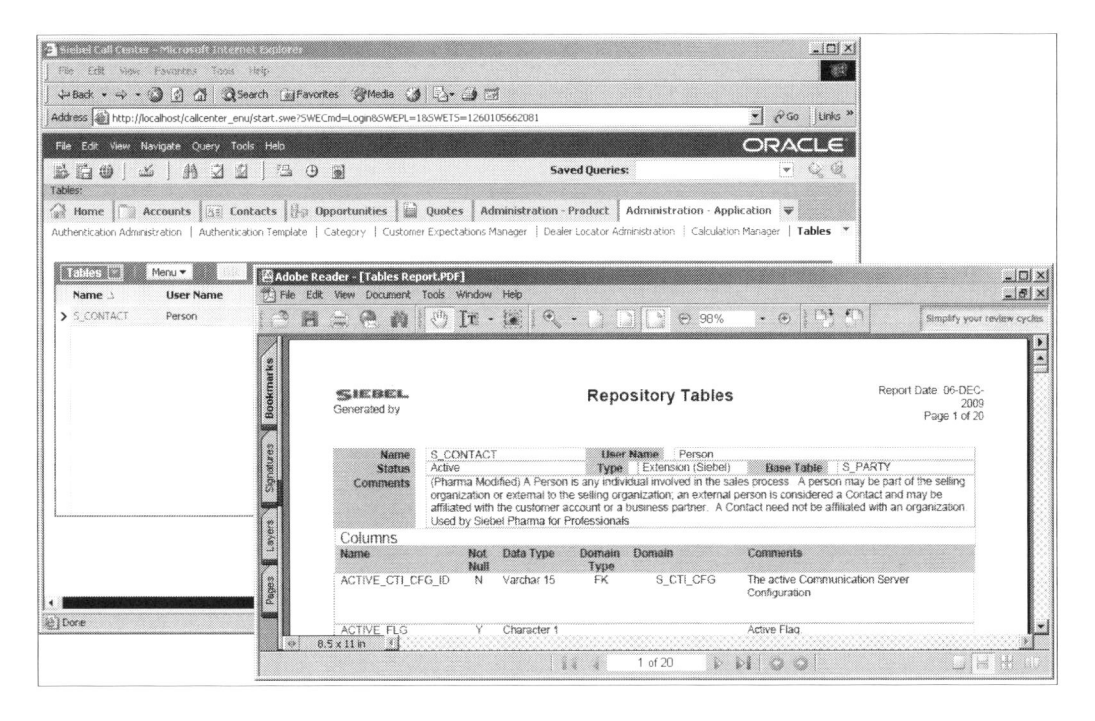

Table reports can be used to provide information about the physical Siebel data model to non-Siebel users.

Assigning BI Publisher roles to the SiebelCRMReports folder

In order to allow users who do not have the XMLP_ADMIN role to view reports, we have to assign the `SiebelCRMReports` folder to other roles such as XMLP_SIEBEL_GUEST.

In the Siebel CRM user administration, non-administrative users should have the XMLP_SIEBEL_GUEST and XMLP_SCHEDULER responsibility assigned to allow them to view and schedule BI Publisher reports.

In the BI Publisher console, we have to navigate to the **Admin** tab and click **the Roles and Permissions** link. Because the roles are synchronized with the Siebel seed responsibilities we find hundreds of roles.

It is a bit cumbersome to find the roles starting with XMLP. Once we locate the XMLP roles, we click the **Add Folders** button for the **XMLP_SIEBEL_GUEST** role and assign the `SiebelCRMReports` folder to the role. We repeat this step for the XMLP_SCHEDULER role. The following screenshot shows the assignment of the `SiebelCRMReports` folder to the allowed folders list for the **XMLP_SIEBEL_GUEST** role:

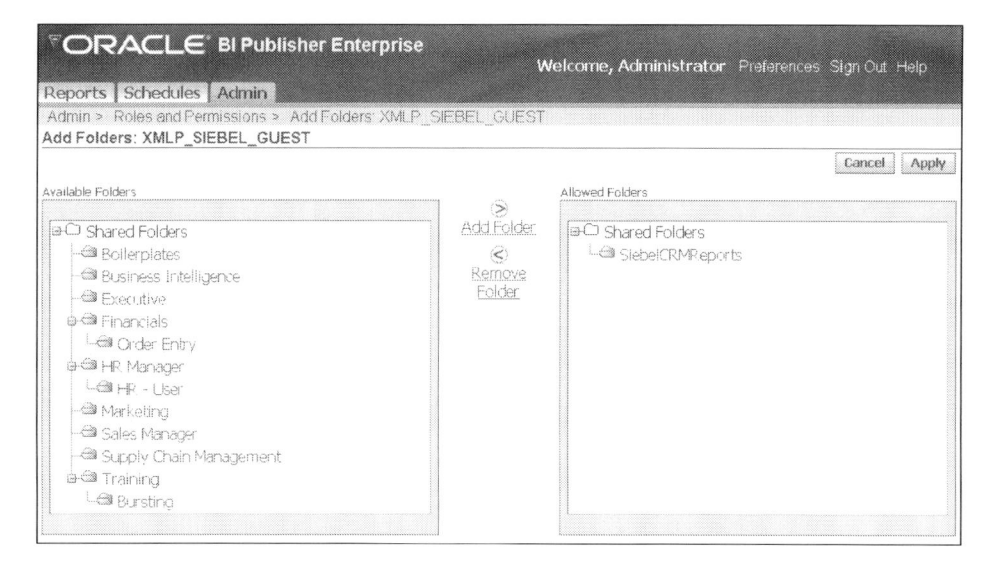

Copying fonts for BI Publisher reports (optional)

To avoid reports being rendered unusable due to missing fonts, we must copy the font definition files to the home folder of the Java virtual machine used by the XMLP Report Server component. The following procedure must be executed on all Siebel Server machines that host this component.

In a Microsoft Windows environment, we use a shell command such as `copy` to copy all files residing in the system fonts folder to the `lib\fonts` folder of the Java Runtime Environment installation. The following is an example command:

`copy C:\Windows\Fonts\*.* C:\jre\lib\fonts\*.*`

It is noteworthy that we must use a shell command on Microsoft Windows machines as the Windows Explorer does not support copy of font definition files.

Configuring the BI Publisher Scheduler (optional)

It is very likely that our company decided to use a patch release of Siebel CRM 8.1 or a later version because of the capability to schedule BI Publisher reports and retrieve them at a later time.

Setting up BI Publisher for scheduling includes tasks to be carried out on the BI Publisher side and procedures to be followed on the Siebel CRM side. In this section, we will discuss the complete procedure to set up scheduling for Siebel CRM reports.

The following tasks have to be completed to set up BI Publisher scheduling:

1. Create the BI Publisher scheduler tables.
2a. For patched versions of Siebel CRM 8.1, we must additionally:
    i. Enter List Of Values data.
    ii. Create a symbolic URL definition for viewing scheduled reports in Siebel CRM.
2b. For Siebel CRM version 8.2 and above we must:
    i. Configure the BI Publisher host name for viewing scheduled reports in Siebel CRM (version 8.2 and above only).
3. For all Siebel CRM versions, these tasks have to be completed to finalize the setup:
    i. Create the `dataservice.wsdl` file from the Siebel inbound web service administration view.
    ii. Verifying BI Publisher scheduling with Siebel CRM.

Creating the BI Publisher scheduler tables

First, we have to enable scheduling for the BI Publisher. In general, this task is accomplished by creating the BI Publisher scheduler tables in a relational database.

We log in to the BI Publisher Enterprise server as an administrator. Then we select the **Admin** tab and click the **Scheduler Configuration** link in the **System Maintenance** section.

The following settings serve as an example for setting up the BI Publisher scheduler tables in an Oracle database.

Parameter	Example value
Database Connection Type	jdbc
Database Type	Oracle 10g
Connection String	jdbc:oracle:thin:@oracle_host:1521:orcl
Username	BIP
Password	BIP
Database Driver Class	oracle.jdbc.OracleDriver

These example values assume that a BIP user account has been created in an Oracle database with the rights to create tables and indices. The connection string is populated automatically and only the host name (`oracle_host` in the example), port number (`1521`) and the service identifier (`orcl`) have to be entered.

We should click the **Test Connection** button to verify that our entries are correct. To create the BI Publisher scheduler tables, we click the **Install Schema** button.

We must restart the BI Publisher server to make the changes complete.

Creating List of Values data to support report scheduling

This step is necessary if we deploy a patched version of Siebel 8.1 such as 8.1.1.1 because of the fact that seed data is not imported when we apply the patch.

In order to support end users in creating scheduled reports, we have to administer the missing List of Values (LOV) data to populate the dropdown boxes in the form applet used to define the schedule.

The following task list guides us through the process of creating the necessary LOV data:

1. Log in to the Siebel Web client as an administrator.
2. Navigate to the **Administration - Data screen**, then go to LOV Explorer view.
3. Create a new record in the **List of Values - Type** list with the name **XMLP_RPT_SCHEDULE_MODE**.
4. In the Explorer applet, expand the new type and click the **Values** folder.
5. In the **List of Values** list applet, create the following records (we might have to use the Columns Displayed command in the applet menu to display the Order column):

Display Value	Order
Run Immediately	1
Run Once	2
Run Daily/Weekly	3

6. In the Applet menu, click **Clear Cache**.

The following screenshot shows the **List of Values** data entered in Siebel CRM 8.1.1.1 to support the BI Publisher scheduling functionality:

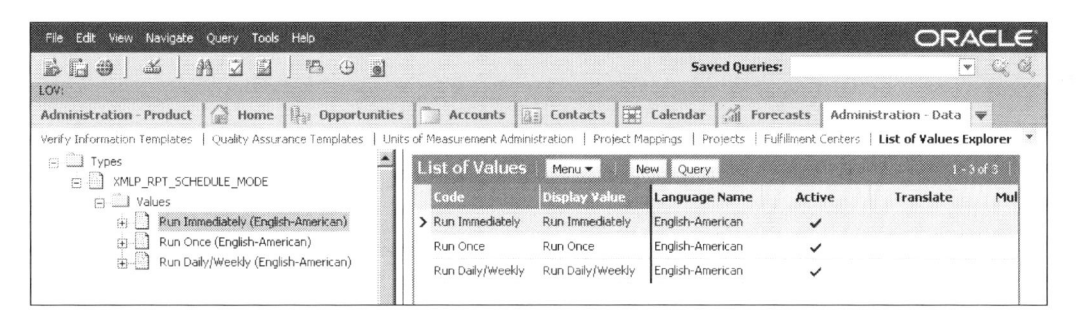

Creating a symbolic URL definition for viewing scheduled reports in Siebel CRM

If we decide to use the scheduling feature for Siebel BI Publisher reports, it is beneficial to add the symbolic URL definition in Siebel CRM to support end users in the effort of reviewing and downloading their scheduled reports from within the Siebel Web client.

Installing Ancillary Siebel Server Software

The Siebel Portal Framework provides a mechanism named Symbolic URLs in order to provide a repository for URL construction. In Siebel CRM 8.1, the seed data for symbolic URLs does not include the definitions necessary for viewing the BI Publisher scheduled reports list.

The following procedure must be executed if we wish to support viewing and downloading scheduled reports from the Report Job List View in patched versions of Siebel 8.1 such as 8.1.1.1:

1. Log in to the Siebel Web client using an administrative account.
2. Navigate to the **Administration - Integration** screen, **Host Administration** view.
3. Create a new record and set the **Name** field to the hostname and port number of the BI Publisher server such as **bip_host:9704**.
4. Set the **Virtual Name** to **biphost**.
5. Using the dropdown box in the list applet, navigate to **the Symbolic URL Administration** view.
6. Create a new record and set the **Name** field to **BIPReportJobListPage**.
7. Set the URL to `http://biphost/xmlpserver/servlet/myhistory`.
8. In the **Host Name** field, select the hostname and port number of the BI Publisher server.
9. Set the **Fixup Name** field to **Default**.
10. Set the SSO Disposition field to IFrame.
11. In the Symbolic URL arguments list, create the following records:

Name	Argument Type	Argument Value
`PreloadUrl`	Command	`http://biphost/xmlpserver/signout.jsp`
`PreloadUrlPerSession`	Command	`True`
`anyname`	Command	`PostRequest`
`id`	Field	`BIPUser`
`passwd`	Field	`BIPPassword`

[222]

We can use the screenshot below to verify our entries:

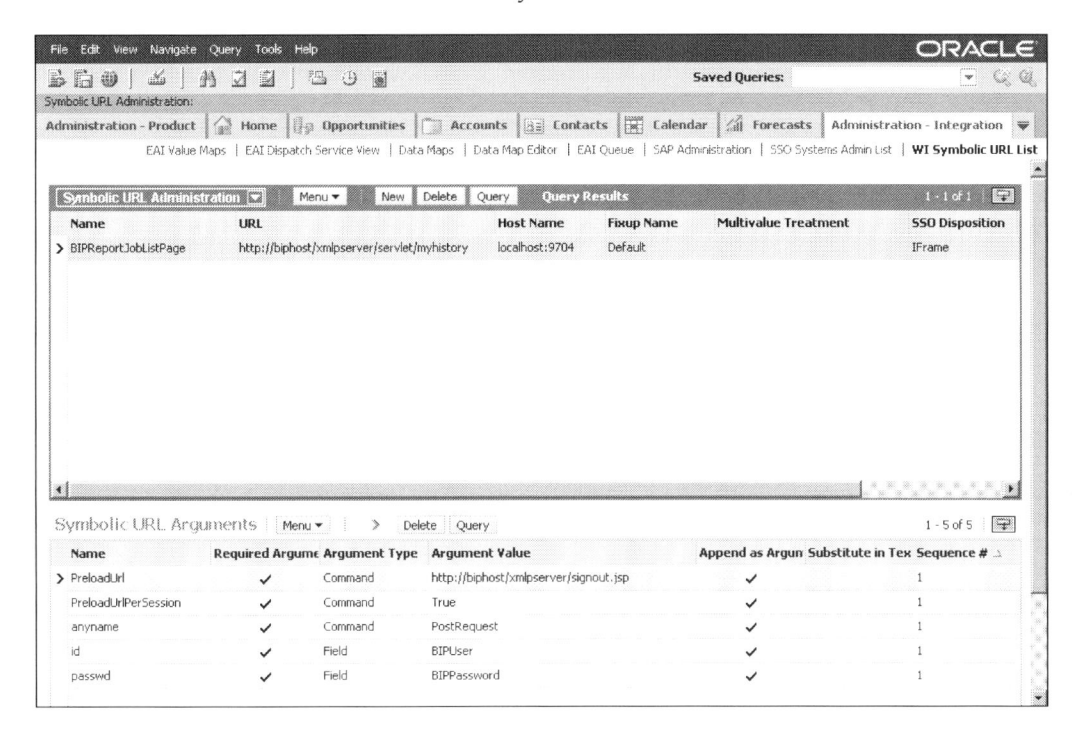

The screenshot shows the **Symbolic URL Administration** view with the symbolic URL **BIPReportJobListPage** and its arguments.

Configuring the BI Publisher host name for viewing scheduled reports in Siebel CRM

As Siebel CRM versions 8.2 and above are shipped with a newer set of seed data, the Siebel database for these versions already contains the symbolic URL definition for the integration of the BI Publisher scheduled jobs list.

However, we must administer the correct BI Publisher host name in the Host Administration list. The following procedure completes this task:

1. Log in to the Siebel Web client as an administrator.
2. Navigate to the **Administration - Integration** screen, **Host Administration** view.
3. Query for the virtual host named biphost.
4. Set the name field to the host name and port number of the BI Publisher server such as bip_host:9704.

Creating the dataservice.wsdl file from the Siebel inbound web service

When the BI Publisher server executes the scheduled report, it has to connect to the Siebel server to obtain the data for the report. The integration mechanism for this connection is the Siebel inbound web service named BIPDataService.

The wsdl (web service definition language) file for this web service must be present on the BI Publisher server. The following procedure guides us through the steps to create and store the wsdl file:

1. Log in to the Siebel Web client as an administrator.
2. Navigate to the **Administration - Web Services** screen, **Inbound Web Services** view.
3. Query for the inbound web service named **BIPDataService**.
4. Verify the address in the service ports list. It should point to the appropriate Siebel web server and the username and password parameters should be correctly set.
5. Click the **Generate WSDL** button on the **Inbound Web Services** list applet.
6. Save the file as `dataservice.wsdl` to a local directory.
7. Copy the `dataservice.wsdl` file to the `bin` directory of the `OC4J` folder on the BI Publisher server machine (an example path would be `C:\BIP\oc4j_bi\bin`).
8. Restart the BI Publisher server.

Verifying the BI Publisher scheduler functionality

To verify that the scheduling functionality of BI Publisher is properly configured, we can use the Tables Report again. This time, we use the Schedule Report command instead of opening the report immediately.

We should follow the procedure below to verify that the BI Publisher scheduler works as expected:

1. Log in to the Siebel Web client as an administrative user.
2. Navigate to the **Administration - Application** screen, **Tables** view.
3. Query for the "S_CONTACT" table, using double quotes to ensure an exact query.
4. Click the **Reports** button and select **Schedule Report**.
5. In the **Report Name** field, select **Tables Report**.
6. In **the Job Name** field enter **Job 1**.
7. Keep the default values such as **Run Immediately** for the **Time** field.
8. Click the **Schedule** button.
9. Close the scheduling dialog box.
10. Click the **Reports** button and select **My BI Publisher Reports**.
11. Click the **My Jobs** link.
12. Verify that a job named **Job 1** exists and has a status of **Running** or **Success**.
13. If the status is **Running**, use the Refresh icon to reload the list until the status is **Success**.
14. Click the Download icon in the **Document** column to view the report.

The following screenshot shows the **My Jobs** view in the **BIP Reports Server** screen:

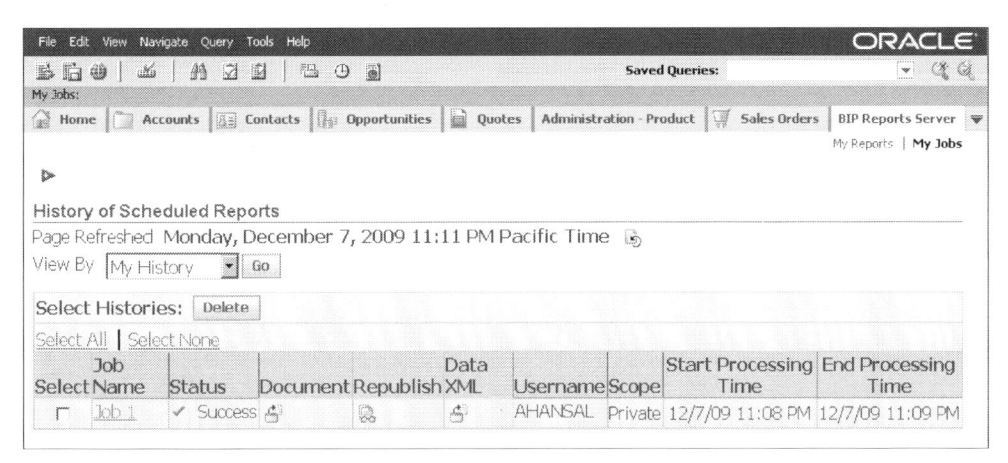

This view uses the Siebel Portal Framework to integrate the BI Publisher web page into the Siebel Web client. End users can verify and download scheduled reports from the list.

> Depending on the Siebel CRM version you are using, follow the necessary steps to configure and verify the integration points between Siebel CRM and Oracle BI Publisher Enterprise server on your demonstration machine.

Summary

In this chapter, we discussed the installation and configuration of two ancillary server software products that enable charting and reporting functionality in Siebel CRM.

The Visual Mining NetCharts server is needed to enable the Siebel chart applets, which allow end users to visualize the data they currently see in the Siebel Web client.

Oracle BI Publisher is the reporting engine that is supported with Siebel 8.1.1 and above. In this chapter, we learned how to install the BI Publisher Enterprise server and how to configure both the BI Publisher product and different versions of Siebel CRM in order to support real-time and scheduled reports.

In the next chapter, we will learn how to configure Siebel Load Balancing and multi-lingual environments.

8
Special Siebel Server Configurations

In this chapter, we will discuss additional server configuration processes that are typically executed in Siebel CRM environments. The first half of the chapter is dedicated to load balancing and failover security. For these purposes, administrators must know how to install and configure multiple Siebel servers in an enterprise.

The second half of the chapter discusses the installation and configuration steps for multilingual Siebel CRM environments. In total, we will cover the following topics:

- Installing and configuring additional Siebel servers
- Configuring Siebel Load Balancing
- Installing additional language packs
- Supporting Multilingual List of Values (MLOV)

Installing and configuring additional Siebel servers

While having only a single Siebel Server is a common scenario for demonstration or development environments, there are several good reasons to deploy more Siebel Servers in other Siebel environments such as test or production environments.

Special Siebel Server Configurations

Among these reasons are the following:

- Scalability, load balancing, and performance considerations
- Failover security
- Deployment of application configurations with minimal downtime

The following diagram depicts a Siebel Enterprise with two Siebel Servers:

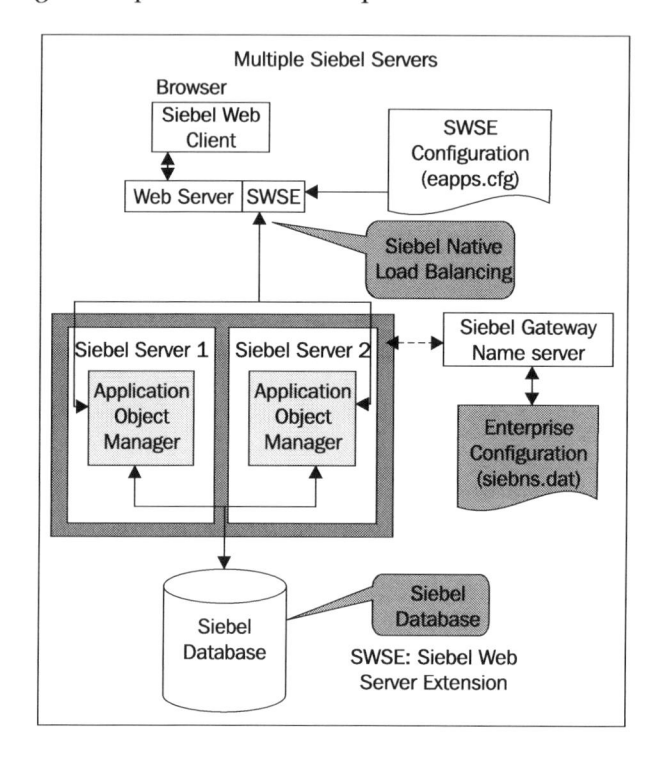

Both servers host the same object manager. Siebel Native Load Balancing is enabled, distributing the load evenly between the servers.

When the engineers at Siebel Systems drafted the first design documents in the early 90s, they had large global corporations with thousands of end users in mind. This is one of the reasons why the Siebel server infrastructure is so scalable. It is an easy computation that the more servers we have, the more end users we can support in a timely fashion. However, the load on these servers' CPUs and memory has to be evenly distributed.

An additional benefit of distributing Siebel software on more than one hardware unit is a higher level of failover security. When one node fails—for example due to a malfunctioning power supply—end users might lose their current session but can log on to the other nodes and continue to work with minimal loss of productivity.

There are situations such as the deployment of new configurations where we have to shut down and restart servers. If we have more than one server, we can support a rolling server restart scenario, which means that only one server is down at a time while the other servers are still operational.

Planning the installation of additional Siebel Servers

Before we install additional Siebel servers in an existing enterprise, we should ensure that the planning documentation is updated accordingly. Each Siebel server should have a specific purpose that translates to the enablement of specific component groups on that server. For example we could plan to install a production enterprise with four servers as follows:

Server Number	Server Role	Component Groups
1	Object Manager	Call Center
2	Object Manager and Application Deployment	Call Center, ADM
3	Mobile User Synchronization	Siebel Remote
4	Integration	EAI

In order to implement the above plan, we would need to provide four server machines and configure server 1 and 2 for load balancing (as both host the same component groups).

In the following section, we will discuss the process of installing and configuring additional Siebel servers in an enterprise as well as the load balancing configuration process.

Installing additional Siebel Servers

If we intend to use more than one Siebel Server, it is recommended to install and configure the additional servers on separate hardware units. Only then will we have all the benefits such as hardware failover security. However, it is technically possible to configure multiple Siebel servers on the same hardware unit. This scenario should remain reserved only for small demonstration, training, or evaluation environments.

Special Siebel Server Configurations

Installation and configuration of Siebel server software has been discussed in great detail in Chapters 3 and 4. There are no major differences when we repeat these processes. The following table shall serve as a guide for the process of installing and configuring additional Siebel servers into an existing Siebel enterprise:

Step	Description	Tasks
1	Use the InstallShield wizard to install the Siebel Server.	Follow the steps in Chapter 3, section *Installing the Siebel Server*.
2	Ensure that the Siebel Enterprise is operational.	Verify that the Siebel Gateway Name Server for the Enterprise is started.
3	Ensure validity of parameters.	Verify that the planning documentation is up to date and contains the correct values for the new Siebel Server.
4	Use the Siebel Configuration Wizard to configure the new Siebel Server.	Follow the steps in Chapter 4, section *Configuring the Siebel Server*.

For installation and configuration of a new Siebel server on Linux or other UNIX-based operating systems, we should follow the instructions in Chapter 5. As discussed in the previous chapters, Siebel servers—like all other server software in Siebel CRM—could also be installed in unattended mode. The benefit of an unattended installation is the avoidance of errors due to the repetitive nature of the installation and configuration of Siebel servers on different machines.

Verifying the successful Siebel Server installation and configuration

Once the new Siebel Server is installed and configured, we should complete the following verification steps.

On Microsoft Windows, a new service should be visible in the Windows Services console. The service should start without errors. On Linux and other UNIX-based operating systems, we should also be able to start the service.

If errors occur during the start up of the new Siebel Server service, we should consult the server's log directory. It is recommended to use the Siebel Configuration Wizard to remove the server and retry the configuration after the cause of the error is eliminated.

Once the service is started, we can log on to the Siebel Server Manager command line using a command similar to the following from the `BIN` subdirectory of the Siebel Server or Siebel Gateway Name Server installation folder.

```
srvrmgr /g appsrvrgw1 /e SIEBELEVAL /u SADMIN /p TJay357D
```

In this command, `appsrvrgw1` is the host name of the machine where the Siebel Gateway Name Server resides. `SIEBELEVAL` is the name of the enterprise and we use `SADMIN` as the username and `TJay357D` as the password to log on.

At the command prompt, we enter the following to get a list of servers in the enterprise:

```
list servers
```

Alternatively, we can shorten the result set by adding the show command followed by column names:

```
list servers show SBLSRVR_NAME, SV_DISP_STATE
```

As a result, we should see all Siebel Servers in the enterprise and their current state of operation. We can now verify that the server we just configured is operational. The screenshot below shows the output of the `list servers` command at the srvrmgr command line prompt:

```
srvrmgr> list servers show SBLSRVR_NAME, SV_DISP_STATE

SBLSRVR_NAME    SV_DISP_STATE
------------    -------------
Eval_1          Running
EVAL_AUTO       Running
EVAL_AUTO2      Not available

3 rows returned.
```

The Siebel servers **Eval_1** and **EVAL_AUTO** are running while server **EVAL_AUTO2** is not available because it has not yet been configured.

About configuring multiple Siebel Servers on the same physical machine

As discussed above, it is technically possible—albeit not recommended for environments other than simple demonstration, training, or evaluation enterprises—to configure multiple Siebel servers on the same physical machine.

To accomplish this, we can even skip the installation of the Siebel server software, but we must use the Siebel Configuration Wizard to complete the configuration of additional servers.

Special care has to be taken when configuring the port numbers for the **Siebel Connection Broker Component**. This component is running on every Siebel server and occupies a port. The default port number is 2321. So when we install a second server on the same physical machine, we must configure the Connection Broker port number to a value other than 2321. Incrementing the number is recommendable, so 2322 would be the next port number.

If we have a situation where we intend to use multiple Siebel servers to support synchronization of mobile clients' databases, we have to follow the same port numbering schema for the **Siebel Synchronization Manager** port.

All deviations from default port numbers have to be documented diligently in order to inform other team members.

> If your demonstration machine has enough physical memory to support it, you can follow the steps to install and configure a second Siebel server in the enterprise. Alternatively — because it is only a demonstration system — you can skip the installation and use the Siebel Server configuration wizard to configure a second Siebel Server from the same installation folder as the first Siebel server. However, you must ensure that the Connection Broker Port for the second server is set to a number other than 2321.
>
> In order to support a load balancing demonstration (see next section), enable the Call Center component group as you did for the first server.

Configuring Siebel load balancing

When two or more Siebel servers host the same component such as the Siebel Call Center Object Manager, we have to complete the procedure described in this section to allow a round-robin load balancing strategy to be applied when user sessions are established.

About Siebel load balancing

Siebel CRM provides three levels of load balancing:

- Single Siebel Server
- Siebel Native Load Balancing
- Third-Party Load Balancing

These options are displayed during the configuration of the Siebel Web Server Extension (SWSE), which has been discussed in Chapter 4. The screenshot below shows the SWSE Configuration Wizard's dialog **Select a Load Balancer**:

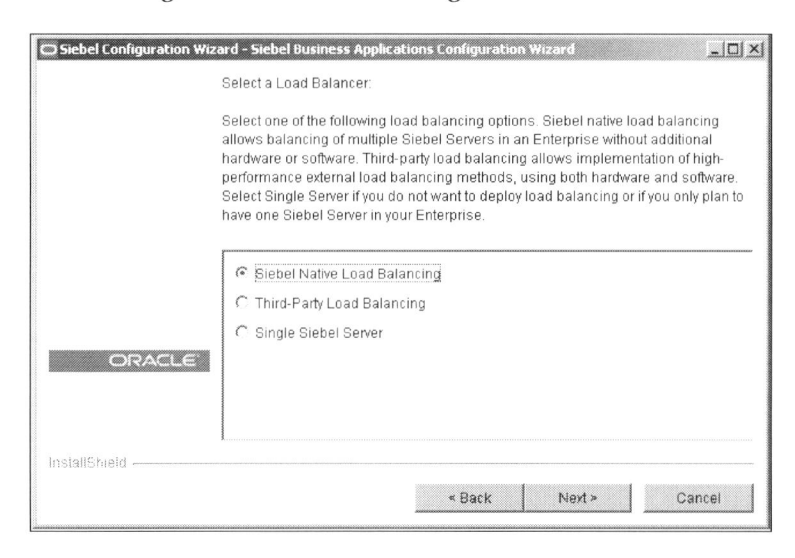

In the following, we will discuss the three options.

Single Siebel Server

When this option is chosen, all entries in the `eapps.cfg` file, which resides in the SWSE's `bin` folder, point to the Connection Broker Port on the same Siebel Server. Any additional server would have to be entered manually by altering the ConnectString parameter.

The following screenshot shows the sections for Siebel Service **[/service_enu]** and Siebel Call Center **[/callcenter_enu]** in the SWSE configuration file (`eapps.cfg`):

In order to use the second Siebel server on the same machine for the Siebel Service application, the administrator has modified the port number for the Siebel Connection Broker port to 2322.

Modifying the `eapps.cfg` file directly is error-prone and requires a restart of the Siebel Web Server, which leads to system downtime. It is therefore recommended to create a backup of the `eapps.cfg` file before manipulating it.

Siebel Native Load Balancing

When two or more Siebel servers host the same component and should take the load of the user sessions evenly, then we should configure the SWSE for Siebel Native Load Balancing. This process is described in detail later in this section.

Siebel Native Load Balancing is a software-based round robin strategy to evenly distribute user sessions across multiple Siebel servers. It relies on a file named `lbconfig.txt` that contains the information about the physical host names and Connection Broker port numbers of all Siebel servers that participate in the load balancing strategy.

Third-Party Load Balancing

For large enterprises with user numbers in the tens of thousands, the software-based Siebel Native Load Balancing might not be sufficient. In this case, hardware load balancers can be used to optimize the distribution of sessions. The System Requirements and Supported Platforms document lists the supported vendors and systems for Third-Party Load Balancing.

Configuring the SWSE for Siebel Native Load Balancing

The process of configuring the SWSE for Siebel Native Load Balancing consists of two main steps:

1. Creating the load balancer configuration file.
2. Reconfiguring the SWSE.

In the following, we will discuss both steps in detail.

Creating the load balancer configuration file

The load balancer configuration file (`lbconfig.txt`) contains the information that the SWSE needs to apply the load balancing algorithm to the incoming session requests.

The creation of the `lbconfig.txt` file is accomplished through a command at the Siebel Server Manager command line prompt.

We navigate to the Siebel Server's BIN folder and enter a command similar to the following to log on to the Gateway Name Server and open the Server Manager command line:

`srvrmgr /g appsrvrgw1 /e SIEBELEVAL /u SADMIN /p TJay357D`

In the above example, we connect to the Siebel Gateway Name Server residing on the `appsrvrgw1` machine and log on as SADMIN to the SIEBELEVAL enterprise.

At the srvrmgr command prompt, we enter the following command to generate the load balancer configuration file:

`generate lbconfig`

The command has no output message. To verify the generation of the `lbconfig.txt` file, we navigate to the Siebel Server's ADMIN subdirectory and locate the newly generated file.

The following screenshot shows a portion of the load balancer configuration file generated by the `generate lbconfig` command at the Siebel Server Manager command line:

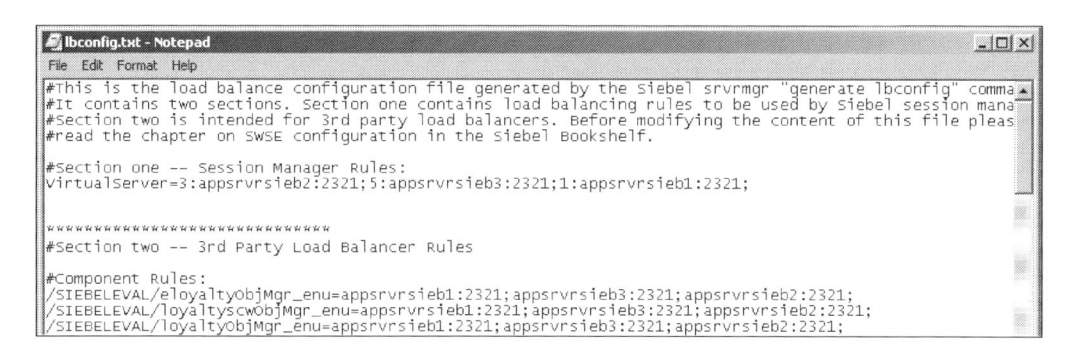

```
#This is the load balance configuration file generated by the Siebel srvrmgr "generate lbconfig" comma
#It contains two sections. Section one contains load balancing rules to be used by Siebel session mana
#Section two is intended for 3rd party load balancers. Before modifying the content of this file pleas
#read the chapter on SWSE configuration in the Siebel Bookshelf.

#Section one -- Session Manager Rules:
VirtualServer=3:appsrvrsieb2:2321;5:appsrvrsieb3:2321;1:appsrvrsieb1:2321;

*****************************
#Section two -- 3rd Party Load Balancer Rules

#Component Rules:
/SIEBELEVAL/eLoyaltyObjMgr_enu=appsrvrsieb1:2321;appsrvrsieb3:2321;appsrvrsieb2:2321;
/SIEBELEVAL/loyaltyscwObjMgr_enu=appsrvrsieb1:2321;appsrvrsieb3:2321;appsrvrsieb2:2321;
/SIEBELEVAL/loyaltyObjMgr_enu=appsrvrsieb1:2321;appsrvrsieb3:2321;appsrvrsieb2:2321;
```

To finalize this step, we must copy the file to the location of the SWSE logical profile, which by default is the ADMIN\Webserver directory of the Siebel Gateway Name Server installation folder.

Reconfiguring the Siebel Web Server Extension

In order to configure the Siebel Web Server Extension (SWSE) for Siebel Native Load Balancing, we have to remove the existing configuration and apply the new configuration. For both tasks, we use the Siebel Configuration Wizard for the SWSE.

Special Siebel Server Configurations

The following table describes the process to remove an existing SWSE configuration on Microsoft Windows. The process on Linux or other UNIX-based operating systems is similar:

Step	Description	Tasks and Example Values
1	Start the Configuration Wizard.	Click the **Siebel Web Server Extension Configuration** shortcut in the Windows start menu that has been created by the Siebel installer.
2	Select configuration mode.	Select **Configure Product in Live Mode**. Click **Next**.
3	Select configuration task.	Select **Remove the SWSE Configuration** Click **Next**.
4	Confirmation	Select **Remove Selected Siebel Web Server Extension.** Click **Next**.
5	Summary	Review the summary information. Click **Next**.
6	Do you want to execute configuration?	Click **Yes**
7	A large number of command windows are opened as the configuration wizard removes the SWSE configuration and deletes existing virtual directories from the web server.	Wait for all command windows to close.
8	Execution results are displayed.	Click **OK.**
9	The wizard jumps back to the configuration mode selection page.	Select **Exit Configuration Wizard.** Click **Next**.

Once the current configuration is successfully removed, we can continue by applying the new SWSE logical profile.

The following table guides us through the process:

Step	Description	Tasks and Example Values
1	Start the Configuration Wizard.	Click the **Siebel Web Server Extension Configuration** shortcut in the Windows start menu that has been created by the Siebel installer.

Step	Description	Tasks and Example Values
2	Select configuration mode.	Select **Configure Product in Live Mode**. Click **Next**.
3	Select configuration task.	Select **Apply an SWSE Logical Profile**. Click **Next**.
4	Select a load balancer.	Select **Siebel Native Load Balancing**. Click **Next**.
5	SWSE logical profile location.	Browse for or enter a path to the directory specified during the SWSE logical profile configuration. Click **Next**.
6	Final Tasks	Review the information about EVT. Click **Next**.
7	Summary	Verify the selections and values you provided. Click **Next**.
8	Do you want to execute configuration?	Click **Yes**
9	A number of command windows are opened as the configuration wizard applies the SWSE logical profile.	Wait for all command windows to close.
10	Execution results are displayed.	Click **OK**.
11	The wizard jumps back to the configuration mode selection page.	Select **Exit Configuration Wizard**. Click **Next**.

The configuration wizard has now generated new virtual directories and a new set of SWSE configuration files (`eapps.cfg` and `eapps_sia.cfg`).

Validating the eapps.cfg file

In order to ensure correct operation of Siebel Native Load Balancing, we must open the newly generated `eapps.cfg` file in the `BIN` subdirectory of the SWSE's installation folder.

In the **[ConnMgmt]** section, we should check that the **EnableVirtualHosts** parameter is now set to **true**. The **VirtualHostsFile** parameter must typically be modified to point to the correct file (the default path is to a `.cfg` file but the lbconfig file has a suffix of `.txt`).

The screenshot below shows the **[ConnMgmt]** section of the modified `eapps.cfg` file:

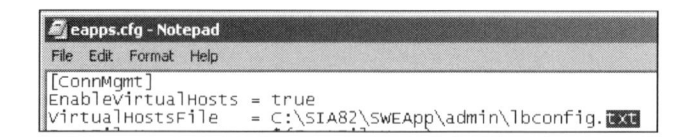

```
[ConnMgmt]
EnableVirtualHosts = true
VirtualHostsFile   = C:\SIA82\SWEApp\admin\lbconfig.txt
```

The **VirtualHostsFile** parameter has been changed to point to the `lbconfig.txt` file in the `admin` subdirectory of the SWSE installation folder.

To finalize the reconfiguration of the SWSE, we must restart the web server service.

Verifying the successful load balancing configuration of the SWSE

In order to verify the successful load balancing configuration of the SWSE, we can open multiple sessions at once and verify their distribution across the servers.

A good practice is to open Microsoft Internet Explorer several times as a separate process (avoid using the "New Window" feature). In each browser window, we navigate to the URL that directs us to the Siebel Application Object Manager. In our example we open the URL for Siebel Call Center in American English.

```
http://appsrvrweb1/callcenter_enu
```

When the login page appears, we can log in with any valid user account (SADMIN should always work). This process is repeated until we have a number of open sessions for the same object manger (Siebel Call Center). These windws must be kept open.

At the Siebel Server Manager command line, we can enter a command similar to the following to verify the distribution of sessions across the servers:

```
list active sessions for comp sccobjmgr_enu show SV_NAME, TK_DISP_RUNSTATE, OM_LOGIN
```

In the above example, we only want to see the Siebel Server name, the status of the sessions, and the user login name for all active sessions of the Siebel Call Center object manager. The following screenshot shows the result for the `list active sessions` command at the srvrmgr command line prompt:

```
srvrmgr> list active sessions for comp sccobjmgr_enu show SV_NAME, TK_DISP_RUNSTATE, OM_LOGIN

SV_NAME     TK_DISP_RUNSTATE   OM_LOGIN
-------     ----------------   --------
Eval_1      Running            AHANSAL
EVAL_AUTO   Running            SADMIN
EVAL_AUTO   Running            SADMIN

3 rows returned.
```

We can observe that three sessions are running. Two sessions are hosted by the **EVAL_AUTO** server and one is hosted by the **Eval_1** server.

In the case of errors, we must carefully review all steps and consult the log files of both SWSE and object managers.

> On your demonstration machine, follow the steps described in the above section to configure the SWSE for Siebel Native Load Balancing.

Installing additional language packs

To accommodate end users in non-English speaking countries, Oracle provides language packs for Siebel CRM software. Siebel 8.1.1 supports 22 languages and locale variants as per the following list:

Language	Three letter code	Siebel Description
Arabic	ARA	Arabic (Saudi)
Simplified Chinese	CHS	Chinese (Simplified)
Traditional Chinese	CHT	Chinese (Traditional)
Czech	CSY	Czech
Danish	DAN	Danish
Dutch	NLD	Dutch (Standard)
English	ENU	English (American)
Finnish	FIN	Finnish
French	FRA	French (Standard)
German	DEU	German (Standard)
Hebrew	HEB	Hebrew
Italian	ITA	Italian (Standard)
Japanese	JPN	Japanese
Korean	KOR	Korean
Polish	PLK	Polish
European Portuguese	PTG	Portuguese (Standard)
Brazilian Portuguese	PTB	Portuguese (Brazilian)
Russian	RUS	Russian
Spanish	ESN	Spanish (Modern)
Swedish	SVE	Swedish

Language	Three letter code	Siebel Description
Thai	THA	Thai
Turkish	TRK	Turkish

In the following section, we will discuss the process of obtaining and installing additional language packs.

> For several reasons, including the fact that not all system messages are translated, we should always install the English language pack first and then add other languages. This ensures that we can safely access all functionality even if language dependencies cause erroneous behavior on the Siebel application.

Downloading Siebel CRM language packs

If we need to download additional language packs, we do so by navigating to the Oracle E-Delivery website at http://edelivery.oracle.com. As discussed in Chapter 2, we must use a registered account and then select the Siebel CRM software packages for the operating system platform we need. The section that contains all the language packs for Siebel CRM 8.1.1.0 is named *Siebel Business Applications (with Translations) Media Pack 8.1.1.0 Release*. For Siebel server software, we need to download the respective Language Extension Pack separately. Siebel client software packages typically contain all language packs.

Even if we select an operating system type in the E-Delivery search, the language extension packs contain the installation archives for all platforms. It is therefore beneficial for both download time and disk space to use download management software such as Free Download Manager (http://freedownloadmanager.org), which allows for selecting just the contents in the download archive that we need, as shown in the following screenshot:

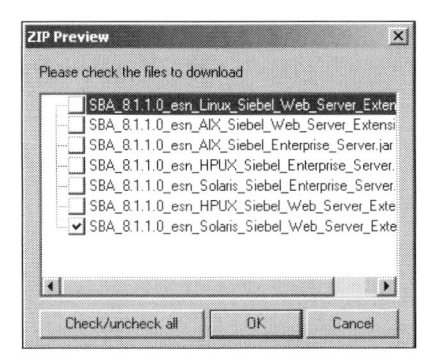

Adding language packs to existing Siebel installation images

Once we have downloaded the language extension packs for Siebel server software, we must use an Oracle recommended unzip tool to extract the installation packages (.jar files). We should ensure that the .jar files are transferred into the folder we use to store the base installer archives.

The Siebel Image Creator is used to extract the new content into the existing Siebel installation image folders. The following table describes the necessary steps to complete this process on Microsoft Windows operating systems:

Step	Description	Tasks and Example Values
1	Start the Siebel Image Creator.	Double-click the **Windows_ImageCreator.exe** file.
2	The Welcome dialog is displayed.	Click **Next**
3	Display of options.	Choose **Add language(s) to an existing image.** Click **Next**.
4	Specify the directory to which the installer images should be copied.	Example: **C:\Siebel_Install_Image** Click **Next**
5	Language selection.	For example, select **DEU - German (Standard)**. Click **Next**.
6	Progress of the file extraction process is displayed.	Wait for completion. Note: In case the installer cannot locate the .jar file, a prompt appears to navigate to the folder that contains the archive.
7	Success message is displayed.	Click **Finish**

Special Siebel Server Configurations

We can now verify that the Image Creator has extracted the language-specific files into new subdirectories of the Siebel installation images. The following screenshot shows the Siebel installation image for the Siebel Enterprise Server software containing four language specific subdirectories for German (deu), English (enu), Spanish (esn), and Russian (rus), created by the Image Creator:

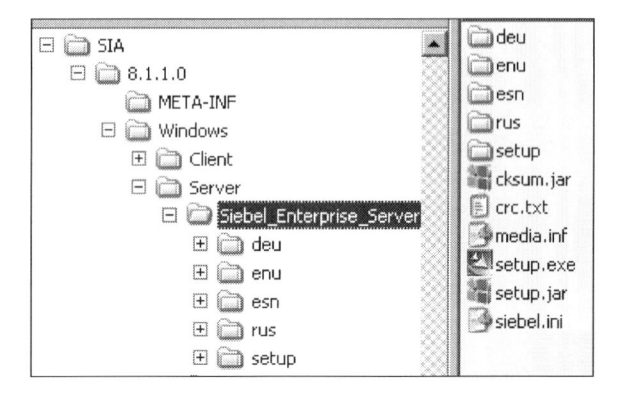

> Use the instructions in the previous section to download additional language packs for the Siebel Enterprise Server and add them to the existing Siebel installation image.

Installing additional language packs for Siebel Enterprise Server software

The following table guides us through the process for Microsoft Windows operating systems. Similar steps have to be completed on Linux or other UNIX-based operating systems. This process has to be repeated on each machine that hosts Siebel Enterprise Server software.

Step	Description	Tasks and Example Values
1	Start the InstallShield Wizard.	Double-click the `setup.exe` file in the `Siebel_Enterprise_Server` folder.
2	The Welcome dialog is displayed.	Click **Next**.
3	Setup has detected one or more existing versions.	Select an existing instance to add language packs to.
		Click **Next**.

Step	Description	Tasks and Example Values
4	Select Languages	Select one or more languages. Click **Next**.
5	The installation progress is displayed.	Wait for the installation to finish.
6	The Configuration Wizard for the Siebel Server is invoked by the installer.	Click **Cancel** to close the Configuration Wizard. Using the configuration wizard to add language support for a Siebel server is discussed later in this section.
7	The InstallShield wizard success dialog is displayed.	Click **Finish**.

The installer copies the files necessary for language-specific functionality into the existing installation folders. In addition, files that contain language-specific seed data and repository metadata are extracted into the Database Server Utilities (dbsrvr) directory.

The installation of additional language packs includes procedures to enable the language support for a specific Siebel server as well as the import of the above mentioned data files into the Siebel Database. The language pack installation is only complete when we execute these tasks:

- Add language support for Siebel servers
- Import language-specific seed data into the Siebel database
- Import language-specific repository metadata into the Siebel database
- Updating multilingual List of Values (MLOV) data

In the following section, we will discuss the procedures in detail.

Adding language support for a Siebel Server

If the Siebel server has been installed separately from the other Siebel server software products—also known as "stand-alone" installation—we must execute the Siebel Configuration Wizard to add language support to it.

In other words, we use the configuration wizard to generate additional language-specific component definitions, such as a Call Center Object Manager for German, and associate it to the Siebel Servers on the machine that the wizard is executed on.

The following table describes the process to add language support for a Siebel Server on Microsoft Windows operating systems. Similar steps must be executed on Linux or other UNIX-based operating systems.

Step	Description	Tasks and Example Values
1	Start the Configuration Wizard.	Click the **Siebel Server Configuration** shortcut in the Windows start menu.
2	Select configuration mode.	Select **Configure Product in Live Mode**. Click **Next**.
3	Configuration Wizard Welcome Page	Select **Add Language Support for the Siebel Server**. Click **Next**.
4	Gateway Name Server Authentication user name and password.	User Name: **SADMIN** Password: **TJay357D** Click **Next**.
5	Gateway Name Server hostname and port number.	Hostname: **appsrvrgw1** Port: **2320** Click **Next**.
6	Siebel Enterprise Name	Enterprise Name: **SIEBELEVAL** Click **Next**.
7	Deployed Languages	Select one or more languages to add. Click **Next**.
8	Summary	Verify the selections and values you provided. Click **Next**.
9	Do you want to execute configuration?	Click **Yes**.
10	Execution results are displayed.	Click **OK**.
11	The wizard jumps back to the configuration mode selection page.	Select **Exit Configuration Wizard**. Click **Next**.

This process must be repeated on all machines that host a Siebel server. We will discuss verification steps later in this section.

Importing language-specific seed data into the Siebel database

The second post-installation step of adding language packs to an existing Siebel server installation is to import language-specific seed data into the Siebel server database.

Like any database-centric activity, this task is executed by the Siebel Upgrade Wizard, which is invoked by and reads the output of the Siebel Database Configuration Wizard. Details about the Siebel Upgrade Wizard are given in Chapter 4.

The following table entails the detailed steps and example entries for importing language-specific seed data using the Siebel configuration wizard on Microsoft Windows-based operating systems. Similar steps will have to be executed on Linux or other UNIX-based operating systems. This process must be repeated once for each additional language.

Step	Description	Tasks and Example Values
1	Start the Configuration Wizard.	Click the **Database Server Configuration** shortcut in the Windows start menu.
2	Siebel Server directory.	Provide the path to the Siebel Server's installation directory.
		Typically, the default can be kept.
		Click **Next**.
3	Siebel Database Server Utilities directory.	Provide the path to the Siebel Database Server Utilities installation folder.
		Typically, the default can be kept.
		Click **Next**.
4	Database Platform	Select **Oracle Database Enterprise Edition.**
		Click **Next**.
5	Task selection.	Select **Install Database.**
		Click **Next**.
6	Action selection.	Select **Add a language to an existing Siebel Database**
		Click **Next**.
7	GRANTUSR.SQL	Select **GRANTUSR.SQL has been run...**
		Click **Next**.
8	Select Base Language.	Select **English (American)**
		Note: English should always be chosen as the base language.
		Click **Next**.
9	Select Language to add.	Select **German (Standard)**
		Click **Next**.

Special Siebel Server Configurations

Step	Description	Tasks and Example Values
10	ODBC Data Source Name	Enter **SIEBELEVAL_DSN**
		Note: This is the name of the System DSN generated during configuration of the Siebel Enterprise.
		Click **Next**.
11	Siebel Database User Name and Password	User Name: **SADMIN**
		Password: **TJay357D**
		Click **Next**.
12	Siebel Database Table Owner and Password	Table Owner: **SIEBEL**
		Password: **dQ7JXufi**
		Click **Next**.
13	Repository Name	Keep the default (**Siebel Repository**)
		Click **Next**.
14	Oracle parallel indexing	Keep the default (**Does not use...**)
		Click **Next**.
15	Security group and log output directory	Keep the defaults.
		Note the log output directory will become a subdirectory of the Siebel Server's LOG directory.
		Click **Next**.
16	Apply configuration changes.	Select **Yes apply configuration changes now**.
		Click **Next**.
17	Summary	Review the summary information.
		Click **Next**.
18	Do you want to execute configuration?	Click **Yes**.
19	The Siebel Upgrade Wizard is displayed.	Click **OK** in the Siebel Upgrade Wizard dialog.
20	During the installation process, several command windows are opened.	Ensure that you do not close or make selections in any of the command windows.
		Wait for the Siebel Upgrade Wizard to complete.
21	The configuration wizard displays a message "Execution successful".	Click **OK** to confirm successful execution of the configuration wizard.
22	The configuration wizard jumps to the Siebel Server directory selection.	Click **Cancel** in the Siebel Configuration Wizard dialog.

Step	Description	Tasks and Example Values
23	Confirm exiting the configuration wizard.	Click **Yes**.
24	Siebel Upgrade Wizard displays "Complete".	Click **OK** in the Siebel Upgrade Wizard dialog.

The Siebel Upgrade Wizards executes the following steps during the process:

- Install language-specific seed data
- Deactivate non-multilingual List of Values (MLOV) seed data

We will discuss details of these steps next.

Installing language-specific seed data

Some data used by Siebel applications is localized. The most prominent representatives of localized seed data are List of Values (LOV) records that contain the values displayed in the static pick lists across the Siebel user interface. The following screenshot shows the **Account Type** field in the Siebel user interface as an example for a static pick list that contains preconfigured values in American English that the end user can choose from:

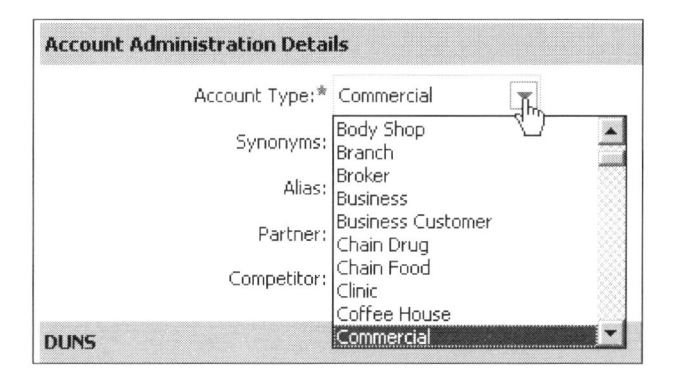

The Siebel Upgrade Wizard invokes the necessary utilities to import the translated seed data from flat files into the Siebel database.

Deactivating non-multilingual List of Values (MLOV) seed data

Even if translated seed data for static pick lists is imported by the Siebel Upgrade Wizard, the localized content is in most cases not yet available to the end user because additional configuration steps are required. In order to avoid problems with static pick lists such as values for multiple languages appearing in the user interface at the same time, the Siebel Upgrade Wizard ensures that the correct updates are made to deactivate the List of Values seed data that has not yet been configured for Multilingual List of Values (MLOV). The following screenshot shows the List of Values administration view in the Siebel Web client after the import of German seed data:

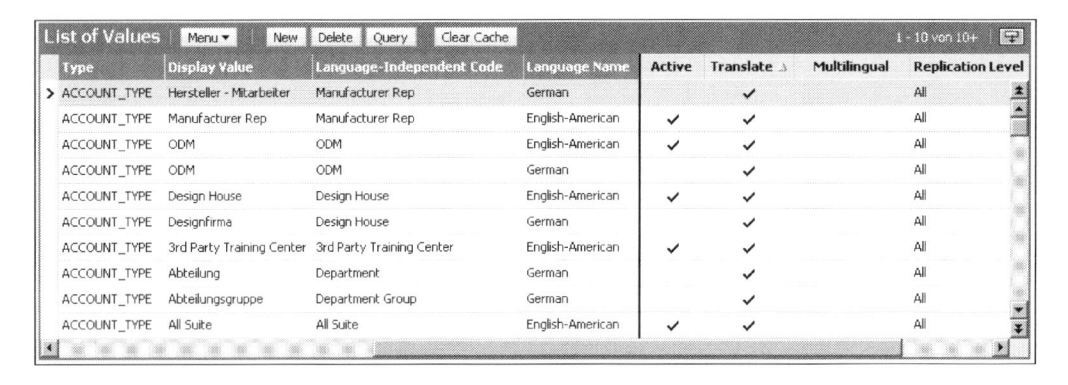

Type	Display Value	Language-Independent Code	Language Name	Active	Translate	Multilingual	Replication Level
> ACCOUNT_TYPE	Hersteller - Mitarbeiter	Manufacturer Rep	German		✓		All
ACCOUNT_TYPE	Manufacturer Rep	Manufacturer Rep	English-American	✓	✓		All
ACCOUNT_TYPE	ODM	ODM	English-American	✓	✓		All
ACCOUNT_TYPE	ODM	ODM	German		✓		All
ACCOUNT_TYPE	Design House	Design House	English-American	✓	✓		All
ACCOUNT_TYPE	Designfirma	Design House	German		✓		All
ACCOUNT_TYPE	3rd Party Training Center	3rd Party Training Center	English-American	✓	✓		All
ACCOUNT_TYPE	Abteilung	Department	German		✓		All
ACCOUNT_TYPE	Abteilungsgruppe	Department Group	German		✓		All
ACCOUNT_TYPE	All Suite	All Suite	English-American	✓	✓		All

We can observe that the German translations for the Account Type pick list are inactive (the Active flag is not set).

Importing language-specific repository metadata

The Siebel metadata repository supports the localization of messages, labels, and captions displayed in the Siebel user interface. To enable easier and consistent development, the **Symbolic String library** is the major building block of repository localization. The screenshot below shows the Symbolic String object definition in Siebel Tools with German (DEU) and American English (ENU) translations:

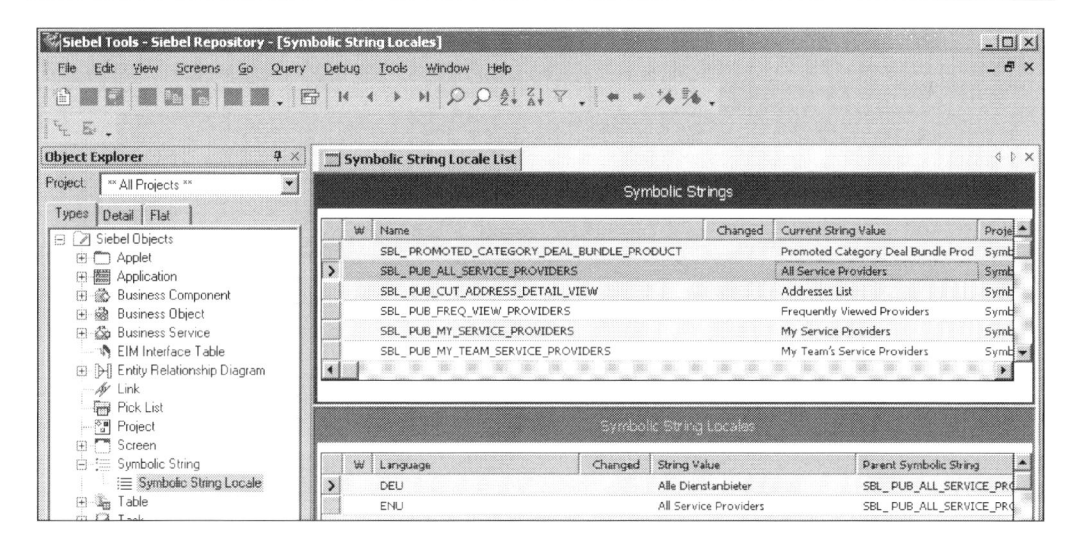

Symbolic Strings serve as a common library of reusable, translatable strings that are used for labels, captions, and messages across all Siebel applications.

The following table describes the process to import language-specific repository metadata into the Siebel database using the Siebel Configuration Wizard and Siebel Upgrade Wizard:

Step	Description	Tasks and Example Values
1	Start the Configuration Wizard.	Click the **Database Server Configuration** shortcut in the Windows start menu.
2	Siebel Server directory.	Provide the path to the Siebel Server's installation directory.
		Typically, the default can be kept.
		Click **Next**.
3	Siebel Database Server Utilities directory.	Provide the path to the Siebel Database Server Utilities installation folder.
		Typically, the default can be kept.
		Click **Next**.
4	Database Platform	Select **Oracle Database Enterprise Edition**.
		Click **Next**.
5	Task selection.	Select **Import/Export Repository**
		Click **Next**.
6	Action selection.	Select **Add a language to an existing Repository**
		Click **Next**.

Special Siebel Server Configurations

Step	Description	Tasks and Example Values
7	Select Language to add.	Select **German (Standard)**
		Click **Next**.
8	ODBC Data Source Name	Enter **SIEBELEVAL_DSN**
		Note: This is the name of the System DSN generated during configuration of the Siebel Enterprise.
		Click **Next**.
9	Siebel Database User Name and Password	User Name: **SADMIN**
		Password: **TJay357D**
		Click **Next**.
10	Siebel Database Table Owner and Password	Table Owner: **SIEBEL**
		Password: **dQ7JXufi**
		Click **Next**.
11	Repository Name and import file.	Keep the default (**Siebel Repository**)
		Verify the path to the import file represents the language (for example DEU)
		Click **Next**.
12	Oracle parallel indexing	Keep the default (**Does not use...**).
		Click **Next**.
13	Security group and log output directory.	Keep the defaults.
		Note the log output directory will become a subdirectory of the Siebel Server's LOG directory.
		Click **Next**.
14	Apply configuration changes.	Select **Yes apply configuration changes now**.
		Click **Next**.
15	Summary	Review the summary information.
		Click **Next**.
16	Do you want to execute configuration?	Click **Yes**.
17	The Siebel Upgrade Wizard is displayed.	Click **OK** in the Siebel Upgrade Wizard dialog.
18	During the installation process, several command windows are opened.	Ensure that you do not close or make selections in any of the command windows.
		Wait for the Siebel Upgrade Wizard to complete.

Step	Description	Tasks and Example Values
19	The configuration wizard displays a message "Execution successful".	Click **OK** to confirm successful execution of the configuration wizard.
20	The configuration wizard jumps to the Siebel Server directory selection.	Click **Cancel** in the Siebel Configuration Wizard dialog.
21	Confirm exiting the configuration wizard.	Click **Yes**
22	Siebel Upgrade Wizard displays "Complete".	Click **OK** in the Siebel Upgrade Wizard dialog.

Enabling multilingual List of Values

Every time we add an additional language pack to the Siebel server infrastructure, we must ensure that existing records are correctly updated to reflect the new localized List of Values data.

Enabling multilingual List of Values requires additional configuration steps to be carried out by developers in Siebel Tools. This configuration is out of the scope of this book but an example shall be given using one of the preconfigured multilingual List of Value types, namely the BI Publisher Report output type. The following screenshot shows the definition of the **OUTPUT_TYPE** column in the **S_XMLP_REP_TMPL** table in Siebel Tools.

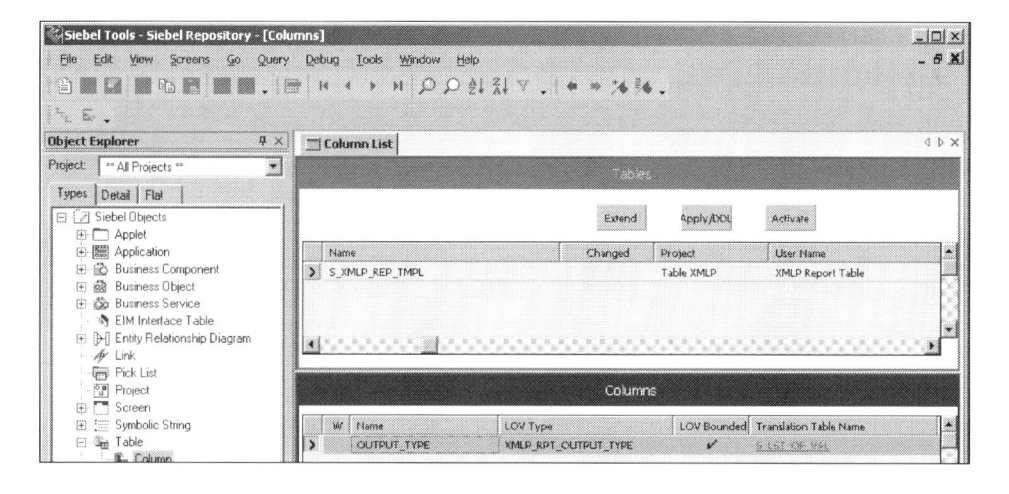

We can observe that the **LOV Type** for the column is set to **XMLP_RPT_OUTPUT_TYPE** and the **LOV Bounded** flag is active. In addition, the **Translation Table Name** property is set to **S_LST_OF_VAL**, which is the name of the table that holds all List of Values entries. These settings enable the Siebel application to dynamically look up translated values in static pick lists depending on the language of the object manager.

Special Siebel Server Configurations

The settings in the above example have been preconfigured by Oracle engineering and similar settings must be applied to other columns by developers if enabling multilingual List of Values for the respective static pick list is a necessary requirement.

The following screenshot shows the **List of Values** entries for the BI Publisher Report output type pick list in the Siebel Web Client:

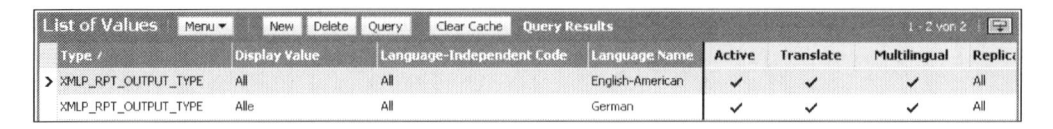

Type	Display Value	Language-Independent Code	Language Name	Active	Translate	Multilingual	Replic
XMLP_RPT_OUTPUT_TYPE	All	All	English-American	✓	✓	✓	All
XMLP_RPT_OUTPUT_TYPE	Alle	All	German	✓	✓	✓	All

Both the German and English-American entry are set to active because the process of enabling multilingual List of Values has been completed successfully.
Note: "XMLP" or "XML Publisher" is the old product name for Oracle BI Publisher.

The following table describes the process of using the Siebel Configuration Wizard and Siebel Upgrade Wizard to update the Siebel database for multilingual List of Values. This process must be repeated for each language pack installation and after each MLOV configuration carried out by developers.

Step	Description	Tasks and Example Values
1	Start the Configuration Wizard.	Click the **Database Server Configuration** shortcut in the Windows start menu.
2	Siebel Server directory.	Provide the path to the Siebel Server's installation directory.
		Typically, the default can be kept.
		Click **Next**.
3	Siebel Database Server Utilities directory.	Provide the path to the Siebel Database Server Utilities installation folder.
		Typically, the default can be kept.
		Click **Next**.
4	Database Platform	Select **Oracle Database Enterprise Edition.**
		Click **Next**.
5	Task selection.	Select **Run Database Utilities.**
		Click **Next**.
6	Action selection.	Select **Multilingual List of Value Conversion.**
		Click **Next**.

Chapter 8

Step	Description	Tasks and Example Values
7	Action selection.	Select **Translate**.
		Click **Next**.
8	Select base Language.	Select **English (American)**
		Click **Next**.
9	ODBC Data Source Name	Enter **SIEBELEVAL_DSN**
		Note: This is the name of the System DSN generated during configuration of the Siebel Enterprise.
		Click **Next**.
10	Siebel Database User Name and Password	User Name: **SADMIN**
		Password: **TJay357D**
		Click **Next**.
11	Siebel Database Table Owner and Password	Table Owner: **SIEBEL**
		Password: **dQ7JXufi**
		Click **Next**.
12	Repository Name	Keep the default (**Siebel Repository**)
		Click **Next**.
13	Oracle parallel indexing.	Keep the default (**Does not use...**)
		Click **Next**.
14	Security group and log output directory.	Keep the defaults.
		Note the log output directory will become a subdirectory of the Siebel Server's LOG directory.
		Click **Next**.
15	Apply configuration changes.	Select **Yes apply configuration changes now**.
		Click **Next**.
16	Summary	Review the summary information.
		Click **Next**.
17	Do you want to execute configuration?	Click **Yes**.
18	The Siebel Upgrade Wizard is displayed.	Click **OK** in the Siebel Upgrade Wizard dialog.
19	During the installation process, several command windows are opened.	Ensure that you do not close or make selections in any of the command windows.
		Wait for the Siebel Upgrade Wizard to complete.
20	The configuration wizard displays a message "Execution successful".	Click **OK** to confirm successful execution of the configuration wizard.

[253]

Special Siebel Server Configurations

Step	Description	Tasks and Example Values
21	The configuration wizard jumps to the Siebel Server directory selection.	Click **Cancel** in the Siebel Configuration Wizard dialog.
22	Confirm exiting the configuration wizard.	Click **Yes**.
23	Siebel Upgrade Wizard displays "Complete".	Click **OK** in the Siebel Upgrade Wizard dialog.

The Siebel Upgrade Wizard executes the following steps during this process:

- Validates MLOV inconsistencies
- Fixes referential integrity
- Updates preconfigured MLOV columns to language independent code
- Activates List of Values data for non-base languages

In summary, the Upgrade Wizard updates the List of Values records to an active state for all columns that are defined for MLOV translation in the Siebel Repository. We must remember that the above process has to be repeated if developers modify the MLOV configuration in Siebel Tools.

Installing additional language packs for the Siebel Web Server Extension

The following table describes the procedure to install additional language packs and create language-specific virtual web server directories on the web server hosting the Siebel Web Server Extension (SWSE). This process, similar on Microsoft Windows and Linux or other UNIX-based operating systems, has to be executed on each machine hosting the SWSE.

Step	Description	Tasks and Example Values
1	Start the InstallShield Wizard.	Double-click the `setup.exe` file in the `Siebel_Web_Server_Extension` folder.
2	The Welcome dialog is displayed.	Click **Next**.
3	Setup has detected one or more existing versions.	Select an existing instance to add language packs to. Click **Next**.

Chapter 8

Step	Description	Tasks and Example Values
4	Language selection.	Select one or more languages. Click **Next**.
5	Installation progress is displayed.	Wait for the installer to continue.
6	The **Siebel Configuration Wizard** is launched automatically.	Continue with the next steps.
7	Task Selection	Select **Add Language Support for the SWSE Configuration.** Click **Next.**
8	Deployed Languages	Select one or more languages. Click **Next**.
9	Summary	Review the summary information. Click **Next.**
10	Do you want to execute configuration?	Click **Yes.**
11	Several command windows are opened automatically.	Wait for all command windows to close.
12	Configuration Wizard displays successful execution.	Click **OK.**
13	The InstallShield wizard success dialog is displayed.	Click **Finish.**

As the wizard modifies the SWSE configuration, we must restart the web server service after the successful execution of the language pack installation.

Verifying the successful language pack installation for Siebel server software

In order to verify the successful installation of one or more additional language packs for a Siebel enterprise, we should follow the procedure described below:

1. Restart the Siebel Enterprise
2. Log on to the new application object manager
3. Verify UI translation
4. Verify multilingual List of Values

Next, we will discuss each step in detail.

[255]

Restarting the Siebel Enterprise

In order to make all changes available to each and every process, it is highly recommended to execute a complete restart of the entire Siebel enterprise.
To accomplish this, we follow this procedure

1. Stop all web servers hosting the SWSE.
2. Stop all Siebel servers.
3. Stop the Siebel Gateway Name Server.
4. Start the Siebel Gateway Name Server.
5. Start all Siebel servers.
6. Start all web servers hosting the SWSE.

Furthermore, we must ensure that the processes have enough time to start up properly. We can monitor the CPU usage of the systems and review the log files if we are insecure about the duration and success of the start up procedure.

Logging on to the new application object manager

Once the Siebel enterprise is restarted, we can navigate to a URL that directs us to one of the newly configured object managers. In the below example, we use the German object manager:

`http://appsrvrweb1/callcenter_deu`

Note that we use `_deu` as a suffix, which is the default language abbreviation for German. Once the login page is displayed, we should log in as an administrative user and click the Site Map icon in the application toolbar.
The following screenshot shows a portion of the Site Map of the German version of Siebel Call Center:

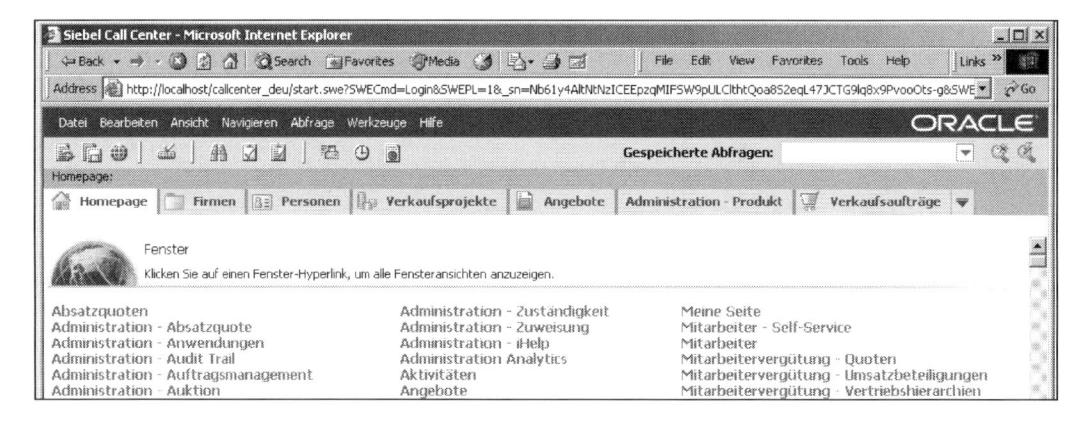

We can verify that all display values like menu item captions, screen tab labels, or site map entries are translated.

> The Siebel object manager only supports one language at a time—specified by the Language parameter. The object manager will read the Siebel Repository File (SRF) from the subdirectory in the OBJECTS folder, which is named after the language code.

Verifying UI translation

In order to verify that all translations are properly loaded, we can press *CTRL + H* to open the Siebel online help page. It should appear in the object manager's language as well. The following screenshot shows a portion of the Siebel online help page of the German version of Siebel Call Center:

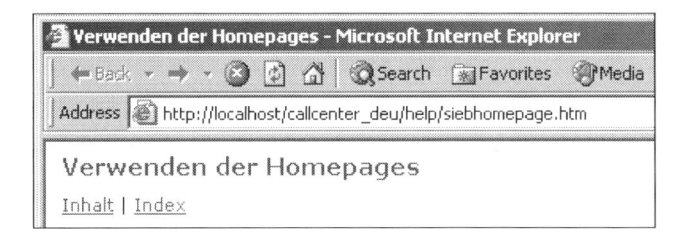

Verifying multilingual List of Values

Several system-related entities such as Assignment Manager rules, BI Publisher report templates, or Server administration are preconfigured by Oracle to support multilingual List of Values.

It is therefore a good idea to navigate to the BI Publisher Template Registration view and verify that the list of values data is translated.

> If you have difficulties navigating between Siebel views in a foreign language, you can use the technical view name in a URL similar to the following to direct the browser to the desired view:
>
> `http://appsrvrweb1/callcenter_deu/start.swe?SWECmd=GotoView&SWEView=Report+Template+Registration+Admin+View`
>
> The SWEView parameter takes the technical view name (which you can obtain using the "About View" option in the help menu or from Siebel Tools) with spaces replaced by plus signs.

Special Siebel Server Configurations

Using the Site Map or the technique described in the *Did you know?* box, we navigate to the BI Publisher Report Template Registration view and verify that the value for "All" in the output type field is translated to the selected language. The following screenshot shows the German translation of the BI Publisher Report Template Registration view:

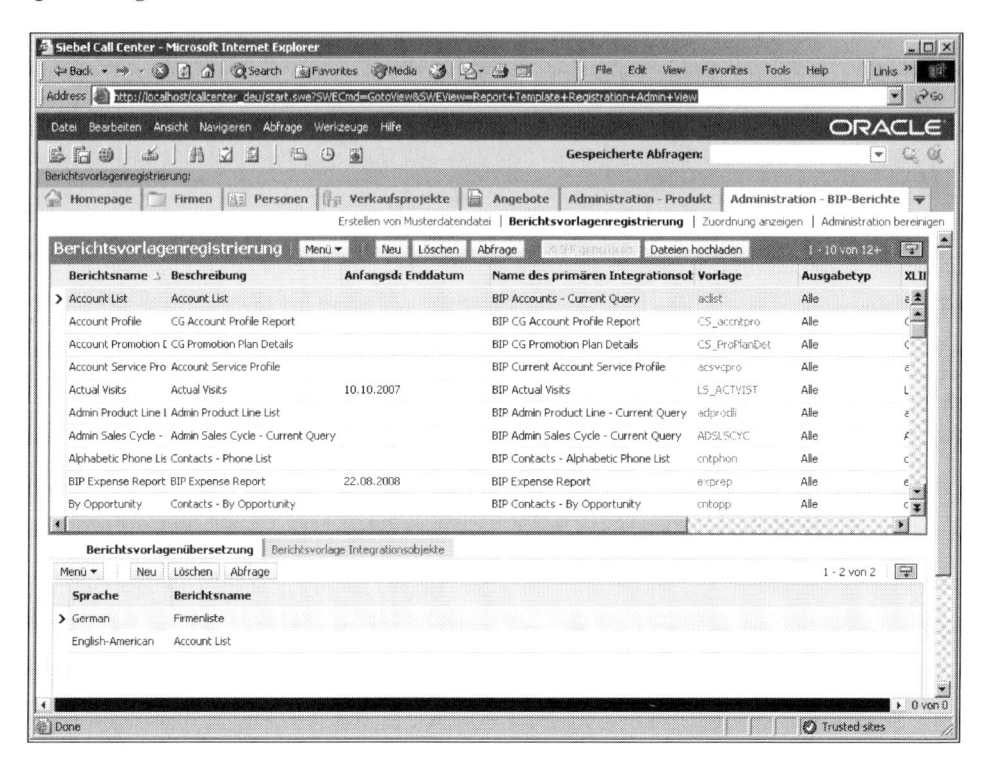

We can confirm that the value **Alle** in the output type field (labeled **Ausgabetyp**) represents the German translation of "All" in the English application. Furthermore, we can use this view to verify the correct import of language-specific seed data by reviewing the data in the lower list applet. It correctly contains the report name to appear in the Report menu in German and English.

> Using the tables in this section as a guide, install one or more additional language packs on your demonstration system. Verify the installation by following the instructions in the above section.

Installing additional language packs for the Siebel Developer or Mobile Web Client

If we wish to provide translated content to the Siebel Developer or Mobile Web clients, we have to use the Oracle Universal Installer to apply additional language packs.

The table below describes the procedure of adding additional language packs to the Siebel Developer or Mobile Web clients:

Step	Description	Tasks and Example Values
1	Start the Oracle Universal Installer.	Double-click the `oui.exe` file in the `Siebel_Web_Client/Disk1/install` folder.
2	The Welcome dialog is displayed.	Click **Next**.
3	Specify the home directory.	Select the appropriate Oracle home from the Name dropdown list and verify the path.
		Note: We must select an existing installation.
		Click **Next**.
4	Prerequisite checks.	The installer performs prerequisite checks. Verify that all checks are passed successfully.
		Click **Next**.
5	Select Languages	For example, select **German**.
		Click **Next**.
6	Summary	Review the summary information.
		Click **Install**.
7	The installation progress is displayed.	Wait for the installation to finish.
8	Success Message	Click **Exit** and **Yes** to leave the installer.

The installer copies language-specific files into the existing Siebel client installation folders and creates new Windows start menu shortcuts for the selected languages.

Verifying the successful language pack installation for the Siebel Developer Web Client

In order to verify the successful installation of an additional language pack for the Siebel Developer Web Client, we can open the Windows start menu for the Siebel Web Client and click one of the newly created shortcuts for the selected language. For example we can launch the Siebel Pharma - DEU shortcut if we installed the German language pack.

We should be able to log in as SADMIN to the Server data source and verify the availability of the application in the installed language.

About language packs for Siebel Tools

Oracle provides language packs for all Siebel applications, including Siebel Tools. Following the procedure for Siebel Developer or Mobile Web clients, we could also install a translated version of the Siebel Tools development environment. However, due to the fact that the user interface of Siebel Tools is then no longer consistent with the documentation and online help, this step is rarely considered.

Summary

In this chapter, we discussed two typical tasks in the life of a Siebel CRM administrator. In the first half of the chapter, we learned how to install and configure additional Siebel servers to ensure high availability, performance, and failover security.

We also discussed how to enable Siebel Native Load Balancing if the same processes are available on multiple Siebel servers.

The second part of the chapter was dedicated to the installation of additional language packs to support localized versions of Siebel applications. We learned how to install and configure language packs for Siebel Enterprise server software, the Siebel database, the Siebel Web Server Extension (SWSE), and the Siebel Developer or Mobile Web Client.

The chapter also clarified the topic of multilingual List of Values (MLOV) and explained the necessary steps to successfully configure the Siebel application to support translated values in static pick lists.

In the next chapter, we will discuss the techniques of Siebel server management.

9
Siebel Server Management

Once the first Siebel servers within an enterprise are installed and operational, we reach the maintenance phase of a project. Being a Siebel administrator, our task list now includes the correct configuration of server and component parameters as well as the ability to identify performance bottlenecks or erroneous situations. This chapter introduces Siebel server management skills such as:

- Understanding servers, components, and parameters
- Using server management screens in the Siebel client
- Using command line tools for Siebel server management

Along with explanations of the tools that an administrator can use to manage a Siebel enterprise, we will also discover typical server management scenarios such as:

- Listing and reviewing information about the Siebel enterprise
- Backing up the enterprise configuration
- Listing and modifying parameters
- Creating and modifying component definitions
- Synchronizing batch components
- Controlling assignment of component groups to Siebel servers
- Setting the start up mode of server components
- Controlling server components
- Creating job templates
- Running jobs for batch and background components

Understanding servers, components, and parameters

As we learned in previous chapters, a Siebel enterprise is a collection of Siebel servers that share the following characteristics:

- Their configurations are stored by the same Siebel Gateway Name Server
- They connect to the same Siebel database and file system

In order to better understand the relationships between the Siebel Servers in an enterprise, their components and parameters, it is best to examine the Enterprise Explorer view in the Administration - Server Configuration screen in the Siebel Web Client.

We can access that view by logging on to the Siebel Web Client using an administrative user account. Then, we navigate to the Site Map, select the Administration - Server Configuration screen and click the hyperlink for the Enterprise Explorer view. The following screenshot shows the partially expanded Siebel Enterprise Explorer tree applet in that view:

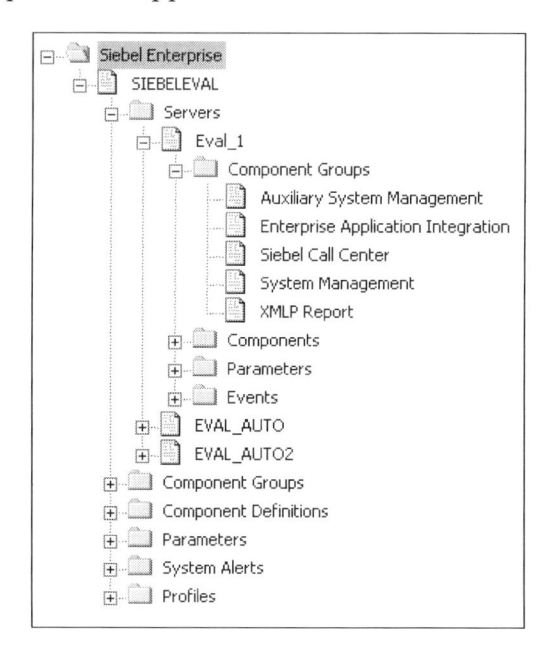

We can observe that a Siebel enterprise consists of the following:

- Servers
- Component groups

- Component definitions
- Enterprise parameters
- System alerts
- Enterprise profiles

Next, we will discuss each of these major building blocks of a Siebel Enterprise in more detail.

Servers

As we can confirm by examining the Enterprise Explorer tree, multiple Siebel servers can be members of a Siebel Enterprise. Each Siebel server has one or more component groups assigned, which results in a list of components that the server hosts.

Furthermore, parameters and event log levels can be set at the server level. In the following sections of this chapter, we will discuss the configuration of Siebel servers in greater detail.

Component groups

A component group is—as the name suggests—a collection of components. Grouping components allows for better manageability. The preconfigured Siebel enterprise for Siebel Industry Applications contains more than fifty component groups. The following screenshot shows the list of component groups for the selected enterprise:

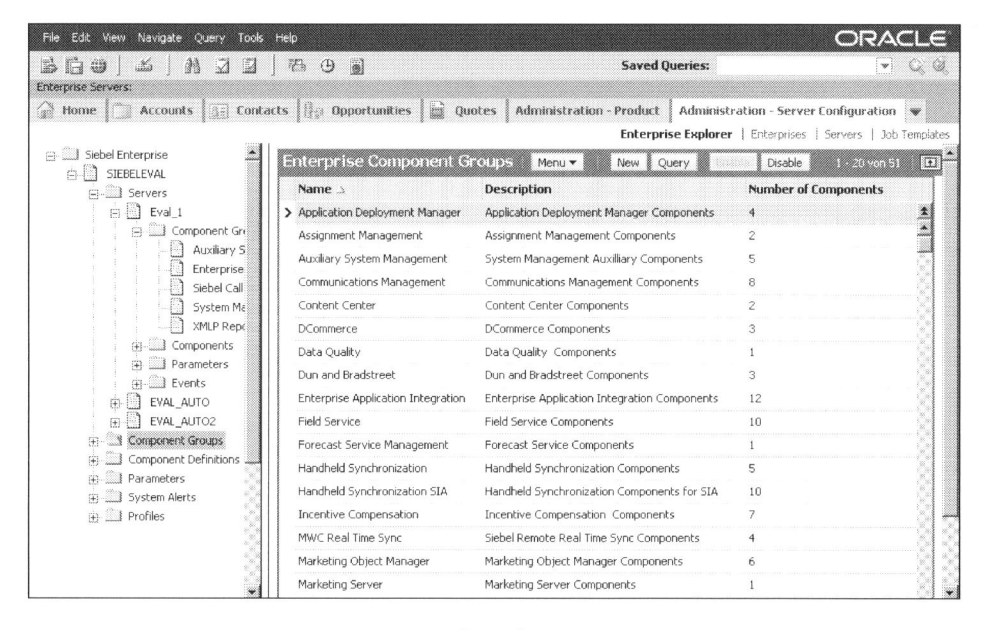

We can click the **Component Groups** folder in the explorer tree to obtain the list as depicted. The components within a component group serve a common purpose, such as supporting the deployment of application configurations (Application Deployment Manager group) or assignment of data to users or organization (Assignment Manager group).

Component groups are the vehicles that enable Siebel CRM functionality—implemented as components—on Siebel servers. Later in this chapter, we will learn how to assign and enable component groups on Siebel servers.

The following table describes the most important component groups—in alphabetical order—available in Siebel CRM version 8:

Name	Alias	Supported Functionality
Application Deployment Manager	ADM	Deployment of configuration changes from source to target enterprises.
Assignment Management	AsgnMgmt	Automatic assignment of data to employees, positions, or organizations.
Auxiliary System Management	SystemAux	System Component Group—enabled by default.
Communications Management	CommMgmt	In- and outbound communication across various channels (Email, Fax, Pager).
Data Quality	DataQual	Integration with third-party data cleansing and enrichment software.
Enterprise Application Integration	EAI	Base components for enterprise application integration (EAI). Supports queue-based transports such as IBM Websphere MQ or JMS.
Field Service	FieldSvc	Siebel Field Service application object manager and support for automated scheduling optimization.
Marketing Object Manager	MktgOM	Siebel Marketing application object managers.
PIM Server Integration Management	PIMSI	Integration with Microsoft Exchange Server.
Search Processing	Search	Integration with third-party search engines.
Siebel Call Center	CallCenter	Siebel Call Center application object managers.
Siebel CME	Communications	Siebel Communications, Media, and Energy application object managers.

Name	Alias	Supported Functionality
Siebel eAutomotive	`eAutomotive`	Siebel eAutomotive application object manager.
Siebel eChannel	`eChannel`	Siebel Partner Relationship Management application object managers.
Siebel eDocuments	`eDocuments`	Generation of office documents such as letters, proposals, or agreements.
Siebel Financial Services	`Fins`	Siebel Financial Services application object managers.
Siebel ISS	`ISS`	Siebel Interactive Selling Suite (ISS) object managers and components.
Siebel Life Sciences	`LifeSciences`	Siebel Life Sciences application object managers.
Siebel Loyalty	`Loyalty`	Siebel Loyalty application object managers.
Siebel Public Sector	`PublicSector`	Siebel Public Sector application object managers.
Siebel Remote	`Remote`	Synchronization with remote clients.
Siebel Sales	`Sales`	Siebel Sales application object managers.
Siebel Universal Customer Master	`UCM`	Siebel Universal Customer Master application object manager and supporting components.
Siebel Wireless	`Wireless`	Siebel Wireless application object managers for support of mobile web-enabled devices.
System Management	`System`	System Component Group—enabled by default.
Workflow Management	`Workflow`	Executing Siebel workflows.
XMLP Report	`XMLPReport`	For generating Oracle BI Publisher reports (XMLP or "XML Publisher" is the old product name for Oracle BI Publisher).

As we can see from the table above, there are many component groups that mainly hold the object manager components for specific Siebel applications while other groups enable cross-application functionality such as integration with external systems or reporting.

The two system component groups (System Management and Auxiliary System Management) are enabled on each Siebel server by default and should never be disabled.

Component definitions

Each component, no matter what specific functionality it implements, is defined only once for the entire enterprise. The result of this is a very high level of reusability. Components can run multiple times on any server within the enterprise but they all inherit their parameter settings from an enterprise-wide template—the **component definition**.

In more technical terms, a component is a type of program with a specific set of parameters that can be instantiated on one or more servers in the enterprise.

> The core Siebel server technology is implemented in the C++ programming language. When the C++ code represented as .dll (dynamic link library) files on Microsoft Windows or .so (shared object) files on Linux and other UNIX-based operating systems is executed, a task is instantiated on the Siebel server. The task is also visible as an operating system process or thread.

In order to examine the component definitions for a Siebel enterprise, we can use the Component Definitions view in the **Administration - Server Configuration** screen of the Siebel Web Client. The out-of-the-box configuration for a Siebel enterprise contains over one hundred component definitions, most of them language-specific. The following screenshot shows the **Component Definitions** view in the **Administration - Server Configuration** screen:

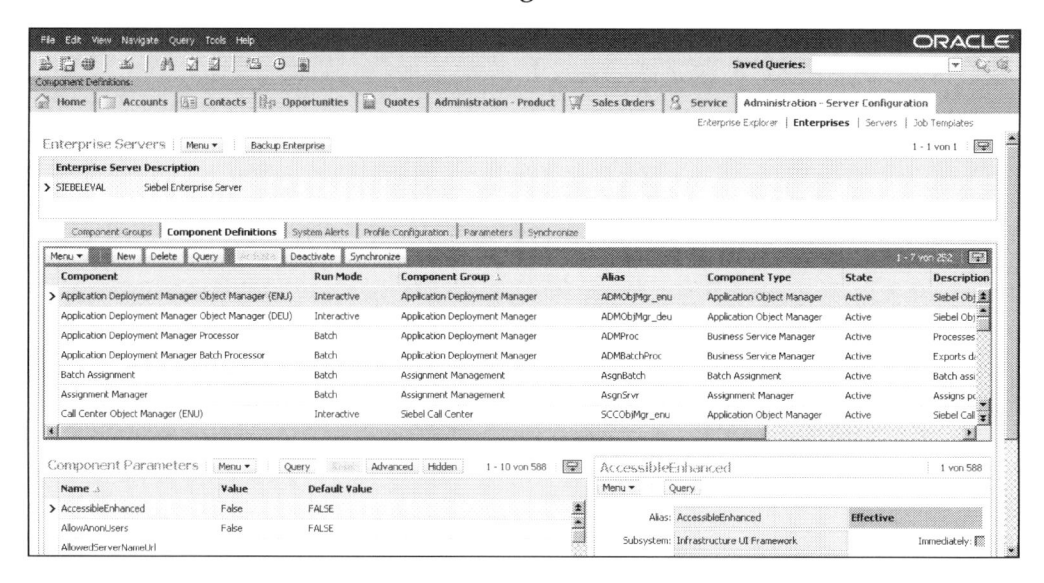

The view displays the list of component definitions for the current Siebel enterprise as well as the parameter definitions for the selected component definition.

A component definition is specified by the following:

- A unique name and alias (short name)
- Run mode
- Component group membership
- Component type
- List of parameters that define the behavior of the component

Next, we will discuss the component definition run modes and component types.

Component definition run modes

The run mode of a component definition drives the general behaviour of the server component. There are three run modes:

- Background
- Batch
- Interactive

A **background** component is defined as a constantly running process which performs tasks that require regular attention. Examples of typical Siebel background components are the various "EAI Receivers" that enable integration with other enterprise applications. We can imagine that if a Siebel application should be able to process incoming data at any given point in time, a receiver must be constantly listening for data sent by an external system. To avoid the component consuming too much CPU time while "waiting", a **Sleep Time** parameter controls the amount of time that the component remains in a "sleeping" state before "waking up" and doing the actual work.

Batch components are typically invoked by an administrator, an end-user initiated workflow, or by schedule. Each task for these components has a defined start time and only consumes CPU and memory of the host machine when it is active. Once the task is complete, the operating system process is finished as well. Examples for batch components are the **Enterprise Integration Manager (EIM),** which supports import, export, delete, and merge of mass data or the **Database Extract** component, which is used to extract the initial database snapshot for mobile clients.

Application object managers are the dominant example for **interactive** components. Their main purpose is to wait for incoming requests from either the end users or external systems and handle the request according to the metadata information in the Siebel repository file (.srf).

Component types

The component type property of a component definition defines both the base functionality of the component and the list of parameters for all components of that type. When we explore the list of component definitions for a Siebel enterprise we find. For example, dozens of component definitions that have a type of "Application Object Manager". Closer inspection of the parameters list for each of these component definitions reveals that they have the same parameters albeit with slightly different values.

The generic component types used to define the majority of components in a Siebel Enterprise are listed below:

- Application Object Manager
- Business Service Manager
- Enterprise Application Integration Receiver

Application Object Managers, as discussed above, serve as request handlers for end users or external systems. The main distinguishing parameters for application object managers are **Application Name** and **Language Code**.

Components of the **Business Service Manager** type allow the Siebel server to execute code implemented as a so-called business service method as a component. The majority of Siebel functionality is implemented as business services. Developers can write custom business services to implement additional functionality. The **Business Service Name** and **Method** parameters distinguish component definitions of this type.

As discussed above, **Enterprise Application Integration (EAI) Receivers** are components that serve as listeners for incoming requests and data from external systems. Siebel CRM supports the following protocols for EAI message exchange:

- MQ (IBM Websphere Message Queuing)
- MSMQ (Microsoft Message Queuing)
- JMS (Java Message Service)
- HTTP (Hypertext Transfer Protocol)
- File
- SOAP (Simple Object Access Protocol)

Apart from the three component types discussed above, we can find many others that are, most of the time, specific for one component definition. These component definitions, such as the **Siebel Connection Broker** or other system-related components, use specialized code to implement their functionality.

Later in this chapter, we will learn how to create additional component definitions, which will deepen our understanding of these major building blocks of Siebel server-side functionality.

Enterprise parameters

Many parameters have the same value for all component definitions. Good examples for enterprise-wide parameters are **Username** and **Password**. They define the name and password of the database account that is used by Siebel processes to connect to the Siebel database.

When these parameters are defined on the enterprise level and are not changed at a lower level such as the server or component level, the value of each parameter is inherited by subordinate members of the hierarchy.

To view the list of parameters for the current enterprise, we can navigate to the **Parameters** view in the **Administration - Server Configuration** screen in the Siebel Web Client. The following screenshot shows the parameter list for the SIEBELEVAL enterprise:

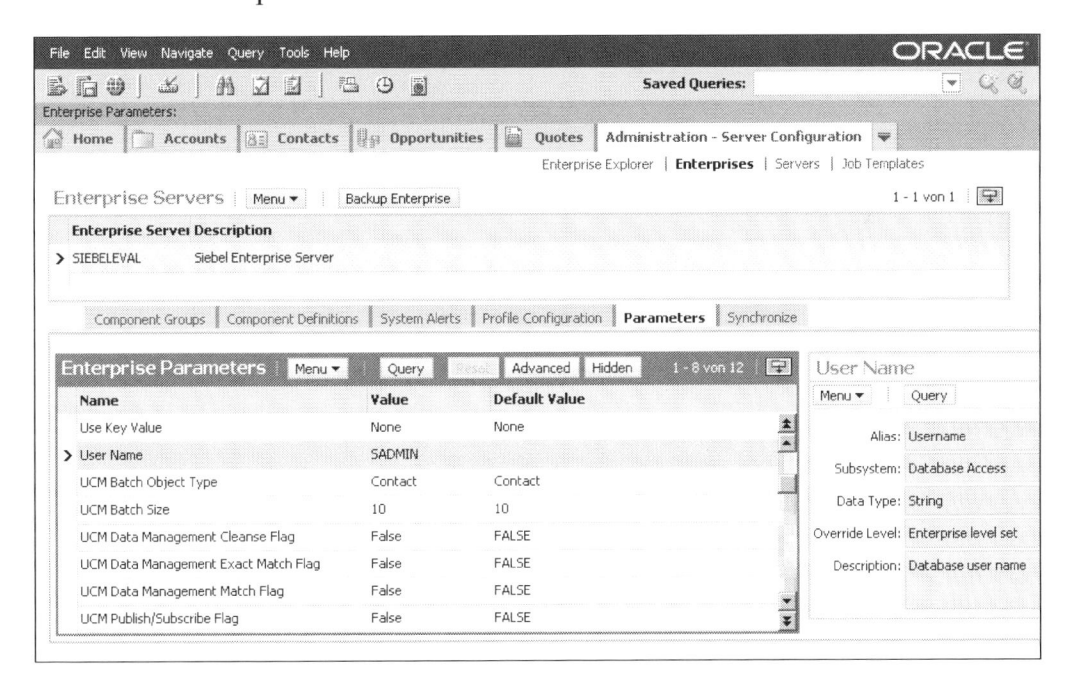

The **User Name** parameter is selected and we can observe by its description that it denominates the database username for connections to the Siebel database.

Enterprise profiles

Enterprise profiles are reusable collections of parameters. A good example is the ServerDataSrc profile which—very much like in a Siebel Developer client's configuration file—contains the information to allow the object manager to connect to the server database.

We can investigate all enterprise profiles for a given Siebel enterprise by navigating to the **Profile Configuration** view of the **Administration - Server Configuration** screen in the Siebel Web Client, which is shown in the following screenshot:

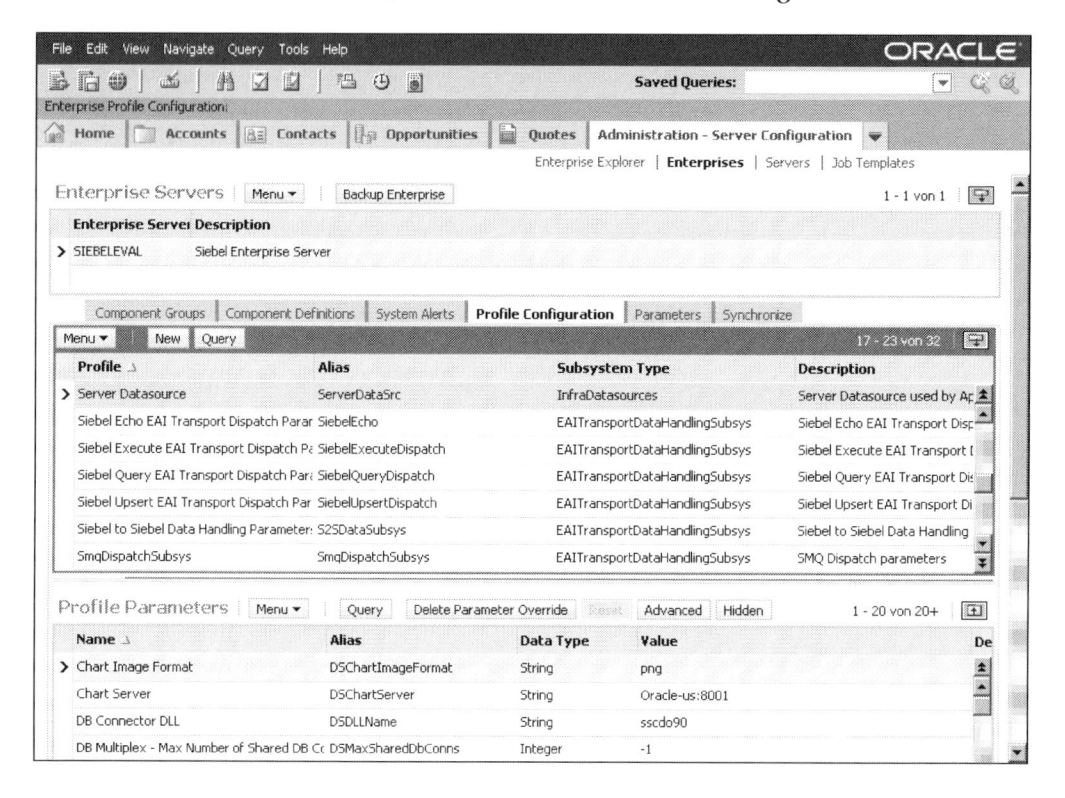

The view displays all enterprise profile definitions for the selected enterprise. The **Server Datasource** profile is currently selected and a part of the list of parameters for this profile is visible. We can observe that the **DB Connector DLL** parameter has a value of sscdo90. A similar parameter (DLL) exists in the **[ServerDataSrc]** section in the Siebel Developer Web client's configuration file. The following screenshot shows the **[ServerDataSrc]** section of the siebel.cfg file, which is the configuration file used for the Siebel Sales application:

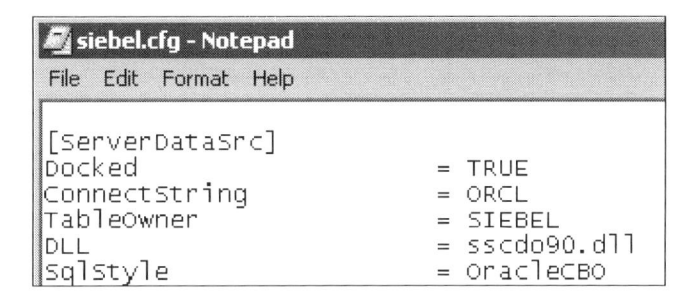

```
[ServerDataSrc]
Docked              = TRUE
ConnectString       = ORCL
TableOwner          = SIEBEL
DLL                 = sscdo90.dll
SqlStyle            = OracleCBO
```

We can observe by comparing the values of the DLL parameters that sections in client configuration files and enterprise profiles serve a similar purpose.

Enterprise profiles are typically referenced by their alias name in server or component parameters. For example, the **Call Center Object Manager** component definition references the **ServerDataSrc** profile in its data source parameters. The following screenshot shows a portion of the Component Definitions view and the **OM - Named Data Source name** parameter for the **Call Center Object Manager (ENU)** component definition:

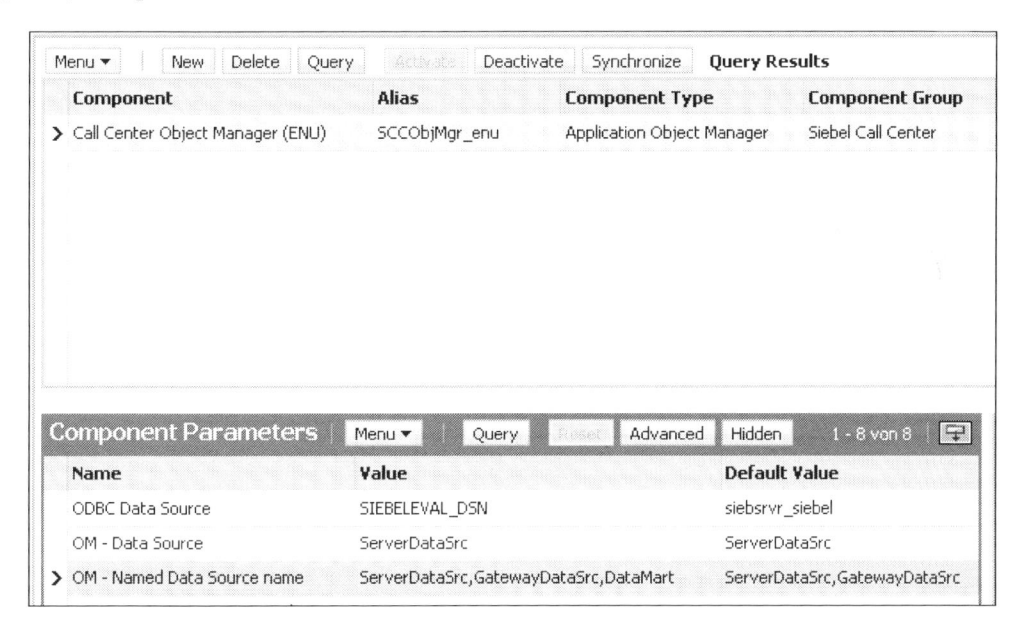

Component	Alias	Component Type	Component Group
Call Center Object Manager (ENU)	SCCObjMgr_enu	Application Object Manager	Siebel Call Center

Component Parameters

Name	Value	Default Value
ODBC Data Source	SIEBELEVAL_DSN	siebsrvr_siebel
OM - Data Source	ServerDataSrc	ServerDataSrc
OM - Named Data Source name	ServerDataSrc,GatewayDataSrc,DataMart	ServerDataSrc,GatewayDataSrc

The value of this parameter is a comma-separated list of names of enterprise profiles that contain the connectivity information. All other application object manager definitions reference the same enterprise profile to obtain the connection information for the server database. Having to set connection parameter for the server database only in one place implements a high level of reusability.

> Enterprise profiles are also known as "named subsystems", which is the term used in the Siebel Server Manager command line utility. The word "named" is an abbreviation for "name daemon" and refers to the Siebel Gateway Name Server service.

System alerts

System alerts are a special type of enterprise profile. Similar to all other enterprise profiles, they are reusable collections of parameters. Their speciality lies within the purpose of defining a list of e-mail recipients—typically administrators—who need to be notified in case of an error situation on one of the servers.

We can find a default system alert definition when we navigate to the `System Alerts` folder in the Enterprise Explorer view of the Administration - Server Configuration screen.

System alerts can be referenced by specifying their name as the value of the **Notification Handler** parameter of the component definition. As a result, an e-mail will be sent to the recipients defined in the system alert profile when the component's tasks exit with an error.

Siebel enterprise hierarchy and parameter inheritance

As we have now discussed the major building blocks of a Siebel enterprise, we find that they are arranged in a specific hierarchy. This hierarchy also defines the inheritance of parameter values from higher levels to lower levels. The following diagram depicts the information available from the Enterprise Explorer view:

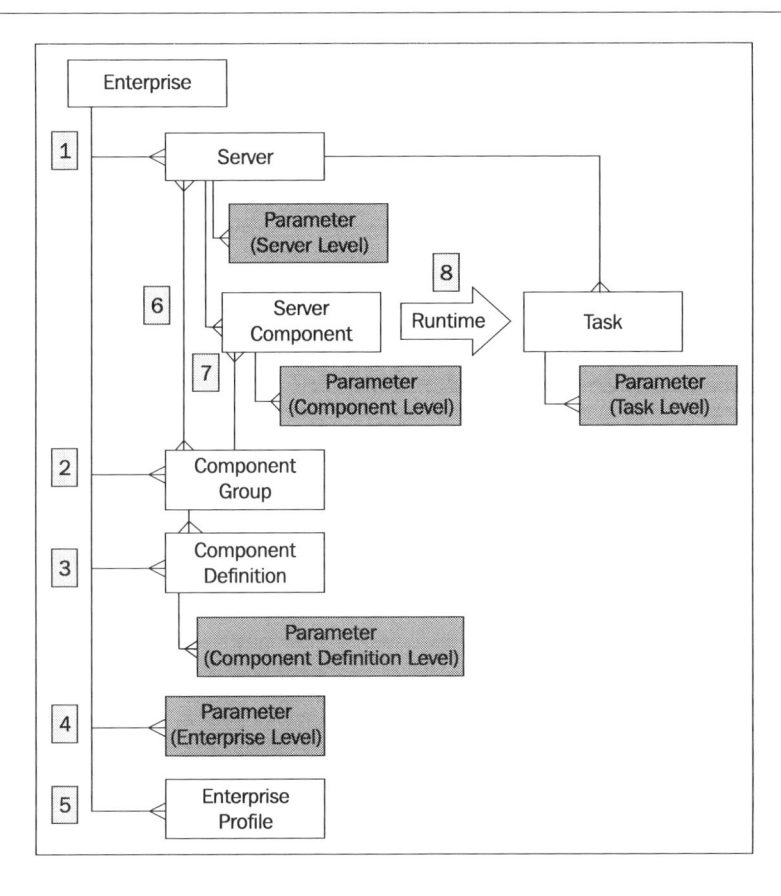

We can summarize our exploration of the Siebel enterprise structure as follows (using the numbers in the diagram):

1. A Siebel enterprise contains one or more Siebel servers.
2. More than 50 default component groups are part of a freshly installed Siebel enterprise.
3. Each component group contains one or more component definitions. Component definitions also define the parameterization of server processes at the enterprise level.
4. Each enterprise has a preconfigured list of global parameters.
5. Enterprise profiles (including System Alerts) are reusable collections of parameters and are typically referenced at lower levels.
6. We can assign multiple component groups to each Siebel server and each component group can be assigned to more than one Siebel server.

7. As a result of the component group assignment, each Siebel server hosts a specific set of components. Component parameters can be individually set on each Siebel server.
8. When a component—representing program code—is executed on a Siebel server, a task is instantiated. We can pass specific parameter values to a task before it starts.

When we observe and rearrange the different levels of parameters in the above diagram, we find the following chain of parameter value inheritance in a Siebel enterprise:

```
Parameter Inheritance in a Siebel Enterprise

    Enterprise
    Parameter
        │
        ▼
    Server Parameter
        │
        ▼
    Component
    Definition
    Parameter
        │
        ▼
    Server
    Component
    Parameter
        │
        ▼
    Task Parameter
```

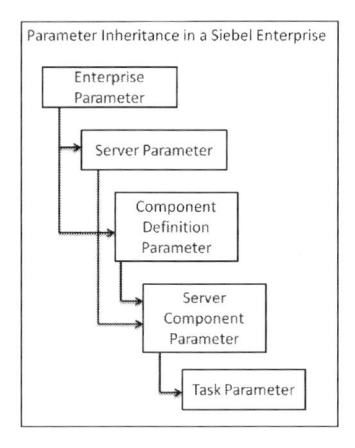

If a parameter with the **same name** exists in a lower level and **has not been changed** at that lower level, it inherits its value from the parameter in the upper level. If we change a parameter at a lower level, for example at the server component level, this is considered a **parameter override**. In that case, the chain of inheritance is broken and the parameter must now be managed on the level that it has been set on.

An administrator must therefore consider any changes to parameters very carefully. In general, setting parameter values at higher levels is recommended in order to avoid repetitive work at lower levels. If for any reason we wish to reestablish the chain of inheritance for a parameter, we must use the **Delete Parameter Override** command from the applet menu. The following screenshot shows the **Notification Handler** parameter at the server level:

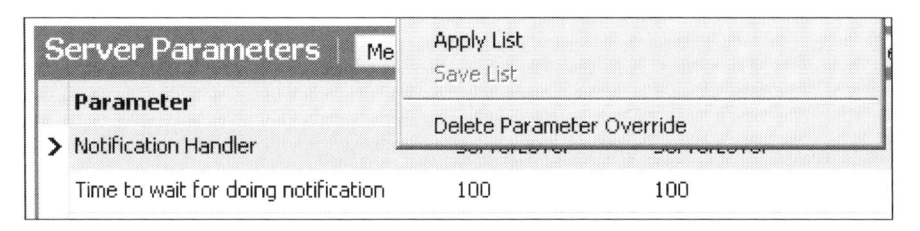

Server Parameters	Me	Apply List
		Save List
Parameter		
> Notification Handler		Delete Parameter Override
Time to wait for doing notification	100	100

The command **Delete Parameter Override** — visible in the screenshot in the context menu — can be used to delete the overridden value at the current level and reestablish inheritance of the parameter value from upper levels.

> On your demonstration system use the Administration - Server Configuration screen in the Siebel Web Client to verify the findings in the previous section.

Using server management screens in the Siebel client

Each standard Siebel application is shipped with two screens that are intended to support administrative users in their daily routine of configuring and managing the Siebel enterprise. The benefit of using a graphical user interface lies within the similarities to other Siebel screens with regard to querying for data, comparing and visualizing data, and so forth. The two screens provided by Oracle are:

- Administration - Server Configuration
- Administration - Server Management

Next, we will discuss the most important aspects of these two administrative screens.

> Even if the look and feel of the server administration views is similar to other Siebel views, the data displayed comes from the Siebel Gateway Name Server. This is a nice showcase for the capability of the Siebel CRM framework to connect to external systems and provide access to their data and functionality via a single user interface.
>
> However, because of the fact that the Siebel Gateway Name Server is not a relational database management system, we may encounter difficulties when trying to use special query techniques such as wildcards or function calls.

Using the Administration - Server Configuration screen

In the above sections of this chapter, we have already used some views of the Administration - Server Configuration screen to verify the hierarchical relationships and properties of a Siebel enterprise's building blocks. We can access the screen by logging in to a Siebel application using an administrative user account and navigating to the Site Map.

In the following, we will discuss the functionality in the different views of that screen.

Backing up the Siebel enterprise configuration

Before making major changes to the configuration of a Siebel enterprise, it is highly recommended to back up the existing configuration. As we learned in previous chapters, the entire enterprise configuration is stored in a text file named `siebns.dat`. The file is managed by the Siebel Gateway Name Server and must not be modified manually.

To allow easy access to the backup functionality, all enterprise list applets in the server configuration views have a button labelled **Backup Enterprise,** as shown in the following screenshot:

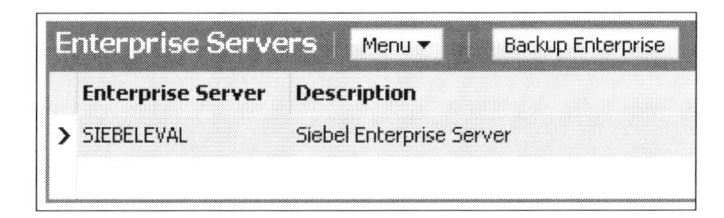

Enterprise Servers	Menu ▼	Backup Enterprise
Enterprise Server	**Description**	
> SIEBELEVAL	Siebel Enterprise Server	

Any time we wish to save the current enterprise configuration, we simply click the button. The browser status bar will display "Backup Enterprise Server is completed successfully" once the backup file is created. We can verify the existence of the backup file in the ADMIN folder (on Microsoft Windows) or the sys folder (on UNIX-based operating systems) of the Siebel Gateway Name Server's installation directory. The filename will have a suffix containing the timestamp of the file creation.

> Because of the sensitive nature of the `siebns.dat` file, the Siebel Gateway Name Server automatically backs up the file frequently. But because it keeps only the last five versions and the backup interval is rather short it is very likely that the last "working" version is overwritten.
>
> For this reason, we should always create a manual backup of the `siebns.dat` file following the procedure described in the above section.

Restoring the Siebel enterprise configuration

If for any reason we have to restore the enterprise configuration to an earlier state, we have to complete the procedure below:

1. Stop all Siebel servers in the enterprise.
2. Stop the Siebel Gateway Name Server.
3. Rename the existing `siebns.dat` file to `siebns.dat.notused` (or similar).
4. Rename the backup file to `siebns.dat`.
5. Start the Siebel Gateway Name Server.
6. Start all Siebel servers.

After the Siebel enterprise is fully started, we should verify that the correct configuration has been loaded by navigating to the Administration - Server Configuration views. We will now discuss these views in detail.

Enterprise Explorer

The Enterprise Explorer view has already been discussed above. Its main purpose is to provide insight into the hierarchical structure of the current Siebel enterprise, which is facilitated by a tree applet.

Even if the modification of data such as enabling or disabling component groups or setting parameter values is supported, the Enterprise Explorer view is typically used in a read-only manner.

Enterprises - Component Groups

By navigating to the Enterprises - Component Groups view, we can access the following information and functionality:

- List of all component groups and their enterprise-wide state (enabled or disabled)
- List of all components for the selected component group
- List of all Siebel servers and the component group assignment and state of the selected component group to each server

The following screenshot shows the Enterprises - Component Groups view in the **Administration - Server Configuration** screen:

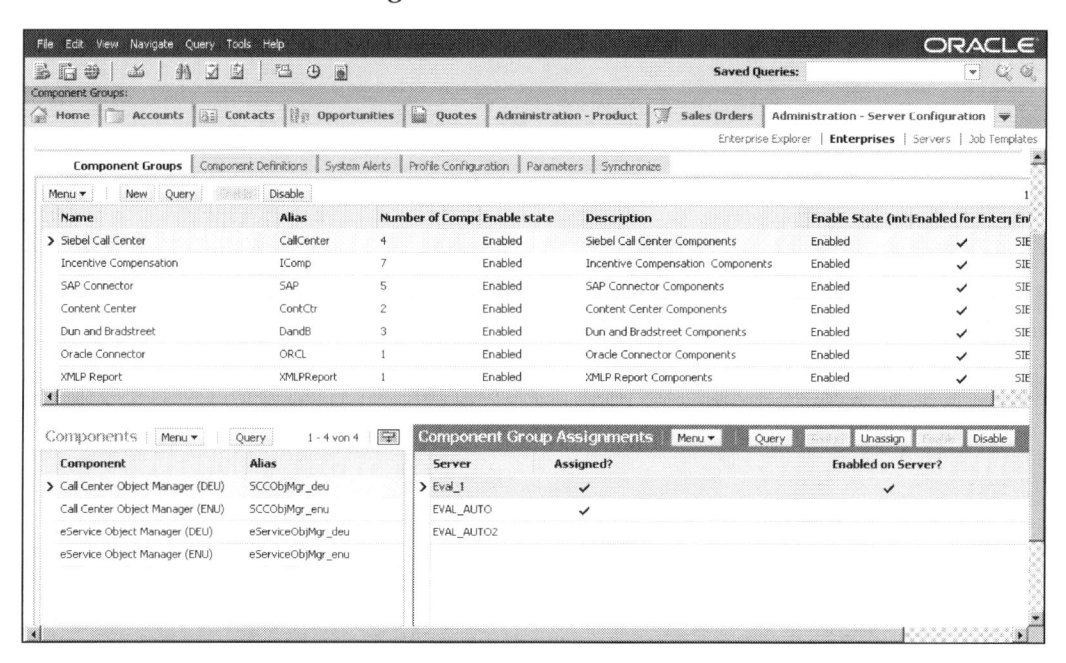

The key functionality of this view is to assign and enable component groups for specific Siebel servers, thus defining the role of each server and the functionality hosted by that server in the enterprise.

A component group must be assigned to a server (the Assigned flag is checked) before it can be enabled. When a component group is assigned but not enabled on a Siebel server, it is still possible to adjust some settings for components on that server. For example, the component start up mode can be set to manual or automatic (component start up modes will be discussed later in this chapter). Only when a component group is assigned and enabled to a Siebel server, can the components within that group execute as tasks on that server.

The following procedure describes the enablement of a component group on a Siebel server:

1. In the Component Groups list, query for the desired component group.
2. Ensure that the correct component group is selected.
3. In the Component Group Assignments list in the lower right of the view, select the desired server.
4. Click the **Enable** button in the Component Group Assignments list to enable the selected component.
5. Restart the system service for the selected Siebel Server.

If we wish to disable a component group on a Siebel server, we must use the **Disable** button in the Component Group Assignments list. Furthermore, we can use the **Unassign** button to remove the assignment of a component group to a Siebel server. When a component group is unassigned, it is also disabled. As a result, the functionality provided by the components of that group becomes unavailable on that Siebel server when it is restarted.

Restarting Siebel servers after changing component group assignments is necessary because of the fact that a Siebel server connects to the Siebel Gateway Name server only once during its start up phase to obtain its configuration.

> All component groups are assigned but not enabled by default for each Siebel server.
>
> Component groups can also be enabled or disabled on an enterprise-wide level. Disabling a component group for the entire enterprise would make the respective components unavailable on all servers after restarting the services.

Enterprises - Component Definitions

The next view in the Administration - Server Configuration screen is the Component Definitions view. In this view, we can examine and modify all component definitions and their parameters for the current enterprise.

The following tasks are typically carried out in this view:

- Deactivating or activating component definitions on an enterprise-wide level
- Creating new component definitions
- Reconfiguring component definitions
- Modifying parameters for component definitions
- Deleting parameter overrides on the component definition level

When modifying parameters in this view, we must consider that—due to the inheritance principle—the new parameter value will affect any component instance of that component definition on any Siebel server where it is enabled.

The moment when the parameter change is effective depends on the parameter type. We can verify this for each parameter in the form applet in the lower-right corner of the view. The following screenshot shows this form applet:

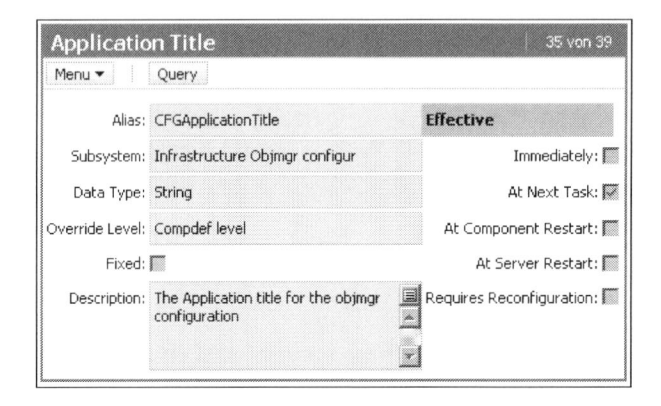

In the above example, the **Application Title** parameter of an application object manager component definition is shown in the form applet. In the **Effective** section in the right half of the form, we can observe that any change made to the parameter will be effective **At Next Task**, which translates to "when a new session is established" for application object managers.

As we can observe on the above screenshot, there are five levels of effectiveness of parameter changes:

- Immediately
- At Next Task (or session)
- At Component Restart
- At Server Restart
- Requires Reconfiguration

While the first four levels are somewhat self-explanatory, the fifth one ("Requires Reconfiguration") might need some more insight. We can use the context menu on the component definition list to access the following commands:

- Start Reconfiguration
- Commit Reconfiguration
- Cancel Reconfiguration

The concept of reconfiguring component definitions means that an administrator can modify one or more parameters of a component definition without affecting current user sessions. We must follow the procedure below to reconfigure a component definition:

1. Select the desired component definition (typically, an application object manager).
2. Right-click the component definition and select Start Reconfiguration.
3. Ensure that the component definition is selected and has a state of "Reconfiguring".
4. Modify the parameter values.
5. Right-click the component definition and select Commit Reconfiguration.
6. Ensure that the component definition state changes to "Active".
7. Allow the server to apply the reconfiguration (approx. 1 minute).
8. Test the reconfiguration by logging in to the application.

The benefit of using the reconfiguration technique is that end users do not have to interrupt their sessions. Existing sessions will use the old parameter set while new sessions will use the modified parameter set. We can use this technique for any configuration change that allows the parallel usage of old and new parameter values.

Enterprises - Parameters

The Enterprises - Parameters view allows us to list and modify all parameters for the selected Siebel enterprise.

When viewing or searching for parameters, we should consider that there are three levels of visibility for parameters and relevant buttons on the parameter lists allow us to switch between these levels. The following screenshot shows the **Enterprise Parameters** list applet as an example for all parameter list applets in the Siebel server configuration screen:

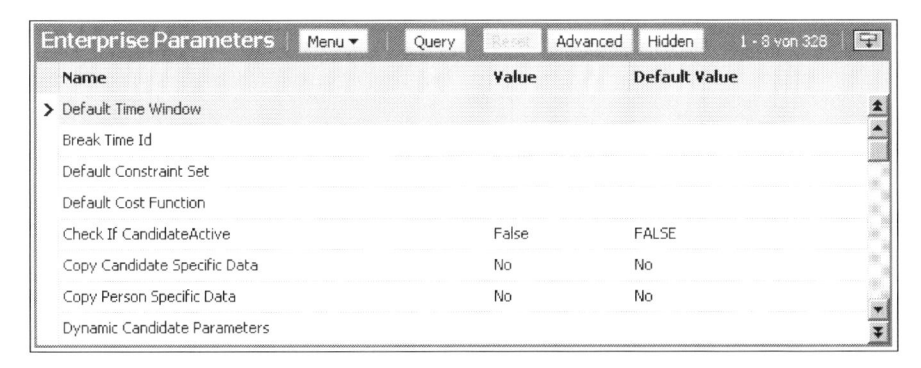

Name	Value	Default Value
> Default Time Window		
Break Time Id		
Default Constraint Set		
Default Cost Function		
Check If CandidateActive	False	FALSE
Copy Candidate Specific Data	No	No
Copy Person Specific Data	No	No
Dynamic Candidate Parameters		

The following table describes how to use the **Reset**, **Advanced**, and **Hidden** buttons to switch between different lists of parameters:

Button	List display
Advanced	Advanced parameters are displayed.
Hidden	Hidden parameters are displayed.
Reset	Normal parameters are displayed (Note: The Reset label is ambiguous, no "reset" whatsoever takes place).

Apart from viewing or modifying enterprise parameter values, this view also provides the ability to delete parameter overrides at the enterprise level.

Enterprises - Profile Configuration

The Profile Configuration view of the Administration - Server Configuration screen allows us to create or modify enterprise profiles. The concept of enterprise profiles—being reusable collections of parameters—has already been discussed in this chapter.

Enterprises - System Alerts

The System Alerts view allows us to modify or create specialized enterprise profiles for Email notification and has already been discussed above.

Enterprises - Synchronize

As described in Chapter 4 during the discussion of the final steps to set up a Siebel enterprise, the definitions of batch components have to be synchronized from the Siebel Gateway Name Server to tables in the Siebel database.

This task has to be executed at installation time and every time when a definition of a batch component has been created or modified. The purpose of the batch component synchronization is to allow administrators to select these components and their parameters from pick lists while creating server jobs.

To synchronize batch components, we must navigate to the Enterprises - Synchronize view and click the **Synchronize** button. We can use the view to verify that the batch component definitions have been successfully synchronized.

Servers view

When we navigate to the Servers view in the Administration - Server Configuration screen, we observe that we can view or modify the following settings for each server in the list individually:

- Set the component start up mode

- View or modify event log levels for servers and individual components
- View or modify parameters for servers and individual components

In the following section, we will discuss the first option in greater detail.

The following screenshot shows the Servers - Components - Events view in the **Administration - Server Configuration** screen:

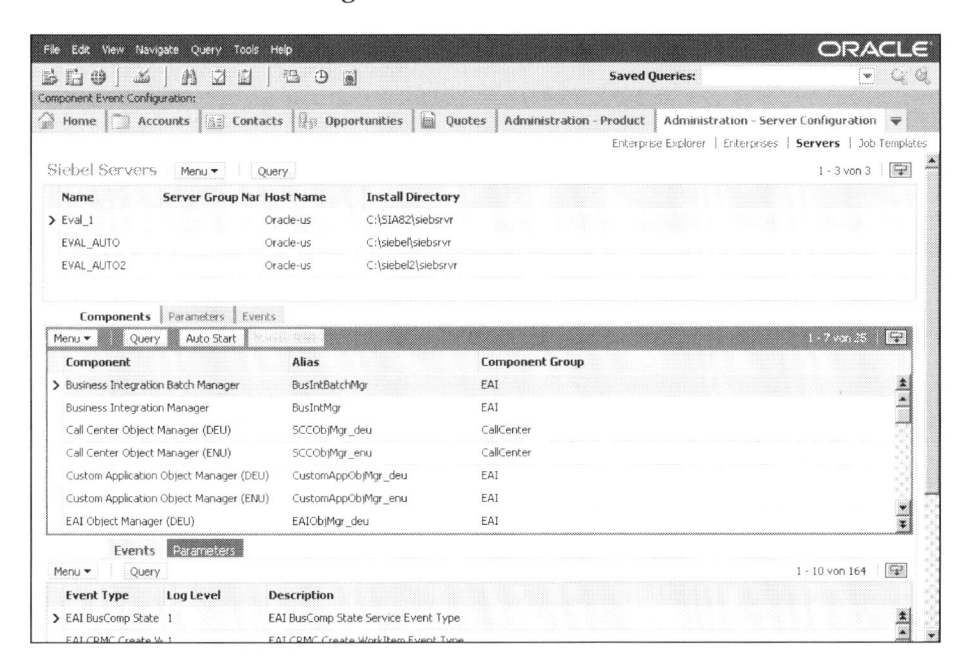

![Screenshot of the Administration - Server Configuration screen showing Siebel Servers list with Eval_1, EVAL_AUTO, and EVAL_AUTO2, and Components tab listing various components like Business Integration Batch Manager, Call Center Object Manager, etc.]

In this view, we can select a server in the upper list and control the component behavior for that server using the startup mode buttons in the Components list or by using the sub views for Events (to set log levels) or Parameters for the selected component.

When we use the middle tabs for Parameters and Events, we can view or modify the parameters and event log levels for the selected server as a whole.

Setting component start up mode

Similar to system services on operating systems, we can configure a server component for automatic or manual start. When the startup mode for a server component is set to "Auto Start" (the default value), the component starts up immediately when its host server service is started. When a server hosts a great number of components, the parallel start up of dozens or even hundreds of processes can consume all CPUs and a lot of memory on the machine. This can severely affect the server start up time.

[283]

In order to avoid this, we should consider setting some of the lesser used components to manual start up mode. For example, the component group EAI contains many "EAI Receivers", which allow integration with queue-based transports such as IBM Websphere MQ or JMS. If we enable the EAI component group on a server only because we need the EAI Object Manager component, we can safely set all other components of that group to manual start. We can accomplish this either in the above mentioned view or via commands at the Siebel Server Manager command line (discussed in the next section in this chapter).

To set a server component to manual start up mode, we can proceed as follows.

1. Navigate to the Servers view in the Administration - Server Configuration screen.
2. Select the appropriate Siebel server in the upper list.
3. Select the component in the middle list.
4. Click the Manual Start button.

Once manual start is enabled, the Manual Start button becomes inactive and the Auto Start button becomes active, allowing us to set the start up mode back to automatic if we need to. By observing the inactive buttons, we can also tell in which start up mode the component currently is.

Setting components to manual start rather than disabling their component definition keeps the component available on the server. Once the server is started, we can use the graphical user interface (GUI) or the command line to manually start the components. This will be discussed later in this chapter.

Setting event log levels

In order to assist the administrator with the task of logging component activity or troubleshooting erroneous behavior of server processes, the Siebel Server framework provides the possibility to set log levels for a great variety of events. Setting event log levels is discussed in detail in Chapter 16.

Job Templates

The Job Templates view in the Administration - Server Configuration screen allows administrators to define reusable job definitions. In the Siebel server framework, a job is referred to as a batch component that is scheduled for execution. When creating jobs "on the fly" an administrator would typically have to manually override a number of parameters. This is a repetitive, time consuming, and error prone activity.

For this reason, the **Job Templates** view allows us to store the parameter settings for a specific type of job and give it a unique name. The following screenshot shows the **Job Templates** view in the **Administration - Server Configuration** screen:

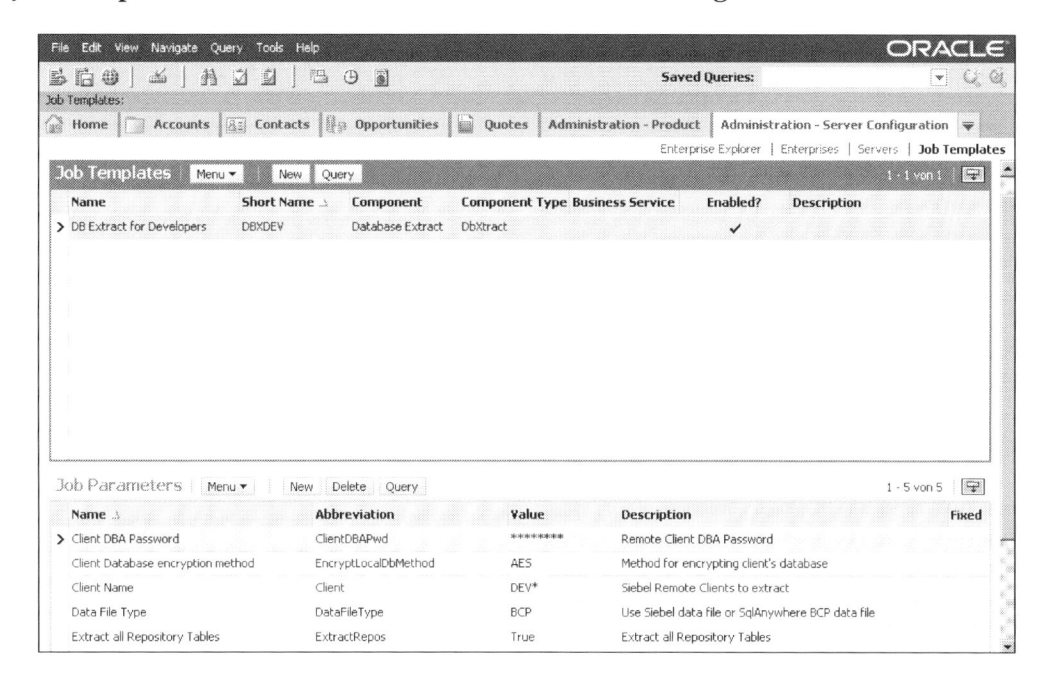

A job template definition is visible. We can observe that several parameters and their values are defined in the lower list applet.

An administrator can now select the job's name from the component dropdown list in the Jobs view in the Administration - Server Management screen. Creating jobs will be discussed in the next section.

> Job templates are stored in the Siebel database and are therefore different from the other server configuration data that is managed by the Siebel Gateway Name Server. For this reason, we can create job templates only from the web client and not via the Siebel Server Manager command line.

Using the Administration - Server Management screen

While the Administration - Server Configuration screen allows us to view or modify the configuration of Siebel enterprise members such as Siebel servers or components, the Administration - Server Management screen is intended to provide insight into the current state of the Siebel enterprise. We will discuss the main views of this screen in the following order:

1. Enterprises
2. Servers
3. Components
4. Tasks
5. Sessions
6. Jobs

This order represents the "natural" hierarchy of the building blocks of a Siebel enterprise.

Enterprises view

The Enterprises view in the Administration - Server Management screen allows administrators to monitor the state of all servers across the enterprise. Furthermore, administrators can review and control the state of components for the selected server and view a list of tasks for the selected server. The following screenshot shows a portion of the Enterprises view:

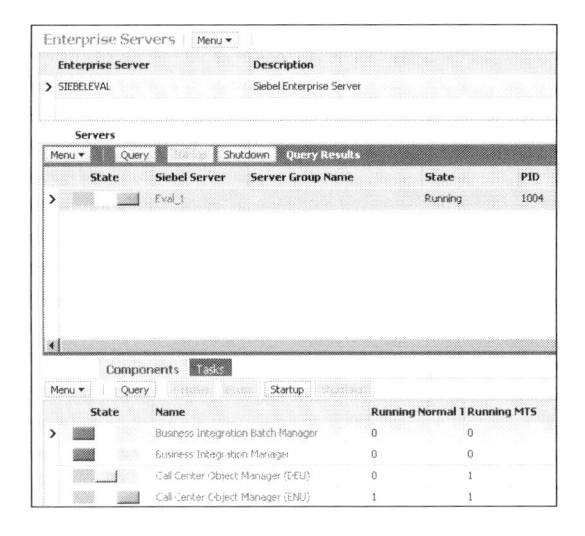

The Server **Eval_1** is in a running state—as indicated by the green traffic light icon and the value of **Running** in the **State** column. The components list for the selected server is also visible. Traffic light icons allow us to quickly verify the state of each component on the server.

About component run states

The following table gives an overview of the run states of Siebel server components:

Run State	Traffic Light Icon Color	Description
Running	Green	The component is fully operational and at least one task is currently executing.
Online	Green	The component is fully operational but no tasks are currently executing.
Paused	Yellow	The component is fully operational. Tasks may be currently executing but no new tasks will be instantiated while the component is in paused state.
Shutting down	Yellow	The component is currently shutting down.
Starting up	Yellow	The component has been started but it is not yet fully operational.
Shutdown	Red	The component has been shut down.
Unavailable	Red	The component has experienced an error, is currently starting up or has reached the maximum number of possible tasks.

Source: *Siebel System Monitoring and Diagnostics Guide, Version 8.1*

```
http://download.oracle.com/docs/cd/E14004_01/books/SysDiag/
booktitle.html
```

Controlling component run states

Each component list in the Administration - Server Management screen features four buttons, which allow administrators to issue commands to control the state of server components. The following buttons are available:

- Startup
- Shutdown
- Pause
- Resume

The following table gives an overview of the functionality of each component control button:

Button	Button is enabled when component is in state(s)	State(s) of the component after command is applied
Startup	Shutdown, Unavailable	Online or Running
Shutdown	Online, Running, Unavailable	Shutdown
Pause	Online, Running	Paused
Resume	Paused	Online or Running

When clicking the respective buttons, we can observe that the component state does not immediately change to the final value. For example, when using the Startup button to start up a component from its shutdown state, the component state changes to "Unavailable" because it takes a certain amount of time for the process to launch.

Because the Siebel views do not typically refresh automatically, we must manually refresh the list by pressing ALT+ENTER. It is generally recommended to refresh the views after issuing commands.

Servers view

The Servers view of the Administration - Server Management screen allows administrators to monitor and control the following for the selected server:

- Siebel server run state
- Object manager and system component sessions
- Component groups and component states for the selected component group
- Tasks
- Log entries and statistics

Components view

Sometimes, it is necessary to review and compare component information across servers in the enterprise. This is why the Administration - Server Management screen contains the Components view.

Featuring the same control buttons as described above, this view displays all components across all Siebel servers in the enterprise. For each selected component, we can review state values and statistics and monitor and control the state of the components' tasks.

Tasks view

Similar to the Components view, the Administration - Server Management screen contains a view that allows administrators to monitor and control all tasks across all Siebel servers in the enterprise. As discussed earlier in this chapter, a task is an instance of a component, present as an operating system process or thread while it executes. The screenshot below shows the **Tasks - Parameters** sub view of the **Administration - Server Management** screen:

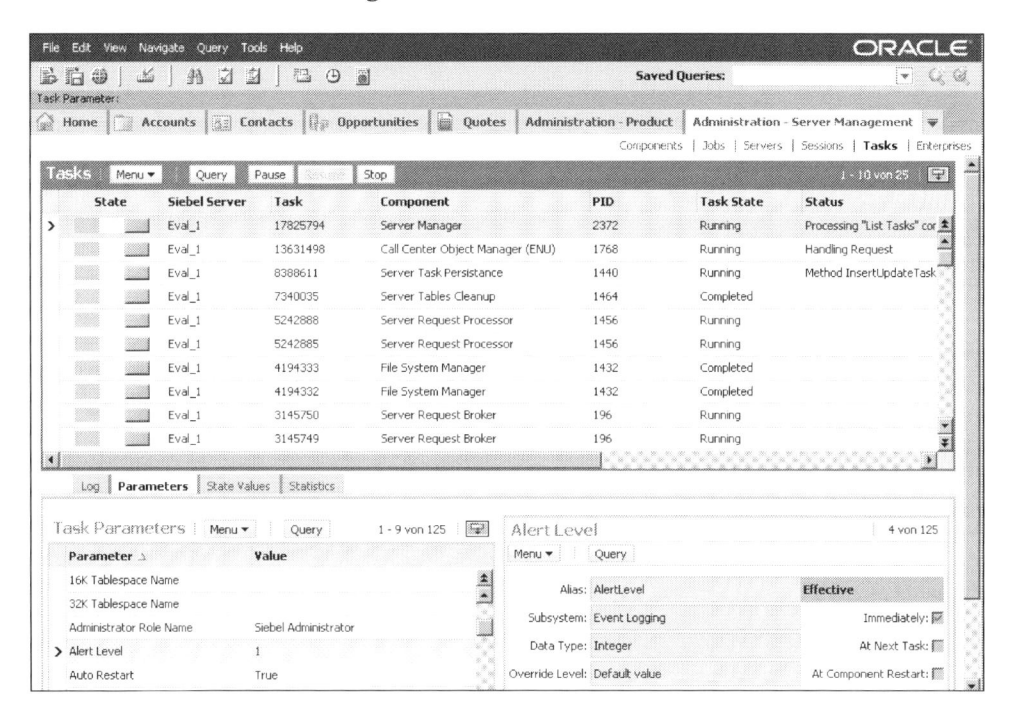

The **Tasks** list applet buttons allow us to control the state of the selected task. It is possible to change parameters for the selected tasks but this is limited to parameters that have an effective level of **Immediately**.

Furthermore, the **Tasks** view's sub views allow us to review log entries, state values, and statistics for the selected task.

Sessions view

Sessions are tasks for interactive components, namely application object managers and system components such as Server Manager and Server Request Broker. For troubleshooting purposes, it might be beneficial to review a flat list of all running, completed, or failed object manager sessions for all end users across all Siebel servers.

Siebel Server Management

This can be accomplished using the Session view. In this view, we can review and monitor all sessions irrespective of their run state. Furthermore, we can list log entries, state values, parameters, and statistics for each session.

Jobs view

As we learned above, a job in Siebel terms is a requested or scheduled task for a batch component. Jobs can be created manually by administrators or automatically by Siebel workflow or other internal services.

The **Jobs** view of the **Administration - Server Management** screen—shown in the following screenshot—allows us to create, submit, and monitor one-time or repeating job requests:

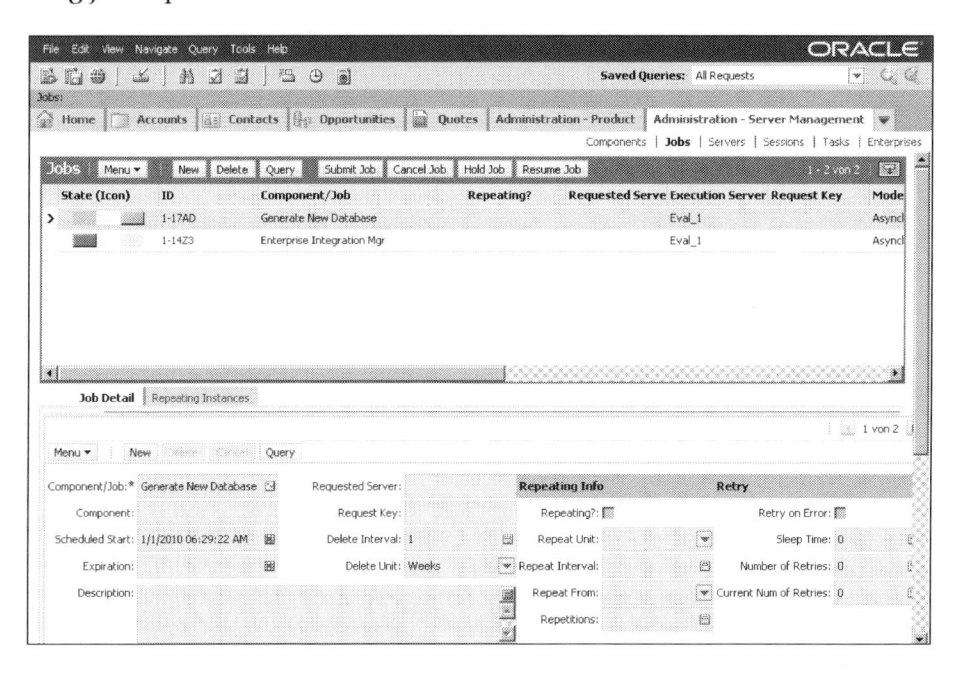

The following table guides us through the process of creating and submitting a job under the assumption that we are already logged in to the Siebel Web Client as an administrative user:

Step	Description
1	Verify that the component we wish to execute is available on at least one Siebel server. If not, we have to enable the respective component group on one of the servers.
2	Navigate to the Administration - Server Management screen, Jobs view.
3	Click New in the Jobs list.

Step	Description
4	Click the select icon in the Component/Job field to open the component pick list.
5	Select either a component or a component job template from the pick list.
6	Optional: Set the Scheduled Start timestamp to a value other than the default value.
7	Optional: Set the Delete Interval and Delete Units fields (using the form applet in the middle of the view) to control the automatic purge of request data from the database table.
8	To define repeating jobs, use the Repeating Info section in the form applet to specify the interval of the repetitions.
9	Optional: To specify the behavior in the case of errors, use the fields in the Retry section.
10	Scroll down to the Job Parameters list at the bottom of the view.
11	For each parameter we need to override at the task level, we create a new record in the Job Parameters list and provide the parameter name and value.
12	In the upper list applet, click Submit Job.
13	Refresh the list by pressing *ALT+ENTER* and monitor the job execution status.
14	For repeating jobs, navigate to the Repeating Instances tab to monitor the instances of the job.

During its life cycle, a job's status field can have different values. The following table describes each job status:

Job Status	Traffic Light Icon Color	Description
Creating	Yellow	The job creation is in progress, changes can be made to fields and parameters.
Queued	Yellow	The job request has been submitted but no tasks are executing yet.
Active	Green	One-time jobs: A task is currently executing for the component defined in the job.
		Repeating jobs: Tasks are executed as scheduled.
Success	Green	The task for a one-time job has been successfully completed.
Completed	Green	All tasks for a repeating job have been successfully completed.
Error	Red	An error occurred during task execution.
Hold	Yellow	A repeating job has been put on hold. Tasks will not execute.
Canceled	Yellow	A job that has been queued or on hold has been canceled.

The Siebel server framework ensures that submitted jobs are executed by routing the job request to the appropriate server. If for some reason the requested component is unavailable, the job remains in queued state until the component becomes available.

For an administrator, it is important to understand that a component might become available just when a Siebel server is restarted. As there could be a large number of queued jobs for that component, the parallel execution of all the requested jobs upon server restart could negatively impact the Siebel server performance.

Using the Cancel Job button, we can cancel jobs that are in a queued or hold state. If we wish to execute the same job without having to specify all parameters again, we must copy an existing job definition using the Copy Record command—or the *CTRL+B* keyboard shortcut. Restarting a job is not possible.

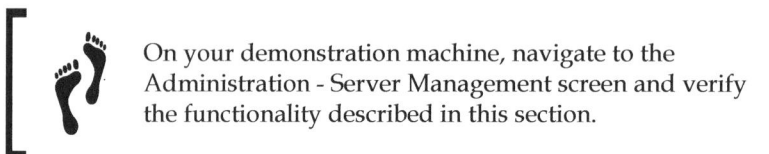

> On your demonstration machine, navigate to the Administration - Server Management screen and verify the functionality described in this section.

Using command line tools for Siebel server management

In the previous section of this chapter, we learned how to use the Siebel Web Client's views—the graphical user interface (GUI)—to perform various tasks related to configuring, managing, and monitoring servers and components within a Siebel enterprise.

Using the GUI has several benefits, such as the easier lookup and visualization of data. However, many administrators prefer to interact with the Siebel servers on a command line basis. Using commands at the command line is typically faster than using a graphical user interface. Furthermore, commands can be placed in script files, allowing administrators to accomplish complex tasks with a single keystroke.

Next, we will inspect the Siebel Server Manager command line utility and its commands. After this section, we will be able to accomplish the same tasks as have been described for the graphical user interface via the command line. These tasks are:

- Listing and reviewing information about the Siebel enterprise
- Backing up the enterprise configuration
- Listing and modifying parameters
- Creating and modifying component definitions
- Controlling assignment of component groups to Siebel servers
- Setting the start up mode of server components

- Controlling server components
- Running tasks for batch and background components

Before we begin, we will explore the basic command line utility, namely srvrmgr, which we must invoke before we can start issuing commands to the Siebel enterprise.

About the srvrmgr command line utility

The **Siebel Server Manager**—its official name—is a command line utility that can be located as an executable file for Microsoft Windows or UNIX-based operating systems. The srvrmgr.exe file (on Microsoft Windows) can be found in the `bin` directories of the Siebel Gateway Name Server, the Siebel server, or the Siebel Developer Web Client installation folders.

We can open a command shell, navigate to the folder containing the srvrmgr executable and simply type `srvrmgr` to obtain a list of required and optional input parameters.

If no parameters are specified, the executable generates a list of parameters.

The following table describes the input parameters for the srvrmgr executable:

Parameter	Description	Required?
/g	Gateway Name Server host name and port number (if different from 2320) separated by a colon.	Yes
/e	Enterprise name (Default: siebel).	Yes
/u	Username	Yes
/p	Password	Yes
/s	Logical Siebel server name to connect to.	No
/z	Name of a server group.	No
/l	Language for status messages (Default: ENU).	No
/i	Path to a text file containing commands.	No
/o	Path to an output file (used only together with /i).	No
/c	Followed by a single command to execute.	No
/m	Enable compression for message exchange with the Siebel Gateway Name Server.	No
/r	Enable encryption for message exchange with the Siebel Gateway Name Server.	No
/b	Used with /i to specify batch mode. The utility will exit on any error.	No
/h	Display the parameter list.	No

A typical command line to connect to a Siebel Gateway Name Server could look like the following:

`srvrmgr /g appsrvrgw1 /e SIEBELEVAL /u SADMIN /p TJay357D`

The above command will establish a connection to the Siebel Gateway Name Server on the `appsrvrgw1` machine, open the configuration store for the SIEBELEVAL enterprise, and authenticate as the user `SADMIN` using `TJay357D` as the password.

> We can omit the `/p` parameter and the password to avoid exposing the administrator's password on the screen or in text files. The srvrmgr utility will then prompt for the password and the keystrokes will not be printed to the screen.

If the information in the command line is correct and the Siebel Gateway Name Server is operational, we should see the Server Manager start up information and the `srvrmgr>` prompt.

Once logged in correctly, we can start issuing commands. Besides the information in the Oracle documentation (Siebel Bookshelf) we can also use the `help` command to assist us with the first steps at the srvrmgr> prompt. Typing `help` at the prompt provides a large list of possible commands.

We can use the `spool` command to write the information of the `help` command to a text file for better readability. At the srvrmgr> prompt, we enter a command similar to the following:

`spool c:\srvrmgr_help.txt`

`help`

`spool off`

The above commands will create a text file on the local C: drive named `srvrmgr_help.txt`. This text file now contains the output of the help command. The `spool off` command turns the spooling off to avoid other information being written to the text file. The screenshot below shows the beginning of the text file with the output of the `help` command:

As we can observe, the first command explained is the `list` command. It must be followed by a keyword such as **component groups** or an abbreviation such as **compgrps**.

The `help` command itself can also be followed by the name of a command we wish to view details about. The following command for example explains the usage of the `list session` command:

`help list session`

The following screenshot shows the output of the `help list session` command at the srvrmgr> command prompt:

```
srvrmgr> help list session

   list [active | hung] sessions
           [ for [ [app] server <server_name> ]
                 [ component <component_name> ]
                 [ login <om_login>            ] ]
```

We can observe that optional keywords such as **active** or **hung** can be inserted between the **list** and **sessions** keywords. In addition, the `list session` command allows the specification of server, component, or user login names. Optional keywords and commands are always put between square brackets in the help text.

Next, we will discuss typical administrative tasks and their srvrmgr command line syntax.

> If you wish to follow along with the examples, use the `help` command frequently to familiarize yourself with the syntax and possibilities of the Siebel Server Manager command line utility.

Listing and reviewing information about the Siebel enterprise

We can use the various `list` commands to review information about the building blocks of a Siebel enterprise. Viewing this information on the command line—or spooling it to files—is similar to using the list applets in the server management views in the Siebel Web Client.

Siebel Server Management

The following table describes the most important `list` commands that we can issue at the srvrmgr> prompt:

Command line	Output
list servers	List of all servers in the enterprise.
list compgrps	List of all component groups and their server assignment across the enterprise.
list compgrps for server Server1	List of all component groups assigned to server Server1.
list compdefs	List of all component definitions for the enterprise.
list comps for server Server1	List of all component, their startup mode and their current status for server Server1.
list params	List of all enterprise parameters and their current values..
list tasks	List of all tasks (running or completed) across all servers in the enterprise.
list active tasks	List of all tasks that are currently running across all servers in the enterprise.
list sessions	List of all object manager and system component sessions (running or completed).
list active sessions	List of all sessions that are currently running.
list named subsystems	List all enterprise profiles—called named subsystems at the Siebel Server Manager command line—for the enterprise.

Note: Server1 is an example of a logical Siebel server name.

As the output of the `list` command can be quite wide, it is recommended to adjust the settings for the command shell to allow more row width.

The `list` command can be used in conjunction with the `show` command to define the columns and their width to use for the output. The following command line serves as an example on how to retrieve only three columns of information about tasks.

```
list tasks for comp SCC% show CC_ALIAS, TK_DISP_RUNSTATE(10), TK_LABEL
```

We can learn from this example that the `show` command must be followed by a comma-separated list of precisely written column names. Column names can be followed by the desired number of characters to display in parentheses.

Furthermore, we can use the percentage sign (%) as a wildcard character to filter the information in the list output as indicated in the above example. The following screenshot shows the output of the example command:

```
srvrmgr> list tasks for comp SCC% show CC_ALIAS, TK_DISP_RUNSTATE(10), TK_LABEL

CC_ALIAS        TK_DISP_RU  TK_LABEL
------------    ----------  --------
SCCObjMgr_enu   Running     SADMIN
SCCObjMgr_enu   Completed   SADMIN
SCCObjMgr_enu   Completed   SADMIN
SCCObjMgr_enu   Completed   SADMIN
SCCObjMgr_enu   Completed   SADMIN
SCCObjMgr_enu   Completed   SADMIN
SCCObjMgr_enu   Completed   SADMIN
SCCObjMgr_enu   Completed   SADMIN
SCCObjMgr_enu   Completed   SADMIN

9 rows returned.
```

Backing up the enterprise configuration

As discussed in previous sections of this chapter, we should consider creating a backup copy of the `siebns.dat` file before we undertake major modifications. We learned that this can be accomplished by pressing the Backup Enterprise button in the graphical user interface (GUI).

At the srvrmgr> prompt, we can use the following command to accomplish the same task:

`backup namesrvr`

The command can be optionally followed by a file path, which allows us to define the location and name of the backup file.

Listing and modifying parameters

In the above sections, we already learned about the `list params` command, which allows us to create lists of parameters at various levels such as enterprise, server, component definition, or component.

If we wish to modify parameters, we have to use the `change param` command followed by the parameter's alias name, an equals sign, and the new value for the parameter. The following is an example:

`change param EnableEAIMemoryMetrics=True for compdef eaiobjmgr_enu`

The above command changes the value of the parameter `EnableEAIMemoryMetrics` of the EAI Object Manager component definition to `True`. We can obtain the alias name of parameters by using the `list params` command.

We can combine multiple parameter-value pairs to a comma-separated list such as in the following example:

```
change param MaxMTServers=2,MaxTasks=100 for comp sccobjmgr_enu server Eval_1
```

Using a command similar to the above, we can change two parameters at once. The example shows how to change the values for the `MaxMTServers` and the `MaxTasks` parameter to `2` and `100` respectively. The change is made for the Call Center Object manager component on the `Eval_1` server.

> The `MaxMTServers` parameter defines the maximum number of multi-threaded operating system processes that can be instantiated for the component. The `MaxTasks` parameter defines the maximum number of threads—or tasks—for the component.
>
> Setting these two parameters allows administrators to adjust the CPU and memory allocation on the Siebel server machines.

Creating and modifying component definitions

Even if it is not a daily task, a Siebel server administrator must be able to create additional component definitions and make the respective components available in the enterprise.

The following example explains how to use the `create compdef` command to create a new component definition for a workflow monitor agent.

> Workflow monitor agents are background components that monitor the Siebel database for certain events and execute the actions defined in so-called workflow policies.

```
create compdef EvalWorkMon for comptype WorkMon compgrp Workflow run mode background full name "Evaluation Workflow Monitor Agent" desc "Created for testing purposes" with param SleepTime=20,GroupName="Assignment Group",DfltTasks=1
```

When we inspect the example more closely we find that the new component definition will have an alias name of `EvalWorkMon`, its component type will be set to `WorkMon` and it will belong to the `Workflow` component group. The run mode will be `background`. The above example also shows how to set the full name and description text for the new component definition as well as how to provide values for some parameters. Setting parameters could also be done in a separate command.

In order to make the new component definition available, we must activate it using the following command:

`activate compdef EvalWorkMon`

The `activate compdef` command sets the component definition's status from `Creating` to `Active`, thus enabling the instantiation of components. However, the new components will not be available on any Siebel server before the server itself is restarted.

It is highly recommended to put complex commands like the above example in text files. The reason for this is that the text file can be saved and reused later to create the same component definition in other environments, which is a very likely scenario.

Furthermore, storing the creation scripts and other frequently used commands in text files allows for easier documentation of changes.

The `read` command can be used to open a text file and execute the commands in that file while we have a Siebel Server Manager session window open. The following example explains how to use the read command:

`read c:\temp\create_custom_compdefs.txt`

Entering this line at the svrmgr> prompt will open the file specified in the path and execute all commands contained in that file.

Controlling assignment of component groups to Siebel servers

The Siebel Server Manager command line also allows administrators to control the assignment and enablement of component groups to Siebel servers.

The following table provides examples for assigning, enabling, disabling, and removing a component group association for a Siebel server:

Command Example	Description
`assign compgrp workflow to server Eval_1`	The command assigns the component group Workflow to the server Eval_1.
`enable compgrp workflow for server Eval_1`	The command enables the component group Workflow on the server Eval_1. Components within this group will be available after server restart.
`disable compgrp workflow for server Eval_1`	The command disables the component group Workflow on the Server Eval_1. Components will no longer be available on the server once it is restarted.

Command Example	Description
`remove compgrp workflow from server Eval_1`	The command removes the assignment of the component group Workflow from the server Eval_1.

As we learned in this chapter, component groups are already pre-assigned to all Siebel servers but not yet enabled. If our task is to enable a component group on a specific server, the only command needed would be similar to the following:

`enable compgrp workflow for server Eval_1`

We must restart the Siebel server for the changes to take effect.

Setting the start up mode of server components

In order to speed up the start up of a Siebel server, it is beneficial to set certain components to manual start up. This will cause the component to be in shutdown state when the server is started, thus consuming no CPU or memory.

The Siebel Server Manager command to set components to manual start up mode is similar to the following example:

`manual start comp sccobjmgr_deu for server Eval_1`

The above command sets the start up mode for the German Call Center object manager on server `Eval_1` to manual.

To set the start up mode to automatic, we can use a command similar to the following:

`auto start comp sccobjmgr_deu for server Eval_1`

To view the current start up mode for a server's components, we can use a command similar to the following:

`list comps for server Eval_1 show CC_ALIAS, CP_STARTMODE`

> To avoid having to specify the Siebel server name with every command, we can use the /s flag with the srvrmgr executable followed by the Siebel server's logical name. During a srvrmgr session, we can use the `set server` command followed by the logical Siebel server name to focus the prompt on that server.

Controlling server components

Similar to using the buttons on the component list applets in the Server management screen in the Siebel web client, we can issue commands at the srvrmgr> prompt to control the state of server components.

The following table describes the commands to control server components. As discussed above, we can use the `set server` command followed by the logical Siebel server name to specify the target server for the commands. The examples in the table assume that the server has been set, and use the English Call Center object manager as the target component.

Command Example	Command applicable when component is in state(s)	Final component state(s)
`startup comp sccobjmgr_enu`	Shutdown	Online, Running
`shutdown comp sccobjmgr_enu`	Online, Running, Unavailable	Shutdown
`shutdown fast comp sccobjmgr_enu`	Online, Running, Unavailable	Shutdown Note: The `shutdown fast` command enforces the shutdown irrespective of the state of tasks for the target component.
`pause comp sccobjmgr_enu`	Online, Running	Paused
`resume comp sccobjmgr_enu`	Paused	Online, Running
`kill comp sccobjmgr_enu`	Any state	Shutdown Note: the `kill comp` command should only be used when the component is hung and there is no other way to shut it down safely.

To verify the current state of server components, we can use a command similar to the following:

`list comps for server Eval_1 show CC_NAME, CP_RUN_STATE`

The above command will write the component name and the current run state of all components hosted by Siebel server `Eval_1` to the console.

Running jobs for batch and background components

While the graphical user interface (GUI) allows administrators to store job templates and repeating job definitions for batch components, the Siebel Server Manager command line only provides commands to start tasks—the server manager term for jobs—immediately. However, if we wish to invoke a task for a background component while the Siebel server is running, the command line is the only location to accomplish that.

In the following example, we use the `start task` command to invoke a task for the Generate New Database component.

```
start task for comp gennewdb with sqlflags=1
```

The above command invokes a task for the Generate New Database component and passes one parameter override to the task.

Using input files

As indicated in this and previous chapters, it is highly recommended to use input files to store complex command combinations. We can use the /i flag with the srvrmgr executable to direct it to read the file at the path following the flag and execute all commands in the file. The following is an example for a command line that invokes the Siebel Server Manager and executes the contents of a text file:

```
srvrmgr /g appsrvrgw1 /e SIEBELEVAL /u SADMIN /p TJay357D /i c:\daily_batch.txt /o c:\daily_batch_log.txt
```

When this command is executed in a command shell, the Siebel server manager will connect to the Siebel Gateway Name Server on `appsrvrgw1` machine, open the `SIEBELEVAL` enterprise configuration store, and log in as user `SADMIN`. The executable will open the `daily_batch.txt` file on the local C: drive, execute all commands in the file and exit on completion. The complete output that would be typically written to the command shell will be directed to the `daily_batch_log.txt` file on the C: drive.

Commands similar to the above can be placed in script files, which can subsequently be registered in a scheduling facility such as the Microsoft Windows task scheduler or cron if we are using Linux or other UNIX-based operating systems.

> On your demonstration machine, use the srvrmgr executable and experiment with the commands explained in this chapter.

Summary

Administering Siebel enterprises, their servers and components is a complex endeavour. Oracle's Siebel CRM provides two built-in tools to assist administrators with their daily tasks regarding server monitoring, maintenance, and troubleshooting.

In this chapter, we explored these tools, namely the server management views in the Siebel web client, which provide a graphical user interface (GUI) and the Siebel Server Manager command line tool srvrmgr.

An introduction to the concepts of the building blocks of a Siebel enterprise was given as well.

Using typical server management scenarios like listing server components and their current run state or creating job requests, we explored the various ways to professionally manage Siebel servers, components and tasks within a Siebel enterprise.

In the next chapter, we will cover the mechanisms of user authentication in Siebel CRM.

10
User Authentication

When we prepare a Siebel environment for productive use, we have to carefully select the technology for user authentication. A typical Siebel CRM deployment caters for hundreds, if not thousands of end users. Their user accounts, passwords, and privileges must be administered in the most professional manner possible. Avoiding redundant user accounts across various systems is the most crucial aspect of professional user administration. In this chapter, we will explore the technical concepts of user authentication in Siebel CRM. The chapter will be structured as follows:

- User authentication concepts
- Database authentication
- LDAP server authentication
- Web Single-Sign-On (SSO)

User authentication concepts in Siebel CRM

We can distinguish three concepts of user authentication in Siebel CRM:

- Database authentication (default)
- Directory server authentication (LDAP or Microsoft Active Directory)
- Web Single-Sign-On (SSO)

While these concepts are supported by built-in functionality, Siebel CRM also supports custom authentication solutions by providing a software development kit (SDK) to develop a custom security adapter.

User Authentication

Before we describe each of the user authentication concepts in greater detail, we should explore the general Siebel CRM authentication architecture and its main building block, the security adapter. The following diagram represents the Siebel CRM authentication architecture and the flow of a user authentication request in two scenarios:

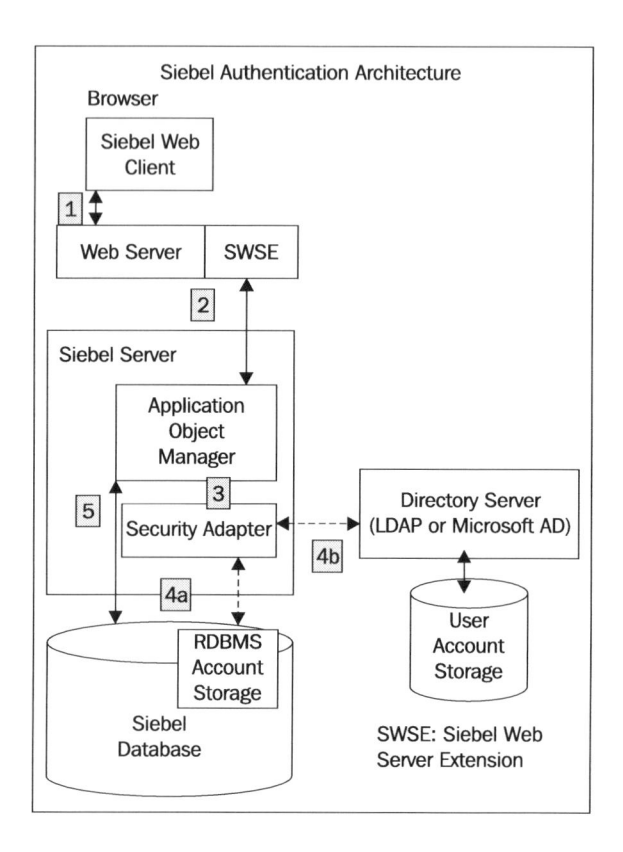

We can describe these two scenarios as follows:

1. The end user provides username and password (summarized as user credentials) on the web client's login page.
2. The Siebel Web Server Extension (SWSE) forwards the login request and the user credentials to the application object manager.
3. Each application object manager is associated with a security adapter, which it invokes in order to authenticate the user.

4a. If the security adapter used by the application object manager is a database security adapter, it connects to a relational database management system (RDBMS) and verifies the user credentials. The RDBMS can be—and is by default—the same that is used to host the Siebel database, but this is not mandatory.

4b. If the security adapter is configured for the Lightweight Directory Access Protocol (LDAP), it connects to a third-party directory server, verifies the user credentials, and retrieves the so-called proxy user credentials. Proxy user credentials are username and password pairs that are also present as an RDBMS account.

5. If the security adapter reports successful user authentication, the application object manager establishes a database connection using either the end user's account (scenario 4a) or the proxy user account (scenario 4b).

> Independent of the database user account being used for the physical database connection, changes to the records in the database are always made on the end user's behalf, thus allowing auditing and usage tracking on an individual basis. Data visibility is also controlled by the end user's account and not the one of the proxy user.

There are several noteworthy details regarding the way Siebel CRM handles user authentication:

- User accounts (including passwords) are always managed outside of Siebel CRM
- Each user must be registered as such and associated with a responsibility in the Siebel application
- The security adapter is a reusable software library that works in conjunction with Siebel server components
- Application object managers and other Siebel server components can be associated with one security adapter at a time
- Developers at customer sites can use the SDK provided by Oracle to write their own custom security adapter to connect to any authentication system

We will now explore the built-in techniques of Siebel CRM user authentication.

Database authentication

Using the account management of a relational database management system (RDBMS) for user authentication is the default configuration of Siebel CRM. For example during the installation of the Siebel database—as discussed in previous chapters—we must create user accounts in the RDBMS that hosts the Siebel database.

This preconfigured behaviour of Siebel CRM is useful during installation and for small evaluation, development, or test environments to which only a limited number of users have access. Production environments will hardly ever use database authentication.

In the following sections, we will explore the preconfigured settings that enable the default database authentication.

Security adapters are defined as enterprise profiles

Each security adapter is implemented as an enterprise profile. As discussed in Chapter 9, enterprise profiles are reusable collections of parameters. They are referenced by their alias name in parameters of other members of the Siebel enterprise such as component definitions.

The following screenshot shows the three preconfigured security adapter definitions in the **Profile Configuration** view of the Administration - Server Configuration screen.

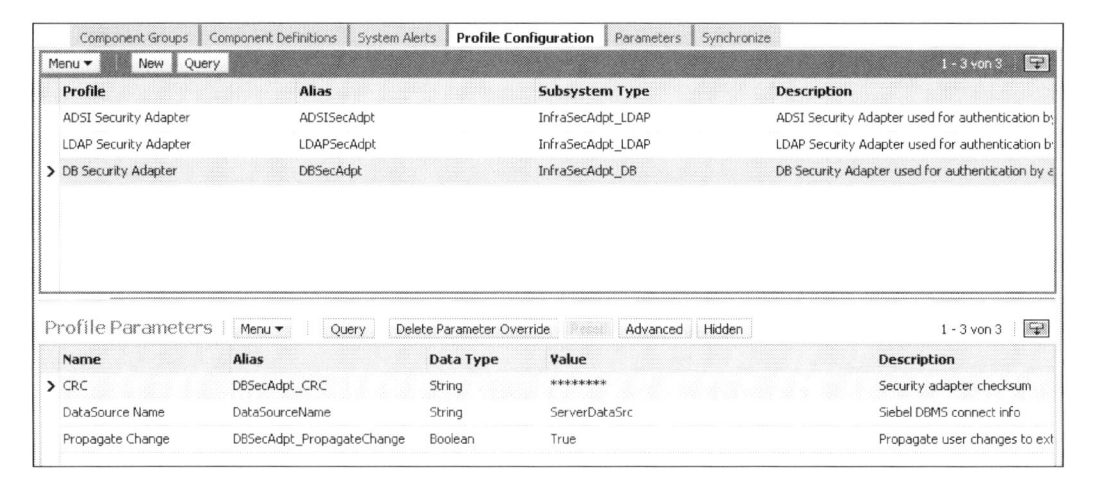

We can observe that the **DB Security Adapter** is selected and is of type **InfraSecAdpt_DB**, which defines a small list of parameters (three normal and one advanced parameter). The **DataSourceName** parameter of the DB Security Adapter profile references the **ServerDataSrc** profile, which in turn provides the physical connectivity information to the Siebel database.

The only advanced parameter in this profile (not visible in the screenshot) is the name of the library file (.dll on Microsoft Windows and .so on UNIX-based operating systems) that implements the security adapter's program logic.

Associating a security adapter with a server component

Each server component that needs to establish user sessions is associated with a security adapter by means of the **Security Adapter Name** parameter.

The screenshot below shows the component definition for the Call Center Object Manager (ENU) component as the selected record in the **Component Definitions** view in the Administration - Server Configuration screen:

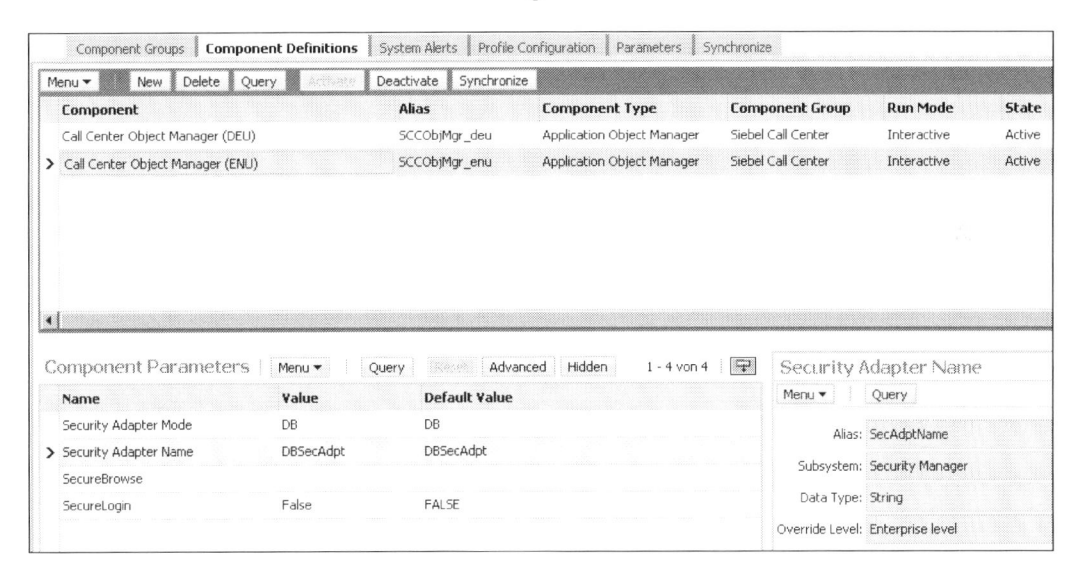

We can observe that the **Security Adapter Name** parameter value is the alias name of the DB Security Adapter profile (**DBSecAdpt**). Furthermore, the **Security Adapter Mode** parameter is set to **DB**, indicating that user authentication is done via a relational database.

Both parameters are set on the enterprise level by default. This can be verified by reviewing the **Override Level** field in the lower-right form applet of the view. The fact that these two parameters are set on the enterprise level—and that their values are therefore inherited downward in the enterprise hierarchy—confirms that database authentication is the default user authentication behaviour for all component definitions.

Managing user accounts for database authentication

If we wish to provide an end user access to the Siebel CRM application by means of database authentication, we must ensure that a database account exists for that user. In addition, the user must be registered in the Siebel application as a user or employee. Registering users or employees in the Siebel application will be discussed in Chapter 12.

Depending on the tool set available for the RDBMS we use, we have the choice how we manage user accounts. In most projects, the database administrator (DBA) is controlling the creation and modification of user accounts in the RDBMS.

The following script example gives us an idea how a new user account is created in an Oracle database. We can use the respective lines in the `grantusr.sql` file in the `ORACLE` folder of the Database Server Utilities installation directory as a guideline for creating our own scripts:

```
create user EVALUSER identified by EVALPWD;
grant sse_role to EVALUSER;
alter user EVALUSER default tablespace SIEBELDB_DATA;
alter user EVALUSER temporary tablespace TEMP;
```

The script creates a new user account with the name of `EVALUSER` and assigns a password (`EVALPWD`) to it.

The `grant` command assigns the role `sse_role` to the user account. This role has been created during the initial Siebel database installation process.

The assignment of the default and temporary tablespaces completes the script. The `SIEBELB_DATA` tablespace has been created during the Siebel database installation process.

Scripts similar to the example above must be executed against the RDBMS in order to create the database account needed to enable database authentication. Alternatively, a DBA can of course use graphical user interfaces to create and manage database user accounts.

Directory server authentication

For Siebel CRM deployments that support hundreds or thousands of users, it is very likely that the administrative overhead of managing user accounts for Siebel applications in the RDBMS is too high. Furthermore, it is more reasonable to use existing centralized user account management systems, which typically provide a higher level of manageability and security than RDBMS account management.

For these reasons, Siebel CRM supports a variety of LDAP (Lightweight Directory Access Protocol) based directory servers as well as Microsoft Active Directory. The following table lists the directory server vendors (in alphabetical order) and their products that are supported with Siebel CRM version 8.1.

Vendor	Product	Supported Protocols
IBM	Tivoli Directory Server	LDAP
Microsoft	Active Directory	LDAP and ADSI
Novell	NDS eDirectory	LDAP
Oracle	Internet Directory	LDAP
Oracle/Sun	Java System Directory Server	LDAP

Source: *Siebel Security Guide, Version 8.1*

```
http://download.oracle.com/docs/cd/E14004_01/books/Secur/
booktitle.html
```

In the following, we will discuss the setup and configuration of LDAP-based authentication for a Siebel application. The high-level process is as follows:

1. Install the directory server (when needed).
2. Install the IBM LDAP client on Siebel server and client machines.
3. Create user accounts in the directory server.
4. Verify the proxy account.
5. Configure the LDAP Security Adapter.
6. Configure server components.
7. Verify LDAP authentication.
8. Configure the Siebel Gateway Name Server for LDAP authentication (optional).
9. Configure Siebel clients for LDAP authentication (optional).

The following diagram depicts the non-optional steps of the process of configuring LDAP authentication:

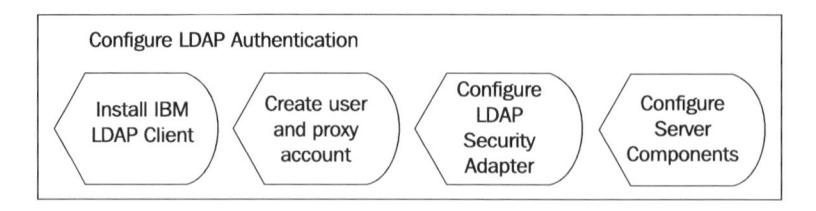

Installing the directory server (optional)

It is very unlikely that a directory server does not exist in the network infrastructure of the company that deploys Siebel CRM or that the existing directory server will not be used for Siebel CRM users.

In that case, we must purchase and install one of the supported directory servers according to the software vendor's instructions. Installing and configuring directory servers is beyond the scope of this book and therefore not discussed.

Installing the IBM LDAP Client

In order to allow the processes on Siebel servers and clients to connect to the directory server, the IBM LDAP Client must be installed on each machine that hosts a Siebel application for which we wish to enable LDAP authentication. The IBM LDAP client must be installed independent of the directory server vendor.

The IBM LDAP Client is delivered as part of the download archives for Siebel CRM on the Oracle E-Delivery website (http://edelivery.oracle.com). If we have not already downloaded the IBM LDAP client installer, we must do so now. The download archive "Siebel Business Applications Version 8.1.1.0 Base Applications for Windows (Part 2 of 2)" typically contains the installer for the IBM LDAP Client.

If we have not already done so, we must also extract the .jar file from the downloaded .zip archive and use the Siebel Network Image Creator to create the installation image files. Downloading Siebel installation archives and using the Siebel Network Image Creator has already been discussed in detail in Chapter 2.

The following screenshot shows the installation image for the IBM LDAP Client after extraction:

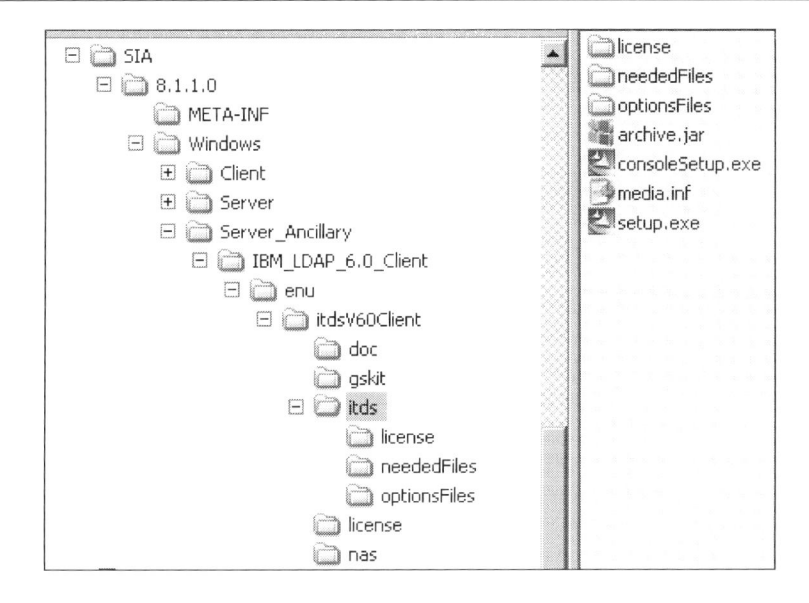

The itds folder (IBM Tivoli Directory Server) contains the installation executables.

The following table describes the process of the IBM LDAP Client installation on Microsoft Windows:

Step	Description	Tasks and Example Values
1	Start the InstallShield Wizard.	Double-click the setup.exe file in the itds folder.
2	Choose a setup language.	Choose **English**. Click **OK**.
3	The welcome dialog is displayed.	Click **Next**.
4	License Agreement	Select **I accept...** Click **Next**.
5	Installation Directory	Keep the default directory. Click **Next**.
6	Feature selection.	Select **Client SDK 6.0** Unselect **GSKit**. Note: The Global Security Kit (GSKit) is only required when client-server communication needs to be encrypted using SSL. Click **Next**.

Step	Description	Tasks and Example Values
7	Summary	Check the information in the summary dialog.
		Click **Next**.
8	The installation progress is displayed.	Wait for the installation to finish.
9	The InstallShield wizard success dialog is displayed.	Click **Finish**.

The installation process on Linux and other UNIX-based operating systems is similar. However, to finalize the installation on these operating systems, we must edit the environment preparation scripts (`siebenv.sh` or `siebenv.csh`) and add the path to the `lib` directory of the IBM LDAP client to the lines that set the library path variables.

The installation procedure must be repeated on each machine that will host a Siebel application that uses LDAP authentication. These could be machines that host any of the following Siebel software units:

- Siebel Gateway Name Server
- Siebel Server
- Siebel Developer Web Client
- Siebel Tools

> If you wish to practice the procedures described in the following sections, you should obtain and install both a suitable LDAP directory server and the IBM LDAP client as described above.

Creating user accounts in the directory server

For each user that should be able to access the Siebel application, a valid and active account must exist in the LDAP directory tree. Typically, as the directory server is most likely already in use for other systems than Siebel CRM, these accounts probably already exist.

To ensure a minimum amount of administrative overhead, a **shared credentials** account should be added to the LDAP directory tree. This special account will carry the information about the so-called proxy database account, a username and password combination that the Siebel application will use for each user to physically connect to the Siebel database.

In addition, the so called **anonymous users** as specified in the Siebel Web Server Extension's (SWSE) configuration file (`eapps.cfg`) must be added to the LDAP directory tree. The anonymous users are typically created during the initial installation phase and allow the application object manager to retrieve, for example, the login page template.

Creating the shared credentials account

Depending on the directory server vendor, there might be different approaches to log in to the directory server administration console and create directory entries. We should follow the vendor's documentation and create a user with attributes similar to the following example:

Attribute	Example Value	Description
First Name	Shared	First name of the shared credential account.
Last Name	Credentials	Last name of the shared credential account.
Common Names	Shared Credentials	Common name of the shared credential account.
User ID	SCredentials	Maps to the **uid** attribute in LDAP.
Password	T67PBhtr	A secure password should be chosen and documented.
E-Mail	type=ServerDataSrc username=LDAPUSER password=BFxR87DT type=GatewayDataSrc username=SADMIN password = TJay357D	The **mail** attribute used to store the proxy account information by default. See below for a detailed explanation.
Description	Shared account for Siebel CRM LDAP authentication.	Optional.

In the above example, we use the E-Mail field to store two parameter triplets, which define the data source and the proxy user account name and password to use to connect to that data source.

```
type=ServerDataSrc username=LDAPUSER password=BFxR87DT
type=GatewayDataSrc username=SADMIN password=TJay357D
```

For each data source that is used by the application, we must define one line similar to the above example. **ServerDataSrc** and **GatewayDataSrc** are the default data sources for a standard Siebel CRM application. Depending on the integration with external systems, the development team might provide additional data source names.

The **type** parameter value must be set to the alias name of a valid Siebel enterprise profile that defines a data source for the application object manager. The **username** and **password** parameter values must be set to a valid user account for the respective data source. In the above example, LDAPUSER is the account that the application object manager will use to connect to the Siebel server database. Therefore, an account with the name LDAPUSER must exist in the Siebel server database. In addition, LDAPUSER must be registered as a user and associated with an appropriate responsibility in the Siebel application.

The following screenshot shows an example shared credentials account defined in the administration console for the SUN Java Directory Server:

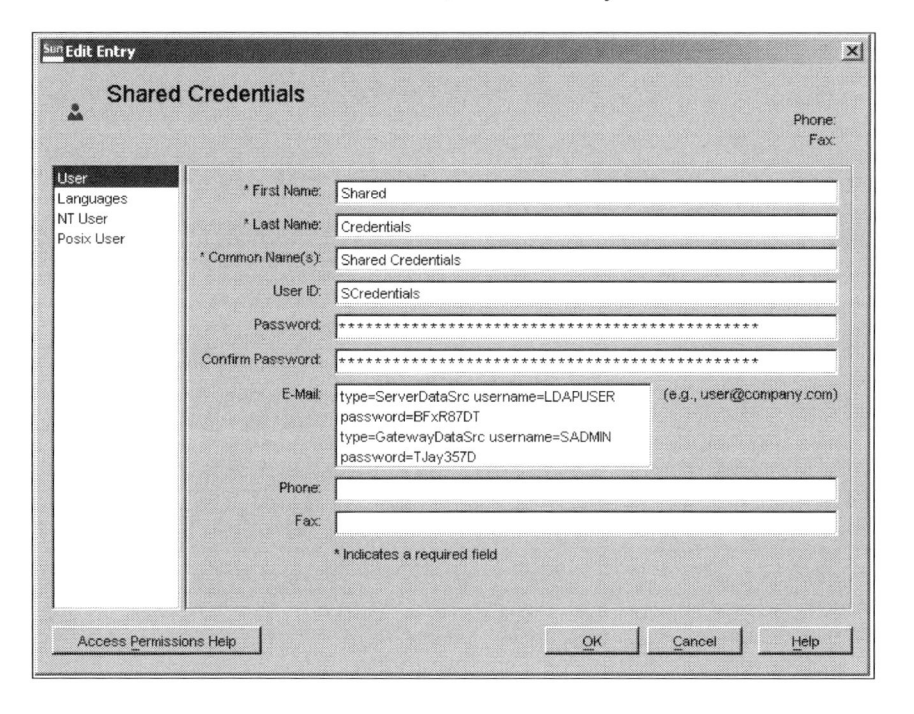

We are free to use any multi-valued attribute to store the proxy account information. However, if we choose a field different from the mail attribute, we must specify that field later during configuration of the enterprise profile for the LDAP Security Adapter.

Creating the anonymous user accounts

Every Siebel application uses an anonymous user account to create the initial object manager session. This session is necessary to provide a user interface to the end user where she or he can enter the login credentials or browse anonymously.

The following screenshot shows the homepage for the Siebel eService application:

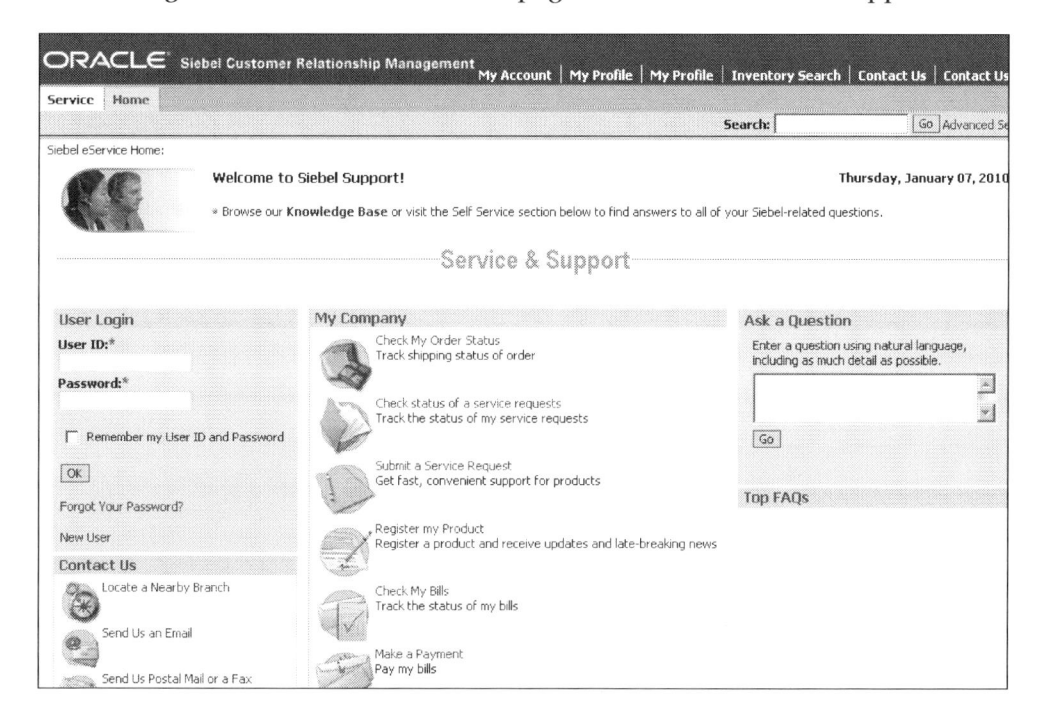

This view is generated by the eService application object manager using the anonymous user account. We can observe that the User Login form in the left column of the page allows the user to authenticate by entering a **User ID** and a **Password**.

Depending on the type of application or the definition in the Siebel Web Server Extension's (SWSE) configuration file (`eapps.cfg`), different anonymous user accounts might exist. We must therefore consult either the planning documentation or the `eapps.cfg` file—located in the BIN directory of the SWSE installation folder—to obtain the list of anonymous user accounts to create in the LDAP directory tree.

The following screenshot shows the section for the **eservice_enu** virtual directory in the SWSE configuration file `eapps.cfg`:

```
[/eservice_enu]
AnonUserName    = GUESTCST
AnonPassword    = wX3P7ChSRrgRJLzxjc3YfgGjjJgx
ConnectString   = siebel.TCPIP.None.None://VirtualServer/SIEBELEVAL/eServiceObjMgr_enu
StartCommand    = SWECmd=GotoView&SWEView=Home+Page+View+(eService)
WebPublicRootDir = C:\SIA82\SWEApp\public\enu
SiebEntSecToken = Dlxk5rwOTLwBo4yYMQ==
```

In the example, the eService object manager will use the **GUESTCST** account as the anonymous account, indicated by the **AnonUserName** parameter's value. We can also observe that passwords are stored encrypted in the `eapps.cfg` file.

If the parameter **AnonUserName** is not present in a virtual directory definition, the parameter definition in the **[defaults]** section of the `eapps.cfg` file applies.

The screenshot below shows the **[defaults]** section of the SWSE configuration file:

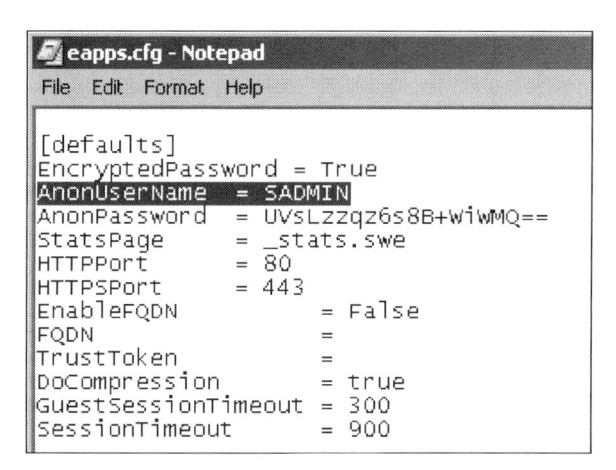

```
[defaults]
EncryptedPassword = True
AnonUserName    = SADMIN
AnonPassword    = UVsLzzqz6s8B+WiWMQ==
StatsPage       = _stats.swe
HTTPPort        = 80
HTTPSPort       = 443
EnableFQDN               = False
FQDN                     =
TrustToken               =
DoCompression            = true
GuestSessionTimeout      = 300
SessionTimeout           = 900
```

We see that SADMIN is used as the anonymous account for each application that has no anonymous user defined in the corresponding section in the `eapps.cfg` file.

With the information collected about anonymous user accounts, we can use the tools provided by the directory server vendor to create corresponding accounts in the LDAP directory.

The screenshot above shows the LDAP directory entry for the **SADMIN** account.

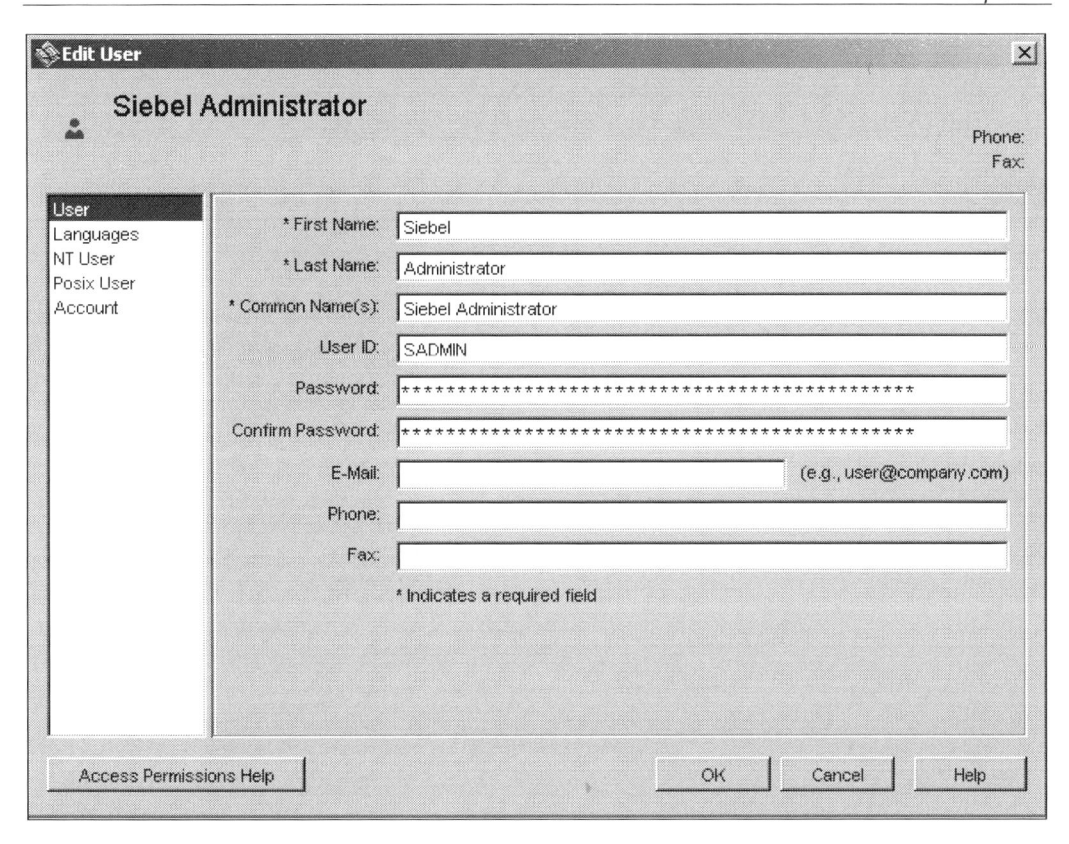

[Screenshot of Edit User dialog for Siebel Administrator]

We can observe that the **E-Mail** field is blank. As we use the shared credentials account to specify the proxy account information, we do not have to repeat this information for the other entries in the directory.

Setting access permissions for LDAP accounts

Depending on our company policy or the security settings in the directory server, we might have to maintain additional security information in the LDAP directory. This information includes allowing users or groups to change, add, or delete directory entries.

For example, if we wish to enable user self registration for customer-facing applications such as Siebel eService or Siebel eSales, we must allow the anonymous user account to create additional accounts in the directory.

We must consult the directory server vendor documentation to understand how to apply the access permissions.

> On your demonstration system, create the necessary LDAP directory entries for the shared credentials account, the anonymous users, and test users.

Verifying the proxy account

Before we configure the server components to authenticate users via the directory server, we must ensure that the proxy accounts specified in the shared credentials account are valid.

We can accomplish this by logging in to the respective data source using the username and password in the proxy account information. For example if we specified **LDAPUSER** as the username for the Server data source, we should be able to log in to the Siebel server database using **LDAPUSER** as the username.

For an Oracle database, we can use the SQL*Plus command line utility to verify the user account. The following screenshot shows the successful login to the Oracle SQL*Plus command line tool using the **LDAPUSER** account:

```
C:\>sqlplus LDAPUSER/LDAPUSER

SQL*Plus: Release 10.2.0.1.0 - Production on Thu Jan 7 02:52:43 2010

Copyright (c) 1982, 2005, Oracle.  All rights reserved.

Connected to:
Oracle Database 10g Enterprise Edition Release 10.2.0.1.0 - Production
With the Partitioning, OLAP and Data Mining options
```

In addition, we should log in to the Siebel Web Client as an administrative user and verify that a corresponding user is registered in either the Users or Employees administration views in the Administration - User screen.

> If not already done, verify the existence of both the database account and the Siebel user or employee for the proxy user you have chosen.

Configuring the LDAP Security Adapter

The LDAP Security Adapter is defined as an enterprise profile. As we learned in Chapter 9, we can use either the server management views in the Siebel web client or the Siebel Server Manager command line to modify parameters of enterprise profiles.

Because of the enterprise-wide implications of switching to directory server authentication, it is highly recommended to use the capability of the Siebel Server Manager command line to read and execute script files. The benefits of storing commands that manipulate the server configuration in a script file are mainly that the changes are documented in the file and the changes can be quickly applied in other Siebel environments.

The following script should serve as an example of how to configure the LDAP security adapter:

```
backup namesrvr
change param ApplicationUser='uid=admin,ou=Administrators,ou=TopologyM
anagement,o=NetscapeRoot',
ApplicationPassword=LdApAdMin,
SharedCredentialsDN='uid=SCredentials,ou=Special
Users,dc=us,dc=oracle,dc=com',
BaseDn='ou=People,dc=us,dc=oracle,dc=com',
Port=15313,
ServerName=osappeval1,
SharedDBUsername=SADMIN,
SharedDBPassword=TJay357D,
SiebelUsernameAttributeType=uid,
UsernameAttributeType=uid
for named subsystem LDAPSecAdpt
spool c:\ldap_config_log.txt
list params for named subsystem LDAPSecAdpt
spool off
```

The above script—stored in a text file and executed via the Siebel Server Manager command line—does the following. Note that line breaks have been added to the script to allow better readability.

The `backup namesrvr` command ensures that the current `siebns.dat` file is copied to a safe backup file.

User Authentication

The `change param` command sets several parameters for the LDAPSecAdpt named subsystem (recall that named subsystem is the term used by the Siebel Server Manager command line for enterprise profiles). The following table describes the parameters:

Parameter	Example Value	Description
`ApplicationUser`	`uid=admin,ou=Administrators,ou=TopologyManagement,o=NetscapeRoot`	A valid distinguished name (DN) that identifies a directory user with sufficient privileges to look up other entries in the directory.
`ApplicationPassword`	`LdApAdMin`	The password for the application user.
`SharedCredentialsDN`	`uid=SCredentials,ou=Special Users,dc=us,dc=oracle,dc=com`	The DN of the user account that stores the proxy account information.
`BaseDn`	`ou=People,dc=us,dc=oracle,dc=com`	The DN of a group where the user accounts are stored.
`Port`	`15313`	The port number that the LDAP directory server is listening on.
`ServerName`	`osappeval1`	The host name of the machine that the LDAP directory server is running on.
`SharedDBUsername`	`SADMIN`	A valid DB user account. Must be a registered Siebel user.
`SharedDBPassword`	`TJay357D`	The password for the shared DB user account.
`SiebelUsernameAttributeType`	`uid`	The LDAP attribute that contains the Siebel user's Login Id.
`UsernameAttributeType`	`uid`	The LDAP attribute used to match with the username provided by the end user.

The `spool` and `list` commands at the end of the script write the new configuration of the LDAP security adapter to a text file for later retrieval. Spooling information to text files is a common practice in Siebel server management.

Configuring server components

For each application object manager that we wish to authenticate its user sessions via the directory server, we have to specify two parameters. Again, we should do this via a reusable script file in order to document the changes. The script could be similar to the following:

```
set server Eval_1
change param SecAdptMode=LDAP for comp sccobjmgr_enu
change param SecAdptName=LDAPSecAdpt for comp sccobjmgr_enu
```

The script switches the focus of the srvrmgr> prompt to the server `Eval_1`. It then modifies the English Call Center object manager instance on that server by changing the value of the parameter `SecAdptMode` to `LDAP` and the `SecAdptName` parameter value to the alias name of the LDAP Security Adapter enterprise profile, namely `LDAPSecAdpt`.

After such changes, the component must be restarted using commands similar to the following:

```
shutdown fast comp sccobjmgr_enu
startup comp sccobjmgr_enu
```

Before restarting application object managers, it is highly recommended—at least on production systems—to verify that no sessions are currently running. Alternatively, end users should be notified before the component is shut down. A command similar to the following can be used at the srvrmgr> prompt to list active sessions for an application object manager:

```
list active sessions for comp sccobjmgr_enu
```

We can notify end users about the imminent shut down, for example by using the Message Broadcast feature of Siebel CRM.

> On your demonstration machine, use the commands described in the above sections to modify the LDAP security adapter enterprise profile and a selected application object manager.

Verifying LDAP authentication

In order to verify that the object manager successfully authenticates both anonymous and registered user logins, we must establish a session by navigating to the application URL in a browser window.

In addition, we can temporarily increase the event log level for the security adapter related events by using a srvrmgr command similar to the following:

```
change evtloglvl SecAdptLog=5,SecMgrLog=5 for comp sccobjmgr_enu
```

This command sets the event log level for the Security Adapter Log and Security Manager Log events to a value of 5 for the English Call Center object manager, thus increasing the amount of information in the object manager's log file.

As usual, we should remember to set the log level back to 0 or 1 once the testing phase is complete.

If we receive an error when trying to access the Siebel application URL, we must check the log file for messages indicating the source of the failure. If we see the login page for the application in the browser window, we should be able to log in using any user account that is currently present in the LDAP directory and registered as a Siebel user.

> After ensuring that all necessary services are restarted, navigate to the application URL on your demonstration machine and verify that you can log in using your test LDAP account (for example SADMIN).

Registering a new user

To verify that the security settings in the LDAP directory allow the registration of new users, we should log in to the Siebel application using an administrative user account such as SADMIN.

We then navigate to the Site Map, select the Administration - User screen and click the hyperlink for the Employees view. In that view we can use the Copy Record command (*CTRL+B* is the keyboard shortcut) and create a copy of the employee record for SADMIN. In the new record, we specify the fields described in the following table:

Field	Example Value	Description
First Name	LDAP	Choose a value that indicates a test purpose.
Last Name	Test	Choose a value that indicates a test purpose.
User ID	TLDAP	Must be unique.
Password	TLDAP	The password field should be writeable when LDAP authentication is properly set up.
Confirm Password	TLDAP	The password confirmation field should be writeable as well.

After setting the field values, we click the Save command in the applet menu (or press *CTRL+S* on the keyboard) to save the record.

Now, we open the administration tool for the LDAP directory and query for the test account using any of the field values that we specified before. We should be able to verify that a new directory entry has been automatically generated upon saving the employee record in the Siebel web client.

The following screenshot shows the newly created directory entry for the test employee account in the directory server administration console:

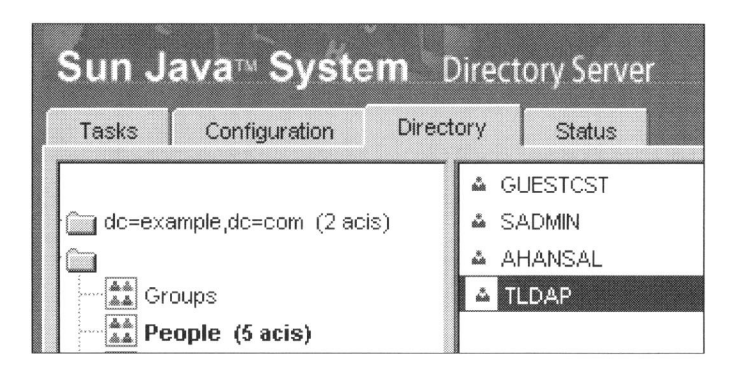

> The `PropagateChange` parameter in the LDAP Security Adapter enterprise profile controls whether changes to the directory entries can be made from the Siebel application or not. When the parameter value is set to TRUE, then the behavior is as described above. If the value is FALSE, then no changes can be made from within the Siebel application.

Finally, we should log in to the Siebel application using the new account to verify the successful configuration for directory server based user authentication for the application object manager.

After successful login, we should see the homepage salutation for the new user. The following screenshot shows the salutation text for the LDAP Test user on the Siebel application home page view:

> My Homepage   Welcome Back LDAP Test.
>
> My Activities

After successful testing, we should consider deleting the test user account in both the Siebel employee administration view as well as the LDAP directory.

> Follow the procedure described above to create a new user from within the Siebel web client.

Configuring the Siebel Gateway Name Server for LDAP authentication (optional)

Similar to the components on the Siebel server, the Siebel Gateway Name Server can be configured to authenticate user sessions via an external directory server. However, this is an optional task and it is very likely that our company decides to keep database authentication as the mechanism for authenticating administrative logins to the Siebel Gateway Name Server.

The main vehicle to provide the authentication information is via the Siebel Gateway Name Server's configuration file. The file is named `gateway.cfg` and can be located in the BIN directory of the Siebel Gateway Name Server's installation folder.

It is recommended to create a backup copy of the `gateway.cfg` file and then set the parameters in the original file according to the examples provided in the following table. Basically, we are setting the same parameters as during configuring Siebel server components, only in a text file.

Section	Parameter	Example Value
[InfraSecMgr]	`SecAdptName`	`LDAPSecAdpt`
	`SecAdptMode`	`LDAP`
[LDAPSecAdpt]	`ServerName`	`osappeval1`
	`Port`	`15313`
	`BaseDN`	`ou=People,dc=us,dc=oracle,dc=com`
	`SharedCredentialsDN`	`uid=SCredentials,ou=Special Users,dc=us,dc=oracle,dc=com`
	`UsernameAttributeType`	`uid`
	`PasswordAttributeType`	`userPassword`
	`CredentialsAttributeType`	`mail`
	`RolesAttributeType`	`cn`
	`ApplicationUser`	`uid=admin,ou=Administrators,ou=TopologyManagement,o=NetscapeRoot`
	`ApplicationPassword`	`LdApAdMin`
	`PropagateChange`	`FALSE`
	`SiebelUsernameAttributeType`	`uid`

All other parameters in the **[LDAPSecAdpt]** section may have empty values.

User Authentication

The following screenshot shows a sample `gateway.cfg` file with the necessary parameter settings to support LDAP authentication for the Siebel Gateway Name Server:

```
[InfraNameServer]
EnableAuditTrail = TRUE

[InfraSecMgr]
SecAdptName = LDAPSecAdpt
SecAdptMode = LDAP

[LDAPSecAdpt]
SecAdptDllName              = sscfldap
ServerName                  = osappeval1
Port                        = 15313
BaseDN                      = ou=People,dc=us,dc=oracle,dc=com
SharedCredentialsDN         = uid=SCredentials,ou=Special Users,dc=us,dc=oracle,dc=com
UsernameAttributeType       = uid
PasswordAttributeType       = userPassword
CredentialsAttributeType    = mail
RolesAttributeType          = cn
SslDatabase                 =
ApplicationUser             = uid=admin,ou=Administrators,ou=TopologyManagement,o=NetscapeRoot
ApplicationPassword         = LdApAdMin
HashDBPwd                   =
PropagateChange             = FALSE
CRC                         =
SingleSignOn                = FALSE
TrustToken                  =
UseAdapterUsername          = FALSE
SiebelUsernameAttributeType = uid
```

> We can encrypt the value of the `ApplicationPassword` parameter in order to avoid security issues. To accomplish this, we must use the encryptstring command line utility, which can be located in the Siebel Web Server Extension's (SWSE) bin directory. For example, to encrypt the string `LdApAdMin` we would type the following at the command line:
>
> **encryptstring LdApAdMin**
>
> The output of the utility is the encrypted string, which can then be copied and pasted to the `gateway.cfg` file.

Since we specified the `RolesAttributeType` parameter with a value of `cn` (referencing the Common Name(s) LDAP attribute), we must add "Siebel Administrator" as a new line entry of the Common Names attribute in order to allow administrators to log in to the Siebel Gateway Name Server. The administrative and sensitive nature of the Siebel Server Manager functionality requires that administrators are assigned the Siebel Administrator role via responsibility administration (for database authentication) or an attribute in the directory entry as described.

The Common Name(s) attribute must contain the full name of the user as well as "Siebel Administrator" in separate lines. Siebel Administrator is the privilege or responsibility that a user must have in order to use the Siebel Server Manager command line.

Of course, we can create or use any other multi-valued LDAP attribute than Common Name(s)—or cn—to store the user role for Siebel Gateway Name Server authentication.

Verifying LDAP authentication for the Siebel Gateway Name Server

In order to verify the successful configuration of the Siebel Gateway Name Server, we must restart the entire Siebel enterprise, which includes the following steps:

- Stop all Siebel Servers
- Stop the Siebel Gateway Name Server
- Start the Siebel Gateway Name Server
- Start all Siebel Servers

After restarting the enterprise, we can use the srvrmgr command line utility and try to log on using one of the user accounts that have the "Siebel Administrator" role assigned in the LDAP directory.

If the login is successful and we can retrieve information from the command line (for example using the `list servers` command), then we have properly configured the Siebel Gateway Name Server to authenticate user sessions via an external directory server.

In the case of errors, we must consult the Siebel Gateway Name Server's log files and verify all configuration steps.

Configuring Siebel clients for LDAP authentication (optional)

If our company's security requirements include directory server-based user authentication for Siebel clients such as the Siebel Developer Web Client or Siebel Tools, we can switch from the default database authentication to LDAP authentication in a similar manner as we discussed for the Siebel Gateway Name Server.

We could simply edit the client's configuration file (.cfg) similarly to the Siebel Gateway Name Server's configuration file. But let us consider the administrative overhead that would arise when we had to make changes to dozens of configuration files on different workstations. To avoid this time-consuming and error-prone process, Siebel CRM clients have the capability to read the authentication information from a centrally stored file, which we can for example place in a shared network folder.

The following process must be completed to enable directory server-based user authentication for the Siebel Developer Web Client or Siebel Tools:

1. Set the SecThickClientExtAuthent system preference to TRUE
2. Create the central authentication configuration file
3. Modify the client configuration file
4. Verify directory server authentication for the Siebel client.

In the following section, we will discuss each step of this process in detail.

Setting the SecThickClientExtAuthent system preference to TRUE

System preferences are enterprise-wide parameters that are stored in the Siebel database. We can view, create, and modify system preferences using either the Siebel Web client or Siebel Tools.

The **SecThickClientExtAuthent** system preference must be set to **TRUE** in order to allow "thick clients"—a term used to describe the Siebel Developer Web Client or Siebel Tools, as they both must be installed locally, hence they are "thick"—to use external authentication mechanisms.

In the Siebel Web client, we navigate to the Administration - Application screen and click the hyperlink for the **System Preferences** view.

In the list, we query for the **SecThickClientExtAuthent** system preference and set the value to **TRUE**. We then step off the record or save the record using *CTRL+S* on the keyboard. The following screenshot shows the **System Preferences** view in the **Administration - Application** screen:

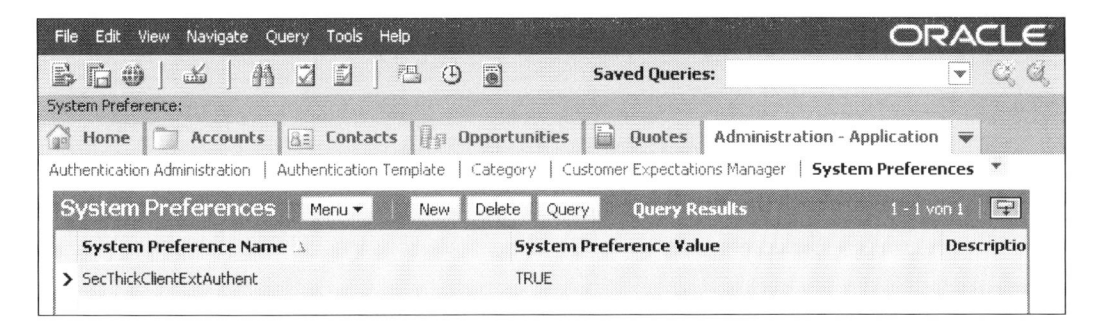

The **SecThickClientExtAuthent** system preference value is set to **TRUE** to support external authentication for the Siebel Developer Web Client or Siebel Tools.

Creating the central authentication configuration file

To avoid repetitive work when changes are made to the directory server infrastructure, we create a new text file and ensure that it can be accessed for reading from all machines that host Siebel clients.

The content of the file is only the [LDAPSecAdpt] section, which usually resides in the local client configuration files. The following table describes the parameters in the [LDAPSecAdpt] section and gives examples:

Parameter	Example Value
ServerName	osappeval1
Port	15313
BaseDN	ou=People,dc=us,dc=oracle,dc=com
SharedCredentialsDN	uid=CCredentials,ou=Special Users,dc=us,dc=oracle,dc=com
UsernameAttributeType	uid
PasswordAttributeType	userPassword
CredentialsAttributeType	mail
ApplicationUser	uid=admin,ou=Administrators,ou=TopologyManagement,o=NetscapeRoot
ApplicationPassword	LdApAdMin
PropagateChange	TRUE
SiebelUsernameAttributeType	uid

We must save the file with no other content but the [LDAPSecAdpt] section in a shared folder. An example file path could be `\\workserver\share1\siebel_ldap.cfg`.

The shared credentials user account in the directory server should not define proxy data sources when used with Siebel clients. We can create an additional shared credentials account and define the following value in the attribute used to carry the proxy connection information:

```
username=SADMIN password=TJay357D
```

The user for the proxy connection must be a registered Siebel user. If security concerns arise because we use SADMIN as the proxy, any other registered user can be used as a proxy user.

Modifying the client configuration file

We must now direct the Siebel client executable to the central LDAP configuration file we just created. This can be accomplished by setting the following parameters in the [InfraSecMgr] section in the client's configuration file (`.cfg`).

Parameter	Example Value
`SecAdptName`	`LDAPSecAdpt`
`SecAdptMode`	`LDAP`
`UseRemoteConfig`	`\\workserver\share1\siebel_ldap.cfg`

If the **UseRemoteConfig** parameter is present, the client executable will ignore the [LDAPSecAdpt] section in the local configuration file and try to read the information from the file defined in the parameter value.

The above applies to Siebel Developer Web Client configuration files and the Siebel Tools configuration file (`tools.cfg`). If the [InfraSecMgr] section is not present, we must create it in the file.

Verifying directory server authentication for the Siebel client

We should now be able to start the Siebel Developer Web Client or Siebel Tools and log in using any user account that is present in the LDAP directory tree.

In the case of errors, we must consult the Siebel client's log file and verify the configuration steps.

> If we have to troubleshoot the local client software we can set the SIEBEL_LOG_EVENTS environment variable to a value of 4 or 5 to increase the amount of information in the client's log file.
>
> However, we must ensure that the environment variable is deleted or set to a value of 0 for normal operation. Higher log levels always affect performance negatively.

Web Single-Sign-On

Web Single-Sign-On allows companies to deploy web-based portal pages from which users can launch other web applications such as Siebel CRM. The typical scenario is that the end user community does not wish to provide login credentials for each web application repetitively. To accommodate this requirement, Siebel CRM supports web Single-Sign-On (SSO).

Web SSO is based on user authentication at the web server level. The web server takes care of authenticating the user. On Microsoft Windows platforms, this is typically achieved with Microsoft Internet Information Services (IIS) and Microsoft Active Directory (AD).

User Authentication

The following diagram depicts the Siebel Web SSO architecture and its authentication flow:

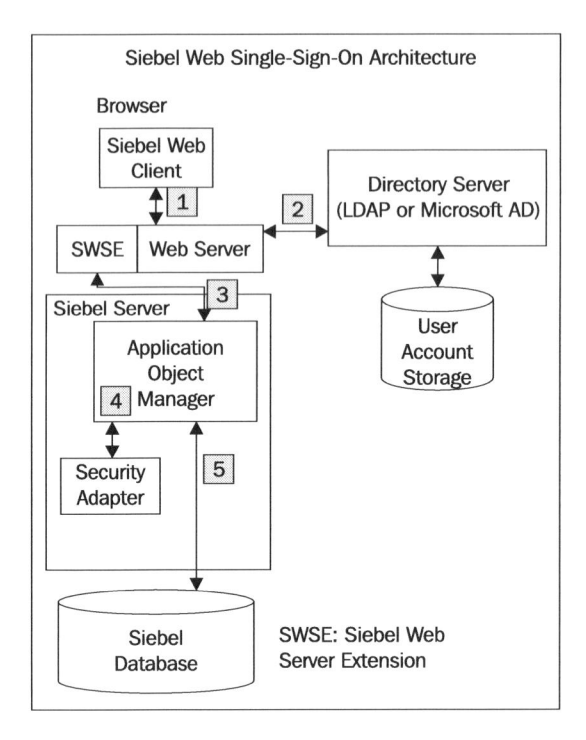

We can describe the authentication flow for Web SSO as follows:

1. The end user accesses the Siebel Web client URL.
2. The web server authenticates the user and passes the username to the Siebel Web Server Extension (SWSE).
3. The SWSE retrieves the trust token from its configuration file and passes it to the application object manager. The trust token is an encrypted string which—when accompanying a user session request—identifies the user as authenticated, or "trusted".
4. The application object manager uses the security adapter to verify the trust token.
5. When the trust token from the SWSE matches the trust token stored in the security adapter enterprise profile, the application object manager establishes a session for the user without prompting for a username and password.

> Web SSO is only supported in conjunction with an LDAP or ADSI security adapter. This is because only the enterprise profiles for LDAP or ADSI security adapters can store the trust token as a parameter.

In summary, the end user experience is such that she or he just has to provide the login ID and password only once, typically when logging on to the Microsoft Windows workstation.

Next, we will describe a simple test scenario that implements Web SSO using Microsoft's Internet Information Services (IIS) as the web server and Windows local user management as the external authentication system. In order to set up Web SSO, the following steps must be executed at least:

1. Create a non-anonymous virtual directory on the web server
2. Create or verify user accounts in the external authentication system
3. Modify the SWSE configuration file
4. Modify the security adapter
5. Verify the Web SSO configuration

Creating a non-anonymous virtual directory on the web server

In our example Web SSO configuration, we will use the web server's built-in authentication capabilities. In order to enforce username and password retrieval when a directory is accessed, we must modify the directory security settings to disallow anonymous access. In the example below we modify the security settings for the virtual directory of the German Siebel Call Center application.

The following screenshot shows the **Directory Security** settings for the callcenter_DEU virtual directory in Microsoft IIS:

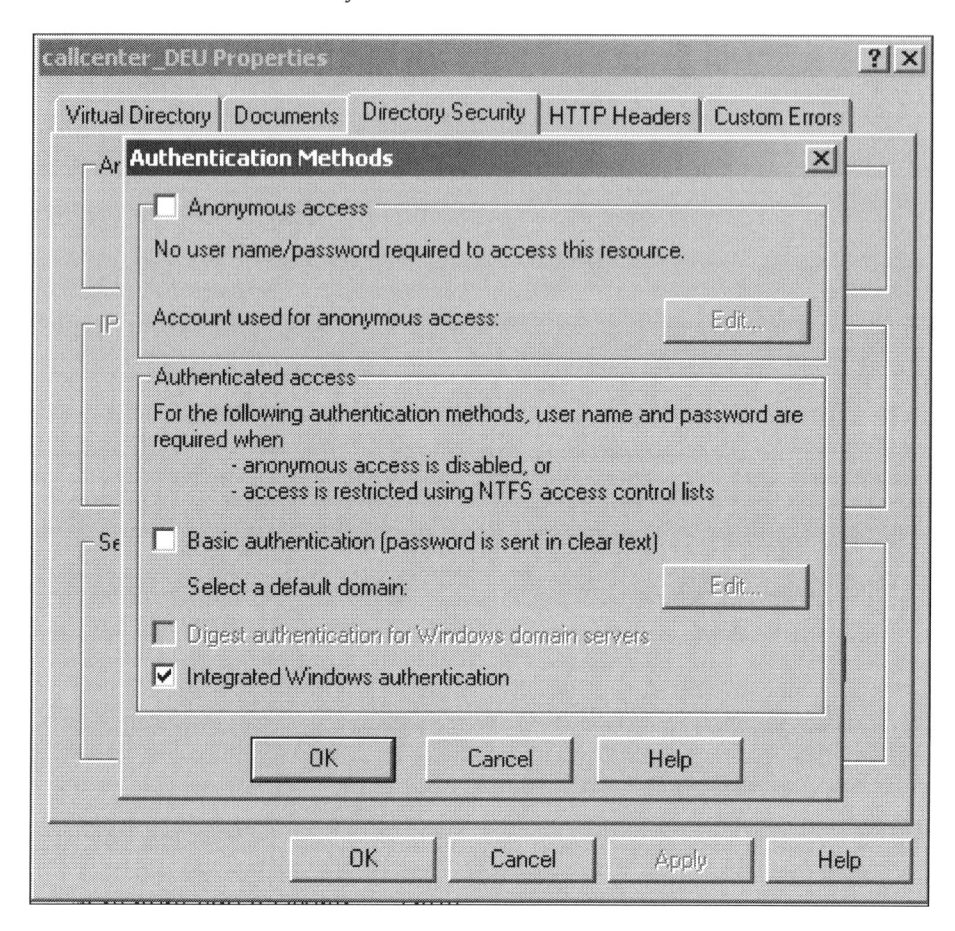

Anonymous access has been disabled. Integrated Windows authentication is enabled. When these settings are applied, only users that are authenticated by Windows (when logging in at the workstation) are eligible to access the virtual directory's content.

Creating or verifying user accounts in the external authentication system

As we are exploring a Microsoft Windows scenario, we must ensure that a Windows account exists for each Siebel user we wish to use as test accounts. In real life production systems, these would typically be created or already present in Microsoft Active Directory. In our simple example, we create a local test user account on the Windows machine using the Local Users and Groups section in the Windows Computer Management console.

The test account must also be a registered user in the Siebel application. If the user is not already registered, we must create a test employee with the same user ID as used for the Windows user account in the Employee administration view in the Administration - User screen in the Siebel Web client.

Modifying the Siebel Web Server Extension configuration file

In order to enable Web SSO for the German Siebel Call Center application, we must edit the Siebel Web Server Extension's (SWSE) configuration file (eapps.cfg). We can locate the eapps.cfg file in the BIN directory of the SWSE installation folder.

Before we start adding parameters to the section, we must create an encrypted representation of the trust token. As explained above, the trust token is a string that is passed from the SWSE to the application object manager to identify the user as already authenticated. For security reasons, the trust token should not be entered in the eapps.cfg file in clear text.

To encrypt the trust token string, we have to use the **encryptstring** utility, which resides in the SWSE's bin directory. In order to encrypt the string HELLO—an example string that we choose as the trust token—we open a command shell, navigate to the SWSE's bin directory and enter the following command:

```
encryptstring HELLO
```

The output of the encryptstring utility is the encrypted representation of the string HELLO. The following screenshot shows the usage of the encryptstring utility and its output:

```
C:\WINNT\System32\cmd.exe

C:\SIA82\SWEApp\BIN>encryptstring HELLO
svHnyKB111UBmUNIBw==
```

User Authentication

We should copy the output string to the clipboard to have it ready for inserting into the `eapps.cfg` file. We open the file with a text editor of our choice and look up the [/callcenter_deu] section that defines the parameters for the German Siebel Call Center application.

We append the following parameters to the section:

Parameter	Example Value	Description
SingleSignOn	TRUE	Enables SSO for the application.
TrustToken	svHnyKBl11UBmVNIBw==	The encrypted representation of the trust token string.
UserSpec	REMOTE_USER	The default variable used by the web server to pass the username.
UserSpecSource	Server	Defines the web server as the source of the UserSpec parameter value.

In addition, we must add or edit the following parameter in the [swe] section of the `eapps.cfg` file:

Parameter	Example Value	Description
IntegratedDomainAuth	TRUE	Must be set to TRUE to support Windows Integrated Authentication.

Source: *Siebel Security Guide, Version 8.1*

```
http://download.oracle.com/docs/cd/E14004_01/books/Secur/
booktitle.html
```

The following screenshot shows a portion of the modified `eapps.cfg` file:

```
eapps.cfg - Notepad
File  Edit  Format  Help
[swe]
Language        = ENU
Log             = errors
LogDirectory    = C:\SIA82\SWEApp\log
ClientRootDir   = C:\SIA82\SWEApp
SessionMonitor  = False
AllowStats      = true
LogSegmentSize  = 0
LogMaxSegments  = 0
DisableNagle    = False
IntegratedDomainAuth = True

[/callcenter_deu]
ConnectString = siebel.TCPIP.None.None://VirtualServer/SIEBELEVAL/SCCObjMgr_deu
WebPublicRootDir = C:\SIA82\SWEApp\public\deu
SiebEntSecToken = ws+Il74vi9kBZj6YMQ==
SingleSignOn = TRUE
TrustToken = jXnmWzaGqMcBbOq8Yg==
UserSpec = REMOTE_USER
UserSpecSource = Server
```

The parameters have been added as described above to support Web SSO for the German Siebel Call Center application.

After modifying the file, we save it and restart the web server service to reinitialize the Siebel Web Server Extension.

Modifying the LDAP security adapter

To finalize the server-side settings to support Web SSO, we must set two parameters of the LDAP security adapter enterprise profile. As usual, we should create a script file and use the Siebel Server Manager command line utility to apply the changes. The command in the file is as follows:

```
change param SingleSignOn=TRUE,TrustToken=HELLO for named subsystem ldapsecadpt
```

This command sets the SingleSignOn parameter value to TRUE, thereby enabling Web SSO functionality for the security adapter. The TrustToken parameter value is set to HELLO, which is the unencrypted trust token string.

After applying the changes, we must restart the Siebel server(s), which host the application object manager for which we wish to enable Web SSO.

Verifying the Web SSO configuration

To verify the successful Web SSO configuration, we log on to the Windows machine using the new test account. Once the user is logged on, we open an Internet Explorer window and navigate to a URL similar to the following for the German Siebel Call Center application:

```
http://osappeval1/callcenter_deu
```

If Web SSO is properly configured, the Siebel application should launch and navigate directly to the application homepage view where we can use the salutation text to verify that the user has been authenticated without the need to provide a username and password in the Siebel login page.

User Authentication

The following screenshot shows the Siebel Call Center homepage with the salutation text for Alexander Hansal:

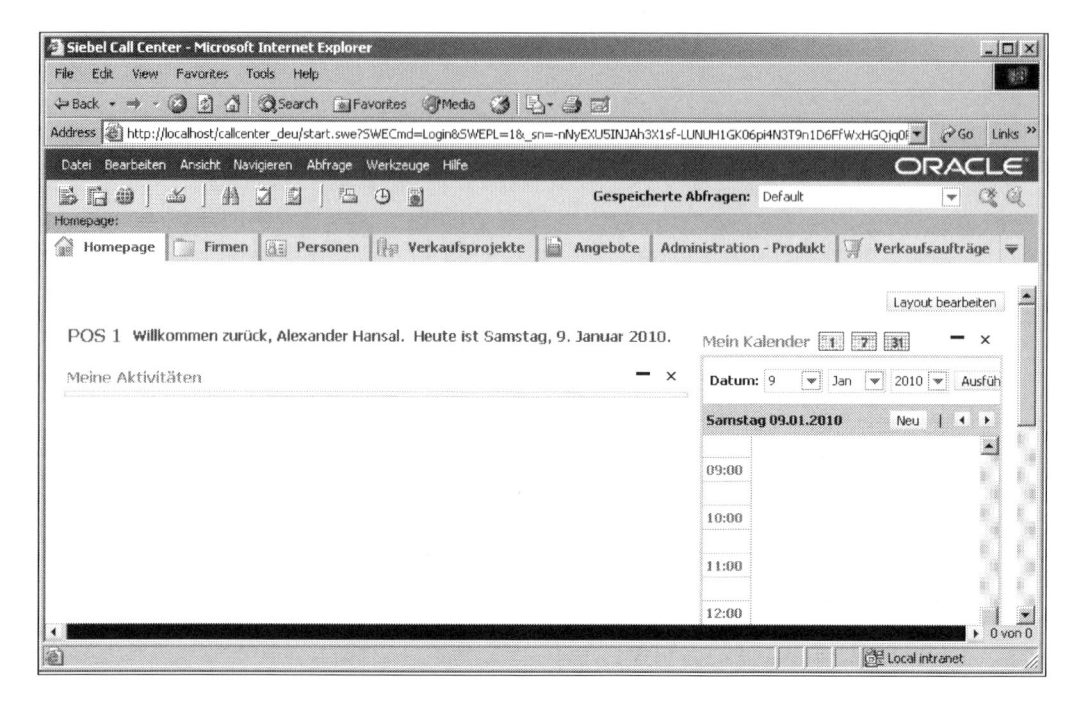

The user has been authenticated by Web SSO. We should consider deleting the test account after successful verification if security regulations apply.

> If you wish to practice setting up Web SSO for a Siebel application, you can do so by following the steps in the above example. You should bear in mind that this is only an example for demonstration purposes and a real life implementation of Web SSO would involve more steps.

Summary

In this chapter, we learned how to switch from the default user authentication mechanism, namely database authentication, to external directory server-based authentication. After exploring the functionality of the security adapter infrastructure, an example configuration for LDAP authentication was discussed.

LDAP authentication is supported for Siebel server software such as application object managers or the Siebel Gateway Name Server. The chapter introduced us to the complete procedure of setting up LDAP authentication for a Siebel application. To support centralized user management for user communities that use "thick clients" such as Developer Web Client or Siebel Tools, we described the procedures to enable LDAP authentication for Siebel clients as well.

To accommodate the requirement to only log in once to the workstation and then access all web applications without having to log in again, we learned how to set up a Siebel application for Web Single-Sign-On.

In the next chapter, we will explore the principles of Siebel user authorization and access control.

11
User Authorization and Access Control

Given the fact that the founders of Siebel Systems Inc. started designing Siebel CRM in the early nineties, and that several hundreds of engineers have been continuously extending the functionality of Siebel CRM, we find today the result of thousands of person-years of innovation. This vast array of functionality for use across various industries will never be made accessible to a single user in its entirety for the simple reason of the confusion and frustration arising from the abundance of information.

The other reason for limiting access to application features and data for end users is data security. This is a major aspect of every software implementation project.

In this chapter, we will explore the mechanisms of user authorization—how we can manage the access to Siebel CRM functionality for large user groups—and the concepts behind data access control. The chapter will be structured as follows:

- Understanding Siebel Access Control
- Controlling access to Siebel views
- Controlling access to customer data
- Controlling access to master data
- Personalized access to features and data

Understanding Siebel Access Control

Siebel Access Control is the final security layer that an end user has to pass in order to get access to Siebel CRM functionality and data. The following diagram depicts the security layers that a user typically has to cross to access application functionality and data:

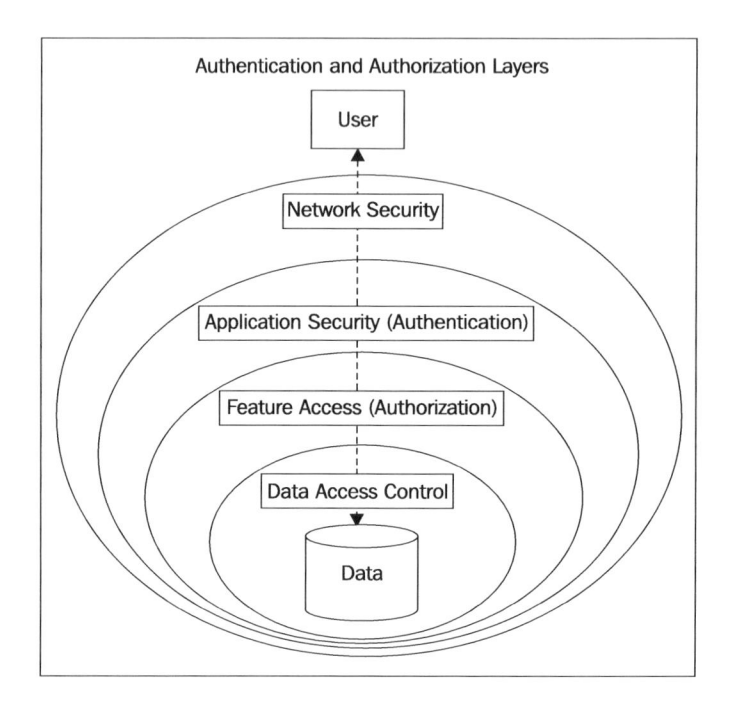

Network security is typically represented by the requirement to log in with a valid username and password to the corporate network using either the workstation logon provided by the operating system or a secure connection via the Internet, for example by means of VPN (Virtual Private Network) protocols.

To access the various applications that a company deploys to its staff, the end user either has to provide security credentials such as a username and password or she or he is authenticated by an integrated mechanism such as Web Single-Sign-On (SSO). **Application security** for Siebel CRM has been discussed in the previous chapter.

Once the user is logged on to the Siebel CRM application, she or he must have access to a set of screens and views, depending on which business processes are part of her or his work assignment. **Feature access**, or in other terms the authorization to use the Siebel views, which a user needs to carry out the assigned business processes, is a vital part of Siebel CRM user authorization and will be discussed in detail in this chapter.

Finally, depending on the position or job entitlement of the end user, **data access control** mechanisms must be in place to ensure that the end user has exactly defined access to the data she or he needs to execute the business processes or is allowed to see. In this chapter, we will also discuss the mechanisms to control access to data in Siebel CRM.

As a Siebel administrator, it's important to understand the mechanisms that define an end user's access to Siebel views and the data therein in order to be able to manage and troubleshoot data security in Siebel CRM.

Controlling access to Siebel views

When we look at a Siebel view from a high level, it has the characteristics of a web page that provides access to data stored in the Siebel database or external systems and the functionality to work with that data. The functionality can range from simple queries in the data set to complex automated steps. Creating a new quote for a customer from the **Account List** View is an example of the latter.

The screenshot below shows the **Account List** View in the Siebel Web client:

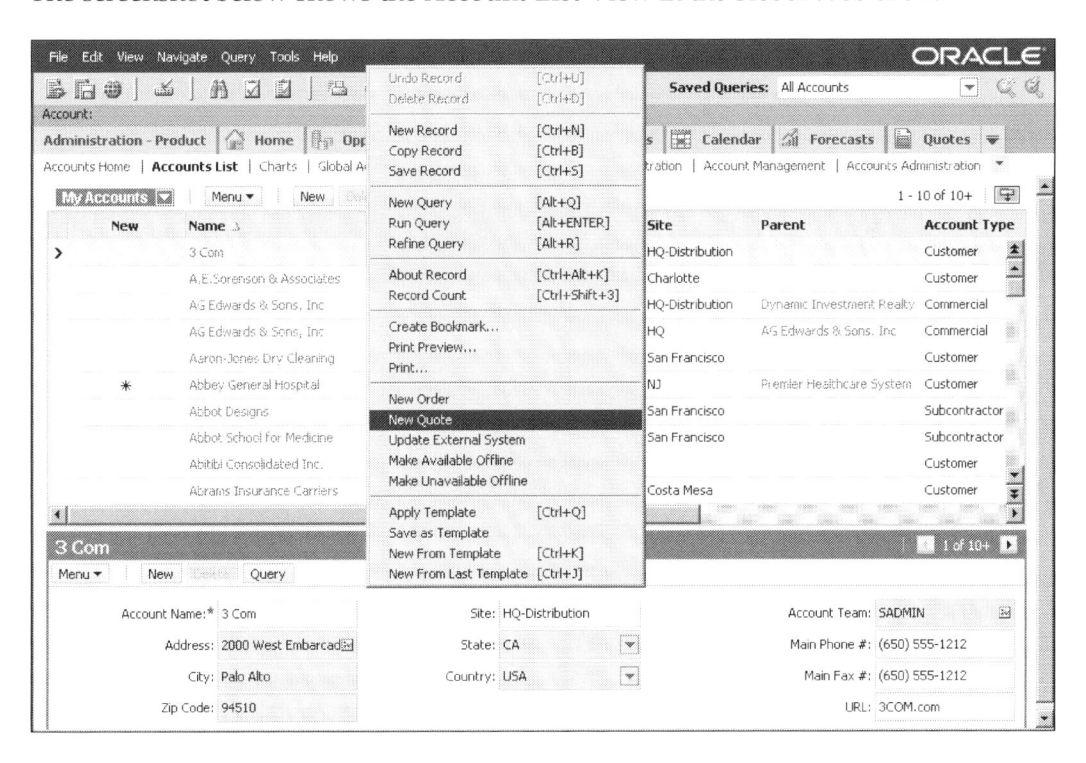

We can observe that the end user has access to account records and that for each record a set of commands is available in the context menu. The **New Quote** command visible in the context menu is an example of functionality beyond simple record querying and manipulation.

The importance of business process analysis

From a business process perspective, a user who is in charge of looking up or creating a customer account and then creating a new quote for the customer needs access to the above described Siebel view. Next, we will learn how business analysts gather this kind of information.

During the early phases of Siebel CRM projects, business analysts conduct workshops with end users to determine the exact definitions of the company's business processes. They then map each step in a business process that should be executed in Siebel CRM to a Siebel view.

The following diagram depicts the relationships between the business process, its steps, and the detailed instructions for each step as well as the mapping of each business process step to a Siebel view:

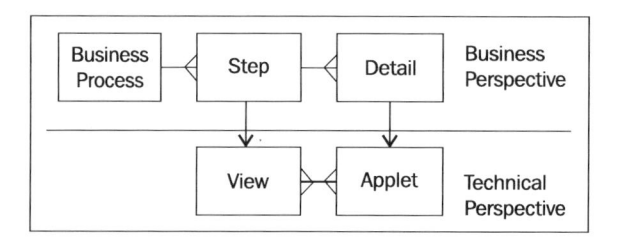

Detailed instructions can relate to applets in the view such as "Click the Query button in the form applet".

When a business analyst performs the business process analysis thoroughly — including the mapping of business process steps to Siebel views — she or he bridges the gap between business and technical perspective, thus providing the foundation for a process-driven CRM project. Process-driven projects are considered more successful and faster than technology-driven projects where user communities are presented with a new application without prior business process analysis.

When the business analysis is completed, we also should find information on which persons in the Siebel CRM user community should execute which business process. The business analysis team can achieve this by adding information about user groups and users to the business process documentation. The following diagram shows how user and group information is related to each business process:

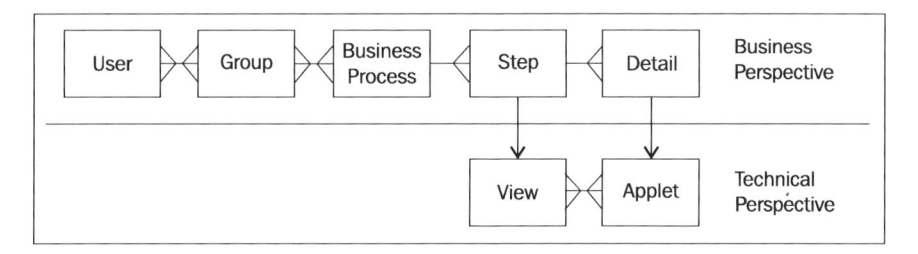

Each business process can be among the daily tasks of many groups, which in turn have one or more users.

When the business process documentation includes the information about the users and groups entitled to a business process, we can easily derive a list of Siebel views that a single user needs to execute her or his daily tasks in Siebel CRM.

The business analysis team can now continue to relate business information to technical information by mapping users and groups to Siebel entities. The following diagram introduces the concept of **Responsibility**:

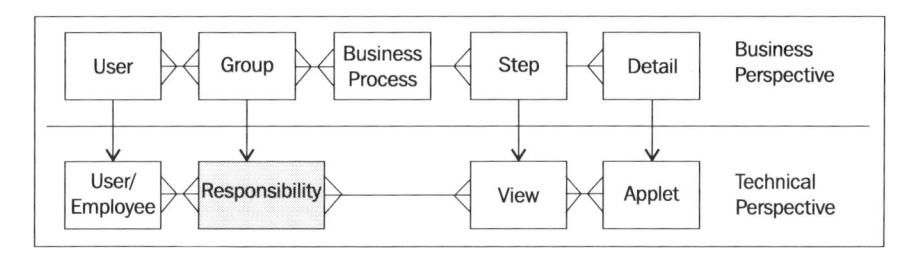

Responsibility is a Siebel entity that represents the main mechanism of controlling access to views for groups of users who share the same business processes.

Using responsibilities to control access to views

As we have learned from the above diagram, a responsibility is a list of users and a list of views at the same time. Each user can be associated with one or more responsibilities. A view can be listed in many responsibilities.

User Authorization and Access Control

Responsibilities are administered in a set of specialized views in the Siebel Web client. Administrators can use these views to modify or create responsibilities and associate them with users and views.

We can access the responsibility administration views by logging in to a Siebel application using an administrative user account, navigating to the **Administration - Application** screen in the site map, and clicking the hyperlink for the **Responsibilities** view. The following screenshot shows the **Responsibilities** administration view:

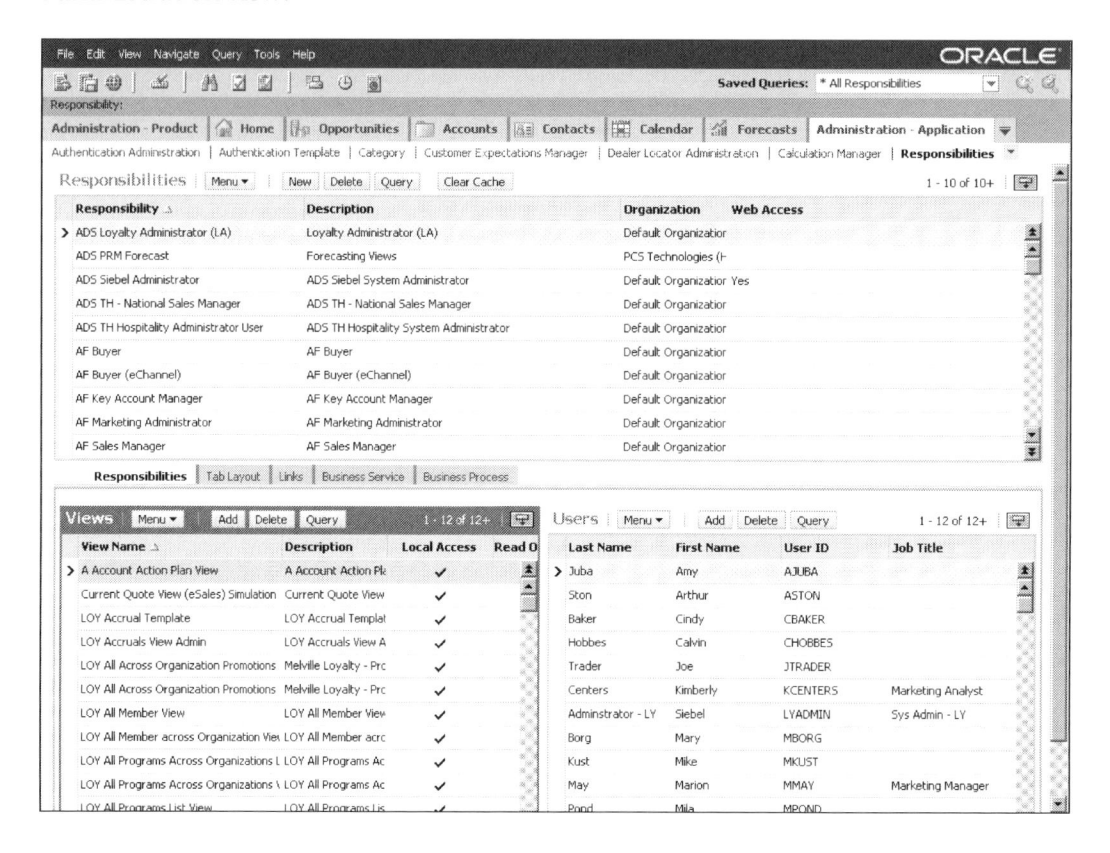

Using this view, administrators can create and modify responsibilities (upper list applet) and associate them with views (lower-left list applet) and users (lower-right list applet).

Working with responsibilities includes various tasks, which can be listed as follows:

- Creating or modifying responsibilities
- Understanding the implications of view access
- Controlling view access on local databases

- Controlling read only behavior of views
- Controlling the tab layout for screens and views

Next we will discuss each task in detail. Example scenarios will be given in each section as well.

Creating or modifying responsibilities

In order to understand how to create or modify responsibilities and how these settings affect the end user experience, we will explore an example scenario. We can use any of the so-called seed responsibilities that are loaded into the Siebel database during the installation process for research purposes.

The following task list guides us through the process of associating a user with a responsibility:

1. Log in to the Siebel application as an administrator.
2. Navigate to the **Administration - Application** screen, **Responsibilities** view.
3. Query for the seed responsibility named "Universal Agent".
4. Use the *CTRL+B* keyboard shortcut to copy the Universal Agent responsibility.
5. Enter a meaningful name for the new responsibility.
6. Navigate to the **Administration - User** screen, **Employees** view.
7. Locate or create a test employee account (not SADMIN). If you create a new employee, you must also ensure that a user account for that employee exists in the authentication system.
8. In the responsibilities list for the test employee, ensure that only the new test responsibility is selected.
9. Open a new browser window and navigate to the Siebel Call Center URL.
10. Log on using the test employee account.
11. Navigate to the site map and compare it to the site map you see in the first session (of the administrative user).
12. Verify that the site map in the test user's session provides a smaller set of screens and views.

The following screenshot shows the site map resulting from the assignment of a copy of the Universal Agent responsibility to a user of Siebel Call Center:

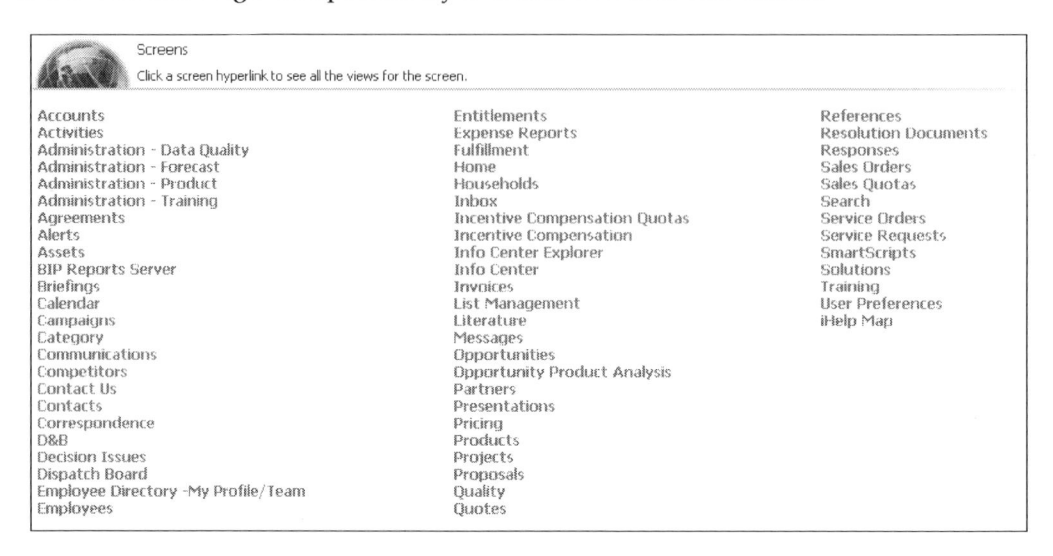

```
Screens
Click a screen hyperlink to see all the views for the screen.

Accounts                              Entitlements                      References
Activities                            Expense Reports                   Resolution Documents
Administration - Data Quality         Fulfillment                       Responses
Administration - Forecast             Home                              Sales Orders
Administration - Product              Households                        Sales Quotas
Administration - Training             Inbox                             Search
Agreements                            Incentive Compensation Quotas     Service Orders
Alerts                                Incentive Compensation            Service Requests
Assets                                Info Center Explorer              SmartScripts
BIP Reports Server                    Info Center                       Solutions
Briefings                             Invoices                          Training
Calendar                              List Management                   User Preferences
Campaigns                             Literature                        iHelp Map
Category                              Messages
Communications                        Opportunities
Competitors                           Opportunity Product Analysis
Contact Us                            Partners
Contacts                              Presentations
Correspondence                        Pricing
D&B                                   Products
Decision Issues                       Projects
Dispatch Board                        Proposals
Employee Directory -My Profile/Team   Quality
Employees                             Quotes
```

The site map shows fewer screens than the Siebel Administrator has access to.

Understanding the implications of view access

Only views listed in the user's responsibilities can be accessed by the user. This means that the following elements of the user interface are only present (or active) when the user has the target view listed in one of his or her responsibilities:

- Tabs and Links
- Hyperlinks in the site map
- Drill down hyperlinks
- Links from screens and application home pages
- View links in iHelp items

In addition, the user will receive an error message if she or he tries to access the view by using a bookmark or direct entry in the browser address bar. Similar error situations can occur when a Siebel workflow or a script tries to access the view on the user's behalf.

As an example, we can verify the site map management by removing the views that belong to the **Administration - Training** screen from the test responsibility. The following task list guides us through the process:

1. If necessary, log in to the Siebel application as an administrator.
2. Navigate to the **Administration - Application** screen, **Responsibilities** view.
3. Locate the test responsibility created earlier.
4. In the Views list, delete the following views:
    - Training Test Run List View
    - Training Test Run Detail View
5. Click the **Clear Cache** button in the Responsibilities list.
6. Log in to Siebel Call Center using the test employee account.
7. Verify that the **Administration - Training** screen is no longer present in the site map.

When conducting the business process analysis for a Siebel CRM project, it is highly beneficial to collect information about the necessary views early in the project. Adhering to high standards of project management ensures that critical information such as which user group has access to which set of views is available when needed.

Controlling view access on local databases

In order to avoid slow performance and network congestion during synchronization of local databases with Siebel Remote, we can control the availability of views in local databases. Typically, views that allow the end user to access large data sets should be made unavailable when the user is working offline. Examples for these views are the "All Accounts" or "All Accounts across Organization views", as well as most administrative views.

The Local Access flag in the view list controls the availability of a view in a Siebel Mobile Web Client. The screenshot below shows the Views list applet in the Responsibilities view in the **Application - Administration** screen with the **Local Access** column.

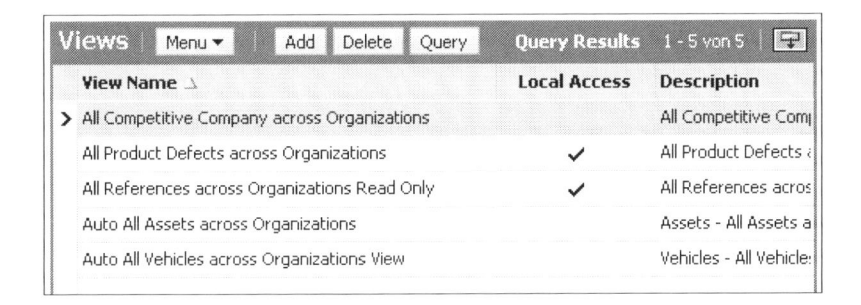

User Authorization and Access Control

Some views in the above screenshot have the Local Access flag unchecked. Mobile users will therefore be unable to access these views. In addition, data that would be visible in these views will not be synchronized to the local database, thus increasing the speed of the overall synchronization process.

Controlling read-only behaviour of views

Under some circumstances, companies want to provide read-only access to data to one group of users while others should still be able to create, update, or delete data. Siebel CRM supports this behaviour by providing a **Read Only View** flag. When this flag is set for a view, all users who have the responsibility containing that view can only access the data in the view in read-only mode. They will not be able to insert, update, or delete records in the view. The screenshot shows the **All Account List View** with the **Read Only View** flag set in the responsibility administration view.

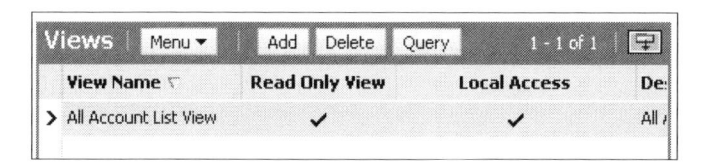

This flag can be set for each view-responsibility association. The setting is only effective when a view is set to read only in all responsibilities that the user is assigned to.

The screenshot below shows the form applet in the **All Account List View** for a user who has the **Read Only View** flag checked in all responsibilities that contain this view:

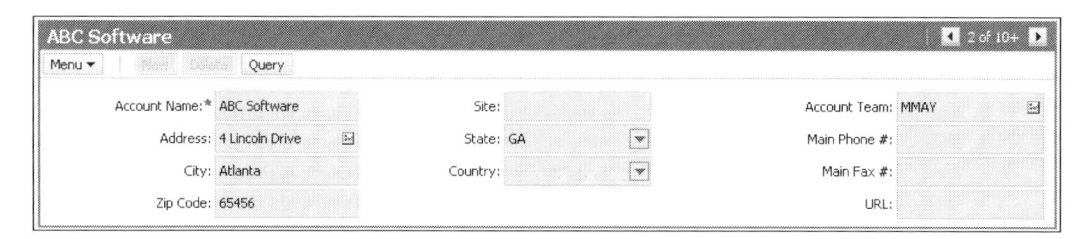

The effect of the setting is that all data fields are greyed out and the **New** and **Delete** buttons are inactive. As a result, the user can not insert, update, or delete records in that view.

[352]

Controlling the tab layout for screens and views

In addition to allowing administrators to control the access to views and their behaviour, responsibilities also allow for defining a default tab layout. In Siebel terms, tabs are clickable items in the UI that allow a user to select either a screen—navigating to the default view for the screen—or a detail view.

We refer to the tab layout as the order of appearance in the screen bar and view bar of the Siebel user interface. The tab layout is controlled by a total of three mechanisms:

- Metadata in the Siebel repository file
- The tab layout for the responsibility
- The individual tab layout for each user

Next we will explore how to modify the tab layout for a responsibility. This task list explains the procedure to change the appearance of screen and view tabs for the Siebel Call Center application:

1. Log in to the Siebel application as an administrator.
2. Navigate to the **Application - Administration** screen, **Tab Layout** view.
3. In the Responsibilities list, query for the responsibility you wish to modify.
4. In the Application list, query for **Siebel Universal Agent** (this is the technical application name for Siebel Call Center).
5. In the Screen Tab Layout list, set the order number for the Service screen to 3.
6. Check the Hide flag for the **Administration - Product** screen.
7. Select the Accounts screen.
8. In the View Tab Layout list, check the Default View flag for the My Accounts view.
9. Click the **Clear Cache** button on the top list applet.
10. Log on to a second session for Siebel Call Center as a test employee who has the modified responsibility as the primary responsibility.
11. Verify the following:
    - The Service screen tab is the third tab from the left
    - The **Administration - Product** screen tab is not visible
    - Clicking the Accounts screen navigates to the My Accounts view

The above procedure serves as an example to demonstrate how the tab layout settings affect the end user experience.

> Use your Siebel demonstration installation to experiment with responsibilities using the information above as guidance.

Controlling access to customer data

When we think about the fact that the Siebel database stores data that is being viewed and modified by hundreds or thousands of employees of a company, potentially thousands of customers and even external companies, we find that efficient filtering of data is a mandatory requirement.

Customer data records such as accounts, service requests, orders, and agreements must be "tagged" with which user group or users can access them. In Siebel CRM, almost every entity can be associated with the following data to enable precise data security:

- One or many users or employees
- One or many positions
- One or many organizations

The following diagram helps us understand the relations between these entities:

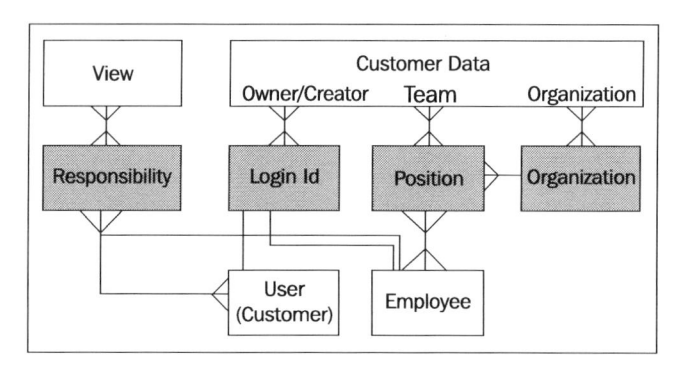

A **user** is a person who can use login credentials (a unique login name and a password) to log in to a Siebel application. A user must be associated with at least one responsibility. Customers who are given access to Siebel data by means of customer facing applications such as Siebel eSales or eService are an example of registered users. A Siebel **employee** is defined as a user who is flagged as an internal employee and is therefore associated with at least one **position**. A position can also be described as a job role in a company and is always part of an organization. **Organization** is a term used in Siebel to describe a part of a company structure, such as an internal department, or an external organization, such as a partner company whose employees are granted access to Siebel applications such as the Siebel Partner Portal.

Each customer data record can be associated with one or more employees or users by storing a reference to the employee or user as a foreign key. The field which allows us to view or modify this relationship in the user interface is typically labelled "Owner".

When we associate a record with one or more positions, this is called a "Team" in Siebel terms. This is because a position can be a group of employees who have the same job within an organizational unit. For example "Call Center Agent" can be a position held by hundreds of employees.

By associating a record to one or more organizations, we can provide a filtering mechanism that allows us to hide information from other companies or departments. This is also called multi-tenancy.

Managing users, employees, positions, and organizations is discussed in greater detail in the next chapter.

In the following, we will describe some scenarios to strengthen our understanding of Siebel access control. All examples can be reproduced using the Siebel Sample Database and the Siebel Mobile Web Client. Chapter 6 of this book discussed how to install the Siebel clients and the sample database.

Controlling record access for a single user or employee

To discover how Siebel customer data records can be efficiently retrieved and filtered for individual users or employees, we can use the Siebel Service functionality. A service request describes a customer inquiry or problem and must be resolved by a single person in the company.

By using a command line (or Windows shortcut) similar to the following, we can launch the Siebel eService application and connect to the Siebel Sample Database using the demo user account of Dana Smith (DSMITH). For convenience, it is recommended to create Windows shortcuts in order to launch the test applications more easily:

```
D:\SIA81\CLIENT\BIN\siebel.exe /c D:\SIA81\CLIENT\bin\ENU\eservice.cfg /d
sample /u DSMITH /p DSMITH
```

> The Demo Users Reference document in the Siebel bookshelf lists all demo user accounts that are provided in the Siebel Sample Database for various Siebel applications. Using demo user accounts for evaluation and research purposes is more beneficial than using the SADMIN account because the demo users and employees are associated with more meaningful responsibilities. This allows us to create test scenarios and evaluate them from the perspective of different application users.

The following screenshot shows the homepage of Siebel eService for Dana Smith, which is displayed when we launch the application as described above:

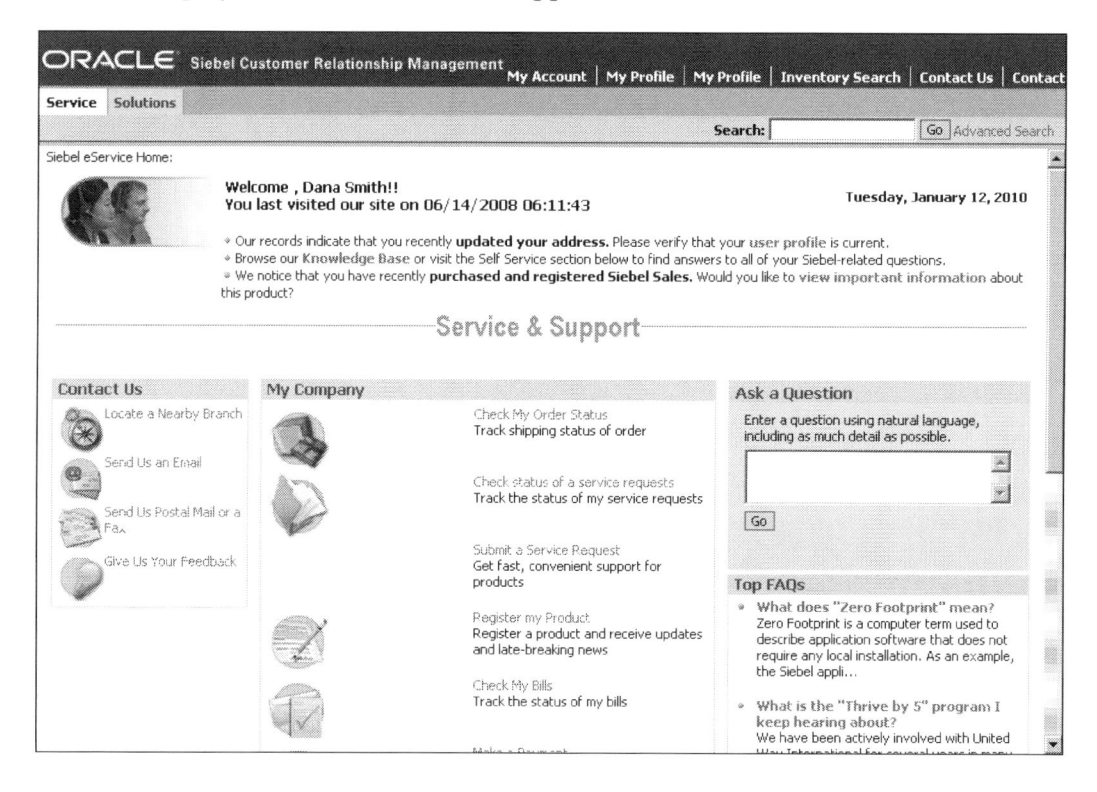

We can now verify that Dana Smith has used Siebel eService before to create service requests. By clicking the **Check status of a service request** link in the **My Company** section of the homepage, we navigate to the list of service requests created by Dana Smith. No other eService user will ever be able to see those service requests because the application logic matches the creator field value of each service request with the ID of the current user to filter the data.

The following screenshot shows the **My Service Request** list for Dana Smith in Siebel eService:

SR #	Status	Created	Summary	Product	Serial #
176914-5064321	Open	1/11/2006 11:38:42 PM	Pothole Repair - 12th St		
176914-5019597	Open	1/9/2006 9:37:20 AM	Issue with pothole		
130258-2579297	Open	4/15/2004 12:22:28 AM	Refferal for benefits		
130258-2566294	Open	4/14/2004 12:58:07 AM	Current housing is being condemned - Knight family requires alternative housing (See Attachment)		
130258-2565934	Open	4/13/2004 10:35:34 AM	Referral for Child Care		
130258-2552053	Open	4/9/2004 1:50:50 AM	Thank you		
130258-2552050	Open	4/9/2004 1:49:52 AM	Re-Schedule Interview		
130258-2552047	Open	4/9/2004 1:47:26 AM	Change in job status		
130258-2552044	Open	4/9/2004 1:46:12 AM	Status of application		
130258-2551854	Open	4/9/2004 12:23:00 AM	Referral		

It is a good idea to note (or copy to the clipboard) the service request number (in the column labeled **SR #**) of the first service request.

We can now use the Siebel Public Sector application to explore the role of the demo user Ashley Cohen (ACOHEN). Siebel Public Sector is just one of many applications that could be used to explore Siebel access control from the perspective of an employee. By using a command line or Windows shortcut similar to the following, we can launch the application and connect to the Siebel Sample Database using ACOHEN as the username and password.

```
D:\SIA81\CLIENT\BIN\siebel.exe /c D:\SIA81\CLIENT\bin\enu\publicsector.cfg /d sample /u ACOHEN /p ACOHEN
```

Once the application is launched, we navigate to the Service screen and click the hyperlink for the My Service Requests list view. In the list, we use the **SR #** column to query for the service request created by Dana Smith. We can paste the service request number from the clipboard.

User Authorization and Access Control

The following screenshot shows the detail form applet in the My Service Request list view displaying the service request created by Dana Smith:

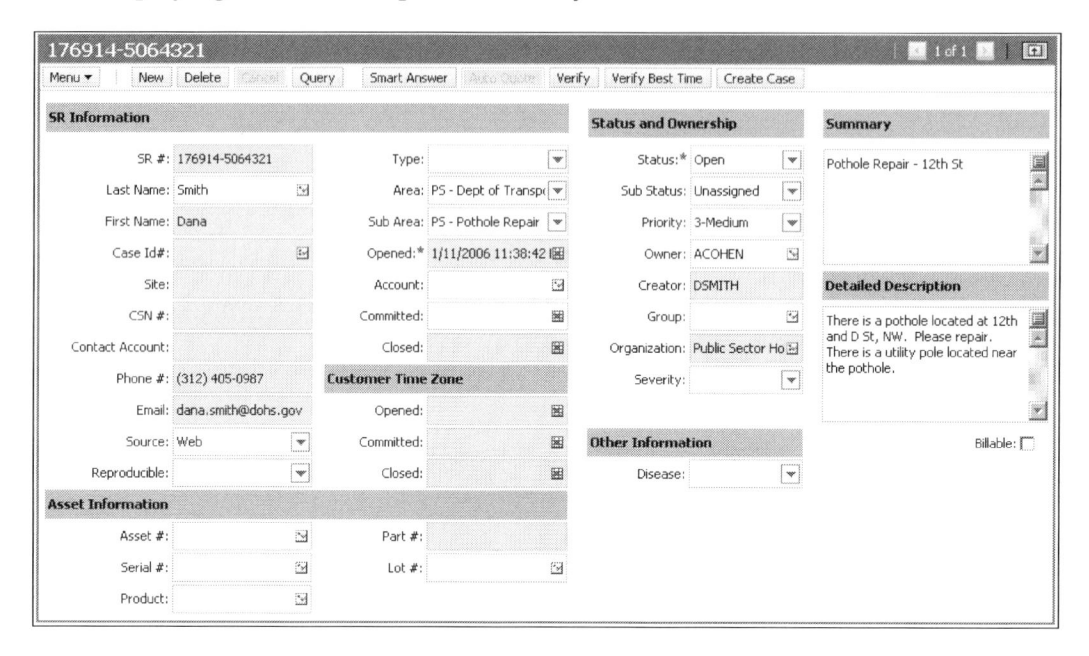

The reason why Ashley Cohen is able to see this service request in the **My Service Requests** list view is that her employee record is associated with the service request record by means of the **Owner** field (fourth field from above in the **Status and Ownership** section) thus indicating that Ashley Cohen is responsible for resolving the service request.

To retrieve all service requests that a user is assigned to, the Siebel application matches the current user's ID with the ID stored in the **Owner** field.

This concludes our example for controlling record access for single users or employees.

Controlling record access for multiple employees

In the following section we will examine a scenario for a record that must be visible to multiple employees. An easy to follow example is in the form of Siebel activities, which are also displayed in the calendar views. We will create a new activity for a meeting and assign a colleague to it. Again, we will use the Siebel Sample Database. We can follow the following task list to accomplish this:

1. Log in to the Siebel Call Center application as the Siebel Administrator (SADMIN) and connect to the Sample database.
2. Navigate to the Activities screen - Activities List.
3. Create a new activity record.
4. Enter a description, for example **Test access control**.
5. Enter a value in the Duration field, for example 60 (minutes).
6. Click the select icon in the Employees field and add Casey Cheng (CCHENG) to the list of selected employees.
7. Step off the record or press *CTRL+S* to save the activity.
8. In the **File** Menu, click **Connect**. The Connect command allows us to log in to the application with a different user account without having to log off completely.
9. In the Login dialog, enter CCHENG as the username and password.
10. Once the session for Casey Cheng is established, verify that the activity is visible in both the My Activities list and the Calendar on the homepage view.

The following screenshot shows the Siebel Call Center homepage view for the demo user Casey Cheng:

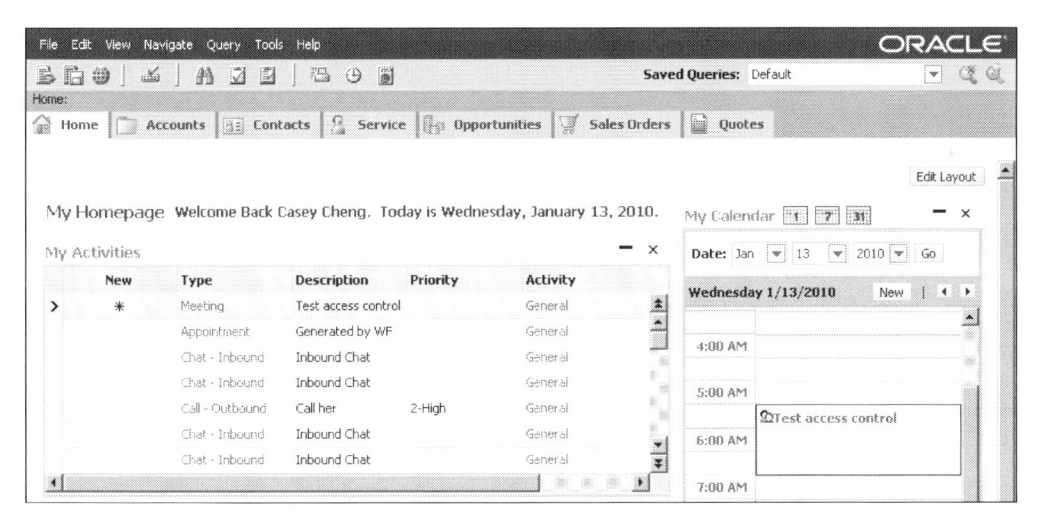

The activity created by the Siebel Administrator user is visible in Casey's activity list and calendar.

Activities are examples for records that can be associated with one or more employees. The Siebel application displays all activities that a user is assigned to because it matches the user's ID with the IDs that are associated with the activity records.

Controlling record access for teams based on positions

Entities such as service requests or activities have a relatively short life cycle. This means that the persons associated with the data will likely work with the record from its creation to completion of the task.

This is different for records such as accounts or contacts that have a much longer lifespan. The people responsible for an account might very well change over the years.

In order to avoid the administrative overhead that would arise from associating individuals with long lived records, Siebel CRM supports the concept of positions. A position is an individual job description in an organization. Each employee must be associated with at least one position that in turn must be associated with an organization. By reading this information, the Siebel application can determine which organization the employee belongs to.

The following example uses the Siebel Sample Database to demonstrate how positions can be used to create sales teams for opportunities and how the association of positions to records influences the visibility of these records.

We can follow the task list below to verify the behaviour of Siebel access control:

1. Log in to Siebel Sales as Terry Smythe (TSMYTHE) connecting to the Sample database.
2. Navigate to the Opportunities screen, My Opportunities list view.
3. Create a new opportunity record.
4. Enter a meaningful name, for example "Test Opportunity".
5. Enter a Revenue amount of 100,000 USD.
6. Step off the record or press *CTRL+S* to save it.
7. Click the select icon in the Sales Team field and verify that Terry Smythe's current position (**HT 20 21 Sales Representative**) has been automatically added to the team.
8. Add the position **HT 20 10 Sales Vice President** to the team by using the functionality of the shuttle applet. Note that this position is held by Nat Sachs (NSACHS).
9. Use the **File** menu's **Connect** command to connect to the Siebel Sales application as Nat Sachs by using NSACHS as the username and password.
10. Navigate to the My Opportunities list view and verify that the record created by Terry Smythe is visible for Nat Sachs.

11. Use the **File** menu's **Connect** command to connect to the Siebel Sales application as Madison Stern by using MSTERN as the username and password.

12. Navigate to the My Opportunities list view and verify that the record created by Terry Smythe is not visible for Madison Stern. This is because Madison Stern's position is not on the Sales Team.

13. Navigate to the My Team's Opportunities list (by using the dropdown in the title bar of the list) and verify that the record created by Terry Smythe is visible for Madison Stern.

The My Team's Opportunities view directs the Siebel application to consider the position hierarchy. Because Madison Stern's current position is registered as a parent position to Terry Smythe's position, Madison can see the opportunity in the My Team's view without the need to explicitly add her position to the Sales Team.

To review the position hierarchy, we use the **File** menu's **Connect** command to connect to the Siebel Sales application as the Siebel Administrator by using SADMIN as the username and password. We can follow this task list to verify the reporting relationship between Madison Stern and Terry Smythe:

1. Log on to the Siebel application as SADMIN.
2. Navigate to the **Administration - Group** screen, **Positions** view.
3. In the form applet, click the **Query** button.
4. Enter "Stern" in the Last Name field and click Go. This retrieves the position that Madison Stern is associated with (**HT 20 20 Sales Manager**).
5. Copy the position name into the clipboard.
6. Run a new query and paste the position name into the Position field. Click Go.
7. Expand the explorer tree on the left side of the view to verify that Terry Smythe's position is a child position of Madison Stern's position, indicating that Madison is Terry's manager.

The following screenshot shows the **Positions** view in the **Administration - Group** screen:

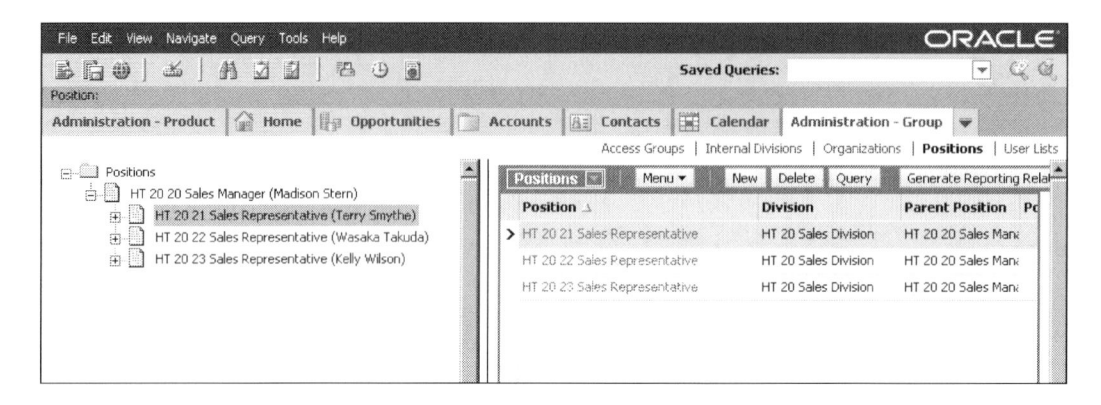

The explorer tree is expanded and displays the reporting relationship between the manager and the sales representatives.

The "My Team's" views allow managers to view all records that are associated to their subordinates.

Controlling record access for different companies based on organizations

Organizations are used in Siebel CRM to represent separate business units that can be associated with records to allow efficient and secure filtering of data. Siebel CRM supports multiple separate hierarchies of organizations. This allows us to define multi-tenant compatible applications.

The following example uses the Siebel Sample Database and demonstrates how two different companies can share information about sales opportunities using the Siebel Partner Portal, a standard interactivity application which runs in a variety of browsers.

We can follow the task list below to discover access control based on organizations:

1. Log on as Siebel Administrator to the Siebel Sample Database using the Siebel Sales application.
2. Navigate to the **Opportunities** screen, My Opportunities view.
3. Create a new test opportunity and enter a meaningful name.
4. Drill down on the opportunity name.
5. Click the **More Info** tab in the middle of the view.

6. Click the select icon in the Organization field.
7. Add the **HT 51 Active Systems - HQ** organization to the list of selected organizations.
8. Step off the record or press *CTRL+S* to save the opportunity.
9. Use a command line or Windows shortcut similar to the following to log in to the Siebel Partner Portal application as Robin Marlow, a manager at Active Systems, an external organization registered in the Siebel database as a partner company.

   ```
   D:\SIA81\CLIENT\BIN\siebel.exe /c D:\SIA81\CLIENT\bin\ENU\scw.cfg
   /d sample /u RMARLOW /p RMARLOW
   ```

10. Click the Check Opportunities for the Company hyperlink in the My Links applet in the middle of the Partner Portal home page.
11. Verify that the opportunity created before is visible to Robin Marlow.

The following screenshot shows the **All Opportunities** list in the Siebel Partner Portal application:

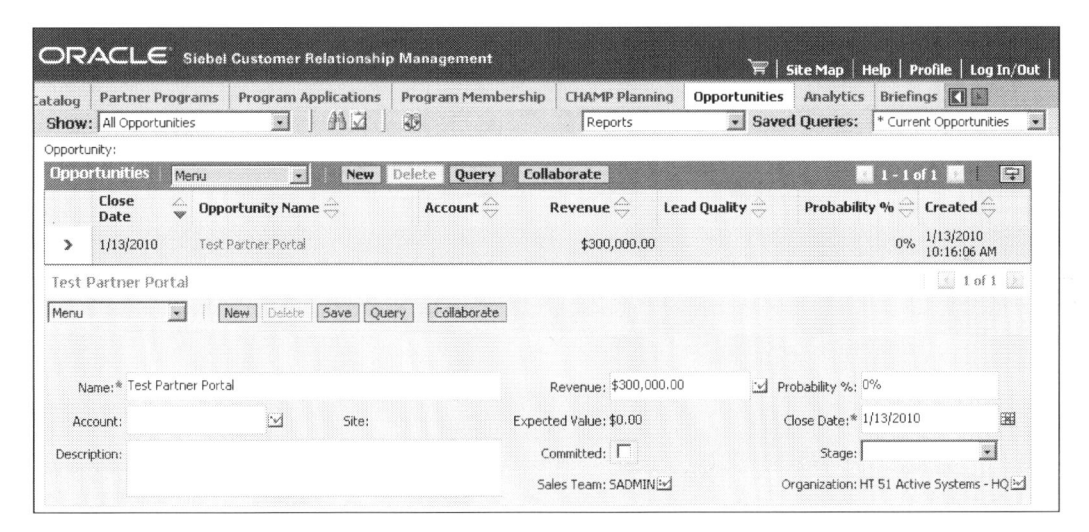

The opportunity displayed can be accessed by the external employee Robin Marlow because his company is registered as an organization in Siebel CRM and that organization has been associated with the opportunity record.

> Follow the scenarios for access control for customer data described in the above section on your demonstration machine.

Controlling access to master data

We have learned above that access to data in Siebel CRM can be controlled for each record individually. On the one hand, this is necessary and required but on the other hand, there is a high level of effort required to manage data visibility on a record-by-record basis.

For this reason, Siebel CRM provides the ability to create catalogs that are divided into categories and grant access on the catalogue or category level. The ability to create catalogs is limited to the so-called **Siebel master data** entities.

Siebel master data can be described as relatively static, authored data such as products or documents. Such records will only be created and modified by a small group of administrators but referenced very often by the business users. Product records are typically grouped to sales catalogs to provide easier presentation and browsing of product data in online portals. Instead of associating each product with a user or group directly, access control takes place at the category or catalog level. The following table describes major Siebel master data entities that we can create catalogs of:

Siebel Entity	Typical Usage	Description
Product	Online Selling	Products can be presented in hierarchical categories. Templates can be used to define the look and feel of the data display.
Literature	Knowledge Libraries	Documents can be uploaded into Siebel. Large amounts of information can be presented in a structured manner.
Solution, Resolution Item	Knowledge Base	Solutions and associated resolution items can be used to store information about how to resolve issues. Typically used in service scenarios.
Training Course, Curriculum	Training Library	End users can use the training catalog to find and register for training classes.
SmartScript	Self Service Wizards	SmartScripts can be designed to guide employees through internal processes.
Competitor, Decision Issues	Sales Library	Competitor information and sales decision issues can be easier located in catalog format.
Event	Event Catalog	Events can be presented in a catalog for easier lookup and registration.

The mechanism to control access to catalogs and categories is an **access group**. An access group is a collection of other groups of people such as user lists, companies, households, or internal divisions. The benefit of access groups is that data visibility is granted independent of the relationship of the members of the group. This is the main difference to classic access control, which is based on the hierarchical nature of organizations or positions.

The following screenshot shows the **Access Groups** view in the **Administration - Groups** screen:

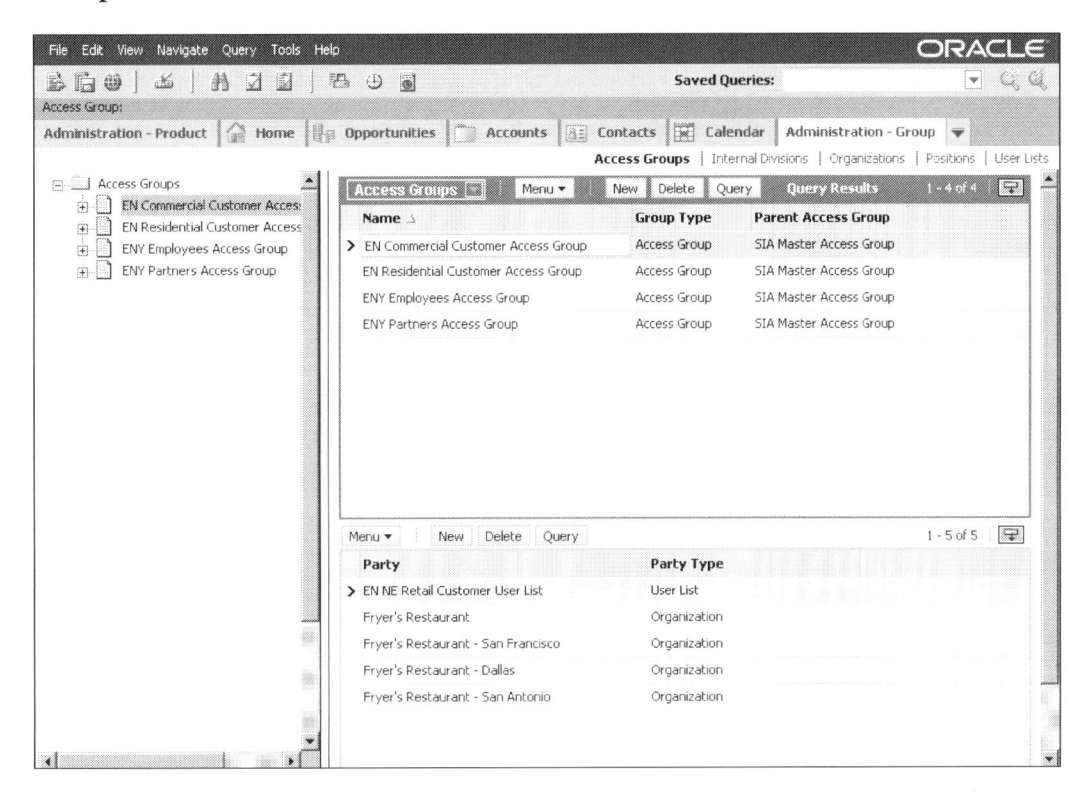

In this view, administrators can create access groups by associating user lists, accounts, internal divisions, positions, and organizations or households without being limited by organizational boundaries.

In the following scenario, we explore how access groups can be used to control access to catalogs and categories in Siebel CRM. The example uses the Siebel sample database. We can follow the following task list to discover access control for master data:

1. Log in to Siebel Call Center as the Siebel Administrator (SADMIN), connecting to the sample database.
2. Navigate to the Administration - Catalog screen, Catalog Administration view.
3. Query for the **Corporate and Business Units** catalog.
4. Verify that the catalog type is set to **InfoCenter**. This makes the catalog available for use in the Info Center screen to provide information for internal employees and partners.

5. Drill down on the catalog name to see the categories for this catalog.
6. Create a new category named Test. Note that the category has the Private flag checked by default. Keep the private flag checked.
7. Click the Literature link.
8. Click the Add button in the Literature list and add a selection of PDF documents to the Test category (use the File Type column to query for pdf as the file type).
9. Navigate to the site map and select the Info Center screen.
10. In the Info Center screen, verify that the **Corporate and Business Units** catalog is visible.
11. Verify that the **Test** category is visible.
12. Click on the Test category.
13. Verify that a list of documents is displayed.
14. Use the browser's back button to return to the administration view for the Test category.
15. Select the Test category and click the Access Group link (not the tab).
16. Click the first access group in the list and verify that the Siebel Administrator position is a member of the group. Note that you are currently logged in as the Siebel Administrator.
17. Click the browser's back button to return to the catalog administration view.
18. Delete both access groups from the Test category.
19. Navigate to the Info Center screen and verify that you can no longer access the Test category. This is because no access group that you are a member of is associated with the private category.

The above scenario demonstrates that when a catalog or a category within a catalog is declared as private, an end user must be a member of at least one of the access groups associated with that catalog or category in order to access the data. Users can not be associated directly to access groups. We can group individual users into user lists, which then can be associated to an access group.

The following screenshot shows the **Info Center** screen in the Siebel Web Client:

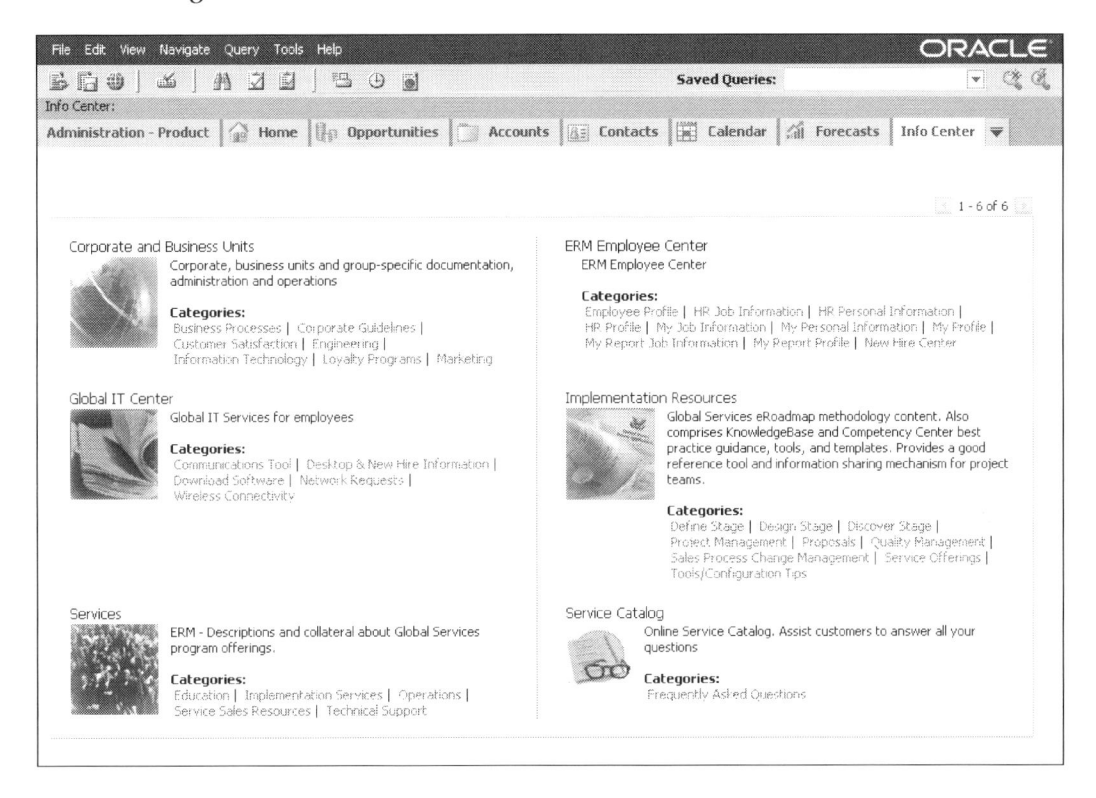

The **Info Center** is a mechanism to provide structured information to internal employees or partner employees whilst maintaining a high level of data security by means of access groups.

Personalized access to features and data

The access control features discussed so far can be considered standard methods to provide usable sets of views and data to end users. However, implementation teams are often confronted with the requirement to filter data based on criteria other than the user's current position. For example, there might be the need to display data of celebrities only to selected employees.

Another requirement could be that experienced users should be able to use a large and complex form applet for data entry whereas new hires should start with a simpler version of the applet.

To support these requirements, Siebel CRM includes the **personalization engine**, which acts as an additional filter layer on views, applets, and records to provide a personalized user experience. The following diagram depicts the various filter mechanisms that limit the user's access to data, views, and applets:

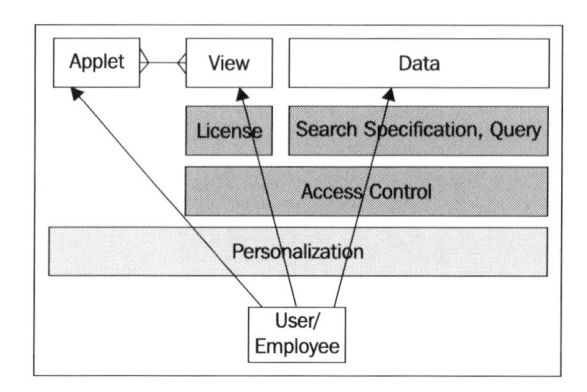

As we can see from the diagram, the Siebel Personalization layer allows us to declare which data sets, views or individual applets inside a view can be accessed by a user or employee.

Next we will explore how access to applets and views or data filtering can be controlled using the Siebel Personalization engine.

Controlling access to applets and views based on personalization

We can use the Siebel Sample database to explore examples of how access to individual applets or views is controlled by Siebel personalization. We can follow the task list below to achieve this:

1. Log in to Siebel Call Center as SADMIN, connecting to the Siebel Sample database.
2. On the homepage view, click the Help menu and select About View.
3. In the About View dialog, verify that the calendar applet is named eCalendar Daily Applet Home Page.
4. Navigate to the Administration - Personalization screen, Applets view.
5. Query for the eCalendar Daily Applet Home Page applet.
6. Verify that a conditional expression (GetProfileAttr('Is Anonymous') = 'FALSE') is defined for the applet.

Conditional expressions are defined in the **Siebel Query Language**. We can click the select icon in the conditional expression field to open the Siebel Expression Designer, which is shown in the following screenshot:

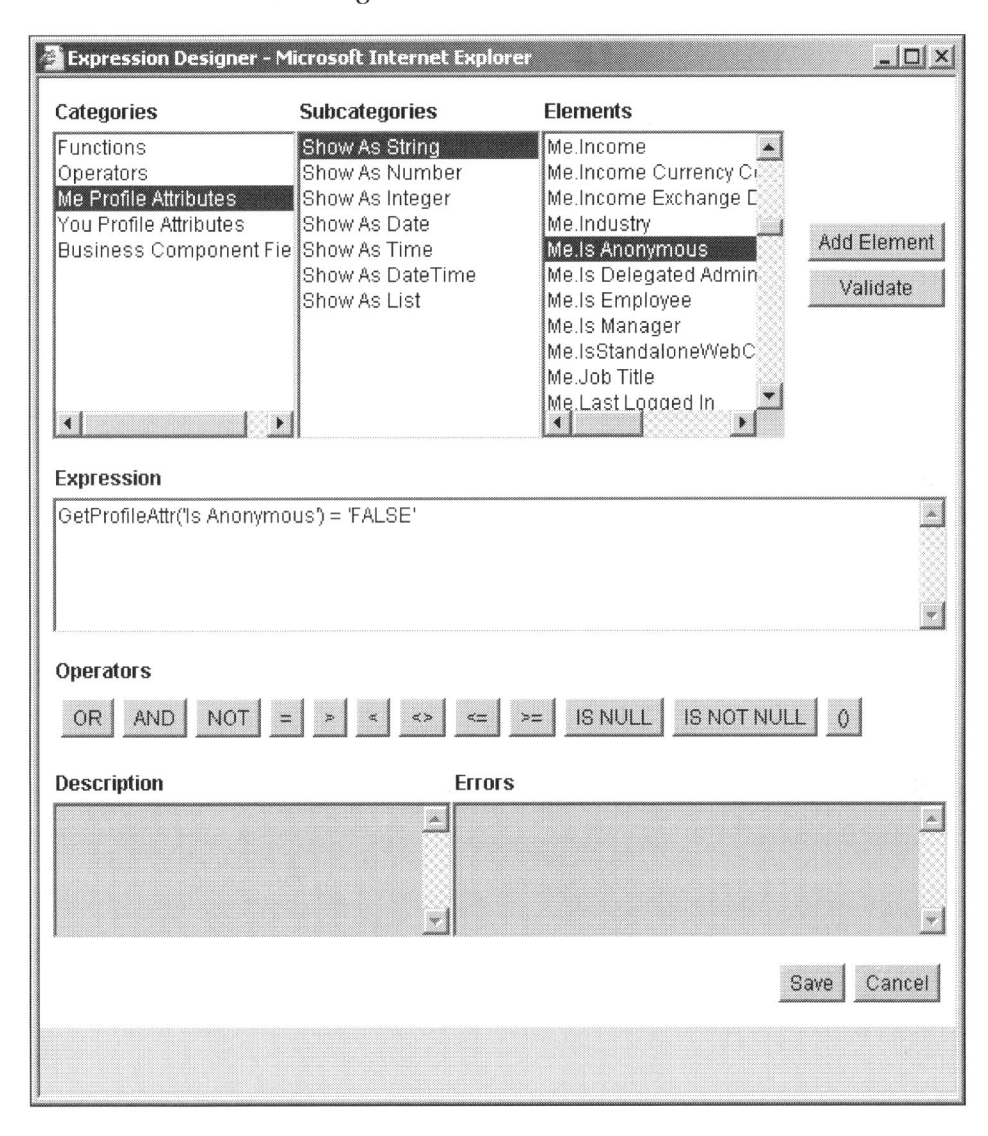

Administrators can use the expression designer to quickly create Siebel Query Language expressions, which the application interprets at runtime to determine whether a condition is satisfied or not.

The personalization engine can use built-in functions of the Siebel Query Language such as `GetProfileAttr()` to read the value of profile attributes—a Siebel term that can be translated as session variables. The "Me Profile" is the profile of the currently logged in user. Under some circumstances, for example during a phone call with a customer, the application can load the "You Profile", which is the set of profile attributes for a secondary user.

Other built-in functions and operators can be selected in the upper text areas of the expression designer. In addition, the conditional expressions can reference fields of the current record to evaluate data-specific criteria.

To continue with our example, the expression `GetProfileAttr('Is Anonymous') = 'FALSE'` compares the value of the current user's "Is Anonymous" profile attribute with the string 'FALSE'. That means, if the value of "Is Anonymous" is 'TRUE'—indicating that the user has not yet been authenticated—the left and right side of the expression will not match and therefore the condition is not met. If a condition is not met, the respective applet will not be displayed.

The fact that we see the Calendar applet in the homepage indicates that we are not an anonymous user. We can test the personalization engine by modifying the expression to `GetProfileAttr('Is Anonymous') = 'TRUE'` and investigating what happens to the homepage view, as shown in the following steps:.

1. Modify the conditional expression for the calendar applet to `GetProfileAttr('Is Anonymous') = 'TRUE'` and save the record.
2. Right-click the list applet and select **Reload Personalization Rules** from the menu. This refreshes the cache of the personalization engine.
3. Navigate to the **Home** screen and verify that the calendar applet is no longer visible.
4. Click the Edit Layout button and verify that the applet is not just hidden but really unavailable to the user.
5. Use the browser's back button to navigate back to the personalization settings for the calendar applet and set the conditional expression back to the original state.
6. Save the record and use the context menu to reload the personalization cache.

A similar mechanism applies when we wish to use the Siebel personalization engine to conditionally remove entire views from the user's current set. For example the Upgrade Kit Application View—a view that allows a mobile user to verify the availability of upgrade kits, which can be synchronized via Siebel Anywhere—can only be used in the Siebel Mobile Web Client. Therefore, a conditional expression is defined for that view in the **Administration - Personalization** screen to check the value of a user profile attribute that indicates whether the current client is a mobile web client (standalone) or a web client.

The following screenshot shows the personalization settings for the **Upgrade Kit Application View**:

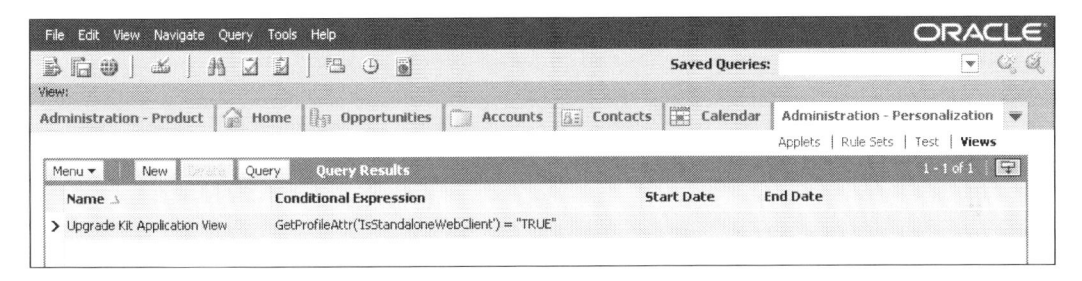

The condition defined by the expression `GetProfileAttr('IsStandaloneWebClient') = "TRUE"` is only met when the user is logged in to the Siebel Mobile Web Client.

Controlling data display based on personalization

The personalization engine's capabilities include the definition of data filter rules and associating them with applets. These rules define the data that the applet displays. We can imagine that—in database terms—the personalization rules add an additional set of WHERE clauses to the SELECT statement generated by the Siebel application.

The following example uses the Siebel Sample Database and the Siebel Automotive vertical application. We will explore how the list of vehicles in the Siebel Dealer portal can be filtered by the car make that the employee is responsible for.

To explore this behaviour, we can follow the instructions below:

1. Log in to Siebel Call Center as SADMIN, connecting to the sample database.
2. Navigate to the Administration - Personalization screen, Applets view.
3. Query for the **Auto Vehicle List Applet**.

4. Verify that the applet is associated with a rule set (check the list applet at the bottom of the view). This rule set (*Make Visibility Rule Set (Employee Login)*) is applied when the conditional expression that accompanies it evaluates to "True".

5. Drill down on the rule set.

6. Select the "Ford" rule in the rules list in the middle of the view.

7. Inspect the Conditional Expression field (visible in the form at the bottom of the view) for the Ford rule. The Ford rule is only applied when the Job Title of the current user starts with the word "Ford".

8. Inspect the Include Expression field for the Ford rule. This is the filter defined by the rule. Only records where the value of the Make field starts with "Ford" are displayed when this rule is applied.

9. Use a command line or Windows shortcut similar to the following to log in to the Siebel Dealer Portal application as Gus Morris (GMORRIS):

   ```
   D:\SIA81\CLIENT\BIN\siebel.exe /c D:\SIA81\CLIENT\bin\enu\
   edealerscw.cfg /d sample /u GMORRIS /p GMORRIS
   ```

10. In the Siebel Dealer Portal, navigate to the site map, select the **Vehicles** screen and click the hyperlink for the Auto Vehicles List view.

11. Observe that Gus Morris can currently see cars of all makes.

12. Click the **Log In/Out** link on the top right of the application to log off and close the Siebel Dealer application.

13. In the Siebel Call Center application, navigate to the Administration - User screen, Employees view.

14. Query for the employee record with GMORRIS as the User ID.

15. Set the Job Title field of Gus Morris to "Ford Dealer".

16. Save the record by pressing *CTRL+S*.

17. Log in to the Siebel Dealer Portal as Gus Morris again.

18. In the Siebel Dealer Portal, navigate to the site map, select the Vehicles screen, and click the hyperlink for the Auto Vehicles List view.

19. Verify that now only Ford cars are visible to Gus Morris.

The following screenshot shows the vehicle list for Gus Morris in the Siebel Dealer Portal application:

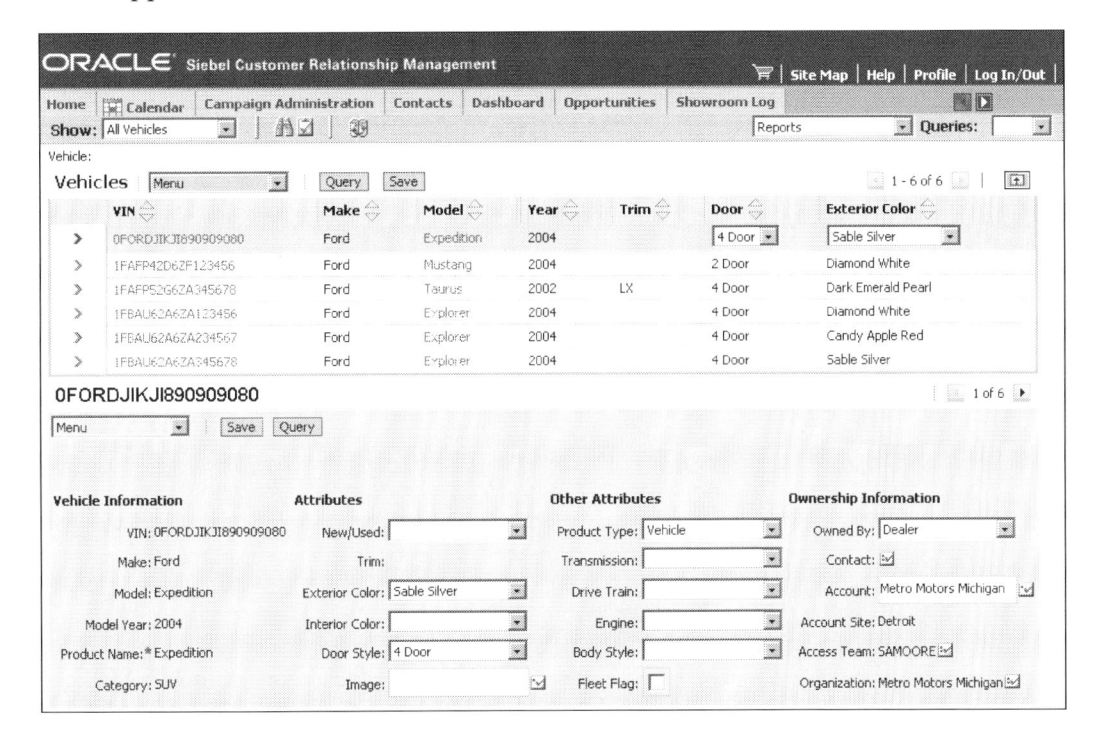

Because Gus' job title starts with "Ford", a rule in the personalization rule set associated with the list applet applies that prevents Gus from seeing vehicles other than Ford.

> Use the Siebel Sample database on your demonstration machine to repeat the scenarios explained in the above section.

Summary

In this chapter, we learned how Siebel access control and Siebel personalization allow administrators to define precise access to application features and data.

We introduced the concept of responsibilities, which allows defining groups of users or employees that have access to the same set of views in order to fulfil their daily tasks as defined by the business processes of their company.

The built-in access control mechanism for data is based on personal ownership or an employee's position within an organization. Specialized views such as the "My" or "All" views exist to invoke the respective filtering instructions.

The Siebel Personalization engine is a powerful filtering layer that allows administrators to define complex expressions, which drive the availability of applets, views, and records.

By using the Siebel Sample Database and various applications such as the Siebel Partner Portal or Siebel Dealer, this chapter also deepened our understanding of Siebel standard functionality.

In the next chapter, we will discuss Siebel user account management.

12
Managing User Accounts

As we have learned in the previous chapter, any person—be it an internal employee, a partner employee, or a customer—who wants to use a Siebel CRM application, must be registered as a user or employee and be associated with at least one responsibility. Data visibility in Siebel CRM is controlled by the **access control layer**, which takes personal data ownership or the user's current position within an organization into account in order to provide secure access to customer data.

It is therefore mandatory for an administrator to understand how to correctly set up and maintain the organizational information to provide end users with the Siebel application features and data they need to do their daily jobs.

In this chapter, we will discuss how to:

- Understand divisions and organizations
- Set up and manage the position hierarchy
- Set up user and employee accounts

Understanding divisions and organizations

Mapping real world entities to technical concepts is one of the key factors for successful software products. It is therefore quite interesting to see how the Siebel design team faced the challenge of bringing the complex hierarchical relationships of large corporations into the Siebel data model.

Managing User Accounts

Early in the analysis phase of a Siebel CRM implementation project, the divisional or departmental hierarchy of the customer is analyzed and documented. The typical diagram type to document the divisions of a company is an organization chart. The following is the organization chart for an example company:

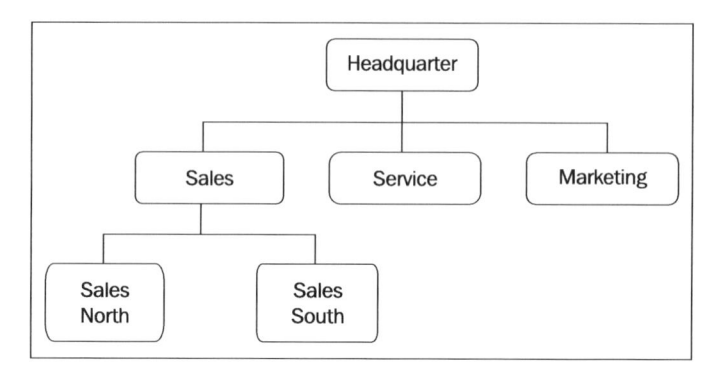

The Sales, Service, and Marketing divisions are subordinate to the Headquarter division. The Sales department has subdivisions, which define the territories (North and South) that the sales force operates in.

Setting up divisions

Once the divisional hierarchy of a company is documented, it must be translated to Siebel administrative data. An administrator uses the **Administration - Group** screen, **Internal Divisions** view—shown in the following screenshot—to enter and manage the division information:

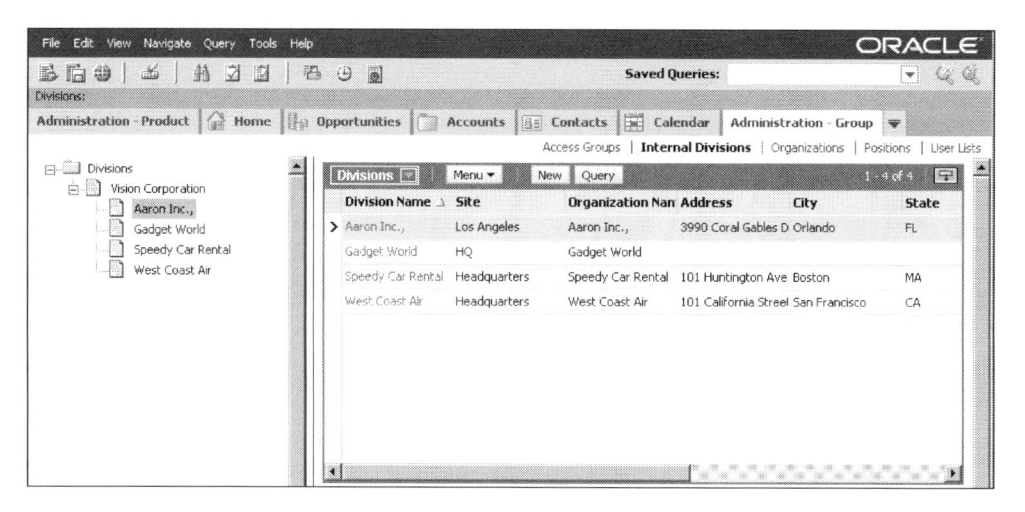

This view allows administrators to enter and maintain information about a company's divisions. The example company visible in the screenshot (Vision Corporation) is part of the Siebel sample database and has four subordinate divisions.

In order to create a new divisional hierarchy, we can follow the steps in the task list below:

1. Log in to the Siebel application using an administrative user account.
2. Navigate to the Administration - Group screen, Internal Divisions view.
3. Create a new record for the top-level division first.
4. Enter address and other information if required.
5. Save the division record.
6. Create a new division for each subordinate division and use the Parent Division field to select the appropriate parent division.
7. Use the explorer applet to verify that the divisional hierarchy represents the organization chart.

The following screenshot shows the explorer applet in the Internal Divisions view after the entry of the data from the example organization chart:

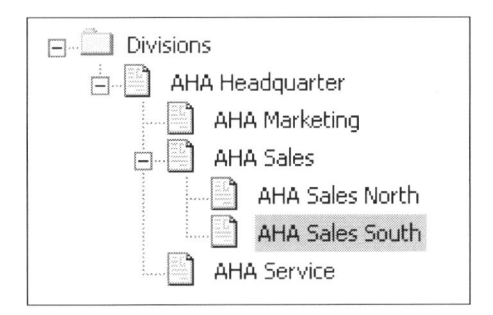

```
Divisions
    AHA Headquarter
        AHA Marketing
        AHA Sales
            AHA Sales North
            AHA Sales South
        AHA Service
```

In order to distinguish the example company from other divisions in the database, the acronym "AHA" was used.

From an administrative perspective, we must be aware of the fact that organizational changes might occur frequently. These changes can include one department becoming subordinate of another, or other departments being detached from the hierarchy in order to become separate companies. Siebel administrators must be informed of these changes in order to be able to adjust the division data in a timely manner.

Managing User Accounts

> In your demonstration environment, use the instructions in the above section to create a division hierarchy. You might want to use the example or create your own divisions.

Setting up organizations

When a division or an entire partner company wants to use the Siebel CRM infrastructure, this is typically accompanied by the requirement to associate data with the division or partner company in order to provide data security.

As we discussed in the previous chapter, records in the Siebel database can be associated with one or more organizations to filter these records for users of the respective organizations.

Siebel administrators can declare a division as an organization. This is done by simply checking the **Organization Flag** of a division. However, this change cannot be undone. Once the division is flagged as an organization and the record is saved, the flag becomes read only, as shown in the following screenshot:

We can decide which divisions within the organization chart should be flagged as organizations depending on the data security requirements defined by the project team. The result is typically a second hierarchy of organizations within the division hierarchy. Once an organization is created, Siebel data such as customer accounts, service requests, and so on can be associated with the organization. The following diagram shows how the divisions named **Headquarter** and **Sales** have been flagged as organizations. They are now part of the organization hierarchy.

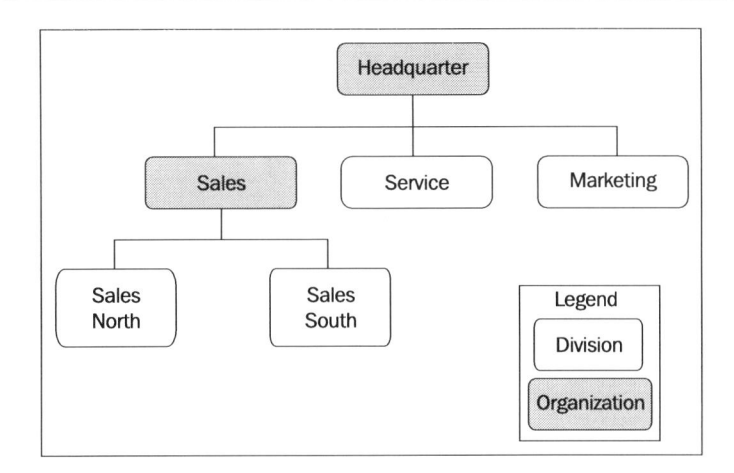

> By default, each new organization becomes subordinate to the "Default Organization", which the position of the Siebel Administrator (SADMIN) is assigned to. If data security policies mandate, we must set the Parent Organization field to an empty value in the Organizations view of the Administration - Group screen.

Even if a division cannot be associated to Siebel data, employees who have a position within that division are automatically associated with the nearest organization that can be located upwards in the division hierarchy.

In the above example, an employee who has a position in the AHA Sales North division will be associated with the Sales organization. The following screenshot shows the AHA Sales North division (note that the Organization Flag is unchecked) in the **Internal Divisions** view:

Managing User Accounts

The **Organization Name** field displays the name of the nearest organization (**AHA Sales**) above the **AHA Sales North** division. Employees who are associated with a position in the **AHA Sales North** division will automatically be associated with the **AHA Sales** organization. They will therefore be able to see data associated with the **AHA Sales** organization and each record they create will be automatically associated with the **AHA Sales** organization.

Similar to divisions, organizations cannot be deleted. When organizational changes require it, a Siebel administrator must detach the non-existing organization or division from all parent records by emptying the parent division field and change the name to indicate the state of the organization or division. For example, the name can be prefixed with "NOT USED" to indicate that the division or organization no longer exists. Furthermore, records that are associated with an organization that no longer exists must be re-assigned to other organizations. This is typically achieved by using the Siebel Assignment Manager.

> Mark at least one of the sample divisions you created earlier as an organization by setting the Organization Flag and saving the record.

Setting up and managing the position hierarchy

Employees are not associated directly with organizations. Siebel CRM uses a mechanism named **positions** to define both the association of an employee to an organization as well as the reporting relationship or hierarchy of the positions.

Positions represent a job entitlement for which people are recruited and subsequently paid. Employees can hold more than one position, for example to take over a colleague's job during vacation or sickness. Positions can also be held by multiple employees, which is unlikely for a CEO position but maybe more likely for sales representative or call center agent positions.

Each position can be assigned as a parent position to multiple child positions, thus enabling the administrator to create the so-called reporting hierarchy, which defines both the career level and the data access rights of an employee who is assigned to the position. The following diagram depicts a typical position hierarchy and indicates that each position must be assigned to exactly one division or organization:

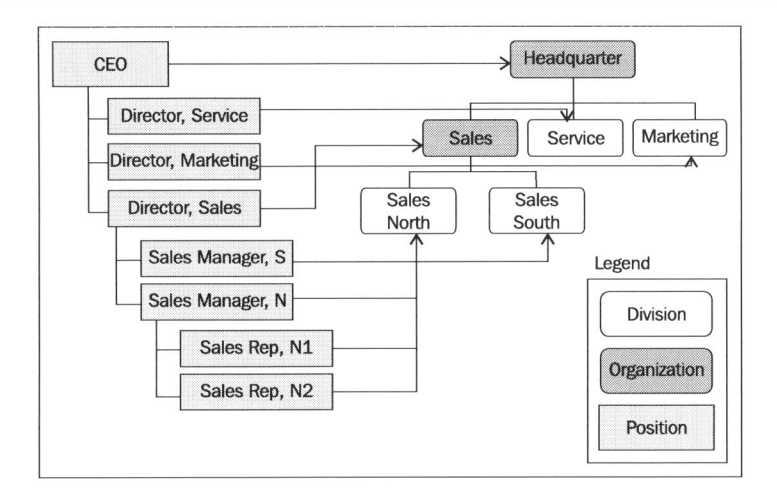

[Organizational hierarchy diagram showing CEO at top, with Director Service, Director Marketing, Director Sales reporting to CEO; Sales Manager S and Sales Manager N under Director Sales; Sales Rep N1 and Sales Rep N2 under Sales Manager N. Headquarters organization contains Sales, Service, and Marketing divisions. Sales division contains Sales North and Sales South. Legend: Division, Organization, Position.]

Positions within a single hierarchy can be associated with divisions or organizations that might be unrelated to each other. This provides a high level of flexibility, which allows administrators to implement almost every organizational setup.

Administrators enter the position hierarchy with guidance from the documents delivered by the business analyst team in the **Administration - Group** screen's **Positions** view, which is shown in the following screenshot:

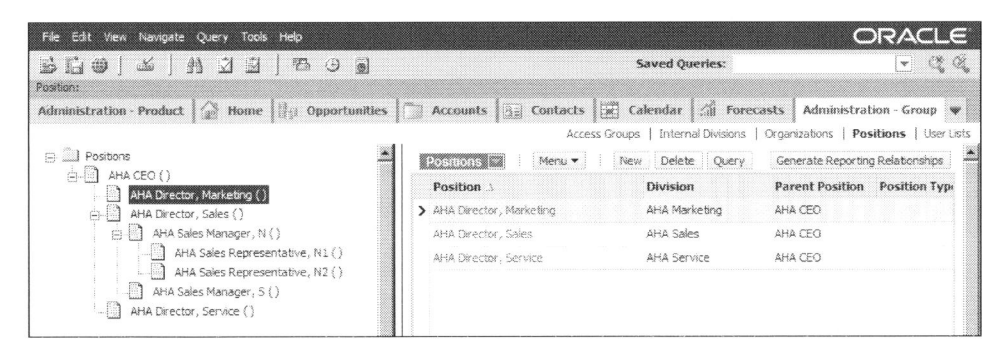

[Screenshot of Oracle Administration - Group screen showing Positions view with hierarchy tree on left (AHA CEO, AHA Director Marketing, AHA Director Sales, AHA Sales Manager N, AHA Sales Representative N1, AHA Sales Representative N2, AHA Sales Manager S, AHA Director Service) and position list on right with Position, Division, Parent Position, and Position Type columns.]

In the above example, the administrator has finished entering the positions depicted in the above diagram. The explorer applet allows administrators to verify the reporting hierarchy defined by the parent position field. The Division field is a mandatory field. It allows an administrator to select any division (marked as organization or not) and associate it with the position.

> Use the example position hierarchy described above to implement sample positions in your demonstration environment.

Multiple positions for an employee

As indicated above, an employee can be associated with more than one position to allow, for example, the implementation of vacation replacement. When an employee holds more than one position, the Siebel application always uses the employee's **primary position** to determine the organization she or he belongs to during login.

In the **User Preferences** screen, the employee can use the **Change Position** view to switch from one position to another. However, in a single session, the employee can only hold one position at a time. The screenshot below shows the **Change Position** view:

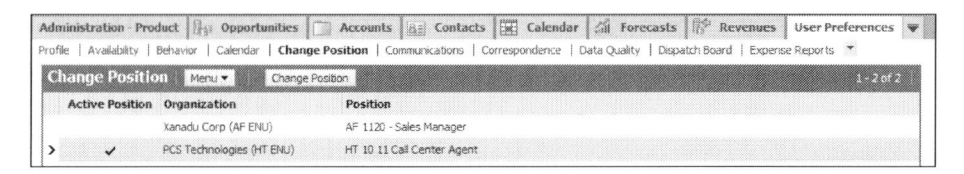

The employee who is currently logged in holds two positions, one of which is marked as the active position. By selecting another position and clicking the **Change Position** button, the employee can switch to the other position, which might result in an association to a different organization.

Once the employee has switched to another position, she or he can use the same views as before but the data displayed will most likely differ because of the Siebel access control layer filtering the data for the employee's current position and organization.

Setting up user and employee accounts

As discussed above, each person who wants to use a Siebel CRM application must be registered as either a user or employee. The difference between user and employee is that employees are associated with at least one position.

User records are typically created for customers who register themselves in customer facing web applications such as Siebel eService or Siebel eSales. The workflows invoked during the user registration process ensure that user records are created and associated with the necessary responsibilities automatically.

In the following, we focus on managing employee accounts. The following task list guides an administrator through the procedure of setting up a new employee manually:

1. Log in to the Siebel application using an administrative user account.
2. Navigate to the Administration - User screen, Employees view.

3. Create a new record and fill in the following fields (at least):
    - **First Name**
    - **Last Name**
    - **User ID** (a unique user identifier for the employee)
    - **Responsibility** (assign at least one responsibility to the employee)
    - **Position** (assign at least one position to the employee)
    - **Time Zone** (if the company deploys Siebel CRM across multiple time zones, associate the correct time zone with the employee)
    - **New Responsibility** (empty this field if the employee is not responsible to create new users or employees).
    - **Password** and **Confirm Password** (these fields are only writeable if directory server authentication is implemented)
4. Save the record.

The following screenshot shows the form applet in the Employees view of the Administration - User screen:

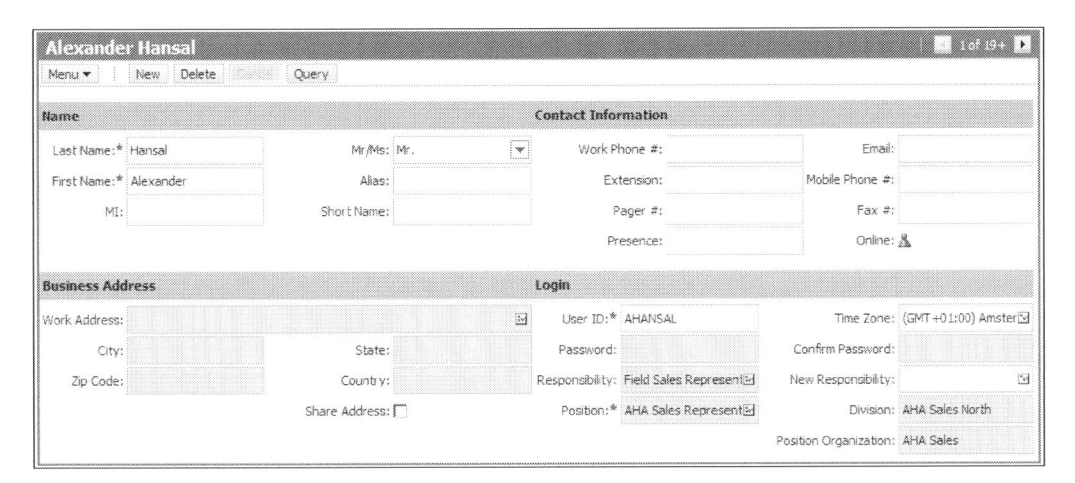

A new employee record for **Alexander Hansal** has been created by the administrator.

> The **New Responsibility** field defines the initial primary responsibility of any new user or employee that is created by the user or employee it is defined for. This is necessary for automated user registration where self-registering customers inherit the responsibility defined in the anonymous user account's New Responsibility field.
>
> The GUESTCST user for example, is used as the anonymous user for customer facing applications and has a "new responsibility" of "Web Registered User", which allows a customer who has registered her or himself to access more views than in anonymous mode.

Creating or verifying user accounts in the authentication system

As discussed in Chapter 10, each employee or user must be authenticated by an external system that is either a relational database management system (RDBMS) or a directory server (LDAP or Microsoft Active Directory).

For Siebel CRM implementations that use database authentication, a user account with the same username as defined in the User ID field must be created in the account management of the RDBMS as discussed in Chapter 10.

If directory server authentication is implemented, the information entered in the Employees view of the Administration - Group screen is propagated to the directory server and a new directory server account will be created automatically for the employee or user.

It is among the Siebel administrator's duties to create or verify the respective accounts in the authentication system.

> On your demonstration system, create a new employee account and ensure that the authentication system is updated accordingly. Test the new account by logging in to the Siebel application using the new employee's credentials.

Summary

In this chapter, we discussed the necessary steps to create the administrative data that allows people to log on to Siebel CRM applications as users or employees.

In Siebel terms, a user is a person who has a responsibility and who can log in to a Siebel application. An employee is a user who has a position within an organization. To enable fully functional data security, administrators must create organizations and positions before they can start creating employee accounts.

The chapter provided insight into the administrative views and the typical administrative tasks to manage divisions, organizations, positions, employees, and users.

In the next chapter, we will learn how administrators can use Siebel Remote to support developers and mobile users.

13
Siebel Remote and the Siebel Development Environment

When Siebel CRM was designed in the mid-nineties, the initial idea was to create a **sales force automation** (**SFA**) system that allowed traveling sales representatives to capture customer data on site and synchronize with the company server later in the day.

This is how Siebel Remote, the module supporting synchronization of mobile client data with the server database, came into existence. Even in a time of ubiquitous Internet access, applications that allow for working with the data offline are still widely adopted. The simple reason behind this fact is that full time wireless access to the company network is still either too costly or impossible to achieve.

Siebel Remote is a module that is used in each and every Siebel CRM project around the world, even if the company never deploys mobile clients. This is because Siebel developers rely on the mechanisms to create and synchronize local databases in order to obtain a secure workspace for application configuration.

In this chapter, we will learn how to support developers and remote users alike with the features of the Siebel Remote module. The chapter is structured as follows:

- Introduction to Siebel Remote
- Setting up mobile clients
- Enabling and configure Siebel Remote server components
- Creating the database schema files
- Extracting data for local databases
- Initializing the local database
- Understanding the Siebel configuration process
- Synchronizing the local database
- Monitoring and managing Siebel Remote users

Introduction to Siebel Remote

As indicated above, Siebel Remote is the result of many years of design and development. In the following, we will explore the fundamental concepts of Siebel Remote.

The following diagram defines the major building blocks of the Siebel Remote architecture:

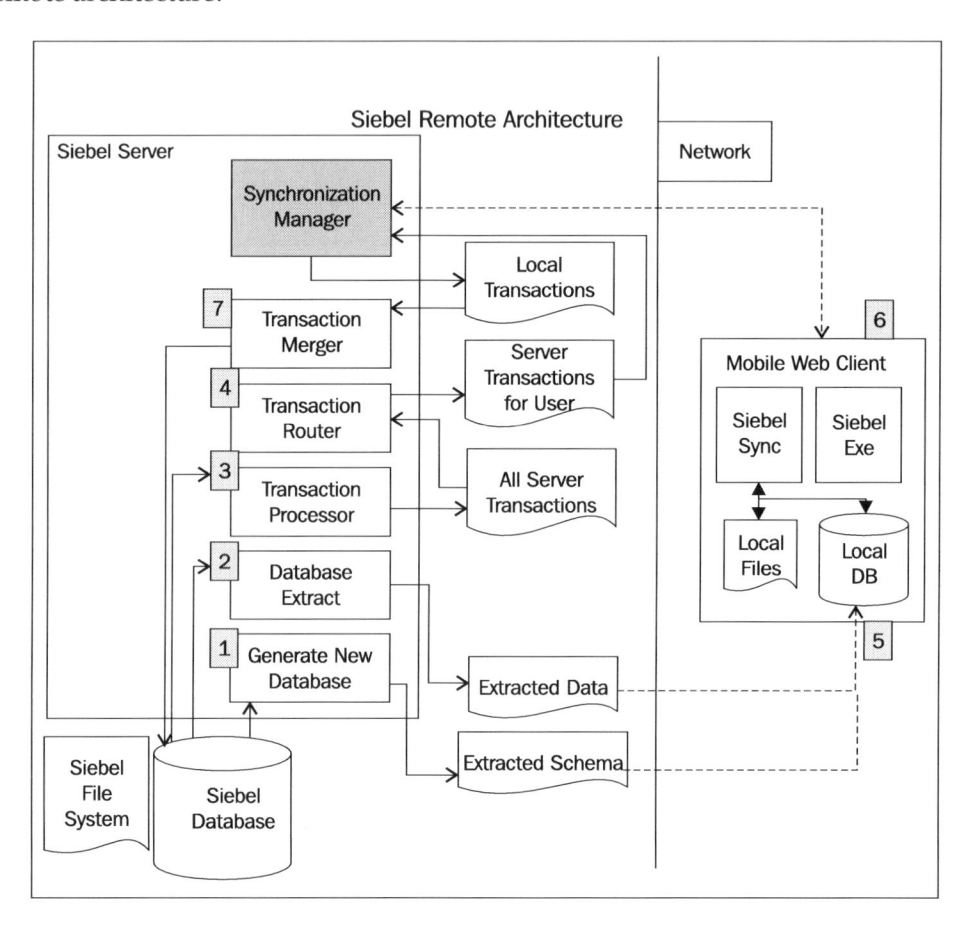

We observe that from a high-level perspective, the architecture consists of Siebel server components, files generated and read by those components, and the Mobile Web Client.

The following table describes the building blocks numbered in the above diagram. Each of the components will be explained in more detail later in the chapter:

Number	Component	Description
1	Generate New Database	A server component that is responsible for reading the current schema of the server database and generate a database template on the Siebel server.
2	Database Extract	This server component extracts the data snapshot for each registered mobile client and stores it as a set of files on the Siebel server.
3	Transaction Processor	A background component that reads a central transaction log table (S_DOCK_TXN_LOG) in the server database and writes the transactions to files on the Siebel server's file system.
4	Transaction Router	This background component continuously reads the transactions extracted by the Transaction Processor and creates individual transaction files for each mobile client depending on visibility and other rules. As a result, each client will only receive a subset of the server data.
5	Local Database Initialization	When a mobile user logs in to the local database for the first time, a network connection is established to fetch the template generated by the Generate New Database component and the data files generated by the Database Extract component. These files are then used by the Siebel Upgrade Wizard on the local machine to instantiate the local database.
6	Local Database Synchronization	When a mobile user synchronizes, a session on the Synchronization Manager component is established via the network. The network connection is then used to transport the server-side transaction files to the mobile client and transport the local transaction files to the server. On the mobile client, the local database is then updated with the server-side transactions.
7	Transaction Merger	This background component continuously reads the transaction files synchronized from the mobile clients and applies the transactions within these files to the server database.

As indicated above, the data synchronization is implemented by the means of exchanging transaction files between the systems rather than establishing direct database connections. The transaction files have a suffix of .dx and are incrementally numbered. Their content is only readable by the Siebel components and consists of individual transactions such as inserting, updating, or deleting a record.

Differences between developers and end users

It is important to understand that both Siebel client types—the Siebel Mobile Web Client and Siebel Tools—can be used in remote mode. The clients differ as much as their users and the way they work with the clients.

Next, we will explore the differences between the way a Siebel developer uses Siebel clients and a local database and the way a typical end user such as a travelling sales representative uses the Siebel Remote infrastructure.

Task	Developer	End User
Initialize the local database.	Can use Siebel Tools or the Mobile Web Client to initialize the local database.	Can **only** use the Mobile Web Client to initialize the local database.
Load repository data into the local database.	It is mandatory for the developer to load repository data into the local database.	End users do **not** have a local copy of repository data.
Work with data.	Uses Siebel Tools to modify or create repository data. Uses the Mobile Web Client to create test data and modify or create administrative data such as Responsibilities for testing reasons.	Inserts, updates, and deletes customer data using the Mobile Web Client.
Synchronize the local database.	Developers typically do not synchronize the local database with the server. The major reason is to avoid inconsistent test data to be inserted into the server database.	End users **must** synchronize on a regular basis to ensure that the changes they made locally are made accessible to other users on the server database.

We can observe that developers need a local database to provide a safe environment to apply and test changes they make to the repository metadata. However, developers do not typically use the synchronization features of the Mobile Web Client.

In the following, we will explore the tasks that a Siebel administrator has to undertake to support developers. Many of the tasks also apply to the deployment of local databases for the remote end user community.

Setting up mobile clients

Registering an employee as a mobile client is the first task in the process of supporting users who need a local database. This procedure is necessary for developers and end users alike.

Administrators register employees as mobile clients in the **Administration - Siebel Remote** screen, **Mobile Clients** view, which is shown in the following screenshot:

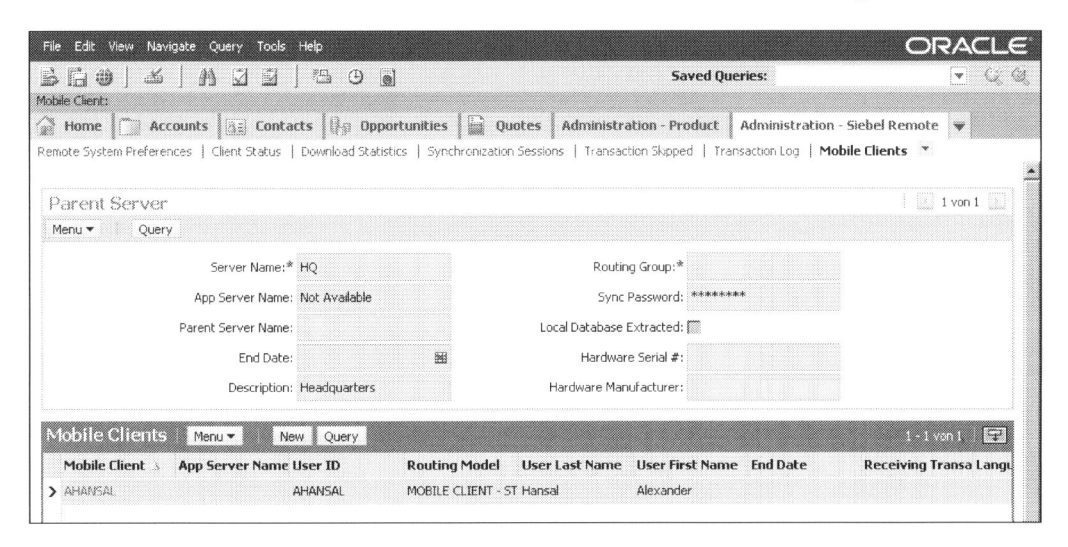

The following steps describe the process of registering a new mobile client:

1. Navigate to the **Administration - Siebel Remote** screen, **Mobile Clients** view.
2. In the Mobile Clients list, click **New**.
3. Enter a name for the mobile client. This is typically the same as the user's login name but can be different from it.
4. Select an employee or enter a user login identifier in the User ID field.
5. Select the MOBILE CLIENT - STANDARD routing model (See the information box below for details on routing models).
6. Save the record.

> Routing models in Siebel Remote define what data is synchronized to the mobile client. For developers who never or rarely synchronize, the standard routing models are sufficient. Specialized routing models exist for scenarios that require smaller amounts of data to be synchronized. For example, the Selective Retrieval routing model only synchronizes records that have been flagged for remote use.

Enabling and configuring Siebel Remote server components

The Siebel Remote component group contains all necessary components to support mobile clients. Administrators must enable this component group on one server in the Siebel enterprise. The Siebel Remote component group consists of the following components:

- Transaction Processor
- Transaction Router
- Transaction Merger
- Synchronization Manager
- Generate New Database
- Database Extract
- Parallel Database Extract
- Replication Agent

The following table describes these components and provides information about the need to enable these components for a Siebel development environment or for mobile end users:

Component	Description	Enable for developers	Enable for mobile users
Transaction Processor	Extracts all record transactions from the server database (table S_DOCK_TXN_LOG) to files in the `txnproc` directory on the Siebel Server.	No	Yes

Component	Description	Enable for developers	Enable for mobile users
Transaction Router	Reads the files generated by the Transaction Processor and generates user-specific transaction files in the outbox directory of the user's docking folder on the Siebel server.	No	Yes
Transaction Merger	Applies transactions in files in the inbox directory of the user's docking folder on the Siebel server to the server database.	No	Yes
Synchronization Manager	Authenticates mobile clients and synchronizes transaction by transporting files from the user's outbox folder on the server to the local inbox and from the local outbox folder to the inbox directory on the server.	Only during local database initialization	Yes
Generate New Database	Reads the schema of the server database and creates a database template in the `dbtempl` folder on the Siebel server.	Only when the server database schema has changed.	Only when the server database schema has changed.
Database Extract	Creates a snapshot of the current data set visible to the user in the outbox directory of the user's docking folder.	Yes	Yes
Parallel Database Extract	This component supports multiple threads to speed up the database extract process for multiple users at once.	Typically not used	Can be used to improve performance of the database extract process.
Replication Agent	Synchronizes a replication server database with the headquarter database.	No	Typically not used.

In order to enable the Siebel Remote component group on a Siebel server, we can use the srvrmgr command line utility. A command similar to the following enables the group on a Siebel server:

`enable compgrp remote for server Eval_1`

The server name `Eval_1` is an example in the above command line.

We must restart the Siebel server once a component group has been enabled. In order to minimize the load on the server's CPU and memory, it is recommendable to use commands similar to the following to set unneeded components to manual start up mode:

`manual start comp PDbXtract for server Eval_1`

The above command sets the Parallel Database Extract component to manual start.

> Siebel Remote supports the concept of replication servers. These servers synchronize against a headquarter server and can have their own group of mobile clients. Given today's ubiquity of high-speed wide area networks, Siebel replication servers are rarely implemented.

Creating the database schema files

After a new installation of a Siebel enterprise and after each change to the schema through developer activity or an upgrade to a newer Siebel version, administrators must run a job for the **Generate New Database** component.

The component is named Generate New Database because it creates a new empty Sybase Adaptive Server Anywhere database in the `DBTEMPL` folder of the Siebel server's installation directory. This empty database contains the same tables and indexes as those that existed in the server database at the point in time when the component was invoked.

We can use either the Siebel Server Manager (srvrmgr) command line utility to start a task for the GenNewDb (its alias name) component or use the Jobs view in the Administration - Server Management screen in the Siebel Web Client.

The following procedure describes how to run a job for the Generate New Database component using the Jobs view:

1. Navigate to the **Administration - Server Management** screen, **Jobs** view.
2. Click **New** to create a new job request.

3. Select **Generate New Database** from the **Component/Job** pick list.
4. Click the Submit Job button.
5. Monitor the Job using *ALT+ENTER* to refresh the Jobs view frequently until the job's status changes to Success.
6. Open the Siebel Server's installation folder and navigate to the `DBTEMPL` folder.
7. Verify that a new subdirectory has been created and that a file `sse_utf8.dbz` exists among other files. This file is a compressed, empty Sybase database with the same tables and indexes as the server database.

The following screenshot shows the **Jobs** view in the **Administration - Server Management** screen:

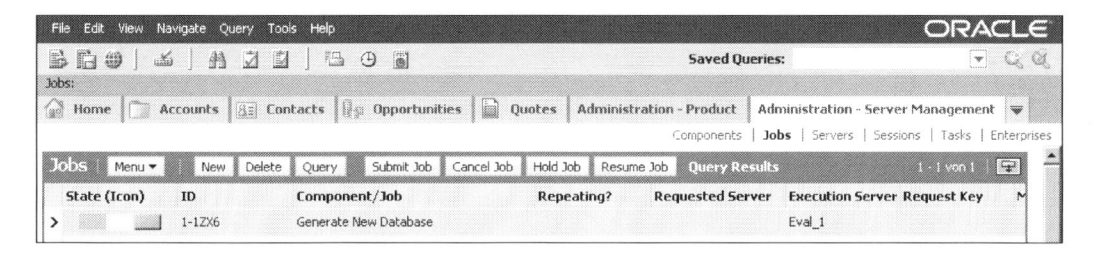

A job request for the **Generate New Database** component is visible in the list.

> Sybase databases have a super user account named DBA. The password for this account is generated by using the first eight characters of the name of the Siebel enterprise. If the enterprise name is shorter than eight characters, the missing characters are replaced by numbers starting at 1.
>
> For example, if the enterprise name is Siebel, the DBA account's password will be Siebel12. Administrators can choose a different password by setting the DbaPwd parameter value before submitting the job request.

Extracting data for local databases

The next step is to extract a data snapshot for one or more mobile users using the Database Extract server component. Before we submit a job request for the Database Extract component, we must verify that the Siebel Remote system preferences are set correctly.

Siebel Remote and the Siebel Development Environment

About Siebel Remote system preferences

We can inspect the system preferences for Siebel Remote by navigating to the **Remote System Preferences** view in the Administration - Siebel Remote screen. The form applet in this view is shown in the following screenshot:

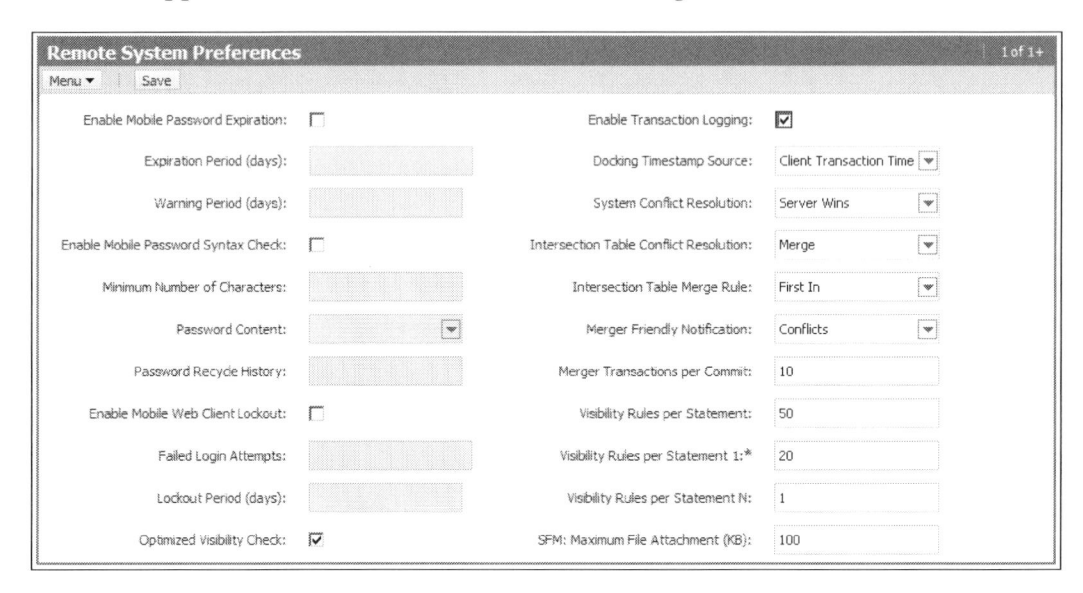

[Screenshot: Remote System Preferences form applet showing fields such as Enable Mobile Password Expiration, Expiration Period (days), Warning Period (days), Enable Mobile Password Syntax Check, Minimum Number of Characters, Password Content, Password Recycle History, Enable Mobile Web Client Lockout, Failed Login Attempts, Lockout Period (days), Optimized Visibility Check, Enable Transaction Logging (checked), Docking Timestamp Source (Client Transaction Time), System Conflict Resolution (Server Wins), Intersection Table Conflict Resolution (Merge), Intersection Table Merge Rule (First In), Merger Friendly Notification (Conflicts), Merger Transactions per Commit (10), Visibility Rules per Statement (50), Visibility Rules per Statement 1 (20), Visibility Rules per Statement N (1), SFM: Maximum File Attachment (KB) (100).]

In the following table, we describe the most important system preferences for Siebel Remote and their impact on the mobile client. In addition we describe the recommended settings for developers and mobile users.

System Preference	Description	Value for developers	Value for mobile users
Enable Mobile Password Expiration	When set to true, the mobile client's password will expire after the amount of days specified in the Expiration Period field. A warning will be displayed as specified in the Warning Period field.	Unchecked. (Local databases for developers do not contain sensitive data.)	Checked. Values for expiration set according to corporate security policies.

System Preference	Description	Value for developers	Value for mobile users
Enable Mobile Password Syntax Check	When set to true, the password chosen by the mobile user will be checked against the rules in the three fields below this flag.	Unchecked. (Developers should be able to choose a password freely.)	Checked. Syntax rules set according to corporate security policies.
Enable Mobile Web Client Lockout	When set to true, the mobile client account will be locked after the specified number of failed login attempts for the specified number of days.	Unchecked. (Due to the possible loss of productivity when a developer is locked out)	Checked. In consideration of corporate security policies.
Enable Transaction Logging	Enables the logging of database transactions to the S_DOCK_TXN_LOG table.	Checked. for database extract. Uncheck once local databases are initialized.	Always checked. Except before major data imports or updates which mandate a new database extract.

Running a database extract job for developers

Because we consider a development environment scenario in this chapter, the following procedure includes instructions to set the security control fields in the Remote System Preferences view to false—as recommended above. The procedure describes how to execute a job for the Database Extract component for a single user or groups of users.

1. Navigate to the **Administration - Siebel Remote** screen, **Remote System Preferences** view.
2. Uncheck the Enable Mobile Password Expiration flag.
3. Uncheck the Enable Mobile Password Syntax Check flag.
4. Uncheck the Enable Mobile Web Client Lockout flag.
5. Check the Enable Transaction Logging flag.
6. Click **Save**.
7. Navigate to the **Administration - Server Management** screen, **Jobs** view.
8. Click **New** to create a new job request.
9. Select Database Extract from the Component/Job pick list.
10. Scroll down to the Parameters list.

11. Create a new parameter record, select **Client Database encryption method** and enter a value of **None**.
12. Create another parameter record, select **Client Name** and enter either an exact mobile client name, a comma-separated list of mobile client names, or use the asterisk (*) wildcard character. For example, specify all mobile clients that start with A by entering A* as the value for the parameter.
13. Create another parameter record, select **Encrypt client Db password** and set the value to **False**.
14. If we wish to extract repository data so that developers do not have to copy it in Siebel Tools, we can set the **Extract all Repository Tables** parameter to **True**.
15. In the upper list applet, click **Submit Job**.
16. Monitor the job using *ALT+ENTER* until the job's status changes to Success.

To verify the successful execution of the Database Extract job, we can navigate to the **docking** folder in the Siebel Server's installation directory. For each mobile client specified in the Client Name parameter, we should now find a subdirectory with the client's name. This directory has an `inbox` and an `outbox` subdirectory.

The `outbox` subdirectory should contain a set of files, which represent the data that was present in the server database when the job was executed. The following screenshot shows the **outbox** folder for the mobile client **AHANSAL** and its content generated by the Database Extract component:

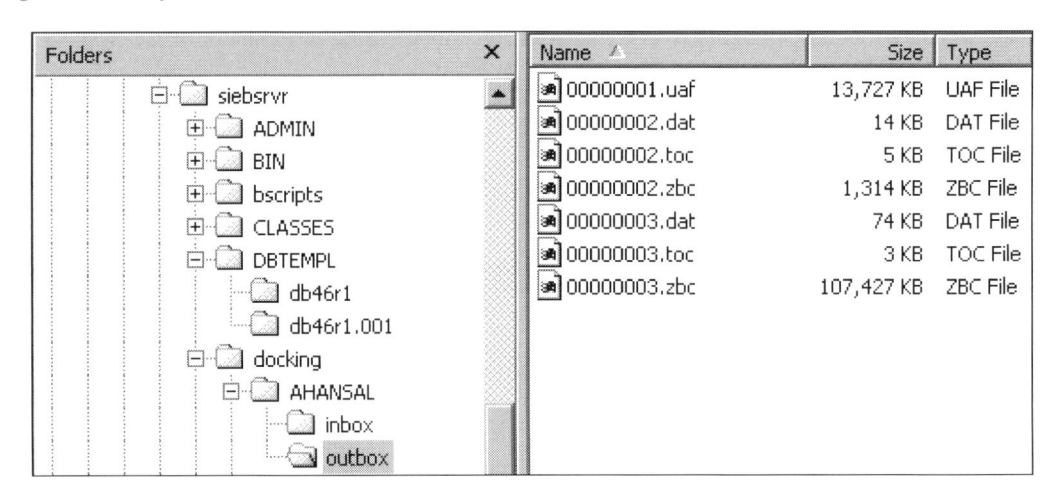

The files in the **outbox** directory contain the data that will be used to initialize the local database.

> On your demonstration machine, use the information in the above sections to register an existing employee as a mobile client, enable the Siebel Remote component group, and execute jobs for the Generate New Database and Database Extract components.

Initializing the local database

The initialization of the local database is a task that is typically carried out by the mobile users or developers themselves. However, it is important for a Siebel administrator to understand the procedure to be able to assist in case of errors.

Prerequisites for a successful initialization of the local database include:

- Establishing network connectivity
- Verifying settings in the client configuration files

Next, we will discuss these prerequisites.

Establishing network connectivity for mobile clients

For the initial download of the files that are needed to initialize the local database and before any attempt to synchronize, the computer that hosts the Siebel Mobile Web Client or Siebel Tools must be able to establish a TCP/IP connection to the Siebel Server machine that hosts the Synchronization Manager component.

Developer workstations are typically stationary and connected to an office network. Laptops are typically used by remote workers. It does not matter which technology (Wireless LAN, VPN or other) is used to establish network connectivity. The only thing that matters is that the computer can connect to the Siebel Server via TCP/IP.

Verifying settings in the client configuration files

Depending on the client used to initialize the local database, settings in one or more client configuration files (.cfg) must be verified. The following parameters in the [Local] section of the .cfg files must be set as described in the table below in order to successfully initialize and synchronize the local database:

Parameter	Description	Example Value
ConnectString	Defines the absolute path to the local Sybase database and includes parameters that are passed to the Sybase database engine.	D:\SIA81\CLIENT\local\sse_data.dbf -q -m -x NONE -gp 4096 -c15p -ch25p Note: The switches control the behavior of the Sybase database engine such as memory allocation.
DockConnString	Defines the hostname and port number where the Synchronization Manager server component is listening. If no port number is specified, the default port number of 40400 is used for the connection.	opsapps4

The following screenshot shows a typical client configuration file with the parameters in the [Local] section correctly set:

```
[Local]
Docked                    = FALSE
ConnectString             = D:\SIA81\CLIENT\local\sse_data.dbf -q -m -x NONE -gp 4096 -c15p -ch25p
TableOwner                = SIEBEL
DockedDBFilename          = CHANGE_ME
DLL                       = sscdw9.dll
SqlStyle                  = Watcom
MaxCachedCursors          = 16
MaxCachedDataSets         = 16
ReverseFillThreshold      = 100
DockTxnsPerCommit         = 500
DockConnString            = opsapps4
ChartServer               = localhost:8001
ChartImageFormat          = png
AutoStopDB                = FALSE
EnterpriseServer          = CHANGE_ME
UseCachedExternalContent  = TRUE
```

> The dbf file specified in the `ConnectString` parameter does not yet exist. It will be created by the Siebel Upgrade Wizard in the initialization step.

Additional configuration file settings for developers

Developers typically use both the Siebel Mobile Web Client and Siebel Tools against the same database. Therefore, the above settings must be applied to the Siebel Tools configuration file (`tools.cfg`) and all client configuration files that are used by the developer for implementation and local testing purposes.

The `ConnectString` parameter must point to the **same** folder across all files. This means that the folder path in the Siebel Tools configuration file must be changed to point to the client installation folder or vice versa In addition, the `LocalDbODBCDataSource` parameter in the `[Siebel]` section of all configuration files used by the developer must point to the name of the same ODBC data source used to access the local database.

Logging in to the local database for the first time

When a mobile user logs in to the local database for the first time, she or he receives a message that indicates that the local database has not been found. This is an expected situation and the user has to acknowledge the message by clicking the **Yes** button in order to connect to the synchronization manager on the Siebel server to download and initialize the local database. The following screenshot shows the notification message:

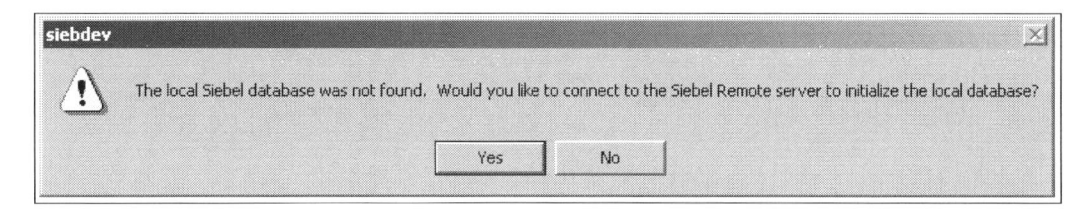

Siebel Remote and the Siebel Development Environment

After clicking the **Yes** button, a dialog box is displayed, prompting for the mobile client name, the username and the **future** password for the local database. The following screenshot shows the Siebel Remote Parameters dialog box:

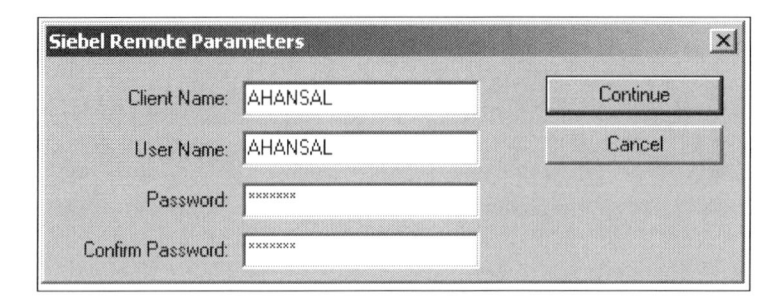

The **Client Name** parameter value must match the name of a registered mobile user. The **User Name** and **Password** parameters specify the login credentials that the mobile user will have to use to log in to the local database after it has been created.

After clicking the **Continue** button, the Siebel Remote software connects to the remote server and downloads the compressed schema and data files over the network to the local computer.

Once the files are downloaded and extracted, the Siebel Upgrade Wizard is invoked. The wizard runs automatically and uses the downloaded files to create and populate the new local Sybase database in the location specified in the `ConnectString` parameter of the client configuration file. The following screenshot shows the Siebel Upgrade Wizard displaying its progress during the local database initialization:

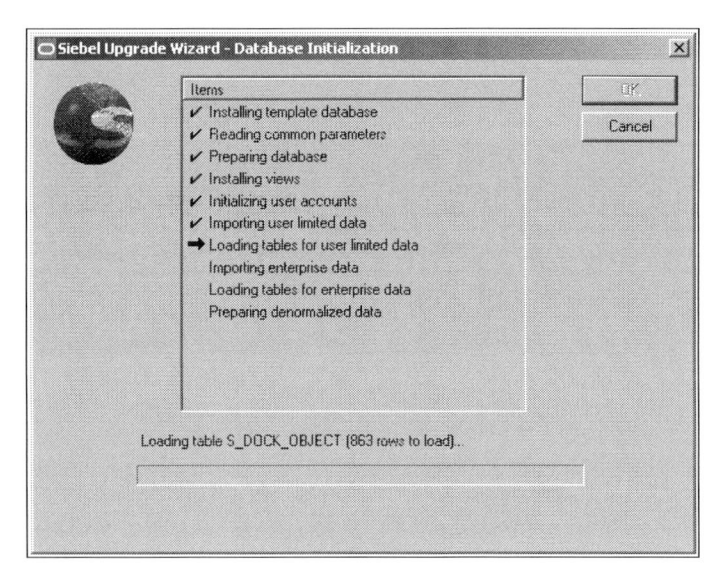

[402]

Once the Siebel Upgrade Wizard has completed all steps, the application is launched and the user is logged in. Developers who used Siebel Tools for the local database initialization will be logged on to Siebel Tools. Mobile users will see the Siebel application's homepage view.

If the database extract job was run using the **Extract all Repository Tables** parameter set to **True**, developers can start working immediately because the repository tables are already populated. If not, the developer will have to complete the process of local database initialization by using the "Get All Projects" functionality provided by Siebel Tools to copy repository data to the local database.

> Follow the instructions in the section above to prepare the client configuration files for your installation of Siebel Tools and the Siebel Developer Web Client. Then, use the client of your choice to log in with the mobile user account you created earlier to the local data source. Complete the process of initializing a local database by following the instructions in the section above.

Understanding the Siebel configuration process

Administrators must be aware of the Siebel configuration process in order to be able to assist developers when problems arise. The following example scenario shall serve to help in understanding the way developers use Siebel Tools to apply configuration changes:

Task	Description	Network Connection Required?
Check Out	When developers need to acquire write access to object definitions in the Siebel repository, they must "check out" the object or the project that contains the object.	Yes
	During the check out process, all selected object definitions are copied from the server database and overwritten in the local database.	
	A flag is set in both databases to indicate the lock and ownership of the developer, thus avoiding that other developers work on the same object at the same time.	

Task	Description	Network Connection Required?
Configure	Developers modify or create object definitions in their local database in order to implement functionality required by the business.	No
Compile	Using the Siebel Tools compile functionality, developers create a new version of the Siebel repository file (.srf) file for their Developer Web Client.	No
Unit Test	Developers use their local instance of the Siebel Developer Web Client against the same local database they use with Siebel Tools. By abiding to this principle, they can test modifications without affecting other developers.	No
Check In	Once the developer has tested the modifications, the object definitions are copied to the server database and the lock flags are unset. Now, all other developers can access the new or modified objects.	Yes

The typical architecture of a Siebel development environment can be described schematically by the following diagram:

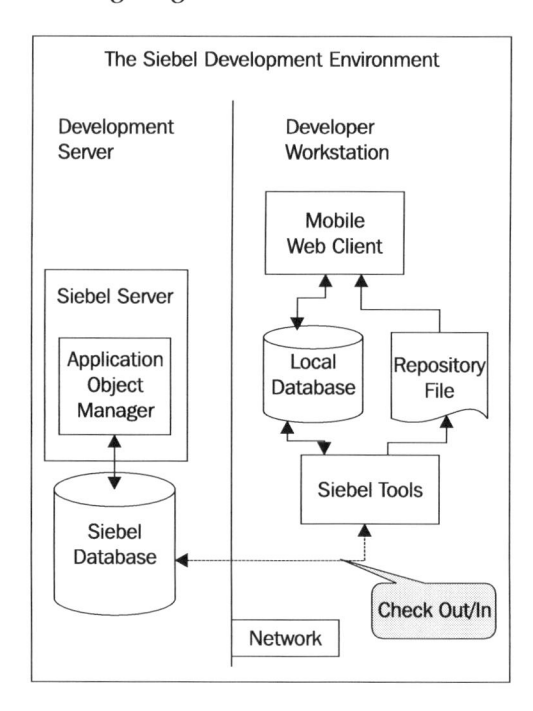

From the diagram, we can confirm that Siebel developers can work on their workstation independent of other developers. As we can observe, Siebel Tools establishes connections to both the local and the server database during the check out and check in processes. It is important to mention that the check out and check in processes never require Siebel Remote server components to be online or running.

Synchronizing local databases

In Siebel CRM projects that support remote end users, administrators must be aware of the synchronization process. After all, there are hundreds or even thousands of local databases that have to be synchronized with the server database on a regular basis.

Siebel CRM offers two approaches to achieve regular synchronization:

- Manual synchronization
- Siebel TrickleSync

Next, we will discuss both approaches and clarify the administrative steps.

Manual synchronization

In order to trigger the synchronization process, a mobile end user must establish connectivity to the corporate network and then select the **Synchronize Database** option from the application's File menu.

The user is then authenticated by the Synchronization Manager component on the remote Siebel server and the Siebel Remote dialog box is displayed, as shown in the following screenshot:

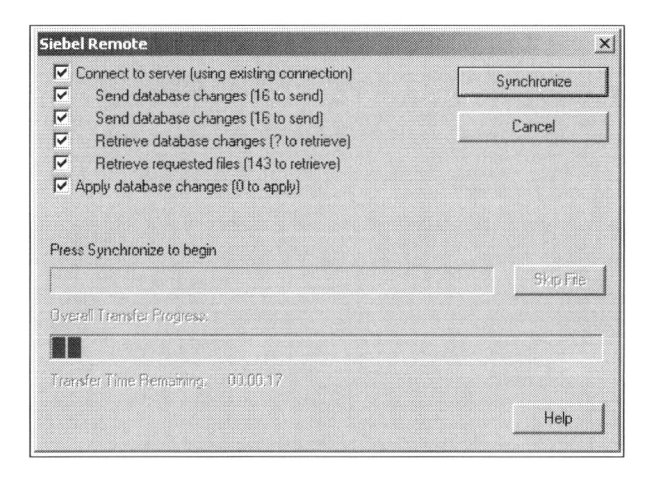

Siebel Remote and the Siebel Development Environment

This dialog box allows the remote user to select what actions should be executed during the synchronization session. In the above example, all actions are selected, including sending, receiving, and applying all changes to the local database and file system.

End users can now click the **Synchronize** button to start the synchronization session. A "two arrows" icon in the Windows system tray indicates a running synchronization session. When end users press the *Shift* key while clicking the Synchronize button, the Siebel Remote window will stay open and display the progress of the synchronization.

Once the synchronization is complete, mobile users can navigate to the User Preferences screen, Remote Status view in order to see details about their recent synchronization sessions.

End users should be encouraged to synchronize at least twice a day—in the morning before they start working and in the evening when they finish working. This ensures that nightly batch jobs on the server environment can process all data sent in from the mobile work force and that the mobile users receive all changes made by the nightly batch jobs before they start working.

Siebel TrickleSync

In order to ease the burden of manual synchronization, Siebel Remote includes TrickleSync. This feature allows administrators and end users (if their responsibility includes the view to make the changes) to control the automatic synchronization of local databases. Synchronization can occur even when the end user is not using the Siebel Mobile Web Client.

An administrator can control the TrickleSync settings for each mobile client in the Administration - Siebel Remote screen, Trickle Sync view. The following screenshot shows the **TrickleSync** settings for a mobile client:

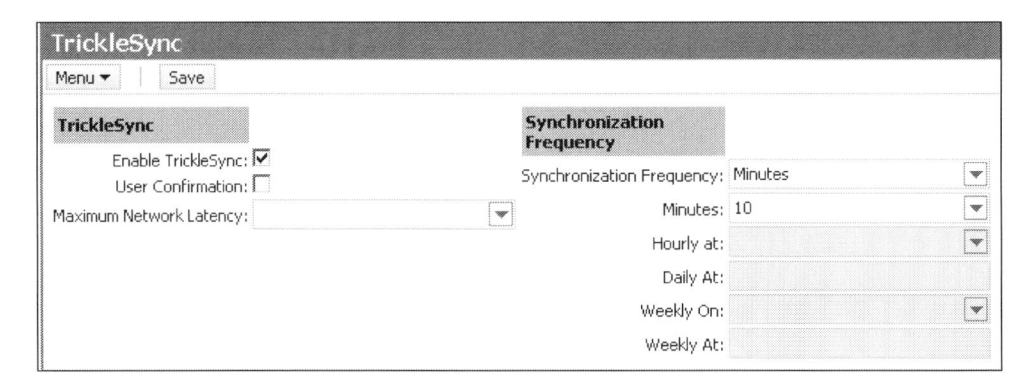

TrickleSync is enabled in the example and the frequency is set to 10 minutes without user confirmation.

TrickleSync is implemented as a separate executable on the mobile client machine named `autosync.exe`. This executable is started automatically with the Siebel Mobile Web Client when TrickleSync is enabled. If administrators wish to synchronize the local Siebel database when the Siebel Mobile Web Client is not open, they must cater for automatic start of the `autosync.exe` program such as placing a shortcut to it in the Windows Startup menu folder.

With Siebel TrickleSync, a high synchronization frequency and therefore high reliability and security of data entered by remote users can be easily achieved.

Monitoring and managing Siebel Remote users

When a company decides to deploy Mobile Web Clients to their remote workforce, administrator positions must be staffed in order to provide smooth operation of all processes related to synchronizing data between the central server database and hundreds or thousands of local databases.

In the following, we will give a brief overview of the most important tasks that a Siebel Remote administrator will have to accomplish:

- Managing the transaction components on the Siebel server
- Monitoring mobile client activity
- Sending messages to mobile users
- Re-extracting local databases
- Deactivating mobile user registrations

Managing the transaction components on the Siebel server

The following server components are critical for flawless processing of data synchronization:

- Transaction Processor
- Transaction Router
- Transaction Merger

- Synchronization Manager

Administrators must ensure that these components are well monitored and that notification mechanisms such as Siebel alert profiles are in place to inform the administrative staff when problems occur.

Apart from the Synchronization Manager, for which full operability is given when its status is either online or running, the other server components in the above list must have a status of running. Otherwise, there is a high risk of backlogged or even lost transactions.

Both the graphical user interface and the Siebel Server Manager command line can be used to monitor and manage the aforementioned server components. The following screenshot shows the **Servers** view in the **Administration - Server Management** screen in the Siebel Web Client:

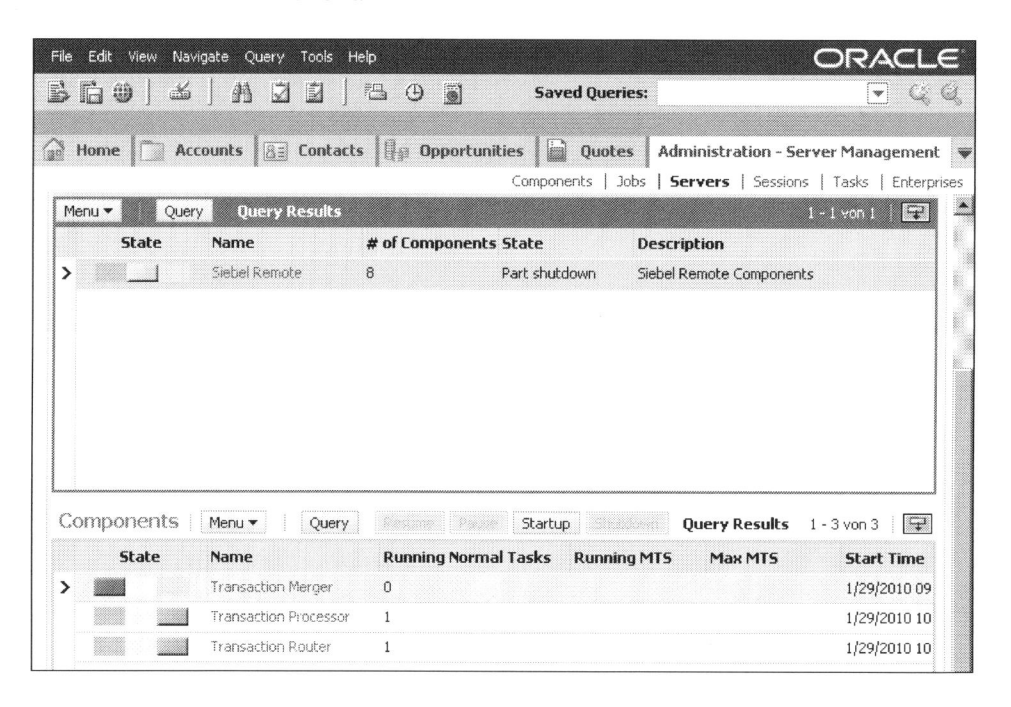

In this view, administrators can verify and change the status of all components enabled on the selected server including the components of the Siebel Remote component group. In the above screenshot, the **Transaction Processor** and **Transaction Router** components are running while the **Transaction Merger** component is not operational.

Monitoring mobile client activity

The Administration - Siebel Remote screen provides various views that an administrator can use to verify and monitor the status and activities of mobile clients. A good example is the Client Status view, which provides information about the database extract, initialization, and current status for each selected mobile client. The following screenshot shows the **Siebel Remote Client Status** form applet in the Client Status view:

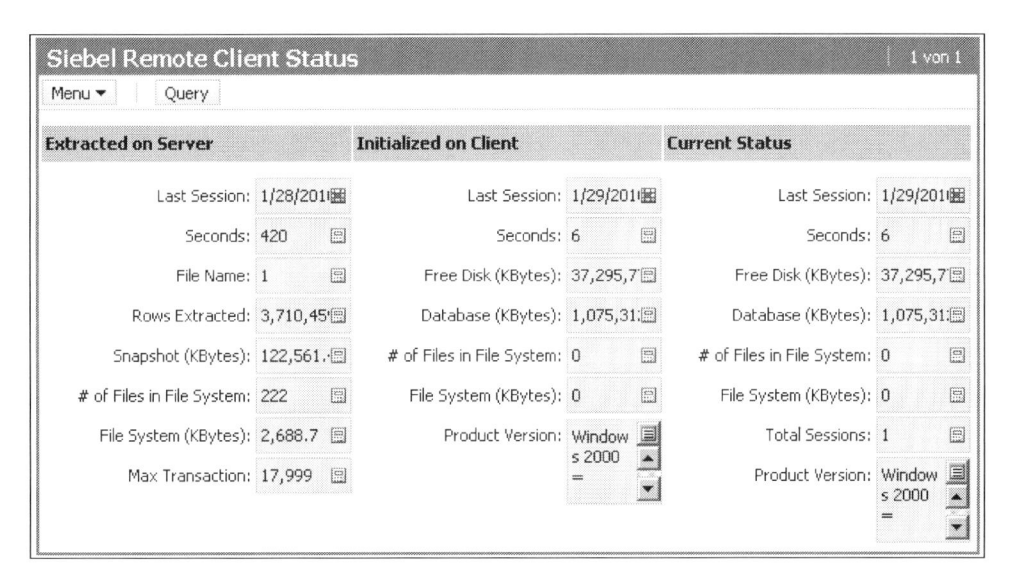

Other views in the Administration - Siebel Remote screen that are useful for administrators are listed in the following table:

View	Description
Download Statistics	Displays information about data downloaded to the selected mobile client during the last synchronization session.
Upload Statistics	Displays information about data uploaded to the headquarter server from the selected mobile client during the last synchronization session.
Synchronization Sessions	Lists all synchronization sessions and their timings for the selected mobile client.
Client Diagnostics	Detailed listing of all operations that occurred during all synchronization sessions.

Sending messages to mobile users

In case administrators need to communicate with mobile users on synchronization-related matters, they can create a file named `motd.txt` (message of the day) in the Siebel server's `ADMIN` directory.

When mobile users synchronize, they will receive the message in the `motd.txt` file. An example is shown in the following screenshot:

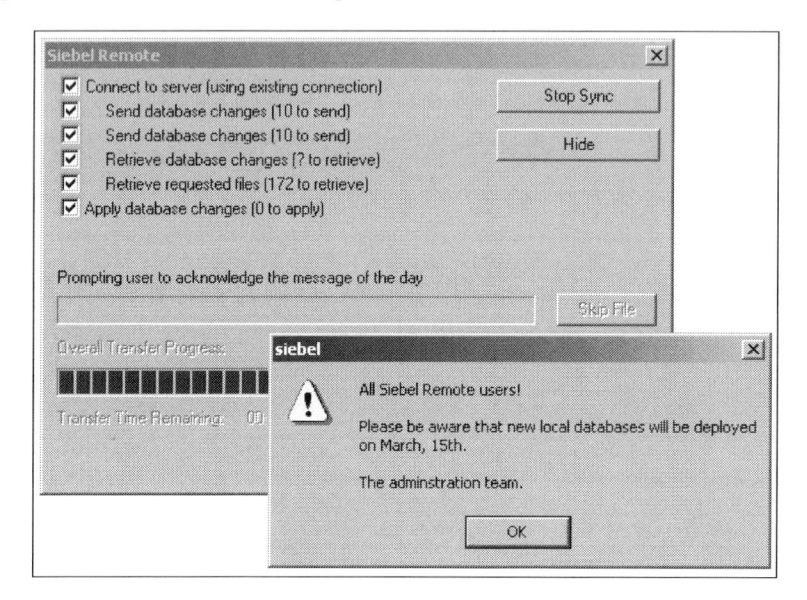

Source: *Siebel Remote and Replication Manager Administration Guide, Version 8.1*

Re-extracting local databases

There are several scenarios that require the repeated extraction of local database snapshots. These scenarios include:

- Database schema changes
- Import or modification of large amounts of data on the server database

In such scenarios, it is faster and more reliable to extract new databases for the mobile user community rather than to synchronize huge amounts of transactions. In the case of mass data changes on the server database such as importing large amounts of records using **Enterprise Integration Manager** (**EIM**), it is even recommended to disable transaction logging completely by unchecking the Enable Transaction Logging flag in the Remote System Preferences view in the Administration - Siebel Remote screen.

This will speed up the import process as a whole because transaction records will not be written to the S_DOCK_TXN_LOG table. On the other side, mobile users will not receive the new or updated records, so the local databases have to be extracted again.

Administrators can simply repeat the Database Extract component job in order to extract new databases. The default value of "True" for the **Save client transactions** parameter ensures that no data is lost when the mobile client synchronizes.

The synchronization mechanism detects the new database and prompts the user to download it. After downloading the files, the Siebel Upgrade Wizard is invoked as usual to create the new local database.

Deactivating mobile user registrations

In case we need to disable a mobile user's account we must ensure that transactions are no longer synchronized to the mobile client. We can accomplish the deactivation of a mobile client by setting the **End Date** field in the Mobile Clients view in the Administration - Siebel Remote screen as shown in the screenshot below:

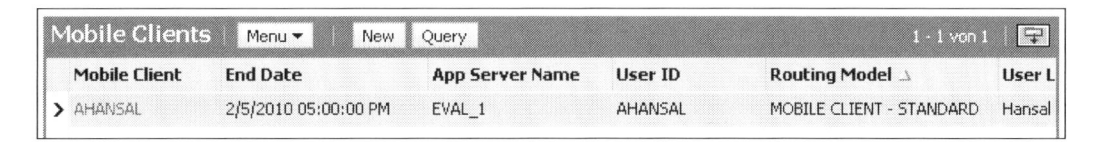

Mobile Client	End Date	App Server Name	User ID	Routing Model	User L
AHANSAL	2/5/2010 05:00:00 PM	EVAL_1	AHANSAL	MOBILE CLIENT - STANDARD	Hansal

The End Date value for the mobile client indicates that no transactions will be synchronized to the mobile client after the 5th of February 2010, 5:00 PM.

In addition to setting the end date, we must stop and start the Transaction Router and Transaction Processor server components in order to refresh their cached information.

To ensure that the mobile client can no longer establish a synchronization session, we must also delete the user's docking directory from the Siebel server.

Summary

The Siebel Remote module enables both the synchronization of hundreds or thousands of mobile clients with a central server database and the creation of local databases for developers.

In this chapter, we have explored the Siebel Remote architecture and described processes for both types of users. We learned how to enable Siebel Remote and extract local database templates and data on the Siebel Server.

To deepen our understanding of the configuration process, we explained the architecture and processes of the Siebel development environment.

Finally, this chapter introduced important procedures related to monitoring and managing remote users.

In the next chapter, we will learn how to install the Siebel Management Server infrastructure.

14
Installing and Configuring the Siebel Management Server Infrastructure

In an ongoing effort to provide a stable and extensible platform for cross-enterprise administration tasks, engineers at Siebel Systems created the Siebel Management Server and Management Agent infrastructure.

At the time of writing this book, two Siebel modules use the Siebel Management Server infrastructure. These features are Application Deployment Manager (ADM) and the Siebel Diagnostic Tool.

Installing and configuring the Siebel Management Server infrastructure is a prerequisite to using ADM to migrate configuration changes between Siebel CRM environments. If our company has licensed the Siebel Diagnostic Tool, we have to install and configure the infrastructure as well.

This chapter introduces the Siebel Management Server infrastructure and focuses on the installation and configuration tasks for the Siebel Management Server and the Siebel Management Agents. The chapter is structured as follows:

- Overview of the Siebel Management Server infrastructure
- Installation and configuration of the Siebel Management Server
- Installation and configuration of the Siebel Management Agents
- Register Management Agents

Overview of the Siebel Management Server Infrastructure

The Siebel Management Server infrastructure, consisting mainly of a single Siebel Management Server and one Siebel Management Agent per Siebel Server, is an open Java-based framework to accomplish administrative tasks that span across all Siebel enterprises. Two features of Siebel CRM currently use this infrastructure:

- Application Deployment Manager
- Siebel Diagnostic Tool

In this chapter, we focus on the installation and configuration of the Siebel Management Server infrastructure. Application Deployment Manager and the Siebel Diagnostic Tool will be discussed in upcoming chapters. It is very important to understand that the Siebel Management Server infrastructure is a generic framework that has been chosen by Siebel engineering to support the two aforementioned features.

The following diagram helps us understand the architecture of the Siebel Management framework:

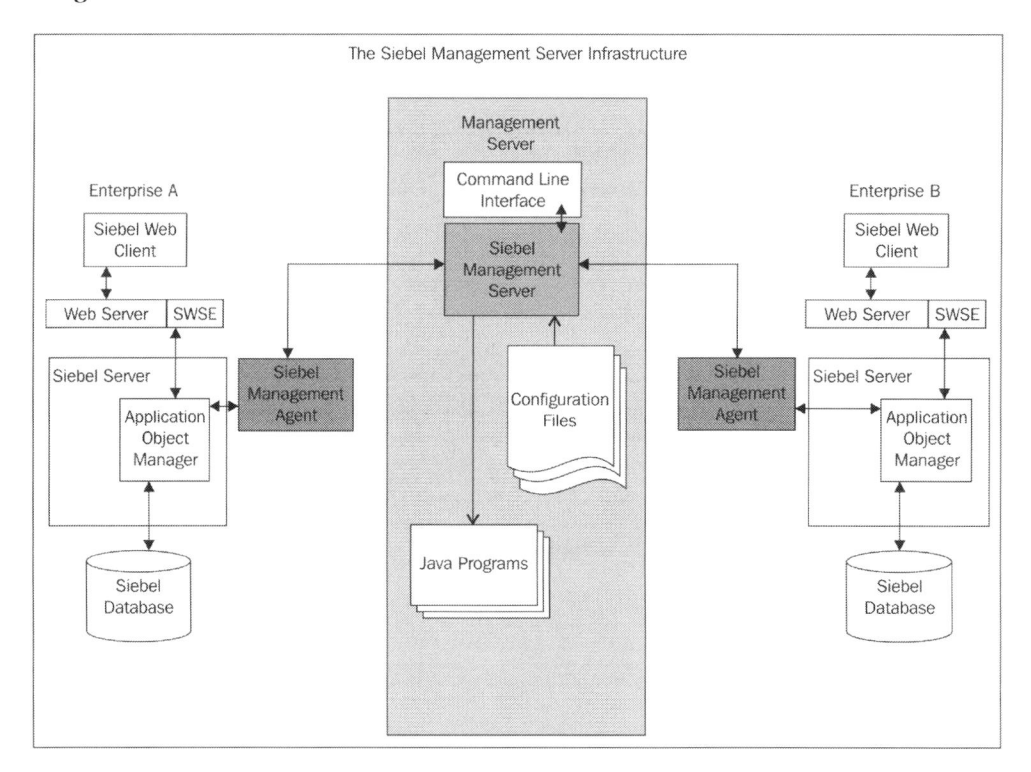

The diagram depicts the building blocks of the Siebel Management Server infrastructure and their relationships to other members of the Siebel Web Architecture.

The Siebel Management Server can be described as a single orchestration service that uses the Siebel Management Agents to access information on the various Siebel servers across all enterprises. One Management Agent is required to be installed for each Siebel Server.

Both the Siebel Management Server and the Agents are written in Java and are implemented as system services. There is no limit in the number of enterprises or Siebel servers per enterprise that can be monitored by a single Management Server.

The Siebel Management Server itself can be accessed by command line tools in order to execute the programs residing on the server and collect their output. Each module that uses the Siebel Management Server—namely Application Deployment Manager and the Siebel Diagnostic Tool—is implemented as a set of files (configuration files, executables, and so on), which reside on the management server machine.

Installing and configuring the Siebel Management Server

The Siebel Management Server installers are available from `http://edelivery.oracle.com`. The process of downloading and extracting the installation images has been described in detail in Chapter 2.

The Siebel Management Server is only supported on Microsoft Windows operating systems. The major reason for this limitation is that it comes preconfigured for the ADM functionality, which includes a small Sybase database for holding ADM-related information. Siebel CRM supports Sybase databases only on Windows platforms.

Prerequisites for the Siebel Management Server

The following prerequisites must be met before we begin with the installation and configuration of the Siebel Management Server:

- Java Development Kit (JDK) 1.5 or higher is installed
- Java Runtime Environment (JRE) 1.5 or higher is installed
- A recent framework (version 5.8 or higher) for the Perl programming language is installed (Perl scripts are used to generate configuration files)

- There is *no* drive mapped using the letter `z:` (to avoid error messages during configuration)
- A Siebel user account is created in all Siebel enterprises with the same username and password (cross-enterprise user account)
- A local service owner account has been created during the Siebel Server installation
- The Siebel Server's `bin` directory is added to the PATH environment variable

About the cross-enterprise user account

The Siebel Management Server uses the same mechanisms of user authentication as all other Siebel CRM software. In other terms, users who want to log in to the Siebel Management Server must be registered as a Siebel user with the following responsibilities:

- MgmtSrvr-Admin (general administrative privileges)
- MgmtSrvr-Deploy&Execute (for ADM deployment)
- MgmtSrvr-Monitor (for Siebel Diagnostic Tool)
- Siebel Administrator

The user must have an account in each authentication system used. If more than one authentication system is used for the different Siebel enterprises, then the user account must have the same password in all authentication systems.

The user account must also be granted the privileges to log on to the Siebel Gateway Name Server. If the Siebel Gateway Name Server or the Siebel Server Manager use database authentication, then the user must be associated with the Siebel Administrator responsibility. If directory server authentication is used, "Siebel Administrator" must be in the list of the account's common name field in the directory.

Adding the Siebel Server bin directory to the PATH environment variable

We must add the path to the Siebel Server's `bin` directory to the Windows system environment variable named Path because of the fact that the Perl scripts, used to register Siebel Management Agents, call the `srvrmgr` executable.

We can use the Properties window for the My Computer icon and navigate to the list of system environment variables. Select the Path system variable and click Edit. Then copy and paste the exact path to the Siebel Server's bin directory at the beginning of the variable value text and add a semicolon after the pasted text.

> If you wish to follow along with this chapter and install and configure the Siebel Management Server infrastructure on your demonstration machine, ensure that the prerequisites described above are met.

Installing the Siebel Management Server on Microsoft Windows

Because the configuration steps require access to executables such as srvrmgr in the Siebel Server's bin directory, it is generally recommended to install the Siebel Management Server on a machine that hosts a Siebel Server installation. As indicated before, the machine must run under a Microsoft Windows operating system.

We start the installation of the Siebel Management Server by double-clicking the setup.exe program in the Siebel_Management_Server folder of the Siebel installation image. The following table describes the steps and dialogs of the InstallShield wizard and the Siebel Configuration wizard:

Step	Description	Tasks and Example Values
1	Start the InstallShield Wizard.	Double-click the setup.exe file in the Siebel_Management_Server folder.
2	The Welcome dialog is displayed.	Click **Next**.
3	Specify the directory to which the application files should be copied.	Example: C:\SIA81\mgmtsrvr. **The directory should already have been specified in the planning document.** Click **Next**.
4	Installation Summary	Check the information in the summary dialog. Click **Next**.
5	The installation progress is displayed.	Wait for the installation to finish.
6	The **Siebel Configuration Wizard** is launched automatically.	Continue with the configuration of the Siebel Management Server.

Installing and Configuring the Siebel Management Server Infrastructure

Step	Description	Tasks and Example Values
7	Siebel Enterprise Name	Example: SIEBELEVAL Click **Next**.
8	Siebel Gateway Name Server	Enter the hostname of the Siebel Gateway Name Server. Note: Choose the machine that hosts the Siebel Gateway Name Server for your first target enterprise. Click **Next**.
9	Siebel User Account	Enter the username and password for the cross-enterprise account created earlier. Click **Next**.
10	Diagnostic Tool User Account	Enter the username and password for the cross-enterprise account created earlier. Click **Next**.
11	RC2 Password Encryption	Select the checkbox. Click **Next**.
12	RC2 Key File and Port Number	Keep the defaults. Click **Next**.
13	Diagnostic Tool HTTP Port	If the default port is already used, change the port number and document it clearly. If not, keep the default (8080). Click **Next**.
14	JRE Home Location	Provide a valid path to the Java Runtime Engine installation. Click **Next**.
15	Authentication Type	Select **Database**. Click **Next**.
16	Security Adapter Configuration File	Copy the file path and use a text editor to open the file. Change the value of the **DSConnectString** parameter to the name of the ODBC data source for the Siebel enterprise. (Hint: Use the Microsoft ODBC Data Source Administrator utility to obtain the correct ODBC data source name.) Save and close the configuration file. Click **Next**.

Step	Description	Tasks and Example Values
17	Secure Sockets Layer	Select **NoSSL**.
		Click **Next**.
18	Windows User Account	Enter the fully qualified name (hostname\account) of a local Windows user account. This should be the Siebel Service Owner Account.
		Hint: use the `hostname` command in a Windows command shell to obtain the correct host name (case sensitive).
		Click **Next**.
19	ADM Default Package Directory	Navigate to the `\adm\packages` folder of the Management Server installation directory.
		Example: `C:\SIA81\mgmtsrvr\adm\packages`.
		Click **Next**.
20	Management Agent Host Name and Port	The configuration wizard allows to configure up to two connections to management agents. Even if we create new configuration files later, we must provide valid values to proceed with the configuration.
		Enter the host name of a Siebel Server you wish to use as a target for ADM deployment.
		Keep the default port (1199).
		Click **Next**.
21	Server Name	Enter the logical name of a Siebel Server that resides on the host you specified in the previous step.
		Click **Next**.
22	Server Type	Select **Siebel Server.**
		Click **Next**.
23	Configure Second Management Agent	Uncheck the flag.
		Click **Next**.
24	Start Management Server	Uncheck the flag.
		Click **Next**.
25	Summary	Review the summary information.
		Click **Next**.

Installing and Configuring the Siebel Management Server Infrastructure

Step	Description	Tasks and Example Values
26	Do you want to execute configuration?	Click **Yes**.
27	Success	The wizard displays successful configuration.
		Click **OK**.
28	Exit the Configuration Wizard	Click **Finish** to close the configuration wizard.

Verifying the successful installation and configuration of the Siebel Management Server

In order to verify the successful installation and configuration of the Siebel Management Server, we should open the Windows Services console and look for a new system service named **Siebel Management Server (port 1099)**. The port number may vary depending on the values we provided during the configuration process. The following screenshot shows the properties dialog for the Siebel Management Server system service created by the Siebel Configuration Wizard:

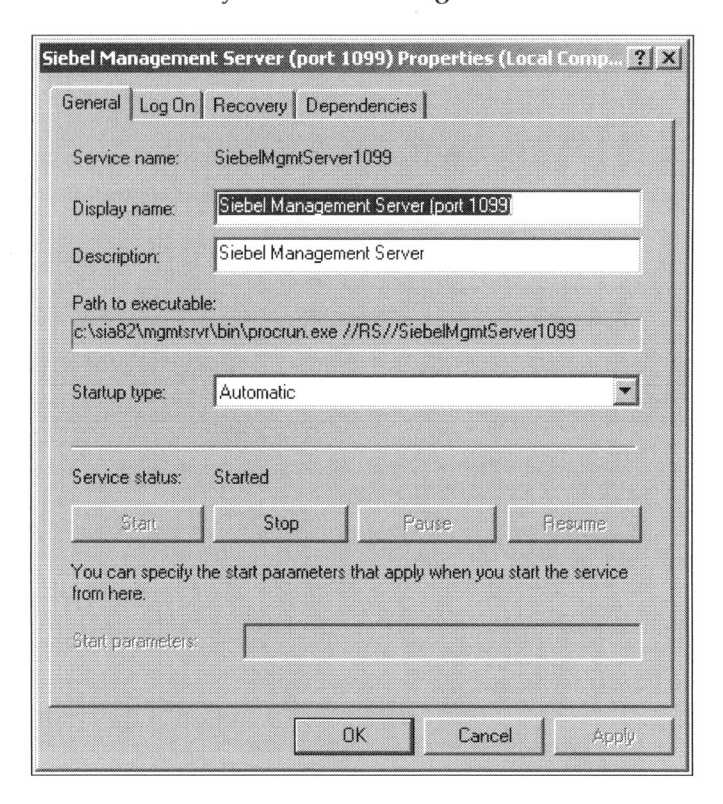

[420]

To further verify the installation and configuration, we should start the Management Server service. Even if no Management Agent is installed at this moment, we should be able to log on to the Diagnostic Tool using the cross-enterprise user account we created earlier.

After starting the Management Server service, we open a browser window and navigate to a URL similar to the following:

`http://hostname:8080/DiagTool`

In the above example, hostname should be replaced with the name of the machine where the Siebel Management Server is installed. If we used a port number other than 8080, it should be changed as well. The browser should display the login dialog for the Siebel Diagnostic Tool, as shown in the following screenshot:

We should be able to log in with the cross-enterprise user account we created earlier.

After login, we receive an error message "Unable to load enterprise / server information...", which is an expected behavior since the configuration of the Diagnostic Tool has not yet been completed.

The presence and successful start of a Windows system service and the ability to log on to the Diagnostic Tool completes the verification steps for the Siebel Management Server installation and configuration.

If the verification steps are not successful, it is recommended to inspect the log files. Before attempting a new installation of the Siebel Management Server, we must remove the system service with the Microsoft Windows `sc` command.

> On your demonstration machine, install and configure the Siebel Management Server according to the instructions above.

Installing and configuring Siebel Management Agents

As indicated above, the Siebel Management Agent software must be installed on each machine that hosts a Siebel Server. The process of downloading and extracting the installation images for the Siebel Management Agent is similar to that for every other piece of Siebel software.

The Siebel Management Agent installers are available for every operating system platform on which Siebel Servers are supported. Installing the Siebel Management Agent is also an option during the installation of a Siebel Server. In Chapter 3, we discussed that it is beneficial not to select this option during Siebel Server installation because a separately installed Management Agent can also be uninstalled separately.

The following table guides us through the process of installing and configuring a Siebel Management Agent:

Step	Description	Tasks and Example Values
1	Start the InstallShield Wizard.	Double-click the `setup.exe` file in the `Siebel_Management_Agent` folder.
2	The Welcome dialog is displayed.	Click **Next**.
3	Specify the directory to which the application files should be copied.	Example: `C:\SIA81\mgmtagent`. **The directory should already have been specified in the planning document.** Click **Next**.

Chapter 14

Step	Description	Tasks and Example Values
4	Installation Summary	Check the information in the summary dialog.
		Click **Next**.
5	The installation progress is displayed	Wait for the installation to finish.
6	The **Siebel Configuration Wizard** is launched automatically.	Continue with the configuration of the Siebel Management Agent.
7	Siebel Server Installation Directory.	Provide a valid path to the Siebel Server installation directory.
		Example: `C:\SIA81\siebsrvr`
		Click **Next**.
8	Siebel User Account	Enter the username and password for the cross-enterprise account created earlier.
		Click **Next**.
9	JRE Home Location	Provide a valid path to the Java Runtime Engine installation.
		Click **Next**.
10	RC2 Password Encryption	Select the checkbox.
		Click **Next**.
11	RC2 Key File and Port Number	Keep the defaults.
		Click **Next**.
12	Authentication Type	Select **Database**.
		Click **Next**.
13	Security Adapter Configuration File	Copy the file path and use a text editor to open the file.
		Change the value of the **DSConnectString** parameter to the name of the ODBC data source for the Siebel enterprise. (Hint: Use the Microsoft ODBC Data Source Administrator utility to obtain the correct ODBC data source name.)
		Save and close the configuration file.
		Click **Next**.
14	Secure Sockets Layer	Select **NoSSL**
		Click **Next**.

Step	Description	Tasks and Example Values
15	Windows User Account	Enter the fully qualified name (hostname\account) of a local Windows user account. This should be the Siebel Service Owner Account.
		Hint: use the `hostname` command in a Windows command shell to obtain the correct host name (case sensitive).
		Click **Next**.
16	Start Management Agent	Uncheck the flag.
		Click **Next**.
17	Summary	Review the summary information.
		Click **Next**.
18	Do you want to execute configuration?	Click **Yes**.
19	Success	The wizard displays successful configuration.
		Click **OK**.
20	Exit the Configuration Wizard	Click **Finish** to close the configuration wizard.

Verifying the successful installation and configuration of a Siebel Management Agent

The first verification step is to look for a new system service. On Microsoft Windows operating systems, we navigate to the Services console and verify that a new service named "Siebel Management Agent (port 1199)" exists. The port number may vary depending on the settings during the configuration. The following screenshot shows the properties for the Windows system service for the Siebel Management Agent:

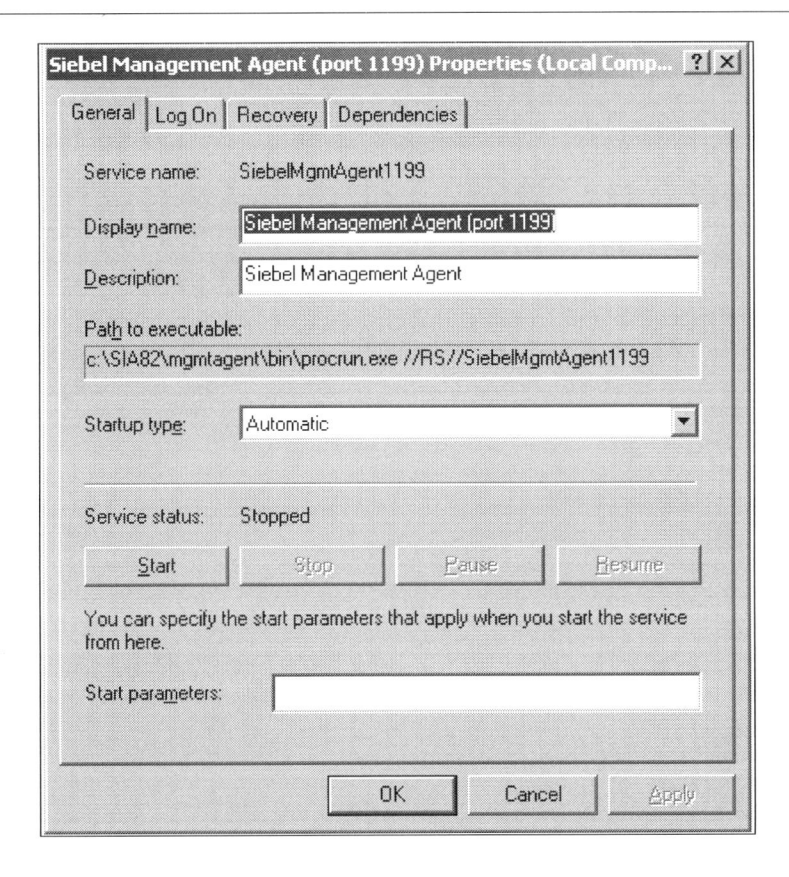

To further verify the successful configuration of the Siebel Management Agent, we should start the system service and inspect the `Agent.log` file in the `log` directory of the Management Agent's installation folder. If the log file does not report an error, we have successfully configured the Siebel Management Agent.

> Use the instructions in the above section to install and configure the Siebel Management Agent on your demonstration machine.

Registering Siebel Management Agents

In order to finalize the configuration of the Siebel Management Server infrastructure, administrators must register all installed Siebel Management Agents. The process of registering Siebel Management Agents is facilitated by two Perl scripts, which have to be executed to generate the configuration files for the Siebel Management Server.

Installing and Configuring the Siebel Management Server Infrastructure

The Perl scripts are located in the `bin` directory of the Siebel Management Server's installation folder. The following table lists the scripts and their purpose:

Perl script	Syntax	Description
`getservers.pl`	`perl getservers.pl -g Gateway -e Enterprise -u Username -p Password -l enu`	Connects to the Siebel Gateway Name Server specified by -g. Collects the Siebel Server listing and writes to a file named like the enterprise.
		Updates the `configuration.globals.xml` file.
`makeagentconfig.pl`	`perl makeagentconfig.pl Enterprise`	Reads the enterprise file and creates or updates the `configuration.agents.xml` file.

The `configuration.globals.xml` and `configuration.agents.xml` files are the main configuration files for the Siebel Management Server. When the Siebel Management Server starts, it reads these files from its `pref\system` folder and tries to establish connections to the Siebel Gateway Name servers listed in the `configuration.globals.xml` file and to the Siebel Management Agents listed in the `configuration.agents.xml` file.

Next we will describe the process of registering Siebel Management Agents. These steps must be executed on the machine that hosts the Siebel Management Server:

1. Create a backup copy of the `configuration.globals.xml` and `configuration.agents.xml` file in the `pref/system` folder of the Siebel Management Server installation directory.

2. Copy the `configuration.globals.xml` file from the `pref/system` folder to the `bin` folder of the Siebel Management Server installation directory.

3. Open a command window and navigate to the `bin` directory of the Siebel Management Server's installation folder.

4. Enter a command similar to the following:

   ```
   perl getservers.pl -g gateway_host -e enterprise_name -u username
   -p password -l enu
   ```

   In the above example, `gateway_host` should be replaced with the host name where the Siebel Gateway Server resides, `enterprise_name` should be replaced with the name of the Siebel enterprise to register, and the username and password must match a valid username and password pair.

The script updates the `configuration.globals.xml` file with information about the Siebel Gateway Name Server and writes information about all Siebel Servers found in the enterprise to a text file that is named after the enterprise.

We must repeat the `getservers.pl` script for all Siebel enterprises we wish to register.

5. In the command window, enter a command similar to the following:

   `perl makeagentconfig.pl Enterprise1 Enterprise2`

   In the above example, two Siebel enterprises (`Enterprise1` and `Enterprise2`) are registered. The `makeagentconfig.pl` script takes a list of enterprise names as the input parameter. It reads the corresponding files (generated by `getservers.pl`) and information about Management Agents and Siebel Servers is written to the `configuration.agents.xml` file.

6. Copy the `configuration.globals.xml` and `configuration.agents.xml` file to the `\pref\system` folder of the Siebel Management Server installation directory, overwriting older versions if necessary.

7. Copy the `configuration.agents.xml` file to the `tomcat\webapps\DiagTool\WEB-INF` folder of the Siebel Management Server installation directory. This is an optional step to enable the Siebel Diagnostic Tool functionality.

8. Restart the Siebel Management Server service.

9. Check the `ManagementServer.log` file in the `log` directory of the Siebel Management Server installation folder for errors.

The registration process must be repeated each time Siebel Servers are added or removed from an enterprise or when an entirely new enterprise has been set up.

> Using the instructions above, execute the Perl scripts to register the Siebel Management Agent on your demonstration machine.

Summary

In this chapter, we learned how to install and configure the prerequisite infrastructure for Siebel CRM modules such as Application Deployment Manager and the Siebel Diagnostic Tool.

The Siebel Management Server is a central cross-enterprise orchestration environment, which connects to the Siebel Management Agents that are installed on each Siebel Server.

The chapter also introduced the procedure to register management agents using the Perl scripts provided by Oracle.

The next chapter will discuss how to use Application Deployment Manager to migrate configuration changes.

15
Migrating Configuration Changes between Environments

A Siebel CRM project typically involves configuring or customizing the CRM application to the customer's needs. Developers work together with system architects and business analysts to implement the requirements demanded by the end user community. During this process, changes are made in various locations such as the Siebel Repository, administrative data such as List of Values (LOV), template files, BI Publisher reports, browser scripts, or graphic files.

Administrators must be able to support the development team by providing reliable migration mechanisms to transport the configuration changes from the development environment to the test and production environments.

In this chapter, we will learn how to use Application Deployment Manager from an administrator's point of view. The chapter is structured as follows:

- Overview of Application Deployment Manager functionality
- Setup of Application Deployment Manager
- Export and package configuration changes
- Deploy ADM packages
- Other migration utilities

Overview of Siebel Application Deployment Manager

Siebel Application Deployment Manager (ADM) is a set of tools that assists Siebel CRM project members with the task of migrating configuration changes from one source Siebel enterprise to one or more target Siebel enterprises.

The configuration areas that ADM operates on are the following:

- Administrative data (Database objects)
- Repository objects
- Files on Siebel servers and Siebel Web Server Extensions (SWSE)

In this section, we will discuss details for each of these areas.

Administrative data (Database objects)

Administrative data are entities that are created and modified by administrators by means of administrative screens in the Siebel Web Client. Examples for administrative data are List of Values (LOVs), responsibilities and views, as well as positions and organizations. The following table lists the major administrative data objects supported by ADM as of Siebel CRM version 8.1:

Major Area	Description	ADM Data Type Name
Access Control	Access groups	AccessGroup
	Divisions	Internal Division
	Organizations	Organization
	Positions	Position
	Responsibilities, associated views and users	Responsibility
Assignment Manager	Assignment manager groups, including assignment manager rules	AssignGroup
Audit Trail	Audit Trail administrative data	Audit Trail Admin
BI Publisher Reports	Report template registration	BIP Report Template Registration
	Report-view associations	BIP View Association
Communication Server	Communication drivers and profiles	ADM CommSrv CM Adapter Administration

Major Area	Description	ADM Data Type Name
Communication Server	Email templates	ADM Comm Package
Document Server	Correspondence templates	Correspondence Template
	Proposal template	Proposal Template
Enterprise Application Integration	EAI data map	EAI Data Map
	Inbound web service	Web Service - Inbound
Field Service	Shift schedule	ADM Shift Schedule
General application features	List of Values (LOV)	LOV
	Predefined queries	PDQ
	State Model	StateModel
iHelp	iHelp item	iHelp
Personalization	Applet personalization	Personalization - Applets
	View personalization	Personalization - Views
Portal Framework	Symbolic URLs	Symbolic URL
Product and Pricing Management	Price lists	PriceList
	Product catalogs	ProductCatalog
	Volume discounts	VolumeDiscount
Runtime Events	Action sets	Personalization - Actions
	Events	Personalization - Events
Siebel Search	Search categories	ADM Search Category
	Search connector settings and parameters	ADM Search Connector
SmartScript	SmartScript	SmartScript
Task UI	Access controlled task	Access Controlled Task
Workflow Policies	Workflow policy	Workflow Policy

A complete list of preconfigured administrative data types can be reviewed and new data types can be registered in the **Data Type Details** view of the **Application Deployment Manager** screen in the Siebel Web Client, which is shown in the screenshot below:

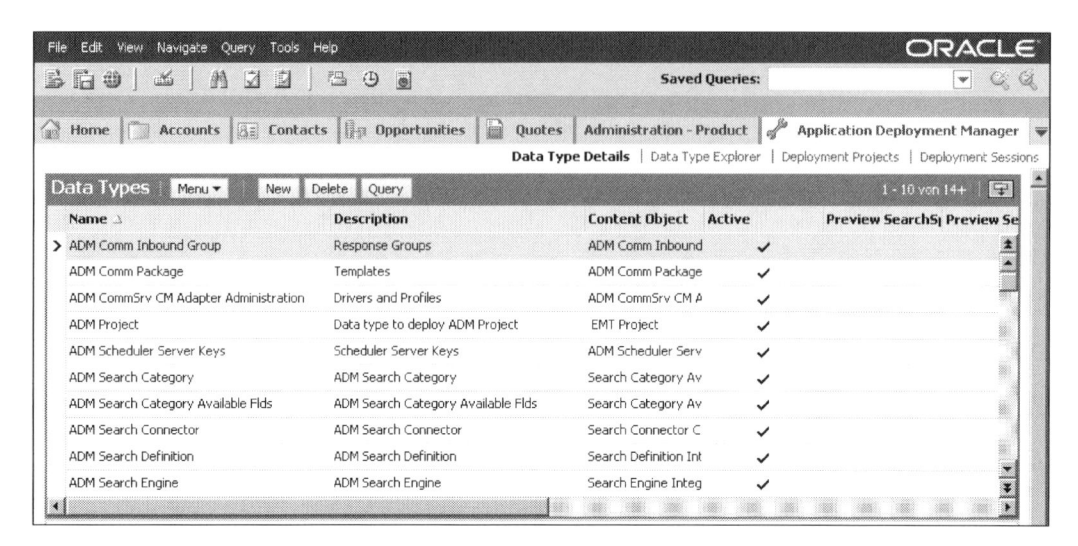

Administrators can use this view to verify whether the administrative data they wish to migrate is supported by a preconfigured data type. New data types can be registered in this view as well.

Registering new data types requires the creation of integration object and content object definitions in the Siebel repository using Siebel Tools, and is out of the scope of this book.

Repository objects

Any object definition that is created or modified in Siebel Tools can be migrated using the Application Deployment Manager functionality.

It is important to understand that this functionality is intended for mid-level releases and hot fixes. To migrate an entire repository, we use the Siebel Upgrade Wizard's "Migrate Repository" utility, which we will discuss later in this chapter.

Files on Siebel servers and Siebel Web Server Extensions (SWSE)

Siebel Application Deployment Manager is preconfigured to support the migration of the following file types between Siebel enterprises:

- Siebel Repository Files (`.srf`)
- Siebel Web Templates (`.swt`)
- BI Publisher Report Templates and related files (`.rtf` and others)
- All file types residing in the `public` directory of the Siebel Web Server Extension (SWSE), including cascading stylesheets (`.css`), graphic files, and browser scripts

The Application Deployment Manager Architecture

The following diagram helps us understand the building blocks of Application Deployment Manager and how it uses the Siebel Management Server framework to migrate configuration changes from a source enterprise to one or more target enterprises:

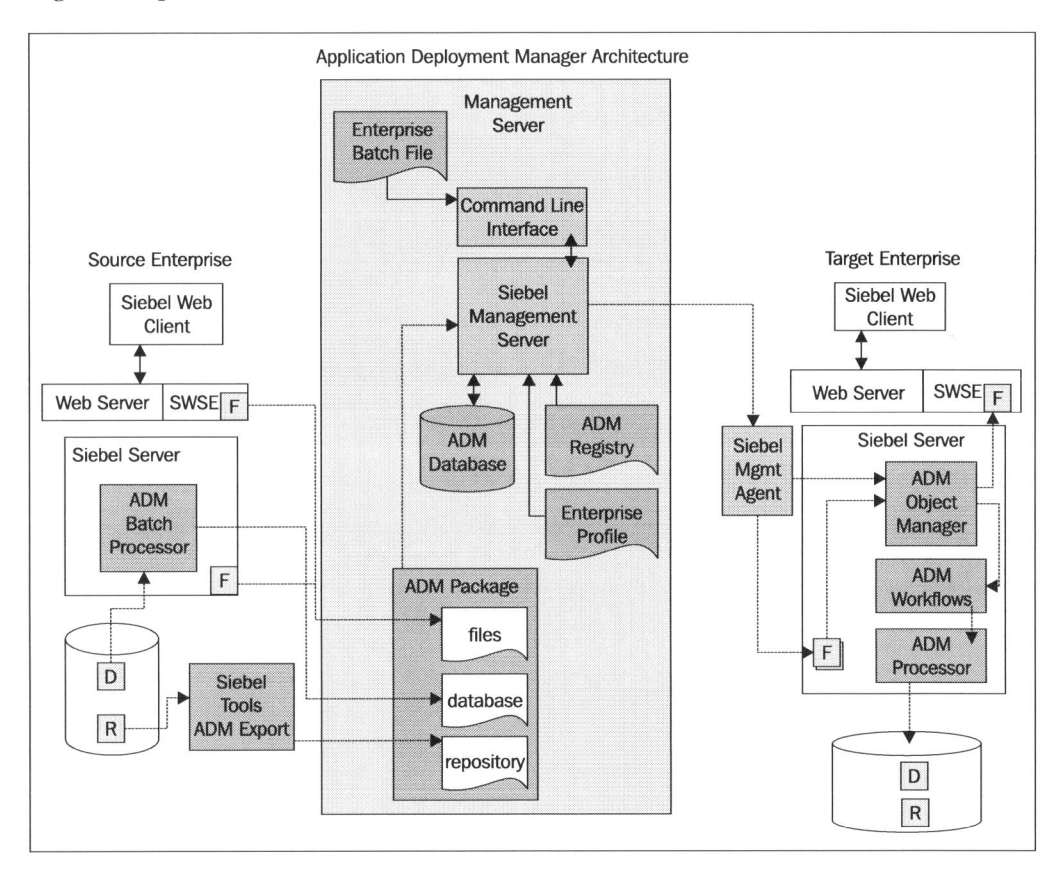

The source enterprise is typically the development environment where changes are made to Siebel repository data (R), administrative data (D), and files (F) on the Siebel Server, and Siebel Web Server Extension (SWSE).

Repository data such as workflow process definitions are exported to a package directory using the ADM-specific functionality available in Siebel Tools.

Administrative data objects—or "Database Objects"—such as List of Values (LOV) are either exported manually using the Administration Deployment Manager screen (not depicted in the diagram) or via the **ADM Batch Processor** server component. The ADM package directory has a subdirectory for database objects.

Files such as Siebel web templates or cascading stylesheets that have been created or changed are copied to the package folder structure using the regular file copy mechanisms of the operating system.

The following major building blocks enable ADM functionality on the Siebel Management Server:

- A Sybase database that holds data about packages and deployment sessions
- The ADM registry, an XML file, which gives details about each deployable data type
- The enterprise profile, an XML file, which contains information about the target enterprise
- The enterprise batch file, which wraps the command line invocations in easy-to-use command syntax

During the deployment process, the Siebel Management Server reads the data in the ADM package folders and uses the Siebel Management Agents on the Siebel Servers in the target enterprise to copy the data objects to their destination.

Two server components, namely **ADM Object Manager** and **ADM Processor,** act on the target enterprise in order to process incoming data and invoke ADM workflows, which write the data to the target database. Repository data and administrative data are processed by these server components.

Files are written to folders on the target Siebel Server by the Siebel Management Agent. Files that belong to the Siebel Web Server Extension (SWSE) are pushed from the Siebel Server to the machine where the SWSE resides.

From the architecture diagram, we can also derive the following
important information:

- The migration process is split into an exporting and packaging procedure, during which data and files are exported and copied to a package folder structure, and a deployment procedure, during which the data and files are moved to the target enterprise.
- Exporting data from the source enterprise to the ADM package folder does not require a Siebel Management Agent nor does it depend on the Siebel Management Server.
- The deployment process is orchestrated by Siebel Management Server functionality.

Next, we will discuss the procedures to set up ADM functionality on the source enterprise, the Siebel Management Server, and the target enterprise.

Setting up Siebel Application Deployment Manager

Setting up ADM functionality involves tasks to be carried out by administrators on all Siebel enterprises and the Siebel Management Server. The following is a list of setup steps for source and target enterprises:

- Enable the ADM component group
- Configure the enterprise profile for ADM
- Enable ADM support for the application object manager
- Activate ADM workflow processes

The following tasks have to be completed on the Siebel Management Server to enable ADM functionality:

- Verify the `adm.cli` file
- Create shared directories
- Create the enterprise profile file and deployment batch files

The setup process should be completed by a test deployment. Next, we will describe each setup step in detail.

Enabling the ADM component group

The ADM component group must be assigned to and enabled for at least one Siebel Server per enterprise. This component group contains the following components:

- ADM Object Manager
- ADM Processor
- ADM Batch Processor

As already discussed in previous chapters, this task can be carried out in the Administration - Server Configuration screen in the Siebel Web Client or by using the Siebel Server Manager (srvrmgr) command line.

The following is an example for enabling the ADM component group using the srvrmgr command line utility:

```
enable compgrp adm for server Eval_1
```

The above command will enable the ADM component group for the server `Eval_1`.

Managing ADM components in source and target enterprises

If the Siebel Server is part of a source enterprise, the following components can be set to manual start to decrease CPU and memory consumption on the Siebel Server machine:

- ADM Object Manager
- ADM Processor

These components are only used on target enterprises. The only component that should be online on a source enterprise is the **ADM Batch Processor**, which has the purpose of automating the export of administrative data from the Siebel database.

Having understood the purpose of the ADM Batch Processor, it is clear that it can be set to manual start on all Siebel servers in target enterprises.

The following is an example that shows how to set the ADM Batch Processor to manual startup mode using the Siebel Server Manager command line:

```
manual start comp ADMBatchProc for server Eval_2
```

This command sets the ADM Batch Processor component to manual startup mode on the Siebel Server named `Eval_2`.

Configuring the enterprise profile for ADM

In order to enable the integration between the Java-based Siebel Management Agent and the ADM Object Manager, an enterprise profile must be configured. We can use the preconfigured **admjavasubsys** enterprise profile. Commands similar to the following, preferably issued at the Siebel Server Manager command line from a script, provide the correct settings for this enterprise profile (named subsystem is the term used for enterprise profiles in the Siebel Server Manager command line syntax).

```
change param classpath=C:\SIA81\mgmtagent\lib\siebelmgr.jar;C:\SIA81\
mgmtagent\lib\admstatussvc.jar;C:\SIA81\mgmtagent\lib\Siebel.jar;C:\
SIA81\mgmtagent\lib\SiebelJI_enu.jar for named subsystem admjavasubsys
```

```
change param dll=C:\jdk1.5.0_09\jre\bin\client\jvm.dll for named
subsystem admjavasubsys
```

The first command in the above example sets the value of the `classpath` parameter of the `admjavasubsys` named subsystem to a semicolon-separated list of fully qualified paths to Java libraries situated in the `lib` directory of the Siebel Management Agent's installation folder.

The second command sets the value of the `dll` parameter to a valid path to the `jvm.dll` residing in the JDK installation folder on the local machine.

After configuring the `admjavasubsys` enterprise profile, we must set it as the default Java subsystem by setting the value of the `jvmsubsys` enterprise parameter to `'ADM Java Systems'` using a command similar to the following:

```
change ent param jvmsubsys='ADM Java Systems'
```

This specific value is documented in the Application Deployment Manager Guide in the Siebel bookshelf documentation library.

Enabling ADM support for the application object manager

Application Deployment Manager uses an existing application object manager for the push synchronization of files from the Siebel Server to the machine where the Siebel Web Server Extension resides.

This functionality must be enabled by setting the value of the `enableadmsupport` parameter to `True` for at least one application object manager in the target enterprise using a command similar to the following:

```
change param enableadmsupport=True for comp sccobjmgr_enu server Eval_2
```

In the above example, the value of the `enableadmsupport` parameter is set to `True` for the English Siebel Call Center object manager on the Siebel Server named `Eval_2`.

As usual, we could also use the graphical user interface (GUI) provided by the views in the Administration - Server Configuration screen in the Siebel Web Client.

Activating ADM workflow processes

We can follow the procedure below to activate the ADM workflow processes. This procedure must be executed once for each enterprise:

1. Log in to the Siebel Web Client using an administrative user account.
2. Navigate to the **Application Deployment Manager** screen, **Data Type Details** view.
3. Click the **Menu** button or right-click anywhere in the list to open the menu.
4. Select **Activate ADM Workflows**.
5. Click **OK** in the confirmation dialog.

This activates all workflow processes needed for ADM functionality on source and target enterprises. The following screenshot shows the **Data Type Details** view in the **Application Deployment Manager** screen:

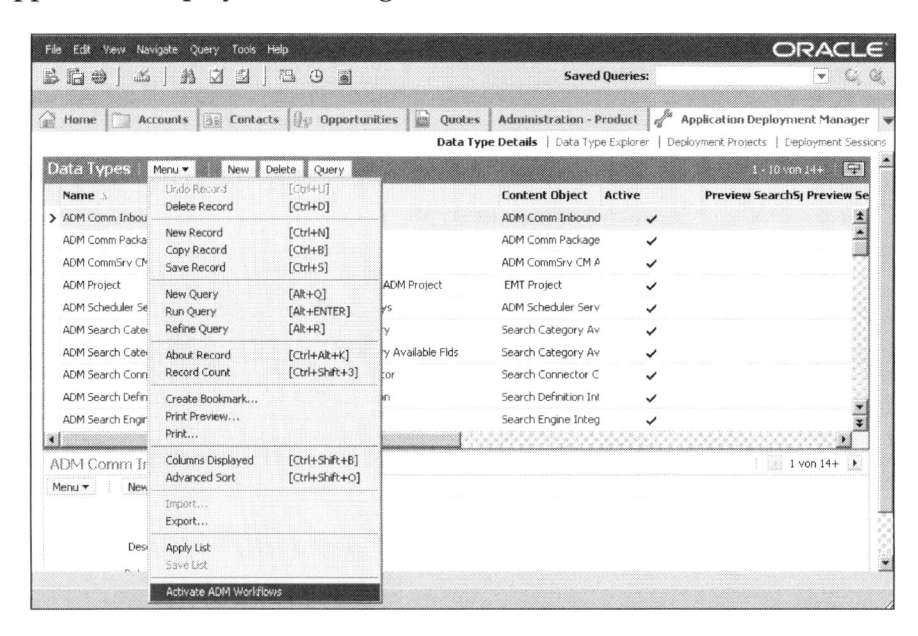

The **Activate ADM Workflows** option in the applet menu is selected.

Restarting Siebel Servers

Because of the enablement of a new component group and several other changes at the enterprise level, we must restart all Siebel Servers that will be hosting ADM server components.

This concludes the ADM setup tasks on source and target enterprises. In the following section, we will discuss the setup steps on the Siebel Management Server.

Verifying the adm.cli file

Under certain circumstances, a file named `adm.cli` is missing in the Siebel Management Server's installation root directory after installation. In order to enable ADM functionality, we must verify that this file exists.

If the file does not exist, we must create a new text file with the following content in the installation root directory of the Siebel Management Server:

```
serverUrl=service:jmx:rmi://localhost/jndi/rmi://localhost:1099/jmx/siebel/MgmtServer
output=xml=.\\adm\\format.xsl
mbean=ADM:type=ADMCommandLineMBean
operation=invoke
```

We write these four lines to the file and save it as `adm.cli`. The Siebel Management Server must be restarted after this procedure.

Creating shared directories

During the ADM deployment process, files are stored temporarily in shared folders to be accessed by the Siebel Management Server and the Siebel Management Agents. In order to secure flawless execution of the ADM deployment process, we must create two shared folders. The ideal location for these folders is the machine where the Siebel Management Server resides. When setting up the share permissions, we must ensure that the system account used to operate the services for the Siebel Management Server and Siebel Management Agents has full read and write permission on the shared folders.

In order to facilitate the exporting and packaging process, it is beneficial to enable file sharing on the `adm\packages` directory in the Siebel Management Server installation folder. For example, we can create a share named ADM_PACKAGES on the `adm\packages` directory.

Creating the enterprise profile and deployment batch files

In order to enable the ADM deployment processes on the Siebel Management Server, an administrator has to generate two files for each target enterprise:

- The enterprise profile file
- The deployment batch file

Both files are generated by a Perl script named `admconfig.pl`, which has to be executed once for each target enterprise. The script is located in the `bin` directory of the Siebel Management Server installation folder and has the following syntax:

```
perl admconfig.pl -e SIEBELEVAL -s 2321 -p C:\SIA81\mgmtserver\adm\packages -r C:\SIA81\mgmtserver
```

The above example shows that the `admconfig.pl` script takes four parameters. The `-e` switch is followed by the name of the enterprise we wish to generate the ADM files for. The `-s` switch specifies the port that the Siebel Connection Broker is listening on. The Siebel Connection Broker is the system server component responsible for forwarding all incoming requests to the appropriate server components. Its default port is `2321`. The `-p` parameter defines the default package location and `-r` is followed by the installation root folder of the Siebel Management Server.

This script reads the file generated by the `getservers.pl` script (which was used to register Siebel Management Agents during the setup of the Siebel Management Server infrastructure) and creates two files in the Siebel Management Server's directory. For the above example enterprise, the file names would be:

- `entprofile_SIEBELEVAL.xml` in the `adm` subdirectory
- `deploy_SIEBELEVAL.bat` in the `bin` subdirectory

The first file, being the enterprise profile file for the SIEBELEVAL enterprise in XML format, must be modified manually. The following table describes the changes we have to make to the enterprise profile file.

As most of the modifications consist of replacing the string "CHANGE_ME" with the qualified agent name, it is beneficial to copy the agent name into the clipboard. The agent name can be obtained from the <ServerInfo> section at the beginning of the file.

We open the `entprofile_<enterprise_name>.xml` file with a text editor of our choice and copy the value of the **AgentName** attribute in the <ServerInfo> section to the clipboard. The following screenshot shows the highlighted value of the **AgentName** attribute (**osappeval_1199**) in the <ServerInfo> section.

```
entprofile_SIEBELEVAL.xml - Notepad
<?xml version="1.0" encoding="UTF-8"?><?mso-infoPathSolution productVersion="11.0.6357"
   <EnterpriseTargetServerInformation>
      <ServerInfo AgentName="osappeval_1199"
      SiebelServerConnectString="siebel://osappeval:2321/SIEBELEVAL/ADMObjMgr_enu"
      ServerInstallDir="C:\SIA82\siebsrvr" />
```

Copying the string between the double quotes into the clipboard eases the tasks described in the table below.

We can now scroll through the XML file and replace all lines that contain the string "CHANGE_ME" as instructed in the table:

Text to modify	Example result/Instructions
`<DeployServer>CHANGE_ME`	`<DeployServer>osappeval_1199`
	Replace *CHANGE_ME* with the fully qualified agent name.
`<DestinationRoot>$SIEBEL_ROOT$`	`<DestinationRoot>C:\SIA81`
	Replace *$SIEBEL_ROOT$* with the root installation folder of the Siebel Server.
`\\CHANGE_ME\upload`	`\\osappeval\ADM_UPLOAD`
	Replace *\\CHANGE_ME\upload* with a valid UNC path to the upload folder.
`<WebServerHosts>http://CHANGE_ME`	`<WebServerHosts>http://osappeval`
	Replace *http://CHANGE_ME* with a valid URL for the web server that hosts the Siebel Web Server Extension (SWSE).
`<ApplicationPath>/callcenter_enu`	If necessary, replace */callcenter_enu* with the virtual directory for the application object manager enabled for ADM.
`\\net\CHANGE_ME\shared;`	`\\osappeval\ADM_SHARED;`
	Replace *\\net\CHANGE_ME\shared;* with a valid UNC path to the shared folder followed by a semicolon.
`<WFPolicyActSrvr>CHANGE_ME`	`<WFPolicyActSrvr>osappeval_1199`
	Replace *CHANGE_ME* with the fully qualified agent name.

> The enterprise profile XML file can also be modified using Microsoft InfoPath. Scripts are provided in the `adm` directory of the Siebel Management Server installation folder to register the enterprise profile file with Microsoft InfoPath.

After saving and closing the file, we must check the validity of the enterprise profile XML file by entering a command similar to the following in a command prompt at the root folder of the Siebel Management Server installation. Note that the Siebel Management Server service must be running for successful execution of the command.

`bin\deploy_SIEBELEVAL valent SIEBMGMT SIEBMGMT`

This command invokes the `deploy_SIEBELEVAL.bat` file (the enterprise batch file for the SIEBELEVAL enterprise) in the `bin` directory of the Siebel Management Server installation folder and passes three parameters. The first parameter (valent) is one of the predefined operations that are implemented in the enterprise batch file. This operation validates the enterprise profile file syntax. The second and third parameters are a valid username password pair for the Siebel Management Server. The following screenshot shows the success message displayed as output of the valent operation:

```
C:\WINNT\system32\cmd.exe

C:\SIA82\mgmt>bin\deploy_SIEBELEVAL valent SIEBMGMT SIEBMGMT
Enterprise Profile Name    entprofile_SIEBELEVAL.xml

All validation succeeded.
```

Error messages indicate invalid syntax of the enterprise profile file. To avoid having to enter the `bin\` path, we can copy the enterprise deployment batch file to the Siebel Management Server's root installation folder.

This concludes the setup procedure for Application Deployment Manager functionality on source and target enterprises as well as the Siebel Management Server.

> Use the setup instructions above to enable and verify ADM functionality on your demonstration machine.

Exporting and Packaging Configuration Changes

As indicated above, ADM supports three different data types—administrative data, repository data, and files—each of which is associated with separate exporting mechanisms.

In this section, we will discuss both the manual and the automated export mechanisms for all data types. We will start with creating the ADM package, a directory structure, which must be populated with data objects.

Creating the ADM package

The ADM package is a folder structure that is created and managed by the **ADM Packager** command line utility (admpkgr). We must use this utility to:

- Create the empty package structure
- Seal the package content with a descriptor file
- Validate the package content against the descriptor file

Next, we will discuss the procedure to create an empty package structure. Sealing and verifying the package is discussed after the exporting procedures.

Creating the empty package structure

As the ideal location for the ADM package is the `adm\packages` folder in the Siebel Management Server's installation directory, the following tasks are typically executed on the machine that hosts the Siebel Management Server. However, the package can also be generated on a different machine and copied to the Siebel Management Server at a later time.

To create an empty ADM package structure, we open a command shell and navigate to the root installation folder of the Siebel Management Server. This is where the admpkgr command line utility is situated.

We use a command similar to the following to create a new empty package structure:

```
admpkgr init C:\SIA81\mgmtsrvr\adm\packages\EVAL_PACKAGE
```

Migrating Configuration Changes between Environments

The `init` command is followed by the full path to the root folder of the new package. As a result of the above example command, a new folder named EVAL_PACKAGE is generated in the `\adm\packages` folder of the Siebel Management Server installation directory. The following screenshot shows the folder structure generated by the ADM Packager:

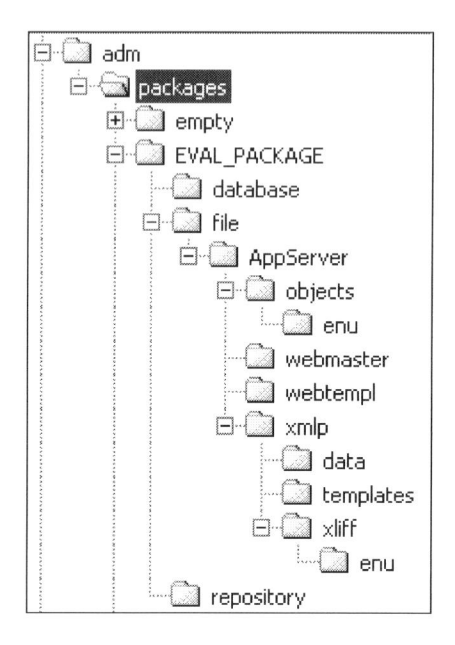

```
adm
└── packages
    ├── empty
    └── EVAL_PACKAGE
        ├── database
        ├── file
        │   └── AppServer
        │       ├── objects
        │       │   └── enu
        │       ├── webmaster
        │       ├── webtempl
        │       └── xmlp
        │           ├── data
        │           ├── templates
        │           └── xliff
        │               └── enu
        └── repository
```

Each package contains three main folders—database, file, and repository. The file folder has subfolders that represent a part of the folder structure of the target Siebel servers.

> In order to generate additional language-specific folders such as "deu" for German or "fra" for French, we can edit the `admpkgr.bat` file using a text editor of our choice. In the file, we locate and modify the line SET LANG_DIR="ENU". The LANG_DIR variable can hold a comma-separated list of three letter codes for the supported Siebel languages
>
> Examples for language-specific data are the localization files (.xlf) for BI Publisher reports.

It is possible to remove unused folders and create new subfolders in the file folder during the export and packaging process.

> On your demonstration machine, use the ADM Packager as described to create an empty package.

Exporting administrative data using the Application Deployment Manager screen

Administrative data such as List of Values (LOV) or responsibilities can be exported from the graphical user interface provided by views in the Application Deployment Manager screen in the Siebel Web Client.

The following procedure describes how to create an ADM deployment project and use it in an ADM export session. Deployment projects are defined once as a list of data objects and the associated filters. They can be reused for multiple export sessions. The example refers to preconfigured List of Values (LOV) data for the Todo Type field in Siebel Activities. The process is similar for each supported ADM data type:

1. Log in to the Siebel Web Client using an administrative account.
2. Navigate to the Application Deployment Manager screen, Deployment Projects view.
3. Create a new (or copy an existing) deployment project.
4. Enter a name for the new deployment project.
5. Ensure that the Export to File and Session Configurable flags are checked.
6. In the lower list applet, click New and select LOV from the Data Type Name dropdown list.
7. Choose Upsert as the deployment method.
8. In the Deployment Filter field, enter [Value]='TODO_TYPE'. This filter ensures that only records for the List of Values type "TODO_TYPE" are exported.

   Alternatively, we can click the select button in the Deployment Filter field and choose one of the existing predefined queries for the respective object. However, because of the fact that predefined queries reference business component fields and ADM operates on integration object components, field name differences can lead to invalid filters when working with predefined queries. Developers can assist in the task of finding the correct field names for the filter specification.

9. Click the **Validate Filter** button in the upper list applet. If no message is displayed, the filter is valid. If an error message appears, correct the syntax of the deployment filter and validate again until no error is displayed.

Migrating Configuration Changes between Environments

10. Click the **Enable** button in the upper list applet. Once a deployment project is enabled, it can no longer be modified. We would have to copy the deployment project record and modify and enable the copied record.
11. Navigate to the Deployment Sessions view.
12. Click the **New** button and select the deployment project created before from the dropdown list in the Project Name field.
13. Press *CTRL+S* to save the record. This populates the lower list applet with the data objects.
14. Click the **Deploy** button in the upper list applet.
15. In the Export dialog box, enter either a valid UNC path or an absolute path to an existing folder where the export files should be written to.

    For example, to write the files to the database folder of the EVAL_PACKAGE package—using the network share created on the `adm\packages` folder—we could specify a path similar to the following:

    `\\osappeval1\ADM_PACKAGES\EVAL_PACKAGE\database`

    In the above example, `osappeval1` is the name of the server where the Siebel Management Server resides and `ADM_PACKAGES` is the name of the network share created on the `adm\packages` directory.

16. Click the **Export** button to start the data export.
17. Verify that the Status field displays a value of Export Completed, which indicates successful export of the data.
18. Navigate to the export folder and verify the existence of three new files. The ADM export process uses the Session ID as a prefix for the files and the data type names—for example LOV—to distinguish the files. The following screenshot shows a completed ADM deployment session and the resulting files in the database folder of the ADM package directory:

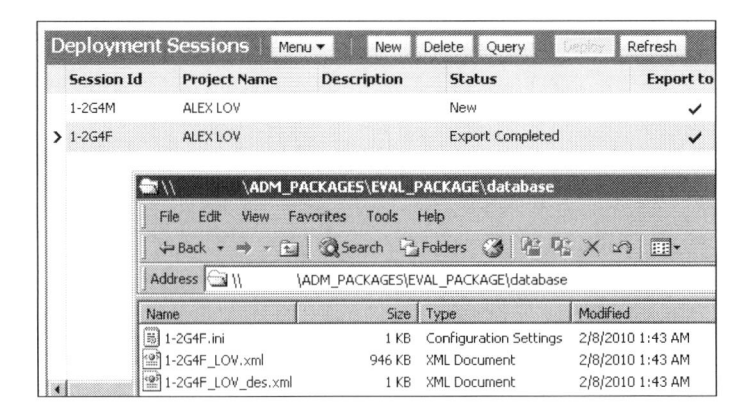

[446]

The file with the `.ini` suffix must be deleted. It does not contain any data for the ADM deployment. The pair of XML files—the data file and an accompanying descriptor file—must be kept as is and must not be modified or renamed.

This process of exporting administrative data using the graphical user interface can be repeated for other data types as often as needed until the set of data to deploy into the target enterprises is complete.

All database export files must be either written directly to the **database** folder of the ADM package or copied there at a later point in time. The latter is a common scenario when project teams use version control tools to keep all modified and new objects until deployment time.

Exporting administrative data using the ADM Batch Processor server component

As we have learned above, the export of administrative data is a manual and therefore time consuming and error prone task. To automate the export, we can use the **ADM Batch Processor** server component.

The ADM Batch Processor is a batch component and is part of the ADM component group. It can be invoked via the Siebel Server Manager (srvrmgr) command line or using the Jobs view in the Administration - Server Management screen in the Siebel Web Client.

Next, we will describe how to invoke the ADM Batch Processor using the Siebel Server Manager command line.

Because of the number of parameters to set, it is beneficial to use an input file that contains the start task command. The following is an example of a command that invokes the ADM Batch Processor and directs it to export List of Values (LOV) data:

```
start task for comp admbatchproc with admpath=\\osappeval\ADM_PACKAGES\
EVAL_PACKAGE\database,

admdatatype='LOV',

admfilter='[Value] = "TODO_TYPE"',

admeaimethod=upsert,

admprefix=LOV_TODO_TYPE
```

> The command must be in a single line. The example above has been broken into separate lines for better readability.

When using the ADM Batch Processor, the following parameters must be set:

- `admpath`: a valid UNC or absolute path where the files should be written to. It is recommended to provide the path to the database folder of the ADM package directory.
- `admdatatype`: the name of the ADM data type
- `admfilter`: the search specification to filter the data
- `admeaimethod`: the EAI method to use when data is imported in the target enterprise; upsert (update or insert operations are carried out automatically), or synchronize (update, insert, or delete operations are carried out automatically)
- `admprefix`: the prefix to be used for the output file names

The ADM Batch Processor writes two files to the specified directory, one file that carries the data and the accompanying descriptor file. For naming the files, the server component uses the value of the `admprefix` parameter and the identifier number of the Siebel server task.

> If we use the ADM Batch Processor server component as in the example above, no deployment project needs to be created in the Application Deployment Manager screen. However, if we wish to use the definitions of a deployment project, we can do so by using the **admproject** parameter and the name of an enabled deployment project as its value. If we use the **admproject** parameter, the only other mandatory parameter is **admpath**.

Exporting repository data using Siebel Tools

In addition to migrating administrative data, Siebel Application Deployment Manager is capable of exporting and migrating repository object definitions from one Siebel enterprise (typically, the development environment) to one or more target enterprises (typically, test or production environments).

As Siebel Tools is the application used by developers to create or modify repository objects, it provides the necessary ADM functionality to export these objects. In the following, we will discuss the techniques to export repository objects using the graphical user interface of Siebel Tools.

ADM supports two scenarios for migrating repository changes:

- Hot-Fix
- Mid-Level Release

In a **Hot-Fix** scenario, a small number of object definitions are typically hand-picked and then exported and migrated to the target enterprise. It is quite common that for example an error has been discovered in a business service method's script, which must be quickly fixed and issued to the production environment in a small timeframe.

A **Mid-Level Release** is considered as a certain time slice in a project, which involves the creation or modification of several dozens of repository objects. A Mid-Level Release represents all changes made to the repository since a certain point in time.

Changes to the database schema, such as the creation of new tables or the addition of columns to existing tables are considered part of a major release and should not be migrated using ADM. The utilities that should be used for these purposes will be discussed in the final section of this chapter.

Exporting repository object definitions for Hot-Fixes

The following procedure describes how to export repository object definitions for a Hot-Fix:

1. Log in to Siebel Tools, connecting to the database that contains the object definitions to export.
2. Navigate to the object definition. For example, click **Business Service** in the Object Explorer pane and then query for the **Siebel Account** business service in the list.
3. Right-click the object definition and select **Add to Hot-Fix...**
4. In the Generate Hot-Fix dialog, specify a label for the Hot-Fix.
5. If you wish to add more object definitions to the Hot-Fix, use the Object Explorer and the list view to select them and repeat the above steps.
6. Once all object definitions are added to the list in the Generate Hot-Fix dialog, click the **Export** button.

A new subdirectory with the Hot-Fix label as its name will be generated in the ADM directory of the Siebel Tools installation folder. It will contain a Siebel Tools Archive file (.sif), an accompanying XML descriptor file, and a log file. All files except the log file must be copied to the **repository** folder in the ADM package directory to complete the export process. The screenshot below shows the Generate Hot-Fix dialog in Siebel Tools:

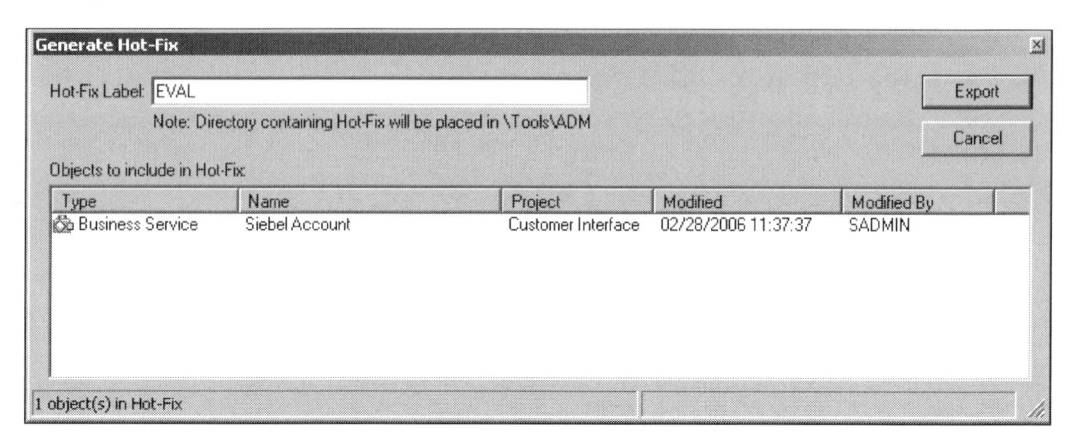

The Hot-Fix has a label of EVAL—the name of the new subdirectory and currently contains a single object definition of type Business Service.

Exporting repository object definitions for mid-level releases

The following procedure describes how we can use Siebel Tools to create a Mid-Level Release. We will specify a start timestamp and then retrieve all object definitions created or modified since then.

1. Log in to Siebel Tools, connecting to the database that contains the object definitions to export.
2. From the View menu, select Options.
3. In the General tab, set the Changed Date to the date and time which defines the begin of the Mid-Level Release.
4. Click **OK**.
5. From the Tools menu, select Generate Mid-Level Release…
6. In the Generate Mid-Level Release dialog, specify a label for the Mid-Level Release.
7. Click the **Generate List** button.

8. Verify that the list is populated with object definitions that have been created or modified after the start date.
9. Optionally, remove object definitions from the list by selecting them and pressing the *Delete* key.
10. Choose an export option. It is recommended to choose "One SIF per object" when the list of object definitions is long to avoid the generation of a single large file.
11. Click the **Export** button.
12. Click **OK** to confirm the success message.

The screenshot below shows the **Generate Mid-Level Release** dialog in Siebel Tools:

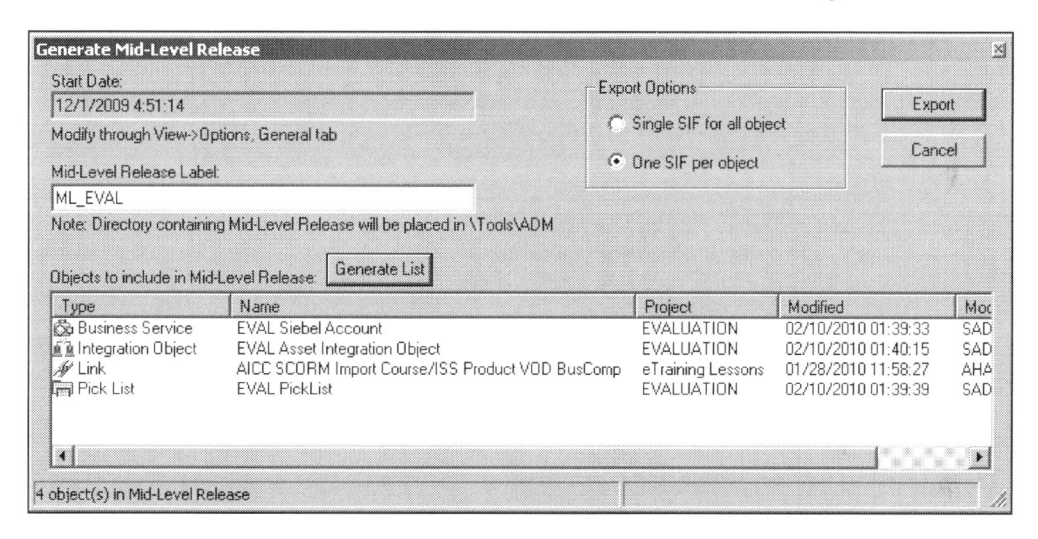

Similar to Hot-Fixes, a new directory with the Mid-Level Release label as its name is generated in the ADM folder of the Siebel Tools installation directory. Depending on the export options, we find either a single or multiple Siebel Tools Archive files (.sif). When we choose to export to one .sif file per object, the utility generates subdirectories for each object type to avoid name conflicts. As usual, they are accompanied by XML descriptor files and .log files.

Copying the .sif and accompanying XML descriptor files to the repository folder of the ADM package directory completes the export of a Mid-Level Release.

Exporting repository data using the consoleapp utility

The two procedures described above—exporting repository object definitions for Hot Fixes and Mid-Level Releases—must be carried out manually in the Siebel Tools user interface. Similar to exporting administrative data automatically using a script, we can leverage a utility named consoleapp to automate the export of repository data to the ADM package.

The consoleapp—"console application"—utility is a generic interface that allows administrators to invoke business service methods from the command line.

The Siebel repository contains a pre-built business service named **Siebel Tools Export Support for ADM**, which supports the automated export of repository data to an ADM package directory.

Source: *Siebel Application Deployment Manager Guide, Version 8.1*

Before we launch the consoleapp command line utility, we must verify that the **DataSource** parameter in the Siebel Tools configuration file (`tools.cfg`) points to the data source that contains the repository object definitions we wish to export.

We can issue a command similar to the following from the Windows command shell to export one or more object definitions:

```
C:\siebel\8.2\Tools_1\bin\consoleapp.exe
"C:\siebel\8.2\Tools_1\bin\enu\tools.cfg" ENU SADMIN TJay357D
"Siebel Tools Export Support for ADM"
Export:Repository=Siebel Repository,
Object_1=EVAL Siebel Account,
Type_1=Business Service,
ExportFile=\\osappeval\ADM_PACKAGES\EVAL_PACKAGE\repository\EVAL_BS_1.sif,
DescriptorFile=\\osappeval\ADM_PACKAGES\EVAL_PACKAGE\repository\EVAL_BS_1_des.xml,
ExportCount=1,
LogFile=c:\temp\adm.log"
```

The above example script has been broken into separate lines for better readability. The syntax of a `consoleapp.exe` invocation is as follows:

```
consoleapp <application configuration file path> <language code>
<username> <password> <Business Service name> <Method name:Param_1=Value_1,Param_2=Value_2,…,Param_N=Value_N>
```

In the example above, the application configuration file path points to the Siebel Tools configuration file (`tools.cfg`). We are using ENU (English - United States) as the language code and SADMIN as the username to log in to the console application.

The business service to be invoked is Siebel Tools Export Support for ADM. The method of the business service is named Export. The following parameters can be passed to the Export method:

Parameter Name	Description	Example Value
`Repository`	Name of the repository to export object definitions from.	`Siebel Repository`
`Object_N`	The Object_N syntax allows for exporting multiple object definitions at once. N is to be replaced by a numeric sequence. The parameter value is the exact name (case sensitive) of an object definition in the repository.	`Object_1=EVAL Siebel Acccount,Object_2=Account List Applet`
`Type_N`	The Type_N parameter value is the exact type of the object definition. It corresponds to the Object_N parameter.	`Type_1=Business Service,Type_2=Applet`
`ExportFile`	Full path to the export file. The suffix must be .sif.	`\\osappeval\ADM_PACKAGES\EVAL_PACKAGE\repository\EVAL_1.sif`
`DescriptorFile`	Full path to the descriptor file. The name must match the name of the export file followed by "_des.xml".	`\\osappeval\ADM_PACKAGES\EVAL_PACKAGE\repository\EVAL_1_des.xml`
`ExportCount`	Number of object definitions to export.	`ExportCount=2`
`LogFile`	Full path to the log file for the export process.	`LogFile=D:\temp\admexport1.log`

As a result of the above command, which should be part of a command shell script, the export file (`.sif`) and accompanying descriptor XML file are written directly to the `repository` folder of the ADM package directory.

The main benefit of using the consoleapp utility is that we have full control over the file names and the output folder. In addition, the command line invocation technique allows us to create any type of shell script or small application to wrap the consoleapp call and parameter settings.

Copying files to the ADM package

As indicated earlier in this chapter, Siebel Application Deployment Manager supports the migration of files from one source enterprise to multiple target enterprises. We must copy files such as Siebel web templates (`.swt`) to the appropriate subdirectory in the `file\AppServer` folder of the ADM package structure.

There is no specialized utility provided by Oracle to copy the files. We must rely on the copy functionality of the operating system or other file transport automation tools such as robocopy or ftp.

The following table provides an overview of the various supported file types and the destination folder in the ADM package directory:

File Type	Comments	Destination Folder
Siebel Repository File (`.srf`)	The `.srf` file is compiled using Siebel Tools once for each deployed language pack. If repository data is migrated, the `.srf` file must be migrated as well. Deployment of `.srf` files is discussed in more detail below.	`file\AppServer\objects\<language>`
Siebel Web Templates (`.swt`)	Siebel Web Templates are typically modified rather infrequently.	`file\AppServer\webtempl`
BI Publisher Report templates (`.rtf`)	Created by report developers.	`file\AppServer\xmlp\templates`
BI Publisher Report Translation files (`.xlf`)	Contain translatable strings in the respective language.	`file\AppServer\xmlp\xliff\<language>`
Files in the `PUBLIC` directory of the Siebel Web Server Extension (SWSE)	All files in the `PUBLIC` directory are supported for migration by ADM.	`file\AppServer\webmaster` Note: appropriate subdirectories must be created manually. Use the existing `webmaster` directory on the Siebel server as a guideline.

About deploying Siebel Repository Files

There are several considerations about deploying the Siebel Repository File (.srf) using ADM.

- ADM cannot be used to deploy a .srf file that already exists on the target server. This is because the file is locked when the Siebel server processes are running.
- ADM is not capable to shut down and restart the Siebel Server components or the entire Siebel Server. This step must be done manually.
- If the ADM package does not contain repository objects or if these objects are of type "Workflow Process" or "Task", it is not necessary to deploy the .srf file.

Most projects therefore abstain from using ADM to deploy Siebel Repository Files. Administrators can follow the procedure below to deploy a new .srf file. The procedure is applicable when there are two or more Siebel Servers in the enterprise and a load balancing mechanism is in place. It provides a safe path with minimal impact on running sessions.

1. Bring all non-system server components such as application object managers to a paused status. This ensures that no new tasks are started for the server components on this Siebel server.
2. Monitor the active sessions on all non-system server components on the Siebel server and wait until the active session count is zero.
3. Shut down the Siebel server service.
4. Copy the new .srf file to the correct language-specific subdirectory in the Siebel Server's object folder.
5. Start the Siebel server service.
6. Verify that the Siebel Server starts up without errors.

Sealing the ADM package

Once the package is populated with all administrative data, repository data, and files that are part of the release, we must use the `admpkgr` command line utility again to generate an XML descriptor file that contains information about the package content.

It is recommended to delete all empty directories from the package structure in order to avoid warnings being displayed during the remaining steps.

A command similar to the following, issued from the Siebel Management Server's root directory, will generate the descriptor file:

```
admpkgr generate C:\SIA81\mgmtsrvr\adm\packages\EVAL_PACKAGE
```

The above command will generate a package descriptor file and an accompanying XML schema definition (.xsd) file in the package root directory.

Once the descriptor file is generated, the package content must not be changed. If changes are made to the package content, we must delete the descriptor file and the schema file and repeat the above command to generate a new package descriptor.

Validating the ADM package

In order to verify that the content of an ADM package matches the package descriptor file, we can use the validate command of the admpkgr command line utility as shown in the following example:

```
admpkgr validate C:\SIA81\mgmtsrvr\adm\packages\EVAL_PACKAGE
```

The above command validates the content of the EVAL_PACKAGE directory against the descriptor file. We should see a message indicating that the package directory was successfully validated. If this is not the case, the package content has been modified and the ADM package is not valid.

> On your demonstration machine, you can use the Developer Web Client and Siebel Tools to create and validate an evaluation package. In the adm\packages directory of the Siebel Management Server installation folder, you will also find a sample package that you can inspect (and deploy).

Deploying ADM packages

In contrast to the somewhat heterogeneous process of exporting and packaging data and files for ADM, the deployment process is driven by a single batch file. This file is generated during the ADM setup and is named deploy_EnterpriseName.bat, where EnterpriseName is replaced with the name of the target Siebel enterprise for which the ADM setup was completed. If we have more than one target Siebel enterprise, there will be one deployment batch file per enterprise.

The enterprise deployment batch file serves as a wrapper for calls to the underlying Java functionality and allows administrators to use a simple syntax for the complete deployment cycle. Below is an example of the syntax of the enterprise deployment batch file.

`deploy_SIEBELEVAL load SIEBMGMT SIEBMGMT EVAL_PACKAGE`

The first parameter passed to the deploy_SIEBELEVAL batch file is the name of the command—`load` in the example—to be executed. The second and third parameter is a valid username and password combination. The fourth parameter is the name of an ADM package directory.

To see a complete list of possible commands and syntax examples, we can use the `help` command:

`deploy_SIEBELEVAL help`

The above command results in the display of the usage information for the deployment batch file including all available commands. If we wish to see a detailed explanation of a specific command such as `load`, we can simply type it after the `help` command.

`deploy_SIEBELEVAL help load`

The above command displays details about the `load` command.

The most important commands and their typical sequence for a successful and safe deployment are described in the following table:

Sequence	Command	Description	Mandatory?
1	load	Reads the package and writes information about the content of the package to the ADM database.	Yes
2	create	Creates a new deployment session for the package. Once a session is created, it must be completed or stopped before another session can be executed.	Yes
3	validate	Validates the state of the target enterprise by establishing connections to the management agents and ADM object managers.	No
4	backup	Reads data that matches the files in the package from the target enterprise and writes it to a temporary backup package. The parameter to do an automatic backup is turned on by default, so this is only mandatory if the automatic backup is turned off and a manual backup is needed.	No

Migrating Configuration Changes between Environments

Sequence	Command	Description	Mandatory?
4	`copy`	The copy command directs the Siebel Management Server to write—and subsequently overwrite—data and files to the target enterprise.	Yes
5	`activate`	The Siebel Management Server reads information from the ADM registry file and directs the management agents to execute business services that activate the data. Examples are the refreshing of caches or the synchronization of the SWSE's public folder.	Yes
6	`restore_session`	This command, which creates a restore session for the given package, is only applicable when we wish to copy a backup package—created with the backup command—to restore the state of the target enterprise before the copy command.	No
7	`restore_copy`	Copies the content of the backup package to the target enterprise.	No
8	`restore_activate`	Activates the content of the backup package on the target enterprise. Note: After this command, the target enterprise is in the same functional state it was before the copy command. This does not mean that all data imported during the copy is deleted. For example, a workflow process would stay in the repository but it would be inactive, hence the term functional state.	No
9	`acknowledge`	The acknowledge command should be issued only after thorough testing. It completes the session by confirming that everything is correct. No restore session is possible after this point.	Yes
10	`status_detail`	There are several status commands available to obtain information about the current state of the deployment session.	No
11	`report`	Creates an HTML report for the package. The report includes performance measurements for every single file in the package.	No

Sequence	Command	Description	Mandatory?
12	delete	Cleans up data about the package and the deployment session in the ADM database. This is only necessary if we wish to use a package with the same name over and over again.	No

The following is a simple example script that gives us the general idea of how the deployment batch commands are used:

```
# load the package
call bin\deploy_SIEBELEVAL load SIEBMGMT SIEBMGMT EVAL_PACKAGE

# create a deployment session for the package
call bin\deploy_SIEBELEVAL create SIEBMGMT SIEBMGMT EVAL_PACKAGE

# display the contents of the package
call bin\deploy_SIEBELEVAL list_detail SIEBMGMT SIEBMGMT EVAL_PACKAGE

# display the status details of the package
call bin\deploy_SIEBELEVAL status_detail SIEBMGMT SIEBMGMT EVAL_PACKAGE

# migrate data to target enterprise
call bin\deploy_SIEBELEVAL copy SIEBMGMT SIEBMGMT EVAL_PACKAGE

# activate data on target enterprise
call bin\deploy_SIEBELEVAL activate SIEBMGMT SIEBMGMT EVAL_PACKAGE

# display the status details of the package
call bin\deploy_SIEBELEVAL status_detail SIEBMGMT SIEBMGMT EVAL_PACKAGE

# create an html report file for the package
call bin\deploy_SIEBELEVAL report SIEBMGMT SIEBMGMT EVAL_PACKAGE

# acknowledge the session
call bin\deploy_SIEBELEVAL acknowledge SIEBMGMT SIEBMGMT EVAL_PACKAGE
```

The script accomplishes the following:

- Calls the load command to write package information to the ADM database
- Calls the create command to create a new session for the package
- Uses the list_detail and status_detail commands to output information about the package content and deployment status

- Uses the `copy` and `activate` commands to copy the package content to the target enterprise and activate it
- Invokes the `status_detail` and `report` commands to obtain information about the session status and runtime information
- Calls the `acknowledge` command to confirm and close the session

Script files similar to that above can be used by administrators to automate the ADM deployment process. As indicated in this section, the deployment process must include a strict testing regimen in order to ensure that the migrated configuration changes do not affect the functionality or performance of the target system in a negative manner.

Other migration utilities

Because ADM is not designed to cover all aspects of the deployment of configuration changes, we will discuss additional utilities for configuration migration as provided by Oracle.

- Siebel Upgrade Wizard—Migrate Repository
- Deployment of enterprise configuration data using the cfgmerge utility

Siebel Upgrade Wizard—Migrate Repository

As indicated during the discussion of repository migration scenarios, we can observe that the capability of ADM for migration of repository changes is limited to either a Hot-Fix or a Mid-Level Release scenario. Both scenarios share the characteristics of having a relatively small number of object definitions and no database schema changes to be deployed.

A major release scenario, including changes of hundreds or thousands of object definitions including object definitions at the data layer such as tables, columns, or indexes is supported by the **Siebel Upgrade Wizard**.

The **Migrate Repository** procedure is provided by the **Siebel Database Configuration Assistant**. The configuration assistant provides a graphical user interface to capture relevant parameter information and then invokes the Siebel Upgrade Wizard, which executes the necessary tasks. The Migrate Repository procedure includes the following tasks:

1. Export the complete repository from the source database to a flat file.
2. Import the data from the flat file to the target database as the new Siebel Repository.
3. Rename the old Siebel Repository in the target database.
4. Synchronize the physical schema of the target database with the object definitions in the data layer of the new repository.
5. Update the schema version information in the target database.

> The Migrate Repository procedure is widely known in the technical Siebel CRM community as "dev2prod" — development to production. The default name for the log file directory created by the Siebel Upgrade Wizard is reminiscent of this old name.

The following table describes the procedure of invoking the Siebel Database Configuration Wizard and executing the Migrate Repository procedure. The example is for Microsoft Windows operating systems.

Step	Description	Tasks and Example Values
1	Start the Configuration Wizard	Click the **Database Server Configuration** shortcut in the Windows start menu.
2	Siebel Server directory	Provide the path to the Siebel Server's installation directory.
		Typically, the default can be kept.
		Click **Next**.
3	Siebel Database Server Utilities directory	Provide the path to the Siebel Database Server Utilities installation folder.
		Typically, the default can be kept.
		Click **Next**.
4	Database Platform	Select **Oracle Database Enterprise Edition**.
		Click **Next**.
5	Task selection	Select **Migrate Repository**.
		Click **Next**.

Migrating Configuration Changes between Environments

Step	Description	Tasks and Example Values
6	Action selection	Select **Read source repository directly from the database**
		Click **Next**.
7	Target environment	Select **The target environment will be offline when migration starts**.
		Note: We must bring the target environment to an offline state before executing the Siebel Upgrade Wizard.
		Click **Next**.
9	Schema changes	Select **There are new schema changes to be applied**.
		Note: Selecting this value ensures that the database schema is synchronized with the data layer object definitions. It is safe to choose even if no schema changes have been made.
		Click **Next**.
10	Select base language	Select **English (American)**.
		Click **Next**.
11	ODBC Data Source Name (source)	Enter **SIEBELEVAL_DSN**.
		Note: This is the name of the System DSN for the source enterprise.
		Click **Next**.
12	Siebel Database User Name and Password (source)	User Name: **SADMIN**.
		Password: **TJay357D**.
		Click **Next**.
13	Siebel Database Table Owner and Password (source)	Table Owner: **SIEBEL**.
		Password: **dQ7JXufi**.
		Click **Next**.
14	Source and target repository name	Keep the defaults ("Siebel Repository").
		Click **Next**.
15	Target Database Platform	Select **Oracle Database Enterprise Edition**
		Click **Next**.
16	Unicode selection	Select **UNICODE Database**.
		Click **Next**.

Chapter 15

Step	Description	Tasks and Example Values
17	ODBC Data Source Name (target)	Enter the name of the System DSN for the target enterprise. Note: We might have to create system DSN entries for the source and target databases on the machine where this process executes. Click **Next**.
18	Siebel Database User Name and Password (target)	User Name: **SADMIN**. Password: **7uxkfl0D**. Click **Next**.
19	Siebel Database Table Owner and Password (target)	Table Owner: **SIEBEL**. Password: **6tOPDD3**. Click **Next**.
20	Index and data tablespace names (target)	Index Table Space Name: **SIEBELDB_IDX**. (Data) Table Space Name: **SIEBELDB_DATA** Click **Next**.
21	Oracle parallel indexing	Keep the default ("Does not use…"). Click **Next**.
22	Security group and log output directory	Keep the defaults. Note the log output directory will become a subdirectory of the Siebel Server's LOG directory. Click **Next**.
23	Apply configuration changes	Select **Yes apply configuration changes now**. Click **Next**.
24	Summary	Review the summary information. Click **Next**.
25	**Target Enterprise Shutdown** (not part of the wizard)	Ensure that all Siebel Servers in the target enterprise are shut down. On production enterprises, ensure that the downtime is either announced well in advance or the migration is executed when no users are active.
26	Do you want to execute configuration?	Click **Yes**.
27	The Siebel Upgrade Wizard is displayed.	Click **OK** in the Siebel Upgrade Wizard dialog.

Step	Description	Tasks and Example Values
28	During the installation process, several command windows are opened	Ensure that you do not close or make selections in any of the command windows.
		Wait for the Siebel Upgrade Wizard to complete.
29	The configuration wizard displays a message "Execution successful"	Click **OK** to confirm successful execution of the configuration wizard.
30	The configuration wizard jumps to the Siebel Server directory selection	Click **Cancel** in the Siebel Configuration Wizard dialog.
31	Confirm exiting the configuration wizard	Click **Yes**.
32	Siebel Upgrade Wizard displays "Complete"	Click **OK** in the Siebel Upgrade Wizard dialog.

Once the Siebel Upgrade Wizard has successfully completed all steps, we should use Siebel Tools—connecting to the target database—to verify that a new Siebel Repository exists.

Depending on the project policies, we must ensure that the necessary tests are completed before we start the Siebel servers in the target enterprise.

Deploying enterprise configuration data using the cfgmerge utility

Siebel Application Deployment Manager is not designed to deploy changes made to the configuration of enterprise parameters, servers, and components. As discussed in Chapter 9, these changes can be made either through the server management screens and views in the Siebel Web Client or through the Siebel Server Manager (srvrmgr) command line utility.

We already know that the storage location of this information is the `siebns.dat` file, which is managed by the Siebel Gateway Name Server.

Because some of the parameters refer to enterprise-specific paths or host names such as the file system path or the chart server host name, we cannot simply copy the `siebns.dat` file from one enterprise to the other.

The **cfgmerge** command line utility is one possible solution to achieving a merge of configuration stores.

The utility compares two `siebns.dat` files—target and source—and produces an input file for the Siebel Server Manager (srvrmgr) command line utility. This file contains the necessary commands to change those parameters in the target environment that have been modified in the source environment. The input file must be reviewed, modified if necessary, and then executed using the srvrmgr command line.

Deploying new component definitions from source to target enterprises

The cfgmerge utility can produce input files on the enterprise level and the individual server level. It can only compare parameters, component definitions, and server components that are already present in both `siebns.dat` files and have the same names in both files.

If we wish to use the cfgmerge utility to deploy new component definitions from the source system to the target system, we have to create them manually in the target system by simply copying and renaming an existing component definition in the graphical user interface or by using a script and then running the utility.

Using the cfgmerge utility

The following list gives an example procedure of how to use the cfgmerge utility:

1. Log in to the Siebel Server Manger (srvrmgr) command line against the **source** enterprise.
2. Use the `backup namesrvr` command to create a backup of the current `siebns.dat` source file.
3. Rename the backup copy to `siebns_source.dat`.
4. Log in to the Siebel Server Manger (srvrmgr) command line against the **target** enterprise.
5. Use the `backup namesrvr` command to create a backup of the current `siebns.dat` target file.
6. Rename the backup copy to `siebns_target.dat`.
7. Copy both files created in the previous steps to a temporary directory on a machine where a Siebel Gateway Name Server is installed.
8. On this machine, open a command shell and navigate to the `bin` directory of the Siebel Gateway Name Server installation folder.
9. Execute a command similar to the following to create the input file at the enterprise level.

```
cfgmerge -l ENU -i D:\cfgmerge\siebns_source.dat,D:\cfgmerge\
siebns_target.dat -e SIEB_DEV,SIEB_TEST -o D:\cfgmerge\DEV_TEST_
ENT.txt
```

The above command invokes the cfgmerge utility. The -l parameter takes a three letter language code. The -i switch is followed by a comma-separated list of the full paths to the file representing the source `siebns.dat` and the file representing the target `siebns.dat`. The -e switch is followed by a comma-separated list of the names of the source enterprise and the target enterprise. The -o parameter value specifies the path where the output file should be written to.

10. Execute a command similar to the following to create the input file at the server level:

    ```
    cfgmerge -l ENU -i D:\cfgmerge\siebns_source.dat,D:\cfgmerge\
    siebns_target.dat -e SIEB_DEV,SIEB_TEST -s Dev_1,Test_1 -o D:\
    cfgmerge\DEV_TEST_SRV.txt
    ```

    The above command is similar to the one that generates the enterprise level output. The difference is the -s switch, which is followed by a comma-separated list of the names of the two Siebel servers to compare.

11. If necessary, we repeat the command for any additional Siebel servers in the source or target enterprise.

12. Review and modify the output files if necessary. It is mandatory to thoroughly review the output files of the cfgmerge utility in order to avoid unwanted changes being applied to the target enterprise configuration.

13. Log in to the Siebel Server Manager (srvrmgr) against the **target** enterprise and execute a command similar to the following to apply the changes:

```
read D:\cfgmerge\DEV_TEST_ENT.txt
read D:\cfgmerge\DEV_TEST_SRV.txt
```

The read command opens the specified file and executes all commands in that file.

The process is completed by shutting down and restarting all services of the target enterprise. If end users are affected by the shutdown, we must of course ensure that the end user community is notified of the downtime well in advance.

Summary

The complete, flawless, and reliable deployment of configuration changes from one Siebel enterprise to another is a complex endeavour that cannot be accomplished with a single tool.

In this chapter, we introduced the major deployment tool, namely Siebel Application Deployment Manager (ADM). The chapter discussed the main steps to enable ADM functionality on the Siebel Management Server infrastructure.

The two main processes of an ADM deployment cycle are the exporting and packaging process and the deployment process. The exporting and packaging process relies on a variety of tools depending on the type of data to be migrated.

The chapter discussed both the manual and automatic possibilities to export and package administrative data, repository data, and files.

The ADM deployment process relies on a single deployment batch file and the commands supported by it. A sample script has been provided in this chapter to demonstrate how the deployment batch file can be used to automate the deployment process.

In addition to ADM, this chapter discussed two other utilities that are widely used for migration of configuration information from source to target enterprises, namely the Migrate Repository process driven by the Siebel Upgrade Wizard, which is used to migrate the entire repository, and apply schema changes to the target database and the cfgmerge utility, which allow administrators to accomplish the comparison and application of changes made to the Siebel Enterprise configuration store in the Siebel Gateway Name Server's `siebns.dat` file.

In the next chapter, we will explore techniques to monitor Siebel Server events and performance.

16
Monitoring Siebel Applications

Complex, enterprise-class applications such as Siebel CRM are based on an interwoven architecture that combines heterogeneous hardware, different network protocols, and software from various vendors.

Often, thousands of end users and dozens of external systems require high-speed access to the system at the same time. Developers modify the configuration in order to meet end user requirements, which adds additional complexity to the overall implementation.

As responsible Siebel administrators, we must be aware of the technical possibilities of monitoring the performance and usage of Siebel CRM applications across the network as well as provide a reliable insight in the case of slow performance. Only by using the tools provided by Oracle correctly, will we be able to respond to possible performance breaches in a proactive manner.

In this chapter, we will elaborate on the following concepts:

- Server Component Event Logging
- Siebel Application Response Measurement (SARM)
- Siebel Diagnostic Tool
- Client Side Logging
- Siebel Usage Collection

Server component event logging

The Siebel Server and the server components it hosts are among the most frequently used processes in a typical Siebel CRM implementation. In the case of error situations or slow performance, we must be able to quickly pin-point the root cause of the problem. One way to do this is to direct the server processes to write more detailed information in their log files.

The Siebel server infrastructure provides a logging model, which is based on event types. We can control the amount of information written to the log file separately for each server component and for each individual event type by choosing a log level for each event type.

The following log levels exist for Siebel servers or individual components:

Log Level	Description
0	Fatal—Only severe errors are written to the log file. Recommended for productive operation.
1	Errors—The default setting; all error messages are written to the log file. Recommended for productive operation.
2	Warnings—Messages with warning characteristics are included in the log file. Recommended to trace configuration issues.
3	Informational—Messages with informational content are included in the log file. Recommended for troubleshooting and debugging.
4	Details—The log file will include detailed information about the process. Recommended for more detailed troubleshooting and debugging.
5	Diagnostic—All message output from the process will be written to the log file. Only recommended when lower levels do not yield the desired output or when requested by Oracle's technical support team.

Source: *Siebel System Monitoring and Diagnostics Guide Version 8.1*

```
http://download.oracle.com/docs/cd/E14004_01/books/SysDiag/booktitle.
html
```

When setting log levels to 2 or higher, we must bear in mind that a higher log level negatively impacts the performance of the Siebel server. In addition, the log files can quickly grow very large in size, clogging the log directories and making it hard to retrieve valuable information.

In the Servers view of the Administration - Server Configuration screen, we can view or modify event log levels for an entire Siebel Server (affecting all components on that server) or individual components. The following screenshot shows the Events list for a selected Siebel Server:

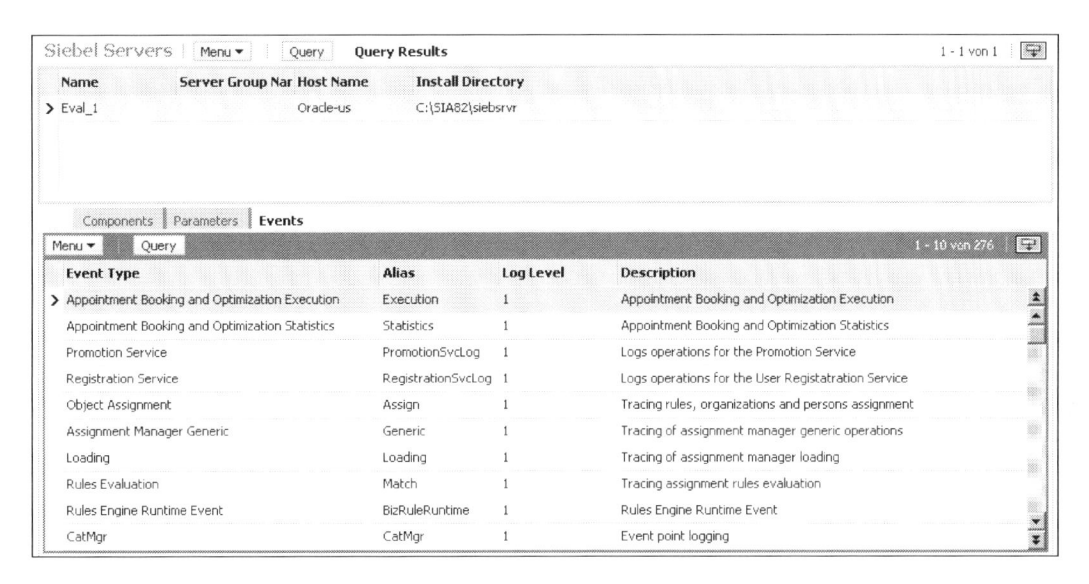

Event Type	Alias	Log Level	Description
Appointment Booking and Optimization Execution	Execution	1	Appointment Booking and Optimization Execution
Appointment Booking and Optimization Statistics	Statistics	1	Appointment Booking and Optimization Statistics
Promotion Service	PromotionSvcLog	1	Logs operations for the Promotion Service
Registration Service	RegistrationSvcLog	1	Logs operations for the User Registatration Service
Object Assignment	Assign	1	Tracing rules, organizations and persons assignment
Assignment Manager Generic	Generic	1	Tracing of assignment manager generic operations
Loading	Loading	1	Tracing of assignment manager loading
Rules Evaluation	Match	1	Tracing assignment rules evaluation
Rules Engine Runtime Event	BizRuleRuntime	1	Rules Engine Runtime Event
CatMgr	CatMgr	1	Event point logging

In this list, we can set the log level for each event type individually. The following table lists some commonly used event types. Oracle recommends a log level of 4 for troubleshooting and 0 or 1 for normal operation.

Event Type	Description
Component Tracing	Various informational messages about parameter values and more.
General Events	Information about event points is written to the log file. Example: a background component enters its sleep interval.
Task Configuration	All parameters for the current task will be written to the log file header.
SQL Profiling	Extended summary of SQL prepare, execute, and fetch statements.
SQL Summary	Writes the timings for SQL statement preparation as well as fetch and execute operations to the log file.
SQL Error	Traces all erroneous SQL statements.
SQL Parse and Execute	Writes all insert, update, and delete SQL statements to the log file.

Event Type	Description
Event to track the flow of a message	For tracking messages exchanged between the Siebel Web Server Extension (SWSE) and the application object manager.
Object Manager Session Operation and SetErrorMsg Log	For capturing user session information.
Event Context	Traces screen, view, and applet names for the user session.
Security Adapter Log	Writes information about the Siebel security adapter to the log file.

Source: *Siebel System Monitoring and Diagnostics Guide Version 8.1*

http://download.oracle.com/docs/cd/E14004_01/books/SysDiag/booktitle.html

If we wish to set the log level for one or more event types, we must execute the following tasks:

1. Verify that the event type and chosen log level is appropriate for the purpose.
2. Navigate to the Events view for either the server or the component level.
3. Select the Siebel server or the individual component.
4. Select the event type.
5. Set the log level to the desired value.
6. Restart the Siebel server or the individual server component.

Any modification of log levels should be documented and the respective log levels—especially on production systems—should be set back to 0 or 1 when no longer needed in order to avoid performance problems.

The Siebel Server's log directory holds all log files that are produced during the server's operation. If log levels have been increased, we will observe more and larger log files depending on our settings. The following screenshot shows the Siebel Server log directory and an open log file for the Call Center Object Manager component:

Chapter 16

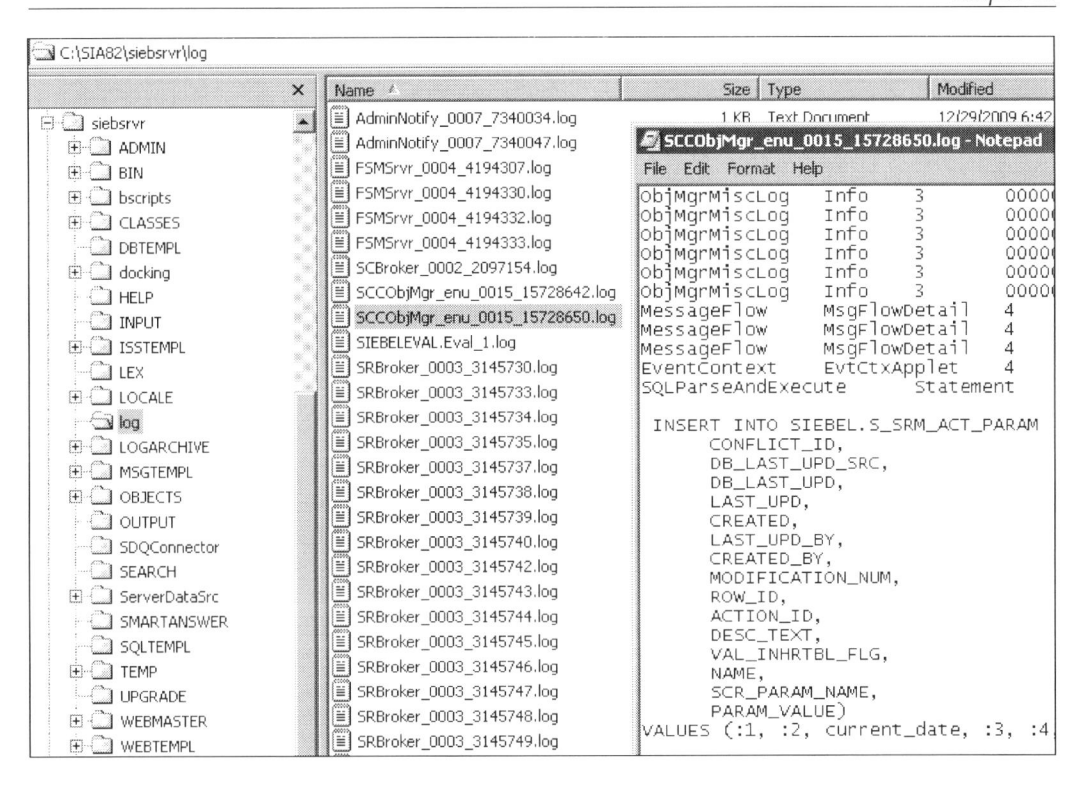

[Screenshot of Windows Explorer showing C:\SIA82\siebsrvr\log directory with log files, and a Notepad window displaying the contents of SCCObjMgr_enu_0015_15728650.log containing ObjMgrMiscLog entries, MessageFlow entries, and an SQL INSERT INTO SIEBEL.S_SRM_ACT_PARAM statement.]

We can observe that detailed information about the session is written to the file, including SQL statements.

> Once a Siebel Server is restarted, the log directory's content is moved to an incrementally numbered subfolder of the LOGARCHIVE directory. We can control the number of archive directories by setting the Log Archive Keep parameter at the server level. This is important to know as the desired log file might reside in a subdirectory of the **LOGARCHIVE** folder rather than in the log directory, because the Siebel Server has been restarted.

Using the Siebel Server Manager command line to set event log levels

As an alternative to using the graphical user interface (GUI) provided by the views in the Administration - Server Configuration screen, we can issue commands or scripts at the Siebel Server Manager (srvrmgr) command line.

The following example illustrates how to set event log levels for an application object manager:

```
change evtloglvl genericlog=5 for comp sccobjmgr_enu
```

The above command sets the log level for the General Events event type to 5 for the English Siebel Call Center object manager.

Using the command line or script files is recommended if we frequently have to change the log level for a larger amount of event types. Scripts can also be used to ensure that log levels are reset back to lower values of 0 or 1 when the troubleshooting process is finished.

> Use your demonstration machine to set the log level for a server component as described in the above section and inspect the resulting log files.

Siebel Application Response Measurement (SARM)

When an end user clicks a view tab to navigate to a new view, a chain of processes is invoked on different machines in order to handle the request. For example, the Siebel Web Server Extension must connect to the application object manager (AOM) on the Siebel server. The AOM will issue an SQL statement to the Siebel database and the Siebel Web Engine (SWE) will put the view layout and data together and render the view.

In order to be able to make exact measurements to determine performance bottlenecks quickly, Siebel engineers have included instrumentation points in the core program code of all Siebel software components.

This feature is commonly known as Siebel Application Response Measurement (SARM). The following diagram explains how SARM works:

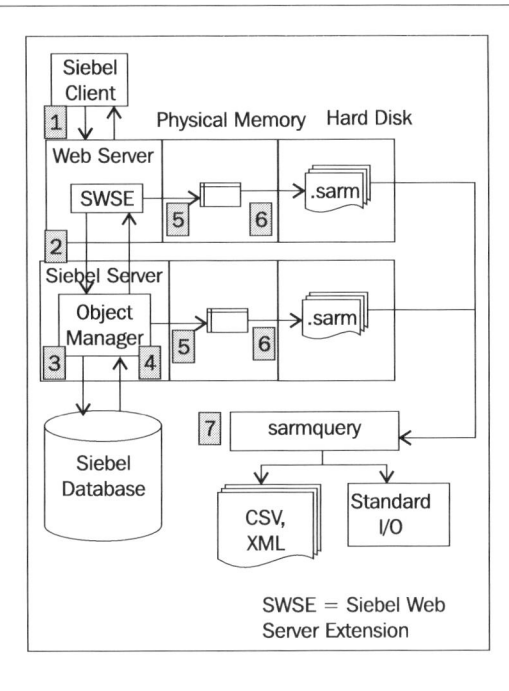

From the above diagram, we can learn the following about Siebel Application Response Measurement:

1. Requests from the web client are processed on the Siebel Web Server Extension (SWSE) on the web server machine.
2. The request is passed on to the application object manager on the Siebel server machine.
3. The application object manager requests data from the Siebel database.
4. The database returns the data.
5. When the Siebel code executes, a buffer in the machine's physical memory is filled with information about each single event.
6. Once the memory buffer is full or a timeout is reached, the buffer's content is flushed to files on the hard disk. These files have a `.sarm` suffix.
7. Administrators can use the sarmquery command line utility to convert the binary content of the `.sarm` files to readable formats such as CSV (comma separated values) or XML. Alternatively, SARM information can be viewed directly at the command prompt.

Next, we will discuss these major administrative tasks related to Siebel Application Response Measurement:

- Enabling SARM
- Managing SARM files
- Using sarmquery to read SARM files
- Automating SARM data retrieval

Enabling SARM

The default behaviour of Siebel software is not to produce `.sarm` files. In order to turn on the production of `.sarm` files, we have to set parameters (for Siebel Servers and their components) or environment variables (for all other variants of Siebel software such as the Siebel Web Server Extension or Siebel clients).

> Even when SARM is "turned off", the memory buffer is always filled with response measurement data. However, the buffer is overwritten once it is full. In the case of an exceptional abort of the program, the buffer is actually flushed to disk to record an image of the last operations (one of which might have led to the error situation). We can find the traces of these flush operations as files with an `.fdr` suffix (= flight data recorder—in analogy to the voice and data recorders used in aviation). FDR files can be opened with the sarmquery utility as well in order to retrieve information about the final operations of the process that crashed.

Enabling SARM for Siebel servers and components

We can use the graphical user interface (GUI) provided by the views in the Administration - Server Configuration screen or the Siebel Server Manager (srvrmgr) command line utility to set the SARM-related parameters. It is recommended to enable SARM only for a specific set of server components rather than for an entire Siebel server in order to keep the performance impact to a minimum.

The following table describes the SARM-related parameters:

Parameter Alias	Description	Example Value
SARMLevel	If set to a value greater than zero, .sarm files are written. A value of 1 produces less information than a value of 2. Value 3 is reserved for Oracle internal use.	2
SARMBufferSize	The amount of physical memory reserved for the SARM buffer (in bytes) for each process instance.	5000000
SARMPeriod	The interval (in minutes) how often the memory buffer is flushed to disk (even if not full).	1
SARMMaxFiles	The maximum number of .sarm files to be produced by each process instance. Once the limit is reached, the oldest file is deleted.	4
SARMFileSize	The maximum size of an individual .sarm file (in bytes).	15000000
SARMThreshold	It is important to set this parameter to the number of milliseconds that define the threshold for "long running" events. Because of the large number of events happening in very short time, we can dramatically reduce the size of the .sarm files by setting this parameter.	100
SARMLogDirectory	It is possible to direct the .sarm file output to any shared or local directory. If not set, the .sarm files will be located in the local log subfolder of the Siebel software installation directory.	\\appsrvr\sarmdata

Parameter Alias	Description	Example Value
SARMUsers	A comma-separated list of user account names to limit the amount of data in the .sarm files. If left empty, .sarm data is collected for all users.	sadmin,siebmgmt,adm

The following procedure describes how we can enable SARM for an application object manager component:

1. Log in to the Siebel Server Manager (srvrmgr) command line using a command similar to the following at the Siebel server's bin directory:

```
srvrmgr /g osappeval4 /e SIEBEL_EVAL /u SADMIN /p TJay357D /s Eval_1
```

The above example command will connect to the Siebel Gateway Name Server on the host osappeval4. The enterprise name is SIEBEL_EVAL, username is SADMIN, and the server to be set at the prompt is Eval_1.

2. At the srvrmgr> prompt, enter a command similar to the following:

```
change param sarmlevel=2,sarmperiod=1,sarmthreshold=100 for comp sccobjmgr_enu
```

The above example command enables SARM at level 2 for the English Siebel Call Center object manager. The memory buffer's content will be flushed once a minute; only events that took longer than 100 milliseconds will be written to the .sarm files. These parameter changes are effective immediately, so no component or server restart is required.

Enabling SARM for other Siebel software units

Because of the fact that only Siebel servers and their components can read the parameters from the Siebel Gateway Name Server's configuration store, we must use environment variables to enable SARM for other Siebel software units such as the Siebel Web Server Extension (SWSE) or Siebel clients such as Siebel Tools or the Siebel Mobile Web Client.

The following table relates the SARM environment variables to the parameters discussed above. Basically, the environment variable's name can be derived by adding the prefix "SIEBEL_" to the parameter name.

Environment Variable	Related Parameter
SIEBEL_SARMLevel	SARMLevel
SIEBEL_SARMBufferSize	SARMBufferSize
SIEBEL_SARMPeriod	SARMPeriod
SIEBEL_SARMMaxFiles	SARMMaxFiles
SIEBEL_SARMFileSize	SARMFileSize

The following procedure describes how to set the SARM environment variables on Microsoft Windows-based operating systems:

1. Right-click the **My Computer** icon and select **Properties**.
2. In the System Properties dialog, click the **Advanced** tab.
3. Click the **Environment Variables** button.
4. In the **System Variables** area, click the **New** button.
5. Enter the correct values in the Variable Name and Variable Value fields and click **OK**.
6. Repeat the previous step for each environment variable you need to set.
7. Restart the application (for example the Siebel Developer Web Client or the web server).

We can verify that SARM is properly enabled by inspecting the log directory of the installation folder of the Siebel software unit. SARM files should appear in this directory after the time specified in the SARMPeriod parameter. The screenshot below shows the Siebel Server's log directory with .sarm files:

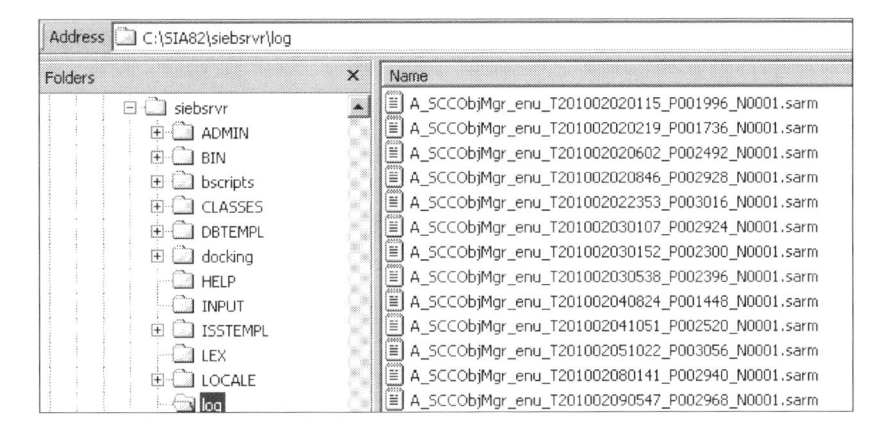

The naming convention for sarm files is as follows:

```
A_<Server component name>_T<Timestamp>_P<Process Id>_N<counter>.sarm
```

If we used the `SARMLogDirectory` parameter to specify a different storage location for `.sarm` files, we must inspect the respective directories.

> Repeat the steps in the previous section on your demonstration machine to enable SARM for at least one application object manager component.

Managing SARM files

It is imperative for Siebel administrators to understand how to create usable sets of `.sarm` files without cluttering the server's hard drives. In environments with hundreds or even thousands of end users, the amount and size of `.sarm` files can grow out of bounds quickly.

The following techniques ensure that we harvest a reasonable amount of information without affecting the overall system performance more than necessary.

Always set the SARMThreshold parameter to a value of 10 or higher. This avoids too much data being written to the `.sarm` files. Because SARM is often used to trace long-running and therefore performance-hampering events, we can ignore the events that execute very fast.

Setting the SARMThreshold for example to a value of 100 reduces the amount of data written to the `.sarm` files by an average of 90%. This can be easily verified by comparing `.sarm` file sizes at different settings of this parameter.

Adjust the amount of `.sarm` files for a single process using the `SARMMaxFiles` parameter. After a short evaluation period, we should be able to determine the ideal number of files. We should always have the amount of files that is needed to cover a typical monitoring period. For example, if we monitor a work day (9:00 am to 5:00 pm) we should set the `SARMMaxFiles` parameter to a number which ensures that `.sarm` files for an individual process do not get overwritten before eight hours.

With regard to reading the `.sarm` files with the sarmquery utility or using the Siebel Diagnostic Tool, the default folder—the log directory of the Siebel software unit—should be kept as the storage location. However, we can use scheduled scripts to copy the `.sarm` files to an archive folder to avoid loss of data.

Using sarmquery to read SARM files

The sarmquery command line utility is the primary means of converting the binary content of the .sarm files to readable output. We can choose between various output formats such as text, XML, or csv files or we can consume the output directly at the command prompt.

We can locate the sarmquery executable in the bin directory of the Siebel server's or the Siebel Gateway Name server's installation folder. In addition, the Siebel Management Agent uses sarmquery to support the Siebel Diagnostic Tool, which is discussed later in this chapter.

When we enter `sarmquery` at a command prompt in the Siebel server's bin directory, the utility reveals the basic usage information. The following screenshot shows the output of the `sarmquery` command in a Microsoft Windows command shell:

```
C:\SIA82\siebsrvr\BIN>sarmquery

sarmquery -copyright      : license and terms
sarmquery -tips           : quick start tips
sarmquery -help           : detail help
sarmquery -macrosyntax    : description of macro syntax language

Note: "sarmquery -output verbose=help.txt -help" will redirect the help
to the 'help.txt' file. Likewise, for -copyright, -tips and -macrosyntax

Synopsis
sarmquery [-quiet] [-flags [value] ]
          [-config key=value ...]
          [-select key=value ...] [-aggregate key=value ...]
          [-histogram key=value ...] [-output key=value ...]
          [-input] <input file specification>

Supports SARM schema version: 20041117
Build Version: 8.2 [22107] LANG_INDEPENDENT
Last Compiled: Oct 20 2009 15:01:41

== sarmquery exited successfully ==
```

It is recommendable to use the information provided to produce text files that contain the information obtained by the **-tips**, **-help**, and **-macrosyntax** options.

For example, a command similar to the following will create a `tips.txt` file with useful first step information in the Siebel server's bin directory:

`sarmquery -output verbose=tips.txt -tips`

Monitoring Siebel Applications

The above command uses the `-output` option followed by the `verbose` key with a value of `tips.txt` and the `-tips` option. This command produces a text file of the standard output of the `-tips` option. We can repeat this command to create a `help.txt` and `macrosyntax.txt` file by modifying the above command accordingly.

The main syntax of the sarmquery utility is as follows:

`sarmquery -option key=value -input <directory or file>`

The sarmquery command line utility accepts several options, which must be preceded by a dash ("-") and followed by a key=value pair. The `-input` option must be followed by the name of either a single `.sarm` file or a directory that contains `.sarm` files. If we use the directory option, sarmquery will scan the given directory and all its subdirectories recursively for `.sarm` files.

The following table describes the major options and example key=value pairs for the sarmquery utility:

Option	Example Key=Value Pairs	Description
-input	..\log D:\sia82\siebsrvr\bin\log \\appserver\sarmdata sarmdata0001.sarm	The -input option must be followed by a relative or absolute directory path or the name of a single `.sarm` file. Directories are always scanned recursively and all .sarm files found are taken into consideration.
-aggregate	area subarea user instance component time=60	The -aggregate option is followed by the name of one of the various preconfigured aggregate levels. It defines how SARM data should be grouped in the output. Except for the time aggregate, the -aggregate option does not require values for its keys.
-select	area=DBC subarea=DBC_EXECUTE starttime="2010-02-20 09:00:00" user=CCHENG	The -select option allows constraining the output of the sarmquery utility using preconfigured keys.
-histogram	resptime=500,1000,2000 cputime=100,200,500,1000	The -histogram option groups the output along the specified keys and values. The value is a comma-separated list of millisecond intervals.

Option	Example Key=Value Pairs	Description
-output	sarm=sarmdata.csv fdr=fdrdata.csv agg=sarmdata.xml verbose=tips.txt	The -output option is followed by one of the preconfigured key values, which indicate what content to write to the output file specified as the value.
-config	file=macros.txt macro=myMacro	The -config option allows to read a sarm macro file and executes one of the macros specified in the file.

Each option or key can be abbreviated as long as the abbreviation is not ambiguous. For example, the following is a valid sarmquery command:

```
sarmquery -i ..\log -agg sub -sel area=dbc
```

The above example uses the -input option (abbreviated to -i), the -aggregate (-agg) option followed by the subarea (sub) key and the -select (-sel) option. The abbreviation technique might come handy while using the command line but we should consider using the full text when creating scripts or macro files for the sake of better readability.

For a complete list of possible keys, we can consult the help file (generated using the -help option) or the Performance Tuning Guide in the Siebel bookshelf.

In the following, we will explore common scenarios for sarmquery:

- Specify the start and end time
- Application performance by area and subarea
- Time histograms
- Identify slow performing objects
- Create SARM output files

Specifying the start and end time

In a typical sarmquery scenario, we most probably want to analyze data from a specific timeframe. In order to do so, we must use the -select option for the starttime and endtime keys in every sarmquery call we make.

We can use a command similar to the following to obtain a list of users who logged on in the specified timeframe:

```
sarmquery -input ..\log -aggregate user -select starttime="09:00:00"
-select endtime="17:00:00"
```

The above command—issued at the bin directory of the Siebel server—will read all `.sarm` files in the Siebel server's log directory and create an aggregate plot for all users who had a session between 9:00 AM and 5:00 PM. If no date is given, sarmquery takes the current day into consideration. If we wish to specify a date, we must use the same syntax as in the example below:

```
-select starttime="2010-05-20 09:00:00"
```

The example specifies 9:00 AM on the 20th of May 2010 as the start time.

The output of the above command is similar to the following:

```
                         Histogram Of Average Response Times
User Name Avg Response(ms) | Average Inclusive Response Time                    # Calls
--------- ---------------- +------------------------------------------------   --------
?Unknown?           42.214 | xxxxxxxxxxxxxxxxxxxxxxxxxxxxxxxxxxxxxxxxxxxx           39
  AHANSAL           33.992 | xxxxxxxxxxxxxxxxxxxxxxxxxxxxxxxxxxx                  7188
   SADMIN            6.377 | .                                                   68880
```

The previous screenshot shows the typical output of sarmquery at the command line. Aggregates are plotted as horizontal bar graphs with the average response time as the scale.

Application performance by area and subarea

When SARM collects event data, it not only collects the timestamp, the user, and response timings but also the area and subarea of the Siebel application infrastructure where the event occurred.

A full list of SARM data collection areas can be found in the Siebel Performance Tuning Guide in the Siebel bookshelf documentation. The following table lists the most prominent areas:

Area	Description
OBJMGR	Events at the object manager layer. Includes business component and business service execution information.
INFRA	SARM data in this area represents the communication of Siebel server software components between each other.
SWEPAGE	This area groups events in the Siebel Web Engine (SWE), which is responsible for the rendering of user interface objects such as applets and views.
SWE	The events in the SWE area contain information on the applet level such as method invocation.

Area	Description
DBC	The DBC area contains events in the database connector layer. It records performance timings for database operations such as fetch, write, and execute.
EAITRANSP	Events in this area allow performance measurement for Enterprise Application Integration (EAI) touch points with external systems.
THRESHOLD	This area groups all events that fall below the value (in milliseconds) of the SARMThreshold parameter.
WORKFLOW	Events related to the execution of Siebel workflow processes.
SCRIPT	Allows performance measurement of the execution of eScript or SiebelVB code.
SEC	Events related to the security management layer. Includes user authentication.
SARM	The timings for SARM operations.

Each area has one or more subareas. We can obtain a comma-separated value (CSV) file listing all areas and subareas using the following command:

```
sarmquery -output map=map.csv
```

The above command produces a text file in CSV format, which describes all available SARM areas and subareas.

Analyzing areas, subareas and instances

We use a sarmquery command similar to the following to get a horizontal bar chart, which helps us identify the area in which most of the process time is spent:

```
sarmquery -aggregate area -input ..\log
```

The above command reads all `.sarm` files from the `log` directory of the Siebel server and produces a chart similar to the screenshot below:

```
                    Histogram Of Percent Times
    Area       Percent | Percentage Of Total Self Times         Response Time(ms)
   --------   -------- +-----------------------------------     ------------------
     INFRA     25.350  | xxxxxxxxxxxxxxxxxxxxxxxxxxxxxxxxxxxxxxxxxxxxx   921900.295
     OBJMGR    23.219  | xxxxxxxxxxxxxxxxxxxxxxxxxxxxxxxxxxxxxxxxxx      844377.543
    SWEPAGE    11.079  | xxxxxxxxxxxxxxxxxxxxx                           402914.472
       SWE     10.453  | xxxxxxxxxxxxxxxxxxxx                            380151.163
       DBC      8.749  | xxxxxxxxxxxxxxxxx                               318163.928
       SRB      8.310  | xxxxxxxxxxxxxxxx                                302203.140
  THRESHOLD    5.881  | xxxxxxxxxxx                                      213865.061
  EAITRANSP    5.669  | xxxxxxxxxxx                                      206177.766
       CSS     0.574  | x                                                 20860.997
       SEC     0.481  | .                                                 17488.999
      SARM     0.233  | .                                                  8490.305
       FSM     0.001  | .                                                    29.043
    SCRIPT     0.001  | .                                                    20.267
```

The above screenshot shows the output of the `-aggregate area` option. The chart lists all areas (sorted descending by the percentage of process time spent in the area) for which events have been recorded in the `.sarm` files. In the above example, 25.35% of the total process time recorded by SARM is spent in events that belong to the INFRA area.

We can "drill down" into each area by using commands similar to the following:

`sarmquery -select area=objmgr -aggregate subarea -input ..\log`

The above command uses the `-select` option to filter the output for the OBJMGR area and creates a bar chart that shows the share of process time spent for each subarea.

We can further "drill down" on the data. For example to see a list of business services that use the processing time, we use a command similar to the following:

`sarmquery -select subarea=objmgr_bsvc_invoke -aggregate instance -input ..\log`

The above command uses the `-aggregate instance` option. The instance key typically provides the name of the object involved. In the case of the subarea `objmgr_bsvc_invoke`, business service names are shown in the instance field.

Time histograms

A common server monitoring scenario is the retrieval of application response data over time. The data contained in the .sarm files can be interpreted in this way using the -aggregate time option. A command similar to the following produces a histogram of the application response time for a specific day:

```
sarmquery -input ..\log -aggregate time=10 -select starttime="2010-02-18 00:00:00" -select endtime="2010-02-19 00:00:00"
```

The above command produces a response time plot at 10-minute intervals (specified by the time=10 key=value pair) over the period specified as the timeframe between the starttime and endtime key values.

Identifying slow performing objects

One of the main purposes of SARM is the quick and easy identification of performance bottlenecks. We have learned above that we can aggregate the response time information by area, subarea, and instance.

By using the correct subarea as a filter criteria in the -select option, we can create response time histograms for objects such as views, scripts, or business services and identify slow performers.

The following example command allows us to identify slow performing views with a build time over five seconds:

```
sarmquery -input ..\log -agg instance -select subarea=SWEPAGE_VIEW_BUILD -select selftime=5000
```

The above command produces a response time histogram for all views that required more than five seconds (specified as 5000 milliseconds in the selftime key value) to build (subarea=SWEPAGE_VIEW_BUILD). The following screenshot shows the output of the example command:

```
                                    Histogram Of Percent Times
                      Instance Name    Percent | Percentage Of Total Self Times       Response Time(ms)
             ---------------------------------+-----------------------------------    -----------------
             Enterprise Server/Server View     15.811 | xxxxxxxxxxxxxxxx                       24627.637
                    Home Page View (WCC)       24.529 | xxxxxxxxxxxxxxxxxxxxxxxxxxxxx          38206.952
               Server Server/Compgroup View     7.883 | .                                      12278.708
      Server Server/Component/Parameter View   10.266 | xxxxx                                  15990.643
   Server Server/Component/State Value View    12.350 | xxxxxxxxxx                             19236.399
      Server Server/Component/Statistic View   29.162 | xxxxxxxxxxxxxxxxxxxxxxxxxxxxxxxxxx     45424.415
```

Views of the server management screens typically take a longer time to build because data is being fetched from the Siebel Gateway Name Server. The high response times for the Home Page View are resulting from the fact that it is the application's start view.

Similar commands can be issued using other areas such as SCRIPT (to identify slow running scripts) or OBJMGR (to identify slow performing business layer objects) or their respective subareas.

Creating SARM output files

The sarmquery command line utility can be used to export the content of the `.sarm` files to various output formats such as plain text, comma-separated values (CSV), or XML. Typically, these files are loaded into third-party software such as Microsoft Excel to further analyze the SARM data sets. We use the `-output` option to create SARM output files.

One of the most prominent output commands can be seen in the following example:

```
sarmquery -input ..\log -output sarm=sarmdata.csv#10000
```

The above command writes the raw SARM data to a series of CSV files. By specifying the suffix `#10000`, after the file name, we determine that each CSV file will contain only up to 10000 rows of data.

The CSV files can then be consumed for further analysis in spreadsheet applications such as Microsoft Excel or business intelligence tools such as Oracle Business Intelligence Enterprise Edition. The following screenshot shows a SARM `.csv` output file opened in Microsoft Excel:

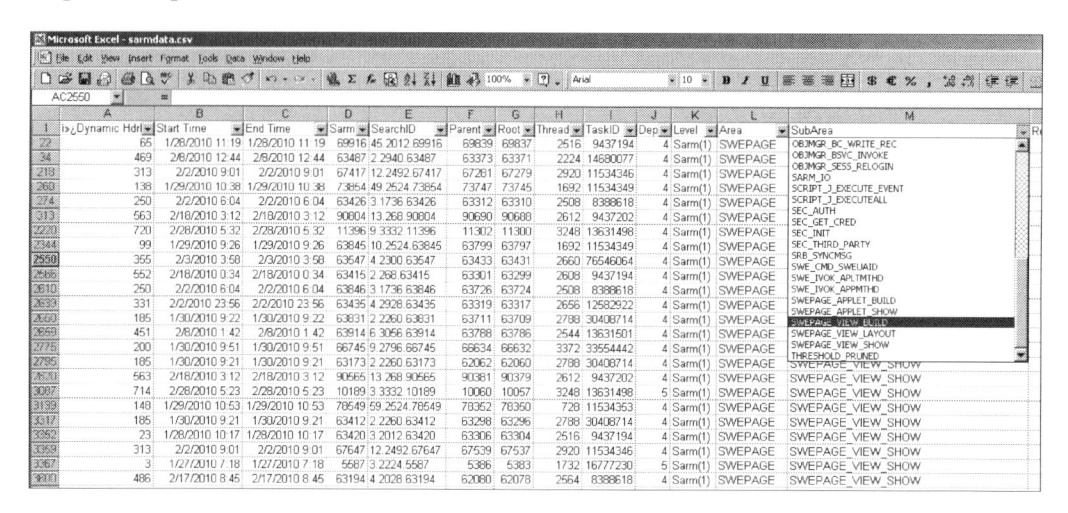

The filter feature of Microsoft Excel allows quick creation of filtered sets of data for easier analysis.

In contrary to the raw data output of the `sarm` key, we can use the `agg` key of the `-output` option to write aggregated information to text or XML files. A command similar to the following yields an XML file containing information aggregated at the area level:

`sarmquery -input ..\log -aggregate area -output agg=area_agg.xml`

The above command uses the `agg` key followed by an XML file name and produces an output similar to the following screenshot.

```
<?xml version="1.0" encoding="UTF-8" ?>
- <xml>
    <sarm version="20041117" />
  + <Group type="Area" name="INFRA" pctCount="0.054" pctSelfTime="25.350" pctInclResp="35.387">
  - <Group type="Area" name="OBJMGR" pctCount="0.316" pctSelfTime="23.219" pctInclResp="25.099">
    - <Statistics>
      + <Self count="4871">
      + <Inclusive count="665">
      </Statistics>
    </Group>
  - <Group type="Area" name="SWEPAGE" pctCount="0.028" pctSelfTime="11.079" pctInclResp="7.157">
    - <Statistics>
      - <Self count="430">
          <TimeFrom>2010-01-27 07:18:08</TimeFrom>
          <TimeTo>2010-02-28 05:33:00</TimeTo>
          <SearchableTimeFrom>2010-01-27 07:18:11</SearchableTimeFrom>
        - <ResponseTime units="ms">
            <Average>937.010</Average>
            <Total>402914.472</Total>
            <Maximum>24627.637</Maximum>
            <Minimum>0.005</Minimum>
          </ResponseTime>
```

The benefit of the XML format is that SARM data can be made available to third-party analysis software more easily.

> After enabling SARM and navigating the Siebel application on your demonstration machine for a while in order to collect data, you can start practicing using the sarmquery command line utility using the above section as a guide.

Automating SARM data retrieval

In order to provide the Siebel CRM project team with fresh and easily readable performance data, we must take the following into consideration:

- Ensure that `.sarm` files are collected and archived according to the monitoring policies of our company. We can use shell scripts to copy `.sarm` files to safe locations so they do not get overwritten by Siebel server processes.

- Create shell scripts, which execute the sarmquery commands that produce the most usable output for our project. We can use the SARM macro language to produce more flexible script files.
- Use a scheduling facility such as the Windows task scheduler to invoke the scripts at a regular basis.
- Provide SARM output files to third-party analysis systems for better visualization of the data.

Siebel Diagnostic Tool

The Siebel Diagnostic Tool is an application that relies on the Siebel Management Server infrastructure to retrieve SARM data from Siebel server machines in one or more enterprises and renders this data as charts and tabular data.

The following diagram describes the architecture behind the Siebel Diagnostic Tool:

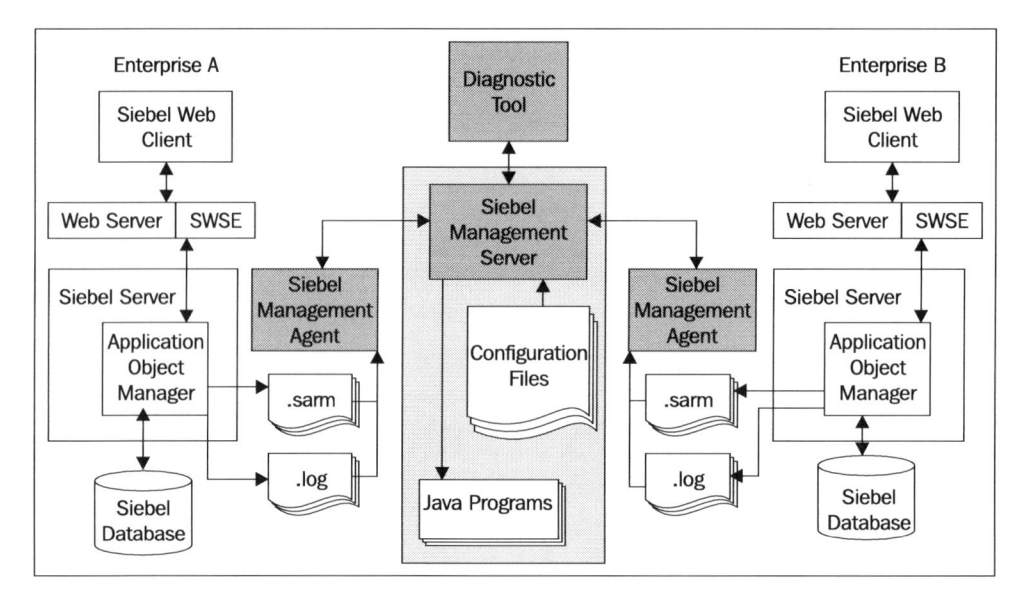

From the above diagram, we can derive the following information:

- Siebel Management Agents—installed on the machines hosting the Siebel Servers—use sarmquery to access `.sarm` files generated by the Siebel processes
- Additionally, the Siebel Management Agents can access the standard `.log` files on the Siebel Server
- The Diagnostic Tool connects to the Siebel Management Server
- The Siebel Management Server communicates with the Siebel Management Agents in order to fulfill data requests from the Diagnostic Tool

The installation and configuration of the Siebel Management Server infrastructure has been described in detail in a separate chapter of this book.

In the following procedure, we will explore the functionality of the Siebel Diagnostic Tool:

1. Ensure that the Siebel Management Agents and Siebel Management Server are started.
2. Ensure that SARM data files are generated on the Siebel Servers.
3. Open a browser window and navigate to a URL similar to the following:

   `http://appserver1:8080/DiagTool`

   The above URL example connects to port 8080 (the default port of the Siebel Diagnostic Tool) on the appserver1 machine.
4. Log in using a Siebel Management user account. The user account is created during the configuration of the Siebel Management Server.
5. In the **Server Performance Analysis** tab, use the form fields to specify a Siebel Enterprise, a Siebel Server Group (optional), a Siebel Server, and (optionally) a server component. We can also specify start and end dates to define a timeframe for the analysis.

The following screenshot shows the **Server Performance Analysis** tab of the Siebel Diagnostic Tool:

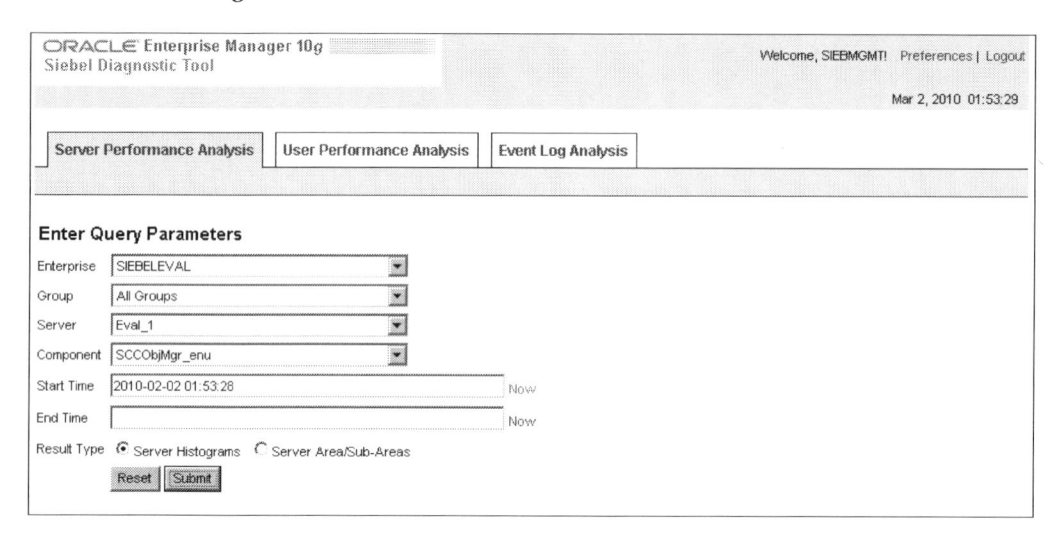

6. Choose a result type (Server Histograms or Server Area/Sub-Areas) and click the **Submit** button.
7. Depending on the selected result type, the server histogram charts or the area/subarea analysis are displayed.

Server Histograms are vertical bar charts displaying the average response times and CPU times for the selected server components, as shown in the following screenshot:

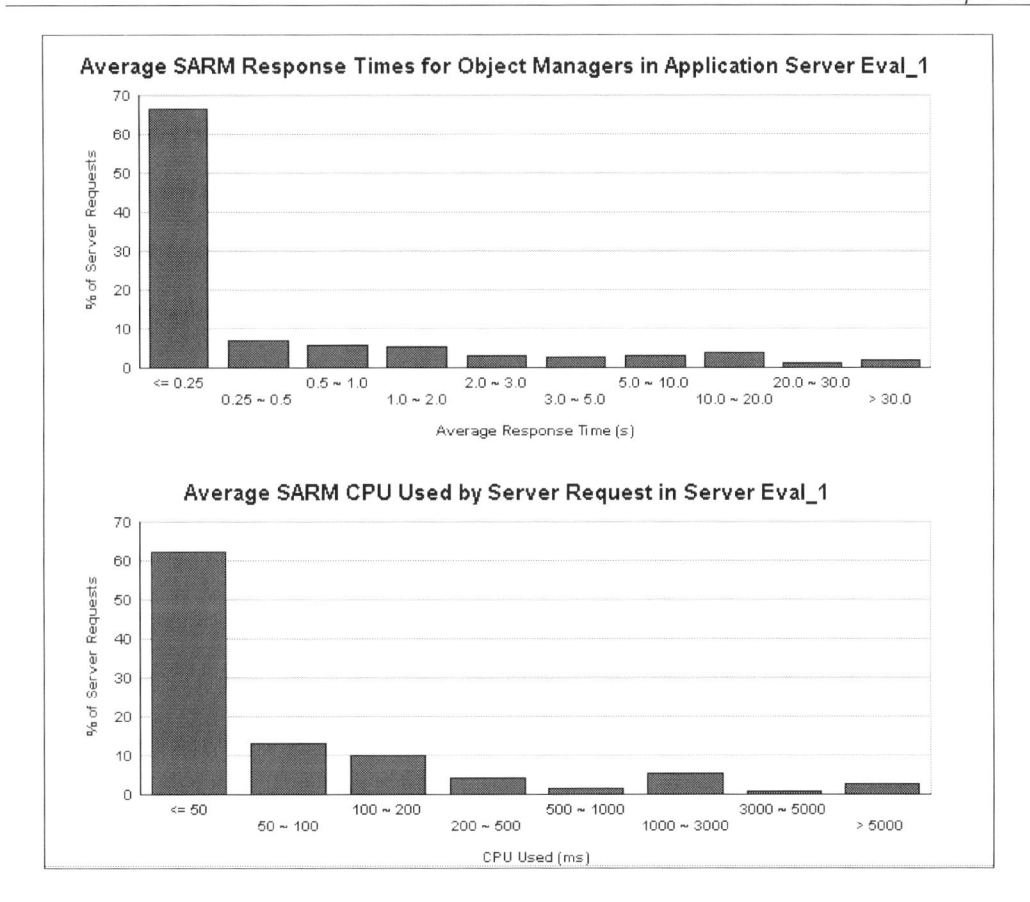

We can click on the bars in the chart to drill down into a detailed view, which displays a list of SARM data entries belonging to the interval group we clicked. We can further drill down by clicking on the SARM ID to see the instance detail.

Monitoring Siebel Applications

If we choose the Server Area/Subareas option for the output, the Diagnostic Tool renders a series of pie charts to visualize the share of each SARM area of the total response time, CPU time, and memory consumption. The pie charts—shown in the following screenshot—are displayed below a table with aggregate SARM information for each area and subarea:

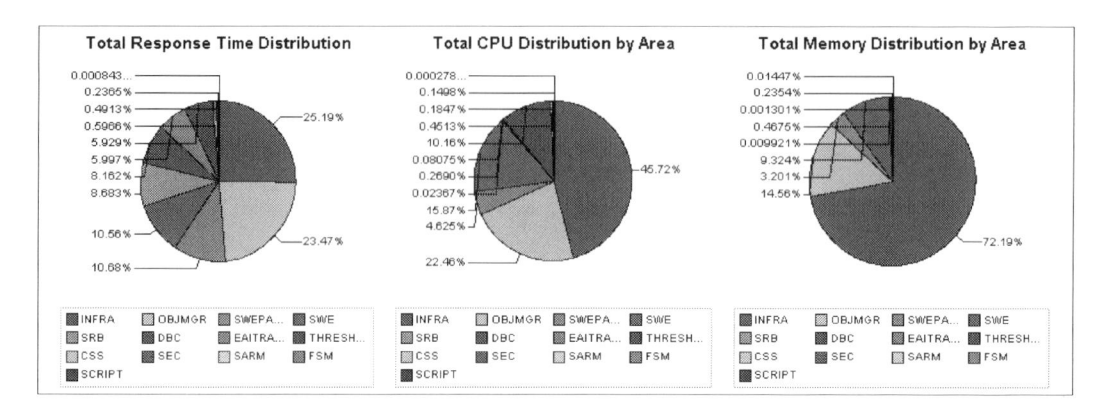

The Diagnostic Tool has two more tabs that allow us to analyze SARM data for specific users (**User Performance Analysis** tab) and to identify erroneous server component behavior (**Event Log Analysis** tab). The data displayed in the **Event Log Analysis** tab comes from the standard .log files produced by the Siebel server components rather than the .sarm files.

> If you have the Siebel Management Server infrastructure installed on your demonstration machine, you can follow the descriptions in the previous section to explore the capabilities of the Siebel Diagnostic Tool.

Client-side logging

Because SARM data collection is limited to machines where Siebel software is installed, it is not possible to collect SARM performance information for Siebel Web Clients. To overcome this limitation, Siebel CRM supports client-side logging for high-interactivity applications.

This feature allows us to identify issues and possible performance bottlenecks occurring on the client machine. For example, a loop in a browser script could slow down the response time on the client machine.

Enabling client-side logging for the application object manager

The following procedure describes how to enable Siebel client side logging for high-interactivity applications. We must set several parameters on the application object manager server component to enable client side logging.

We can use the graphical user interface (GUI) provided by the Siebel server management screens in the Siebel Web Client or the Siebel Server Manager (srvrmgr) command line to set the client side logging parameters for the application object manager as described in the table below.

Parameter	Description	Example Value
ClientSideLogging	Must be set to True to enable client side logging. A value of False turns off client side logging.	True
ClntTraceMode	Must be set to 1 to enable client side logging. A value of 0 disables client side logging.	1
ClntLogFileSize	The maximum size of the log file in megabytes. Minimum value is 50.	50 (default value)
ClntLogArchiveCount	The number of client log files to be archived.	5 (default value)
ClntLogDirectory	A directory on the client machine where the log files should be written to. The directory must be present on the client machine.	D:\temp\siebel_log
ClntTraceUnicode	A value of True indicates that the log file will be written in Unicode.	True

Source: *Siebel System Monitoring and Diagnostics Guide, Version 8.1*

http://download.oracle.com/docs/cd/E14004_01/books/SysDiag/booktitle.html

The following example shows how we can set these parameters using the Siebel Server Manager (srvrmgr) command line utility:

```
change param ClientSideLogging=True,ClntTraceMode=1,ClntLogDirectory
=D:\temp\siebel_log,ClntTraceUnicode=True for comp sccobjmgr_enu server
Eval_1
```

The above command sets the `ClientSideLogging`, `ClntTraceMode`, `ClntLogDirectory`, and `ClntTraceUnicode` parameter for the English Siebel Call Center object manager on the `Eval_1` server thus enabling the logging of client side events on the local `D:\temp\siebel_log` directory.

Enabling client-side logging on the client machine

On the client machines, we have to ensure that the directory specified in the `ClntLogDirectory` parameter exists and that the SEBLCL_TRACEMODE system environment variable is set to 1.

We can use scripts or the Windows Explorer to create the directory and use the Windows System Properties dialog to create the environment variable. It is possible to create additional local environment variables to override the server-side settings.

Reviewing the client log file

When client-side logging is enabled and end users work with the Siebel Web Client, one or more log files will be written to the directory specified by the `ClntLogDirectory` parameter. We can open the log files with a text editor of our choice and use the editor's search mechanisms to identify any erroneous or performance-hampering behavior by the Siebel high-interactivity client.

Because of the performance impact, client-side logging should only be enabled under certain circumstances such as testing or troubleshooting.

Siebel Usage Collection

When a web designer publishes a website, she or he is definitely interested in the number of times a web page is viewed. Likewise, in Siebel CRM applications, the number of times a Siebel view is accessed can provide useful insight.

In order to collect that information, we can use the Siebel Usage Collection feature. The following procedure describes how to enable it:

1. Log on to the Siebel Web Client using an administrative user account.
2. Navigate to the **Administration - Runtime Events** screen, **Action Sets** view.
3. Create a new action set named **Usage Collection**.
4. In the second list applet from above, click the **New** button to create a new action definition.
5. Set the **Name** and **Sequence** fields to 1.
6. Set the Type field to **BusService**.
7. In the form applet at the bottom of the view, enter **Usage Tracking Service** in the Business Service Name field.
8. Enter **EventType=Runtime Event** in the Business Service Method field.
9. Navigate to the **Events** view in the **Administration - Runtime Events** screen.
10. Create a new record and set the **Sequence** field to 2.
11. Set the **Object Type** field to **Application**.
12. In the **Object Name** field, click the select button and select the name of the application you are using.

> If you are unsure about the "technical" application name, you can look up the value of the ApplicationName parameter in the Siebel Developer Web Client's configuration file (.cfg).

13. In the Event field, enter ViewActivated.
14. Set the Action Set Name field to Usage Collection (the name of the action set created earlier).
15. Navigate to the **Administration - Application** screen, **System Preferences** view.
16. Set the system preferences for Siebel Usage Collection according to the table below.

System Preference	Description	Example Value
UsageTracking Enabled	Controls whether Usage Tracking is enabled.	TRUE
UsageTracking Log Time Period	Defines the interval how often a new file is created. Possible values are Hourly, Daily, Weekly, or Monthly.	Daily

System Preference	Description	Example Value
UsageTracking LogFile Dir	The directory where usage tracking log files will be written to. Should be a shared directory for a multi-server installation.	\\appserver1\usage
UsageTracking LogFile Format	Allows specifying the output format of the log files. Possible values are XML, CSV, or W3C.	XML

Source: *Siebel Content Publishing Guide, Version 7.8*

```
http://download.oracle.com/docs/cd/B31104_02/books/ContentPub/booktitle.html
```

Restart the application object manager component.

To verify the correct setup of Siebel Usage Collection, we can log in to the Siebel Web Client and navigate to several views. After a few minutes, an XML file should be present in the directory specified by the `UsageTracking LogFile Dir` system preference.

The entries in the file indicate the username, IP address of the client machine, the time of accessing and leaving the view, and the view name. The screenshot below shows a portion of the Siebel Usage Tracking log file in XML format.

```xml
<?xml version="1.0" encoding="ASCII" ?>
- <events>
  + <event>
  + <event>
  - <event>
      <userid>SADMIN</userid>
      <ipaddr>127.0.0.1</ipaddr>
      <sessid>ZNLk02a0qCX7k1UY6ti8yqzX5Jop.J7W8wPtN8ebZ3QyeVizTr04P-WJSmLAeoih</sessid>
      <type>ViewActivated</type>
      <viewid />
      <name>Account Screen Homepage View</name>
      <rowid />
      <start>03/02/2010 19:12:45</start>
      <end>03/02/2010 19:12:52</end>
      <status>Success</status>
    </event>
```

Summary

In this chapter, we introduced the major techniques for efficient monitoring of Siebel CRM application usage and performance.

Server component log files can be controlled in their content by setting the log levels for certain event types. Administrators can use the Siebel Server Manager (srvrmgr) command line utility or the Siebel Web Client to set the log levels.

Siebel Application Response Measurement (SARM) is the most powerful module when it comes to performance measuring. We learned how to enable SARM and how to interpret the data collected in .sarm files using the sarmquery command line utility. We also introduced the Siebel Diagnostic Tool, which relies on the Siebel Management Server infrastructure and allows us to visualize SARM data across various Siebel enterprises.

In order to identify the root cause for slow performance or errors on the client machine, we can use client side logging for high-interactivity clients. This chapter provided information on how to enable this feature.

A simple but useful way to collect usage tracking information is the Siebel Usage Collection feature, which was also introduced in this chapter.

A
Sample Planning Document

In this appendix, we introduce an example of how to structure a planning document for the installation of Oracle's Siebel CRM server software. Depending on the scope of your project, the information needed might differ.

> For the sake of example and simplicity, passwords in the sample document are written in clear text. In a real life project, we must ensure that no sensitive information is included in the document. Rather, we can use common encryption tools to secure the information or leave references in the planning document about where to get the information.

Database server information

The table below contains information about the relational database management system (RDBMS) to host the Siebel database. We record information about the RDBMS vendor and version as well as the machine hostname and administrative user account. For a typical Siebel CRM installation, we also plan the creation of two tablespaces.

Component/Parameter	Name/Value Examples	Description
Database Server Vendor	Oracle	The example values in this table refer to Oracle Enterprise database.
Database Server Version	11gR1	
DB Server System Account/Password	sys/T67PBhtr as SYSDBA	Needed to connect directly to the database to run the `grantusr.sql` script.
Database Server hostname	dbsrvr1	

Sample Planning Document

Component/Parameter	Name/Value Examples	Description
DB host admin user	Administrator	Needed to connect to the machine remotely.
DB host admin user password	XBXfi8F9	See the note on password examples.
Database Server port	1521	
Database Server SID	ORCL	
Siebel DB index tablespace	SIEBELDB_IDX	This tablespace will hold the indexes of the Siebel CRM schema.
Siebel DB data tablespace	SIEBELDB_DATA	This tablespace will hold the data tables of the Siebel CRM schema.

Siebel File System-related information

The table lists the most important pieces of information we would need to successfully set up the Siebel File System in the form of a shared and secured directory on the network.

Component/Parameter	Name/Value Examples	Description
File System hostname	appsrvrfs1	
File System physical path	D:\SIA811\siebfile	
File System UNC path	\\appsrvrfs1\siebfile	Permissions on the share should be limited to the system owner account.
File System Username	DOMAIN\siebsvc	
File System Password	6thBXur	See the note on password examples.
File System host admin user	Administrator	Needed to connect to the machine remotely.
File System host admin user password	XBXfi8F9	See the note on password examples.

Web server-related information

The planning document must also list information about the web server, which will host the Siebel Web Server Extension. Making this information accessible to the system administrators ensures that they can set up the web server(s) before we launch the Siebel installers.

Appendix A

Component/Parameter	Name/Value Examples	Description
Web Server Vendor	Microsoft	
Web Server Version	IIS 6	
Web Server hostname	appsrvrweb1	
Web Server host admin user	Administrator	Needed to connect to the machine remotely.
Web Server host admin user password	XBXfi8F9	See the note on password examples.

Siebel Gateway Name Server installation and configuration

In order to install and configure a Siebel Enterprise, we must first cater for the Siebel Gateway Name Server. The table below lists sample parameters that we need to know before we install the software:

Component/Parameter	Name/Value Examples	Description
Gateway NS hostname	appsrvrgw1	
Gateway NS host admin user	Administrator	Needed to connect to the machine remotely.
Gateway NS host admin password	XBXfi8F9	See the note on password examples.
Gateway NS installer target directory	D:\SIA811	
Gateway NS port	2320	The default port number (2320) should be kept.
Gateway NS service start	Automatic	The Siebel Gateway Name Server is typically set to automatic start.

Sample Planning Document

Siebel Enterprise Server configuration

As we learned, the Siebel Enterprise Server is not a piece of software. However, it must be configured, so we must plan naming conventions and security strategies for the Gateway Name Server. The table below lists the parameters and example values, which the person configuring the Siebel Enterprise Server will have to provide:

Component/Parameter	Name/Value Examples	Description
Gateway NS Authentication User	SADMIN	
Gateway NS Authentication User Password	TJay357D	See the note on password examples.
Gateway Name Server hostname	appsrvrgw1	
Gateway Name Server port	2320	
Enterprise Name	SIEBELEVAL	Ensure that each Siebel Enterprise has a distinctive name.
Primary Siebel File System	\\appsrvrfs1\siebfile	Reference to the file system information.
Database Platform	Oracle	
DB Table Owner	SIEBEL	
DB Table Owner Password	dQ7JXufi	See the note on password examples.
DB Connect String	ORCL	
DB User Account	SADMIN	
DB User Account Password	TJay357D	See the note on password examples.
Enterprise Security Authentication Profile	Database	

Siebel Web Server Extension logical profile configuration

The installation process will include the placement of configuration settings for one or more Siebel Web Server Extensions on the network. Our planning document must include the following information in order to ensure an uninterrupted installation and configuration process:

Appendix A

Component/Parameter	Name/Value Examples	Description
Siebel Enterprise Name	SIEBELEVAL	
Logical Profile Folder	D:\SIA811\gtwysrvr\admin\webserver	Can be a shared network directory.
Collect statistics	checked	
Compression Type	None	
Encryption Type	None	
HTTP 1.1 Compliant Firewall	checked	
Login Session Timeout	3000	Specified in seconds.
Active Session Timeout	9000	Specified in seconds.
HTTP Port	80	
HTTPS Port	443	
Fully qualified domain name	ourdomain.com	
High Interactivity Login Name	SADMIN	Anonymous user account for employee facing applications.
High Interactivity Login Password	TJay357D	See the note on password examples.
Standard Interactivity Login Name	GUESTCST	Anonymous user account for customer and partner facing applications.
Standard Interactivity Login Password	8icJIPZH	See the note on password examples.
Encrypt SI password	unchecked	
Enterprise Security Token	TZH65ret	This password is needed for specialized URL commands.
		See the note on password examples.
Web Server Statistics Page	monitoring.swe	The default (_stats.swe) should not be kept because of possible security problems.
Deploy SSL?	unchecked	

[505]

Sample Planning Document

Siebel Server installation and configuration

We need to know on which machine(s) a Siebel Server service needs to be present and how it should be configured. We ensure that this information is accessible to all project peers by adding it to our planning document, like in the following example:

Component/Parameter	Name/Value Examples	Description
Siebel Server hostname	appsrvrsieb1	
Siebel Server host admin user	Administrator	Needed to connect to the machine remotely.
Siebel Server host admin password	XBXfi8F9	See the note on password examples.
Siebel Server installer target directory	D:\SIA811	
Gateway Name Server Authentication User	SADMIN	
Gateway Name Server Authentication Password	TJay357D	See the note on password examples.
Gateway Name Server hostname	appsrvrgw1	Ensure that the Siebel Gateway Name Server is running at this point.
Gateway Name Server port	2320	
Siebel Enterprise Name	SIEBELEVAL	
Siebel Server Logical Name	SEBLSRV_1	Ensure that each Siebel Server has a meaningful logical name.
Siebel Server Description	Evaluation Server 1	
Component Groups	Call Center, Remote, ADM, EAI	
Connection Broker Port	2321	
Synchronization Manager Port	40400	
Exchange Server Sync	unchecked	
Server-specific Security Encryption Settings	unchecked	
Server-specific Security Authentication Settings	unchecked	
Register external Oracle ODBC driver	unchecked	

Appendix A

Installing the Siebel database

For each initial Siebel Enterprise installation, the tablespaces must be filled with the Siebel database schema and Siebel seed data. A specialized utility will be launched and an administrator will be expected to provide the following information:

Component/Parameter	Name/Value Examples	Description
Siebel Server Directory	D:\SIA811\siebsrvr	
Database Server (Utilities) Directory	D:\SIA811\dbsrvr	
Action	Install Database	
Install Option	Install Database	
Has `grantusr.sql` been run	Yes (checked)	
Unicode or non-Unicode database?	Unicode	
ODBC DSN	SIEBELEVAL_DSN	
Siebel System Account	SADMIN	
Siebel System Account Password	TJay357D	See the note on password examples.
Table Owner	SIEBEL	
Table Owner Password	dQ7JXufi	See the note on password examples.
Siebel DB index tablespace	SIEBELDB_IDX	
Siebel DB data tablespace	SIEBELDB_DATA	
License Key	<insert license key from file>	License keys must be obtained from Oracle.
Use Oracle parallel indexing?	No	
Security Group	SSE_ROLE	
Log output directory	install	

Siebel Web Server Extension installation and configuration

Our planning document is almost complete. Using a table similar to the one below, we ensure that all necessary values can be entered upon installation and configuration of the Siebel Web Server Extension:

Component/Parameter	Name/Value Examples	Description
Installation Directory	D:\SIA811\sweapp	
Load Balancing	Single Siebel Server	
Siebel Server host	appsrvrsieb1	
Siebel Connection Broker Port	2321	
SWSE Logical Profile Location	D:\SIA811\gtwysrvr\admin\webserver	Could be a network share.

Example topology

The planning document could include a topology diagram similar to the following:

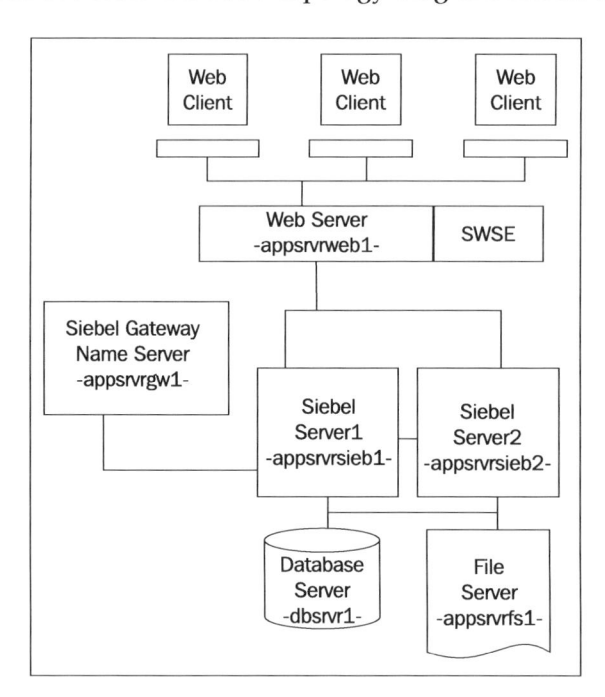

The planned installation consists of:

- The Siebel database residing on the dbsrvr1 host
- The Siebel File System residing on the appsrvrfs1 host
- Two Siebel Servers on host appsrvrsieb1 and appsrvrsieb2
- The Siebel Gateway Name Server on host appsrvrgw1
- The web server with the Siebel Web Server Extension (SWSE) on host appsrvrweb1

The diagram also shows the network paths between the server machines. The three icons for the Siebel Web Client represent the desktop PCs of the end users connecting to the web server machine.

B
Uninstalling Siebel CRM Software

There are several reasons why we might have to remove an existing installation of Siebel CRM software from server or desktop machines. One reason could be that we want to upgrade to a newer version of Siebel CRM and therefore have to uninstall the old version. Another reason might be that server machines are removed or dedicated to other tasks:

This appendix gives an overview of the following processes related to uninstalling Siebel CRM software.

- Uninstall Siebel CRM Server Software on Microsoft Windows
- Uninstall Siebel CRM Server Software on Linux or UNIX
- Uninstall Siebel CRM Client Software on Microsoft Windows

Uninstalling Siebel CRM server software on Microsoft Windows

Depending on the situation, we can uninstall a single Siebel Server instance on a machine or completely remove an entire Siebel Enterprise.

If we wish to uninstall a Siebel Enterprise completely, we should execute tasks in the sequence described below:

1. Uninstall the Siebel Database Configuration Utilities.
2. Uninstall EAI Connectors (if present).
3. Uninstall Siebel Servers.

4. Uninstall the Siebel Management Agents (if present).
5. Uninstall the Siebel Management Server (if present).
6. Remove the Siebel Enterprise.
7. Uninstall the Siebel Gateway Name Server.
8. Uninstall third-party software such as NetCharts server or Oracle BI Publisher if necessary.
9. Delete the Siebel database schema if necessary.

The Siebel Gateway Name Server must be running during the complete process of uninstalling and it has to be uninstalled last.

The Siebel Web Server Extension (SWSE) can be uninstalled independent of the Siebel Enterprise Server software.

To start the uninstaller on Microsoft Windows, we navigate to the Windows Control Panel and select **Add or Remove Programs**. The list contains one or more items for uninstalling Siebel CRM server software. Clicking the **Change/Remove** button initiates the uninstaller executable. The screenshot below shows the **Add/Remove Programs** list of Microsoft Windows:

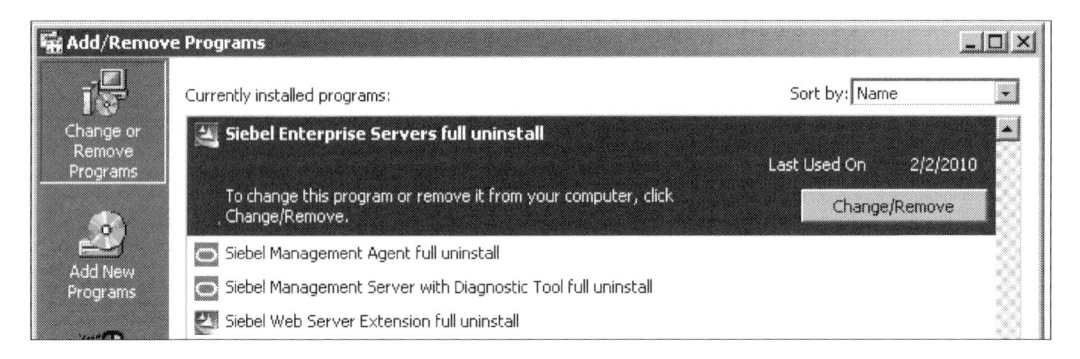

The **Siebel Enterprise Servers full uninstall** item is selected. In addition, the uninstallers for the Siebel Management Agent, the Siebel Management Server, and the Siebel Web Server Extension are visible.

> Alternatively, instead of using the **Add or Remove Programs** feature of Microsoft Windows, we can launch the `uninstaller.exe` program from the `_uninst/ses` folder of the Siebel software installation root folder.

Appendix B

The process of uninstalling Siebel CRM server software on Microsoft Windows is similar for most building blocks of the Siebel Enterprise server infrastructure. The Siebel Configuration Wizard is launched while uninstalling Siebel Servers, the Siebel Web Server Extension, or removing a Siebel Enterprise.

The following table describes the process of removing a Siebel Server from a Siebel Enterprise and shall serve as an example for uninstalling Siebel CRM server software on Microsoft Windows:

Step	Description	Tasks and Example Values
1	Ensure that the Siebel Gateway Name Server is running	Use the Windows Services console to verify that the Siebel Gateway Name Server service is in a running state.
2	Stop the Siebel Server service	Use the Windows Services console or the command shell to stop the service for the Siebel Server you wish to remove.
3	Start the Uninstaller.	Click the Change/Remove button for the Siebel Enterprise Servers uninstaller item in the **Add or Remove Programs** list.
4	The Welcome Page is displayed.	Click **Next**.
5	Select products to uninstall	Select **Siebel Server**.
		Click **Next**.
6	Uninstaller Summary	Review the summary information.
		Click **Next**.
7	The Siebel Configuration Wizard is launched automatically	Continue with the next step.
8	Task selection	Select **Remove Existing Configuration**.
		Click **Next**.
9	Gateway Name Server Authentication	User Account Name: **SADMIN**
		User Account Password: **TJay357D**
		Click **Next**.
10	Gateway Name Server	Host Name: **appsrvrgw1**
		Port Number: **2320**
		Click **Next**.

Step	Description	Tasks and Example Values
11	Siebel Enterprise Name and Siebel Server Name	Enterprise Name: **SIEBELEVAL**
		Server Name: **Eval_2**
		Click **Next**.
12	Confirm removal of Siebel Server configuration	Select **Remove Siebel Server Configuration**
		Click **Next**.
13	Server Removal Options	Select **Remove Siebel Server Windows Service**.
		Unselect **Remove Siebel Server ODBC Data Source**.
		Click **Next**.
14	Confirm removal options	Review the information that the ODBC data source should only be removed when there are no other Siebel Servers installed on the machine.
		Select **Remove Selected Siebel Server**.
		Click **Next**.
15	Summary	Review the summary information.
		Click **Next**.
16	Do you want to execute configuration?	Click **Yes**.
17	Execution Successful.	Click **OK**.
18	The Siebel Configuration Wizard jumps to the start page.	Select **Exit Configuration**.
		Click **Next**.
		Click **Yes** to confirm.
19	The Uninstaller displays a success message.	Click **Next**.
20	Restart Computer options	Select **Yes, restart my computer**
		Click **Finish**.
21	Computer is restarted	Wait until the machine is completely restarted.

Verifying the Siebel Server uninstaller

After the machine has been restarted—via the uninstaller option or manually—we can verify the following:

- The Windows system service for the Siebel server has been removed
- The siebsrvr directory is empty except for custom files, backup files, and log files.

It is recommended that we create a backup archive of the remaining directories before we delete them. This ensures that we still have access to the custom files in case we need them.

Uninstalling Siebel CRM server software on Linux or UNIX

On Linux or other UNIX-based operating systems, the process of uninstalling Siebel CRM server software is the same as on Microsoft Windows operating systems. The only difference is that the uninstaller executable must be launched from a command shell.

To launch the Siebel uninstaller executable on Linux or other UNIX-based operating systems, we open a command shell, navigate to the _uninst/ses folder of the Siebel server software installation root directory and enter the following command:

`uninstaller`

This invokes the uninstaller executable and the same graphical dialogs will guide us through the process of uninstalling as described in the previous section on Microsoft Windows.

If we wish to run the uninstaller in console mode, we must use the following command:

`uninstaller -is:javaconsole -console`

The above command invokes the Siebel uninstaller executable in console mode and the administrator will have to provide the selections and data entries in the command shell.

Uninstalling Siebel CRM client software

Siebel CRM client software such as the Siebel Mobile or Developer Web Client and Siebel Tools are uninstalled using the "Deinstall Products" option of the Oracle Universal Installer.

If the Siebel Sample Database is installed, it should be removed first using the Siebel Uninstallation Manager item in the **Add or Remove Programs** list.

The following table describes the process of uninstalling Siebel Tools or Siebel Mobile or Developer Web Client using Oracle Universal Installer:

Step	Description	Tasks and Example Values
1	Launch Oracle Universal Installer	Navigate to the installation directory of the Siebel client software. In the `oui/bin` subdirectory, double-click the `setup.exe` program.
2	The Welcome dialog is displayed	Click the **Deinstall Products** button.
3	The Inventory dialog is displayed	Select the correct products to remove. For example, select **Tools1** to remove Siebel Tools. Click the **Remove** button.
4	Confirmation	Click **Yes** to confirm.
5	Uninstaller progress is displayed	Wait for the uninstaller to complete.
6	Close the Inventory dialog	Verify that the selected Oracle products have been removed from the inventory list. Click **Close** in the Inventory dialog.
7	Exit Oracle Universal Installer	Click **Cancel** and **Yes** to exit the Oracle Universal Installer.

After the uninstaller process is complete, we should restart the computer. We should then create a backup archive of the remaining installation directories before we finally delete them.

C More Information

You are at the end of the book. Congratulations! However, you might have just started with a steep learning curve. In order to ease the mission of finding additional information about Siebel CRM, this appendix provides details on the following:

- Getting trained
- Finding information

Please note that the Internet addresses in this chapter have been thoroughly revised at the time of writing this book. Given the nature of the Internet, they could have changed in the meantime.

Getting trained

The success of a Siebel CRM project, or any standard software implementation project in general, is linked to the education of the professionals who undertake it. Complex systems like Siebel CRM will not reveal their intricate patterns to naïve consultants (or their managers) who believe in self study or "fast track" trainings.

The money saved on training will be spent equally on project delay. It is paramount for the Siebel professional to expose him or herself to high quality instructor-led training, which is provided, for example, by Oracle University and its training partners throughout the world.

The following website addresses shall serve as an entry point for your personal training plan:

Oracle University: `http://education.oracle.com`

Oracle Partner Network: `http://opn.oracle.com`

Oracle Technology Network: `http://otn.oracle.com`

Finding information

Siebel CRM has been developed under the assumption that customers will employ their own technicians or hire external consultants to install, configure, and manage the software. Documenting the necessary steps to do so and also providing information about the features of Siebel CRM has evolved into what is known today as the Siebel Bookshelf.

The Siebel Bookshelf

Oracle has made the entire Siebel documentation available on its web servers. We can access the documentation library for each version from Siebel 6 and above online or download it from the following Internet address: http://www.oracle.com/technology/documentation/siebel.html

As the bookshelf contains hundreds of megabytes of information in more than 100 individual guides, we can use the online search engine of our choice to locate the information we need.

The following screenshot shows search results for "Siebel Installation" on Oracle Technology Network:

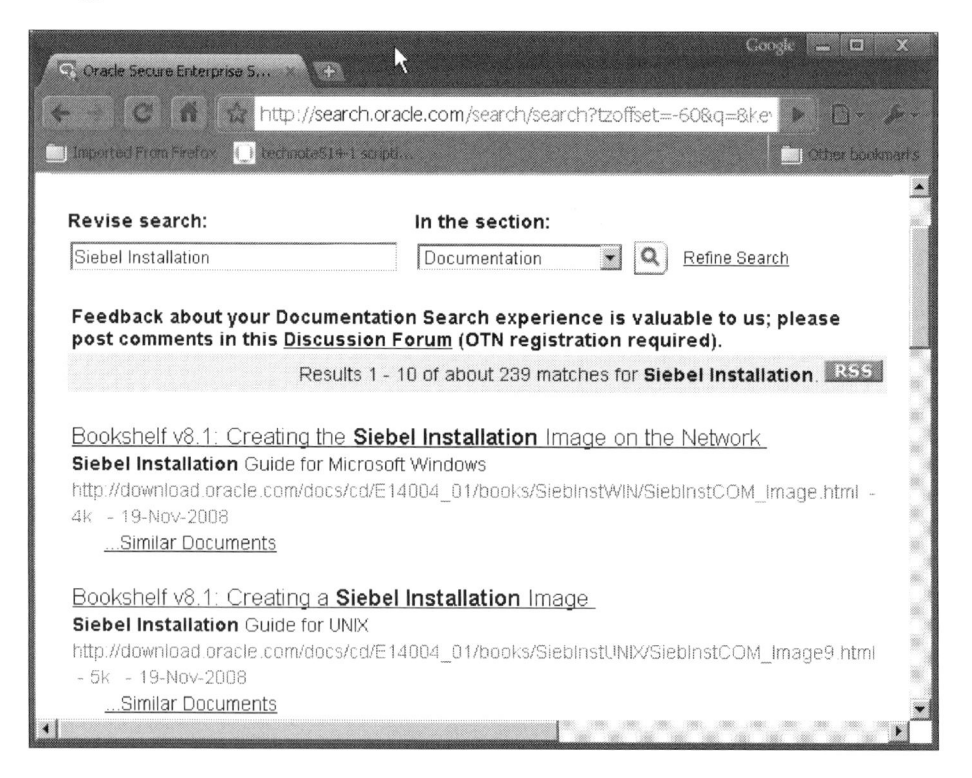

Before we start downloading and installing Siebel CRM, we should ensure that we have read and digested the information given to us by the technical writers at Oracle. Below is a list of recommended Bookshelf guides for the ambitious newbie:

- Deployment Planning Guide
- Developing and Deploying Siebel Business Applications
- Fundamentals
- Going Live with Siebel Business Applications
- Installation Guide (for your operating system)
- Overview: Siebel Enterprise Application Integration
- System Administration Guide

Oracle Forums

Not every trick, bug, or workaround can be found in the official Siebel Bookshelf. While you read these lines somebody encounters a problem or explores some functionality within Siebel CRM. Many Siebel professionals use the Oracle Forums to post questions and findings. Experienced consultants pick up the posts and answer them so the community has a great place to search for information outside the official documentation.

We can access the Oracle Forums here: `http://forums.oracle.com`

My Oracle Support

Customers, partners, and employees of Oracle have access to the Oracle support system, which not only allows for creating service request but also to search the knowledge base of resolved service requests, bulletins, and other documents.

My Oracle Support is a centralized portal for all Oracle products and can be accessed via the URL `http://support.oracle.com`.

The Internet community

Various channels exist to share findings and knowledge on the Internet. Over the past few years, many IT professionals decided to create their own websites, weblogs, or twitter channels to distribute information on Siebel CRM.

A good starting point for our research into this vast amount of information might be Google's blog search: `http://blogsearch.google.com`.

More Information

The author's blog on Siebel CRM and Oracle Business Intelligence can be found at `http://siebel-essentials.blogspot.com`.

Index

Symbols

7zip
  URL 35
-aggregate option 482
-args RECORD=<path to response file> command 45
-args SS_SETUP_INI=<path to response file> command 45
/batchexport parameter 186
/batchimport parameter 186
/bc parameter 186
/b parameter 177, 293
/bv parameter 186
-config option 483
/c parameter 177, 293
/ctsim parameter 178
-d, EVT parameter 63
.dll (dynamic link library) 266
/d parameter 177
/editseeddata parameter 177
-e, EVT parameter 63
/e parameter 293
-fea switch 130
-f, EVT parameter 63
-g, EVT parameter 63
/g parameter 293
-help option 483
-histogram option 482
/h parameter 293
.ini file
  creating, for unattended Siebel server installation 113
  managing, to launch configuration 114
-input option 482
/i parameter 293

-is:javaconsole -console argument 126
-is:javaconsole -console command 44, 45, 69
-is:log <logfile path> command 45
-is:tempdir <directory> command 45
.kb (knowledge base) 107
-l, EVT parameter 63
-l parameter 466
/l parameter 177, 293
/m parameter 293
/m switch 95
-o, EVT parameter 63
-o parameter 466
/o parameter 293
-output option 482, 483
-p, EVT parameter 63
-p parameter 440
/p parameter 177, 293
-q, EVT parameter 63
/r parameter 293
.SAF (Siebel Attachment File) 107
.scm files 127
-select option 482, 486
-select (-sel) option 483
-s, EVT parameter 63
[SIEBELX_DSN] entry 135
@ sign 87
.so (shared object) 266
/s parameter 177, 293
<swe:> tags 16
-t, EVT parameter 63
.ucf file 144
-u, EVT parameter 63
/u parameter 177, 293
/webservice parameter 178
-w, EVT parameter 63
/z parameter 293

A

access control
  data display controlling, personalization based 371-373
  to applets and views, personalization based 368-371
  to catalogs and categories 364-366
  to customer data 354, 355
  to features and data 367, 368
  to master data 364
  to Siebel views 345, 346
access control layer 375
access controlled task 431
access group 364, 430
acknowledge command 460
Action, configuration/parameter 507
activate command 458, 460
Active Session Timeout, component/parameter 505
ADM
  about 413, 430
  adm.cli file, verifying 439
  ADM component group, enabling 436
  administrative data (D) 434
  administrative data (database objects) 430-432
  administrative data exporting, ADM batch processor server component used 447, 448
  administrative data exporting, application deployment manager screen used 445-447
  admjavasubsys enterprise profile 437
  ADM object manager, server component 434
  processor, server component 434
  application object manager support, enabling 437
  architecture 433, 434
  building blocks 434
  classpath parameter 437
  components in source enterprise, managing 436
  components in target enterprise, managing 436
  configuration areas 430
  deployment batch files, creating 440-442
  dll parameter 437
  empty package structure, creating 443, 444
  enableadmsupport parameter 437
  enterprise profile, configuring 437
  enterprise profile, creating 440-442
  files, copying to ADM package 454
  files (F) 434
  files, on Siebel servers 432
  files, on Siebel Web Server Extensions (SWSE) 432
  jvmsubsys enterprise parameter 437
  overview 430
  package, creating 443
  packages, deploying 456-458
  package, sealing 455
  package, validating 456
  repository data exporting, consoleapp utility used 452, 453
  repository data exporting, Siebel tools used 448, 449
  repository data (R) 434
  repository objects 432
  setting up 435
  shared directories, creating 439
  Siebel Repository File (.srf), deploying 455
  Siebel servers, restarting 439
  source enterprise 434
  workflow processes, activating 438
ADM batch processor
  about 436
  admdatatype parameter 448
  admeaimethod parameter 448
  admfilter parameter 448
  admpath parameter 448
  admprefix parameter 448
  parameters, setting 448
  used, for exporting administrative data 447
adm.cli file
  verifying 439
ADM comm package 431
ADM CommSrv CM adapter administration 430
ADM component group
  ADM batch processor 436
  ADM object manager 436

components in source enterprise,
    managing 436
components in target enterprise,
    managing 436
enabling 436
admdatatype parameter 448
ADM deployment processes, enabling
  deployment batch file, creating 440
  enterprise profile file, creating 440
admeaimethod parameter 448
admfilter parameter 448
**administrative data (database objects),
    ADM**
  access controlled task 431
  AccessGroup 430
  ADM comm package 431
  ADM CommSrv CM adapter
      administration 430
  ADM search category 431
  ADM search connector 431
  ADM shift schedule 431
  AssignGroup 430
  audit trail admin 430
  BIP report template registration 430
  BIP view association 430
  correspondence template 431
  EAI data map 431
  exporting, ADM batch processor server
      component 447, 448
  exporting, application deployment manager
      screen used 445-447
  iHelp 431
  internal division 430
  LOV 431
  organization 430
  PDQ 431
  personalization - actions 431
  personalization - applets 431
  personalization - events 431
  Personalization - views 431
  position 430
  PriceList 431
  ProductCatalog 431
  proposal template 431
  responsibility 430
  SmartScript 431
  StateModel 431

symbolic URL 431
VolumeDiscount 431
web service - inbound 431
workflow policy 431
admjavasubsys enterprise profile 437
**ADM object manager, server component
    434**
ADM package directory, file types
  BI Publisher Report templates (.rtf) 454
  BI Publisher Report Translation files
      (.xlf) 454
  PUBLIC directory of the Siebel Web Server
      Extension (SWSE), files 454
  Siebel Repository File (.srf) 454
  Siebel Web Templates (.swt) 454
**ADM Packager command line utility
    (admpkgr) 443**
admpath parameter 448
admpkgr command line utility 455
admprefix parameter 448
ADM processor, server component 434
ADM search category 431
ADM search connector 431
ADM shift schedule 431
AHA 377
American English (ENU) 248
**AnalyticsDataSrc (epharma.cfg only)
    data source 173**
Ancillary Siebel Server Software
  installing 189
AnonUserName parameter 318
applets and views
  access controlling, personalization based
      368-371
Application Deployment Manager. *See*
    ADM
**application deployment manager,
    component groups 264**
application deployment manager screen
  used, for exporting administrative data
      445-447
Application Object Manager (AOM)
  about 14, 268
  ADM, enabling for support 437
ApplicationPassword parameter 322
application shortcuts, Siebel
  /b parameter 177

[523]

/c parameter 177
/ctsim parameter 178
/d parameter 177
/editseeddata parameter 177
/l parameter 177
/p parameter 177
/s parameter 177
/u parameter 177
/webservice parameter 178
Application Title parameter 280
ApplicationUser parameter 322
AssignGroup 430
assignment management, component groups 264
audit trail admin 430
auto start command 211
auxiliary system management, component groups 264

B

background component 267
backup command 457
backup namesrvr command 321, 465
BaseDn parameter 322
Batch components 267
bin directory 148
BIP report template registration 430
BI Publisher 10.1.3.4.1
 new outbound web service, creating 205, 206
BI Publisher reports
 BI Publisher integration for Siebel CRM, verifying 216-218
 BI Publisher roles, assigning to SiebelCRMReports folder 218
 CRM, setting up 202
 fonts, copying 219
 preconfigured reports, uploading 214-216
 Siebel Server components, enabling 210, 211
BI Publisher Report templates (.rtf) 454
BI Publisher Report Translation files (.xlf) 454

BI Publisher Scheduler
 BI Publisher host name configuration, for viewing scheduled reports in Siebel CRM 223
 configuring 219
 dataservice.wsdl file, creating from Siebel inbound web service 224
 follow me instructions 226
 functionality, verifying 224, 225
 List of Values (LOV) data creating, to support report scheduling 220
 symbolic URL definition, creating for viewing scheduled reports 221, 222
 tables, creating 220
 tasks 219
BI Publisher security model
 setting up 213, 214
BI Publisher server
 external file references, enabling 209, 210
 Siebel java libraries, copying 209
BIP view association 430
Business Service Manager 268

C

cascading stylesheets (.css) 433
cfgenv.sh script 128, 136
cfgmerge utility
 used, for deploying enterprise configuration data 464, 465
 using 465
 using, steps 465, 466
change param command 322
CLASSPATH 128
classpath parameter 212, 437
client side logging
 about 494
 client log file, reviewing 496
 enabling, for application object manager 495, 496
 enabling, on client machine 496
ClientSideLogging parameter 495
ClntLogArchiveCount parameter 495
ClntLogDirectory parameter 495, 496
ClntLogFileSize parameter 495
ClntTraceMode parameter 495
ClntTraceUnicode parameter 495

Collect statistics, component/parameter 505
command line mode 36
command line tools, Siebel server management
  background components, jobs running for 302
  batch, jobs running for 302
  component definitions, creating 298
  component definitions, modifying 298
  component groups assignment to Siebel server, controlling 299
  enterprise configuration, backing up 297
  input files, using 302
  parameters, listing 297
  parameters, modifying 297
  server components, controlling 301
  server components start up mode, setting 300
  Siebel enterprise information, listing 295, 296
  srvrmgr command line utility 293
  using 292
comma-separated value (CSV) 485
communications management, component groups 264
component definition
  about 266
  component type property 268
  creating 298, 299
  modifying 298, 299
  run modes 267
  specification 267
component groups
  about 263, 264
  application deployment manager 264
  assignment management 264
  auxiliary system management 264
  communications management 264
  data quality 264
  enterprise application integration 264
  field service 264
  marketing object manager 264
  PIM server integration management 264
  search processing 264
  Siebel call center 264
  Siebel CME 264
  Siebel eAutomotive 265

Siebel eChannel 265
Siebel eDocuments 265
Siebel financial services 265
Siebel ISS 265
Siebel life sciences 265
Siebel loyalty 265
Siebel public sector 265
Siebel remote 265
Siebel sales 265
Siebel universal customer master 265
Siebel wireless 265
System management 265
workflow management 265
XMLP report 265
Component Groups, component/parameter 506
components view, server management screen 288
component tracing, event type 471
component, types
  Application Object Manager 268
  Business Service Manager 268
  Enterprise Application Integration (EAI) Receivers 268
Compression Type, component/parameter 505
configuration areas, ADM
  cadministrative data (database objects) 430
Connection Broker Port, component/parameter 506
ConnectString parameter 173, 174, 233, 400, 401
consoleapp utility
  used, for exporting repository data 452, 453
copy command 458, 460
Copy Record command 292, 324
correspondence template 431
create command 457, 459
cross-enterprise user account, Siebel management server 416
customer data, Siebel access control
  access, controlling 354, 355
  employee 355
  organization 355
  owner 355
  position 355

[525]

record access for different companies based on organizations, controlling 362, 363
record access for multiple employees, controlling 358, 359
record access for single user or employee, controlling 355-358
record access for teams based on positions, controlling 360-362
team 355
user 355

D

database. *See* Siebel database
database administrator (DBA) 310
database authentication
  about 308
  security adapter, associating with server component 309, 310
  security adapter, defined as enterprise profiles 308, 309
  user accounts, managing 310
Database Extract component 267
database extraxt, Siebel remote components 393
Database Platform, component/parameter 504
database schema files
  creating 394, 395
Database Server hostname, component/parameter 25, 501
Database Server information
  about 501
  Database Server hostname, component/parameter 501
  Database Server port, component/parameter 502
  Database Server SID, component/parameter 502
  Database Server Vendor, component/parameter 501
  Database Server Version, component/parameter 501
  DB host admin user, component/parameter 502
  DB host admin user password, component/parameter 502
  DB Server System Account/Password, component/parameter 501
  Siebel DB data tablespace, component/parameter 502
  Siebel DB index tablespace, component/parameter 502
Database Server port, component/parameter 25, 502
Database Server SID, component/parameter 25, 502
Database Server (Utilities) Directory, configuration/parameter 507
Database Server Vendor, component/parameter 25, 501
Database Server Version, component/parameter 25, 501
data display
  controlling, personalization based 371-373
Data Manager (DM) 15
data quality, component groups 264
data quality connector 51
DataSourceName parameter 309
DataSource parameter 452
data sources
  AnalyticsDataSrc (epharma.cfg only) data source 173
  configuring, for Siebel client 172, 173
  GatewayDataSrc data source 172
  local data source 172
  sample data source 172
  ServerDataSrc data source 172
DBC area 485
DB Connector DLL parameter 270
DB Connect String, component/parameter 504
dbenv.sh script
  creating 139
  executing 141
  modifying 139
DB host admin user, component/parameter 25, 502
DB host admin user password, component/parameter 25, 502
DB Security Adapter profile (DBSecAdpt) 309
DB Server System Account/Password, component/parameter 25, 501

DB Table Owner, component/parameter 504
DB Table Owner Password, component/parameter 504
DB User Account, component/parameter 504
DB User Account Password, component/parameter 504
delete command 459
Delete Parameter Override command 274
Deploy SSL, component/parameter 505
DescriptorFile parameter 453
developers
  and end users, differences 390, 391
  configuration file, settings 401
developer web client. *See* Siebel developer web client
directory server
  user accounts, creating 314
directory server authentication. *See also* LDAP authentication
directory server authentication
  IBM LDAP cient, installing 314
  IBM LDAP client, installing 313
  LDAP authentication, verifying 324
  LDAP security adapter, configuring 321-323
  server components, configuring 323
  Siebel clients, configuring for LDAP authentication 329, 330
  Siebel Gateway Name Server for LDAP authentication (optional), configuring 326-29
Disable External Reference parameter 209
divisions
  about 375
  AHA 377
  divisional hierarchy creating, steps 377
  example company , distinguishing 377
  follow me instructions 378-380
  organization chart, for company 376
  organizations, setting up 378-380
  setting up 376, 377
DLL parameter 174, 437
DockConnString parameter 173, 400
DSChartImageFormat parameter 195
DSChartServer parameter 195
dynamic link libraries (dll) 15

E

EAI Connector
  for COM Data Control 58
  for Java Data Bean 58
  for Microsoft BizTalk Server 57
  for OLE DB 57
  for Oracle 57, 58
EAI data map 431
EAI method 448
EAI Object Manager 210
EAITRANSP area 485
eapps.cfg file, Siebel native load balancing
  validating 237, 238
employee 355, 382
employee account
  managing 382
  new employee, manual set up 382, 383
enableadmsupport parameter 437, 438
EnableVirtualHosts parameter 237
Encryption Type, component/parameter 505
Encrypt SI password, component/parameter 505
enterprise application integration, component groups 264
Enterprise Application Integration (EAI) Receivers 268
enterprise configuration
  backing up 297
enterprise configuration data
  deploying, cfgmerge utility used 465
  new component definitions from source to target enterprises, deploying 465
enterprise explorer view, server configuration screen
  about 277
  component definitions view 279, 280
  component definitions view, reconfiguring 281
  component groups view 278, 279
  parameters view 281, 282
  profile configuration view 282
  synchronize view 282
  system alerts view 282
Enterprise Integration Manager (EIM) 267, 410
Enterprise Name, component/parameter 504

[527]

enterprise parameters 269
enterprise profiles 270, 271
Enterprise Security Authentication Profile, component/parameter 504
Enterprise Security Token, component/parameter 505
enterprise server. *See* Siebel enterprise server
EnterpriseServer parameter 173
enterprises view, server management screen
  about 286
  component run states 287
  component run states, controlling 287, 288
  Siebel server components, run states 287
Environment Verification Tool (EVT), installation on Microsoft Windows
  system configuration, checking 61-64
event context, event type 472
event type, Siebel server
  component tracing 471
  event context 472
  Event to track the flow of a message 472
  general events 471
  Object Manager Session Operation and SetErrorMsg Log 472
  security adapter log 472
  SQL error 471
  SQL parse and execute 471
  SQL profiling 471
  SQL summary 471
  task configuration 471
EVT parameters
  -d 63
  -e 63
  -f 63
  -g 63
  -l 63
  -o 63
  -p 63
  -q 63
  -s 63
  -t 63
  -u 63
  -w 63

Exchange Server Sync, component/parameter 506
exit command 195
ExportCount parameter 453
ExportFile parameter 453
Extract all Repository Tables parameter 398

F

field service, component groups 264
file system. *See* Siebel file system
File System host admin user, component/parameter 502
File System host admin user password, component/parameter 502
File System hostname, component/parameter 502
FileSystem parameter 174
File System Password, component/parameter 502
File System physical path, component/parameter 502
File System UNC path, component/parameter 502
File System Username, component/parameter 502
FQDN (Fully Qualified Domain Name) 82
Fully qualified domain name, component/parameter 505

G

GatewayDataSrc data source 172
gateway name server. *See* Siebel gateway name server
Gateway Name Server Authentication Password, component/parameter 506
Gateway Name Server Authentication User, component/parameter 506
Gateway Name Server hostname, component/parameter 504, 506
Gateway Name Server port, component/parameter 504, 506
Gateway NS Authentication User, component/parameter 504

Gateway NS Authentication User Password, component/parameter 504
Gateway NS host admin password, component/parameter 503
Gateway NS host admin user, component/parameter 503
Gateway NS hostname, component/parameter 503
Gateway NS installer target directory, component/parameter 503
Gateway NS port, component/parameter 503
Gateway NS service start, component/parameter 503
general events, event type 471
generate new database, Siebel remote components 393
GetProfileAttr() 370
getservers.pl, perl script, Siebel management agents 426
getservers.pl script 440
grant command 310
grantusr.sql file 138
grantusr.sql script 84
  executing 87
graphical mode (GUI) 36
graphical user interface (GUI) 111, 474
grep command 130

H

handheld synchronization 51
hardware prerequisites, Siebel CRM installation 26, 27
help command 294
help list session command 295
High Interactivity Login Name, component/parameter 505
High Interactivity Login Password, component/parameter 505
High-Interactivity mode. *See* HI mode
HI mode 19
hot-fix, ADM
  about 449
  repository object definitions, exporting 449, 450

HTTP 1.1 Compliant Firewall, component/parameter 505
httpd.conf file 151
HTTP (Hypertext Transfer Protocol) 268
HTTP Port, component/parameter 505
HTTPS Port, component/parameter 505

I

IBM LDAP client
  downloading 312
  installing, on Microsoft Windows 313, 314
iHelp 431
inbound web service. *See* Siebel inbound web service
INFRA area 484
init command 444
Installation Directory, component/parameter 508
Install Option, configuration/parameter 507
integrated development environment (IDE) 182
IntegratedDomainAuth parameter 338
interactive component 267
internal division 430
internet community
  URL 519

J

Java Data Bean (JDB) 51
Java integrator 51
Java Runtime Environment (JRE) 163
Java Software Development Kit (SDK) 200
JMS (Java Message Service) 268
jobs view, server management screen 290, 292
job templates view, server configuration screen 284, 285
jvmsubsys enterprise parameter 437

K

key
  license key 110

L

LANG argument 126
LANG=ENU argument 69
language pack installation, for Siebel developer web client
  steps 259
  verifying 260
language pack installation, for Siebel enterprise server software
  language-specific repository metadata, importing 248-251
  language-specific seed data, importing into Siebel database 244-247
  language-specific seed data, installing 247
  language support, adding for Siebel server 243, 244
  multilingual List of Values, enabling 251-254
  multilingual List of Values, verifying 257, 258
  new application object manager, logging on to 256, 257
  non-multilingual List of Values (MLOV) seed data, deactivating 248
  Siebel enterprise, restarting 256
  steps 242
  tasks, executing 243
  UI translation, verifying 257
  verifying 255
language pack installation, for Siebel mobile web client
  steps 259
language pack installation, for Siebel tools 260
language pack installation, for Siebel Web Server Extension (SWSE)
  steps 254, 255
language packs, Siebel CRM software
  adding, to existing Siebel installation images 241, 242
  downloading 240
  installing, for Siebel developer or mobile web client 259, 260
  installing, for Siebel enterprise server software 243

installing, for Siebel Web Server Extension (SWSE) 254, 255
list 239, 240
language-specific repository metadata
  importing 248
language-specific seed data
  importing, in Siebel database 244-247
  language-specific seed datainstalling 247
LDAP authentication
  access permissions, setting for LDAP accounts 319
  anonymous user accounts, creating 317-319
  configuring, steps 312
  directory server (optional), installing 312
  follow me instructions 314
  for Siebel gateway name server, verifying 329
  IBM LDAP client, installing 312-314
  LDAP security adapter, configuring 321, 322
  new user, registering 324-326
  proxy account, verifying 320
  server components, configuring 323
  shared credentials account, creating 315, 316
  Siebel clients, configuring 329, 330
  Siebel gateway name server (optional), configuring 326-329
  user accounts, creating in directory server 314
  verifying 324
LDAP (Lightweight Directory Access Protocol) 311, 384
LDAP security adapter, directory server authentication
  configuring 321-323
LDAP security adapter, Web Single-Sign-On (SSO)
  modifying 339
LD_LIBRARY_PATH 127
license key
  about 110
  follow me instructions 39
  obtaining 38
License Key, configuration/parameter 507
License List link 33
list active sessions 296

list active tasks 296
list command 295, 323
　list active sessions 296
　list active tasks 296
　list compdefs 296
　list compgrps 296
　list compgrps for server Server1 296
　list comps for server Server1 296
　list named subsystems 296
　list params 296
　list servers 296
　list sessions 296
　list tasks 296
list compdefs 296
list compgrps 296
　for server Server1 296
list comps for server Server1 296
list_detail command 459
list named subsystems 296
list_ns command 130, 153
list params 296
list_server command 153
list servers command 148, 149, 296, 329
list sessions 296
list tasks 296
LIVE mode 126
ln command 156
load balancing, component/parameter 508
load command 457, 459
local database
　database extract job, running for developers 397, 398
　data, extracting for 395
　initializing 399
　re-extracting 410
　Siebel remote system preferences 396, 397
local database, initialization
　client configuration files, settings verifying in 400
　configuration file settings, for developers 401
　logging in 401-403
　network connectivity, establishing for mobile clients 399
local database, synchronization
　manual synchronization 405, 406
　Siebel TrickleSync 406, 407

local data source
　about 172
　ConnectString parameter 173
　DockConnString parameter 173
　EnterpriseServer parameter 173
　RequestServerName parameter 173
LogFile parameter 453
Logical Profile Folder, component/parameter 505
Login Session Timeout, component/parameter 505
log levels, Siebel server
　0 470
　1 470
　2 470
　3 470
　4 470
　5 470
Log output directory, configuration/parameter 507
log parser 88
LOV 431

M

makeagentconfig.pl, perl script, Siebel management agents 426
marketing object manager, component groups 264
master data, Siebel access control
　access, controlling to 364-367
　competitor 364
　curriculum 364
　decision issues 364
　entities 364
　event 364
　literature 364
　product 364
　resolution Item 364
　SmartScript 364
　solution 364
　training course 364
Microsoft Active Directory (AD) 333, 385
Microsoft Internet Information Services (IIS) 333, 335
Microsoft Windows
　Siebel diagnostic tool 421, 422

Siebel management server, installing 417-419
mid-level release, ADM
 about 449
 repository object definitions, exporting 450, 451
migration utilities 460
mobile clients
 registering, steps 391
 setting up 391
mobile web client. *See* **Siebel mobile web client**
MODE argument 126
MODEL_FILE argument 69
MODEL_FILE parameter 127
MSMQ (Microsoft Message Queuing) 268
multilingual List of Values (MLOV)
 enabling 251-254
 seed data, deactivating 248
 verifying 257, 258
multiple Siebel servers
 configuration, verifying 230, 231
 configuring 229
 configuring, on same physical machine 231
 follow me instructions 232
 installation, planning 229
 installation, verifying 230, 231
 installing 227-229
 installing, steps 230
My Oracle Support
 URL 202, 519

N

NetCharts server. *See* **Visual Mining NetCharts server**
New Responsibility field 384
non-anonymous virtual directory, Web Single-Sign-On
 creating, on web server 335, 336
non-multilingual List of Values (MLOV) seed data
 deactivating 248
Notification Handler parameter 272

O

object manager component 51
Object Manager Session Operation and SetErrorMsg Log, event type 472
Object_N parameter 453
OBJMGR area 484
ODBC DSN, configuration/parameter 507
ODBC settings
 verifying, odbcsql used 141
odbcsql
 used, for verifying ODBC settings 141
Oracle BI Publisher
 about 197
 enterprise server, downloading 199
 enterprise server, installing 200
 enterprise server, prerequisites 200
 features 197
 installation, verifying 201, 202
 integrating, in Siebel CRM 198
 Oracle's Business Intelligence Suite Enterprise Edition (OBI EE) 197
Oracle BI Publisher enterprise server
 downloading 199
 follow me instructions 202
 installation, verifying 201, 202
 installing 200
 prerequisites 200
Oracle Business Intelligence Enterprise Edition (OBI EE) 189, 197
Oracle database installers
 downloading, URL 30
Oracle E-Delivery website
 about 32
 URL 32
Oracle forums
 URL 519
Oracle Partner Network
 URL 517
Oracle Siebel CRM Documentation Library
 URL 203
Oracle Technology Network website
 URL 118, 517
Oracle Universal Installer (oui.exe) 165

[532]

Oracle University
  URL 517
Oracle XML Publisher. *See* Oracle BI
    Publisher
organization 355
Organization Name field 380
organizations
  setting up 378, 380
OTN license agreement 30
outbound web service. *See* Siebel outbound
    web service
Override Level field 310
owner 355

P

package
  ADM package, creating 443
  ADM package, files copying to 454
  empty package structure, creating 443, 444
parallel database extract, Siebel remote
    components 393
parameters
  listing 297
  modifying 297
password parameter 316
patches
  applying, for Siebel server software 65
  applying, to Siebel client software 186, 187
PATH 127
PDQ 431
perl script
  getservers.pl 426
  makeagentconfig.pl 426
personalization - actions 431
personalization - applets 431
personalization - events 431
personalization - views 431
PIM server integration 52
PIM server integration management,
    component groups 264
planning document
  about 24
  information 26
  sample 25
  topology diagram 508, 509
Port parameter 322

position 355
position hierarchy
  follow me instructions 381
  managing 380, 381
  multiple positions, for employee 382
PriceList 431
PrimaryEnterprise parameter 174
Primary Siebel File System, component/
    parameter 504
ProductCatalog 431
PropagateChange parameter 326
proposal template 431

Q

query language, Siebel 369

R

RECORD mode 126
Register external Oracle ODBC driver,
    component/parameter 506
Relational database management systems
    (RDBMS) 10
remote search support 51
replication agent, Siebel remote
    components 393
report command 458, 460
repository. *See* Siebel repository
repository data, ADM
  exporting, consoleapp utility used 452, 453
  exporting, Siebel toos used 448
  repository object definitions exporting, for
      hot-fixes 449
  repository object definitions exporting, for
      mid-level release 450, 451
repository objects, ADM 432
repository parameter 453
RequestServerName parameter 173
response file
  creating, for Siebel configuration wizard
      113
restore_activate command 458
restore_copy command 458
restore_session command 458
RolesAttributeType parameter 328
run modes, component definition
  background component 267

batch component 267
interactive component 267

S

sales force automation (SFA) system 387
sample data source 172
SARM
　about 474
　application performance, by area 485, 486
　application performance, by subarea 484, 486
　data collection areas, list 484, 485
　data retrieval, automating 489, 490
　enabling 476
　enabling, for application object manager component 478
　enabling, for other Siebel software units 478-480
　enabling, for Siebel servers and components 476, 477
　files, managing 480
　files reading, sarmquery used 481-483
　output files, creating 488, 489
　parameters 477, 478
　slow performing objects, identifying 487
　time histograms 487
　working 475
SARM area 485
SARMBufferSize parameter 477
SARMFileSize parameter 477
SARM files reading, sarmquery used
　about 481
　application performance, by area 484, 485
　application performance, by subarea 484, 485
　areas, analyzing 485, 486
　instances, analyzing 485, 486
　options 482, 483
　SARM data retrieval, automating 489, 490
　SARM output files, creating 488, 489
　slow performing objects, identifying 487
　start and end time, specifying 483, 484
　subareas, analyzing 485, 486
　time histograms 487
SARMLevel parameter 477
SARMLogDirectory parameter 477, 480

SARMMaxFiles parameter 477, 480
SARMPeriod parameter 477
sarmquery command line utility
　application performance, by area 484, 485, 486
　SARM data retrieval, automating 489, 490
　SARM output files, creating 488, 489
　slow performing objects, identifying 487
　start and end time, specifying 483, 484
　time histograms 487
　using, to read SARM files 482, 483
SARMThreshold parameter 477, 480
SARMUsers parameter 478
Save client transactions parameter 411
Schedule Report command 224
SCRIPT area 485
SEA 34
search processing, component groups 264
SecAdptMode parameter 332
SecAdptName parameter 323, 332
SEC area 485
security adapter log, event type 472
Security Adapter Mode parameter 309
Security Adapter Name parameter 309
security adapters, database authentication
　associating, with server component 309, 310
　defined, as enterprise profiles 308, 309
Security Group, configuration/parameter 507
selftime key value 487
server. See Siebel server
Server component event logging
　about 470
　Siebel server manager command line using, to set event log levels 474
　Siebel server manager command line, using to set event log levels 474
server components
　controlling 301
　start up mode, setting 300
server components, directory server authentication
　configuring 323
server configuration screen
　enterprise explorer 277

Siebel enterprise configuration, backing up 276
Siebel enterprise configuration, restoring 277
server data sources
  configuring, for Siebel developer web client 174
ServerDataSrc data source 172
server management screen
  about 286
  components view 288
  enterprises view 286
  jobs view 290
  servers view 288
  sessions view 289, 290
  tasks view 289
ServerName parameter 322
servers 263
server-side synchronization for Exchange (SSSE) 52
Server-specific Security Authentication Settings, component/parameter 506
Server-specific Security Encryption Settings, component/parameter 506
servers view, server configuration screen
  about 282, 283
  component start up mode, setting 283, 284
  event log levels, setting 284
servers view, server management screen 288
service owner account
  creating 30
  follow me instructions 32
session command 295
sessions view, server management screen 289, 290
session timeout values 81
set server command 213
SharedCredentialsDN parameter 322
SharedDBPassword parameter 322
SharedDBUsername parameter 322
shared directories
  shared directoriescreating 439
show command 148, 296
SIA 34, 69
Siebel 7.0 8
Siebel 8.2
  Siebel outbound web service, configuring 208, 209
Siebel access control
  about 344
  application security 344
  customer data, access controlling to 354, 355
  data access control 345
  feature access 344
  master data, access controlling to 364-367
  network security 344
  Siebel views, access controlling to 345, 346
Siebel Administrator (SADMIN) 108
Siebel Application Deployment Manager. *See* **ADM**
Siebel Application Response Measurement. *See* **SARM**
Siebel authentication architecture 306, 307
SIEBELB_DATA tablespace 310
Siebel Bookshelf 518, 519
Siebel Call Center application 103
Siebel call center, component groups 264
Siebel charts
  verifying 196
Siebel client
  data sources, configuring 172
  server management screens using 275
Siebel client configuration file
  about 170, 171
  ApplicationName parameter 171
  ApplicationSplashText parameter 171
  RepositoryFile parameter 171
Siebel clients for LDAP authentication, configuring
  about 329
  central authentication configuration file, creating 331, 332
  client configuration file, modifying 332
  directory server authentication for Siebel client, verifying 332
  directory server authentication, verifying 332
  SecThickClientExtAuthent system preference, setting to true 330, 331
Siebel client software
  and user groups 161, 162
  patches, applying 186, 187
Siebel CME, component groups 264

[535]

Siebel configuration process 403, 404
Siebel configuration wizard
  response file, creating 113
Siebel configuration wizard, on Linux
  starting 141
  steps 142, 143
Siebel Connection Broker Component 232
Siebel Connection Broker Port, component/
    parameter 508
Siebel CRM
  BI Publisher host name configuration, for
      viewing scheduled reports 223
  connectivity, configuring 194
  fix pack SIF files, importing 204
  Oracle BI Publisher, integrating 198
  reporting facility 197
  Siebel Enterprise Applications (SEA) 34
  Siebel Industry Applications (SIA) 34
  SISNAPI (Siebel Internet Session Network
      Application Programming Interface),
      21
  symbolic URL definition creating, for
      viewing scheduled reports 221, 222
  synchronization, ways 405
  version, differences 202, 203
  Visual Mining NetCharts Server
      installation, planning 191
  Visual Mining NetCharts Server
      installation, preparing 191, 192
  Visual Mining NetCharts Server
      installer, installing 191
Siebel CRM 8.1
  database system vendors 10
  products 10
  version 10
Siebel CRM client software
  uninstalling 516
Siebel CRM, information finding
  about 518
  internet community 519
  My Oracle support 519
  Oracle forums 519
  Siebel Bookshelf 518, 519
Siebel CRM installation
  hardware, prerequisites 26, 27
  license key, obtaining 38
  planning 24

planning and preparing process 24
planning document 24
planning, information 26
sample planning document 25
service owner account, creating 30
Siebel database, preparing 28, 29
Siebel deployment, sizing 27
Siebel file system root folder, creating 32
Siebel image creator 36, 37
Siebel installation archives, downloading
    3-34
software, prerequisites 26, 27
Siebel CRM language packs. *See* language
    packs, Siebel CRM
Siebel CRM server software
  installing, process 41
  Siebel gateway name server, installing
      46-48
  Siebel server installer 42
  uninstallation on Microsoft Windows,
      verifying 515
  uninstalling, on Linux 515
  uninstalling, on Microsoft Windows 511
  uninstalling, on UNIX 515
Siebel CRM server software configuration,
    on Linux
  Siebel enterprise, configuring 131, 132
  Siebel gateway name server, configuring
      128
  Siebel gateway name server, installing 119
  Siebel server, configuring 146, 147
  SWSE, configuring 149
  SWSE logical profile, configuring 135-138
Siebel CRM server software configuration,
    on Microsoft Windows
  administrative Siebel user accounts,
      creating 108-110
  license keys, applying 110
  process 68
  server components, synchronizing 111
  Siebel database schema, installing 83, 84
  Siebel enterprise, configuring 73
  Siebel enterprise server installation,
      verifying 101, 102
  Siebel file system seed files, copying 107
  Siebel gateway name server, configuring 70
  Siebel server, configuring 95-97

Siebel server installation, finalizing 106, 107
Siebel server software configuration, in unattended mode 112
Siebel server software installation, in unattended mode 112
Siebel software configuration wizard 68-70
SWSE, configuring 98-100
SWSE logical profile, configuring 79-82
system service owner account, setting 106, 107

Siebel CRM server software installation, on Linux
Siebel database schema, installing 138
Siebel database server utilities, installing 123
Siebel enterprise server installation, verifying 152
Siebel gateway name server, installing 118
Siebel server, installing 121, 122
Siebel software configuration wizard, using 126
SWSE, installing 124, 125

Siebel CRM server software installation, on Microsoft Windows
patches, applying 65
Siebel database server, installing 53, 54
Siebel EAI Connector support files, installing 56
Siebel Environment Verification Tool (EVT), system configuration checking with 61-64
Siebel gateway name server, installing 46-48
Siebel server installer 42, 43
Siebel server, installing 49-52
support files for Siebel EAI Connectors, installing 57, 59
SWSE, installing 60

Siebel CRM server software uninstallation, on Linux 515

Siebel CRM server software uninstallation, on Microsoft Windows
steps 511-514
verifying 515

Siebel CRM server software uninstallation, on UNIX 515

Siebel CRM, setting up for BI Publisher reports
about 202
BI Publisher integration, verifying for Siebel CRM 216-218
BI Publisher roles, assigning to SiebelCRMReports folder 218
BI Publisher Scheduler (optional), configuring 219
BI Publisher security model, setting 213, 214
external file references, enabling for BI Publisher 209, 210
fix pack SIF files, importing 204
fonts, copying 219
new outbound web service, creating for BI Publisher 10.1.3.4.1 205, 206
preconfigured reports, upgrading 214-216
Siebel CRM version, differences 202, 203
Siebel inbound web services, importing 207
Siebel java libraries, copying to BI Publisher server 209
Siebel outbound web service, configuring for Siebel 8.2 or higher 208, 209
Siebel server components, enabling 210, 211
XMLP Java subsystem, parameters setting for 212, 213
XMLP responsibilities, creating 208

Siebel database
about 10
Action, configuration/parameter 507
Database Server (Utilities) Directory, configuration/parameter 507
Follow me instructions 30
installing 507
Install Option, configuration/parameter 507
language-specific seed data, importing 244-247
License Key, configuration/parameter 507
Log output directory, configuration/parameter 507
ODBC DSN, configuration/parameter 507
preparing 28, 29
Security Group, configuration/parameter 507

[537]

Siebel DB data tablespace, configuration/
    parameter 507
Siebel DB index tablespace, configuration/
    parameter 507
Siebel Server Directory, configuration/
    parameter 507
Siebel System Account, configuration/
    parameter 507
Siebel System Account Password,
    configuration/parameter 507
Table Owner, configuration/parameter 507
Table Owner Password, configuration/
    parameter 507
**Siebel database schema installation, on
    Linux**
  about 138
  database configuration, environment
      preparing for 139
  dbenv.sh script, creating 139
  dbenv.sh script, executing 141
  dbenv.sh script, modifying 139, 140
  ODBC settings verifying, odbcsql used 141
  Siebel configuration wizard, starting 141
  Siebel gateway name server, restarting 144
  Siebel upgrade wizard, starting 144
  verifying 144
**Siebel database schema installation, on
    Microsoft Windows**
  about 83
  additional user accounts, adding 85, 86
  data, verifying 94
  default passwords, modifying 85
  grantusr.sql file, executing 84
  grantusr.sql file, preparing 84
  grantusr.sql script, executing 87
  log parser 88
  Siebel database task, steps 91
  Siebel log parser, using 92, 93
  Siebel upgrade wizard 87, 88
  Siebel upgrade wizard, restarting 94, 95
  steps 89, 90, 91
  tablespace names, entering 84
  tables, verifying 94
  verifying 92
**Siebel database server utilities installation,
    on Linux**
  about 123

follow me instructions 124
steps 123, 124
**Siebel database server utilities, installation
    on Microsoft Windows**
  features 54, 55
  steps 53, 54
  verifying 55
Siebel DB data 25
**Siebel DB data tablespace, configuration/
    parameter 502, 507**
Siebel DB index tablespace 25
**Siebel DB index tablespace, component/
    parameter 502**
**Siebel DB index tablespace, configuration/
    parameter 507**
Siebel deployment
  sizing 27
Siebel developer web client
  about 159, 161, 162
  additional data sources, setting up 175
  and Siebel mobile web client, differences
      160
  ConnectString parameter 174
  data sources, configuring for Siebel client
      172, 173
  DLL parameter 174
  FileSystem parameter 174
  follow me instructions 170, 178
  installation, verifying 168-170
  installing 165, 166
  installing, steps 166, 167
  language pack installation, verifying 260
  language packs, installing 259
  predeploy.htm file 168
  PrimaryEnterprise parameter 174
  server data sources, configuring 174, 175
  Siebel application shortcuts, creating
      177, 178
  Siebel client configuration file 170-172
  SqlStyle parameter 174
  TableOwner parameter 174
  uninstalling, Oracle universal installer used
      516
Siebel development environment
  architecture 404, 405
Siebel diagnostic tool 413
  about 490

architecture 490, 491
Event Log Analysis tab 494
follow me instructions 494
functionality 491
Server Performance Analysis tab 492
User Performance Analysis tab 494
Siebel EAI Connector support files, installation on Microsoft Windows
EAI Connector, for COM Data Control 58
EAI Connector, for Java Data Bean 58
EAI Connector, for Microsoft BizTalk Server 57
EAI Connector, for OLE DB 57
EAI Connector, for Oracle 57
steps 59
Siebel eAutomotive, component groups 265
Siebel eChannel, component groups 265
Siebel eDocuments, component groups 265
Siebel enterprise
information, listing 295, 296
information, reviewing 295, 296
Siebel Enterprise Application Integration (EAI) 20
Siebel Enterprise Applications. *See* **SEA**
Siebel enterprise configuration, on Linux
about 131
follow me instructions 135
ODBC Data Source, verifying 134, 135
steps 132-134
verifying 134
Siebel enterprise configuration, on Microsoft Windows
about 73
additional tasks 77, 78
finalizing 106
follow me instructions 78, 102
naming conventions 76
Siebel administrator, logging as 102, 105
steps 74-76
verifying 78
Windows system services, starting 101, 102
Siebel enterprise hierarchy 272
Siebel enterprise installation, on Microsoft Windows
finalizing 106
Siebel Enterprise Name, component/ parameter 505, 506

Siebel Enterprise security token 82
Siebel Enterprise Server. *See* **Siebel server installer installation, on Microsoft Windows**
Siebel enterprise server
about 12
InstallShield Wizard 44
Siebel enterprise server configuration
about 504
Database Platform, component/parameter 504
DB Connect String, component/parameter 504
DB Table Owner, component/parameter 504
DB Table Owner Password, component/ parameter 504
DB User Account, component/parameter 504
DB User Account Password, component/ parameter 504
Enterprise Name, component/parameter 504
Enterprise Security Authentication Profile, component/parameter 504
Gateway Name Server hostname, component/parameter 504
Gateway Name Server port, component/ parameter 504
Gateway NS Authentication User, component/parameter 504
Gateway NS Authentication User Password, component/parameter 504
Primary Siebel File System, component/ parameter 504
Siebel enterprise server configuration, on Linux
finalizing 154
finalizing, steps 154
Siebel enterprise server configuration on Linux, finalizing
non-root user file, creating 156
services, configuring for automatic start 155
siebel_server file, copying to to init.d folder 156
siebel_server file, editing 155

siebel_server file, permissions setting
    for 156
soft links, creating 156
Siebel enterprise server installation, on Linux
finalizing 154
finalizing, steps 154
follow me instructions 154
SADMIN, logging on as 154
services, starting 152
Siebel gateway name server, starting 152, 153
Siebel server, starting 153
verifying 152
web server, starting 153
Siebel enterprise server installation on Linux, finalizing
follow me instructions 156
non-root user file, creating 156
services, configuring for automatic start 155
siebel_server file, copying to to init.d folder 156
siebel_server file, editing 155
siebel_server file, permissions setting for 156
soft links, creating 156
Siebel enterprise server software
language pack installation, verifying 255
language packs, installing 243
multilingual List of Values, verifying 257, 258
new application object manager, logging on to 256, 257
restarting 256
UI translation, verifying 257
Siebel Environment Verification Tool (EVT). *See* **Environment Verification Tool (EVT), installation on Microsoft Windows**
siebel.exe file 160
Siebel file system 11, 12
Siebel file system-related information
about 502
File System host admin user, component/parameter 502

File System host admin user password, component/parameter 502
File System hostname, component/parameter 502
File System Password, component/parameter 502
File System physical path, component/parameter 502
File System UNC path, component/parameter 502
File System Username, component/parameter 502
Siebel file system root folder
creating 32
follow me instructions 32
Siebel financial services, component groups 265
Siebel gateway name server
about 9, 13
Gateway NS host admin password, component/parameter 503
Gateway NS host admin user, component/parameter 503
Gateway NS hostname, component/parameter 503
Gateway NS installer target directory, component/parameter 503
Gateway NS port, component/parameter 503
Gateway NS service start, component/parameter 503
Siebel gateway name server configuration, on Linux
about 128
follow me instructions 131
steps 129
verifying 129-131
Siebel gateway name server configuration, on Microsoft Windows
follow me instructions 73
steps 71
verifying 72, 73
Siebel gateway name server, for LDAP authentication
configuring 326-329
verifying 329

Siebel gateway name server installation,
    on Linux
  about 118, 119
  follow me instructions 120
  steps 119, 120
Siebel gateway name server installation,
    on Microsoft Windows
  sabout 46
  follow me instructions 48
  steps 46, 47
  verifying 48
Siebel gateway name server, Siebel
    database schema installation on
    Linux
  restarting 144
  siebenv.sh file, executing 145
  siebenv.sh file, modifying 145
  starting 145
  stopping 145
  verifying 146
Siebel image creator
  command line mode 36
  follow me instructions 38
  graphical mode (GUI) 36
  language packs, installing 241, 242
  used, for creating Siebel installation
      image 36, 37
Siebel inbound web service
  dataservice.wsdl file, creating 224
  importing 207
Siebel Industry Applications. See SIA
Siebel installation archives
  downloading 32-34
  download management tool used 34
  follow me instructions 36
Siebel Installation Guide for UNIX
    (Version 8.1)
  URL 118
Siebel installation image
  creating, Siebel image creator used 36, 37
  follow me instructions 242
  language packs, adding 241, 242
Siebel installer
  executing, in unattended mode 115
Siebel ISS, component groups 265
Siebel load balancing
  configuration of SWSE, verifying 238, 239

follow me instructions 239
levels 232
Siebel native load balancing 234
Siebel native load balancing, SWSE
    configuring for 234
single Siebel server 233
third-party load balancing 234
Siebel loyalty, component groups 265
Siebel management agents
  about 52, 422
  configuration, verifying 424, 425
  configuring, steps 422-424
  follow me instructions 427
  getservers.pl, perl script 426
  installation, verifying 424, 425
  installers 422
  installing, steps 422-424
  makeagentconfig.pl, perl script 426
  registering 426, 427
Siebel management server
  adm.cli file, verifying 439
  application deployment manager 415
  architecture 414, 415
  configuration, verifying 420, 421
  cross-enterprise user account 416
  deployment batch files, creating 440-442
  enterprise profile, creating 440-442
  follow me instructions 417
  infrastructure 414
  installation, verifying 420
  installers, URL 415
  installing on Microsoft Windows 417-419
  prerequisites 415
  shared directories, creating 439
  Siebel diagnostic tool 415
  Siebel server bin directory, adding to PATH
      environment variable 416
Siebel mobile web client
  about 159, 161
  and Siebel developer web client, differences
      160
  language packs, installing 259
  local data source, configuring 173
  uninstalling, Oracle universal installer
      used 516
Siebel native load balancing
  about 234

[541]

eapps.cfg file, validating 237, 238
load balancer configuration file
    (lbconfig.txt), creating 234, 235
SWSE configuration, removing 235, 236
SWSE, configuring 234
SWSE, reconfiguring 236, 237
Siebel outbound web service
  configuring, for Siebel 8.2 or higher
    208, 209
  creating, for BI Publisher 10.1.3.4.1 205, 206
Siebel Partner Portal application 20
Siebel personalization layer
  about 368
  access to applets and views, controlling
    368-371
  data display, controlling 371-373
Siebel public sector, component groups 265
Siebel query language 369
Siebel remote
  about 387, 388
  architecture 388
  developers and users, differences 390, 391
Siebel remote architecture, building blocks
  about 389
  database extract 389
  generate new database 389
  local database initialization 389
  local database synchronization 389
  transaction merger 389
  transaction processor 389
  transaction router 389
Siebel remote components
  database extract 393
  enabling 392
  enabling, on Siebel server 394
  generate new database 393
  parallel database extract 393
  replication agent 393
  synchronization manager 393
  transaction merger 393
  transaction processor 392
  transaction router 393
Siebel remote system preferences
  about 396
  enable mobile password expiration 396
  enable mobile password syntax check 397
  enable mobile web client lockout 397

enable transaction logging 397
Siebel remote users
  about 407
  local databases, re-extracting 410
  messages, sending to mobile users 410
  mobile client activity, monitoring 409
  mobile user registrations, deactivating 411
  transaction components on Siebel server,
    managing 407, 408
Siebel repository 38
Siebel Repository File (.srf)
  about 433, 454
  deploying 455
Siebel Repository File (SRF) 15
Siebel sales, component groups 265
Siebel sample database
  about 162
  follow me instructions 181
  installation, verifying 180, 181
  installing 178
  installing, steps 179
  Siebel tools, verifying 185
**SIEBEL_SARMBufferSize, environment
    variable 479**
**SIEBEL_SARMFileSize, environment
    variable 479**
**SIEBEL_SARMLevel, environment variable
    479**
**SIEBEL_SARMMaxFiles, environment
    variable 479**
**SIEBEL_SARMPeriod, environment
    variable 479**
Siebel server
  about 13, 14
  Application Object Manager (AOM) 14
  Component Groups, configuration/
    parameter 506
  configuration parameters 15
  Connection Broker Port, configuration/
    parameter 506
  Data Manager (DM) 15
  Exchange Server Sync, configuration/
    parameter 506
  Gateway Name Server Authentication
    Password, configuration/parameter
    506

Gateway Name Server Authentication User, configuration/parameter 506
Gateway Name Server hostname, configuration/parameter 506
Gateway Name Server port, configuration/parameter 506
installation and configuration 506
language support, adding 243, 244
log levels 470
Register external Oracle ODBC driver, configuration/parameter 506
restarting 439
Server-specific Security Authentication Settings, configuration/parameter 506
Server-specific Security Encryption Settings, configuration/parameter 506
Siebel Enterprise Name, configuration/parameter 506
Siebel Repository File (SRF) 15
Siebel Server Description, configuration/parameter 506
Siebel Server host admin password, configuration/parameter 506
Siebel Server host admin user, configuration/parameter 506
Siebel Server hostname, configuration/parameter 506
Siebel Server installer target directory, configuration/parameter 506
Siebel Server Logical Name, configuration/parameter 506
Siebel Web Engine (SWE) 15
Siebel Web Templates (SWT) 16
Synchronization Manager Port, configuration/parameter 506
Siebel Server components, BI Publisher reports
  enabling 210, 211
Siebel server configuration, on Linux
  about 146
  steps 146-148
  verifying 148, 149
Siebel server configuration, on Microsoft Windows
  about 83, 95
  steps 96, 97
  verifying 98

Siebel Server Description, component/parameter 506
Siebel Server Directory, configuration/parameter 507
siebel_server file
  copying, to init.d folder 156
  editing 155
  permissions, setting 156
Siebel Server host admin password, component/parameter 506
Siebel Server host admin user, component/parameter 506
Siebel Server host, component/parameter 508
Siebel Server hostname, component/parameter 506
Siebel server installation and configuration 506
Siebel server installation, on Linux
  features 122
  follow me instructions 122
  steps 121, 122
  verifying 122
Siebel server installation, on Microsoft Windows
  about 49
  data quality connector 51
  features 50
  finalizing 106
  follow me instructions 52
  handheld synchronization 51
  Java integrator 51
  object manager component 51
  PIM server integration 52
  remote search support 51
  Siebel management agent 52
  steps 49
  verifying 52
Siebel server installer installation, on Microsoft Windows
  about 42
  console mode used 44-46
  GUI mode used 44
Siebel Server installer target directory, component/parameter 506

[543]

Siebel Server Logical Name, component/
      parameter 506
Siebel server management
  command line tools, using 292
Siebel Server Manager command line 436
Siebel servers (additional)
  configuration, verifying 230, 231
  configuring 229
  installation, planning 229
  installation, verifying 230, 231
  installing 227-229
  installing, steps 230
  multiple Siebel servers, configuring on
      same phsical machine 231, 232
Siebel servers and components
  SARM, enabling for 476-478
Siebel server software
  patches, applying 65
Siebel server software configuration, on
      Microsoft Windows
  .ini file, modifying 114
  in unattended mode 112
  response file, creating for unattended
      configuration 113
Siebel server software installation, on
      Microsoft Windows
  .ini file, creating 113
  .ini file, creating for unattended installation
      113
  .ini file, modifying 114
  installer, executing in unattended mode
      115
  in unattended mode 112
  patches, applying 65
Siebel software configuration wizard, on
      Linux or UNIX
  MODEL_FILE parameter 127
  preparing, to run 127, 128
  using 126, 127
Siebel software configuration wizard, on
      Microsoft Windows 68-70
Siebel software units
  SARM, enabling for 478-480
Siebel System Account, configuration/
      parameter 507
Siebel System Account Password,
      configuration/parameter 507

Siebel System Monitoring and Diagnostics
      Guide Version 8.1
  URL 470, 472
Siebel System Requirements and Supported
      Platforms document
  URL 26
Siebel tools
  about 162
  configuring, for Siebel sample database 185
  configuring, steps 183
  installation, verifying 184
  installing, steps 182, 183
  language pack, installation 260
  shortcuts, creating 185, 186
  uninstalling 516
  used, for exporting repository data 448, 449
Siebel tools export support
  about 453
  DescriptorFile parameter 453
  ExportCount parameter 453
  ExportFile parameter 453
  LogFile parameter 453
  Object_N parameter 453
  Repository parameter 453
  Type_N parameter 453
Siebel tools, shortcuts
  /batchexport parameter 186
  /batchimport parameter 186
  /bc parameter 186
  /bv parameter 186
Siebel upgrade wizard
  about 87, 460
  migrate repository procedure 461
  migrate repository procedure, executing
      461-464
  Siebel database configuration wizard,
      invoking 461
Siebel upgrade wizard, on Linux
  starting 144
Siebel usage collection
  abling 496, 497
  system preferences, setting 497, 498
SiebelUsernameAttributeType parameter
      322
Siebel views, Siebel access control
  access, controlling 345, 346
  Account List View 345

[544]

business process analysis, importance 346, 347
New Quote command 346
read only behaviour, controlling 352
responsibilities, creating 349, 350
responsibilities, modifying 349, 350
tab layout for screens and views, controlling 353
user responsibilities 347-349
view access, implications 350, 351
view access on local databases, controlling 351, 352

Siebel web architecture, building blocks
browser 19
diagrammatic representation 9
directory structure 8
relational database 8
Siebel database 10
Siebel enterprise server 12
Siebel file system 11, 12
Siebel gateway name server 9, 13
Siebel server 13, 14
Siebel servers 9
Siebel user interface 19
Siebel web server extension (SWSE) 17, 18
Siebel Web Server Extension (SWSE) 9
web browser 9
web server 9, 16, 17

Siebel web client
about 110, 161
follow me instructions 164
prerequisites 162

Siebel web client, prerequisites
database client software, for developer web clients 162, 163
installing, with administrative user rights 163
Internet Explorer, security settings 163
Java Runtime Environment (JRE) 163
software recommendations 164

Siebel Web Engine (SWE) 15, 474
Siebel Web Server Extension. *See* **SWSE**
Siebel Web Templates (.swt) 433, 454
Siebel Web Templates (SWT) 16
Siebel wireless, component groups 265

siebenv.sh file
  executing 145
  modifying 145
siebns.dat file 131
siebsrvr directory 122
SI mode
  about 19
  Siebel Partner Portal application 20
single Siebel server, Siebel load balancing 233
SingleSignOn parameter 339
SISNAPI (Siebel Internet Session API) protocol 81
SISNAPI (Siebel Internet Session Network API) 77
SISNAPI (Siebel Internet Session Network Application Programming Interface), 21
sleep 20 command 211, 213
Sleep Time parameter 267
SmartScript 431
SOAP (Simple Object Access Protocol) 268
software prerequisites, Siebel CRM installation 26, 27
spool command 294
spool off command 294
SQL error, event type 471
SQL parse and execute, event type 471
SQL profiling, event type 471
SqlStyle parameter 174
SQL summary, event type 471
srvrmgr command 195, 324
srvrmgr command line 447
srvrmgr command line utility 394
srvrmgr executable, input parameters
  /b 293
  /c 293
  /e 293
  /g 293
  /h 293
  /i 293
  /l 293
  /m 293
  /o 293
  /p 293
  /r 293
  /s 293

[545]

/u 293
/z 293
Standard Interactivity. *See* **SI mode**
Standard Interactivity Login Name,
    component/parameter 505
Standard Interactivity Login Password,
    component/parameter 505
start_ns script 130
start_server command 153
start up mode, server components
  setting 300
StateModel 431
status_detail command 458, 459
stopapa command 153
subarea (sub) key 483
SWE area 484
SWEPAGE area 484
SWEView parameter 257
SWSE
  about 9, 17, 18
  additional language packs, installing 254, 255
  configuration 508
  configuration, removing for Siebel native load balancing 236
  configuration, verifying 238, 239
  configuring, for Siebel native load balancing 234
  installation 508
  Installation Directory, component/parameter 508
  load balancing, component/parameter 508
  Siebel Connection Broker Port, component/parameter 508
  Siebel Server host, component/parameter 508
  SWSE Logical Profile Location, component/parameter 508
SWSE configuration file, Web Single-Sign-On (SSO)
  modifying 337, 338
SWSE configuration, on Linux
  about 149
  steps 150, 151
  verifying 151, 152
  web server, preparing 149

SWSE configuration, on Microsoft Windows
  about 98
  follow me instructions 101
  steps 99
SWSE installation, on Linux
  about 124, 125
  follow me instructions 126
  steps 125
SWSE, installation on Microsoft Windows
  follow me instructions 61
  steps 60, 61
SWSE logical profile configuration
  about 504, 505
  Active Session Timeout, component/parameter 505
  Collect statistics, component/parameter 505
  Compression Type, component/parameter 505
  Deploy SSL, component/parameter 505
  Encryption Type, component/parameter 505
  Encrypt SI password, component/parameter 505
  Enterprise Security Token, component/parameter 505
  Fully qualified domain name, component/parameter 505
  High Interactivity Login Name, component/parameter 505
  High Interactivity Login Password, component/parameter 505
  HTTP 1.1 Compliant Firewall, component/parameter 505
  HTTP Port, component/parameter 505
  HTTPS Port, component/parameter 505
  Logical Profile Folder, component/parameter 505
  Login Session Timeout, component/parameter 505
  Siebel Enterprise Name, component/parameter 505
  Standard Interactivity Login Name, component/parameter 505
  Standard Interactivity Login Password, component/parameter 505

Web Server Statistics Page, component/
parameter 505
SWSE logical profile configuration, on
Linux
about 135, 136
follow me instructions 138
steps 136, 137, 138
verifying 138
SWSE logical profile configuration, on
Microsoft Windows
about 79
follow me instructions 83
steps 79-81
SWSE, parameters 81, 82
verifying 82, 83
SWSE Logical Profile Location, component/
parameter 508
SWSE, parameters
about 81
application-specific statistics, collecting 81
compression type 81
contact user account 82
employee user account 82
FQDN (Fully Qualified Domain Name) 82
session timeout values 81
Siebel Enterprise security token 82
symbolic URL 431
Synchronization Manager Port,
component/parameter 506
synchronization manager, Siebel remote
components 393
system alerts 272
system management, component groups
265

T

TableOwner parameter 174
Table Owner Password, configuration/
parameter 507
task configuration, event type 471
tasks view, server management screen 289
team 355
third-party load balancing 234
THRESHOLD area 485
Tools with German (DEU) 248

transaction merger, Siebel remote
components 393
transaction processor, Siebel remote
components 392
transaction router, Siebel remote
components 393
TrickleSync 406, 407
TrustToken parameter 338, 339
Type_N parameter 453
type parameter 316

U

unattended mode
.ini file, creating 113
Siebel installer, executing 115
unset server command 213
user 355, 382
user account
about 382
anonymous user accounts, creating 317-319
creating, in authentication system 384
creating, in directory server 314
divisions 375
follow me instructions 384
in external authentication system, creating
337
in external authentication system, verifying
337
managing, for database authentication 310
shared credentials account, creating 315,
316
verifying, in authentication system 384
user authentication
database authentication 305
database authentication 305
directory server authentication 311
handling 307
Web Single-Sign-On 333
Web Single-Sign-On (SSO) 305
UseRemoteConfig parameter 332
user groups
and Siebel client software 161, 162
UsernameAttributeType parameter 322
user responsibilities, Siebel views
creating 349, 350
modifying 349, 350

[547]

read only behaviour of views, controlling 352
tab layout for screens and views, controlling 353
view access, implications 350, 351
view access on local databases, controlling 351, 352
UserSpec parameter 338
UserSpecSource parameter 338

V

validate command 457
VirtualHostsFile parameter 237, 238
Visual Mining NetCharts server
  about 189
  connectivity from Siebel CRM, configuring 194
  file, creating for Siebel 194
  installation, planning 191, 192
  installation, preparing 192
  installation, verifying 193, 194
  installer, installing 191
  installing, on Windows 192, 193
  project folder, creating for Siebel 194
  Revenue by Month by Account chart in Siebel Sales 190
  Siebel Charts setup, verifying 196
  Siebel enterprise parameters, setting 195
vmoptions parameter 213
VolumeDiscount 431

W

web architecture. *See* Siebel web architecture, building blocks
web browser 9
web server 9, 16, 17
Web Server host admin user, component/parameter 503
Web Server host admin user password, component/parameter 503
Web Server hostname, component/parameter 503

web server related information
  about 502
  Web Server host admin user, component/parameter 503
  Web Server host admin user password, component/parameter 503
  Web Server hostname, component/parameter 503
  Web Server Vendor, component/parameter 503
  Web Server Version, component/parameter 503
Web Server Statistics Page, component/parameter 505
Web Server Vendor, component/parameter 503
Web Server Version, component/parameter 503
web service - inbound 431
Web Single-Sign-On (SSO)
  about 333
  architecture flow 334
  authentication flow 334
  configuration, verifying 339, 340
  IntegratedDomainAuth parameter 338
  LDAP security adapter, modifying 339
  non-anonymous virtual directory, creating on web server 335, 336
  SingleSignOn parameter 338
  SWSE configuration file, verifying 337-339
  TrustToken parameter 338
  user accounts in external authentication system, creating 337
  user accounts in external authentication system, verifying 337
  UserSpec parameter 338
  UserSpecSource parameter 338
WORKFLOW area 485
workflow management, component groups 265
workflow policy 431
workflow processes, ADM
  activating 438

X

XMLP Java subsystem
　parameters, setting 212, 213
XMLP report, component groups 265
XMLP Report Server 210
XMLP responsibilities
　creating 208

Z

ZLIB compression 81

Thank you for buying
Oracle Siebel CRM 8 Installation and Management

About Packt Publishing

Packt, pronounced 'packed', published its first book "Mastering phpMyAdmin for Effective MySQL Management" in April 2004 and subsequently continued to specialize in publishing highly focused books on specific technologies and solutions.

Our books and publications share the experiences of your fellow IT professionals in adapting and customizing today's systems, applications, and frameworks. Our solution based books give you the knowledge and power to customize the software and technologies you're using to get the job done. Packt books are more specific and less general than the IT books you have seen in the past. Our unique business model allows us to bring you more focused information, giving you more of what you need to know, and less of what you don't.

Packt is a modern, yet unique publishing company, which focuses on producing quality, cutting-edge books for communities of developers, administrators, and newbies alike. For more information, please visit our website: `www.packtpub.com`.

About Packt Enterprise

In 2010, Packt launched two new brands, Packt Enterprise and Packt Open Source, in order to continue its focus on specialization. This book is part of the Packt Enterprise brand, home to books published on enterprise software – software created by major vendors, including (but not limited to) IBM, Microsoft and Oracle, often for use in other corporations. Its titles will offer information relevant to a range of users of this software, including administrators, developers, architects, and end users.

Writing for Packt

We welcome all inquiries from people who are interested in authoring. Book proposals should be sent to author@packtpub.com. If your book idea is still at an early stage and you would like to discuss it first before writing a formal book proposal, contact us; one of our commissioning editors will get in touch with you.

We're not just looking for published authors; if you have strong technical skills but no writing experience, our experienced editors can help you develop a writing career, or simply get some additional reward for your expertise.

Middleware Management with Oracle Enterprise Manager Grid Control 10g R5

ISBN: 978-1-847198-34-1   Paperback: 350 pages

Monitor, diagnose, and maximize the system performance of Oracle Fusion Middleware solutions

1. Manage your Oracle Fusion Middleware and non-Oracle middleware applications effectively and efficiently using Oracle Enterprise Manager Grid Conrol
2. Implement proactive monitoring to maximize application performance

Oracle Coherence 3.5

ISBN: 978-1-847196-12-5   Paperback: 408 pages

Create Internet-scale applications using Oracle's high-performance data grid

1. Build scalable web sites and Enterprise applications using a market-leading data grid product
2. Design and implement your domain objects to work most effectively with Coherence and apply Domain Driven Designs (DDD) to Coherence applications

Please check **www.PacktPub.com** for information on our titles

Printed in Great Britain
by Amazon.co.uk, Ltd.,
Marston Gate.